The Chief Rivals of Corneille and Racine

The Chief Rivals of Corneille and Racine

TRANSLATED INTO ENGLISH BLANK VERSE
WITH INTRODUCTIONS

BY

LACY LOCKERT

Nashville

THE VANDERBILT UNIVERSITY PRESS
1956

THE CHIEF RIVALS OF
CORNEILLE AND RACINE

To three much-prized friends:

MRS. W. F. PEIRCE
lately of Ithaca, New York, and

DR. C. MAXWELL LANCASTER
of Vanderbilt University, both of whom have helped
me greatly in my translating of these plays, and

DR. HUNTER KELLENBERGER
of Brown University, who has always appreciated the
importance of having some knowledge of the minor
French dramatists of the seventeenth century.

CONTENTS

PREFACE ix
SOPHONISBE .... *Jean de Mairet* 1
LA MARIANE .... *Tristan l'Hermite* 55
SAÜL .... *Pierre Du Ryer* 107
SCEVOLE .... *Pierre Du Ryer* 159
VENCESLAS .... *Jean Rotrou* 211
COSROES .... *Jean Rotrou* 267
LAODICE .... *Thomas Corneille* 319
LE COMTE D'ESSEX .... *Thomas Corneille* 373
ANDRONIC .... *Jean-Galbert Campistron* 423
MANLIUS CAPITOLINUS .... *Antoine de La Fosse* 467
RHADAMISTE ET ZENOBIE... *Prosper Jolyot Crébillon* 511
ZAÏRE .... *Voltaire* 555

PREFACE

No great period of drama can be properly understood by knowing its major figures alone. These major figures themselves cannot be properly understood without some knowledge of the plays of their lesser contemporaries. This has long been realized in regard to Elizabethan drama and Shakespeare; and there have been many single-volume collections of Elizabethan plays for both the college student and the general reader.

The same is not the case in regard to the great period of French drama, the so-called "classical" period of the seventeenth century. There, only the major figures—Corneille, Molière, and Racine—have received much attention. Most college professors of French, even, have read few of the plays of the minor dramatists of that century; the very names of those dramatists are almost unknown; and even the best of their plays are little read, even in France. Yet the reasons for having some acquaintance with Shakespeare's fellow-dramatists can be applied to argue with no less validity that anyone interested in French-classical drama should know something of those who wrote in rivalry with Corneille, Molière, and Racine.

There is a serious obstacle, however, to one's doing so. There are no modern collections of the best dramas of the lesser French-classical playwrights; these dramas can be found only in very old, out-of-print editions or in small, scholarly reprints of single plays, and they are often unobtainable in any form. That situation makes it difficult (if not impossible save in universities with exceptional libraries) to give courses in French comparable to courses in Elizabethan drama such as are commonly given to advanced students of English; and there have been no English translations of any of these plays for English readers whose knowledge of French is inadequate or totally lacking, yet who are interested in drama and would like a proper orientation in this important period of its flourishing.

No doubt the greatest need is for a well-chosen collection of some of these plays, printed in modern French. For me, however, the editing of such a volume would be an impractical and uncongenial task. The next-best thing if not quite the best—and a thing which also needs to be done in any case—is to bring out a collection of these plays translated into English verse; and this I accordingly do.

Perhaps, indeed, such a volume is of not much less value for English-speaking people. It makes these plays accessible for one who has little or no French, as a reprint of the French text could not do; and it affords opportunity for a fairly adequate knowledge of these plays even to one who could read them in the original and would prefer to do so, but who cannot find copies of the French plays themselves. Plays need lose very little in translation, except their poetry if they are poetic; and it happens that the verse of the minor French-classical dramatists is nearly all very commonplace, rising to real poetry only with Rotrou and to a less extent with Tristan l'Hermite. We read—we may even study intensively—Ibsen in English; almost none of us knows Norwegian, yet without it we feel competent to judge his work and actually to write about him.

There is one special circumstance in which a collection of translations like this one would be more useful even to teachers and students of French than would reprints of the originals. Undergraduate classes in Corneille, Molière, and Racine may be composed of pupils who do not read French fluently yet whom the instructor may wish to enlighten as much as possible about all the literary aspects of their subject. Such classes could be assigned several or all of the plays in this volume, as collateral reading, to afford a background against which to see the great men of the period more clearly; a few hours devoted to reading these plays in English would supply enough of this background, whereas for such students to read the plays in French would require far too much time to be at all practicable.

An adequately representative collection of both the tragedies and the comedies of the lesser French-classical dramatists would exceed the limits of any single volume. I have therefore restricted the scope of this book to the field of tragedy; it aims to make available in translation the best work of the chief rivals of Corneille and Racine.[1] In addition to ten tragedies written in the great age of the seventeenth century, it contains two from the eighteenth, the most famous play of each of the two most famous writers of tragedy, Crébillon and Voltaire, in that period of decline. These two plays, forming a sort of appendix to the others, are included for purposes of comparison, to show what French-classical tragedy presently

[1] A companion volume of the best seventeenth-century French comedies outside of Molière is eminently to be desired. I hope someone will undertake it.

became and how even the best specimens of it then produced compare with the best plays of much less celebrated, minor dramatists of the great age.

As for the ten seventeenth-century tragedies, I have tried to select the ones that are at the same time the best and the most representative. Where my judgment, as to which these are, does not agree with the general opinion of specialists in this little-known field, I have explained in the case of Rotrou's *Saint Genest* and Thomas Corneille's *Ariane* my reasons for rejecting them; in the case of *Venceslas* I would not leave out a play which has really striking excellences as well as some small reputation beyond that of its fellows, though it seems to me unsatisfactory as a whole. I should have liked to include two examples of purely romanesque tragedy: Thomas Corneille's *Timocrate,* the most noted of the usual highly complicated sort, and Quinault's *Astrate,* the most noted of the simpler ones. But *Laodice* has enough of the characteristics of that type of play to give the reader some idea of it; and besides practical considerations of space there is the question of whether a wholly romanesque tragedy would be found readable today. As the collection stands, it contains no seventeenth-century play (unless *Venceslas*) which is not decidedly good, and it omits no tragedy by any minor French-classical dramatist of the seventeenth century which I think can rightly be pronounced good—except Campistron's *Tiridate* and perhaps Péchantré's *Géta. Tiridate* has unpleasantly morbid subject matter—it deals with a brother's incestuous love for his sister—and its author's work is sufficiently exemplified by *Andronic.* I could wish, however, that both *Tiridate* and *Géta* might be made available in English—and of course also in French—as well as *Timocrate* and *Astrate, Saint Genest* and *Ariane,* some play of La Calprenède's, Du Ryer's *Lucrèce* and *Esther,* Tristan l'Hermite's *Mort de Sénèque* and *Mort du Grand Osman,* and perhaps Rotrou's *Laure persécutée.*[2] There is quite enough material, it will be

[2] This last play, a light tragi-comedy, might more fitly appear in a collection of comedies. The three plays named immediately before it would be of especial interest to compare respectively with Racine's *Esther, Britannicus,* and *Bajazet.* Similarly, La Calprenède's *Mort de Mithridate* or his *Comte d'Essex* would be interesting, the former as a predecessor of Racine's *Mithridate,* the latter as a predecessor of Thomas Corneille's *Comte d'Essex.* The *Mariamne* of the pre-"classical" Alexandre Hardy might well be included in such a collection, alike for its own merit, for comparison with Tristan l'Hermite's subsequent *Mariane,* and in view of

seen, to compose a desirable second volume, equal in size to this one, of minor French tragedies of the period.

In the brief introductions to these translated plays, I have condensed and quoted freely from my not yet published book, *Studies in French-classical Tragedy*. As to dates of plays, I have accepted the conclusions of Henry Carrington Lancaster recorded in his great *History of French Dramatic Literature in the Seventeenth Century*.[3]

---

its author's importance as an enormously prolific, transitional figure in the history of French drama.

[3] Baltimore, 1929-1940.

Sophonisbe

(SOPHONISBA)

By
JEAN DE MAIRET

INTRODUCTORY NOTE

Jean de Mairet was born at Besançon, of bourgeois parents, in 1604. He received a good education, to complete which he went to Paris in 1625; in that same year he wrote his first play, *Chryséide et Arimand,* a tragi-comedy based on an episode in d'Urfé's interminable pastoral romance, the famous *Astrée.* He became intimately acquainted with Théophile de Viau, author of a celebrated tragedy on the story of Pyramus and Thisbe, and with Théophile's protector, the Duc de Montmorency, whom Mairet followed in an expedition against the Huguenots. He took part in a naval battle won by the duke, and later was his secretary at Chantilly. After the execution of Montmorency in 1632, Mairet became a dependent of the Comte de Belin, the patron also of the dramatist Rotrou and of the great actor Montdory; Richelieu and others also favored Mairet.

Meanwhile, his pastoral tragi-comedy *Sylvie* (1626) won him great fame; and in 1630 he attempted in his *Silvanire* to conform pastoral drama to the "classical unities" of time, place, and action, as then understood. The play was not successful, but its preface was an important document of dramatic theory. After a comedy, *les Galanteries du duc d'Ossonne* (1632), Mairet applied the same principles to tragi-comedy in *Virginie* (1633) and finally to tragedy in *Sophonisbe,* produced in 1634.

This version of the story of Sophonisba and Masinissa as told by Livy and Appian, about which it is said that more plays have been written than about any other subject, is notable as being the first genuine French "classical" tragedy. Its scene, though not limited to a single spot, is laid within the walls of one city and almost entirely in one edifice; its events take place in twenty-four hours (one afternoon and the next morning) though these hours are indeed full-crowded; its action is indubitably unified. The love-element is of primary importance. The interest is centered chiefly in the minds of the characters rather than in physical events; physical violence does not occur on the stage (except for the suicide of Masinissa at the final "curtain") but is reported by messengers; long speeches of a highly rhetorical cast abound. Thus all important features of French-classical tragedy are to be found in this play.

It enjoyed an immense success, which continued for many years, and this it to no small extent deserved. Even in the latter part of the eighteenth century, it was one of three tragedies by lesser seventeenth-century playwrights—the others were *Venceslas* and *Scévole*—which Marmontel selected as examples of dramatic masterpieces. Though its earlier acts drag somewhat and there are instances of the crudity characteristic of the earlier years of a dramatic art not yet perfected (just as in the work of the predecessors of Shakespeare in England), the issues posed and the conflicts depicted have a universal appeal, concerned as they are with primary human emotions. The portrait of Sophonisba as a woman not without conscience but mastered by a love which she cannot control is not so satisfactorily drawn as a later, more sophisticated dramatist might have drawn it; but the repeated suggestions of patriotic considerations in the midst of her love and the devotion which she inspires in her servants are clever touches, and the characters of Masinissa, Scipio, and Laelius are well portrayed. The last two acts, dealing with the vain efforts of Masinissa to save his wife and with his grief over her loss are hardly surpassed in French-classical tragedy outside of Racine and the best plays of Corneille. The greatest defect in this drama is that though Sophonisba is of necessity its central figure—for Masinissa does not appear till Act III—she has a passive role throughout these later acts, which are the most important part of the play; the struggles and decisions are Masinissa's, not hers.

Many echoes of *Sophonisbe* occur in important French tragedies written in the next few years. For example, in the *Cid*, Don Diegue's hair, like that of Syphax, has, we are told, "grown white beneath his helmet"; in *Horace* as in *Sophonisbe*, it is stated that love does not usually develop in times of violence and fear, and in both of these plays a combat is reported piecemeal by successive messengers; in Tristan's *Mariane* (1636) as in *Sophonisbe,* the origin and credibility of dreams are discussed.

The later career of Mairet was an inglorious one. His *Marc-Antoine* and *Solyman* (1635) are inferior to *Sophonisbe.* In the controversy over the *Cid,* none of Corneille's enemies exhibited greater jealousy or malice. The foremost figure among French dramatists before the appearance of that great play, Mairet must have realized that he could not compete with its author in serious drama. Thereafter, he returned to tragi-comedy and produced four examples of it: *l'Illustre Corsaire* in 1637, *le Roland furieux* in 1638, *Athénaïs* in 1638, and *Sidonie* in 1640—all quite poor. In 1640 he abandoned play-writing for politics, and presently was banished from Paris by Mazarin. He returned to Besançon, where he lived to a great age, a remote observer of the flourishing of the dramatic type which he had helped to inaugurate. He died in 1686.

CHARACTERS IN THE PLAY

SYPHAX, *King of Numidia.*
SOPHONISBA, *his wife.*
SCIPIO, *a Roman consul, commander of the Roman army.*
LAELIUS, *his lieutenant.*
MASINISSA, *a prince of Numidia and enemy of Syphax, holding a command in the army of Scipio.*
PHILO, *a general of Syphax.*
CALIODORUS, *a servant of Sophonisba.*
PHENICE, *a handmaiden of Sophonisba.*
CORISBA, *another handmaiden of Sophonisba.*
PHILIP, *an officer serving under Masinissa.*
ARISTO, *a Roman soldier.*
Other Roman soldiers.

The scene is laid in Cirta, a city of Numidia.

The accent falls on the first syllable in the names of all these characters except "Phenice" (three syllables), "Corisba," and "Aristo," in whose names the accent falls on the second syllable.

Sophonisba

ACT I

Scene One

A large room in the palace of SYPHAX. SYPHAX *and* SOPHONISBA
are discovered.

SYPHAX.   False woman! To have dealings with my foes—
Is this the love which thou hast promised me?
Is this the faith which thou hast given me?
Is this the reverence which is owed to marriage?
Ungrateful Sophonisba, hast thou lost
So soon the memory of Syphax's love?
Whate'er the difference between our ages,
With countless grounds for doubt and for offense
Which more suspicious husbands well might find,
Have I done aught that put thee to annoyance?
Hast thou not always had, as sovereign queen,
Every freedom which thou e'er hast wished?
Yet thy caprice, inimical to my interests,
Foully betrays my honor and thine own.
   Thou knowest that to gratify the hatred
Thy nation hath had always for the Romans
I turned from friendship with that mighty people,
By which my realm had flourished hitherto.
Save for thy counsels, followed to content thee,
For which my ruin is my just reward,
Men would not see me broken as I am
And blindly groping amidst clouds of woes.
My crown would sit securely on my brow;
For Rome and Fortune both would be my friends.
But having robbed me of my kingly glory
And prosperous estate, thou still couldst rob me
Of honor; thou couldst still, to cap the climax
Of wickedness, begin a love affair
With Masinissa. I am willing for thee
To deem me burdensome and my grey hairs
A target for the scorn of thine own youth.
Hate me if so thou wilt, abhor my person;
But how, pray, have my crown and people wronged thee
To make my foe the object of thy longings?

7

Canst thou find none with whom to take thy pleasure
Unless thou winnest this Numidian prince
Who makes thee wholly shameless and perfidious?
Thou canst not love him without hating me,
Connive with him without betraying me.
    I know, unhappily, only too well
The occasion whence thy love for him was born.
Thou'st loved him ever since that fatal day
When Hasdrubal, thy sire, betrothed thee to him,
And when the poison of thy darted glances
Made me embark on this accursed marriage.
How fortunate were I in my misfortune
If the same torches which then lighted us
To the nuptial couch had lighted us to the tomb!

SOPHONISBA. Ah, my lord, would to heaven thou wouldst hear me!

SYPHAX. What couldst thou say, brazen-faced, shameless woman?

SOPHONISBA. That which would spare me these abusive words.

SYPHAX. Thou couldst, if I had neither mind nor eyes.
Or, if I know not what is thy handwriting,
Convict me still of error and false statements.
I will be satisfied when thou clearest thyself.
Then do it, if thou canst, and I shall thank thee.

                                [He shows her her letter.
Wilt thou disown these shameful characters,
Furtherers and proof of thy adulterous love?

SOPHONISBA. No, they are mine, sir; I cannot deny it,
Nor do I seek to justify myself
By a bold stroke of obvious effrontery.
'Tis true, I erred; but it was in imprudence,
In lack of cleverness, and in having hidden
From thee a noble purpose I conceived,
Of which mine own lips should indeed have told thee.

SYPHAX. O gods! hast thou lost all sense and all shame?
Thy fault, thou tellest me, lay in concealing
Thy noble purpose to commit a sin!
Oh, answer as imprudent as insensate!
Explain, explain thy dubious motive better.
Excuse, make not more heinous, thine offense,
And do not soil thy fame, but wash it spotless.
Think what thou sayest, and think that never ear
Hath heard of folly to match thine. Recover
Thy wits, then, after thy mad loss of them.

SOPHONISBA. Thou graspest ill the meaning of my words.
I mean to say, sir, to express it clearly,

That ne'er hath any flame of unchaste love,
Whate'er thou thinkest, been kindled in my bosom,
That I have written with a different object,
And that 'tis thus that I intend to prove
My innocence if thy Majesty will let me.

SYPHAX. Speak, madam, speak; and, if thou canst, establish
Thy innocence to the degree thou shouldst.
That is the greatest pleasure thou couldst give me,
But I how justly fear thou canst not do it.

SOPHONISBA. My lord, thou seest to what extremity
The Roman armies have reduced thee now:
Thy realm laid waste, thy capital besieged,
The enemy encamped before our gates,
The courage of our best troops ebbing fast,
Our outworks carried and our walls assailed.
Thou seest that 'tis no more within the power
Of man to beat back these proud Romans. I,
Who am a Carthaginian, of the true
Blood of Hasdrubal, never have beheld
Or feared an evil worse than this wherewith
Fate will afflict me if this hated people
Should make of me a slave. I have believed
That 'twould be well to gain for myself elsewhere
An arm which could at need preserve my freedom.
Therefore did I write to Prince Masinissa,
Hiding beneath a feigned love my design;
And to prove better to thee that the truth
Is what I tell thee, let thy Majesty
Note, if it please thee, how I disregarded
The flower of the chief men of Italy,
Both the great Scipio and the wise Laelius,
And sought to assure myself of the assistance
Of one who shares with us the name of Libyan.
   That, sir, is in a few words the real cause
Of my mistake which makes me appear guilty;
But after all, heaven, which I call to witness,
Knows well that I am anything but that.

SYPHAX. Think, rather, that the gods, the foes of perjurers,
Will in this way avenge my wrongs and theirs,
And that they some day soon will punish thee
For thy disdain alike of them and me.
I will treat thee, if thou wilt, as pure and modest;
But recollect that a prophetic voice
Tells thee through me that, before long, disaster

Will be the outcome of thy amorous intrigues.
The only reason I now let thy offenses
Remain unpunished is that I would rather
Heaven should avenge me than myself take vengeance
With sword or poison.

SOPHONISBA.   What! does thy suspicious
Nature reject my explanations, then?
O gods!

SYPHAX.   Disguise more cleverly thy schemes,
With whose false colors thou canst not deceive me.
Go, go, lest on thee shall mine anger fall.
Farewell. I wish no more to see or hear thee,
Thou faithless, heartless, most ungrateful woman!
Begone, and shed far from me thy feigned tears,
And leave me all alone here with my grief.

                        [*Exit* SOPHONISBA.

   Heaven, couldst thou better show thou hatest me than
By putting in my bed this shameless Helen—
Rather, this pestilence, this fatal brand
Whose flame hath set my house on fire already!
What king without a wife so vilely false
Could have ill fortune comparable to mine?
Curst be forever the place, day, and hour
In which her lovely sight awoke my love!
Though I should in one day have lost three battles
And given up to the foe a hundred strongholds,
I still would have lost less than when her beauty
Bereft me of all sense and liberty.
Ever since this mistake darkened my life
Ill fortune hath fast followed on its heels.
There is no misery that has not assailed me.
More than my body hath my spirit aged.
Since then, my judgment is beyond doubt poorer
And seems to have lost its former confidence.
All that I undertake results in failure
Whether from bad luck or from bad devising.
O thrice and four times ill-starred marriage rites,
Which made my last years' course calamitous!

Enter PHILO.

PHILO.   Sire, we await only thy Majesty
To launch the attack in the impending combat
On Masinissa. Even now his legions,
Grown bold from their too great success, have planted

Far from their camp their banners, floating proudly;
And thine own troops, drawn up outside the city
In battle array, swear to re-enter it
Only as victors who have taken vengeance.
While their souls pant to take it, is the time
To lead them to the encounter they desire,
Lest by this being deferred they fruitlessly
Lose that fierce ardor which brings victory.

SYPHAX.　Come, then; and may, please heaven, a brave death
Release me soon from such a wretched lot!

PHILO.　What, sire! And since when hath thy stricken spirit
Allowed misfortune to o'erwhelm thy manhood?
Why is it that in thy words and on thy face
Are manifested things of evil omen?
Thou hast not yet been so ill used by Fate
That thou'rt reduced to longing now for death,
And though up to this time contrarious Fortune
Hath done us all the harm that it could do us,
Still we must hope its fickleness will make it
Come over to thy Majesty.

SYPHAX.　　　　　　　　Ah, Philo,
Do not forget that Fortune is a woman
And howsoever Syphax may entreat her
She is for Masinissa and would rather
Follow a young prince than one old already.
But that is not the reason for my fear
And the great woe with which my soul is smitten.
My life is subject to more grievous dangers,
Believe me, and not all my foes are strangers.

PHILO.　How now, my lord, hath someone in thy household
Been guilty of disloyal practices?

SYPHAX.　Yes, I am loathed by those of mine own house
Who ought, most naturally, to cherish me.

PHILO.　Then thou must needs drown promptly in their blood
Their perfidy and their ingratitude.
The right course, in this case, is to forestall them;
Thy safety lieth in their punishment.
But who are these ingrates, these treacherous hearts,
Who can conceive such murderous intentions
Touching the worthiest king in all the world;
And why are they not killed, since they are known?

SYPHAX.　Because in killing them I would kill myself,
Who, traitors though they are, excuse and love them.
That is the reason why I should be pitied:

For having still a little love for her
Instead of punishing her with scorn and hatred.

PHILO. Her? . . .

SYPHAX.   Yes, Philo, 'tis of the Queen I speak;
And I would fain entrust to thy discretion
A woe which I keep hidden from all others.
I in my hands have proofs which will convince thee
That if my soul is shaken, 'tis with good cause,
And that the fear bred by a conquering foe
Is not what makes my face and spirit downcast.
Behold this shameful letter—its handwriting—
And learn and pity, both at once, my plight.
(*He reads*) "See what misfortune my soul undergoes.
The stories of thy magnanimity
And valor force me now to love my foes
With feelings stronger than mere amity."
    And wouldst thou have believed that 'neath such beauty
Lurked such disloyalty and heartlessness?

PHILO.   Certainly heaven hath not yet made a soul
Which would remain unshaken 'neath such blows,
And it is natural that thine showeth today
So much distress at such a great misfortune.
But, sire, thou must reflect that 'tis for great men
To bear great trials and that wives are women.
Let us with brave hearts rush to remedy
The nearest and the most important danger.
Bethink thee, to o'erthrow the Roman power
Is to o'erthrow the aims, too, of the Queen—
Whom it is well meanwhile to watch most closely
With the most vigilant eyes that can be found.

SYPHAX.   Come, Philo, let us go whither Fate calls me
And may my death content a faithless spouse.
    Thou, Masinissa . . .

PHILO (*to himself*).   Gods! How pale he is!

SYPHAX.   To make thee a gift worthy of a foe
And wish worse things for thee than sword or flame,
I would have Sophonisba be thy wife!   [*Exeunt.*

Scene Two

Another, smaller room in the palace. SOPHONISBA *and* PHENICE
are discovered.

SOPHONISBA.   Ah, the truth is that he betrayed my trust,
Phenice, that he gave the King my letter,

12

And his imprudence . . .

PHENICE.   Madam, rest assured
That nowise hath the eunuch been to blame,—
That he did not lack faithfulness to thee
Nor cleverness nor even constancy,
When he was taken by surprise. Then doubt
No more his proved reliability,
And learn just how the thing befell. Already
This hapless man, without the least delay,
Was ready from the walls to issue forth
And from one sleeping army steal to the other
When, by his own ill luck as well as thine,
As day was breaking he fell into the hands
Of African horse—a roving squadron of them—
Who stripped him in their midst as a deserter
And vied in searching him so carefully
That one of them espied the paper fastened
In his robe's hem, where we had hidden it;
And all, to profit by this accident,
Then brought him to the King, with it unopened.
Thus the poor eunuch, to his rage exposed,
Deserveth to be pitied and not censured.
That is the way in which what happened happened.

SOPHONISBA. But Masinissa does not know my thoughts.
This glorious conquerer has yet to learn
The sorry treatment which he brings on me,
How much the love I cherish for him will cost me,
And how on his account I risk my honor.
Gods! oh, how nearly I would crown my wishes
If he but realized my feelings towards him!
I would at least be sure, beyond all question,
Of whether he was grateful or ungrateful.
Phenice, thinkest thou if he knew that he
Possessed my heart, he would give his to me?
Have I, in thy opinion, enough charms
To win one bred amidst the clash of arms?

PHENICE. Only too great, too great, madam. I doubt not
That this young conqueror to those charms will yield,
For Syphax hath been seen, in his life's evening,
To have like passion for so fair a face—
He whose hair 'neath his helmet hath grown white,
Seeking the honors glory promised him.
Believe full surely that if Masinissa
Saw thee in all the beauty that is thine,

13

He would be mad if he did not exchange
War's laurels for love's myrtles instantly
If his heart's freedom be not lost elsewhere,
Leaving him cold to any other love—
For, to be frank, we have no indication
Whether or not he hath remained indifferent
Amid the many fair ones that Spain boasteth.

SOPHONISBA.   O gods! how this thought troubles and affrights me!
How I would suffer if my love, deluded,
Found Masinissa's heart already given!
Truly, whenever my insensate mind
Has wished to dwell upon this dread idea,
I blenched, Phenice, each time, and my soul's
Confusion hath borne witness to mine anguish.

PHENICE.   But, madam, after all, this love's disclosure
Will surely cause thy shame and my undoing.
The King showed, by the way he stormed at thee,
That all thy answers have not satisfied him,
And when he hath returned here from the battle,
Which stayed the tempest of his wrath, I fear
That on thee will its utmost fury fall.

SOPHONISBA.   Far from it. All too well I know love's power
To be afraid the King will do me harm.
The love he hath for me will not allow him
To shame me on account of a mere letter.
He in reproaching me for my offense
Hath punished it; and had he wished to slay me,
He would have done so then and there. Herein
My fault is still more to be blamed, that I
Basely deceive a husband who adores me.
But some mysterious fate, stronger than I,
Against my will constraineth me to wrong him.
I myself countless times have been astounded
At my heart's passion and my destined lot.
Once more this morning I shed tears in thinking
Of the unknown fatality which hounds me.
Reflecting on the greatness of mine erring,
I scarcely could believe that this was I
Or that in such a time of sore distress
I have been able to have thoughts of love.
Alas, it seems that to requite my sins
Love kindled in my breast unlawful flames;
For generally or always hath it happened
That love is born in times of peace and comfort,

14

But that it should be born midst war's alarums—
Its torch be lit when all around is weeping—
Is such a prodigy that its occurrence
Forebodes a most unusual destiny.

Enter CORISBA.

CORISBA. Madam, all waits, both for the sacrifice
    And for the public prayers.
SOPHONISBA.   Come, then, Phenice,
    And lest I pray 'gainst mine own welfare, I,
    In worshipping the gods, shall ask naught of them.

                                              [*Exeunt.*

ACT II

The larger room, as in I, i. SOPHONISBA, PHENICE, *and* CORISBA
are discovered.

PHENICE. The entire city is upon the walls,
    Whence one, as in a theater, can watch
    The battle; and thy Majesty, so please thee,
    Could see it also without going far.
SOPHONISBA. Nay, I feel too great fear, and am too much
    Distressed, to watch this mortal, dubious combat
    Where Mars and Fate decide the destiny
    Of both the African and the Latin peoples.
    But if ye fain would view this tragic sight
    Equally without danger and unhindered,
    Go to the summit of the highest tower,
    Whence the whole plain can on all sides be seen,
    And one or the other now and then come down
    To let me always learn those ills I dread.
    For howsoever hard may Syphax fight,
    So little is my hope I deem him lost,
    Such strange calamity dogs our common aims.
CORISBA. Fortune oft changes in an instant, madam,—
    Oft makes those happy whom it hath made weep
    And curbs its malice for those who can endure.

                      [*Exeunt* PHENICE *and* CORISBA.
SOPHONISBA (*alone*). O wisdom! and O reason! beloved lamps
    Of guidance, shed on me your wonted light,
    And do not let my heart, unvigilant,
    Pray secretly for its own enemy,
    Nor let its passions make me wish today

Safety for those who would destroy me! Vainly,
However, I call back my feeble reason;
For 'tis an aid which can avail no longer,
And I must needs obey that god who bids me
Follow the counsels that his madness gives me.
    I cannot doubt that at this very moment
Through which I pass with soul wracked by such torment,
This youthful hero plans and toils alone
To win a battle and therewith my crown,
And that he would delight in capturing me
To be a trophy in the Romans' triumph.
Yet though I needs must ardently desire
To preserve honor at my life's expense,
How sure it is that I would die of sorrow
If by some sword of ours he found his grave!
    O ye brave men who perish beneath our walls,
Making a shield and rampart of your bodies
To stand firm 'gainst all efforts of proud Rome,
How ill do ye employ your signal valor
In my behalf, who ne'er was worthy of it!
Wherefore so many combats, great and famous,
With so much prowess expended and resisted,
If all your courage, far from pleasing, only
Offends her whom ye loyally protect,
Since her self-interest, now transformed by love,
Favors the leader of the opposing army!
What serves it you at such cost to defend
The gates and towers within which is your queen,
If she e'en now so madly loves her conqueror
That in her heart she ever keeps his image?
What serves it to defend what hath surrendered?
Would ye preserve her freedom who hath lost it?
Rather, brave subjects, arm yourselves 'gainst me,
Who am your king's most mortal enemy,—
Who make my heart the shrine and the retreat
Of him who strives for your complete defeat.
Return ye from the fray, victors or vanquished,
To crush me 'neath the weight of your great shields—
Me, who betray my name, good fame, and country
To love idolatrously Masinissa.
    O fatal meeting, O unhappy moment,
In which Fate let me see his comely face!
What pride or what ingratitude towards heaven
Could have brought on me such a punishment?

Of what crime against Love could I be guilty
That he hath sworn my ruin with my foes'?
If my o'erthrow redounded to his glory,
He could augment that by another victory.
But who can know whether on this occasion
He does not seek it less than my confusion?
Must this crime, Sophonisba, be committed:
To love a Masinissa, thy land's mortal
Enemy, a friend of Rome, whose valor
Gives me the death-blow in my last misfortune?
For at this instant, while I grieve and sigh,
Syphax, it well may be, hath lost his kingdom,
And very soon . . .

Re-enter PHENICE *and* CORISBA.

                          But here my handmaids are
Again, all pale, who from the tower have come.
Their fear breeds mine. No matter; let us hear
What I must needs know and yet dread to learn.
        And what, then, have ye seen?
CORISBA.   The fiercest battle
One e'er will see.
SOPHONISBA.   O gods! How my heart throbs
And tells me even now that we are beaten!
PHENICE.   That is what we, assuredly, cannot tell thee;
For in addition to the fact that distance
So great showed all things poorly to our eyes,
There was a dense cloud, too, of dust and smoke,
Preventing us from seeing either army.
All we could spy was, shining in the air
Out of the dust, a series of brief flashes
Which darted in long shafts of flickering light
From the well-polished steel of their bright arms.
Amid these went up cries from time to time,
Mingled and muffled with the combatants' blows,
The dreadful noise of which, striking our ears,
Hath filled us with a terror never equaled.
CORISBA.   Thus neither my companion nor myself
Could longer look upon this dreadful sight.
That is the reason why we have come down,
O'erwhelmed with horror, trembling with affright.
SOPHONISBA.   What of the populace?
CORISBA.   The populace?
They are upon the walls, lifting to heaven

17

Their cries and eyes, as much to demonstrate
Their wonted cravenness as to encourage
Our soldiers to fight well. Many of them
Can be seen going through the streets, to pray
In the temples, which stand open, so that Cirta,
Within the entire circuit of its ramparts
Is one vast picture of confusion and fear.
But after such great trials, perhaps the gods
Will change today our fortunes for the better.

SOPHONISBA. Alas, Corisba, Fate hath vowed my ruin,
And human power collides with that of heaven.
The gods, whom doubtless my good fortune wearied,
Are not yet satisfied by my past misfortunes,
And I myself dare prophesy to myself
That they reserve for me still something worse.
The dreams that I have had the last few nights
Foretell for me no ordinary woes,
And what assures me better of their truth
Is that I who, far from believing in dreams,
Have always held them lying and absurd,
Produced by an excess of heavy vapors,
Cannot prevent myself from crediting
These last ones, which are all of evil omen.

PHENICE. Madam, our passions, of their own will, alone
Create these visions, without aim or sequence.
Our fancy, while we sleep, imagines them
According to what mood is dominant.
If we have anxious thoughts throughout the day,
The night's dreams will needs be unhappy also.
Thou indeed hast not, in thy present plight,
Dreamed of festivities and feasts and dances.
Thy spirit, restless, sad, and full of care,
Will not present thee with such gracious visions.
Then dread no more these specters of the mind,
And do not think thou seest what will befall thee
In such dim mirrors, which, though deceptive, bring
On credulous folk genuine calamities.
But I hear someone at the door, I think.
Shall I go open it?

SOPHONISBA.   Go; it is the bearer
Of the news, good or bad, which I await.

PHENICE *opens the door. Enter* CALIODORUS.

CALIODORUS. The King, Phenice!

PHENICE. Gods! What do I hear?
But please, for fear of frightening the Queen,
Conceal from her at first what brings thee hither.
CALIODORUS. I will, if I but can; yet much I fear
That such a clear and acute mind as hers
Will soon discover it.
SOPHONISBA. How now, Caliodorus!
Does the ill fate of old pursue us still?
Has the same evil fortune we so often
Experience ended the fight badly for us?
Speak. As scant hope is left me of good fortune,
I shall expect from thee only grim tidings.
CALIODORUS. Madam, it is too true that heaven in anger
Smites us again today indubitably,
And that 'tis difficult to vanquish Fate
When she would fain display her fiercest hate.
Certainly never hath the hope to see
Our valor raise again our stricken kingdom
Flattered with fairer prospects of success
Our troops or made them fight more confidently.
Fortune at first smiled on our glorious efforts
Wherewith we covered the whole field with dead.
Two powerful legions, both superbly armed,
Accustomed at all times to victory,
Could not sustain the onset of our forces,
Recoiled upon their fellows, throwing them
Into confusion, and thus by their panic
Lost their proud claims to being invincible.
From this initial triumph more than ever
We boldly advanced all our line of battle.
The King in front, unsparing of his person,
Led us into their camp, abandoned to us
After resistance so irresolute
And feeble that we might have judged that they
Had wished it to be nothing more than this,
And that it was a master stroke, naught less,
Of stratagem, as the event soon showed.
For now, instead of finishing their glorious
Task that would crown our brows with victory,
Our soldiers broke their ranks imprudently
And fell to burning and to plundering
The camp, nor, glutting thus their greed for booty,
Perceived how much thereby their ardor cooled.
While they were thus engaged, the foe had rallied.

19

On one side Masinissa, on the other
Laelius, giving us no chance to re-form
Our lines, fell on us like two raging torrents.

SOPHONISBA. Why hide from me the dagger that will kill me?
No, no; I needs must die; the fight is lost.

CALIODORUS. Thyself hast said it, madam; and 'tis true.
Indeed—if I must tell thy Majesty
All—should the Romans, as it is too dire
To think, conserve better than we the fruit
Of victory, they as easily will enter
Cirta as if they found there not one soldier.
The terror-stricken populace will open
The gates when their first cohorts are seen coming.

SOPHONISBA. The King is dead, then, or a prisoner?

CALIODORUS. Of all the public woes, that is the greatest.
Yes, while he was displaying the utmost valor,
This hapless monarch's life-thread was cut short.

SOPHONISBA. Nay, rather was he happy in not having
Lived to be at the mercy of his conquerors.
What an ill fate it is, to save one's life
When death is something to be so desired!

PHENICE. Madam, in such a great and urgent peril
Thou shouldst exhibit a resourceful nature
And realize that in thy present plight
Thou needs must instantly resolve on flight.
In such a situation tears are vain
And loss of time is not repaired again.

> *[Loud cries are heard outside.*

SOPHONISBA. Gracious gods! What sound, mingled with the people's
Laments, awakens new fears in my soul?

CALIODORUS. Wait, if it please thee, madam; I will see
Whence comes this tumult.

SOPHONISBA.   Yes, learn what it means.

> *[Exit* CALIODORUS.

(*To her handmaids*) O ye, the brave companions of my trials,
Must my misfortunes make you, too, unhappy;
And must the affection which ye feel for me
Reduce your fortunes to where now I see them?

CORISBA. Ah, madam, lament only *thy* ill fortune,
And let it be common to us with thee.
In that alone hath Fate been kind to us
And willing to treat us as we desire.
This selfsame rigorous lot apportioned to us,
Suffered for thee, pleases and gratifies us.

As we had part in thy prosperity,
We ought to bear adversity with thee.
SOPHONISBA.   Oh, marvels of love, loyalty, and virtue,
Worthy of a different fate, a different mistress!

Re-enter CALIODORUS.

CALIODORUS.   Madam, 'tis no time to dissimulate
Or keep from thee what cannot be concealed.
The city hath surrendered, or soon will do so,
And thence arose the noise we lately heard.
Masinissa himself stands before
Our walls, where all from all sides flock to see him.
SOPHONISBA.   Then must I call my courage to mine aid
And shun by death the shame of servitude.
Come, which of you will lend me, now, an arm?
Which of you will at need be kindest to me?
(*To* CALIODORUS)   Thou, faithful subject, if my accomplished
ruin
Still leaves to me the rank of queen o'er thee,
Employ thy sword to do this act of love.
To take my life now is indeed to love me.
Dispatch, and wait not till Rome hath the chance,
By humbling me, to triumph over Carthage.
CALIODORUS.   In such commands as this, my heart protests
That it will ne'er obey thy Majesty.
SOPHONISBA.   Alas! how can I hope to cure mine ills
If mine own people now refuse to help me?
PHENICE.   As one can doubt not that the most desperate ills
Have in death always a sure remedy,
Death is also the last which one should try
And ought to be reserved for the worst evils.
For my part, I believe that thou shouldst think not
Of death, but turn to thine own charms for aid.
Thou art in need of little artifice
To make thee pleasing in Masinissa's eyes.
Attempt to win his love.
SOPHONISBA.   Would to the gods . . .
PHENICE.   Remember, he is young and of a race
Which, in all Africa, is the most famous
For falling in love suddenly and wishing
To be loved. Pray thee, in the gods' name, try
What power o'er a Numidian's heart the glance
Of beauty hath. Test this, for our love's sake.
SOPHONISBA.   I expect nothing from my charms, Phenice.

2 1

To trust to them is useless and absurd.
'Twere better to rely upon my hand
And by a brave deed, worthy of my courage,
Find a safe harbor in the storm's despite.
But to content thee, I will force myself
To follow a base course which will serve naught.

ACT III

Scene One

An open space, or square, inside the city walls. MASINISSA,
PHILIP, *and Roman soldiers are discovered.*

MASINISSA.   Thanks to the gods, our signal, crowning victory
Gives me back all my former glorious honors.
Dead is that barbarous and base usurper
Who was the source and cause of so much strife.
Heaven hath by his downfall shown the world
That ill success follows an unjust war.
O ye to whom I owe my royal state,
Workers and witnesses of my good fortune,
Believe, dear comrades, whose victorious arms
Have cleared my path to my ancestral throne,
That your long toil which seats me safely there
Does not, I deem, deserve to be forgotten.
I well know what reward is due your service
And that ingratitude is the worst of sins.
But there is left us still one deed to do,
To bring me glory in the highest degree.
PHILIP.   Great-hearted leader, use us as thou wilt;
And if thou hast yet loftier ambitions
So that Syphax's realm doth not content thee,
Aim higher still, and we shall follow thee.
With the approval of the Senate, thou
Canst undertake to lead us even farther
Than Alexander went. Four legions love thee,
And they can win thee lands as wide as his,
Yielding in naught to those old phalanxes
Which saw so many seas and distant regions.
MASINISSA.   Resistless Romans, I shall not refuse
The aid of these brave hearts and mighty arms,
Which, throughout all the world, in righteous causes,
Take away crowns and give them, at their will.

I know your love for me; I know it hath
Made me king in a realm increased by half.
Truly ye could, if ye desired to do so,
Render all Africa subject to my sway.
But these kind feelings which ye have for me
Must to an even better use be put,
To achieve a greater thing—what I desire
And now propose to you.

PHILIP.   Only command us
And say what must be done.

MASINISSA.   Go straight to the palace
And carry it by storm, if the report
That it resists be true—not that the place
Is in itself of such importance that
It absolutely must, without awaiting
The morrow, be at once taken by force
At our blood's cost, but because Sophonisba
Is there with all her retinue, brought to bay.
I fear that waiting till tomorrow morning
Would be injurious to the Latin empire;
For if this African queen, as shrewd as she
Is fair, should save herself by some new ruse,
Ye'd always have in her a dangerous foe
And would have only half won and half conquered.
Besides, this queen's incomparable beauty
Should with its marvel make our triumph perfect—
As it would not be unless thus embellished,
Nor would your valiant deeds appear as great.
    Then let us go forthwith to attack this place
Defended by the weak, base populace.
If blood must needs be spilled in storming it,
Distinguish between citizens and soldiers,
And spare if possible the few brave souls.
Respect the Queen, above all, and her women,
And for the sake of both their sex and their
Rank, let them suffer no indignity.   [*Exeunt.*

Scene Two

The larger room. SOPHONISBA, PHENICE, *and* CORISBA *are discovered.*

SOPHONISBA. Once more I say, Phenice, let me use
While I yet can, a sure cure for my woes.
The one I am to employ, besides being shameful,

23

Hath a most dubious prospect of success.
The power of my glance, if I must try that,
Offers less help than what my hand can give me,
Which is the promptest, surest aid of all,
And the most worthy, too, of a proud heart.
A single dagger-blow my blood can drain
And end my troubles almost without pain.
Ah, but for thee I would ere this have fled
The shame and misery of captivity!

PHENICE.   Possess thyself, please, of a little patience,
And of thy loveliness make trial. Learn
The power of it, and what it can accomplish.
How know this, save by putting it to the test?

CORISBA.   Indeed, the disbelief in it which Madam
Feels, can come only from not having tried it.

SOPHONISBA.   Forget not in what straits I am, Corisba,
And judge thereby, like me, what I can do.
Though yesterday I were the living picture
Of quite the most exquisite beauty seen
In nature, how could I still have today
An extreme beauty when in extreme distress?
With charms no longer more than commonplace,
I could accomplish nothing or but little,
So that I, after all, deem I had better
Trust to my hand than to my glance for succor.

CORISBA.   If thy glance, madam, hath not enough allurement,
Thy hand, when the worst comes, will still be strong
Enough to sink a dagger in thy breast.

SOPHONISBA.   But I may wish too late to use it, then
Having, perhaps, no blade to kill myself.

PHENICE.   What a sword cannot do, grief will accomplish.
So many different roads there are to death
That he who does not find it, does not wish to.
Thou must—so please thee, madam—resolve to live
And freedom take from him who took thine from thee.
I do not know that he at sight of thee
Will burn with love or tremble out of reverence
Or will believe that thou wouldst win the apple
Of Paris from all in Capua and in Rome.
However, misery hath not bedimmed
Thy bright eyes nor thy loveliness of color.
Thy tears have flowed, but thou art one of those
Whom a sad, piteous look makes fairer still.

Thy lifeless glances will arouse compassion.
Which love doth oft attend and kindness always;
For there is nothing like the amazing power
O'er gallant hearts of beauty in distress.
Certainly Masinissa hath a breast
Of stone if thy perfection cannot touch it,
And he is crueler than the Hyrcanian tiger
If in the least he plays the tyrant towards thee.

Enter CALIODORUS.

CALIODORUS. Masinissa, madam, is in the great court,
Which might be taken for a temple where
Everyone comes for refuge, so much do
His efforts to prevent all violence
And outrage give assurance to the hearts
Of the most terrified. Moreover, he
Appears so kindly that thy Majesty
Should hope much from his magnanimity.
      But now the royal stair resounds, meseemeth,
With the loud clash of bucklers.
SOPHONISBA.   Ah, Phenice,
      I tremble!
PHENICE.   Yet 'tis now that thou must be
Confident, and with shafts he cannot parry
Assail him. When he enters here, address him
Straightway with those words which necessity
Will put upon thy tongue, whereof soft glances
And frequent sighs will be the truest aids
And the most eloquent. A young man is won
Especially by the sweetness of the eyes,
Gestures, and tones. Then let thy Majesty
Refuse not to beset her conqueror
With all her charms.
SOPHONISBA (*lifting her eyes to heaven*). Here, mighty god of love,
Is an occasion great enough to leave
A memorable example of thy power.
Work now a miracle, that mortals may
With prayers and incense throng about thine altars.
Act, and I vow a splendid temple to thee
As the restorer of the African cause!

MASINISSA, *with soldiers behind him, appears at the door.*

MASINISSA.   Soldiers, await me; do not enter farther.
    This place of royalty should not be thronged.
                      [The soldiers withdraw.
    Even as her grief, her beauty shows her to us.
    She comes to meet us with a sad, slow step.
                    [He advances towards her.
    Madam, I know that it is to renew
    Or to increase thy griefs to speak of them,
    And that I would do better to keep silent
    Than to console thee for the woes I cause thee.
    Thy gods and mine, though, from whom naught is hidden,
    Know that 'tis with regret I have undone thee,
    And that in some wise my good fortune irks me
    Because it comes to me by thy ill fortune.
    But in as much as Fate, to show she hates thee,
    Hath not left matters to my choice, regard it
    As good that both my mouth and heart swear to thee
    That thy distress touches me very deeply
    And that I would make less thy cares and sorrows
    If sharing them with thee could make them less.
    Since I was not permitted to prevent them,
    I shall at least attempt to lighten them;
    And if I cannot do that, I will see to it
    In any case that thou shalt have no new ones
    And that thou shalt be treated as a queen,
    Not as a captive. Let thine anxious soul
    Be reassured, then, and consider how
    I or my soldiers can allay thy woe.
SOPHONISBA.   It is most rightly, O magnanimous victor,
    That all the world resounds with praise of thee.
    Thy qualities of rare worth show me why
    Disaster obstinately dogged our house.
    Their brilliance is so great that even Fortune,
    Blind though she is, hath learned of them and loved them,
    And acts so wisely when she favors thee
    That she thereby proves that she hath good judgment.
    But unless that inconstant Being, as
    The just reward of such exceptional virtues,
    Adds to thy prosperous estate much greater
    Blessings than those that she hath taken from us,
    Thou wilt obtain far less than thou deservest.
    Many conquerors by sheer prowess bring
    Nations beneath their sway, but very few

Know how to conquer hearts, and truly merit
The scepter they have won. To thee alone
Doth it belong to do both things. The power
To do so is peculiar to a soul
Like thine. 'Tis fated that the kings of foes
Are at first loathed by those they have subdued,
Whereas thy courtesy, O kindly victor,
Hath wrought in me no common miracle.
Though thy good fortune forces me to murmur,
I beg the gods to cause it to continue,
And thou wilt ne'er attain to supreme greatness
Till thou hast all that I desire for thee.
The gifts which Fate gives thee at my expense
Are not the reason for the tears I shed.
I see thy good luck without hate or envy,
And only mourn the ill luck of my life,
Which is so much the worse that, having robbed me
Of everything—hope, peace, success, and freedom—
To make my destiny at all points piteous,
It robs me of the means to win thy credence.
In circumstances such as mine, I seem
Suspectable and little worthy of trust
But, having not much more to hope or fear,
I would do ill to flatter or to feign,
And I would hate myself if I should purchase
The realm of Syphax by unworthy conduct.
PHENICE (*aside to* CORISBA). Companion, he is won!
MASINISSA.   O gods,
        what marvels
Enchant at the same time mine eyes and ears!
Certainly no one ever had such bliss
As I now feel at being esteemed by thee.
Mars hath no laurels whose glory is a prize
So dear to me as praise from lips so lovely.
But never will my happiness be perfect
If no act followeth thy gracious words,—
If thou dost not prove thy esteem is real
By giving me a chance to serve thee somehow.
Command me, then, madam, and learn today
The absolute power thou hast o'er Masinissa;
And may all evil fortune henceforth hound him
If wheresoe'er he can he doth not serve thee
Both honestly and without reservations.

SOPHONISBA. Great king, since thou must have a hapless subject
  Towards whom to show thy magnanimity,
  To make thy good will towards me not be fruitless,
  I shall ask of thee what is not unmeet.
PHENICE (*as before*). The victory is ours, if I know aught.
SOPHONISBA (*continuing*). No, I wish neither power nor possessions
  From thee; I ask not, from thy generous hands,
  For my lost scepter nor its royal pomp.
  I swear unto the gods that, if I had them,
  With all my heart I would bestow them on thee.
  But if thy sympathy with human misery
  Makes thee feel pity for a dolorous queen,
  Lately the ornament of her rank, but now
  An object for compassion, grant to me
  One of two things: that never shall the Tiber
  See me a slave, or that I shall die free.
  We beg thee—my misfortunes and I beg thee—
  As thou art African, as thou art a sovereign
  Whose majesty is always sacrosanct,
  Let not my shame be publicly displayed;—
  (*Kneeling*) Yes, by the throne which I had and which thou
      hast,—
  By these thy sacred knees, wet with my tears,—
  By these thy valiant hands, always victorious,—
  By all thy deeds, which are so glorious!
MASINISSA. Gods! Must a victor die beneath the blows
  Of those whom he hath vanquished? Madam, rise.
SOPHONISBA. Nay, sir; not till my tears win what I ask for.
MASINISSA. Thou wilt obtain something yet greater still:
  A heart which beauty never hath subdued
  Before, and which thine now hath ravished from me.
SOPHONISBA (*rising*). In this my plight I cannot but submit
  To the insulting cruelty of thy conduct;
  But know that never did a generous conqueror
  Distress with words of mockery the vanquished.
MASINISSA. Ah, madam, cherish not this false belief
  Whose error both wrongs me and offends thee.
  Judge better the respect a prince must feel
  For thee, and see the power of thy beauty.
  Too much I glory in thy conquest of me
  To disavow it or to keep it secret.
  Boast of achieving with thy glance alone
  What neither fire nor darts could ever do.

I set a captive queen free, it is true;
But I deprive myself of liberty.
My fervent transports and my sighs, not feigned,
Will show thee clearly what is my complaint.

SOPHONISBA. My vanity would be absurd indeed,
Or I would be extremely credulous,
If I believed that in my present state,
A prisoner, forsaken, full of woe,
My bosom swollen with sighs, and mine eyes drowned
In tears, I still preserved beauty and charm
Sufficient to arouse an ardent love.

MASINISSA. 'Tis true that pity was what first I felt,
But as the sun follows Aurora's footsteps,
The love which followed it, and still follows it,
Made in one instant in my burning heart
The greatest change that love hath ever caused.

SOPHONISBA. It is too violent to be long-enduring.

MASINISSA. Yes, for my death is certain before long
If thou wilt not console with kindlier treatment
A man who henceforth cannot live without thee.

CORISBA (*aside to* PHENICE). How, more and more, his soul becomes
ensnared!

MASINISSA. Give me one of two things: death or thy mercy.
We beg this of thee, I and my heart's passion,
Not as I am a conqueror and a king,
For love hath made me lose both of these titles,
But by my sad fate, whereof thou art mistress,
By my blood set on fire, my ardent sighs,
My raptures, my desires, so sudden, fervent,
By thine own glances, shafts of light and flame,
Which I have felt pierce my soul's inmost depths,
By those dark tyrants whose decrees I reverence,
Those conquerors of conquerors, thine eyes, rulers
Of kings, and by that reason thou tookest from me,
Give me the pity that I have given thee,
Or if thy wrath must in my blood be drowned,
Take thou this sword and slay me at thy feet,
The victim of my love and of thy hate.

SOPHONISBA. Nay, rather would thy death increase my woe;
But pity, O great king, thy fate and mine,
Who am constrained to repay good with evil.
I pity thee, and I am to be pitied
For kindling a fierce flame I cannot slake.

MASINISSA. Thou either hast no heart or it is hard.

SOPHONISBA. Nay, 'tis because I have too much of one
    That I speak thus to thee.

MASINISSA.   Thy words conceal
    A meaning which I cannot understand.

SOPHONISBA. Yet they are easy to be understood.
    The tragic situation I am in
    Prevents me from responding to thy love.
    The widow of Syphax is all too ill-starred
    To wed with Masinissa in a second
    Marriage, and too good blood flows in her veins
    For her to do aught unbecoming of her.
    Fortune in all its anger hath indeed
    Taken my crown but not my lofty heart.
    I know that as my conqueror and master
    Thou canst do with me whatsoe'er thou wilt,
    But I thus far have deemed thy soul too noble
    Even to think of such a crime.

MASINISSA.   So deem it
    Still, madam, and know well that on this point
    I and thy trust in me will not deceive thee.
    To show thee that 'tis by fair means that I
    Wish to achieve my acme of all joy,
    As Syphax is no more, it rests with thee
    To have for lawful husband Masinissa.

SOPHONISBA. What queens on earth, of the most perfect beauty,
    Have e'er deserved the honor which thou doest me?
    O miracle of favor and good fortune,
    Which puts a captive in her sovereign's bed!

MASINISSA. Since thou wilt make me of all men the happiest,
    My intense ardor and this present time
    Do not allow me greatly to defer
    The most extreme bliss for which one could hope.
    Hence deem it well that in the usual manner
    The nuptial torch should blaze for us today,
    As much to speed the attainment of a blessing
    So dear to me as on account of other
    Reasons which could prevent my having it,
    Whereof I needs must now say nothing to thee.
    In the meantime, let me freely take one honest
    Kiss as a pledge of that faith which the god
    Of marriage fain would have from thee and me.

                                  [He kisses her.

O rapturous kiss of nectar and of flame,
What ecstasy thou bringest to my soul!
　Madam, if thou permittest, I shall go
Unto my soldiers, and when I have given
Orders to them, I will return at once.
Farewell; 'tis plain to thee from my wan face
That leaving thee is leaving mine own self.

　　　　　　　　　　　　　　　[Exit MASINISSA.

SOPHONISBA.　O miracle of love, unparalleled!
PHENICE.　Perhaps thou'lt follow my advice again?
SOPHONISBA.　Ah, the truth is, Phenice, such a marvel
　Makes me quite rightly wonder if I am
　Awake, or if a lying dream beguiles me.
PHENICE.　Madam, Numidia's king is so in love,
　His fervor is so great, thou needest not fear
　That anything but death could quench its fires.
　Truly, herein the providence of the gods
　Against our will hath done all for the best.
　If he this morning had received thy letter,
　Thine aims would not have been so well achieved.
　If he had only known that thou didst love him,
　Thou'dst have in him a lover, not a husband.
　Be very certain that thy modesty
　Hath of his passion caused the larger half.
　Then persevere; cease not to play thy role
　Till the task undertaken be concluded.
　Afterwards, when thou art his wedded wife,
　Thou canst reveal to him thy earlier love
　That he may cherish thee with more fervent ardor,
　Seeing that thou lovest him and not his greatness.
　Let us go, then, to finish the preparations
　Needed to re-establish thy position.
　But wherefore, madam, standest thou musing thus?
SOPHONISBA.　Phenice, I know not what is to happen
　To me; but howsoever sweet the present
　Moment which my good fortune sends to me,
　My heart by no means tastes a perfect joy.
　Syphax hath not yet had his funeral rites,
　And I am lighting a new marriage torch!
　Truly, the memory of his affection,
　Joined with a sense of what is unbecoming,
　Wakens in me remorse, almost repugnance.
CORISBA.　Madam, 'tis true in other circumstances

Thou wouldst indeed with justice have such feelings.
But think to what a plight thou art reduced;
Necessity, naught else, governs thy course.
A thousand reasons of State, of which thou knowest,
Are the excuse and the criterion
For what thou doest. Those of thy rank are always
Exempt from letting their conduct be affected
By all such thoughts.

SOPHONISBA.   Let us, then, go and strive
To save ourself from slavery, and let us
Yield to the stern claims of necessity.

ACT IV

Scene One

The smaller room, as in I, ii. MASINISSA *and* SOPHONISBA *are discovered.*

MASINISSA.   However great good fortune I have owed
To favors of kind Fate, which smiles upon me,
This is the greatest that hath e'er been mine.
Yes, madam, truly I am more enraptured
To learn that thou returnest my love than I
Would be if I had conquered the whole world.
I love far more when knowing I am loved;
My love grows greater for a heart that loves me.
With even the fairest wife, if she is cold
The maddest ardor lessens and grows weary.
Lawful delights should be reciprocal,
And love should be repaid by love alone.
Yes, even as one wave creates another,
A sigh of love incites an answering one.
When two souls are by marriage bonds united,
A kiss should be returned as soon as given;
And consequently the best wife is always
One who exhibits the intensest love.
In wedlock her own fervor shows her virtue,
And to restrain it is of ill repute.
For my part, though my love was such already
That no one else's was as violent,
My passion for thee hath increased two-fold
Since I have learned of thy great love for me.

SOPHONISBA. I would needs have the voice of eloquence
    Itself, to make thee know how much I love thee.
    Enough that since my love for thee is all
    Too great, there are no words that can express it.
    However—and it is of this that I
    Am mortally afraid—thou mayest imagine
    That my love, which is really unalloyed,
    Hath some self-interest mingled with its flame;
    But I call heaven to witness that my heart
    Sees Masinissa only, not his crown;
    And were our fortunes, good and bad, reversed
    I would for him do what he did for me.
MASINISSA. For proof of what thou sayest, I need only
    My happiness.
SOPHONISBA.   But thine own worthiness . . .
MASINISSA. By the by, how, when, and why was the love
    Born which thou hast for me? Pray, let me have
    The joy of hearing that. Wilt thou not?
SOPHONISBA.   Most
    Willingly. I am going to tell thee of it
    Thou knowest that we at one time were about
    To be united in a marriage which
    Was not accomplished. That ill-fated monarch
    To whom heaven pleased to sacrifice my youth
    Then caused my father, pliant to his wishes,
    To thwart the sacred troth which binds us now;
    Yet in the hope to be some day thy wife
    I had conceived a secret love for thee
    And in my soul nursed that sweet malady,
    Whereof time, as the years passed, would have healed me
    If the strange accident of which thou shalt hear
    Had not rekindled this flame amid its ashes.
    Dost thou recall the day when Syphax led
    His men against the Massessilians?
    That day was filled so full with glory for thee
    That thou indeed shouldst keep the memory of it;
    For the defeat we suffered at thy hands
    Brought thee unto the fosse before our ramparts,
    Where I beheld thee fight so valiantly
    I even then felt enough good will towards thee
    To wish that no unfortunate success
    Of ours should end before mine eyes thine exploits.
    But when, from the high tower where I was,

I saw thee with thy helmet's visor raised,
Which thou hadst left up for the sake of coolness,
And I could thus behold at no great distance
That face in which the Thracians' god and Love
Mingled such daring with such graciousness,
Then I began to be false to my country;
Then was my heart disloyal to my people;
I felt my breast pierced with a shaft of flame
So that of all mortals I was the most
Grievously smitten. It is true that now
My wound is salved by him who gave it to me,
And that the curing of it which ensues
Will make me bless him for it all my life.

MASINISSA.   Certainly I in such degree am happy
That my good fortune rouses my misgivings.
So great I find it in my future prospects
That I am dazzled by it, if not afraid.
One's happiness is like the ocean tides
In that it mounts yet higher or subsides,
But if the gods will needs, as is their custom,
Make the bitter follow the sweet, may I
Alone, if possible, drink all the gall
Which on us may by heaven's anger fall!

Enter ARISTO.

What does this soldier, clad in Roman armor,
Want of us? How now, my good friend, Aristo,
What brings thee here? And what is Scipio doing?

ARISTO.   Sir, he has just arrived and by my mouth
Bids thee to come to him.

MASINISSA.   Where didst thou leave him?

ARISTO.   In the large room near by, where only Laelius
Is with him.

MASINISSA.   I will go there in a moment.

[*Exit* ARISTO.

SOPHONISBA.   I expect naught good of this summons of thee.
The name of Scipio presages evil
For me.

MASINISSA.   O gods!

SOPHONISBA.   And why, sir, dost thou change
Countenance? What reason hast thou to be
Disturbed?

MASINISSA.   None, save not liking to leave thee.

SOPHONISBA. A change so quick betokens something else,
　　And thy dismay hath a quite different cause.
　　Tell me the truth. Fearest thou the power of him
　　Who sent for thee, and whom thou art to face?
MASINISSA. The truth is that I fear that this stern man
　　Will thwart our happiness or make it less.
　　I see my fate about to be decided,
　　Knowing that Scipio has come to undo
　　Our holy union. That was why I wished
　　To hasten it, for when it once was formed
　　He could do nothing but accept it. He
　　Will be less angry than if I had waited
　　To have our marriage rites till after he
　　Forbade them. He beyond all doubt will beg me,
　　Press me hard, bid me with cruel threats, to leave thee;
　　But may I be hurled living into hell
　　If ever I consent to be so base.
SOPHONISBA. Nay, rather may I lose the light of day
　　Than see my love bring ruin unto thee.
　　If Scipio, as we can doubt not, wishes
　　To part us twain whom marriage hath made one,
　　Thou must needs do all that is possible
　　To turn his hard heart from its ruthless purpose;
　　But if naught can, I beg of thee at least,
　　In the name of all those gods who of our nuptials
　　Were witnesses, and by the holiness
　　Of conjugal love, to save the dignity
　　Belonging to my royal station. I
　　With all the fervor in my power conjure thee
　　Ever to hold in memory what I am
　　To thee. Let not thy wife be led in chains
　　Some day in triumph through the streets of Rome.
　　I speak to thee no longer as I did
　　Yesterday, as the widowed wife of Syphax
　　And subject to thy mandates. Well do I
　　Know that the tie which links our hearts doth fuse
　　Our interests likewise indistinguishably,—
　　That any hurt to me will hurt thee, also,
　　And 'tis o'er both of us that Rome would triumph.
MASINISSA. Too much I love thee and too proud am I
　　To suffer such indignities without
　　Killing myself. But 'twill not come to that.
SOPHONISBA. I know Scipio, how severe he is.

MASINISSA.   I give my word to thee that Rome in no case
 Will e'er behold a captive Sophonisba.
SOPHONISBA.   Thou swearest this to me?
MASINISSA.   I swear this to thee.
SOPHONISBA.   Go, then. My mind hath now been set at rest.

[*Exeunt.*

Scene Two

The larger room. SCIPIO *and* LAELIUS *are discovered.*

SCIPIO.   But thou, who from a long and close acquaintance
 Shouldst best know this inconstant soul, what cure
 Seems to thee surest for his malady?
 Is it compulsion, or is it, rather, kindness;
 And which of these two should I now employ?
LAELIUS.   The one oft loses what the other gains.
 I think the latter will accomplish most.
SCIPIO.   *I* think the former will succeed the better.
LAELIUS.   Yet kindness is the best balm one can use
 To salve the sickness of a noble mind.
SCIPIO.   But when a noble mind is reft of reason,
 This remedy is useless or untimely.
 What Masinissa did is such sheer folly
 That I can scarcely even conceive of it.
 It shows so great derangement of his wits
 That by his blindness he is exculpated.
 Far from supposing we with no great trouble
 Can tear this Paris from his Helen's breast,
 I fear his marriage will augment his frenzy
 And make its error harder to correct;
 And the same mood which prompted such a step
 Will lead him, in his madness, to defend it.
 Herein we see to what extremity
 This fatal love of his would carry him.
  But look: he comes, sad and irresolute.
 Let us try kindness ere we try compulsion.
 I think that meanwhile 'twould be well advised,
 In policy and for our peace of mind,
 To go, thyself, and take the time and trouble
 To see to it that our guards are quietly
 Placed to secure the person of the Queen.

Exit LAELIUS. *Enter* MASINISSA.

36

Well, my dear Masinissa, is there under
The sun a king with happiness like thine?
Good heavens! in the course of one same day
Regain a kingdom and contract a marriage?
For my part, I scarce deem that one unaided
By magic could go further or more nimbly.
Certainly when the story of these marvels
Came to the ears of Laelius and me,
Both of us, moved by the same friendship for thee,
Exclaimed, "Great gods! this is too much by half!"
Truly, thou couldst without harm to thy glory
Have been contented with a single conquest.
'Twas needless to achieve at the same time
Two things so notable and so important.

But this, perhaps, is an unfounded rumor
Which the whole army hath believed too quickly.
I, with my judgment until now suspended,
Will never credit this reported marriage
Till that which fame alleged concerning it
Hath by thine own avowal been confirmed.
Rid us, then, of all doubt, and thyself tell us,
If thou wilt, what the situation is.

MASINISSA.   Common sense would not let me hide from thee
    That which the whole world very soon will know.
Both heaven and earth require me to reveal
A precious secret of which both were witness.
Indeed, I would impose upon thy patience
If I did not speak candidly to thee.

    It is true, Scipio, that Sophonisba
And I have exchanged marriage vows, and we
Are linked together by a bond so sacred
That none could without sin undo its knot.
I plainly see that thy stern soul already
Condemns my love and my impulsiveness—
So much the more as thou hast yet to learn
Love's mastery o'er a heart which it hath conquered.
I would be fortunate in my misfortune,
Had I a judge who once had been in love;
But having instead a Scipio for my judge,
What can I hope for? where will be my refuge?
And of what arguments must I make use
If he knows not the mighty power of love,
Which alone caused my fault and doth excuse it?

And what indulgence can I expect from him
If by his feelings he judges those of others?

SCIPIO. True, I have always kept myself, heart-free,
From falling into the snares that have ensnared thee,
And always I avoided those mad passions
Which lead one on a path opposed to that
Of noble deeds. It is not that my breast
Contains a heart of stone, impenetrable
By any arrows with which love assails it.
The hand that fashioned thine, fashioned mine, too,
And only manhood renders it impervious.
'Tis with this shield one must protect oneself,
And my example should suffice for thee.

Ah, my dear Masinissa, thou shouldst have
Defended thyself better than thou hast.
I know that histories from of old are full
Of the mad loves of some of the best generals;
But where among the most unmeasured of them
Can one be found equal to thine in madness?
Masinissa in one day sees, loves,
And weds. Hath aught so frenzied e'er been told of?
Yet more, his passion hath so blinded reason
In him that he hath climbed into the bed
Of his worst enemy, of Syphax, a tyrant
Who with unrighteous sword usurped the crown
Of his slain father. Surely, if to avenge
Our nearest and dearest we must wed the widows
Of tyrants, thine whose deaths he wrought have all
The satisfaction which they could desire
From such a vengeance.

                          Everyone, 'tis true,
In what concerns him renders an account
Unto himself and does as he may wish,
And therefore thou hast thought it possible
That in this matter all was optional for thee.
But it can hardly be, in my opinion,
That thou wert not mistaken in regard
To that. Perhaps thou thinkest Sophonisba
Is by this marriage thine. Who gave her to thee?
By what authority dost thou take the booty
Which is the property of the Latin empire?
Dost thou not really know what belongs to it
Or that it gave thee back thy heritage?

By whose permission hast thou done this thing?
Nay, our ally, nay, come now to thy senses.
The briefest madness always is the best.
Leave Sophonisba, then; surrender her
At once. 'Tis thus alone thou wilt recover
The honor and the peace which thou hast lost.

MASINISSA. What peace of soul, what honor, can a husband
Have who abandons, O great gods, his wife!

SCIPIO. Thou couldst not wed her; she belonged to us;
Hence all regard this marriage as null and void.

MASINISSA. Both might and right bid me to yield her to you.
She is indeed yours, but I ask her of you.

SCIPIO. I would be guilty of an unpardonable
Crime if I gave thee such a fatal gift.
To accord it unto thee, consumed by passion,
Would be to give the shirt of Nessus to thee.

MASINISSA. If 'tis permitted me to account as gifts
To you my services given from my youth,
And if unto these past ones I may add
All that I fain would do for you hereafter,
I in my misery now conjure thee by them:
Take not the guerdon of my love from me!
Not that my whole life of past services
Hath not already been too well rewarded,
But of what use are honors and possessions
If I am reft of what I prize the most?
I know that when I beg what is denied me
I beg a treasure infinitely precious.
However, 'tis for Rome alone to grant me
A thing which is of value without equal.
Then by these hands I kiss, feet I embrace,
Vouchsafe to me this crowning act of grace.

SCIPIO. Nay, stand up, Masinissa, and remember
To keep unstained the honor of thy station.
Yes, as thy friend who pities thy misfortunes,
I would accord all things, alike, to thee;
But on the other hand, as thy general who
Regrets and blames in thee this frenzy blind,
I say, for the last time, I must refuse thee
That which thine evil genius asks of me.
The reasons why I do this are so weighty
That naught can change this fixed decision, which
The safety of the commonwealth requires.

MASINISSA. O fatal verdict, tyrannous decree!
    Why could my breast, bared to so many blows,
    And my poor body, covered o'er with wounds
    Of which thine own eyes formerly were witness,
    Not win for me a worthier recompense!
    Have men so often seen me, spear in hand,
    Do battle for the greatness of Rome's empire
    To see me beg with tears for what my shed
    Blood and my feats of arms have merited?
    But he who saw them makes so little of them
    That 'tis to be presumed he hath forgot them.
    Look, look, then, on the scars of these old wounds,
    Vain marks of honor graven by the sword!
    Would that ye wounds might be as once ye were
    When ye made this unhappy body fall.
    See if by changing into bleeding mouths
    Ye cannot soften his relentless will.
    O gods! naught moves him! Heart that ne'er hath loved,
    Insensible alike to prayers and pity!
       [He ceases to speak, and walks apart, back and forth in
        silence.

SCIPIO (*to himself*). Let us for awhile leave him, sunk in gloom,
    And then avail ourselves of Laelius' tact.
    Good! he comes seasonably.

Enter LAELIUS.

LAELIUS.   Well, hath he yielded?
SCIPIO. Thou seest how, walking with great strides, he muses.
    Farewell. I now will leave you; try, I pray thee,
    Gently to calm the tempest of his fury.
    Being of violent nature, he could fly
    Into a passion, and I had best not hear him.
                              [Exit SCIPIO.

MASINISSA (*in reverie*). No, I will do nothing about it. All
    Is settled, or sheer power will constrain me.
LAELIUS (*to himself*). These words cut short by his redoubled sighs
    Show that his mind is greatly agitated.
    The tragic thoughts in which I see him plunged
    Increase his frenzy and his gnawing grief,
    So he must speedily be diverted from them.
    But what . . .
MASINISSA.   No, Scipio; I cannot consent.

LAELIUS (*to himself*). The greatness of his grief blinds and deludes
   him.
   (*To* MASINISSA) What, sir! canst thou not tell thy friends
   apart?
MASINISSA (*startled*). Ha! 'Tis true, Laelius, that I thought I spoke
   To that inexorable man.
LAELIUS.   He has just gone.
   He pities thy misfortune.
MASINISSA.   Oh, how absurd!
   He pities my misfortune, and he it is
   Who causes it! How rarely is a true
   Friend found!
LAELIUS.   Believe me, Scipio really loves thee.
   He loves thee, and 'tis in this situation,
   Above all, that his fondness is displayed
   For thy protection. Think, I pray, without
   Losing thy self-control, what is this great
   Treasure of which he wishes to deprive thee?
   It is the widow of a king who oft-times
   During his life sought cruelly to take thine,
   Employing against thee both steel and poison
   After he had destroyed thine entire house.
   As for her, she according to report
   Is a quite lovely thing; but let us see
   Her nature and the harm that she hath done.
   Before the poison of her enchanting glance
   Had ranged old Syphax among those who loved her,
   Was not this king, his perfidy aside,
   The greatest that Numidia e'er had seen?
   And when they were by wedlock's tie united,
   Was e'er calamity equal to his?
   She would not rest until, to gratify
   Her hatred, he deserted mighty Rome
   And by this rashness drove those to destroy him
   Who formerly had been his friends and loved him.
      O thou whose virtues, bravery, and prowess
   Are what we cherish most benevolently,
   Judge whether without grounds we fear today
   That the same reef will shipwreck thee, like him.
MASINISSA. Be absolutely certain, my dear Laelius,
   That of all sins I hate ingratitude
   The most, and that there is no woman's beauty,
   No wedlock's faith, that e'er could alienate me

From you. I am indebted to the Senate
For all I have, and I know how much mightier
The power of Rome is than that of Carthage.
Nay, nay, good friend, assure thou Scipio
Of the sincerity of my devotion.
Tell him that never will this innocent queen
Turn me from friendship with the Roman people,—
That sooner might one take the stars from heaven.
Make him have pity on a wretched lover.
Attempt to soften for me his stony heart.
Thou art my sole hope.

LAELIUS.   I will do my best.

[*Exit* MASINISSA.

(*Alone*) Poor, blinded lover, who dost not realize
That love beguiles thee with its delusive charms,
Truly I pity thee, though in this marriage
Thy wilfulness hath brought thee to this plight.

A C T   V

Scene One

The larger room. MASINISSA *is discovered, alone.*

MASINISSA.   How much the gods, perfect although they are,
Display inconstancy in the gifts they give us!
How easy it is to see from my life's woe
That our prosperity excites their envy
And that they grant no pleasure without pain,
For fear that someone who is wholly happy
Might be like them! Vainly in mortal lives
Will any promise themselves certain bliss
If I today show that the selfsame sun
Which yesterday saw my unmatched good fortune
Can find me now the saddest man on earth
Before its chariot sinks beneath the waves.
    What do the power and name of king avail me
If in my own realm I must obey others?
What do these laurels on my brow avail me
If they cannot ward off the lightning's bolt
With which this deadly foe to love's desires,
This dour nature which itself loves no one
And cannot sanction or suffer love in others,
Is going to blast my honor and my joy?

And what will boldness, what will courage avail me
If in this worst of plights my hands are tied?
    Alas, if as I won by force of arms
This treasure-trove of beauty and of charms,
It likewise could by force of arms be kept,
What would I not do that I might retain it?
Had I to slay Andromeda's dire monster,
My woe would in my strong arm find its cure.
Had I to go among the dead, too, following
The steps of Hercules, to try my prowess
And bring my beloved thence as he did Theseus,
My love would make that task easy for me.
But having to oppose a monster ever
Reborn, a harpy fierce, a ravening eagle
Whose spread wings cover our whole hemisphere,
What could I do? what could I undertake
Not beyond human power and endeavor?
Shall I o'ercome alone the might of Rome—
Alone do what in sixteen years of war
Hannibal could not do on land or sea?
No, no, such thoughts are vain, my Sophonisba.
Our fate is one whereof we are not master.
Mercy, naught else, can make thee mine. Except
For that, my hope hath nothing to sustain it.
    Possibly Laelius hath succeeded better
Than I dare hope . . . O great gods! here he is,
Come to pronounce for me my final sentence.
Up, my heart! arm thyself with fortitude
Against the blow.

Enter LAELIUS.

                        How now, dear Laelius, is it
To death that I must go? Wilt thou announce
My shipwreck or safe harborage to me?
LAELIUS.   Sir, with regret I am the intermediary
And the sad bearer of a grim decree.
I have been charged to tell thee and command thee
To leave, or to hand over, Sophonisba
As an act necessary to the interests
Of the Roman people. Now consider what
Thou wishest to do.
MASINISSA.   I wish to kill myself
And by my death to teach all monarchs never
To follow your ways or governance, cruel men,

Who in the name of public policy
Use with impunity a tyrant's power,
And who, to show ye can do what ye please,
Treat your allies as though they were your foes.
LAELIUS *(to himself)*.   Lct us not answer him, that his passion's flame
May burn out in such transports and his frenzy
Grow less because it hath free utterance.
MASINISSA.   Oh, if the past could be lived o'er again,
I would not let myself serve as the target
Of the severity of your haughty temper,
Proud people, who deem not that ye have triumphed
Till some poor king be crushed beneath his chains.
'Tis for this reason, public be it or private
(For possibly a single man conceived it),
That I, bowing to power, must give up something
Without which I wish naught and hope for naught.
Yes, Laelius, it increaseth a man's glory
That as a slave my wife should walk through Rome
And that, to please his vanity, he should thus
Triumph at once o'er Syphax and o'er me.
O fortunate old king, whose life-thread snapped
Just when he would have fallen into your hands,
And miserable me to learn today
How heavy is your yoke even for the victors!
Then let him seize, carry off, and drag with him
This desolate and pitiable queen.
His triumph must have all embellishments.
I strive no longer—I vainly strove—against it.
Enough! if I can do naught to prevent it,
Let my death save me from that shameful sight.
LAELIUS *(to himself)*.   The violence of his feelings must be pardoned;
But let us speak, now he has given vent to them.
   Sir, wert thou able by the power of curses
To make thy rage and sorrow less intense,
I would advise thee to continue them
Until thy sufferings were diminished by them,
Denouncing before me our empire's yoke.
I would consent, and even declare it worse.
But I cannot permit thee to blame wrongly
A man who pities thee and dearly loves thee,
And whose ambition is not beyond measure
As thou believest in thy blinded soul.
Thou knowest, and time will make thee recollect it,

The reason that forces him to disoblige thee.
I shall not state it; I have already done so.
Therefore, judge better of so fine a man
Than to imagine that from vanity
He wished to treat thee with indignity.
He knows thy brave heart, values it too highly,
Loves thee too much, in short, to seek thy shame.
He wishes thee only to give up her
Who will undo thee if thou dost not undo her,
And since he loves thee and since thou didst wed her,
She will not be led in his triumph.

MASINISSA.   Then
For what does Scipio mean to destine her?

LAELIUS. That is for thee thyself now to divine.
Thou knowest the last orders from the Senate,
According to which, if she were taken prisoner,
It was enjoined expressly on us both
That we should send her, without fail, to Rome.
Consider now if 'tis not thy desire
To save her honor at her life's expense;
And make no more complaint, for, to be frank,
Thy friend, in letting her die, does thee a kindness.

MASINISSA. What kindness, gracious gods!

LAELIUS.   It is the greatest
That he can grant and that the occasion calls for.
Sir, raise again, then, thy sore-stricken spirit,
And make a virtue of necessity.

MASINISSA. Ah me! what virtue could I make of it
Which would not be absurd or ill-becoming?
Wouldst thou fain have me show a placid face?
Shall I still render thanks to the great judge
Whose dreadful sentence brings my fate upon me,
Or shall I kiss the hand that murders me?

LAELIUS. The highest virtue that is asked of thee
Is to endure an ill that pains us all.

MASINISSA (bitterly). I must endure it, for my helplessness . . .

LAELIUS. I mean to say, endure it patiently;
For I have pointed out to thee that thus
Thou wilt achieve a victory o'er thyself;
And Rome, the Senate, and all Italy,
Wherewith thy throne henceforth will be allied,
Will cherish thee still more if for their sake
Thou wilt resign thyself to this misfortune.
Bethink thee, if thou wilt, of thy last conquests,

Thy once precarious state, thy present safety.
Wilt thou not own that thou wouldst be ungrateful
And little or nowise solicitous
For thy realm's good if by some violence
Thou shouldst compel us to abate our kindness
Towards thee? What a calamity for thee
And all the Romans if 'twere necessary
For them to unmake with their own hands their most
Considerable and perfect work! But let us
Assume that in this case the Senate wrongs thee.
What! for one sorrow that it causes thee
Now, will a hundred kindnesses it did thee
Be wasted? Rail not, then, against our ways
Nor governance.
MASINISSA.   O gods, how cruel they are!
Indeed 'tis true: I would be most ungrateful
If I were heedless of the Senate's favors;
But I would be less than a man—a savage—
If I did not quake at the task ye set me.
Let us not talk of that. My choice is made.
It truly must be mine, when it is Rome's.
O wretched husband! O ill-fated wife!
LAELIUS.   Sir, think of her no more.
MASINISSA.   Then tear my heart out;
But that were vain, for I would still think of her
In the midst of hell.

                  Enter CALIODORUS.

LAELIUS (*to himself*).   What would this messenger?
'Tis certainly the Queen who sends him hither.
He must be kept from seeing her again.
CALIODORUS (*to* MASINISSA).   Sire, when thou readest this letter I now
            give thee,
Thou wilt have learned the reason for my coming.
MASINISSA (*taking the letter and reading*).
"If naught can soften the stern hearts of those
Whom by my courage I have made my foes,
Rather than in their triumph be led a slave
I ask the gift thou sworest to let me have."
      Yes, I am now obliged to keep my oath.
I shall bring what I promised, for time presses,
And death alone can end thine evil fortunes.
LAELIUS.   Sir, give it only by another's hand.
      To see her will increase thy grief.

MASINISSA.   No matter.
LAELIUS. Heed me.
MASINISSA.   No, Laelius, I must take it to her.
LAELIUS. Thou shalt not do so. This is wasting time.
MASINISSA. Why?
LAELIUS.   'Tis a thing thou art forbidden to do,
    Lest again seeing her will make worse thy pain.
MASINISSA. I yield, then. Let Fate do its will with me.
        (*To* CALIODORUS)   Observe, my good friend, how with all my
            greatness
        I am not able to behold her face.
        O ye gods! will ye let unrighteous power
    Thus tyrannize so freely o'er your children?
LAELIUS (*to himself*). He, with his violent nature, constantly
    Loses all self-control. He certainly
    Is to be pitied in his blindness. I
    Fear some derangement of his stricken soul.
    See him, there—how he broods!
MASINISSA.   The die is cast.
    This friend will bear to her my fatal gift.
    Come, Laelius, thou shalt see me give it to him.

                                            [*Exeunt.*

Scene Two

The smaller room. SOPHONISBA, PHENICE, *and* CORISBA *are discovered.*

PHENICE. Madam, thy anxious, apprehensive mood
    Is too ingenious in alarming thee.
    The least thing troubles thee: a dream, a shadow,
    A raven that croaketh—all make thee afraid.
SOPHONISBA. Phenice, credit me: I have reached a pass
    Which ought to terrify the stoutest heart.
    The bad thing which awaits me is so monstrous,
    The signs vouchsafed me of it are so portentous,
    And all so clearly indicates my fate
    That thou, who seekest to reassure me, wilt
    Be shocked by them.
                        Thou knowest that yesterday
    Evening, when marriage united us, at two
    Different times the marriage torch went out,
    That on this very morn a stricken ewe
    Escaped from the priest's hands and from the temple,
    And when 'twas brought back for the mortal blow,

Lightning consumed the victim and the altar.
Two ominous birds in the dread hours of darkness
Disturbed my sleep with melancholy cries;
Again on this same morn at about sunrise
A most appalling dream awakened me.
The bleeding figure of the hapless Syphax
With these sad words appeared to me: "Ungrateful
Woman, I come back from eternal night
To tell thee that misfortune still pursues thee.
The righteous anger of a husband flouted
Asks thee of hell, to which thy sin doth call thee.
Farewell; thy sensual desires will bring thee
To shipwreck in the harbor. So I told thee
In life, and now in death I tell thee so."
    Then of a truth did sleep give place to fear;
And I on waking found myself ice-cold
Till in the King's embraces, counterwise,
Fear wrought in me that which love would have wrought.

CORISBA. 'Tis true that these are omens, beyond question,
Which are the harbingers of tragic fortunes;
But may the all-powerful father of the gods
Turn the fulfilment of them on our foes.

SOPHONISBA. What gives me most grounds for anxiety
Is the extreme length of this conference.
The King is taking too long to return
For me now to be able to believe
He won permission to have me as his wife.
    But here that man is from whom I shall learn
Whether life shall be left me or snatched from me.

Enter CALIODORUS, *bearing a letter and a cup.*

CALIODORUS. How sorry I am to be the instrument
Of Fate's fell wrath!

SOPHONISBA.   Come forward without fear.
Show me that letter; give me that cup to drink
By which I shall escape the shame of bondage.
             [*He gives her* MASINISSA's *letter. She reads:*
"Since we must needs obey necessity,
  Accept from me this deadly draft, which is,
  Of all I had, the one thing left me. This
Is the last proof of my true love for thee."
    O gods! with how great joy this gift would fill me
If I could kiss the hand that sends it to me!
Tell me, good Caliodorus, and in naught

Deceive me: hast thou done as thou wert bidden?

CALIODORUS.　Madam, thou wouldst thyself think, hadst thou seen him,
That like his love his sorrow knoweth no bounds.
The hue of death, which o'er his face is spread,
Shows with what agony his soul is wrung.
　　"My friend," he said to me, "go tell thy mistress
That Rome refuses to let her be my wife
And with a kindness that is hard to bear
Supplies the poison which thou wilt offer her.
It brings unto the heart a death so swift
That pain is ended almost instantly."
　　Then he embraced me, and he whispered to me
In order that the Romans might not hear him:
"I swear to her," he said, "that the Fates' hands
Would have put *me* first in the Stygian bark,
Were it not that when I died, our common foes
Would have forgotten what they promised me.
Let her, then, be assured that a death worthy
Of her will show her soon that I am faithful
To her."
　　　　　　　　With these last words he swooned away.

CORISBA.　O wondrous evidence of perfect love!

PHENICE.　O cruel Romans! O relentless heaven!

SOPHONISBA.　Thus is my dreadful dream fulfilled at last.
Ye see now that I was not wrong when I
Applied all those dire omens to myself.
But 'tis as sweet to die as 'tis to live,
Since Masinissa hath sworn to follow me.
　　Show, then, dear husband, thy love's loyalty
And after I am dead wait not a moment.
Yes, I am cruel because too much I love thee!
I fear so greatly that some Roman lady
By the command of Rome, a tyrant to us
Both, might hereafter take my place with thee.
　　I beg of thee, Corisba, and of thee, too,
Phenice, do me a favor ere I die.
Will ye not promise to?

CORISBA.　　　　　　　　Oh, madam, do
But speak. Command us.

SOPHONISBA.　　　　　　　Since ye so prefer it,
I then command you, as your queen and mistress,
To keep so well suppressed the grief ye feel
That ye will by no tears nor cries make less
The honor that should attend a death so noble.

Is it not very greatly to my glory
That though my life hath been obscure, Rome fears me?
Our conquerors are vanquished if we prove
That they dread us much more than we dread them.
Come, then, and let us waste in talk no longer
The time required for deeds of more avail.
Let us free Rome from all the anxiety
And woe that Hasdrubal's daughter might have caused her.
                              [*She drinks the poison in one draft.*
PHENICE.   O gods! Now is it that we are quite undone.
SOPHONISBA.   Certainly, if the Romans could have heard thee,
        They would have reason to think the harm which they
        Did us afflicts us sorely. No, no, let us
        Show them that if they can do nothing worse,
        We have no reason to fear their empire's sway,
        And let us rob them of the joy and pride
        Which would delight them if they knew our sorrow.
            But death will in a brief space close my lips.
        Help me, my children; bear me to my couch;
        And let me at least die in the same bed
        Wherein last night my marriage was consummated.
                                            [*Exeunt.*

Scene Three

The larger room. MASINISSA, SCIPIO, *and* LAELIUS *are discovered.*

SCIPIO (*to* MASINISSA).   The fact is that herein thy fortitude
        Is such that it should crown thee with undying
        Glory. Do not doubt, therefore, that the Senate
        And Rome will recompense thee marvelously
        Some day for thy behavior. Sophonisba
        Is not the only woman in the world.
        There still are others, worthy of thy love,
        And when thy judgment is itself again,
        Then wilt thou bless the evil that befell thee—
        If one can call "evil" a widowerhood
        Which I wished for thee only for thy good.
MASINISSA.   My "good"! O just gods!
SCIPIO.   Thou wilt yet see better
        The reasons why 'twas needful, and my motives.
        Laelius has, I believe, explained them to thee,
        When he discharged the task he undertook;
        But now thy renewed transports make me question

If he could do this or if thou couldst hear him.
LAELIUS (*to* SCIPIO). Sir, his greater self-control and quietness
    Show that his wits have been regained a little,
    Nor do I doubt he will confess, some day,
    That this love would have brought disaster to him,
    And that we wrought for his fair fame alone.
    But thou, too, sir, shouldst put aside these memories,
    Banish these cares, find elsewhere some diversion,
    And unto happier subjects turn thy thoughts.
SCIPIO (*to* MASINISSA). The overthrow of Syphax leaves thee something
    Able to occupy one's entire mind.
    A new realm furnishes a task sufficient
    To need the whole of its king's time and care.
    This is a work so worthy that thy heart,
    Engrossed, will soon be healed of the wound dealt it,
    And Laelius and I shall see thee censure
    Thyself for the blind passion that found voice.
MASINISSA (*aside*). I will outwit you ere this day is over.

Enter CALIODORUS.

CALIODORUS. O courage past belief! O mortal sorrow!
MASINISSA. Ah gods! The Queen is dead.
CALIODORUS.   Yes, sire; 'tis true.
    Alas! no poison ever worked so swiftly.
MASINISSA. Now, then, my masters! seems it good to you
    That, not being able to see her ere her death,
    We should at least have her brought here before us?
    Yes, ye will find the spectacle so sweet—
    It is so vital to your nation's good—
    That I shall gain my prayer.
SCIPIO (*aside to* LAELIUS).   He must be humored.
MASINISSA. Then let us see this treasure of grace and beauty,
    My good friend; let it be brought here at once.
CALIODORUS. If 'tis thy Majesty's wish that thou be shown
    This piteous object, it is here, close by.
    Her chamber door is scarce two paces hence,
    And from this very spot thou canst look on her
    Merely by drawing aside this tapestry.
SCIPIO (*aside to* LAELIUS). I fear that seeing her will wake his frenzy.
             [*The inner chamber is revealed. Exit* CALIODORUS.
MASINISSA. O sad sight: O despair! Behold ye now,
    Thou Roman consul, and thou, too, his lieutenant,
    If I have given you the blind obedience

Which your authority claims of helpless me.
Was I rebellious, think ye, or too slow
In carrying out your ruthless mandate? Leave
Yourselves no grounds for fears or for suspicions.
See that her death is nowise merely feigned.
See how the rose and lily of her coloring
Are overspread by wintry hues of death.
Note well her fast-closed eyes; note everything
So long as ye can harbor any doubt.
But heeding not her eyes or coloring,
Ye need to look at nothing but my sorrow.
Ye need but to observe the grief that wracks me,
To know that Sophonisba now is dead.
   Yes, she is dead, and by her murder I
Have wished to be, myself, quits with your Senate.
If recompense for favors can be measured,
This one act pays with usury that Senate.
By this act, which proclaims your cruelty,
I have put love and beauty in the tomb
That by her death ye might be well assured
Ye have no more to fear nor I to hope.
Tell me no longer, then, I were ungrateful
And little solicitous for my realm's good
If I compelled you by some violence
To abate your kindness to me. For myself
I care henceforth for naught. As for my realm,
I in my grief make you a present of it.
When ye have robbed me of all wish to live,
Neither your gifts nor honors do I covet.
Seize the whole world, from one end to the other;
I ask for none of it, yield it all to you.
Restore to me only the one thing given me
By love, by marriage, and by destiny.
In one word, give me her whom ye all feared,
And I shall be richer than you and happier.
Give me back Sophonisba!

SCIPIO.   Let us leave him,
Laelius. Our presence aggravates his madness.
We see that he has neither knife nor poison.
Let him with his laments assuage his woe.

                        [*Exeunt* SCIPIO *and* LAELIUS.

MASINISSA (*alone*).   O miracle of beauty, Sophonisba,
Soul of my soul, whom still I scarce dare call
By the sweet name of wife, because too briefly

SOPHONISBA

The chaste delights of Hymen and of Juno
Lasted for me to give that name to thee!
Once living source of love and eloquence
Whereon death now hath set the seal of silence,
Fair lips, fair eyes, so full of charm, which I
Saw for too long or else too short a time
For my heart's peace! have ye now lost that magic
Which steals away men's hearts, enchants their ears?
Bright sun, which an unrighteous Senate feared,
Whose sight the Roman eagle could not bear,
Hath all thy radiance therefore become darkness?
Therefore art thou wrapped in eternal shadows
Where death and Fate henceforward shall confound
Thy morn and eve, with nevermore a noon?
Sad bed, proud bed, thou witness in one day
Both of my nuptials and of my bereavement,
Did heaven, determined to undo me, have
To take away so soon the bliss thou gavest me?

   O happiness, snatched hence as soon as tasted,
What has become of thee now, Sophonisba?
But gods! how void of reason is my question,
Since mine own hand furnished her with the poison
Which makes her on that somber shore await me
Whereon my soul shall find her soul again!
'Tis there, cruel Senate, that your haughty mandates
No more will make unhappy monarchs tremble.
A dagger cheats your tyranny despite you
And grants me the heart's ease which ye deny me.

   Yet in my death, ye too ambitious people,
I call the wrath of heaven down upon you.
May ye encounter, be it in peace or war,
Every misfortune on both land and sea,
The Tagus and the Po revolt against you
And take from you the things of which ye robbed them,
Mars make of Rome a second Troy and give
Your wealth as booty to the Carthaginians,
And the last Roman end with his own hand
Before long the existence of his race!

   But to waste time in empty lamentations,
And to indulge one's grief with words, befits
Those base hearts which the hope of being healed
Dominates rather than the wish to die.
Die, hapless prince, and with a bold hand close

SOPHONISBE

The last act of this woeful tragedy!
> [*He draws a dagger concealed under his robe.*

Herein hath Sophonisba gone before thee,
And since thy efforts could not stay her, give
Thyself at least the joy of following her,
And cease to die of grief by ending life.
Show that the sternness of a pitiless Roman
Hath power o'er a lover, but not o'er love.

> [*He kills himself.*

La Mariane
(MARIAMNE)

By
TRISTAN L'HERMITE

INTRODUCTORY NOTE

The poet and dramatist known as Tristan l'Hermite was christened François and took the name of Tristan only when approaching manhood. Of ancient and noble family, he was born about 1601, in the province of Marche, in central France. He became in early childhood a page of Henri de Bourbon, illegitimate son of Henry IV, and was brought up in the royal family. He was throughout his life a dependent of one or another exalted personage, being first and longest a gentleman in attendance upon the Duc d'Orleans, sole brother of Louis XIII, and at a later period in the service of the Duc de Guise. In youth he was something of a scapegrace, and a disastrous passion for gambling never relaxed its hold upon him. Repeatedly he seemed on the point of attaining an assured position and financial security, but in every case some turn of fate, the death or misfortune of a patron, or some indiscretion of his own, dashed his hopes. His poems and plays, however, brought him considerable fame, and he was made a member of the French Academy in 1649. Never robust, and of especially poor health after his very serious illness at the siege of Montauban in 1621, he died of consumption in 1655.

Tristan early displayed a taste for literature and an aptitude for verses. He wrote many amatory and occasional poems, sometimes in his own interests, sometimes for others. Among the contemporaries of Corneille and Racine, he was an honorable second to Rotrou in poetic ability. As a dramatist, his position is unique. He stands with Rotrou and Du Ryer above all the others who wrote during Corneille's youthful prime; but unlike either of these prolific playwrights his dramatic output was small; and whereas they worked along lines in the main similar to Corneille's, it was Tristan who first wrote tragedies of a somewhat different type, with simple rather than complex action, and with characters controlled by the emotions (especially love) rather than by the intellect, and in verse which aimed at smooth beauty rather than rhetorical elevation—and hence he has been called "a precursor of Racine." Moreover, three of his seven or eight plays—three of his five tragedies—anticipate subjects of Racine's: *la Mort de Chrispe* (1644), a poor play, precedes *Phèdre* in treating of a queen's guilty passion for her step-son, who loves someone else; many years before *Britannicus* and *Bajazet*, *la Mort de Sénèque* (1643) and *la Mort du Grand Osman* (1646-7), in both of which excellent and inept work are intermingled, found themes respectively in Nero and his times and in contemporaneous Turkish history. Tristan's departures from the conventions of French-classical tragedy are bolder than Racine's, alike as regards his subordination of incident to the study of character, his realism of utterance, and his concern for "local color." He had very little ability in plot-construction, however, and hence and because of his emotional power and his interest and skill in characterization and his mingling of good work and bad it will be observed that he has something of the excellences and defects of an Elizabethan dramatist. He was in England for several months in 1634, and also perhaps in his youth; no one has ever suggested that he made any acquaintance with English drama then, but if he did so, it would explain much.

His best play was his first. Based as it was on a tragedy of Alexandre Hardy's by the same name, which itself was of considerable merit, Tristan's *Mariamne*—or, more properly, *"la Mariane,"* as it was originally called—had no chance to be spoiled by its author's weakness at plotting. This drama appeared in 1636, several months before the *Cid,* and, largely because of the brilliant creation of the role of Herod by the great actor Montdory, enjoyed a sensational success which even that of Corneille's masterpiece could not eclipse. Like the *Cid* and *Sophonisbe,* it was written before the old "multiple stage," with several different settings for changes of scene, was replaced by the single "set" used on the later French-classical stage. Its fifth act, occupied almost entirely with Herod's mourning, is the last reminiscence of the concept of tragedy which had been held in sixteenth-century France: that a tragedy was not the depiction of a disaster, but mainly a rhetorical lament over a disaster which takes place at or near the beginning of the play.

Certain weak details in *la Mariane,* such as the failure to explain how its heroine really happened to learn of Herod's secret orders for her to be killed in case of his death, and the suddenness of his jealous convictions, are also a result of its early date, when dramatic technique had not yet been mastered. But it continued to hold the stage throughout the seventeenth century and to be considered a very notable play; "and, indeed," says H. C. Lancaster, "it deserved to be so considered, for it placed the struggle within the soul of the leading person and emphasized the study of passion, thus preparing the way both for Corneille and for Racine." [1]

The story of Herod and Mariamne, told by Josephus, has been the theme of many dramas. Incomparably the finest of them is Friedrich Hebbel's *Herodes und Mariamne* (1848).

[1] *A History of French Dramatic Literature in the Seventeenth Century*, Part II, Baltimore, 1932, p. 55.

CHARACTERS IN THE PLAY

HEROD, *King of Judea.*
MARIAMNE, *his wife.*
PHERORAS, *brother of Herod.*
SALOME, *his sister.*
ALEXANDRA, *mother of Mariamne.*
THARES, *captain of the guard.*
DINAH, *maid of honor to Mariamne.*
NARBAL, *a nobleman of the Court of Herod.*
SOHEMUS, *a minion of Herod.*
Gentleman in attendance upon Alexandra.
Cup-Bearer of Herod.
A Eunuch.
Two Judges.
The Grand Provost.
The Keeper of the Prison.
An Usher.
Guards, etc.

The scene is laid in Jerusalem.

The names "Pheroras," "Sohemus," and "Hyrcanus" are accented on the second syllable. In "Hasmonean" the accent is on the first and third syllables, in "Malichus" on the first syllable.

Mariamne

ACT I

The scene represents a room in the palace of HEROD. *King*
HEROD *is discovered on a couch, asleep.*

HEROD *(awakening with a start).* Malignant ghost who troublest
    my repose,
No further speak thy contumelious words!
Go into night eternal, envious shade,
And do not thus intrude to asperse my life.
I am enough aware of how to reign well
Without thy coming in vain wrath to teach me,
And I have made mine empire much too strong
To dread the woes thou comest to predict.
I shall guard well against all accidents
Which, because unforeseen, destroy the unwary.
  But lo, my brow is damp, and I am breathless.
My spirit has found it in this sleep so hard
To disabuse itself of vexing errors
That I am deeply stirred with rage and horror.
Ho, there!

Enter THARES *and* PHERORAS.

THARES.   What wouldst thou, sire?
HEROD.   Ah, 'tis Pheroras.
PHERORAS.   I had been told that thou wert still asleep.
HEROD.   Thou must have heard me when I spoke so loudly.
Just now I was awakened with a start
By the most dolorous and dreadful vision
That could forebode a tragic accident.
PHERORAS.   And have the blackest dreams which possibly
Can be invented, power enough to daunt thee—
Thee who canst overwhelming strength defy
And who so little fearest genuine dangers?
Visions like these never have consequences.
HEROD.   My soul is shaken by the dreams I wove.
Therefrom comes ever an unwelcome thought
Which only can forewarn me of misfortune:
It is the presage of some adverse thing.
PHERORAS.   This ought not to be deemed inevitable.
Such apparitions are like shapes of cloud;

A darkling picture 'tis, of men and beasts,
Which makes nor good nor evil come to pass.

HEROD (*to himself*). When thou wert snatched from us by hostile
    Fate,
My noble elder brother, brave and loyal,
I learned of thy mishap by the same means;
Just in this way was I warned of thy death.
Upon the Jordan's banks I had cruel visions
Which came ere the report of this sad news.

PHERORAS. For my part, I have often noticed dreams
Without their presage ever being fulfilled;
And as I heard a Rabbi say, one day,
The best way is to expect naught from them.

HEROD. What learnèd reasons did this Doctor give
Who holds that every dream is but a lie?

PHERORAS. He said the humour regnant in our bodies
Inclines us, sleeping, to see certain objects.
Phlegm, which is moist and cold, mounts to the brain,
And thereto representeth mist and water;
Bile, yellow and burning, subtle in its nature,
Depicteth naught but towns ablaze and battles;
Blood, which contains air and which hears spring's call,
Makes the least fortunate have pleasant dreams;
Its exhalation sweet forms only roses,
Objects of cheer, and things agreeable;
And melancholy with its vapors black,
Where fear and sadness dwell perpetually,
Which can show naught but somber images,
Makes us see specters, sepulchers, and shadows.
'Tis thus that each of us can find in sleep
Secret evidence of his temperament.

HEROD. Thus one ought to dream always the same thing.

PHERORAS. Our dreams proceed sometimes from other causes.
Just as some of them represent our humours,
Others quite often show our character.
A man with noble soul, even in repose,
Disdaineth Fortune, maketh his goal honor.
A thief, anticipating what awaits him,
Encounters officers or gets some booty.
Likewise the usurer in sleep goes over
With eyes and hands the money which he hoards;
The lover, biased by his fears or wishes,
Suffers from harshness or doth taste delights.

HEROD. Such explanations scarcely satisfy me.

MARIAMNE

These well-known principles result in little.
Thou thyself knowest that Egypt saw aforetime,
In the momentous dreams interpreted
By Joseph, some with image blithe or ominous
Announcing benison or heaven's wrath.

Enter SALOME *and* SOHEMUS.

Howe'er that be, Pheroras, hearken to mine,
No matter what it augers, good or evil.
SALOME. Does it please thee that I, too, should hear this dream,
Which is, when all is said, but a vain picture—
But a confused enigma traced in sand?
HEROD. Then do not interrupt when I begin.
    The light and sounds of dawn spread o'er the world
And when the sun which riseth from the billows
Raises light vapors to the brain and causes
Those dreams that are most vivid and least false,
After a thousand obstacles of some sort,
Pointless encounters and chimeras vain,
I found myself alone in lonely woods
Where horror neighbored with obscurity,
When through the shadows came a plaintive voice
Which in most dolorous tones cried: "Mariamne!"
    I hastened towards the spot whence came the noise,
Following most fain the love which guided me
And even seemed to have lent me wings that I
Might sooner reach that miracle of beauty.
    To a pool's bank at length my footsteps led me,
Whereof I found the water red with blood.
There came from overhead a peal of thunder;
I felt the solid earth shake 'neath my feet;
And on this shore environed with affright
Mine eyes beheld the young Aristobulus.
SALOME. Ah, heavens! I would, if thou, have died of fear.
My blood at this tale freezes in my veins.
PHERORAS. I feel the same horror through all my bones.
HEROD. Then hearken to the rest, and let me speak.
He now had no tiara on his head
As in the solemn days of our great feast,
When, too resplendent in his rich attire,
He made the Jews declare outspokenly
That such a glorious and noble person
Deserved to wear the mitre and the crown.
I recognized him only by his voice;

He seemed but freshly taken from the billows,
His body swollen with water he had swallowed,
His hair, all dank, fallen o'er his countenance;
The waves had quenched the light within his eyes,
Which he in death had lifted to the skies;
It seemed the effort of a cruel struggle
Had left its horror painted on his face,
And that with dark blood this was covered over,
And that his mouth, though open, lacked life's breath.
    His words were insults from the very first,
Mortal reproaches, but all full of fraud.
He launched against me many imprecations—
Yes, went so far as to heap curses on me—
Spoke to me of my harsh course towards his father,
Charged me with all the woes of our past wars.
In short, I saw that he had grown rebellious,
And finally lifted up mine arm to strike him;
But when I thought thus to requite his insults,
I found but air and not his face before me,
So that, o'erwrought with violence and horror,
I woke with a loud cry. That was my dream;
Well, then, how seemeth it to thee, Salome?
What sayest thou?

SALOME.   I? I say it makes me tremble.
PHERORAS. I shall not hide the fact it frightens me.
SALOME. It is some warning sent to thee by heaven.
HEROD. The warning is so hard, though, to decipher
    That it could not have troubled me more vainly.
SALOME. Perhaps the State is threatened with some change.
HEROD. What Fate hath written cannot be erased;
    Willing or not, the resolute soul must needs
    Do that which its omnipotence hath bidden.
    One cannot 'scape from out its secret toils;
    We run into them straighter, trying to shun them.
    The man whom Destiny hath made to prosper
    Is like the ship saved from a hundred storms,
    Which, subject still to the caprice of chance,
    May founder in the roadstead or the port.
    But who can daunt me? What more need I fear,
    Having attained to such a peak of fortune?
    Nothing hath power enough now to destroy me
    Unless the sky falls, crushing me beneath it.
    I can succumb only in some disaster
    Whose stroke will overwhelm the universe.

The Hasmoneans all are in the grave,
And a new monarch is seen on the throne,
Who 'neath his laurels keeps his crown and head
Forever sheltered from the tempest's fury.
    I well know what support Augustus promised,
Wishing to number me among his friends,
And I am in such favor with his Genius
That it assures me against calumny.
Those whom he loves the best among his courtiers
Prize quite as much my merits as my gifts;
And I have many secret reasons why
The Jordan need not fear the Tiber's wrath.
    To flout misfortune on all other sides,
I am enough supplied with strength and courage.
Let Parthia, Arabia, and Armenia
All threaten my frontiers with thirty legions;
With a swift army I shall go to meet them
And make their plans miscarry to their shame.
I shall pursue them into their own land,
Humiliating them by such invasion,
Till they accept my terms of peace, confessing
That 'tis not profitable to attack me.

SALOME.   The kings that neighbor thee know well thy valor
They have made trial of it from thy youth.
They will incline an ear to better counsels,
And their ambition will choose other courses.

HEROD.   Not fifteen years were mine when I took arms
And went to seek out death 'mid war's alarums,
And since that time, my hand with many a deed
Hath subdued nations and made kings bend low.
    What combats I have fought, what battles won!
What fortresses surprised and ramparts carried!
Upon a spacious plain, when Ceres' harvest
Enriched the plowlands with its golden blades,
One scarce hath seen more of dense swathes than I
Have seen opposed to me of bristling spears
Which flew in splinters everywhere I smote
In the fierce ardor wherewith I did reap them.

PHERORAS.   Thy gallant exploits find no parallel.
Julius, whate'er men say, helped more by heaven
And with less combats and less varied labors,
Made himself hailed the master of the world.
Thou hast surmounted many obstacles
And all thy life is full of miracles.

HEROD. In my position I would be too happy,
If I were not afflicted with love's tortures,
With love's perpetual flame, fierce beyond measure,
Which keeps my soul incessantly in torment;
Or if I could prevail against a coldness
That checks the even flow of my success.
    Imperfect happiness! Untimely harshness!
I have for my companions Love and Fortune:
They never leave me; they attend my steps;
But one is kindly to me, and one not.
One makes me ruler now o'er a whole nation;
And one denies to me a heart I sue for,
A heart o'er which I cannot gain dominion
Though I possess the body that it beats in.
    Blind deities, dispense more equal favors;
Vouchsafe me fewer laurels and more roses;
Let me have more joy, and be less renowned,—
Be not so much feared, and be loved the more.
    It is with reason that my mood is somber:
My glory is but a dream, my pomp a shadow,
If, when the whole world fears the might thereof,
I burn with a desire still unappeased.

SALOME. Since Mariamne in thy bed is entered
And so assiduously is made an idol,
Thy house is opened to continual sorrows;
Ye both are seen but tearful and complaining.

HEROD. My plaints are always juster than her tears.
Why showeth she so many charms to me,
So many virtues, such divine attractions,
To share my couch and still to love me not?
Can two parts of one whole accord so ill,—
One whole be made of parts so contrary,—
I feel so keenly and she feel so little,—
Her heart be frozen and my heart all flame?

PHERORAS. After thou hast acquired thy fame in war,
Which makes thee envied to the ends of the earth,
In peace thou yieldest to invisible blows
And 'tis thy wish that all should pity thee.

HEROD. Great men have had the fault that I am charged with,
Alike in centuries past and in our times.
Love is so fatal to the highest worth
That from its woes no hero is exempt.
He who derived his great strength from his hair
Could nowise turn from that beguilement sweet,

And the young shepherd who became a great king
Was in his latest years more mad than I.
Antony failed in manhood 'neath this yoke
And was by less refulgence blinded more,—
To follow Cleopatra renounced fortune
And sailing thus, made shipwreck of his honor.
All *my* intent is without shame or crime;
The flames consuming me are lawful flames;
I wish for naught for which I can be censured;
For I love only her whom I should love.

PHERORAS.   If in the raptures of your wedded love
The ardor of the Queen and thee were equal,
Who would be able to condemn thy feelings
Or would desire to oppose this heat of passion?
But lo, thy reason is in truth asleep.
Thou takest pride in loving an enemy
Who, to requite thee for thy tenderness,
Applies her mind only to slander thee.

SALOME.   This error verily deserves reproaches.
What pleasure dost thou find in cherishing
A rock, a source of ever-flowing tears,
And one wherein thy love awakes no feeling?

HEROD.   If that divinest object of my worship
Is but a rock, that rock is alabaster,
A reef delectable, where one sees gleaming
All that which nature fashions to attract me.
No rubies are so crimson as her lips,
Which scent like ambergris whate'er they touch.
Her eyes so brightly shine that, in my judgment,
They must be ranked at least as bright as diamonds.

PHERORAS.   That loveliness, though, ought to be disdained
Which is not joined with excellence of soul.

HEROD.   All of her coldness springs from purity,
But she is kind despite her haughty temper.
When Parthia took Hyrcanus and Phaselles,
I owed my own escape to her leal counsels.
Without this clear sign of her secret love
I would have lost at once both crown and life;
Yea, 'twould have meant my death, and false Antigonus
Would on my corpse have mounted to my throne.
    My obligation to her moves me deeply
And makes me easily pardon her disdain.
I see great hauteur in her divine beauty,
But rarely are there roses without thorns.

And then it is quite right, to tell the truth,
She should keep some formality between us:
Her ancestors are many glorious kings;
She might be called the daughter of our masters.

SALOME. And so she acts. All in the palace know
She speaks of us as though we were her servants;
And therefore still must we do naught but smile
However many things one comes to tell us
Wherein her heart, ungrateful, fervently
Declareth against thee her black intent.

HEROD. We are not able, with propriety,
To put such faith in the reports of servants;
Just as self-interest makes them flatterers,
Our easy credence can make liars of them,
And lying is indeed common enough
To petty folk whose souls are mercenary.

SALOME. My folk have neither heart nor wit to invent
All that they come to tell me of the Queen.

HEROD. Acquaint us with the nature of these outbursts.

SALOME. She speaks of thee in an insulting manner
Which is too horrible to be revealed
And yet which 'twould be criminal to hide from thee;
Calls thee at each breath author of her woes,
The land's oppressor, murderer of her sires,
And feeds her anger with a thousand reasons
To make the populace revolt against thee.

HEROD. Judea today, submissive to my yoke,
Finds happiness only in its obedience.
It cannot be stirred up so easily.
And I will not believe all this so lightly.
I know Mariamne—know she is too wise
Thus to lose self-control and use this language.
If great folk hearkened to all things that are told them,
Imposture would have too much power with them,
Within the Court would ceaseless strife be seen,
And a new household needs be found each day.

PHERORAS. Touching the present matter, to act wisely,
Thou needst not believe all nor neglect aught.

HEROD. I soon shall see her, indiscreet but lovely.
I shall reproach her for these secret insults;
And yet her mouth, with but a single kiss,
Though she had uttered them, will atone for all.
Hark to one word, Sohemus.

[*He whispers in* SOHEMUS' *ear.*]

SALOME (*aside to* PHERORAS).   Unheard-of weakness!
　　　He is bewitched; the spell is all too plain,
　　　But we must set ourselves to act adroitly
　　　To dissipate the power of this enchantment.
PHERORAS.　Madam, his love is verily a sickness
　　　For which the remedy required is time.
　　　Today our counsel is not seasonable.
　　　His malady's poison makes him deaf to reason.
HEROD (*having finished whispering, aloud to* SOHEMUS).
　　　Observe well, in delivering this message,
　　　Above all both her voice and her expression—
　　　If she grows pale of hue, or flushes crimson.
　　　I will hear her answer when I leave the council.

ACT II

Scene One

The scene represents the Queen's apartments. MARIAMNE *and*
DINAH *are discovered.*

MARIAMNE.　I would accept thy counsel, were it reasonable.
　　　But what! wouldst thou that I should love a monster
　　　Who comes to me wet with my kindred's blood?
DINAH.　Pretend to love him, if thou lovest him not.
　　　Thou oughtest in this case to constrain thyself.
　　　To feign well is an art most excellent
　　　When one is driven to the extremity
　　　Of being unable to act as one may wish.
MARIAMNE.　I? I constrain myself? though of a birth
　　　Which without danger can use every license,
　　　And which without abuse of this authority
　　　Rules my desires only as honor bids?
　　　My heart belie itself and find a merit
　　　In pleasing a Scythian's, a barbarian's heart—
　　　My kindred's murderer?
DINAH.　　　　　　　Speak lower, madam!
MARIAMNE.　If this my body is captive, yet my soul
　　　Is not! I leave constraint to servile folk.
　　　I come of sires too many who wore crowns
　　　To have my thoughts and visage ill accord
　　　And to become a slave to please a tyrant.
　　　Let Herod trouble me with love or hate,
　　　Thou'lt ever see me live and die a queen.
DINAH.　Madam, the whole palace is full of spies,

Who night and day watch thee at every turn.
For some time since, Salome hath kept paid
For this task certain of the maids and pages;
Ever they come to listen at thy door
For all thy words, which they report to her.
MARIAMNE.   No matter; let them listen at their pleasure.
They shall hear naught that will be pleasing to them.
DINAH.   Hath the King done some new thing which doth vex thee,
To cause the scorn which thou hast for him now?
MARIAMNE.   What! canst thou think the tragic history
Of my dear kindred is forgot by me?
Ever the aged Hyrcanus and my brother,
Both murdered, come to afflict me with sad cries.
Be it when I sleep or be it when I wake,
Their plaint resoundeth ever in mine ears.
They ever stand before my tearful eyes;
I see them, all blood-boltered and disfigured;
They come to me to tell their piteous fortunes;
They come to me to show their mortal wounds,
And seek to crown my woes with their reproaches
That every night I sleep beside their murderer.
     This miscreant must encompass my destruction.
He hates all of my blood, hates all my race.
He is not satisfied with having slaughtered
A venerable old man, a holy priest,
Who lent to him his power and his alliance,
Placing full confidence in his support,
Nor yet with having snuffed out in strange fashion
His innocent brother-in-law, a winsome boy,
The young Aristobulus—oh, when I
Think of it, grief destroys my self-control,
My heart so chokes me that I cannot speak,
And my sad soul is ready to take flight.
     He scarcely had attained his eighteenth year
And something notable was apparent in him.
His charm, his comeliness, his speech, his bearing,
Ravished the hearts of all at the first sight.
He had my hair; he had my features—was
The picture of me, as I the image of him;
Heaven had placed within his soul those treasures
Which corresponded with so fair a body,
And on this youth the grace of God had fallen
To enhance the honor of the Maccabees.
The man who bore our portraits to the Nile

Declared, quite rapturous o'er his loveliness,
That here in Palestine a man was hailed
Peer of the gods who are adored in Rome.
The people who beheld him in the Temple,
Enchanted, marveling at his aspect, blessed him
Aloud, and this cruel tyrant felt such envy
That he cut short the fair thread of his life.
This bright ascending sun which the Court worshipped
Was, like the day-star, plunged beneath the wave,
But did not rise again in pristine beauty,
For 'twas drawn thence death-darkened evermore.
    And, after that, shall I caress the monster
Who has just robbed my closest kin of life?
Sooner let fire consume me, or let water,
Its opposite, make my brother's fate be mine!

DINAH.   All these strokes of misfortune, now quite past,
Ought to be blotted from thy memory.
Must this sad picture needs at every word
Renew for an old injury thy weeping?
Needs must thy spirit in thy fairest years
Wander so sadly in the midst of tombs?
Madam, give over all such thoughts as these.
Thy heavenly beauty is affected by them.
Thy face, which rivaleth the loveliest flowers
Hath been made wet too long by streams of tears.
Time and good sense beyond all question urge thee
To banish woe that will cut short thy days.
Wrongs have been done thee, but, to speak quite frankly,
Much care is taken to console thee for them.

MARIAMNE.   How?

DINAH.   The King loves thee.

MARIAMNE.   Loves me? Oh, thy folly!

DINAH.   He sighs continually when thou art absent.
He names thee every hour, counts all thy steps.
Is this not love?

MARIAMNE.   What! art thou ignorant
That his false heart is full of artifices;
That my destruction hangs on his mere whim;
That, if he thought he ran the smallest risk,
He would at once command that I be slain?
Such is the chief care of this ardent love,
And 'twas this charge he laid upon Sohemus
When he set forth, full sore afraid, for Rhodes—
If he should find the death there he deserved.

DINAH. That act was truly cruel and tyrannous.
    I ask no more what hath offended thee.
    The inhuman mandate of this jealous spirit
    Shows that he loves himself much more than thee.
    But since thou hast survived that deadly peril,
    As thou dost love thyself better than him,
    Feign. Thou wilt some day see thy precious children
    With crowns upon their heads, happy and prosperous,—
    That is, if by behaving badly towards him
    Thou dost not wreck, with thy disdain, their fortune.
    Cast not aside the care which should preserve them.
    The King awaits thee; thou must go and see him.

> SALOME *appears at the door of the room.*

MARIAMNE. I will go; but 'twill be to make known to him
    That he is a foul murderer, villain, traitor,
    And that I recognize no law nor duty
    Which can oblige me henceforth to behold him.
    My mind is made up.
DINAH.   Heavens! My whole body
    Trembles.
MARIAMNE.   Why?
DINAH.   All is lost. Salome heard us.
    How I loathe these malicious, prying natures!

> [*Exit* DINAH, *hastily.*

MARIAMNE (*to* SALOME). Come nearer to us. Thou wilt hear us better.
SALOME. I was about to go, thinking my presence
    Unwelcome, for it seemed that thou wert angry.
MARIAMNE. By righteous wrath my words were animated.
SALOME. Wrath is a passion which inspires thee always.
MARIAMNE. And always do I bear uncommon hardships.
SALOME. Thou hast some woes better than thy deserts.
MARIAMNE. I think that naught appears in my behavior
    Which can deserve the ill treatment I receive.
SALOME. Oh, yes! thy lot is greatly to be pitied;
    But others, also fair, are ill contented.
MARIAMNE. Naught hast thou in *thy* lot which is not good.
SALOME. Of *thy* ills thou art conscious; I am of mine.
MARIAMNE. Is thy proud soul dissatisfied with thy fortunes?
SALOME. Other and many things there are to vex me.
    But when I came, what saidst thou of the King?
MARIAMNE. I complained of him, as he does of me.
SALOME. I cannot guess thy great cause for complaint.
MARIAMNE. 'Tis that his spies impose on me constraint.

SALOME. Innocence never feareth witnesses.

MARIAMNE. More peace were mine if they intruded less.

SALOME. Thou shouldst inform the King how this doth vex thee.

MARIAMNE. Thou shouldst inform him also of his weakness.

SALOME. If he hath any weakness, as thou thinkest,
It scarce appeareth in the course he steers.

MARIAMNE. The sad estate to which I am reduced
Is the most striking consequence of that course.

SALOME. Thou wouldst remark less imperfection in it
If thou hadst not so much aversion for him.

MARIAMNE. I have hate only for his fearful guilt.
All upright folk have the same feeling towards him.

SALOME. If so, they speak in very low tones of it.

MARIAMNE. Because they fear death; and I do not fear it.

SALOME. Thou goest too far, a trifle; for thou shouldst,
Meseemeth, respect more the tie which binds you.

MARIAMNE. I know quite well enough the respect owed
To him; I am not ignorant whence ye sprang.

SALOME. But I am ignorant whence this hate thou showest
Springs.

MARIAMNE. My ill feelings do not concern thee.

SALOME. And yet, if there had grown some breech between you,
About this matter I would offer thee
Myself and my most humble services.

MARIAMNE. Good offices enough thou always doest me.

SALOME. I do far less of them than thou deservest.

MARIAMNE. Heaven will take note of thy kindly acts.

SALOME. The honor of serving thee too much repays me.

MARIAMNE. Each of us knows well what she thinks of this.

SALOME. Thou goest to see the King?

MARIAMNE.   Yes, I go thither
To have speech with him which will please him not.

SALOME. Thou wilt say naught to him which can displease him.
He loves thee wholly—even thy very anger.

MARIAMNE. And I, whom he hath made a thing for pity—
I hate him wholly, even his affection.   [*Exit* MARIAMNE.

SALOME (*alone*). Haughty and scornful woman, dauntless-hearted,
Do not imagine that I have no feelings.
Nay, nay, I am not one of those base spirits
Who find it easy to endure a slight.
Remember that I ne'er receive an insult
Which I do not repay with interest soon.
Salome knows full well how to show kindness,
But is not ignorant of the art of vengeance.

We have not long to suffer her caprices.
My scheme is death to all her artifices.
I won, a short time since, the first Cup-Bearer,
Who must against her cast the shaft I fashioned,
A black shaft, which, freighted with fear and sorrow,
Shall give a credulous heart a mortal wound,
Confuse its feelings, and cause ardent love
To change in an instant to a burst of rage.
   This man is a fit tool; he is my creature,
And gladly puts his life in hazard for me.
Quickly must this good plan be carried out
That on his breast the secret may not weigh
Nor he go warn a third who might betray us
Nor, pondering it too much, himself grow cold.
But do I not behold him coming hither?
Already in this design fear masters him;
He wears a gloomy sadness on his brow.

Enter the Cup-Bearer.

THE CUP-BEARER. May I say one word more unto thy Highness
    About the carrying out of thy command?
SALOME. Yes, I shall listen to thee. Speak, then, boldly.
THE CUP-BEARER. Madam, in serving thee I challenge tortures;
    I walk where on each side are precipices,
    Along a slippery path where one false step
    Will surely make my destination death.
    The King need have only a single thought
    To light again the flame of his past love;
    One sweet remembrance of his fond affection,
    A glance full laden with the darts of pity,
    The least emotion which may waken in him,
    A tear, a sigh, will smite me and o'erthrow me.
    I see a thousand dangers; but I flout them
    All, for my blind obedience is thine,
    And thou assurest me, too, that by this work
    I risk death for myself to save my country.
SALOME. If thy shut eyes express to me thy faith,
    With open hand I would most fain requite thee.
    Thou wilt both make thy fortune and win glory
    Which equaleth the honor of a victory.
    Thou savest thy sovereign from a dire mishap;
    Thou keepest all of us from certain shipwreck;
    And in this project into which I lead thee
    Light is the labor, weighty the reward.

Thou undertakest this task by my commission;
Thou doest thy part therein vouched for by me.
'Tis I who bring thee forward, who stand thy surety,
Who shall set going and impel the wheel.
Thou knowest well the King gives credence quickly
And that he hath a mind which I can mould.
Thy story will surprise a soul distrustful,
Credulous, prone to rage, and most impatient.
Thus wrought upon, if thou wilt do thy duty,
He shall gulp down the hook without perceiving it.
The snare is subtle which I set to catch him,
Nor will the power be his to guard against it.
 Then for thy surety thou shalt be informed
That Mariamne works for us, herself.
Her heart, filled with the venom of new anger,
Aids us in our conspiracy against her.
E'en now she briefly gave me to understand
That she was going to the King, to flout him.
Thou know'st in what way he endures an insult;
Then make it serve thee well in this connection.
All smiles on our designs; all meets our wishes.
The time is fitting; seize it by the forelock.
THE CUP-BEARER. These cogent arguments would make assured
The soul most timid and most wavering.
But since thy Highness and the heavens have wished it,
My heart is quite resolved about this matter.
All that restrains me is that I shall stand
Before a great prince and a mighty ruler
Who knows what one would fain say, ere one says it,
And who can recognize a trickster's heart.
 Madam, be pleased to inform me in a few words
Of the best way in which I can beguile him.
Vouchsafe for my behavior some small lessons
That my attempt may have a happy outcome.
SALOME. 'Tis needful in thy story that with great skill
Thou, to deceive him best, deceive thyself, too.
Imagine the whole thing with artless thoughts
As if in very truth it had occurred;
Then, having stamped this picture on thy brain,
Let tongue and visage act accordingly.
 I cannot give thee any better lesson
Than: always tell the thing in the same way;
Believe, thyself, the horror thou'dst make believed;
And when thou speakest, take care thy memory fail not.

Use words like these: "My lord, from time to time
The Queen has asked me touching a love philter
Which she would like to mix in what thou drinkest,
That thus thou mightest be made to love her more;
But well I knew how much thou dotedst on her.
I found this philter of obnoxious odor;
And marked, while she solicited me about it,
That she was ill at ease and seemed confused;
Hence, being moved by zeal and loyalty,
I come to inform thy Majesty thereof,
That, lest she might employ some other agent,
Thou mayest be forewarned 'gainst evil chance."

THE CUP-BEARER.   I deem these words most suitable to move him,
And I hope, madam, in this to do my duty.
SALOME.   The Queen will have retired, now, to her suite.
Bear, then, this message with a voice assured,
And thou shalt find me present. Wilt thou do it?
THE CUP-BEARER.   Yes, madam, though I should meet death thereby.
[*Exeunt* SALOME *and the Cup-Bearer, severally.*

Scene Two

The scene represents another room in the palace. Enter HEROD
driving out MARIAMNE.

HEROD.   Go; go; I mean to keep the oath thou heardest.
Go quickly from my chamber; come no more there.
A heart inexorable when I beseech thee?
Ingrate, my love is turned to savage fury,
And henceforth all its shafts, plucked from my heart,
Shall become serpents to requite thy cruelty.
Thy scorn reveals to me a wish for vengeance,
Which I intend to watch most carefully.
Henceforth all things thou doest shall be suspect—
No more indulgence from me nor respect!—
And if thou ever shouldst in this black mood
Launch a dart at me sullying my fair fame,
I shall repel it so that all may know
That one must not lack reverence for one's king.

Enter SALOME. *Exit* MARIAMNE.

SALOME.   What is the cause that stirs thee so to anger?
HEROD.   The one that ever gives me naught but woe.
SALOME.   It is perhaps the Queen, then, with her cruelty,

For those harsh ways of hers are nowise new.

HEROD.   Thou hast guessed well; yes, 'tis that heartless woman—
The last affront that I will bear from her.

SALOME.   Thou wilt say that afresh still, every day.

HEROD.   Nay, her disdain hath quite destroyed my love.
I hate her now, even as the pestilence,
Finding that she is heaven's scourge for me.

SALOME.   May I know what infuriates thee so?

HEROD.   I mean to tell thee. Do but seat thyself.
Most fain to see her, not without impatience,
I had called for her with great urgency,
When she, ungrateful, deeming it compulsion,
Obeyed me only so as to offend me.
In vain I treated her with all the address
With which a perfect lover wins his mistress;
For, striving fruitlessly, despite my pains,
I ever found my deference roused her scorn.
My whole love hath availed but to displease her;
Her eyes blazed with a hate that had no warrant;
And in her exhibition of cruel frenzy
She hath said such opprobrious things to me
That, being unable to endure their insult,
I drove her from me forcibly at last.
That is what angers and disturbs me so.
Such is her madness. Tell me if I am wrong.

SALOME.   Yes, thou art wrong, and her ingratitude
Was sure to afflict thee with yet crueler treatment,
Since, without fear of dangerous consequences,
Thou angerest her unceasingly with kindness.
She is a monster of most thankless pride,
To whom thy graciousness gives too free rein.
If heaven's favor averts not the shafts,
Her malice finally will make away with thee.

HEROD.   Being so well informed of her ill will,
I can prevent attempts upon my life.

SALOME.   I have my doubts. Our sex is most vindictive
And fertile of device when turned to treachery.
The tigress that beholds her young borne off
Should less be dreaded than an angry woman.
Prithee note how, rightly afraid for thee,
I speak against my sex for thy protection.

HEROD.   So many watchers shall I set around her
That her offended spirit, after this quarrel,
Will have no means for taking any course

Without my being advised of it at once.
She had best always keep her lips closed tightly;
Else . . .

Enter an Usher. He advances.

What is this?

SALOME.   He comes to tell thee something.

Enter the Cup-Bearer and THARES.

THE USHER.   One of thy cup-bearers, stopped at the door,
    Desires to have speech with thy Majesty,
    Protesting that it is a weighty matter
    Concerning which he should inform thee promptly.

HEROD.   A weighty matter? Well, let him approach.
    What may this matter be?

SALOME.   I cannot guess.

HEROD.   He is speechless.
    (*To the Cup-Bearer*)   What hast thou to tell me of?

THE CUP-BEARER.   A plot against thee and thy kingdom, too.

HEROD.   Come, tell me the whole story of it, clearly.
    [HEROD *and the Cup-Bearer talk together in whispers.*

SALOME (*to herself*).   If the end corresponds to the beginning,
    Victory is ours, and our new stratagem
    Will be disastrous to this haughty woman.
    We tilt i' the lists, and soon our brows shall be
    Crowned, mine with laurel, and with cypress hers.

HEROD (*loudly*).   Oh, damnèd treason! Oh, black perfidy!
    Oh, deadly woman! Oh, plague abominable!
    She tried to win thine aid to poison me—
    Me, who would fain lose all to gain her love!
       These words of thine must be confirmed, or thou
    Puttest thy life indeed in jeopardy.
       What, ho! come hither, Captain of the Guards.
    [THARES *approaches him.*

    (*To* THARES)   Take thy companions, silently and swiftly.
    Go find the Queen in her apartments. Tell her
    A matter hath now come before the Council
    In which I think her presence necessary.
    Do not forget this message; go directly;
    Thyself escort her; do not leave her side.
    For if thou failest herein, on thy head be it!

THARES.   I shall discharge a faithful servant's duty.

Enter PHERORAS. *Exit* THARES.

PHERORAS (*to* SALOME). Madam, what moves the King? He seems
    confounded.
SALOME. We shall soon know; but he has told me naught.
PHERORAS. Mark how he comes to us with look quite changed.
HEROD. The Queen hath stopped at nothing to destroy me.
SALOME. Thou spurnedst always our devoted counsels.
HEROD. I much regret that they have not been followed.
    But seeing the peril, I in truth dare say
    Ye will approve the order I shall give.
    I must forestall those who desire revenge,
    And must act instantly to meet the danger.
    Come to the trial I shall hold today.
    (*To the Cup-Bearer*) Do not go hence, for thou art needful
    to me.

A C T I I I

The scene represents the Council Hall of the palace. HEROD
addresses his assembled Council.

HEROD. Seeing the ghastly wound in the State's body,
    Let us remove the part where gangrene showeth,
    Wisely oppose an antidote to the poison,
    And fail not in severity towards treason.
    What! is my criminal not led in yet?
    To make her hasten, someone run to meet her.
    On this occasion I wish to question her
    And expedite her trial to be adjudged.
    But here is she, who comes with as much boldness
    As if I waited to implore her grace.
    One would say, from her measured steps, she proudly
    Contemns my justice and makes light of death.

Enter MARIAMNE, *the* Cup-Bearer, PHERORAS, SALOME, *two*
Judges, the Grand Provost, and THARES.

(*To* MARIAMNE) Advance, unhappy queen. Well, thou vile
    woman,
    To whom I gave a portion of my soul,
    And who, by right alone of this fond worship,
    Shared with me all my glory and my grandeur,
    That which thy anger planned hath quite miscarried,
    Thy pitfall is exposed, thy mine discovered,

And having taken me for their target, justly
Thou findest that thy shafts rebound point-foremost.
Wouldst thou fain palliate this crime, now bared,
Which heaven's justice hath revealed to us?
MARIAMNE. Words of such ambiguity are dark
And therefore well befit the blood in *thy* veins.
HEROD. Insolent woman! darest thou speak thus to me?
MARIAMNE. Darest thou accuse me of ridiculous crimes?
HEROD. Yes, merely of attempting thy King's life!
MARIAME. This crime is very new; 'tis just invented;
But never have thy wits lacked artifices
To slay the innocent with pretense of justice.
HEROD. Death will make all these biting words less sharp
Which wound my honor and rob me of my peace.
This ingrate, far from proffering excuses,
Can speak no word without insulting me.
(*Pointing to the Cup-Bearer*) But see the witness to thy
black crime, plotted
'Gainst my life, 'gainst the body politic.
For her confusion, let her be confronted . . .
Already, seeing him she grows red with shame.
(*To the Cup-Bearer*) Come to confirm thine honest story here
And tell how artfully my death was planned.
But let the naked truth be shown, and do not
Either diminish or increase the crime.
THE CUP-BEARER. Sire, let a thunderbolt fall on my head
If I have not told all just as it happened.
HEROD. Come, and repeat it, then, and testify
To facts which she denies so impudently.
Speak!
THE CUP-BEARER. If the duty of a faithful subject
Allowed me to conceal a thing so weighty,
Madam, I would be sought for vainly now,
But the King's safety forces me to harm thee.
Forgive me, pray, if I have revealed all.
MARIAMNE. What, wretch?
THE CUP-BEARER. The poison thou spakest of to me.
MARIAMNE. Monster that camest from hell 'gainst innocence,
Darest thou indeed, with such assurance, lie?
Thou wouldst receive the fruit of thy black deed
If thou wert not upheld by those that schooled thee.
Thou shouldst be tortured for false testimony,
But thou art safe: my judge is thine accomplice.
I pardon thy bad faith right heartily.

Thou servest those more wicked than thyself.
This outrage is suborned and nowise irks me.
Thou art not the most base of all my foes.

HEROD. Thou shouldst try better to defend thyself
Touching a crime abhorred of earth and heaven.
To answer what this witness testifieth,
Thou must deny or else confess the fact.

MARIAMNE. It will be hard, either by force or skill,
For one to make me own a supposed crime;
And were it not for my ill fortune, I
Am of a blood too noble not to dread
Being suspected of it by anyone.
My heart, which Fate afflicts to the uttermost,
Suffers from treacheries, but commits them not;
And yet its grounds to do so would be ample
Were it obliged to err by thine example.

HEROD. And what example hast thou of like treacheries?

MARIAMNE. Treacheries unnumbered have I, countless cruelties,
The murder of a grandfather—and brother.

HEROD. At this foul charge I scarce withhold mine anger.
Thou wilful Cerberus, fatal to my House,
Thou know'st well how to spew forth poison 'gainst me.
But uselessly doth thine envenomed mouth
Emit its aconite at my fair fame.
That is so pure naught hath the power to stain it,
And without sacrilege one could not touch it.
I laugh at this thy rage; and these vain slanders,
That seek to wound me, wound thyself alone.
This insolent reproach clashes with truth
And clearly shows the rancor that thou feelest.
Thus is thy perfidy made plain enough;
This statement will suffice for thy destruction.
　　　[*He gives a sign to* THARES *to lead* MARIAMNE *aside while
　　　he collects the verdicts.*
My friends, pronounce that which the law decrees
Where crimes are those committed against kings.
Dispatch. My rights must be accorded me.
Justice desires it; and I ask it of you.

PHERORAS. I hold that this crime is beyond forgiveness.

SALOME. Death is too little for its punishment.

FIRST JUDGE. Unless thy Majesty inclines to mercy,
The crime is mortal; the law bids that she die.

SECOND JUDGE. Or that she be at least confined to prison,
In case the poison cannot be established.

LA MARIANE

HEROD (*looking angrily at the Second Judge*).
  The matter seems established well enough.
  What! have we not most certain proof thereof?
  Are not past crimes and present utterances
  Sufficient to make manifest the fact?
  The accusing witness is a man untainted,
  The old attendant who waits on me at table.
  What instrument more meet could she have chosen
  To execute her horrible desire?
  To plot this villainous deed, was she compelled
  To speak of it aloud in public places;
  And was not this a quite sufficient agent
  If she could have corrupted him with gold?

MARIAMNE.   Go on, go on, cruel monster; do not soften.
  Thou renderest me a service pleasing to me.
  Thy hand, relentless to take life from me,
  Is kinder to me than thy love hath been.
  Thy passion goes with my desire herein.
  Threatening my life, thou fillest me with hope.
  I ought to bless thy mood inexorable,
  For I shall go from death to life immortal.
  My head, which must be severed by thine order,
  Shall in the skies be freighted with a crown,
  The shining jewels of which are not a burden,
  And which no base usurper can tear from me.
    If I regret even now so stern a sentence,
  It is because I have a mother's feelings.
  I leave my babes, and I am grieved for them.
  These hapless children of a wretched father
  Sprang from a stem of such estate that it
  O'ershadowed the four quarters of the earth.
  These little orphans shall deserve men's pity—
  Sweet, precious objects of my tender love,
  Whom a cruel step-mother (for so 'tis likely)
  Shall soon maltreat in the most ruthless manner.
                    [*She wipes her eyes with a handkerchief.*

HEROD.   At just that moment when my wrath was keenest
  My heart is softened by her trickling tears.
  It seems that Love, becoming her accomplice,
  Strips from mine eyes the bandage Justice wears,
  That, seeing her, I may be moved to grant her
  The pardon that he asks of me for her.
  I find my soul inclining toward compassion.
  Thou askest mercy for her, Love; I grant it.

But touch her, too, and vouchsafe to accord me,
A boon which I shall ask at the same time.
From henceforth may her heart, its crime repenting,
Show to my kindness more appreciation
And cease to treat me with injurious pride,
Which else some day must bring us to our graves.
Make her see that I love her as I love
Myself; and if it still be possible,
O Love, make her love me.

> [*At a sign from* HEROD, *all withdraw except* THARES, *the*
> *Grand Provost, and* MARIAMNE.

(*To* MARIAMNE) Be pleased to dry
Thine eyes, O thou most rare and charming creature!
The King yields place unto the lover, now.
My justice might submit thee to my laws,
But my affection could not suffer it.
I am too deeply touched by thy least sorrow.
I find my heart sore wounded when thou weepest.
I stay this sentence, for my greatest rage,
In doing justice on thee, harmeth *me;*
And if I should not stay thy doom at once,
I know that I would seek, with thee, a grave.
I would die of thy death, and thine own death-pangs
Would be the ministers to attain thine object!
See in what truth my fate depends on thine,
And if I vex thee when I fain would serve thee,—
If thou conceivest some cruel wish to harm me,—
Use no more poison to abridge my life.
If the desire is thine to speed my end,
Thou needest but show me that thou dost not love me;
Thou needest but tell me of thy secret hate,
And soon my death will satisfy thee fully.
But confess all to me, and make it seen
That thou wouldst now resume thy wifely duty,
And that thy heart, in genuine remorse,
Detests with horror a detestable crime.

MARIAMNE.   Well do I know this vein, sweet and deceitful,
And how thy soul is skilled in treachery.
Thou wastest too great pains to dig my grave;
A single ruse sufficeth to destroy me.

HEROD.   Wicked one, then thou thinkest me a deceiver
And all this boldness springs but from thy fear.
Doubt not thy pardon; it is ratified.
I keep my word when I have given it.

     Cease to pain me with thy unhappiness.

MARIAMNE. Nay, rather make my life and woes to cease.
    My people all are gone; I long to follow them.

HEROD. What! dost thou wish to die to cut short *my* life,
    And, ruthless still to claims of every sort,
    To seek thy king's death for the second time?
    Though thou art ice and although I am flame,
    Heaven hath linked my soul unto thy soul.
    The fair thread of thy days cannot be snapped
    Without mine being snapped at the same time.

MARIAMNE. However, when *thy* life hath reached its end,
    I shall in truth be ill assured of mine,
    For the precautions of thy careful love
    Will make me, if they can, die the same day.
    That, certainly, is a mark of tenderness!

HEROD. Thy words are dark. I cannot understand them.

MARIAMNE. Let us not lose time in vain talk. The thing
    Is but too recent.

HEROD.   I cannot recall it.

MARIAMNE. When thou didst basely fear Augustus' justice,
    Was not my death resolved on and found meet?

HEROD. Augustus'? Ah, that word tells me enough—
    What animates thee, and what injures me.
    I know the cause, now, of thy fierce disdain,
    And the vile way in which my men betray me.
    Sohemus hath held secret converse with thee?

MARIAMNE. He told me naught of this, but well I know it.

HEROD. Ah, vile Sohemus, to deceive thy master!
    (*Turning to the Grand Provost*) Go instantly to seize upon
     this traitor.
    Let him be brought to me all laden with fetters,
    Giving him now no time to save himself.
    Let those suspected of conspiring with him
    Be thrust in separate dungeons this same hour.
    Be quick, and let the torturers not spare them.

THE GRAND PROVOST. My lord, I will do everything thou biddest.

HEROD. The eunuch of the Queen is her accomplice.
    Let him immediately be brought before me.
    It was with his consent that I was wronged,
    But he will answer to me for what was done.

           [*Exit the Grand Provost.*

    O curst event! O hard fatality!
    Wherefore did I not die when I was young?
    Seeing to my hurt so many ills assembled,

With rage and horror I am quite distraught.
Frenzy hath seized me, and at this cruel outrage
I am beside myself; it leaves me maddened.
(*To* MARIAMNE)   Sohemus told thee, about this, the truth;
But his unfaithfulness hath had what wages?
His station in my Court was very high.
He did not risk his life for a mere nothing.
Thou couldst not dazzle him with shining treasures.
Thou couldst not tempt him save with thy fair body.
He guarded it, and he was its possessor
When he revealed to thee this weighty secret;
Thy favors were the bounty he received.
Lift not thine eyes; answer what I have said.
Didst thou with other recompense content him?

MARIAMNE.   Believe all that thou sayest, all that thou thinkest.

HEROD.   Yes, yes, I wish to, and to make thee feel
A sharp repentance for this perfidy.

MARIAMNE.   Life canst thou rid me of, not innocence.

HEROD.   Ah, I shall have this satisfaction, surely:
Thou shalt no longer laugh o'er having shamed me.
I suffered the affront but now seek vengeance.
Thou threw'st me in chains, threw'st me in burning flame;
Stabb'dst my soul, torest my heart out of my breast;
But flatter not thyself with this vain thought,
That thou couldst do with safety so much evil.
Death is e'en now prepared to take thee hence.

MARIAMNE.   'Twill come less quickly than I would desire it,
And, offered thus to end my weariness,
Can make me dread nothing but its delay.

HEROD.   Thy constancy shall have the test of tortures.
But here thy lover is, with his dear charms.
I shall amuse myself with him at once.
(*To* THARES)   Conduct her to the tower, and do not leave
her.

Enter SOHEMUS *and the Grand Provost. Exeunt* MARIAMNE *and*
THARES.

(*To* SOHEMUS)   Accursed cause of my unbearable plight,
What led thee basely to betray my trust,
And pushing thine audacity to the point
Of utterly disdaining death, reveal
A secret which was so important to me?
Answer. Thou knowest well what wrong thou didst me.

SOHEMUS.   Alas, my lord! This crime was mine through weakness.

'Twas by imprudence and by thoughtlessness
That I sinned thus against thy Majesty;
But the repentance swift to seize my heart
Ought to efface the memory of my deed.
O Prince, as great in mercy as in might,
Pardon a fault committed by mischance.

HEROD. Is it not, then, a traitorous spirit's act
Which sows dissension in the royal house?
And is it a slight wrong, unworthy of wrath,
To bring a wife to try to slay her husband?
Darest thou still say a word in thy defense?
Thy false excuse aggravates the offense.
It would be better for thee to hide nothing.

SOHEMUS. Sire, I have erred too much to attempt excuse.
I am too guilty when I have displeased thee.
I have no arguments against thine anger;
And in the peril in which I plunged myself
I hope for safety only through thy mercy.

HEROD. Yes, but by means which are not ordinary
I learned the secret of this whole affair.
If thou wouldst fain excuse thy monstrous deed,
Confess that it was love that made thee do it.
'Tis well known what charms Mariamne hath.
Thou hast beheld the splendor of her beauty,
Nor couldst resist the power of her glance,
And this it is which overwhelmed thy senses.
Yes, by such means the Queen hath caused thy crime.
But that my grace may be exhibited
Towards thee, inform me by a full confession
The birth and history of this thy passion.
Foundest thou in her soul some slight resistance?
What course was thine before thou wonnest thy will?

SOHEMUS. These strange words so amaze me that I cannot
Hold them in mind precisely, or their meaning.
I fain would understand, but cannot do so.

HEROD. Thy love being secret, this bolt well may stun thee.
But come, collect thy wits and tell me all.

SOHEMUS. O Prince, thou honor and marvel of our days,
Can one think that a soul so fair and noble
Conceiveth suspicions most unworthy of it,
And that a king of such rare intellect
Errs in his judgment, troubling his heart's peace?
What I am charged with makes my fortunes piteous.
If I accused my own self of this crime

Would anyone believe me guilty of it?
How could Sohemus even think of such things
Unless he had completely lost his mind?
And had he fallen into such distemper,
Who would believe a slave's soul was so daring
That he would love a queen and would disclose
To her a rashness which would mean his death,—
And furthermore, a queen so chaste and wise
That she could be a pattern for the age?
Thou dost great wrong to her with such suspicions.

HEROD.   Traitor, thou tirest me with thy disquisitions.
Thinkest thou to clear thyself, praising thy partner,
And with a subtle charm to lull my justice
To sleep?

SOHEMUS.   If I spoke otherwise, I would seem, surely,
A liar.

HEROD.   Let this speech-maker be slain!

SOHEMUS.   Blood which must cry for vengeance will be shed.

HEROD.   Dispatch the faithless wretch immediately!
Is the eunuch here, too?

THE GRAND PROVOST.   Yes, sire. Here he is.

HEROD.   He likewise must be slain at the same time.
He was in this plot also, the vile beast
Who could not pass for either man or woman!

Enter the Eunuch. Exit SOHEMUS.

(*To the Eunuch*)   Horror of nature, scorn of heaven itself,
Monster devoid of sense, pernicious reptile,
I placed the rarest treasure in thy charge,
Of which I rightfully could be a miser.
But thou didst lend assistance to the robber,
Serve as the furtherer of my utmost hurt;
Thou wert the accomplice of this fine adulterer,
Knewest of the intrigue, yet toldest me naught.
When in my bed Sohemus slaked his love,
Thou drewest the curtains and keptest watch all round.
Didst thou so well manage my absences?

THE EUNUCH.   Sire, an all-powerful God who knoweth the guiltless
Hath means to make thy Majesty aware
How I have served thee with fidelity.

HEROD.   Fidelity, wretch?—Let him be dragged away
And even to death be plied with tortures! He
Will 'neath the cruelest torment confess all
If he is not sustained by some enchantment.

ACT IV

Scene One

The scene represents a room in the palace. HEROD, SALOME, *and* PHERORAS *are discovered.*

HEROD. The faithful spirit, watching ceaselessly
The charge which heaven committed to his care,
Guards well my safety, making me disperse
The ills with which Fate would envelop me.
This heavenly minister every hour inspires me
To do what should bring good unto mine empire,
And when I find myself in the worst danger,
He flies to aid me, comes to free me from it,
Preserves my life, and fortifies my throne.
Amid the battle, his wing shelters me,
And with celestial, unexpected help
Leaves me triumphant when I was thought lost.
Truly, the faithful care with which he guides me
Protects me always when disaster seeks me,
Be it by open war, be it by treason,
At Rome, on a campaign, or in my home.
   Now I anew have thanks to render to him,
Touching this vile attempt ye have just learned of.
This is the best work of his care. Without him
Ye would no more have brother now nor king.
If he had not inspired this faithful man,
A deadly ambuscade would have surprised me.
The love which blinded me would have prevented
My knowledge of this fresh-lit conflagration,
By which I was about to be consumed,
And, laughing at my death, a wicked wife
Would share my scepter with her paramour.
Without this warning, Herod would be destroyed.

SALOME. Already to this end the snare was set.

PHERORAS. Had but the revelation been delayed,
Mariamne would have carried out her purpose.

HEROD. Ah, how I suffer at this cruel outrage—
Wrath in my heart and shame upon my brow!
And with whatever rigor I may treat her,
My fury never will be satisfied.
   Yet my desire now to avenge myself
Must needs expose me to another danger.

I strike at mine own breast in threatening her.
My own destruction is bound up with hers.
I can be sure that, if I quench that light,
I shall see naught else lovable or lovely.
Howe'er I be consoled, howe'er diverted,
My heart will carry its anguish everywhere;
At every hour remorse will torture me,
A vulture come to tear me without cease.
    O God, why did she have to be unfaithful!
Less treacherous or less fair thou shouldst have formed her.
Her shafts of charm or else of cruelty
Ought not to have found lodgment in my breast;
Nor should I have beheld, at misery's peak,
My thoughts divided in two adverse factions.
    I would that I were still of name unknown,
Did not stand in the station I have reached,
Had still to clamber up to glory's temple,
Had still to gain my earliest victory,
Could find myself e'en as I was at birth,
So be it this ingrate heart might be proved guiltless.
SALOME.   Such intense feelings of a genuine love
Aggravate her offense and make her fouler;
For her ingratitude is a foul baseness
Worse even than murder or unchastity.
    Seeing the blackness of this traitorous soul,
Everyone pities thee and murmurs at her.
But let not all these vain regrets consume thee.
The earth must be made rid of her; and reason,
Showing her hate and her hypocrisy
To thee, will rid thy mind then of its sorrows.
HEROD.   Justice impelleth me to punish her. . . .
What! cause to perish her I loved so much?
Can I resolve to shatter a fair temple
So dear to me and quite beyond compare?
My spirit rebels at this and stands aghast.
SALOME.   Respectest thou so much a shrine profaned?
Murder, adultery, and ungrateful pride—
Have they not stripped it of all sanctity?
HEROD.   The adultery is not o'er well confirmed.
Sohemus died protesting it was false.
PHERORAS.   He thought that by denying it he had
More chance of thy according him some mercy.
SALOME.   What, cannot this perfidious act confound thee?

Dost thou behold it only to forgive it?

[She pretends to weep.

Thou'rt willing that her hate at last be glutted
And that she should destroy thee and thy race.
Obey thy feelings; we all agree thereto.
We needs must be resigned to perish with thee.

PHERORAS.　Thy heart is by a fearsome spell constrained
To take this piteous course against thyself.

HEROD.　Not so! The course to which I fain would hold
Preserves her but to punish her the better.
Dealing death to her, I would end her misery.
A long imprisonment would be more severe.
Thus ever would chagrin, regret, and shame
Give to her soul a secret punishment,
Her memory picture ever to her thoughts
Her disgrace now and all my favors past,
And showing her crime unto her, and my love,
Put her to torture, night and day alike.

PHERORAS.　With this compassion whereof we are suspicious
Thou seekest to show praise-worthy clemency.
But thinkest thou that the plans she makes to rob
Thine eyes of life's sweet light would ne'er bear fruit;—
That heaven, creating obstacles, would always
Work miracles for thy security?
Remember, when its warnings are neglected,
It oft abandons those it hath protected.

SALOME.　Since thou so lovest the cause of thy misfortunes,
Thou shouldst not, then, have had this matter aired.
The late proceedings can but exacerbate
A heart which, though indulged, yet could not love thee.
What will it not do, after this great insult,
If even thy favors only stirred its wrath?

PHERORAS.　When one would smite a powerful enemy,
Let one not think of half-destroying him.
On such occasions, indiscreet compunction
Exposes a man's life to his foes' vengeance.
If, after one offends, one does not pardon,
Then when offended, one hates to extremes,
And whatsoe'er the oath of reconcilement,
The affront bides in the heart—is ne'er forgotten.
Perjured Hyrcanus might have proved this to thee:
That miserable old man, unfit to rule,
That last dishonor of that wicked race,
Who lived in exile on the Euphrates' bank

And whom thy kindness with a pious care
Caused to be brought back with such honor here.
Could all thy goodness to him turn him from
The lust to avenge his nephews and his brother?
And had not one among his servants warned thee
How he was forming an alliance with Malichus,
Would he not finally with a treacherous ambush
Ruthlessly have repaid thy kindly treatment?

SALOME. Couldst thou preserve, devoid of apprehension,
This leaven of revolt and of sedition
Whose angry thoughts are but of injuring thee
And whose fell spirit burns for thy destruction?
If chance should bring Augustus to his grave
And show the populace some hint of change,
They would have her for pretext to revolt,—
Would come and snatch this Fury from thy clutches,
And we should see her hasten, torch in hand,
To burn the palace and lay thee in the tomb.
When this Erinnys, out of hell, to harm thee
Would in the State have formed a powerful cabal,
Thou with regret wouldst know that thou shouldst have
Forestalled her plottings when thou couldst have done so;
Thou wouldst repent of having been unwise,
But it would be too late.

HEROD.   Well, kill her, kill her!
It will be needful instantly thereafter
To inform Caesar by a special courier,
For fear lest malice, with its trickery,
Will do me some bad offices with him,
And make me seem, concealing the real truth,
A prince suspicious, unjust, and violent.

Scene Two

The scene represents a prison. MARIAMNE *is discovered.*

MARIAMNE. To increase the wrong which uncurbed violence
        Hath done to innocence
Despotic power holds my body penned;
But in whatever peril by ill fate,
        I have this recourse yet:
My heart will none the less endure until the end.

This day shall bring my life-term to its close.
        I see well that my woes
Labor effectually to dig my grave,

And that a cruel tyrant who abuses me
    Falsely of crime accuses me,
That some excuse to commit a new crime he may have.

Let him do what he will; ready am I
    (So as to satisfy
This monster) to make payment of my head.
Whate'er the horror be that death can show,
    Let it appear, and lo,
I shall advance to meet it wholly undismayed.

'Tis time that heaven should sunder me anon
    From that fell, savage one.
His spirit and mine have little common ground.
Virtue that breathes amid the stench of sin
    Such torment finds therein
As he who lips to lips unto the dead is bound.

O sovereign Power, Creator of the earth,
    Who, ever since my birth,
Hast sent me fortune whereof tears are bred,
My soul turns only to thy grace divine.
    Lord, may it soon be mine
To go from midst life's thorns, on flowery fields to tread.

But what noise do I hear? Doth heaven not heed?
I have beguiled myself with this last hope
When I have spent the fairest of my years
In wearing till now such hard and heavy fetters.

       Enter the Keeper of the Prison.

THE KEEPER OF THE PRISON (*in tears*). Thou art awaited in the
    lower hall,
    Madam. That is the King's hest.
MARIAMNE.   God, I thank thee!
    (*To the Keeper*)   Why seemest thou so distressed in speaking
    to me?
THE KEEPER OF THE PRISON.   Because I saw the populace assembled
    Outside, whose cries and tears are of ill omen
    Unto thy Majesty.
MARIAMNE.   The people are
    Not wise to torture and afflict themselves
    About a blessing which my friends should wish me.
    But they may tire of waiting for me there.
    Tell them for me I shall go down to them.

Ere seeing them, I would speak with those that serve me
And what few things are mine divide among them.

[*Exeunt.*

Scene Three

The scene represents a street. Enter ALEXANDRA *and her Gentleman in attendance.*

ALEXANDRA. Thou wilt be led to slaughter, spotless victim.
　　　　Thou goest to death, thou, who hast done no crime.
　　　　And sprangest thou from the blood of kings so many
　　　　To be seen punished by this unjust doom?
　　　　Oh, savage sentence! Oh, unrighteous judgment!
　　　　Oh, ruthless violence! Oh, tyrannous power!
　　　　　Thou base, cruel Arab, who now showest no pity,
　　　　Thou makest thy rage be felt by thy pure helpmate;
　　　　But heaven's grace, converted into wrath,
　　　　Can strike ere long the other of the twain.
　　　　A God who from on high sees our hearts' secrets
　　　　Will punish thee for all thy cruelty soon.
　　　　On a not far-off day his justice, stirring,
　　　　Will on thy head avenge wronged innocence.
　　　　If he has feet of wool, his arm is iron,
　　　　And 'tis for such as thou that he made hell.
　　　　　O great God, I invoke thee in my anguish:
　　　　Take but the daughter; spare, I pray, the mother!
THE GENTLEMAN IN ATTENDANCE. Madam, 'tis here that she will have
　　　　　　to pass.
ALEXANDRA. I see the spot where I should post myself.
　　　　Only be careful that thine eyes display not,
　　　　At the sad sight, tears that would do me harm.
　　　　Let us compose our faces for this meeting
　　　　Nor show by them that we have wept; for now
　　　　We needs must shun the tempest, falsify
　　　　Our feelings, and hide what is in our hearts.

　　　　　[ALEXANDRA *and the Gentleman in attendance take their
　　　　　stand on one side of the scene.*

Enter, on the other side, MARIAMNE, DINAH, *and* THARES.

THARES. Madam, against my will I do this office,
　　　　And with regret perform the fatal task;
　　　　But my obedience and a soldier's honor
　　　　Herein compel me necessarily.
MARIAMNE. For thy compassion little need have I.

Both by constraint and of free will I die.
Lead me without a qualm to meet my death.
Herod desires it, and I do not fear it.
If, at my going hence, I somewhat grieve,
It springs from pity for the babes I leave,
Who in disfavor and neglect will be,
On my account, treated unworthily.
They are without support, but, O great God,
I hope that thou wilt be their stay and father,
And that to guide them in this perilous time
Thine own high providence will watch over them.
Grave on their hearts the love and fear of thee.
Make them burn always with a holy zeal.
Let each hold steadfastly a heart resolved
To die a thousand times ere they offend thee.
Let no excess of sorrow or of joy
Deflect their footsteps from the heavenly path,
And if oppressed because they keep thy Law,
Let them live blamelessly and die like me.
    And thou, cruel monster, most unnatural soul,
Who always art athirst for innocent blood:
Because thy cruelty knows not how to soften,
I shall pour out for thee what will refresh thee.
To quench thy thirst and end my misery I
Shall give thee all the blood within my veins.
Drink it, thou savage tiger, but suppose not
That thy vile charges will survive my death,
Or that the overflow of thy black bile
That blots my life out can blot out mine honor,
Or that some day our seed with crime will charge me
Wherewith I am not stained by thought or deed.
    Time, which brings truth, howe'er concealed, to light,
Will make my spotless innocence apparent,
And the precipitancy of my trial
Defeats by its excess my persecution.
    The blind rage of the war thou wagest upon me
Shall destroy what of me is only earth,
But my immortal soul and glorious name,
Despite the activities of thy mad spirit
And all thy family joined in plots against me,
Will none the less have everlasting life.
    But I behold my mother. She waits here
To vouchsafe unto me a last farewell.
Would that her heart could set bounds to its grief

And that she felt for me less tenderness!
Let me go comfort her and give to her
Both my last tear and also my last kiss.
That can be quickly done.
THARES.   Hasten, then, madam;
For I would bear the blame for this delay.
Strict are my orders, and I must obey.
MARIAMNE. Thou'lt see the words between us will be few.
(*To* ALEXANDRA) Madam, I am constrained to change my
      home,
But I am going to dwell in one far better,
Where no fierce wind nor malice quite as fierce
Stirreth up storms in air or human hearts;
Where innocence is known to eyes unblinded;
Where the fell hand of tyrants hath no power;
Where, for its steadfastness' reward, the soul
Tasteth fair fame and immortality.
   All this ill fate I have is to mine interest.
I am resolved to pass hence without shrinking.
Take comfort, then, and give me thine embrace.
Farewell, farewell, madam, for I shall leave thee.
ALEXANDRA. Fulfil thy fate, vile and unhappy woman.
This death is too small payment for thy crime.
In justice, it should be atoned in flames,
Or on the cross thy body should be hanged.
Go, monster cruel, unmatched in Africa;
Go and receive the price of thy black deed,
Thine effort thus to poison barbarously
A husband who hath always loved thee dearly.
Wife without conscience, thou new Danaid,
Inhuman, traitorous, faithless murderess
Who fain would basely seek her sovereign's life,
I know thee not; thou art not sprung from me,
For of such treason am I incapable.
MARIAMNE. Thou shalt live blameless and I die dishonored.
THARES. Let us go, madam; let us go.
MARIAMNE.   Which way?
THARES. Hither.
DINAH.   Ah, heaven! what constancy! what cruelty!
                    [*Exeunt all but* ALEXANDRA.
ALEXANDRA. Oh, vile device! Oh, heartless stratagem!
Better had I been reckoned her accomplice.
To avoid death, must I needs have recourse
To this grim subterfuge that I shall die of?

My sad, cold heart, which is girt round with horror,
Aches 'neath the blows which grief deals unto it.
My soul shall pay for this excess of woe;
Unto my bed—rather, my bier—I go.

ACT V

The scene represents HEROD's *apartment in the palace.* HEROD
is discovered.

HEROD.   Serpent covered with flowers, deadly viper,
Jaundiced daughter of love, who killest thy father,
Unsleeping dragon with a hundred eyes
Who takest all amiss, seest all awry,
Insatiable monster, horrible jealousy,
Which with unnumbered errors cloudest my fancy,
Hast thou not fully satisfied thy rage?
Hast thou not gnawed upon my heart enough yet?
Vex me no longer, thou ill counselor,
Perfidious spy, and false interpreter,
Who troublest both my peace and my good sense,
And makest me slay the guiltless without scruple.
Have I not yet appeased thee, killing Sohemus
And terrifying even Mariamne?
   "Terrifying"—nay, do not deceive thyself.
Thy lips have spoken the order for her death;
And like a criminal and like one found guilty,
She has been led at once to execution.
Her beauty is no longer in the world,
Or treason worketh and I am betrayed;
Yet 'tis my death if I have been obeyed.
My life is threatened if indeed she lives,
And I must follow her if she be dead.
Oh, bitter pain! Oh, torment without equal!
I see on all sides naught but misery;
And whatsoever paths my thoughts pursue,
I find there always either fear or sorrow.
   Let us go seek to learn what fate is hers,
And if that fair head hath not fallen yet,
Change by a signal act of gracious mercy
This dismal ceremony to her triumph.
But one of my men comes, and I behold
My wretchedness writ on his face in tears.
That alone tells me all.

MARIAMNE

Enter NARBAL.

NARBAL.   Ah, what is done
Consigneth to the tomb the sum of virtue.
Honor and constancy and piety
Have with that loveliness now ceased to live.
HEROD.   What evil maketh thee weep thus?
NARBAL.   Great cause
For mourning.
HEROD.   What? Hath Mariamne died?
NARBAL.   Yes, sire. Thy queen is numbered with the dead.
They but a moment since struck off her head.
                           [HEROD *swoons.*
He is transformed at once. He is o'ercome.
The shock hereof will bring him to his grave.
This is the sad result which all foresaw.
    Open thine eyes! regain thy senses, sire!
HEROD (*reviving*)   Hath Mariamne swelled the ranks of death?
Is that which was my sun, then, but a shadow?
Still in its eastern sky this orb of beauty
That lights my soul hath lost its light? Thou sayest
That Mariamne hath lost the light of day?
And the world's torch yet moveth through the heavens?
Men saw it once turn back upon its path
For the mere sake of an accursed feast,
And now it finds it cannot have like horror
Though it hath seen its counterpart extinguished!
    Day-star that knowest naught and feelest naught,
It is all blindly that thou givest light!
If the immortal hand that formed thee of flame,
In shaping thee had with a soul endowed thee,
Thou wouldst be more responsive to my suffering,
Wouldst make thy bed thy sepulcher, and establish,
By thy eclipse, throughout the universe
The selfsame horror that now reigns in me!
    Did Mariamne taste death's bitterness?
Death has no empire where her charms hold sway.
I know this master-work is like its Maker
And cannot be at once divine and mortal.
What! in so brief a time hath man destroyed
The fairest temple virtue ever had?
Hath man shut up in the grave's narrow space
Love's sanctuary and the Graces' home?
Have the bright stars that were her eyes been quenched,

And hath the lilies' hue now left her cheeks?
Is all this treasury of wonders wasted?
Is my celestial oracle made silent?
Is my whole wealth in this way taken from me,
And will what was my all henceforth be nothing?
Nay, nay, that is a thought which, lacking reason,
Must never find a place in my belief. . . .
Sayest thou this masterpiece of heaven hath perished?
NARBAL. Sire, the sad blow was dealt before mine eyes.
HEROD. Tell me in full the piteous story of it.
I cannot doubt it, nor can I believe it.
NARBAL. When warning had come to her in the tower
That a stern doom would force her exit from it,
The dread recital of the fate decreed her
Shook every heart, but not her constancy.
For, scorning her ill fortune, she made it clear
That this fierce shock had not the power to move her.
She nowise uttered timid sentiments;
Her eyes were dry among so many weeping;
And joyful glances that lit up her charms
Showed well that death was not displeasing to her.
When she had made bequests of certain jewels
To those she loved best of her maids of honor,
And when she had embraced them and enjoined them
Neither to follow her nor to shed tears,
She bent her steps, more gay, more fair than erstwhile,
Whither the scaffold mournfully was waiting.
None ever saw her show a nobler pride.
Upon her face was written scorn of death.
Never more glorious appeared a queen
Of the Amazons in victory and triumph.
The people following her all burst out sobbing,
Awed by her courage, pitying her misfortune.
Many folk even said amid the press
That this great princess perished without cause,
And that her soul, noble beyond all others,
Could never have conceived a single baseness,
And that thou wouldst regret her charms in absence,
And that her blood poured forth would cost thee tears
As soon as thou wert told that she was dead.
HEROD. Ah, had I only shunned what they foresaw!
NARBAL. Her mother, when she spoke to her, through fear
Changed from real pity to feigned condemnation.
Resourceful to avoid the least suspicion

That she in any way was her accomplice,
She hid the feelings nature gives a mother
And rejoiced seemingly at her daughter's fate;
But our great queen, even when afflicted thus,
Fathomed her artifice and was not distressed,
But, passing on, replied to her vain insults
With but a modest smile and a low bow.

HEROD. Ah, I am quite pierced through with shafts of pity.
My heart, to hear these words, is cleft in twain.
What! in this sad estate her mother blamed her,
And only her own virtue took her part?
Tell all the rest.

NARBAL.   When once upon the scaffold,
She joined her hands, lifted her eyes on high,
And on her knees besought the divine Power
That plain to all might be her innocence
And that her children ne'er might be reproached
For crimes by which her soul had been untainted,
Protesting that it was through calumny
That she was seen to suffer ignominy,
And that thou hadst believed in thy blind rage
Things which the very thought of made her shudder.
She called to witness the angel hierarchies
That she had not committed such vile deeds,—
Found hope that heaven would teach thee better, that
Regret that she thus died would make thee mourn,
And that thou still wouldst some affection show
For the young orphans left by a great princess
Who, though ill-fated, bore her sufferings bravely,
Who lived without spot and knew how to die.

   After these words, uttered with flame-like fervor,
She sought to recommend to heaven her soul,
Which was prepared to mount there with its virtues;
Then did she bare her neck, and spake no more;
And when the executioner saw her ready,
With a swift flash of steel he struck her head off.
Thereupon a great cry was heard all round,
Which through the welkin rang heart-breakingly,
And from the eyes of all the people gushed
At once, as from a thousand fountains, tears
Warm as the blood that spurted from her veins.
Thus was it that thy noble wife did perish
While a whole world was like to die with pity.

HEROD. To have deprived of life such loveliness—

Oh, cruelty unknown to the cruelest hearts!
A barbarous Sarmatian could not do it,
A Scythian could not think of it unquailing.
What river or what sea can ever wash
The blackness of this horrid crime away?
What savage mountain or what lonely cavern
Can be the asylum of my impious soul?
Will I find in earth's midmost depths a refuge
Where my sin may have shelter from the thunder;
Where I can bide with neither pain nor fright;
Where I shall not drag my hell after me?
　But think I to have comfort in my woe?
What, live still, and with Mariamne dead?
This fair one gone, and I to fail to follow her,
As if I did not know the roads to death?
　　　　　　　　　　[He seizes upon NARBAL'S *sword.*
Ha! this one is the shortest. Let this blade
With one stab wound my heart and heal my soul.
Lend it to me, I pray, for this good purpose,
Or bury it in my breast, if thou preferrest.

NARBAL.　Oh, sire, have done with these extremes of passion!
　　　　　　　　　　[He takes the sword from HEROD.

HEROD.　This is but to delay the doom thou broughtest me.
Hast thou not dealt me my death-blow already?
Thou toldest me that the Queen is in the tomb.
Thinkest thou that I without her will dwell here?
Make her alive again, or let me die.
I cannot bear so crushing a remorse;
I would pay forfeit for her innocent blood.
　　　　　　　　　　[He tries again to seize the sword.
Withhold not from me my just punishment.
I needs must kill myself, since *I* killed *her.*

NARBAL.　Sire!

HEROD.　　　Oh! I am the author of this murder.
'Twas *my* mouth armed the executioner's hand;
My mouth, the servant of my kindled rage,
With but a single word closed hers forever.
　Ah, mouth bloodthirsty, full of cruelty,
My sorrow proves thou didst betray my heart.
Fatal interpreter of my maddened spirit
Which, to my woe, wast able to speak my thought,
Serve me more suitably in doing thine office,
And give the antidote after the poison!
　Ye down-trod people, witness of my crimes,

Who hold in so great love your lawful sovereigns,
Show a true consequence of such ardency
And to requite my deed employ your zeal.
Come, come, avenge upon an impious tyrant
The death of your pure, lovely Mariamne.
Punish my most unjust severity.
Hasten to bury daggers in my heart.
Appease today with blood of mine the ghost
Of your wronged, innocent queen whom I but now
Have sacrificed unto my cruel hate.
But ye therefor do nothing, timorous nation
Who dare not take a noble course of action.
Ye are too full of fear to win fair fame.
Ye do not wish to live in history
Or by an act of loyalty and courage
Be signalized unto posterity.

    Observer of their baseness and my crime,
O heaven, that seest the wrong done innocence,
Shed on this land misfortunes infinite;
Punish these slaves who have not punished me;
Let them be objects of thy chastisements;
Make them to float in gore, to swim in tears;
Send Scythians and Geloni marching 'gainst them,
And if 'tis possible yet more cruel monsters,
Who have no qualms, taking them unawares,
In blood to leave them, and their homes in ashes;
Grant that their dearest babes may be borne off
And dashed to death on rocks by barbarous hands,
Their wives and daughters raped before their eyes,
Famine and pestilence devour their households,
And their proud Temple, amid these disasters,
Be overthrown even to its foundations.

    Should aught remain of their accursed race,
May they be only objects of disgrace,
People whom Fate abandons to misfortune.
Make them abide in shame and amid sorrows.
Let them find always naught but ignominy.
Let them be everywhere oppressed, and wander
Forevermore, scattered, o'er all the world.
Let them at every turn be cursed and hounded,
And everywhere alike be warred upon,
No longer own a single inch of earth,
And, as the objects of thy execration,
Receive no pity when their woes are told of.

Rain fire and brimstone down upon their heads.
Make all Jerusalem naught but an abyss—
An abyss only, only a sink of horror,
Of which the very name alone is fearsome.
    Is Mariamne dead, then—snatched from me—
And am I left alive still to despair?
Death, in my woe I beg for thy compassion.
Come and take all, where thou hast taken half!

Enter SALOME, PHERORAS, *and* THARES.

SALOME.   Narbal, how doth the King?
NARBAL.   Madam, he is only
    Torturing himself. His sorrow is so keen,
    So very strong, that if thy wise aid doth not
    Divert its course, thou soon wilt see his end.
SALOME.   Have tidings from Augustus come to him
    Or some change in his fortunes given him cause
    For woe?
NARBAL.   Nay, madam.
SALOME.   What, then, troubles him?
NARBAL.   The Queen's death.
PHERORAS.   Ah! 'Tis even as I supposed.
SALOME.   He grieves too much o'er proper grounds for joy.
PHERORAS.   Great tact is needful in accosting him.
    His wrath thereat is to be apprehended.
SALOME.   Not so. His spirit needeth to be chided.
PHERORAS.   See how he comes this way, with madness in him.
    A thousand sad thoughts keep him company.
    Pallid he is of hue, and his eyes roll.
    Observe his bearing and judge of his condition.
SALOME (*to* HEROD).   My lord, thy mood is very melancholy.
HEROD.   It is because I have too many cares
    Of State, but I would fain take some slight rest
    Today.
SALOME.   That would be well.
PHERORAS.   It would be fitting.
HEROD.   To speak without reserve, what doth distress me
    Is that I have not seen the Queen at all
    Since yesterday. Bid her from me to come
    Hither.
SALOME.   His mind wanders. He has forgotten.
HEROD.   Send somebody to fetch her. Do me this kindness.
PHERORAS.   Alas, my lord, how can one satisfy thee?
HEROD.   Let her be told that I would speak with her. . . .

Is it so hard? Does no one wish to go?
SALOME. Can she speak unto thee, and can she hear thee?
Her body is cold; it soon shall be but dust.
HEROD. What! Mariamne dead? Oh, hostile Powers!
Fate snatched her hence, and ye have let this be?
Ye have permitted, then, this sad event
Without requiring that all nature mourn?
What! her cold body hath been buried, then,
And still the world is not annihilated?
Have ye, then, shattered the fair harmony
Which ye had given to her soul divine?
Have ye, then, stopped her mouth—closed her bright eyes—
And not destroyed the fabric of the skies?
Cruel in this wreckage, second to none other,
Ye should have begun that of all the earth,
Swept the whole universe from its foundations,
Shuffled the heavens with the elements,
Broken the curb of the seas, snuffed out the light,
And reduced all to its original chaos.

    Is Mariamne clay? Does the tomb's shade
Receive the ruins of a masterpiece
So lovely? Give thy grief scope, use thy hands,
Tear out thy hair, make ravage of thy cheeks,
Compel thy servants to effect thy death,
Or die of sorrow that thou canst not die.
Do not console thyself, most wretched monarch.
PHERORAS. Forget this loss. It cannot be repaired;
And shouldst thou set thy mind to think upon it,
Thou thyself wouldst not wish it reparable.
SALOME. Thou wilt say, some day, that this notable deed
Was for thy State a necessary evil.
HEROD. Stubborn to do me harm, source of my ills,
Dare ye console me, ye who have murdered me?
By your bad offices ye made me give
This mortal blow to all I took delight in.
'Twas ye inspired me with this fatal purpose.
'Twas ye set torturers within my breast.
Go, hellish pair! begone, accursed breed!
Or I shall treat you after your deserts.

      [*Exeunt, hastily,* SALOME *and* PHERORAS. HEROD *turns to*
        NARBAL *and* THARES.

    And ye, my true friends and my servants dear,
Who do not come like these, traitors nor flatterers;
Who make distinction 'twixt my crown's high state

And me, and keep your zeal for me alone;
Ye who have always loved me honestly—
Unite the griefs ye feel with mine, and let us
Mingle our tears and without cease lament
The death of that divine and most fair princess.
But she is nowise dead; she lives in heaven,
And her rare virtues throne her midst the gods.
A temple must be built to this fair being
Which will forever signalize her worth,—
A temple which will seem a work immortal,
Where her bright image will be o'er the altar.
Yea, I would have her feast established here,
And everyone observe it, or else die.

NARBAL (*to* THARES). The woe he suffers is beyond compare.
The sorrow in his soul obscures his reason.

THARES. His words show clearly he hath lost his senses.

HEROD. I cannot any longer bear her absence.
This lengthy separation drives me frantic.
Tell her for me that she must come to see me.
By her mere presence she can make me happy.
I will forgive her all when I behold her;
Her eunuch shall be granted his full freedom
When I have learned her will concerning him.

NARBAL. The greatness of his grief beclouds his fancy.

THARES. In consequence, he might be deemed insane.

HEROD. When I command, my words are not obeyed.
Did I speak too low to be understood?

NARBAL. What wouldst thou, sire?

HEROD.   That someone should go quickly
To make the Queen come. . . . Ah! I am too indulgent!

NARBAL. Thou askest for the Queen? Alas, sire!

HEROD.   Why not?

NARBAL. Nothing is left of her but her fair name.

HEROD. Her name alone is left? Can she be dead?

NARBAL. I have brought thee the sure news thereof already.

HEROD. Ah, Narbal! I begin to recollect it.
That which afflicts me comes again to punish me,
And my sad memory, conjuring up its image,
Becomes on this point faithful to my hurt.
It is too diligent to present to me
What appears to me only to torment me.
Errors which cause in me remorse so keen,
Violent deeds, ye are too clear before me,
And show too well to my confounded senses,

In the evil that I did, the good I lost.
  But I behold the Queen! She is in that cloud.
A band of blood is round her naked throat.
She mounts to heaven, full of majesty.
Her grace is greater, even as her beauty.
The throng of blessed spirits encircles her;
One offers her a palm, and one a crown.
She turns on me her glances innocent
To observe the hugeness of the pain I feel.
  O beauteous Mariamne, hear my words!
Thou whose divine sight troubles and consoles me,
Theme of my thoughts, object of my desires,
Minister to my joys and miseries,
Despite so many foes who warred upon thee
Thou conqueredst, dear and mighty spirit, on earth;—
And dost thou in a chariot of fire
Depart today and from before our eyes
Vanish, to go and triumph in the skies?
Taste the sweet fruit which midst so many fears
I made thee water, with both blood and tears;
But oh, forget thy woes which came through me;
Fair angel, grant thy persecutor pardon!
I should have prized thee above all things else.
Never shouldst thou have walked except on roses,
And thy great virtues and thy peerless charms
Ought always to have ruled over my will,—
Instead of which, consumed with anger blind,
I treated thee indeed most barbarously;
But I have come to accuse myself to all,
And truly woe like mine ought to appease thee.
If great my sin, if horrible my crime,
I feel repentance keen and real therefor.
  Marvel of beauty, thou of matchless honor,
Who, soaring hence, bear'st all my joy away,
Pure guest of heaven, dear theme of my lament,
Do not imagine that I feign my sorrow.
To go and tell thee what is my repentance,
My soul is poured out with my tears. Behold
The flood of grief which makes it desolated,
And how, to follow thee, it takes its flight.

                              [He sinks to the ground.

THARES.   Strength fails him, and his color paleth. He
  Hath fainted. Let us carry him to a bed.
  Perhaps he will regain his senses when

Water is thrown upon his face.

NARBAL.   O Prince,
Piteous in thy great sorrows! lo, thou art
Thyself the architect of thy misfortunes.
Thy love, suspicions, fear, and anger have
Dimmed thy fair fame and caused thy miseries.
Thou canst administer laws to many nations,
Yet knowest not how to reign o'er thine own passions.
But rarest spirits oft commit great crimes,
And kings are often slaves unto themselves.

Saül

(S A U L)

By

PIERRE DU RYER

INTRODUCTORY NOTE

Pierre Du Ryer was born about 1600 and died in 1658. Though of the petty aristocracy, he was in financial straits during a large part of his life, all of which was passed in Paris or its suburbs. He evidently received an excellent classical education, and was doubtless encouraged to write by his father, himself an impecunious poet and a secretary to the King. Pierre succeeded to this office in 1621, and in 1633 took similar employment under the King's half-brother, the Duc de Vendome. By this time he had married an adoring and capable but uneducated middle-class woman (who bore him at least four children) and had become one of the new generation of playwrights who now appeared upon the termination of the long career of Hardy. After the Duc de Vendome's fall and flight to England in 1640, Du Ryer seems to have had no patron but supported himself and his family as best he could by his plays and his translations from the classics. The latter kind of work, which he had begun to publish as early as 1634, proved the more lucrative and eventually absorbed all his energies. Plays and translations alike were done too hastily, under pressure of need; but notwithstanding this fact his productions in both fields of endeavor were greatly admired in his own times, and in 1646 he was elected to membership in the French Academy under extremely gratifying circumstances.

Among the contemporaries of Corneille's prime, Du Ryer is generally ranked with, and next to, Rotrou. He had considerable originality, an instinct for realism, constructive skill, and some capacity for drawing character. A frequent inability to achieve sufficient emotional intensity in his plays and a lack of style are his greatest faults; his verses at best are dignified, somewhat austere rhetoric, not poetry. His fondness for the rhetorical device of syntactic parallelism is notable.

His earliest plays, and more than half of all his plays, were tragi-comedies—thirteen out of a total of twenty-three dramas; but his best work is in his tragedies, of which there were six. The first of these, *Lucrèce,* was written in 1636, before the *Cid;* its construction and characterization are surprisingly good for so early a play. *Lucrèce* and Jean de Marait's *Sophonisbe* were the chief examples of dramas based on Roman history which Corneille had as models when he turned to that field for subjects. In *Alcionée* (1637) Du Ryer produced a tragedy with a plot simpler than any other until

Racine's *Bérénice*. The situation of its heroine is essentially that of the Infanta in the *Cid*, which had just appeared. It scored a great success.

His third tragedy, *Saül* (1640), was not nearly so popular—a fact which is not surprising, for it is dominated by a single role and is lacking in movement and variety. But it is a meritorious study of a man verging upon melancholia and possessed by a "fixed idea" that he is doomed; and neither its inept second act nor its too static quality as a whole can keep this play, in view of its third and fifth acts especially and of the sobriety and truth of its depiction of human emotions, from ranking among the very best dramas by the contemporaries of Corneille and Racine.

Saül, like *la Mariane* and the *Cid*, was produced on the old type of stage, with multiple sets instead of a single scene. The picturesque setting of Act III is of the sort to which tragi-comedy had accustomed Du Ryer.

CHARACTERS IN THE PLAY

SAUL, *King of the Hebrews.*
JONATHAN, *son of Saul.*
MICHAL, *daughter of Saul.*
ABNER, *Saul's chief captain.*
PHALTI, *A Hebrew courtier and officer.*
THE WITCH OF ENDOR.
The ghost of the prophet SAMUEL.
ACHAS, *the armor-bearer of Jonathan.*
The Armor-Bearer of Saul.
Two other sons of Saul.

Saul

ACT I

The scene represents the tent of SAUL. SAUL, MICHAL, JONA-
THAN *and two other sons of Saul are discovered.*

SAUL.   Cease, my dear children, to console a father
Whom heaven hath made the target of its wrath.
When with such rigor strikes its angry arm,
A sudden death is only a release.
Flee from my sight, then; flee from one most wretched,
Lest his fate crush you if ye seek to aid him,
And lest the just wrath of a vengeful God,
Falling on him, will fall upon you also.

MICHAL.   What! wilt thou lay aside that lofty courage
Which keeps the diadem upon thy brow,
Refuse to conquer and to live for us,
And on this day give up thyself for lost?

SAUL.   Ah, do not force me to confess my weakness.
Yes, I have lost all hope; my courage fails me.
When heaven abandons one who is assailed,
He is abandoned by his courage, too.

JONATHAN.   What circumstance, what fearful, ominous thing
Displayeth in thy realm the wrath of heaven?
Is it that the people in revolt against thee
Bear arms against the throne whereon thou sittest?
Is it that they murmur against that obedience
With which the supreme power should be honored
And which, maintained e'en without fear of laws,
Is the chief stay of royal greatness? Truly
Do the Philistines war with thee; but have they
Borrowed the thunderbolts of the living God?
Have they so much good fortune, so much valor
That one cannot behold them without quailing?
How many, many times have these barbarians
Launched a rash expedition in Judea?
Where and how often, smitten by thy hand,
Have they not found that heaven is on our side?
What with their lands flame-ravaged, and their armies
Crushed, have they not enriched us oft with booty?
In short, may not one say that they bring hither
Not so much war and terror as proud spoils,

113

And that these folk, subdued so frequently,
Pay tribute, as it were, by their defeats?
  Is this a situation, then, to affright us?
In fleeing from us, have they learned to conquer?
Nay, nay, e'en now repenting their invasion,
They are, by fear of being vanquished, vanquished.
They know the spirit burning in our breasts;
We mean to conquer, being wont to conquer,
And if one mounts from glory to more glory,
From victory, too, one goeth on to victory.
In any state to which we are reduced,
The habit of winning is a potent help.
  What can disturb us, then? With what sad fears
Can we be justifiably assailed?
Ah, sire, forgive my feeling as I do,
But nothing frightens us like thy dismay.
'Tis only from the troubled mind thou showest
That our foes' strength can be increased, and by
This perturbation thou canst take from our
Victorious land victory and all its spirit.
Let fear go where the enemy are gathered;
Whenever a king quails, his throne is shaken,
And all too late he knows, when he succumbs,
A shaken throne already is half-fallen.
See in thy children, see in their brave hearts,
The certain presage of a deathless triumph.
In glory's bosom they were ever nurtured.
I am the least of them, yet always conquer.

SAUL. Alas, in you I find all things propitious,
But in myself only sad auguries.
The proof of those ills that are destined for me
Is I, is my own soul, is Saul confounded.
A secret voice from place to place pursues me,
Threatens me, terrifies me, everywhere.
Each hour, each moment, hath more awesome made it
Till now at last it thunders in my heart.
Let a proud enemy attack my realm,
Let there be leagued with him a hundred princes,
Let him array against me many peoples
At whose ferocity the whole world trembles;
'Tis not their rage that I await with dread,
'Tis heaven's hostility, 'tis God that daunts me.
Alas, that Sovereign Judge have I consulted
To know the issue of what so disturbs me;

But I learned naught, either by the voice of dreams
Which do not lie, coming to us from heaven,
Or by the holy voice of honored priests
Who often have declared the future to me.
Trembling, I have consulted then the prophets;
Still mute are these mouth-pieces of the Lord.
Their ghastly silence fills me with dismay;
I find a secret horror overtakes me,
And surely deem that God, who deigned to shield me,
Hath now abandoned him whom he will hear not.

JONATHAN. Let us hope better, sire. A thousand voices
Hath heaven for use when it replies to kings.
If it spake not by these familiar means
Which can be vitiate by their own shortcomings,
It favoreth thy prayers and thine intents
By its preserving of thy subjects' fealty.
Is it possible that their strong and active ardor
Could be maintained if heaven did not consent?
And can it be that heaven would keep it thine
If heaven today hath lost the will to aid thee?
This holy bond, this union of domains,
Reveals a God who gives to kings protection;
It is a sign of love which gleams above them;
It is the voice which doth presage good fortune;
And in despite of mists, despite of storms
Which often break over the noblest heads,
This is a light divine which shows to sovereigns
That heaven loves them and preserves their realms.

SAUL. Yes, now I know what heaven declares to me
If its response lies in a nation's ardor.
My people love my sway. I can perceive
Augury of great good in their devotion . . .

Enter ABNER.

But what would Abner? It seems he is dismayed.
What new bolt menaces my throne? Speak out.

ABNER. Jerusalem forgets her loyalty.

SAUL. What blow is this thou dealest me? What sayest thou?
Speak out.

ABNER.   Jerusalem, e'erwhile so faithful,
Seems to have lost all reverence and devotion.

SAUL. A people so belovèd could revolt?

ABNER. If they have not yet left their loyalty,
They have, at least by murmuring, besmirched it.

SAUL. O wretched prince! O people, O vile people!
Unstable, blind, and hapless is a king
Who conceives hope and bases it on you.
They have repented, then, of seeming faithful.
They murmur, sayst thou? Say they are rebellious,
Because from murmurings to insurrection
One may compute only a single step.

ABNER. This evil can be rectified. 'Tis new-born.

SAUL. This evil is great as soon as it is glimpsed.
But dost thou know the source of their defection?

ABNER. The source of all a people's acts is folly.
I sought to learn the causes of their crime.
But one speaks vainly when a madness grips them.
The populace, when it departs from fealty,
Can no more reason than it can hear reason.

MICHAL (*while* SAUL *strides back and forth*).
Ah! his grief stabs my heart! Ah, brother mine,
His manner shows what great dismay he feels.

SAUL. Nay, nay, it must be. Go, go, Jonathan,
Dear, stalwart buttress of my sad dominions.
Go, then—nay, nay, bide here. Alas, what would I?
Art thou my foe? Am I thine adversary?
How hast thou wronged me that thou meritest
Exposure to a rebel people's blows?
If, when I serve it, it abandons me,
Trampling the reverence that it owes my crown;
If it disdains me—me, me, its defender—
How can this monster's fury spare my children?

JONATHAN. Divest thyself, sire, of a father's love
That shows thee dangers where thine interest calls me.
E'en though I there should find misfortune, can
I serve thee better than where danger reigneth?
But we debate too much a thing that must be.
Too great delay might be disastrous for thee.
Perhaps this evil, that begins its course,
May be just now still able to be cured,
And while we talk of it (oh, dreadful thought!)
It may increase and grow incurable.
Then do not harm thyself by staying me.
To lose one moment now is to lose much.

SAUL. Shall *I* go where this flame is seen enkindled? . . .
But I am needed to inspire my army.
Go, then, and seek indeed to calm this tumult
Before the foe can reap the fruit thereof.

    Go, my dear Jonathan, and obey my hest
    Not so much as necessity. 'Tis this
    That sends thee far away, plucked from mine arms.
JONATHAN. Who goeth to serve his king is not sent far
    Away. Sire, doubt not that my presence, only,
    Will quell the mutineers' proud insolence.

                  [*Exeunt* JONATHAN *and* ABNER.

SAUL. My people in revolt! A wretched people
    Which I from ignominy led to glory—
    A people naught but slaves and miserable
    And only through my toil grown formidable,
    Which knoweth not its king whose mighty deeds
    Unnumbered have each day surpassed its wishes,
    And unto which, without me, the whole earth
    Would be a prison or else a sepulcher,
    And which, with so much evidence of my kindness,
    By its rebellion doth requite my care!
    Ah, this thought kills me! Ah, the people, brood
    Ungrateful, a dread monster towards its friend!
    Too much indulgence shown it, makes it lordly.
    Too much prosperity makes it overbearing.
    It needs must be abased, it must be curbed;
    Unless it feareth, it maketh itself feared.
MICHAL. In David there is help.
SAUL.   David, thy husband?
    His very name excites my wrath. Ne'er speak
    Of him to me.
MICHAL.   Thou knowest his services.
SAUL. Ne'er speak of him to me. I know his wiles.
MICHAL. Ah, sire, his foes' achievement and delight
    Is that suspicion which it seems hath seized thee;
    But although ever admirable is virtue,
    Trust but its enemies and it is guilty.
    It comes from heaven, which hath made it triumph;
    Believe its enemies, it comes from hell.
SAUL. Now I would judge. . . .
MICHAL.   What! thou suspectest *me?*
SAUL. The name of "father" is a holy name
    And I believe that it is reverenced.
MICHAL.   Yea,
    Sire, 'tis reverenced. To deem otherwise,
    Is to consign me to the rack when guiltless.
    But as 'twould be my shame and misery
    To be suspected by my king and father,

I would find glory, for my husband's sake,
In being suspected save by thee alone.

SAUL. If David still loves either wife or master,
This gathering storm will make him come to us.
His country will be shown his generous nature,
His wife his love, I his fidelity.

Enter PHALTI.

Phalti, what is thy news?

PHALTI. The foe advances,
Everywhere dreaded were it but for their daring.
They burn, sack, slaughter, think to crush resistance
And deem they vanquish those who made them tremble.
But what most lends them strength is . . .

SAUL. Let thy news
Be heard. Speak. 'Tis my wish.

PHALTI (*indicating* MICHAL). But . . .

SAUL. I command thee.

PHALTI (*to* MICHAL). Consider, madam, in my trying position,
My duty and compulsion to obey.
If the unhappy words which thou wilt hear
Strike thy heart where it is most sensitive;
If those words bring confusion unto thee,
'Tis common rumor that, despite me, speaks them.
(*To* SAUL). Yes, sire, and this I say unwillingly,
And keener is the sorrow to my soul
Than if, self-loathing, I accused myself,
David—since one cannot imagine it
And therefore spare my tongue this sad report—
David now marches with thine enemies,
Supporting those whom once he conquered for thee.

SAUL. O base deserver of eternal hatred,
I thought thee wicked—not a rebel, though.
But the revolt in which thy guilt appears
Proves that the worst is to be feared of miscreants.
I have received this ingrate in my family,—
Have even shared my power with him. What thing
Can stay the course of traitorous, thankless men
If even such honors can in no wise stay it?
No, no, we cannot doubt, now, that my ruin
Is the intention of his sinful course
And that the rage of a rebellious people
Results from nothing but his wickedness.

MICHAL. Sire!

SAUL.   We no more can doubt it. His behavior
Shows it. The guilty wretch has planned this crime—
Conceived it, shaped it, nursed it in my Court,
And only now revealed it openly,—
A foe less cruel, less treacherous, less base
When he declared it than when he concealed it.
Now, now, defend thy gallant husband. Dream
That he protects thee, that he fights for us.
Dream that he cherishes thee and thinks of thee
When he assails the throne where reigns thy father.
If love alone prescribes his conduct for him,
To make thee queen, himself must he make king!
Yes, David fain would rule. This recreant plotter
Believes crime lawful if it leads to empire.

MICHAL.   David is great of heart, and not a monster.

SAUL.   Great he must needs be, with this great design.
But say no more of him; 'tis time he died.
Whoe'er speaks for a rebel, shares his guilt,
And insurrection is the only crime
Which kings who wish to reign can never pardon.

MICHAL.   If he be guilty, sire, 'tis time he died;
His wife herself would give him up to justice.
But though I speak not for him, his past service
Defends him well enough against suspicions
That are unfounded, or at least deserves
For its renown aforetime that the judgment
Which lays this crime to him should be suspended.
Ah, sire, a king will make his subjects wretched
If he believes too quickly what is charged
Against them; he will arm the hands of envy,
Will give them power o'er the fairest life,
Exhibit Vice tricked out in gorgeous vestments,
And make his Court the reef that Virtue strikes on.
   That Phalti hath spoke thus, does not surprise me,
Nor that he shows a savage hate of David.
He loves me, and believes that if he pictures
David a criminal and a malcontent,
He will inspire in thee that selfsame secret
Hatred which makes him try to ruin David,
And that from such a hatred 'twill be easy
To lead thee to contrive against his life.
Thus Phalti strives, and all his toil is only
To make his king be his hate's instrument,—
Only to win, against all right and reason,

A prize for his base love and for his treason.
View us, then, with an eye at least not hostile.
Do not so soon believe in David's guilt.
Must he be to his prince an odious sight
When only those that envy him accuse him?
See who it is that strikes at and defames him:
His honor's foe, and his wife's would-be lover!

SAUL.   Thou owest him hate if thou art loyal to me.

MICHAL (*looking at* PHALTI).   I hate all subjects who betray
        their king.

PHALTI.   I serve him well.

SAUL.   Let us inspect the army.

                    [*They go out, leaving* MICHAL *alone.*

MICHAL.   How easily deceived! how mazed his soul!
        Or, say, how his aversion, that blind impulse,
        Easily makes him believe false reports
        To think thus, without effort, David guilty!
        Such facile credence plainly shows much hate. . . .
        But what do I myself think? Ah, my heart,
        What doest thou? Thinkest thou David's virtue lapsed
        And that he bears, himself, on this sad soil
        The tragic torch wherewith the war is kindled?
        The frequent shameful outrage that was done him
        May put in question his fidelity;
        But not less do his virtues testify
        That whoso doubts him doeth him one more outrage.
        But woe! the best of men can turn, though shuddering,
        His resolution into sinful rage.
        A mighty spirit is angered, riseth up,
        Goeth too far, does that which it detesteth.
        O David, once revered by those that love thee!
        O David, dreaded now by those that love thee!
        Unhappy source whence my lament proceedeth!
        My hope aforetime, now become my fear!
        When I defend thee in such evil case,
        Art thou an innocent or a guilty man?

A C T   I I

The scene is the same. Enter SAUL, PHALTI, *and* ABNER.

PHALTI.   Whence comes now this new darkness which reveals
        Nothing but ghastly pictures to thy sight?
        Thou hast seen the camp, thy captains and thy soldiers

Fired with one spirit, marching as one man.

SAUL. I fear for Jonathan, and when I consider
The awesome rage of a rebellious people,
My luckless son, cast down from his high station,
Bathed in his blood, appears before mine eyes.

ABNER. The people love him. Be not troubled thus.

SAUL. The people can soon change from love to hate.
But a still greater, more insistent thing
Engenders worse confusion in my soul.
The woe which sorest doth oppress me is
The fearsome silence of enangered heaven.
The tokens of its wrath are everywhere;
I see the people of my realm seditious,
My foes grown stronger, even in my army.
Dread of a secret poison mounts within me.
Those who should aid me now conspire against me;
The enemy of their prince is now their sovereign,
And perhaps prospering in their fell designs,
They rule by silent knavery in my camp.

PHALTI. David was to be feared when by thy side.
Now his ill deeds 'gainst thee are plainly seen.
Do not regret that thou hast lost this traitor;
A traitor really serves thee by unmasking.

SAUL. Truly I see on all sides only woes.
If hostile heaven is deaf, though, to my sorrows,—
If by its silence now it would confound me,—
Let us seek voices elsewhere that can answer.
Know, then, . . . but understand that ye must hear me
Not to give counsel but to do my bidding.

PHALTI. Whate'er thy august power shall please to order,
We shall not answer thee save by obedience.

SAUL (*to himself*). What step do I resolve? Nay, I debate
Too much. Hell is the aid that I must try.
(*To the others*) Let someone, then, be found who can by
charms
Show what success is to attend mine arms.
Help the most hard beset of hapless kings.
Someone find such a one. . . . What? Thunderstruck?

ABNER. Oh, sire, what plan is this!

SAUL. It is a sin,
But need will render it legitimate.
'Tis the last hope of an unfortunate ruler,
Who to himself is cruel and dangerous now,--
Who in the grief with which his soul is full

Cares not if it be heaven or hell that answers.
More laden with woes than any slave with chains,
If I find heaven deaf, I will ask of hell.

PHALTI. Oh, sire! this deed will bring thy doom upon thee.

SAUL. This deed must needs be done this very night.

PHALTI. But, sire . . .

SAUL. Obey, and do not answer me.

PHALTI. Thou hast had punished with a cruel death
All those whose souls by practice of black magic
Have held communication with the Pit.
How is one to be found . . .

SAUL. Go. Do but search,
And yet beware if thou canst search in vain.
Cloak what thou wishest.

Enter MICHAL.

PHALTI. But here is . . .

SAUL. What would she?

MICHAL. Vouchsafe that I appear where duty calls me
And that I win grace of thy Majesty
To speak a single time to thee with freedom.
I shall rouse, doubtless, both the hate and envy
Which are foul foes of a good life's fair days;
But well I know that a just, free-souled king
Will not condemn an act that aims at justice.
Thus in my spirit, which wavers in suspense,
Hope is increased and fear diminishes.
If I should dread my voice might stir thine anger,
Thy soul is just and 'tis for thee I speak.
Yes, with whatever paroxysms my grief
Finds words, my interest, sire, is not what moves me,
Except thus: that the interest of kings
Is that of those who live beneath their sway.
David was pictured to thee in such black
Colors that his own wife doubted his honor,
But soon his virtues, which could not be stained,
Pierced through the darkness that would fain conceal them.
Ah, sire, thou turnest from thine afflicted daughter;
But give not up thine own offended cause,
And leave it not for envious spirits to think
A king doth side with them in their injustice.
If my free speech seems criminal to thee,
For its excuse, think of my zeal at least.
Let realm, let kinship speak to thee for me,

And let the name of "Father" move my king.
　If the suspicion of a crime, and not
Thy hate, hath armed thy sovereign hand 'gainst David,
Let but thy Majesty, who didst deign to exalt him,
At least recall him to make proof of him.
Should he obey and come, he is shown faithful;
Should he obey not, he is shown rebellious.
Thus thou wilt learn if thou hast been betrayed,—
If David hath been guilty or but hated.
Thus, despite all misfortunes, dangers, shipwrecks,
Which follow closely the most noble hearts,
I ask for David, not to see a husband,
But to behold him die, fighting for thee.
If for his king he dies, I will love the battles
That lead him to illustrious obsequies;
And when I see him on his noble bier,
The cause he died for will console my grief.
Yes, as my king is dearer than myself
To me, I seek to expose for my king's sake
Him whom I love. Let David show once more
That he can vanquish giants and kings for thee;
Or let him, in his death, give thee a token
That wrongly did his sovereign lord suspect him.
What other proofs wouldst thou of constancy
And faith than a man's blood shed for his king?

SAUL.　I can approve when a wife shows her courage
In championing a husband wronged by Fate.
I can approve when she tries gallantly
To succor her unhappy father. One
And the other purpose is a noble purpose,
And not to heed her would be most unjust.
Thus left to overcome the woes thou feelest,
I ever hear thy words without vexation.
I have sought grounds—I even till now have sought them—
To make thy plea the stronger and the better.
I have spoken in my heart for thee and David;
My justice long hath held my wrath suspended.
But vainly doth my favor strive for David;
His own deeds speak against him. I should also
Desire for the best interest of my realm
That I could use his arm without suspicion;
But can I make use of a guilty hand
Which adds the deed itself to the suspicion?
Have done, then, with the care thou hast for me.

As a wife thou actest; I act as a king.

MICHAL. Sire, in accusing him, one wrongs thee also,
Since 'tis desired to make thee trust imposture.
Though David hath been painted recreant,
He is in Ziklag, full of loyal ardor;
And there he waits for thy command to call him
And let him prove again to thee his zeal
And finally show that through all adverse fortune
He treasured still his fealty unto thee.
(*Turning to* PHALTI) Thou who assailest him, and whose
black envy
Strives to besmirch the brightness of his life,
If really thou believest that base designs
Arm his felonious hands against his king,—
If, having accused him, thou believest him rebel,—
Ask his return, feign to be anxious for it.
Thy questioned honor seemeth to force thee to it.
If David failed,—if David is a traitor,—
He will do what thou wishest, not dare appear.
Then will thy virtue be seen great and shining,
And whoso blames thee amiss will praise thee justly.
But fear of a result against thy wishes,
Despite thy passions, maketh thee keep silent.
Thou fearest innocence, and I now excuse it
That David's rival does not speak for him.

SAUL. Thou goest too far. If Phalti hopes to win thee,
Know that to me his hope is not displeasing.
Know that I wish success for him. But David
Is leal, thou sayest, and not amid our foes.
Doth not the fact that he hath served this prince
Formerly who now layeth waste the land
Condemn him? Who compelled him to go hence?
What proper reason made him leave my sight?
Was it in order to preserve his life?
My grace could have assured him against harm.
Was it in order to increase in honor?
Honor would bid him to find blessings here.
He did not, therefore, choose this ill-judged flight
To make secure a life that here was threatened;
He did not flee from an unkindly sovereign
To satisfy a soul that craved high honors.
What did his voluntary going prove, then,
Save that he was beginning to be recreant,—
That his proud heart was weary of obedience,—

That he who flees his king embarks on treason?
Even had he foreseen some great disgrace
About to follow threatening rumors of it,
Yes, even in such a plight could he have rightly
Sought an asylum with mine enemies?
No, no, he should have waited for the tempest
To fall on him if nowhere else was shelter.
If he had loved and reverenced loyalty,
He would have died ere let his own be doubted.

PHALTI. If with such evil he hath smirched his life,
Must one accuse thereof my hate or envy?
Would he would offer us his days and life-blood
And that indeed his aid might be accepted!
Would he would give his king the greatest proof
That can distinguish any faithful heart!
Does it seem henceforth that one should not hear
A fealty doubted which he put in question?
And what can a magnanimous prince decide,
If to cause doubt is to commit a crime?

MICHAL. Ah, sire!

SAUL.   Enough!

MICHAL.   Yes, sire, it is enough.
David is guilty if thou hatest him.
O happy Phalti, triumph in this hour.
All smiles on thee; all sorrow dwells with me.

PHALTI. I feel no triumph in another's woes,
And David's fall touches me keenly, too.

MICHAL. He deserves death, if the King please to trust thee.

PHALTI. His deeds alone determine his repute.

MICHAL. His deeds alone, all splendid as they are,
Alarm thee for thyself, not for the State.
Love of his country is the holy flame
With which his heart is kindled. To serve well
Is glory to him; to conquer is his wont.

SAUL. Thou failest to show respect.

MICHAL.   Yes, sire, I do;
But in thus failing to, I think I serve thee,
For I reveal to thee an aid thou needest,
An aid as sure as 'twould be efficacious.

SAUL. David mine aid! what hath he done so great
That may not well have been the fruit of chance?

MICHAL. Ah, sire, if David hath displeased thee, I
In speaking of his great deeds would displease thee.
He were not joined with thine illustrious blood

                              Had not his arm deserved such high reward.

SAUL.   Let him not boast of this exalted bond,
          For I can show him how 'tis not deserved
          And that one ceases to be joined with kings
          When one rebels or trenches on their rights.
          I promise thee the prize thou seekest, Phalti.
          I give it thee.

MICHAL.   What! Even while David lives
          And when he never hath abandoned me?

SAUL.   The traitor hath besmirched his fame forever.
          Know this: that he is dead, since he is guilty.

MICHAL.   Ah, father, if he had committed crimes
          So heinous that they were beyond all pardon,
          The tie that joins us is so strong and sacred
          That scarce can death itself destroy or break it.

SAUL.   To break it, is a most exceptional act.
          Men cannot do it, but a king can do it;
          And by this means I wish to make it seen
          That kings and death have one and the same power.
          But Phalti, do my bidding and thy task.
          Seek thou knowest what, without delaying longer.
          Let me not wait uncertain, but ere nightfall
          May the fair fruit of thy good care appear.

PHALTI.   I go, my lord.   [*Exit* PHALTI.

SAUL.   Ah woes, ah woes too cruel,
          Can ye not lessen, or be mortal things?

ABNER.   But here is Jonathan.

              Enter JONATHAN *and two other sons of Saul.*

SAUL.   Well, what shall we learn?

JONATHAN.   I have appeased the anger of the people.

SAUL.   Whence came their frenzy?

JONATHAN.   From a false report
          That David, who they know is true, hath been
          Spurned.

SAUL.   But what would they have?

JONATHAN.   They ask for David.

SAUL.   That wretch, that coward, whom a crime tears from us?
          Then to content the blinded populace
          I must, forsooth, be lavish of my grace!
          Then I must bear it, to the shame of kings,
          That my rebellious subjects govern me!
          No, no, let all the poisons bred by discord
          Expend themselves in fury 'mid this people;

Let it renounce that duty laid upon it
By heaven; we have vanquished mightier foes.
Let it revolt to David as it wisheth,
Make him an idol in its monarch's place;
Despite the crimes of those that hound me, I
Will hurl down idol and idolaters.—
Wouldst *thou* act so at variance with honor?
JONATHAN. Consider the extremity of thy cause.
'Tis sometimes courage and nobility
To compound somewhat with necessity.
SAUL. Recall a traitor, whence our troubles rose?
JONATHAN. Nay, sire, but David. Thus, sire, say my brothers.
SAUL. Is this the counsel of a noble spirit?
JONATHAN. This is the counsel that will prosper thee.
In every situation the wise counsel
Is always noble, always honorable.
SAUL. This care unparalleled doth not surprise me.
A friend of David needs must give such counsel.
JONATHAN. David I love, for he loves thee, my father.
Pleading to thee for him, I plead for thee.
SAUL. What! mine own children enemies of their race,
Abandoning their father, honor, station?
My subjects in revolt ask for a rebel,
And mine own children second their demands!
What evils have not been prepared for me?
I see my children among those that plan them!
This Jonathan, of old a thunderbolt,
Needeth a chief to lead him into war,—
Needeth a chief to guide his valiant arm,
As oft triumphant as it joined in combat.
This Jonathan, in love with fame, desireth
To owe his triumph to another's hand.
What spell, what poison, what chill slothfulness
Hath stripped from Jonathan both strength and courage?
JONATHAN. If this did not concern the common cause,—
If there were need to save my fortunes only,—
In peace, in war, incapable of fear,
I would wish none but me to fight for me.
As many a time mine arm hath gained the victory,
Mine arm alone today would make me glorious.
But when one cannot safely run a risk,—
When one sees all in flames,—when all needs guarding,—
When a throne totters near a precipice,—
When one must triumph or must perish wholly,—

When all the State hangs on one single effort,—
The mightiest king is never strong enough.
'Tis never shameful for the noblest hearts
To seek assistance against mighty storms,
But too great confidence in their own powers
Has all too often wrought their shame and sorrow.
　Charge me who will with trembling in my soul,
My deeds themselves acquit me of this charge.
A threatened State must not too greatly trust
Its strength or fortune; one that is no more
Than strong enough is never strong enough.
If thou shouldst go to seek for alien forces
Wherewith we might repulse our common foes,
Perhaps the State, perhaps ourselves would have
Thereby disgrace together with the help:
But David is thine own; he seeks thee, loves thee;
He is among thy sons even as myself.
How dims it, then, the glory of the King,
Who shall be conqueror henceforth, I or David?
Another for my prince may win the victory;
If I have fought well, my renown is ample.

SAUL.　What! thou still perseverest? What say'st thou, Abner?
Is this the counsel that I should be given?
Hold'st thou 'gainst me with a contrarious people?

ABNER.　I would not dare to speak, lest I displease thee.

SAUL.　Thou askest for David.

ABNER.　　　　　　　　It is necessary.
Who asks for him doth serve thy Majesty.

SAUL.　Then all betray me. Good, bring David back.
Ye wish for his return, let the wretch have it.
If thus one sets a knife against my throat,
I can use David to requite this scheme.
Since 'tis desired to owe to him our victory,—
Since he must take away from you the glory,—
Since from your shame he will acquire renown,—
I take revenge on you when I recall him.

MICHAL.　Thus thou beginnest to o'ercome a foe
Soon to be brought to thee, dead or in chains.

SAUL.　What! David will return? Doth not this publish
That without him henceforth we cannot reign?
Doth not this show that fear constraineth us?
Doth not this set forth plainly our own weakness,
And tell the proud and all-too-well-pleased foe
That victory, if he will attack, awaits him?

What, David will return and I must know
That need hath forced me thus into surrender?
Although unto the last extremity
I be reduced, must I reveal this need?
Nay, nay, to indicate the ills which threaten
Is not to know the principles of kingship;
And those who cannot hide wherein their States
Are troubled, are unworthy potentates.

JONATHAN. Those principles are properly applied
By altering one's practice when 'tis best.

SAUL. True, Jonathan, quite true; but mark thou, one
Must needs have reigned to know when one should do it.
Ah, my sons, ye whom victory oft hath welcomed
Ought to be strong enough to guard your honor.
Shall it be said some day in later ages
That Saul would not have reigned except for David?
No, no, that would besmirch your noble courage.
Haste, haste yourselves to gain the mastery,
And make it said midst a triumphant nation
That Saul would not have reigned, had he been childless.
I shall believe that I am to be envied
If I should owe my greatness unto those
That owe their being to me. If I must owe
My scepter and my rank to anyone,
Let it be to my sons, to mine own blood.

JONATHAN. Well then, we needs must show that we can fight,
That those who conquer us must fall with us,
And that 'tis for thy sons the happiest fate
To win the field for thee or die for thee.
Come, brothers, let us follow this ambition,
To end this war in triumph or end our lives.
'Twill be no vain loss of a luckless blood
To shed it for his sake who made it ours.
In life or death, let us give noble proof
That we deserved our birth from a king's loins.
On this occasion all is sweet, all fair,
Be it a victor's fame or the dread tomb.

SAUL. Children too much beloved, ye ask for David
Of a fond sire; well, let him be recalled.
Let us have yet this shame, this shame, today,
That without him we could not reign or conquer.
               [*He contemplates his children.*
(*To himself*) If evil fate makes disposition of them,

At least 'twill not be said their father caused it.
JONATHAN.   Blessed decision, which will make us happy!
MICHAL.   Haste we to David! Let us lose no time.

A C T   I I I

*The scene represents wild country in the hills, not far from
the camp of* SAUL. *At the back, on one side is the mouth
of a cave, almost concealed by trees and bushes; on the
other a glimpse of the plain, with the lights of the camp
in the distance. It is dusk, and grows dark as the Act proceeds.* JONATHAN *and* ABNER *are discovered.*

JONATHAN.   Oh, what a dire misfortune for our land!
     David is not to come.
ABNER.   That was my news.
     "Go quickly," the King bade me. "Go tell Jonathan
     That David can be useful to use elsewhere;
     That he can aid this realm, now sore assailed,
     On our frontier as well as in our army;
     And that 'tis necessary for our peace
     That on all sides the State should be defended.
JONATHAN.   'Tis but a pretext, serving that distrust
     Which will abate no jot of unshared power.
     'Tis but a pretext, serving that desire
     Which honor and ambition feed in one.
     He looks on glory as a precious thing
     Whereof he fears that David will partake
     (And that is true), as if he did not know
     That after all great deeds are done, the glory
     Of subjects is entirely their king's.
     But what think we to do, that thus are helpless?
     The evil spirit that possesses him
     Is stronger than men are. In vain do we
     Point out to him the shore and the safe harbor;
     He hugs the reef that is to give him death.
     He deems his children are his enemies;
     He fears to heed their salutary counsels;
     He takes their good advice for baleful profferings—
     Ah, certain presage of disaster! When
     A king is going to perish,—when heaven forsakes him,—
     That, my dear Abner, is the sign it gives
     Thereof. But if we must go down with him
     Into the grave, let us at least select
     The noblest road there. Since with our sole arm

Our king is satisfied, let us try to rise
Higher than he expects us. Keep thy heart
Loyal to him and gallant. Make of it
The greatest treasure of a luckless prince.
If this is not thy king who speaks to inspire thee,
This is his son who speaks, appeals to thee.

ABNER.   I hear respectfully and regard alike
The voices of my sovereign and his son;
But to preserve a gallant, loyal heart,
I hear my duty and my zeal, naught else.
I would betray them, I would render them
Suspect, were 't needful to appeal to me.

JONATHAN.   I urge thee, my dear Abner, on to glory,
Just as one does a victor on to victory.
But let us seek the King.
                                                He comes!—disguised,
Alone with Phalti!

Enter SAUL *and* PHALTI.

SAUL.   Can they have espied me?

JONATHAN.   Oh, sire!

SAUL.   Enough! Abner perhaps hath told thee
What I determined for the kingdom's good,
And I have since provided means and orders
By which Jerusalem is to be kept loyal.

JONATHAN.   I would not doubt that fealty, by thy wisdom,
Hath been restored where insolence held sway,
And that thy purposes, inspired by heaven,
Are at the same time practical and noble.
But seeing thee, sir, divested of those tokens
Which make kings reverently recognized,
One would be wrong in such a situation
If one were unperturbed and unastonished.

SAUL.   Be not astonished. What thou seest me do
Is but the consequence of fruitful counsel.
Abner could have explained it. He knows all.

ABNER.   Yes, sire, but Abner is not indiscreet.
Since this was learned without commands to tell it,
The law I had to set myself was silence.

JONATHAN.   Have I not, then, deserved to know this plan?
Thinkest thou a secret ill befits my breast?
When 'tis to serve thee, when 'tis necessary,
My sword can shine out and my tongue keep silent.

SAUL.   I have consulted heaven. It did not answer.

I mean to see if hell will hear me better.

JONATHAN. Thou! consult hell? Thou! apply to those miscreants
Condemned by thee thyself to flames well-merited?

SAUL. Censoriousness offends me in this crisis.

JONATHAN. It is not, sire, that I oppose thy will,
But these diviners . . .

SAUL.   Trouble not thyself.

JONATHAN. Having already felt thy heavy hand,
If fear does not conceal them from thy Highness,
They will deceive thee with false, flattering words.

SAUL. She whom I seek will not behold my face
And cannot recognize me in this garb.

JONATHAN. That is the reason, then, for thy disguise!

SAUL. Yes, 'tis the reason for this altered aspect.
Thus have I laid aside the signs of greatness
To hide beneath this cloak a hapless monarch.
This is, perhaps, a sinister, dire omen—
No matter, let us go where 'tis decreed.
If the dread justice of offended heaven
Must cause a hideous downfall of my throne,
At least when I have learned of this sad fact
I shall prepare myself to perish nobly.
If heaven's hate makes my ruin ignominious,
My courage at least will make it glorious,
And all kings threatened with an end like mine
Can wish with honor for my destiny.

JONATHAN. Ah, may the horror of a plan so fatal
Be manifested, sire, to thy soul's vision!
To await with constancy what heaven decrees,
Is to prepare one's self to perish nobly.
If we must die, let us die guiltlessly,
Leaving our innocence graven on our tomb.
Shall we expect to find a glorious death
When we shall perish held in hate by heaven?

SAUL. My course is chosen.

JONATHAN.   But 'tis sacrilegious.

SAUL. If 'tis so, if 'tis wrong, the wrong relieves me.

JONATHAN. It can beguile thee, but 'twill finally harm thee.

SAUL. Peace shall at least be mine while it beguiles me.

JONATHAN. Would that one guiltlessly might turn to magic!
Is it thought that demons can foresee the fortunes
Of war, th' outcome of battles, and the events
On which depend our woes and our contentment?
What ray of light that shows what will befall us

Enables them to divine things to come?
If all that shall be in all times, all places,—
In short, the future,—is in God's hands alone,
Can it be that hell, the place of blasphemy,
Knows that which passeth in the breast of God?
That is a vile thought which we ought to banish.
If devils knew the future, they would be gods,
Or midst their torments that rebellious brood
Would at least share with God his power divine.
And even if they, stealing through the cosmos,
Could see laid bare the secrets of the future,
Would those who are man's greatest enemies
Declare unto us aught that would be helpful?
If they tell good things, 'tis a lure they spread
Before our feet to lead us into evil.
If they tell bad things, horror and confusion,
'Tis to make desperate him who doth consult them,
And by the madness which besets his heart
To bring him to the ills they have foretold.
   Flee, then, from this abyss to which thou goest
To plunge thyself therein. Thou turnest to hell;
What aid canst thou expect of it, if in
The extremity in which thy life is threatened
'Tis of thine enemies thou beggest help?
But after all, in knowing by what fate
We shall behold the course of our lives' end,—
In knowing if our lot be fair or baleful,—
Do we advance the good, retard the evil?
Is one the sooner happy, or less soon
Unhappy? May one 'scape the inevitable?
It is enough to fight as a brave man
And leave to heaven the issue of good fortune.

SAUL.   Thy words, my son, have sunk into my soul.
Thou blamest my purpose, and myself I blame it.
It fills my bosom rightfully with terror;
It covers me with shame, whelms me with horror.
I know my sin and that which leads me to it;
In brief, I know but cannot do my duty.
A power which mine is strengthless to resist
Drags me dismayed whither I blush to go.

JONATHAN.   What, sire . . .

SAUL.   Thou harmest me in trying to help me.
I must, I must press on, though to my downfall.

JONATHAN.   Knowing the risk?

SAUL.   Go, go, take thyself hence.
That is thy father's and thy king's command.
Further speech will offend me.
JONATHAN.   Then I must yield.
At least I have tried to be of service to thee.

[Exit JONATHAN.

SAUL.   Thou, Abner, stay. . . . At last, night comes. Then lead me,
Phalti, where I shall learn what I would know.
PHALTI.   The wise woman who was summoned to thine aid
Awaits us in a wood hard by this valley;
But since thine edicts have struck terror in her,
She hath told me that she greatly fears the King.
She is apprehensive, and believes I bring
Either folk strangers to him or scarce friends.
Thou must remember, then, having come hither,
To use thy garb to help deceive her eyes.
SAUL.   May we but see her! Yet is she indeed near?
PHALTI.   Vouchsafe to enter the opening in yon rock.
This yawning hole, where night eternal reigns,
Is the place chosen for our magic spell.
I go to inform her that 'tis time for her
To come.
SAUL.   Go; let thy speed match my impatience.

[Exit PHALTI.

ABNER.   And thinkest thou truly to find succor thus?
SAUL.   And thinkest thou always to oppose me, vainly?
ABNER.   Who thus opposes, serves thee—is thy friend.
SAUL.   And who thus serves me, digs himself a pitfall.
ABNER.   Would I not plunge therein to keep thee from it?
SAUL.   Thy zeal is blind. It leadeth thee astray.
ABNER.   For my king can I do less?
SAUL.   I must be cruel.
If I wish poison, let it be prepared
For me; when I am seen to seek my grave,
Let it be opened for me; and if I
Would fain die, let me be allowed to die.

[Exit ABNER.

But here this woman is. Come, come, and let us
Learn if my fortune is to rise or fall.

Enter THE WITCH OF ENDOR.

(Addressing her)   Thou that with such full knowledge of
great matters
Art able to foretell both war and peace;

Thou who hast given so many proofs of power
That thou art famed more widely than kings are:
Alas, if wretched people still are blest
With the ability to move kind hearts,
Be not astonished if an unknown man
Prays that thy favor now descend on him.

THE WITCH OF ENDOR. Sir, to obtain my favor and my efforts
It is enough that one has need of them.
But thou'rt not unaware of what great tempests
Our heads are threatened with by wrath of Saul.
Thou knowest the edicts he hath framed against us,
How many of my sort have felt his anger
And that thou dost expose me to the same
Ruin when thy affliction begs my aid.

SAUL. I know indeed the edicts of this monarch.
I know still better how to requite boons.

THE WITCH. I shall not serve thee mercenarily.
To hide me from the King is the sole wage
I ask.

SAUL. Drive from thy heart all fear and dread.
Thou wilt be sheltered from the King's pursuit.
Though by an unjust and deplorable fate
The oath of one so wretched wins no credence,
That which thou takest from me in my misfortune
Is no less sacred than a king's pledged word.

THE WITCH. I place my trust entirely in thy care.

SAUL. I place my hope entirely in thee.

THE WITCH. What can I do to serve thee?

SAUL. Spare no efforts.
Call Samuel back from the empire of the dead.

THE WITCH. What, Samuel! Samuel!

SAUL. Samuel, that prophet
Who was the noblest spokesman of God's will.
Call back this great man and the selfsame voice
That formerly gave hope or fear to kings.
Yes, if the matchless power of thine art
Can raise the dead, let Samuel be raised.

THE WITCH. Samuel will show the power of mine art.
Let me withdraw into this cave, apart.
There I must secretly perform the mysteries
To serve the purpose that shall now be mine.

SAUL. Go, then. [*Exit the* WITCH *into the cave.*
(*To himself*) But what am I doing? Ah, stay thy steps,
Henceforth committed to the road of death.

Use the light given thee; fly and shun this crime
While still a feeble gleam shows thee the Pit.
Late cometh the remorse which stirs me, yet
'Tis swift enough if it can profit me.
Friends, let us go. . . . But what do I say in fear?
Nay, let us follow whither ill fate guides us.
Begone, remorse, begone from my wracked heart!
Vainly thy visions have thus frightened me.
Thou hast thy birth in naught but human weakness;
Thou troublest only those distressed by shadows.
Think not to move me again or govern me.
Fear and remorse do not beseem a king.
Let my design be vile and pass for a crime;
Since it can help me, I account it lawful.
If in the end 'tis followed by good fortune,
'Twill seem to those who blame it laudable. . . .
   How long a time this woman makes me wait,
Or else how long it seems to my impatience!
Let us go see.
             But whither would I go,
Blind that I am! Do I desire to merit
My sorrows by my crimes? Do I desire
To merit by my crimes the storm that heaven
Suspends, with thunder fraught, above my head?
What do I? What shall I do? Oh, hapless prince,
Goaded by heaven, by hell, and by thyself!
Thou crime-engendered in a smitten soul,
O healthful offspring of a God that slays us,
Remorse, transport me from this fatal spot
Where even now all hell is bared before me.
If I must die, must die, let a brave death
Signalize my misfortune, not my crime.
Let it draw tears down on my sepulcher.
Let it be death instead of punishment.
Yes, let me tear myself from this loathed place
And be unfortunate without being guilty.

Enter the WITCH.

THE WITCH.   Sir.
SAUL.   Ha! What is 't I do? Well, shall we see him?
THE WITCH.   Already the earth is rent, and opes before thee.
    I see.
SAUL.   What dost thou see? What? Peace or war?
THE WITCH.   I see, I see a God rising from the earth,

But his divine voice, reaching to mine ears,
Tells me at the same time thou art the King.
Alas!

SAUL.   Be not afraid.

THE WITCH.   Ah, sire!

SAUL.   I swear,
If I have any power, that power will shield thee.
What form has that one who is shown to thee?

THE WITCH.   The form of an old man, full of majesty.

SAUL.   Ah, by this noble mien I recognize him,
Whom an unhappy king respected always.

The GHOST *of* SAMUEL *appears at the mouth of the cave.*

THE GHOST OF SAMUEL.   Why, oh, why makest thou so many wicked
Efforts to rob me of the peace which heaven
Gives to the dead?

SAUL.   Thou who beholdest my plight,
Pure spirit, sainted spirit, grant me pardon
For my woe's sake and for constraining thee.
If I have sinned in this extremity,
That sin was born of my necessity.
Alas, on all sides danger girds me round;
Mankind pursues me; heaven abandons me,
Unless its hand, grown kindly to me, fain
Would give me succor by the sight of thee.
Thus desperate in relation to the earth
And to the immortal arm that hurls the lightning,
I seek thine aid, and turn to thee to learn
The fortune that awaits a woeful king.

THE GHOST.   If heaven pursues, if heaven abandons thee,
Thinkest thou to find elsewhere thy crown's support?
Deem'st thou a spirit divested of its body
Hath power to oppose the will of heaven?
Remember that a living God once raised thee
Out of the dust, to set thee in that station
Where a man wields the thunderbolt; remember
That he did set thee on a throne of worship
To which thy boldest prayers did not aspire;
And then remember the ingratitude
With which the thankless Saul repaid his bounty.
Recall that heaven is the foe of evil,
And that thou wert ungrateful when 'twas generous.
Recall the crimes with which thy life is stained,
And thou wilt see how vengeful heaven must loath it.

Think of the sinless ones thy hest hath slain
Because they shielded innocence from thee,—
Because within the circuit of their city
The hapless David found a kind asylum.
Think of how many times my voice hath warned thee,
And to foresee the future, scan the past.

    Heaven laid commands on thee; thou wast rebellious:
Thou pledgedst thy faith thereto; thou wast unfaithful:
And thy rebellion and thy faithlessness
Have lit the fires that shall descend upon thee.
Thou from thy throne shalt fall, and, do thine utmost,
The persecuted David shall mount thither—
That David odious to thee alone
And ever the beloved of earth and heaven—
David, the one sure healer of thine ills,
Whom thine own people were inspired to ask for
To be thine aid—yes, David, driven from thee
By thine injustice, shall most gloriously
Assume the throne from which thou shalt descend,
And kings shall learn by thy dread overthrow
That he who reigns a tyrant, needs must die
For his sins' sake.

SAUL.   I gained the crown to lose it.
Heaven gave it to me; heaven can take it from me.

THE GHOST.   But still 'tis not enough for heaven, which
Abandons thee, to snatch away thy crown.
It will deliver thee to those same foes
Whom its all-powerful arm so oft hath bowed
To thee. It wishes thy defeat and ruin
To exalt a king who was thine adversary.
It wishes still, still hostile unto thee,
To end thy life's course with a fearful death.

SAUL.   Well, I shall die, then. 'Tis for me a victory
To end my life together with my glory.

THE GHOST.   Do not suppose, however, hapless monarch,
That even these many ills are all thy woes.
In bringing thee to a deplorable end,
Heaven makes thee undergo the penalty
That is a sinner's due. In robbing thee
Of a throne whereon thou livedst lawlessly,
Heaven makes thee undergo the punishment
That is a bad king's due. But for a climax
Of horror, of anguish, and of misery,
Heaven wishes to expose thee to a father's

Pangs, and by one same blow to punish in thee
A sire, a criminal, and a wretched king.
Think not to leave, then, to thy budding offspring
The honor or expectation of the throne
Thou losest; dream not thou shalt live again
In sons whom thou hast seen so oft return
In triumph; but know, thou wretch, that thou shalt see them
Fall, 'neath the burden of *thy* crimes, as victims.
Before another night makes dark the skies,
Know that thy sons shall die before thine eyes.

SAUL. Alas! that is the blow that overcomes me.   [*He falls.*

The GHOST *of* SAMUEL *sinks. Enter* ABNER *and* PHALTI.

ABNER. Ah, sire!
THE WITCH.   Ah, take again thy stricken powers.
PHALTI. Sire!
SAUL.   Fearful specter, fly not hence without me,
A father still more wretched than a king.
But this dread phantom, wrapt about in flame,
Goes from my sight to sink into my heart.
Yes, this wan demon, this my mortal foe,
Makes now within my soul his hell and mine.
My children are to die! O grief! O madness!
O impious curiosity cruelly punished!
My sons shall die! O thou, whoe'er thou art,
Samuel or demon, foul or sacred voice,
Blot out, in going hence, the light yet left me.
Visit on me the doom of hell or heaven,
I shall die too well punished, since in these throes
I have already felt my children's death.
Sad hopes of all my life, too piteous sons,
By being my children, must ye then be guilty?
The sins of Saul, unworthy of his rank—
Are these linked to his seed as to his soul?
Ye love me, as sons do; ye pity me.
Is it a crime to love and pity your
Father? Still, what misfortunes equal mine?
"Thy sons," I have been told, "shall die, shall die."
Justice of heaven, that hath no part in kinship,
Cut short my days before I murmur at thee.

A C T   I V

The scene represents the tent of SAUL. PHALTI *and* ABNER *are discovered.*

PHALTI (*speaking to one of* SAUL'S *retinue outside*).
Go to the Princess and inform her that
She must come quickly; that the King would see her.
   Abner, the King tries vainly to show courage.
His soul's woe is revealed in his appearance.
He fain would see his children, whom he thinks
About to die, and I now go to seek them
At his express command. Shall I reveal
To Jonathan the outcome of those spells
Which threaten us with such a great disaster?
Knowing the step which Saul resolved upon,
He will desire to know its consequences.

ABNER. Concerning this, use thy discretion.

PHALTI.   Abner,
'Tis needful he should be informed. He hath
The strongest influence over the King's mind,
And can at least dispel his mortal terror.

ABNER. Take in all things the course which best will serve him.

PHALTI. Well then, I shall go seek for these poor princes.
                             [*Exit* PHALTI.

ABNER. Ah, how great woes illusions can produce!
What tears the anguish of the King foretells us!
But he comes.

Enter SAUL.

SAUL (*to his retinue*). Wait here.
          (*To* ABNER) Abner, I confess
That I now learn how weak a father is.
O bond of nature, jealous of thy power,
Didst thou within this heart put love so strong
Only to be, thyself, O pitiless thing,
The eternal punishment of a king and sire?
Ah, heaven's hate, my fatal enemy,
Would harm me little in stripping me of honors
If that bond did not aid the wrath of heaven
To make this evil greater and more grievous.

ABNER. Wilt thou, then, always cling to this delusion?

SAUL. I cannot lose the horrible impression.

ABNER. Sire, the ghost, doubt not, was an evil spirit

Which sought, in troubling thee, to work thy ruin
And which had only borrowed Samuel's guise
To seem more sacred to thy Majesty.
What, sire! canst thou believe that after death,
Whereof the instant terminates perforce
A good man's miseries, the most righteous souls
Could e'er be happy if compulsive spells
Could reach them? Far from having peace eternal
Which no unpleasantness might ever alter,
Would those who triumphed in a noble death
Not be dependent on the powers of hell?

SAUL. I thought like thee, dear Abner, that a fraud,
The work of devils, wrought the woe I suffer.
At least, the better to resist my foes,
I wished to be beguiled by this opinion;
But whether I turn my gaze or thoughts upon
My place as monarch or my place as father,
It is my duty to neglect not this one;
It is my duty to neglect not that one.
Therefore will I attempt, a piteous father,
To save my children, whom I love so dearly.
Therefore will I attempt, a hapless monarch,
To leave the realm to noble, princely heirs.

ABNER. None could blame that which prudence counsels.

SAUL.   But

What can I hope from it?—alas, what help?
If heaven creates those ills which now I fear,
Can prudence be my rampart and support?
It can defeat the plots of mortals, but
It can do naught against the thunderbolt.
It can o'ercome rebellious spirits, but
It falls beneath the shafts which heaven looses.
Can I expect, then, by the care whereof
I am still capable, to turn aside
The dreadful workings of celestial doom?
If heaven opposes me with stony face,
I cannot soften it save by submission.
With all my efforts, what can I accomplish?
A man against a God! That is too much.
    Die, die, my children; but when I say "die,"
Is 't for our land that ye are to expire?
If to doom *you* is only to lose *that*,
What end will the death serve that ye will suffer?
To expose you unavailingly to death,

Where evil is still certain to ensue,
Is not to be a father, but inhuman.
If a sire sometimes hath sufficient courage
To leave his children to the tempest's fury,—
Can sometimes wish to see them rush into it,—
'Tis then not sure that they must perish there.
Hence let us do our best to save our seed.
Heaven oft-times punishes by threats alone,
And ne'er forbiddeth, like a wrathful tyrant,
That one should try to save himself when threatened.
In short, one should try all before despairing;
That is a sovereign's duty, and a father's.
If we in this extremity strive vainly,
Let us at least leave nothing still untried.

ABNER. Sire, whatso heaven . . . But here the Princess is.
SAUL. Hide from her, if thou canst, the grief thou feelest.

Enter MICHAL.

MICHAL. Not thy hest only, father, but a fear
    Natural and great now brings me to my king.
SAUL. Drive from thy soul the fear that troubles it.
MICHAL. Before thee, and for thee, my fear redoubles.
    'Tis for none other; 'tis for thee alone
    For whom I dread the blows of angered heaven.
SAUL. Why, what then fearest thou?
MICHAL.   Sire, one must fear all things
    When the King's safety seems thus to constrain us.
    If heaven hath till now disdained thy prayers,
    Refusing answer to thy woeful accents,
    Perhaps now, when misfortune is at hand,
    To save thee thence, it speaketh by my lips.
      Thy Majesty, whom heaven sustains, vouchsafe
    To hide thee from thy subjects' eyes today.
    Do not go forth; great evil threatens thee.
    Do not go forth to meet it; let it pass.
SAUL. What hast thou brought to light?—what fell designs?
    Are they the enemy's? Are they my subjects'?
MICHAL. Neglect naught; whatsoever may be said,
    All must seem great on which a kingdom hangs.
SAUL. Tell us, then, of this evil.
MICHAL.   And the smallest
    Advice is often helpful when 'tis followed.
SAUL. Who hath disclosed to thee so dread an evil?
MICHAL. Ah, sire, a dream, a terrifying dream,

Makes me today fear for thy Majesty
All the misfortunes that should most be dreaded.
Alas! I saw thee . . .

SAUL.   I can weigh this fear
By which I see thee still so sorely smitten.
As thou art woman and as I am king,
'Tis worthy of thee, but of myself unworthy.
In thee it springs from natural affection,
But it would be in me a shameful weakness.
Hide myself in my camp? When but to see me
Inspires my men with vigor and respect,
However keen the shafts which might assail me,
That were the evil thy dream makes thee dread.

MICHAL.   But hear at least this vision full of horror.
See if it comes from heaven or from my fear.

SAUL.   'Tis not my custom, when my heart is troubled,
To let a woman's dreams prescribe my course.

MICHAL.   To save us, heaven employs every means
And by the humblest instrument can help us.

SAUL.   Thy natural anxiety annoys me.
If heaven inspired thee to give aid to me,
'Twould touch my heart to make me hearken to thee.
But learn now, daughter and devoted wife,
Both why thou seest me and why I called thee.
Thou hast cleaved to me enough, striven too much for me,
And too long hast in vain displayed thy virtues.
If reason never has o'ercome mine anger,
Heaven will avenge the wrongs thy father did thee.
Go to Jerusalem, and wait there for peace.
Thy father and thy spouse are pleased with thee.
Thy ardent zeal hath satisfied the claims
Alike of conjugal and filial love.
Go, then; delay no more; go, but find comfort
Since kindly heaven preserves thee for a king.

MICHAL.   Me, for a king, sir? Then thou still believest
That by ambition David stains his honor.

SAUL.   Let him aim at a throne—he should, he can,
Since heaven itself thus wills, to punish me.

MICHAL.   What sayst thou, father: heaven desire a crime?

SAUL.   All that which heaven desires is right and proper.
But it would make my chains a load less heavy
By leaving thee some share of my lost greatness.
Go, then, to await elsewhere the good it grants thee.
My woes will be diminished if they cause it.

Let David reign in peace (if true it is
That peace can ever enter a king's breast);
Let his all-conquering arm extend his boundaries;
Let him surpass me in the lore of princes
And standing more securely amid dangers
Than I, have equal power and die happier.

MICHAL. Father!

SAUL.   Go, go!

ABNER.   But here is Jonathan.

Exit ABNER. *Enter* JONATHAN. MICHAL *stands apart and listens
in silence.*

SAUL (*to himself*). What can keep heaven from taking him from me?
(*To* JONATHAN) Where are thy brothers? Do they not follow
thee?
What stays them?

JONATHAN.   They are following me, I think.
But whence these cares of which thou showest the signs?

SAUL. Daily do monarchs with fresh cares contend.
Know, then, that tidings which have just been brought me,
Being for our good, are not to be neglected.
I have just been warned that certain miscreants
Within Jerusalem weave secret webs,
And very soon new waves of storm will rise
Unless my power and care stamp out their plots.
'Tis needful, then, that either thy stout heart
Or thy mere presence should allay this tempest,
And that the sight of thee, whom heaven doth favor,
Should take all hope from these rebellious spirits.
I know that to confine thee within walls
When honor calls thee to the thick of battles,
Is to impose on thee more cruel hardships
Than if one ravished victory from thy hands.

JONATHAN. I cannot now conceal my weakness from thee.
Herein obedience is an act that wounds me.
This is indeed a harsh thing to command.

SAUL. What matter where one serves one's king, or father?
Be it in the camp, or be it in the city,
The place means naught provided one is useful.
In peace, in war alike—the time means naught—
To please one's king is equally an honor.

JONATHAN. Whether to fame or slavery I march,
If 'tis thy hest, I do not deem it harsh.
But, father, I have stilled this rising tempest.

SAUL. It is reborn, though, greater and more fierce.
JONATHAN. If 'tis reborn more fierce, thy presence only
    Can stay effectively its violence.
    Triumph thou in the city, and thy son
    With Fortune's aid will likewise triumph outside.
SAUL. Elsewhere thou'lt serve me best, elsewhere find glory.
JONATHAN. Yet what is dreaded may be but a rumor.
SAUL. Oppose me not. My knowledge is well grounded.
JONATHAN. Yet if one saw this day that fatal day
    Shine forth whereon it is my fate to die,
    Think'st thou thy cares would save me from my death
    Better inside of walls than 'mid the battle?
    Let me go hence, it follows me to the city,
    And it can make our care vain everywhere.
SAUL. But wherefore holdest thou this sad speech with me?
    I know that death pursues us everywhere
    And is a tyrant that rules all the earth,
    Sometimes in peace is crueler than in war,
    And often doeth his bloody deeds in secret
    Where one would think his blows would least be dreaded.
    Thus seeing him work so many evils, I
    Should fear to lead thee to them, not protect thee.
    Is it to show concern about thy safety
    To leave thee in the midst of factious rebels?
    Alas, when I require thee to obey me,
    Perhaps I help to rob thee of thy life.
JONATHAN. Father, do not believe a lying phantom
    Which has no power except to frighten one.
SAUL (*to himself*). Does he, then, know . . .
               (*To* JONATHAN) What sayst thou? Feign
      no further.
    Of a new ill is some new presage had?
    What hath been seen, what feared?
JONATHAN.   Thou knowest, father.
SAUL. What do I know? . . . What have I seen? . . . What?
JONATHAN.   Nothing!
    Whatever makes thy days so sad, so somber,
    'Tis to have seen nothing when one sees shadows.
    Suppress the cares, then, which thou hast for us.
SAUL. Ah, wretched Phalti, who deservest my wrath!
    'Tis he, then, who now wounds me mortally.
    'Tis he, then, who hath told thee this dire news.
JONATHAN. Sire, he hath nowise erred, making it known,
    Far from a crime, he hath but done his duty.

He knoweth well that fear or hope is vain
When a fiend prophesieth joy or pain.
But thy soul, stronger than our words, already
Hath found its aid in its own understanding.

SAUL.   Be it Samuel who discloses my abasement,
Or be this but a demon's empty threat,
'Tis not thereon that thou shouldst fix thy thought.
Thou shouldst forget all else when I give orders.
Whatever help thine arm can give the State,
Thou oughtest to hear naught but thy sovereign's voice.
Obey, obey; even in my sore need
I love thee when obedient as much
As when a conqueror. Though thou shouldst lead me
To glory's peak, wed victory to my throne,
With all its charms 'twould be offensive to me
If given me by a disobedient hand.

JONATHAN.   Sire, through thy love the voice of parenthood
Tempts thee, but monarchs should be deaf to it.
Its counsels are but subtle frauds which they
Should disregard like flattery. To send
Thy sons away, to fear for them the tempest,
Will this not chill the courage of thy soldiers—
Not give with thine own hands the surest blows
By which our enemies will triumph o'er us?

SAUL.   To inspire alike the army and the realm,
The example of the King today sufficeth.
Must I risk all I love in one encounter?
Wouldst thou that staking all, I should keep nothing?
After a thousand noble, glorious conquests
Can I not fall or lose one victory?
If I know how to reign, should I neglect
To safeguard help which serves me if I need it?

JONATHAN.   If thou dost love the realm as it loves thee,
Preserve thyself for such extremity.
Kings should safeguard their persons till the last,
Risking all else before they risk their lives.
Remember, sire, that thy life-days are ours,
That kings are given us that they may preserve us,
And that a king who seeks to preserve others
Must first of all seek to preserve himself.
Wouldst thou preserve thy House that is to be?
Wouldst thou increase the power thereof hereafter?
Preserve thy kingdom in this time of fear,
Since his whole kingdom is a monarch's House.

I know well that a sovereign's noble sons
Are treasures unto him and truly assets,
But they are transient, perishable assets
Which he should hazard to save greater ones.
Seek then to save thy most admired distinctions.
Victory and honor are kings' best possessions.
To live with glory and to reign triumphant
They should endanger friends and wives and children.

SAUL. What! by refusing to obey wouldst thou
Give proof to me that I am powerless now?
Doth heaven ere death, to which thou rushest with me,
Deprive me both of fatherhood and kingship?
Let it heap martyrdom on martyrdom
For me, load me with horror, snatch empire from me,
But show at least, by carrying out my projects,
That while thou livest I shall have some subjects.
Try for at least a day to forget this courage
The excess of which once served and now insults me.

JONATHAN. Rather, concerned for honor more than us,
Forget for one day that I am thine offspring.
Whatever a fair fortune did for me,
I should be loath to have thee for my father
If the vain love my father cherished for me
Prevented me from dying for my king.
What! shall thy humblest subjects win the glory
Of seeking death or victory for their sovereign,
And thine own children, pitiable creatures,
Obtain less honor than thy humblest subjects?
Shall danger follow thee in the midst of battles,
And we in sloth bide behind wretched walls?
Ah, a king's children would be born to misery
Could they not show that they are nobly born!

SAUL. Then heaven decrees that I must needs make war
With blows more terrible than its thunderbolts.
Alas, it is a wretched king's good fortune
To see about him gallant sons; and I
Justly complain, despite this, that I find
In mine own offspring hearts too noble; and by
A strange fate, that is stripped of all good things,
I even am tortured by their worthiness.
Seekest thou to augment a grief unbounded?
Wouldst thou, then, wound me by thy very courage?
Too brave sons! Heaven, to what dost thou reduce me,
Thus making me desire less virtue in them?

JONATHAN.   To what, my father, doth my cruel fate
    Reduce me, making me desire thy hate?
SAUL.   However, since my peace means naught to thee,
    We must not make thy strength and courage languish.
JONATHAN.   Oh, sire, where rushest thou?
SAUL.   I content thy zeal.
    I lead thee into war, where valor calls thee.
JONATHAN.   Do not expose thyself. Keep thy life safe.
SAUL.   Shouldst fear for us, not fearing for thyself?
    Canst thou imagine that this frightful specter
    Would be a fraud for thee and true for me?
    If futile is its threat, as I believe it,
    'Tis futile for ourself, even as for thee.
JONATHAN.   Yes, father, and 'tis not this paltry specter
    Which makes me dread for thee alone the danger.
    I fear the stroke of chance, which in the battle
    Smiteth indifferently kings and soldiers.
    How is there need, because a demon threatened
    Thy life, to expose it to a storm's fierce buffets?
    Dost thou thyself desire in one cruel moment
    To make the threat come true by rushing headlong?
SAUL.   What, then! because a demon threatens me,
    Must I lack spirit, must I become ice-cold?
    Nay, I must show, and even by thus exposing
    Myself, that I can scorn a demon's threats.
    Could I myself offer base evidence
    That in consulting hell I feared the storm,—
    That Saul, afraid, sought knowledge of his fate
    Because he wished by flight to escape from death?
    Let death this day cut short my thread of life;
    I will go meet it to avoid disgrace.
    To expose one's self in war to ghastly struggles,
    Of life uncertain, and of death uncertain,
    And of the outcome in Fate's hand uncertain,
    Betokens ordinary courage only.
    To rush to battle, though, sure of one's fate,—
    To rush to battle, certain of one's death,—
    To see this, to embrace it, when 'tis needful
    To fire his followers' hearts by his example,—
    Is given to kings alone, great-hearted kings,
    For whom shame is alone a dreaded evil.
      Go. I no more restrain thee. I was wrong,
    I will confess, to have shown my love to save thee.
    I must remember I am of a station

In which I owe the realm my sons and life-blood.
A love so strong and dear must be o'ercome.
A king is not a true king when too good
A father. Go, then, to seek out thy tomb
For thy contentment. I shall be consoled
If thou diest nobly. Take thy poor brothers with thee.
Be heaven's instrument to crown my sorrows.
Thus for the realm's sake do I give thee up.
Perish to save it, or with honor perish.

JONATHAN.   Our actions shall proclaim the blood we sprang from.

Enter PHALTI.

SAUL.   But I see Phalti. I will slay this traitor.
Where are my children, where, thou loose-tongued man,
Who knowest so little of a secret's value?

PHALTI.   My lord, I fain would make thee understand
The weighty reasons which could justify me;
But strong though one's desire be for one's good,
Thy interest is more dear to me than mine.

SAUL.   Seest thou that death at hand which heaven decrees me?
Comest thou to tell me of my sons' destruction?

PHALTI.   Sire, to obey thy Majesty, they came
Apace to find thee; but when they beheld
The enemy e'en now prepared for battle,
Beheld him charge, beheld him beat down all,
They deemed they could in this extremity
Defer obedience to thy Majesty.

SAUL.   Let us yield, yield to heaven, before whose fury
Unleashed, our care is powerless when its shafts
Assail us. Is the fight joined?

PHALTI.   Sire, 'twould seem so.

SAUL.   Come.

JONATHAN.   Nay, forbear.

SAUL.   When all is hazarded?
Having no longer aught to save but honor,
Come, come, let us contest the victory
At least. Flee, Princess, from this spot so fell,
And if we perish, be consoled. Farewell.

[*Exeunt all, hastily.*

ACT V

The scene represents a partially wooded hillside on the skirts of the battlefield. Enter PHALTI.

PHALTI (*speaking to soldiers not in view*). Stay, fugitives, let honor
    stay your flight
Since everywhere alike the tempest breaks.
Stay, fugitives, avenge your princes dead;
Make at the least some effort to avenge them.
But I speak vainly, fright so masters them.
Honor hath no appeal, with fear so strong.
Princes, sad objects of celestial wrath,
With you hath died the power of the Hebrews.
Ah, why have I not shed what blood is left me,
Not to survive so fatal a misfortune!
Why do ye see me not, O outraged princes,
In that sad state in which I see you stretched?

Enter ABNER.

    Abner, where fliest thou?
ABNER.   Phalti, I despair.
Death reigns on all sides, and on all sides woe.
Alas, I seek in vain, despite all efforts,
To form some small band of the fleeing soldiers.
In vain I plead with them, threaten them vainly.
Their courage is no more; chill dread appals them;
And unless heaven ere long assumes our cause
Its people will be seen in chains of slavery.
PHALTI. Is the King saved out of this general shipwreck?
ABNER. He is where the ardor of his courage bore him—
Dead or else prisoner.
PHALTI.   And Jonathan?
ABNER. He followed him. What of his other sons?
PHALTI. All are lost, Abner.
ABNER.   What! how sayest thou?
PHALTI (*indicating two sons of the King*). See for thyself what I can
    tell thee of.
ABNER. O frightful spectacle! O hapless kingdom!
Ah, Phalti, from this blood that we see flow,
Let us fear all the woes that were foretold us.
But by what chance are they within this coppice?
PHALTI. Finding them almost dead amid the carnage,
I carried them here to this peaceful spot,

In which the hand of death has closed their eyes.

ABNER.   Alas!

PHALTI.   I hear a noise.

Enter JONATHAN *and* ACHAS.

ACHAS *(to* JONATHAN*)*.   But see, thy wounds!

JONATHAN.   I know some other ills, and pangs more bitter

PHALTI *(to* JONATHAN*)*.   My lord, how doest thou?

ACHAS *(to* PHALTI*)*.   All wounded, dying,
He still would fain rush to meet death half-way.

JONATHAN.   Since I must die bereft of victory,
Let me at least die where I sought for honor.
Tell truly of this body slashed and bleeding
In the fierce carnage whence thine arm hath dragged it.
Grant that my death may be a field of battle.
'Tis there that death holds naught which doth afflict me.
Still to support a throne which is to fall,
Let us display our valor or despair.
Perhaps my blood will serve to this advantage,
That 'twill bring courage back to the confounded
Soldiers and to good purpose will inspire
Their hearts with rage on seeing the horror of it.

PHALTI.   My lord, think of thyself.

JONATHAN *(becoming delirious)*.   O grief too cruel!
I see the King in danger, calling to us,—
See him without defense, about to perish,—
And my unhappy arm can aid him not!
Alas, of all the woes whose weight o'erwhelms me,
This is the keenest; it alone lacks cure.

ABNER.   Do not depict new sorrows to thyself.
If heaven is for us, what do evils matter?
Someone has saved the King.

JONATHAN.   I would believe it
If I knew less the fervor of his courage.
Ah, if alive, he fights on, weak or strong;
And if he fights no more, is dead or dying.
Ye, then, who know him either slain or helpless,
Rush to his aid, or rather to avenge him.
Oh, that I cannot . . .

ABNER.   Voice and senses fail him.
O day too dreadful, day foreseen too little!

PHALTI.   But I perceive, far off, some of the foe,
Who seem to be approaching this lone spot.
Let us attempt to turn their fatal footsteps

From our dead princes and our dying prince.
Thou, Achas, bide here.   [*Exeunt* PHALTI *and* ABNER.
JONATHAN (*reviving*).   What, do I still see?
　　Would ye assuage the evils that devour me?
　　Defend your king.
ACHAS.   Ah, my lord, here he is!
JONATHAN. Let me behold him. Nay, remove me hence,
　　And lest the pain that I endure be greater,
　　Divert his glance from me who now am dying.

　　ACHAS *helps* JONATHAN *to a less conspicuous spot, and then*
　　　himself hastens away. Enter SAUL *and his Armor-Bearer.*

SAUL.   At last thou seest a king hurled from his throne.
　　Heaven fought against me; heaven has overthrown me.
　　Vile enemies have ravished victory from me.
　　The shame of Israel makes today their glory,
　　And heaven—ah, woe!—desires that I be left
　　To see and savor this calamity.
THE ARMOR-BEARER.   Thou hast lost nothing if despite this tempest
　　Thou still preservest thine illustrious courage.
SAUL.   Alas, all is adverse to hapless monarchs!
　　Courage is vain when heaven is against them.
　　Where are my children? O celestial wrath,
　　If thou canst soften, treat me but as a father.
　　　　　[*He sees the bodies of two of his children.*
　　What do I see in this clump? blood? . . . Oh, wretched!
THE ARMOR-BEARER.   Ah, sire, withstand the rigor of this blow.
SAUL.   O crown of all mine ills! O lightning, tempest,
　　Finish thy stroke upon my guilty head.
　　Is there some woe whose pangs I know not of?
　　Have I not drained the whole of heaven's anger?
　　Whether I suffer as a king or father,
　　What evil henceforth can increase my sorrows
　　If I behold my sons the prey of death,
　　My foes victorious, my realm o'erthrown?
THE ARMOR-BEARER.   Hope at least that amid such dire misfortunes
　　Jonathan is a blessing that is left thee.
SAUL.   Instruct me, rather, to endure the torments
　　Of which thou seest yet only the beginnings.
　　Would that I might forget this fearful doom
　　Whose dread fulfilment I perceive already!
　　Would that I might forget that fateful voice!
　　If vainly I should hope, still I would hope—
　　Would hope at least that heaven, which assailed me,

Might yet preserve for me my last rich treasure,
And that the safety of one gallant son
Might yet console me for the loss of two.
But I no longer hope—What sight appears?
I need but fear an ill to see it born.
Jonathan!
JONATHAN.   Ah, woe!
SAUL.   Jonathan, is it thou?
My sons, who give my heart such poignant pangs,
For whom among you must mine eyes first weep?
Alas, these here are dead, the others die!
Crumble, my throne, crumble, for all I care;
Avaunt with horror from a wretched king.
My loss of greatness does not make my misery;
I am a wretched king because a father.
    O thou whose bravery no less than my fate
So horribly hath hurled thee to thy death,—
O thou for whom my heart could be so anxious,
Should I now, Jonathan, blame or pity thee?
Were the commands I sought to give thee needless?
Shouldst thou have heard thy courage, not my voice?
But wherefore blame thee in this common shipwreck
For having heard my voice less than thy courage?
If heaven urged thee on, how couldst thou hear me?
If heaven urged thee on, how could I stay thee?
Dear Jonathan, 'tis thou whom I should pity;
'Tis heaven . . .
JONATHAN.   Ah, nay, sir!
SAUL.   Then I must be patient.
Well, let us bear our ills without a murmur,
Though men have murmured at less weighty sorrows.
O hapless father!
JONATHAN.   O yet more wretched son
Who cannot aid a father in his anguish!
But sire, save thyself; thus comfort me.
Nations lose nothing till they lose their king.
Since with my strengthless arm I cannot serve thee,
Let me at least with my last accents serve thee.
It may be, heaven with anger satisfied
Offers to thee this moment for thy safety.
SAUL.   What! Think of safety when I lose a kingdom,
When heaven pursues, when Jonathan is dying?
JONATHAN.   My death is honorable, like my wounds.
Wouldst thou fain sweeten it? Ah, save thyself!

SAUL. A king who hath naught more to lose but life
    Cannot too soon lose that nor its desire.

JONATHAN. A king who still is free and great of heart
    Ever may conquer those who conquered him.
    Save thyself.

SAUL.   All forbids thy father's safety,—
    The earth and hell and heaven in its wrath.
    This body itself, this body which thou wouldst save,
    This body which thou wouldst bear off from the foe,
    This body pierced with blows, whose strength departeth,
    Forbids his safety by its own great weakness.

JONATHAN. Achas, call Abner, bid him come to help!
    Oh, sire . . .   *[He falls back, dead.*

SAUL.   Ah me! this moment ends his life.
    He is dead, *they* are dead, unhappy victims—
    Dead, what is worse, by reason of my crimes!
    Children ill-starred, I do not weep for you
    For having tasted of the pangs of death.
    Alas, your death bears witness to your manhood;
    'Tis worthy both of you and of your courage.
    'Twas for your country that ye should have died,
    And 'tis for her that men have seen you die.
    This death is lovely, then—worth more than life.
    'Tis not to be lamented, but desired,
    And such that happy and victorious kings
    Could well have wished it, too, for their own sons.
    Nay, nay, I do not mourn to see your blood
    Lie spread out on the ground by chance of war;
    But if despair doth seize upon my heart,
    Drive reason from my mind, and conquer me,
    It is because I see that of your ruin
    My crimes alone have been the origin,
    And that by the most huge of all misfortunes
    A father's punishment hath slain his children.
    Fearful the sentence of relentless heaven,
    Which kills three guiltless youths to smite one sinner,
    And which, to crush me 'neath a crueler weight,
    Seems once, at least, to do what is not justice!
    Pitiful objects, my delight this morning,
    Since ye by will of heaven are now my torment,
    Is it at least permitted me to hope
    That we may have in death one sepulcher?
    Ah, greatness always dangerous, always longed for,
    Everywhere fatal, everywhere adored,

Winsome illusion, flattering and seducing,
Thou'rt courted, sought, and lo, thy fruits are these.

> [*He points to his sons.*

   Whoever in a kingdom hath his trust,
Let him, in me, consider how it passeth.
Let him judge if a king's lot be so fair.
Morn finds him on the throne, eve in the tomb,
Yea, so brought low that when he yields his life
He scarcely even doth expect a grave;
He scarcely even can for his repose
Hope that the earth will clasp and hide his bones.
O heaven, when thou conferrest regal state,
Is it thy love thou showest or thy hate?
Since a throne holds so much adversity,
Heaven, dost thou love us when thou leadest us to it?

THE ARMOR-BEARER. My liege, on all sides danger threatens thee.
I see the enemy not far away.
Thou art pursued; attempt to save thyself.
If heaven abases thee, it can upraise thee.

SAUL. Judge by the onsets that earth makes upon me
How heaven in wrath has left me and disdained me.
But since I needs must die, and all resistance
Is futile, why may I not die sword in hand?
But loss of blood makes mine arm ineffectual;
Courage is helpless in so weak a body.
Midst all disasters, for my crowning anguish,
'Tis not vouchsafed me, then, to perish nobly.
But if cruel Fate deprives me of this honor,
Snatch from the foe their fruits of victory.
Let not thy king, worse racked than if in hell,
Die by their hands or fall into their clutches.

THE ARMOR-BEARER. Command, and I obey. What must I do?

SAUL. Open the grave and make me descend thither.
Yes, speed the death to which thou seest me hasten,
And let me die at least when 'tis my wish.
Make my days end, for fear a savage king
Should add his laughter to the ills he brews me.
To fall before a monarch who attacked me
I deem less bitter than his mockery.

THE ARMOR-BEARER. Sire!

SAUL.   Lend thy hand to my enfeebled strength.
Here, here my heart is. Make an end, strike, kill me.
Show by obedience to my last command
That to the tomb I bear my kingliness.

SAÜL

THE ARMOR-BEARER. Ah, sire, command of me things that are lawful.

SAUL. To kill me is a kindness.

THE ARMOR-BEARER.   'Tis the greatest
Of crimes.

SAUL.   If at thy hands it is a crime,
Thy sovereign will absolve thee when thou doest it.

THE ARMOR-BEARER. Permit . . .

SAUL.   Make answer only with thy sword.

THE ARMOR-BEARER. Sooner with mine own blood it shall be stained.

SAUL. Must I today, through thy cruel loyalty,
Be a base slave or die by mine own hand?
Rather wouldst thou a proud, victorious foe
Should make my shame enhance his glory's brightness,
Or, with my last wrath turned against myself,
My sword should render me a ghastly sight?
Reft of all aid and racked with so great anguish,
What prospect sure have I but death or chains?
And with a fate so sore and so immediate,
Which ought a king to choose, the chains or death?
Ah, drive me not to this extremity,
To die by mine own hand, to kill myself!
Strike; here is that with which to act before me.
I lend thee here a blade; lend me thine arm.
As thy last service, spare thou me a crime.
Helpless to save me, save at least my fame.
Reflect that in my plight my greatest blessing
Consists in perishing by loyal hands. . . .
    What! thou dost fear to strike, both seeing my weakness
And seeing so near the enemy who hunt me?
To abandon to triumphant foes thy prince—
Is that a less crime than to pierce his heart?
Which hand dost think is kinder to a monarch,
The one that slays him or the one that binds him?
Learn, learn, thou fool, that better is a king
In a fair coffin than in odious fetters.
Learn, learn that any wise and steadfast sovereign
Loves like his throne an honorable tomb. . . .
    But I do ill to claim and beg of thee
That which mine own despair can win for me.
Since heaven ordains that I shall fall, 'tis needful
That Saul should be the load 'neath which Saul sinks.
My sons, why had I not at least the comfort
Of dying while able still to doubt your death?
But vain are such complaints; and to complain

156

Thus vainly, I myself prolong my pain.
O ye proud foes who follow after me,
To whom, as a great blessing, my disaster
Is pledged, if ye, sped 'gainst us by the hand
Of heaven, have triumphed o'er a mighty army,
Learn from this blow that snatches a king from you
That Saul alone can triumph over Saul.   [*He kills himself.*
THE ARMOR-BEARER.   Ah, sire! . . . He hath fallen on his sword.
            He is dead.
O Fortune, who had cheated him and whom
He cheated! But with such calamities,
Slaughter and panic on all sides, to follow
My king is the most kindly fate for me.

Scévole

(SCAEVOLA)

By
PIERRE DU RYER

INTRODUCTORY NOTE

After *Saül*, Du Ryer again made use of a Biblical subject, this time with more action and more complication—and with decidedly greater popular favor. His *Esther* (1642) is interesting for its anticipation of Racine's lyrical drama of the same name. There is little similarity between the two plays, however, except that which naturally results from their having a common source. Racine's *Esther* greatly excels Du Ryer's in poetic beauty and religious fervor, but is much less dramatic. Du Ryer's, like Racine's, follows the Book of Esther at the expense of unity. It has two successive themes, the triumph of the heroine over Vashti and her frustration of the murderous designs of Haman against the Jews; and, as in Racine, Haman's compelled honoring of Mordecai is an episode introduced solely because it is a famous feature of the Bible story. But it is doubtful whether Du Ryer ever did better work than some of the scenes dealing with the contest between Esther and Vashti for the King's favor; and, everything considered, his *Esther* is one of the better plays of its immediate times.

Scévole, however, enjoyed a success unapproached by anything else that he wrote. Its date is about 1644, only a few years after Corneille's *Horace* and *Cinna,* which Du Ryer now palpably imitated and sought to rival with a Roman play of his own. Like *Horace, Scévole* deals with a story found in Livy, and is full of the martial spirit and patriotic ardor of early Rome; and like *Cinna* it depicts a good monarch's clemency and abounds in discussions of political principles. Its imitation of Corneille is a source of both weakness and strength in it.

Having as its model other plays rather than life, it is one remove further from reality than its author's other tragedies. In *Scévole*, as too often in French-classical dramas, everyone is represented as being in love who possibly can be, and lovers are quick to believe the worst of each other. At times the resounding rhetoric of Corneille becomes mere bombast in Du Ryer's hands; the turgid description of Horatius at the bridge can be defended as contributing to Porsena's admiration for Rome, but its details are absurd. Scaevola paints a highly colored picture of the dire straits to which the beleaguered city has been reduced by famine; it is her last remaining day of life, he says; but if he fails to kill Porsena, three hundred other Roman youths are to attempt the task— successively! His revelation of their purpose, though part of the original legend, somewhat stultifies the play, in which the emphasis, till this point, has been on the Romans' suppression of self in the interests of Rome—but now Scaevola tries to pay his personal debt of gratitude to Porsena by betraying, while there is still no prospect of peace, the plans of his countrymen which, he himself has said, alone can save her.

On the other hand, there is no other tragedy of Du Ryer's so well constructed, so vigorous, and so full of action. He has hardly portrayed any other character with such vividness and economy of effort as the exiled King Tarquin, embittered, savage, arrogant, doubting the gods and their justice, and so churlish that he eventually alienates the temperate, magnanimous Porsena, who is almost equally well portrayed. To make his play acceptable in monarchial France, the author cleverly perverts history to represent the Romans distinguishing between tyrants like Tarquin and upright sovereigns like Porsena, and abhorring only the former.

Of all the tragedies of the seventeenth century written in deliberate imitation of Corneille, *Scévole* was the best and the most successful. It more nearly catches the tone and spirit of Corneille's Roman dramas than does any other. These facts and its comparative fame among the plays of Du Ryer would tend to create an impression that in tragedy he was primarily a disciple of Corneille. The truth is, rather, that he was himself a pioneer. In *Saül* and *Esther* he struck off independently; *Saül,* especially, is an original contribution to tragic drama. *Lucrèce* had preceded Corneille in treating a Roman subject. *Scévole* really stands apart from the rest of Du Ryer's work, with somewhat different faults and merits. In spite of its success he apparently did not care to do anything more of the sort. He went back instead to his earlier field of tragi-comedy, upon which his one subsequent tragedy, *Thémistocle* (1646-7), verges.

CHARACTERS IN THE PLAY

TARQUIN, *lately King of Rome, deposed for his crimes and driven from the city.*

PORSENA, *King of Etruria, who has espoused the cause of Tarquin.*

ARUNS, *son of Porsena.*

MARCELLUS, LICINIUS, *two captains in the army besieging Rome.*

JUNIA, *daughter of that Brutus who had led the insurrection against Tarquin.*

FULVIA, *a female attendant of Junia.*

SCAEVOLA, *a Roman patriot.*

Soldiers and attendants of Porsena.

The scene is laid in the camp of the army of Porsena, before Rome.

Scaevola

ACT I

The scene represents an open space before the tent of PORSENA,
in his camp before Rome. TARQUIN *and* PORSENA, *with his
retinue, are discovered.*

TARQUIN. What! always put the end off in a war
    Which ought to interest all the kings on earth
    To unite their power—and their cruelty, even—
    To avenge a king on his rebellious people!
    Thou sawest the crime by which the rage of one man,
    Brutus, aroused the insolence of Rome;
    Thou sawest the results of his black deeds,
    For thou beheldest me driven from my domains.
    Yet this day, Porsena, thou, thou thyself,
    Who sawest me fall from mine exalted station,—
    Whose help hath been offered so many times
    To restore Tarquin to the roll of kings,—
    Thou finally . . .
PORSENA.   What have I done, not furthering
    This help which mine affection gives thy vengeance?
    To place the scepter in thy hands once more,
    Do not my soldiers throng the Romans' fields?
    Have I not made appear before their walls
    All the dread aspect of war's Demon-god?
    Rome, which opposed to me its haughty ramparts,
    With horror sees them shaken everywhere;
    Indeed, in this war I am seen in person
    Fighting, not for myself, but for thy crown.
    Is this not evidence that I share thy sorrows?
    Is this not nobly with thy woes to grapple?
    And is not this to give enough clear proof
    That whoso injures one king, injures all kings?
TARQUIN. Yes, Porsena, 'tis true thy generous care
    Shows itself nobly for a hapless monarch.
    Yes, through thine aid this rebel Rome already
    Seeing its ramparts breeched, beholds its ruin.
    Its tottering walls are ready to give way.
    There needs but one more blow to make them fall,
    But thou deferrest this great blow which could
    Reseat an ill-starred ruler on his throne—

Deferrest this great blow which I await,
And givest a breathing-space to these new Titans.
Let us force, force at last, their proud defenses.
Let one brave onset spare me many a battle.
To make the victory and its joys complete,
We must behold this rebel city buried
Beneath its walls o'erthrown.

PORSENA.   If 'tis sufficient
For subjugating this insurgent city
That we should make it see the imminence
Of its destruction,—if these enemies
Of kings can be compelled to come, repentant,
And to submit themselves unto thy sway,—
Why, carrying it by storm, when all is rage,
Wilt thou go ruin thine own heritage?
Why, with the savageness that wrath inspires,
Wilt thou go cast to earth walls that are thine?
What can this give to thine offended soul
But the dire wreckage of a ravaged Rome?
Will this be to regain a mutinous realm—
To win back nothing but its ruined remnant?
Wait but a space, for that which heaven decrees.
Whene'er a king insists on punishing
His people, that disastrous war is fatal
Alike e'en to the one and to the other.
Ne'er hath a sovereign who desires fair fame
Gained a glad victory over his own subjects
By force of arms, and his harsh treatment of them
Soweth the sad seeds of a new revolt.
What though the criminal insolence of the rebels
Abuseth the time of respite given them?
Then we can give free scope to the law's wrath;
Then we can brandish a king's thunderbolt;
And if till now the fate 'neath which thou laborest
Fosters the crime of Rome and of the Romans,
Here let our swords write that insurgent peoples
Are never long the favorites of Fortune.

TARQUIN.   Indeed! If *thy* people, yes, if Etruria
Had risen against thee with the selfsame frenzy,—
If by the blackest treason's deadly blow
Thou hadst been driven from thine own dominions,—
If thou hadst been compelled to go in tears
To other lands to beg their princes' aid,—
Couldst thou accept the counsel which thou givest me

In favor of the insurrectionists?
Surely, a king who uses this mild language
Knows not the burden of such mortal outrage;
Surely, he ne'er hath known the agony
Of having had a throne and losing it.
No, no, to punish this atrocious crime
The cruelest war hath all too little fierceness;
And when conspiring subjects must be tamed,
The bloodiest triumph is the most assured.
 By the misfortunes of my rebel subjects,
Thy subjects should be taught to remain loyal.
Thou thyself oughtest to counsel me to use
The harshness meet to avenge a hapless prince;
Thou thyself oughtest to throw off all restraint
To instruct thy subjects and with fear acquaint them,
And show, in brief, by thy severity
What thou wouldst do to them if they rebelled.
Give back my former greatness, then, to me.
Strengthen thy power in restoring mine.
To offer pardon where it is not asked for
Is to lend boldness to ungrateful miscreants;
'Tis to make Rome believe two kings were lacking
In might against her, after her resistance,
And that to win and rule her we desire
To pardon her, when we cannot punish her.
If we must pardon her, we must, yes, *must*
Wait till the torch is ours which can reduce her
To ashes; we must hold her people helpless;
They needs must be in chains and see that they
Are standing on hell's-brink. Then will a gracious
Pardon crown us with glory, if pronounced
From a triumphal car, if it is not
A consequence of necessity but of
A fine impulse of generosity.
PORSENA. To end so long a strife, since thou hast less
  Love for my counsel than for mine aid in arms,
  I shall contend no more.
TARQUIN.   Thus, then, presuming
  That thou wouldst do all for my satisfaction,
  And seeing in my men the ardent courage
  Which oft is presage of the best success,
  I have acceded to their wish and let them
  Today attack the foes' bridge.
PORSENA.   If thy heart's

Ease, like thine honor, doth consist in quelling
Thy subjects who resist thee insolently,
Whatever Fate decrees for the days left thee,
I find my glory in giving thee assistance.

Enter MARCELLUS.

TARQUIN.　Here are some tidings.
　　　　　　　　　　　　　What ho, then, Marcellus!
　　What have we done?
MARCELLUS.　　　　　　　Possibly taken Rome.
TARQUIN.　Taken Rome?
MARCELLUS.　　　　　　And I come, expressly sent
　　To tell thee what our first attempts accomplished.
TARQUIN.　Now will ye learn, ye infamous, rebellious
　　Populace, how the gods espouse our cause!
　　　　But thou, go on, Marcellus; inform us how
　　The city fares and what your arms have wrought.
MARCELLUS.　At the same moment when against the bridge
　　Two of our cohorts marched and 'gainst yon gates,
　　The Romans, fired with a last spark of valor,
　　Made a sortie, and battle then was joined.
　　Thus each of the two sides tried the same thing;
　　Thus each of the two sides surprised the other;
　　But such keen ardor animated them
　　That neither side betrayed astonishment.
　　By both a courage hath been manifested
　　Which seemed to promise an advantage to them;
　　And victory knows not whither to incline,
　　For both alike appear to have deserved it.
TARQUIN.　But finally . . .
MARCELLUS.　　　　　　　But finally victory
　　Views with a favoring glance the cause of justice.
　　The Romans, weakened by their heavy losses,
　　Slowly give way before our latest efforts.
　　But . . .
　　　　　[*With a gesture he indicates* ARUNS, *who now enters.*
TARQUIN (*to* ARUNS).　Rome is ours, then?
ARUNS.　　　　　　　　　　　No, no.
TARQUIN.　　　　　　　　　　　Well, Marcellus!
ARUNS.　Yes, 'twas long thought that we had won the city.
　　The Romans' flight made us vainglorious.
　　We were upon the bridge—victorious
　　Already, we thought, and Rome a slave already
　　Before she yielded, of her citizens

The funeral pyre or tomb. But at that instant
Fate seemed to be repentant, as it were,
For having favored the more righteous cause.

TARQUIN. O heaven, who betrayest me, art thou just,
Then, to forsake a king for his vile subjects?
Dost thou deserve our prayers?

PORSENA.   I am astounded.
Tell us the rest, my son.

ARUNS.   The rest is truly
Heroic. When the foe's defeat and flight
Appeared to give us Rome, now faced with ruin,
Horatius, who led her forces' remnant,
Turned to them, gestured with his hands, spoke stoutly
To them, besought them, urged them to uphold
The fortunes of the State, giving their lives;
But public welfare is a weak incentive,
Disdained when every man fears for himself.
Horatius vainly tried to stay these dastards.
Terror swept them away, and lent them wings.
   They flee; they leave him there; without supporters
He stands alone, for Rome and for himself.
Yet firm he stands, nor shows to us his back.
One would say heaven sustains his valiant heart,
Or that the destiny of Rome assembles
In him the strength and swords of those who fled.

TARQUIN. What! all alone against us, and unaided,
This leader of the rebels still resisted?

ARUNS. Alone resisted, aided by his arm,
Upon the swaying bridge, which 'neath his feet
Was being felled; for to the town he cried
Amid the fight: "Hew down, hew down the bridge.
Mine arm is my protection." Then, casting on us
His furious glances, he to combat challenged
The victors; he reproached them, like a hero,
With shameful slavery endured; he boasted
His liberty, showed its advantages,
And by its false charms, which he made them savor,
Tried to corrupt those whom he could not conquer.
At last his boldness flamed so gallantly
That like some marvel it amazed our army,
And this amazement, felt by every soldier,
Caused, as it were, a truce amid the strife.
Thus, for a moment, our best captains, in
Their admiration for Horatius,

Forgot their hate; they looked at one another
And lingered still, ashamed to attack one man,
Who all alone confronted them; but finally,
Yet more ashamed that one man stayed them, they
Assailed him with unnumbered shafts at once.
His buckler caught these, and on high he held it
And made us feel the fear he should have felt.
Where'er our people's courage carried them,
His strength or cleverness opposed them; scarcely
Have I believed the evidence of mine eyes:
We rushed from all sides, he was everywhere.
Yes, everywhere we go, there is Horatius,
And with himself alone he fills the bridge.
This foe has certainly astonished me.
This foe has certainly taught me to love him.
At least I feel regret that such fine daring,
So worthy of love, was in a rebel's heart.

TARQUIN.   What! could none strike him down?

ARUNS.   In vain from all sides
Our soldiers launched a storm of darts against him;
'Twould seem the gods, blind partisans of our foes,
Turned aside all the shafts we sped at him,
And, to make notable his every blow,
Guided the missiles which he hurled at us.
But if this war of one against ten thousand
Is a fame-worthy marvel full of marvels,
The end of his magnificent fight is truly
Another miracle in Rome's behalf.
When finally all our warriors, who had been
Confused by such great daring, were about
To try to bear Horatius down with numbers,
The bridge collapsed, and with a mighty crash
Behind him fell into the Tiber's waters.
The air resounded with it, our onset ceased,
And Rome uplifted cries of jubilation.
Horatius then cast on the waves a glance,
And, as though ready to find there his grave,
He said: "God of the Tiber, aid my efforts.
Receive a soldier who defends thy freedom."
He plunged while yet he spake.

TARQUIN.   And did the Tiber
In wrath not swallow up this precious rebel?

ARUNS.   Nay, sir; the gods, delighted by his courage,
Bore him unharmed to the other bank. In spite

Of all our shafts with which he was assailed,
They with his safety recompensed his valor;
For he dared do alone a gallant deed,
Which will receive less credence than esteem.
One would have said, to see him ride the waves,
His shield itself availed him as a boat,
And that, in showering darts on him, we only
Gave him a favoring wind to waft him faster.
One would have said that when he fell, the very
God of the billows, like another dolphin,
Received him on his back, and that the water,
A friend to such brave daring, was a crystal
Chariot, whereon in triumph went Horatius.
    Thus did the broken bridge, by falling, aid him
And cut the course short of our victory.
Thus can we say, even with honor, that
Over the Romans we prevailed, but that
Horatius balked our steps and aims, and vanquished
The vanquishers of Rome and of her people.
TARQUIN (*to* PORSENA). The wickedness of Rome, so near her fall,
    Triumphs, then, o'er the power of two kings?
Oughtest thou to suffer it? Does not this great
Humiliation fall even upon thy brow?
No, no, let us not let this faithless city
Glory in the success which flatters it.
Let us o'erpower these rebels. Do not tell me
That 'tis mine own chattels that I destroy.
In the sad lot to which the gods consign me
I seek revenge as much as my lost crown.
PORSENA. Wait but a little longer. Let us learn
    If Rome, as we are told, verges on famine.

Enter LICINIUS.

    (*To* LICINIUS) What is it?
LICINIUS.   A Roman lady has been taken.
PORSENA (*to* TARQUIN). Sir, we must question her.

                                    Licinius,
Let her be brought here.   [*Exit* LICINIUS.
                  Fright may well be able
To drag forth from her what we wish to know.
TARQUIN. What do I see! Ah, my rage, can I hold thee
    In?
PORSENA. Gods! The daughter of Brutus!

SCEVOLE

Enter JUNIA, *attended by* FULVIA.

                     (*To* JUNIA)   Come. Fear nothing.

JUNIA. I obey, Porsena, and pay thee this
Respect, because Fate puts me in thy power.
But ne'er presume that a disgraceful terror
Could leave its impress upon Brutus' daughter,
Unless her honor, seeing its assassins,
Should fear wherever Tarquins may be seen.

TARQUIN. Proud, proud!

JUNIA.   Thy crimes confer that name on thee.

PORSENA. Show the respect here which one owes a crown.

JUNIA. I have as much for thee, sir, as I owe thee.

TARQUIN. I shall teach thee, rebel, to respect thy king!

JUNIA. Strike! I await thy blow. I offer thee
My head before thy hand is ready for it.
At least, this deed, of such a flagrant nature,
Will everywhere confirm men's judgment of thee.
At least, this deed will justify the hatred
The Roman people cherish for their tyrant.

PORSENA. To persecute thee was not our intention.
Thy prison will be kind; thou'lt be well treated;
Among thy foes thou findest thine asylum.
But tell us in what state the city was
When thou didst leave it.

JUNIA.   I was not in Rome,
But had just gone thence when your legions came
To invest it. Then, far removed, mine own mistress
And prizing freedom like a father's blessing,
I was taken in a temple, where I offered
Prayers, I shall not conceal it, against thee
And for the Roman people.

PORSENA.   The just gods,
Who avenge crime, thus punish instantly
Unrighteous prayers.

JUNIA.   Nay, the just gods have granted
My prayers; Horatius triumphs, and hath repulsed thee.
But understand that Rome is verily
Unconquerable, that famine hath no terrors
For her, and that she will not lack for food
So long as e'er the Romans lack not hands.
This folk, the foe of thine, for honor's sake
Will feed themselves with one hand and will fight
With the other.

SCAEVOLA

PORSENA.   Thou displayest their wickedness,
    Thinking to praise them.

JUNIA.   To make good my words,
    Ready are they to sally forth.

TARQUIN.   We waste
    Our time in fruitless speech. We must have recourse
    To profitable deeds.   [*Exit* TARQUIN.

JUNIA.   So my mere presence
    Hath driven away this mighty king! And so
    The power of dead Brutus lives in me.
    Tarquin, and thou, Porsena, arm all men
    'Gainst Rome; but Rome, to save herself from all
    Of you, required only a single man.
    If by great deeds my father showed that only
    One Roman was enough to drive away
    A hundred tyrants, what hath Horatius done?
    He hath instructed you that only one
    Roman is needed to defend a realm.

PORSENA.   At least thou art allowed, despite our power,
    To flatter with so great a hope thy country.

JUNIA.   But meanwhile, sir, accord unto my prayers
    What courtesy owes to thy prisoner,
    And in my heart confirm that glorious fame
    Which even among us Romans decked thy name.
    I am thy prisoner—true; this I admit;
    But merit thou, by noble solicitude,
    The praise accorded thee. I do not ask
    For such good treatment that I needs must doubt
    Whether I am in prison. Make our treatment
    Resemble punishment. To restrain us better,
    Load us with countless chains. We seek from thee
    But a captivity where, like one's body,
    One's honor is secure.

PORSENA.   This prayer is seemly
    And lovable in thee, and not to hearken
    Unto it, is to hate honor itself.
    So, to bring peace to thy perturbèd spirit,
    I leave thine honor in thy virtue's keeping,
    And, to assure thee by excess of kindness,
    Thyself I leave, paroled, in thy word's keeping.
    Is that a sure guard?

JUNIA.   Yes, sire; and my pledge
    Will guard me better far than a king's soldiers.

PORSENA (*to* ARUNS). My son, take care of her; and 'mid her woes,

Compel her, despite Rome, to love her foes.

ARUNS. I find in this command my entire pleasure.

[Exit PORSENA.

(*To* JUNIA)   Thus I have half of what I wished most fondly.
Two of the Romans were so dear to me
That for their sake I feared our prosperous fortunes:
Thou, Junia, who of old my love didst kindle
And now art still the object of my longings—
Thou, for whom I have burned with secret fires . . .

JUNIA. Do nothing, sir, that can bring blame on thee.
This love which thou dost proffer me is too much;
Compassion is enough for the unfortunate.
But who else is it that doth make thee pity
The destiny of the Romans?

ARUNS.   A true friend,
A gallant friend, whose good help rescued me
From danger, once, by which my life was threatened.
I glimpsed him somewhere, full of noble daring,
Fighting among the men led by Horatius;
But alas! suddenly, after these brave efforts,
I saw him fall, perhaps to join the dead.

JUNIA. What sayest thou, sir? Might this be Scaevola?

ARUNS. 'Tis he, none other, Junia. Ha! these words
Disturb thee?

JUNIA.   Oh, alas! Sir, should I not
Weep for a bulwark of the Romans, whom
Fate layeth low? But lend us now the help
Which we in our distress had from thy father.

ARUNS (*giving his arm to her, tenderly*).   Do not be downcast; thy
        captivity
Will have no fewer charms than liberty.   *[Exeunt.*

ACT II

Scene One

The scene represents another part of the camp of PORSENA.
JUNIA *is discovered, alone.*

JUNIA. O love of country, strong, fair bond, which ought
Alone to bind a Roman woman's heart!
O love of country, pray, forgive me if
The love of Scaevola reigns there with thee.
O mother of Romans! Rome, so near to slavery!

174

SCAEVOLA

Ah, when thy children go to give their lives
For thee, thou shouldst at least, as the reward
Of their fidelity, permit that one
Should weep with thee for those who die for thee.
If thou, thus on the brink of the abyss,
Canst let none grieve for any ills but thine,—
If thou canst nowise suffer it that my feelings
Should make my tears flow at my lover's death,—
At least thou wilt consent that in our common
Woe I should weep the loss of thy defender.
O Scaevola! O great soul where manhood reigns!
If I with coldness have withstood thy love,—
If that love which thy noble heart preserves
Ne'er made my lips avow love's flame in mine,—
Thou shouldst be satisfied, after long yearning,
When between Rome and thee I share my tears.

Enter FULVIA.

FULVIA. Madam!
JUNIA.   What is it, Fulvia? Why this joy?
FULVIA. 'Tis for what doth concern thee, what some god
    Sends thee.
JUNIA.   Is poor Rome's liberty assured?
    Or noble Scaevola brought back to life?
FULVIA. At least he is in the camp.
JUNIA.   Porsena's camp?
    Is he a prisoner, then?
FULVIA.   He is free, and scatheless.
JUNIA. Thou thinkest thou sawest him, but thine eyes were blurred.
FULVIA. Madam, I saw him; we had speech together.
    But as he deemed thou wert in some safe place,
    Sheltered from the misfortunes threatening Rome,
    When from my words he learned of thy disaster,
    His grief seemed such that death were little worse.
JUNIA. Where didst thou find him?
FULVIA.   On a path that leads
    From the Tiber to the quarters of Porsena.
JUNIA. And what did Scaevola say unto thee?
FULVIA. When he had learned of thy mischance, he cried:
    "Gods, from whom I expect a miracle,
    Should ye have given me this obstacle?"
JUNIA. Explain these words, which seem to have burst forth from him.
FULVIA. Not understanding them, could I explain them?
    He is, moreover, armed not like a Roman

But as the soldiers are of Porsena.

JUNIA.   And why?

FULVIA.   His answer misbecomes his manhood.
"To save myself, Fulvia," he said.

JUNIA.   What sayest thou?

FULVIA.   What I do not believe.

JUNIA.   To save himself,
Fulvia! To give not Rome his blood and life!
Rid, rid my heart of this uncertainty.
Go on, or say naught if the rest is shameful.

FULVIA.   Some people then appeared on the same path,
And robbed us of all chance of talking further.
Full of anxieties, we left each other,
But I believe his steps were bent this way.

JUNIA.   To save himself, thou sayest? Thou didst not see him!
His courage contradicts those craven words.
Would Scaevola basely disguise himself?
Would he to such protection owe his life?
Would he, whom honor guides, conceal himself
In the shadow of the buckler of his foe?
Thou sawest but a fiend, wearing his shape,
Who seeks to stain his name when he is dead.
O might his high worth, so well known in Rome,
Shine like the sun to dissipate this cloud!
Come back, come back, O Scaevola; or if some demon
Makes thee thyself serve to defame thy honor,
Return into the coffin where I thought thee.
Better to weep thy death than weep thy shame!
For thou art dead to Rome and me alike
If for thyself some baseness makes thee live.
As well henceforth . . .

Enter SCAEVOLA.

FULVIA.   But, madam, here he is.

JUNIA.   Mine eyes, my faculties, do ye deceive me?

SCAEVOLA.   Is it thou whom I see?

JUNIA.   Nay, is it thou
Or some illusion that appears before me?
I know thee not, clad in this shameful armor.
Far from assuring me, it frightens me.

SCAEVOLA.   O gods, who fire me to so great an effort,
Was it necessary to confront me with
So great an obstacle?

JUNIA.   Fearest thou that I
Shall stay thee?
SCAEVOLA.   Yes, I fear thy presence.
JUNIA.   Gods!
Cometh he to confirm a horrible
Idea?
SCAEVOLA.   What sayest thou, Junia, and on what
Foundation couldst thou build unworthy thoughts?
JUNIA.   What sayest *thou*, Scaevola, and what honorable
Excuse can justify these arms for which I
Blame thee?
SCAEVOLA.   A brave deed, worthy of a shrine.
'Twill make Rome free and Scaevola immortal.
I walk now in the footsteps of thy father.
His courage is at every turn the torch
That lights me; but his daughter here doth seem
A hindrance that puts off a great occurrence.
JUNIA.   I, I a hindrance to a noble venture?
Thou woundest me, Scaevola, and insultest me.
Goest thou to danger? I will lead thee thither.
Goest thou to do a great deed? I will second
Thine arm. But really, dost thou love me? Wouldst thou
Prove it? Then let me share a peril which
Brings glory.
SCAEVOLA.   Alas! I shall attempt a deed
Which is to signalize me. But perhaps
Thy blood, thy blood will pay for it.
JUNIA.   Well, wouldst thou
Pity me if my life paid for a deed
Worthy alike of glory and of envy?
What! is a maiden's blood, in thy opinion,
Too high a payment for a mighty act?
If thou art capable of such a thought,
Thou knowest not what a memorable feat
Is worth. Now let us talk.
SCAEVOLA.   But, Fulvia,
Go and see whether there are any eyes
Or ears near by to take us by surprise.
JUNIA (*to* FULVIA). Go.
         [FULVIA *withdraws to stand and keep watch some little dis-*
              tance away.
         (*To* SCAEVOLA)   But fear no surprisal meanwhile. This
Place is respected like a place of freedom.
There are no eyes that watch me in the camp.

I am free in prison, my pledged word my keeper.
That is my solace amid all my woe,
A favor which to Porsena I owe.

SCAEVOLA. To Porsena?

JUNIA. To this king who is an honor
To sovereigns; who deserves, in short, to be
The Romans' friend. What! Scaevola is dazed
And marveleth that a gallant foe be praised?

SCAEVOLA. If thou canst praise him as thy kind protector,
Wilt thou endure the hand that seeks his death?
I come to dig the grave of Porsena
As the foundation of Rome's greatness. Judge
If this high deed will put thy life in danger.

JUNIA. It stuns me, Scaevola, and thou shouldst think so.
Not that I dread a fearful death, if that
Of Porsena will really profit Rome.
I wish thine arm to carry out thine aims.
Dost thou believe this king's death serves our people,
And deemest thou not that, far from shielding them,
His ashes will beget untold avengers?

SCAEVOLA. If from his blood should spring a myriad monsters,
Rome will beget as many Herculeses
To deal with them.

JUNIA. Is Rome reduced to such
Dire straits that she must seek a remedy
As dire?

SCAEVOLA. Tomorrow needs must be the end
Of her, if she receives not aid today.
Tarquin no longer fights now for a city;
He fights now for a great necropolis,
So sad and hapless is the fate of Rome.
Famine there causeth its most dread results.
Nature hath no fatality wherein
Necessity doth not find nourishment.
In brief, the Roman people use for food
All that can help to make them die. And thus
Everywhere tragic spectacles are seen
Of public misery and private woes.
There the son, tottering with distress and weakness,
While burying his father, falls beside him.
There the babe dies a piteous, lingering death
Upon his dying mother's breast, drained dry—
And she, beholding this cruel sight, herself
Dieth at the same time of grief and hunger.

SCAEVOLA

One seeth everywhere death or death's image;
It is in every heart or countenance;
And such is thy dear land's extremity,
It seemeth but a dwelling place for ghosts.
  Yet this predicament, so fraught with anguish,
Still hath not overcome our Roman courage.
Even the rabble suffers without quailing;
It craveth liberty, or else a tomb.
Everyone, fired with noble anger, seemeth
To have inherited thy father's virtues,
And fain would show that Rome, stripped of all else,
Hath no more citizens than she hath heroes.
Old men have been beheld, drooping and feeble,
Whom age hath made of no help in the war,—
Have been beheld, I say, under the stress
Of fervent feelings, to offer their own bodies
For the nourishment of younger warriors,
As if they hoped, changed into *their* flesh, still
To be the soul and the defense of Rome.

JUNIA. O great hearts! . . . But alas! with naught to hope for,
Thou puttest thyself in peril and furtherest nothing.

SCAEVOLA. Nay, we shall both derive advantage from it:
I dying for Rome's sake like a brave man,
And thou seeing no more a stubborn lover
Whom thy cold glance so oft hath doomed to death.
If I could never win thy love, which I
Sought by the fairest deeds that mark my life,
Let me, a prey to unexampled woes,
Deserve my country's love by dying for her.

JUNIA. Alas!

SCAEVOLA.   Dost pity Porsena?

JUNIA.   Ah, Scaevola!
    (*Aside*) Ah, Junia! hast thou, then, found him again
    When he will lose his life?

SCAEVOLA.   What! will the daughter
Of Brutus now forget her Roman virtue?
Is she to strive thus for our adversary?
If Porsena hath ere now shown that his heart
Burned fiercely with love's flame, satisfy thou
My doubts: shall I believe that to preserve
His love thou dost for him today oppose me?
Wouldst thou fain spare him, then, to gain the crown
With which his passion bargains for thy person,
And which thy heart, noble when nobly harsh,

Had spurned as something which corrupts great souls?
Since when prefer the empty name of "Queen"
To names adorable of "free" and "Roman"?
Can a throned enemy possess, then, charms
Which Rome, thy people, and thy country have not?

JUNIA. Rightly offended by these words, must I
Deem that the ardor which impels thy heart
And this great plan, so dangerous to thee,
Springs from a jealous, not a generous, spirit?
But if it be successful, to our country
It is the same, be it born of rage or courage.

SCAEVOLA. Yes, it is true I love thee; but suppose not
That a caprice of love leads here my footsteps.
Know, then, that seeing the city threatened so
And equally beset, inside and out,
I in my heart, anxious for Rome, conceived
That I would seek her freedom or my death.
But to be sure that neither hate nor envy
Should with its touch blacken my life's fair fame,
I went straight to the Senate, which I found gathered
To alleviate the woes that wracked the people.
I asked to speak; I told them my intention;
'Twas heard; it pleased; the Senate authorized it;
And to find means as to the time and place
To leave Rome and to come into this camp,
We thought of the sortie in which renowned
Horatius hath just made dim the luster
Of all the heroes of his race. So, favored
By this disguise, I went amid the foe
Securely; I have borrowed this their semblance
In order that I might go easily,
And without being known, thus reach the heart
Of Porsena. Is it, then, in thine opinion,
To go in blind rage, when the hest I follow
Of a great senate? If thou wouldst condemn
This noble attempt, dost thou condemn not Rome
That authorizes it?

JUNIA.   But really, tell me,
What is thy object here?

SCAEVOLA.   I seek the glory
And the salvation of the Roman people.

JUNIA. If one can gain such great advantages
Without our welfare causing so great havoc,
Would the Senate's cruelty be such that laurels

Could please it not, unless bedewed with gore?
And art thou, Scaevola, so sanguinary
That thou desirest a foe's needless blood?

SCAEVOLA. No, Junia; and my blood would by my hands
Flow, were my blood sufficient to save Rome.

JUNIA. Then let my words strive, before thee, against
This mighty king, for Rome, for Scaevola.
For such great aims, thou dost deserve at least
Efforts to save thee from thine imminent peril,
And the good treatment which I owe to Porsena
Bids me at least defer his death a little.
When I have tried to turn aside his fate,
I shall have made an effort, at any rate,
To pay my debt. In brief, if this prince will not
Profit by my advice, 'twill be his fault
That I shall not have paid it; then thine arm,
Inspired alike by glory and by danger,
Can triumph o'er him but a moment later.

SCAEVOLA. Wilt let thy soul be charmed by trifling favors?
Beware the foe who treats thee liberally.
Our duty to our country sanctions all things,
And Rome will fall if Porsena lives on.

JUNIA. But I may e'en through him keep Rome from falling.
If this prince loves me, if he shows he loves me,
Why for my country shall I not accept
This love enkindled by my scant attractions?
If I have any charms, answer me, please,
Can they serve better than to serve my country?
Put off, then, the achievement of thy purpose,
Or I shall think thee cruel, or think thee jealous,
And deem thy courage but insensate frenzy
Which jealousy alone breeds in thy bosom.

SCAEVOLA. What! thou dost wish my fame's delay?

JUNIA.   I wish it.

SCAEVOLA. What power those words have o'er a lover's heart!
Well, to obey thee I shall risk my honor.
But thou—what wilt thou do?

JUNIA.   Achieve the victory.

FULVIA. Someone is coming. Away!

JUNIA (*to* SCAEVOLA).   Go. Avoid them.

[Exit SCAEVOLA.

I seek to save him. Gods, do not oppose me!

[Exeunt JUNIA *and* FULVIA.

SCEVOLE

Scene Two

The scene is the same as in Act I. Enter PORSENA, TARQUIN,
and retinue.

TARQUIN. What! thou'rt dismayed?

PORSENA.   I am indeed dismayed
    At the dread omens given us by the victim.
    One need not cease to be called "great" or "glorious"
    For being alarmed when heaven threateneth.

TARQUIN. What! thou'rt dismayed? This great, strong spirit fears
    An empty presage, fears a beast's dead body?

PORSENA. What! art thou not afraid? And thou it is
    Whom heaven in hate and anger menaces!
    Ne'er hath a fearsome, baleful sacrifice
    Testified better to the wrath of heaven.
    And yet, despite these warnings from on high,
    Thou wouldst risk three assaults, for no good reason.

TARQUIN. Let the gods at their pleasure rule the thunder,
    And let them leave earth's governance to kings.
    Valor and strength and a courageous heart
    Oft change sad omens to auspicious omens.
    Dost thou conceive, then, that a slaughtered beast
    Holdeth our fortunes hidden in his belly,
    And that the foul entrails of animals
    Are a fair temple where the Fates are heard?
    These superstitions and all this great mystery
    Are fit to cozen the common folk alone.
    Thereby doth one urge on or stay their steps
    According as which may serve their sovereign's good;
    But kings ought to despise laments and baseness,
    And be above all weakness such as this.
    They have the omens of good fortune in them
    According as they are mighty and are valiant.

PORSENA. Ah, Tarquin! words like thine insult the gods
    And all the more portend those ills I dread.

TARQUIN. If these gods, whom thou fearest, give aid to rebels,
    Are they, then, our protectors? are they really
    Divinities? When their vain omens favor
    Crimes, when they cast down lawful thrones—these idols,
    These gods, these vile deceivers of mankind—
    Do they not teach us how to break their altars?

PORSENA. Thou goest too far, Tarquin, too far!

TARQUIN.   If I

SCAEVOLA

Went too far, Porsena, perhaps I should
Suffer e'en now the punishment therefor.
PORSENA. And thy disaster will today perhaps
Show to the world that thou dost suffer it.
TARQUIN. Thou art too pious for a noble king.
PORSENA. Thou art too little so for a stricken king.
TARQUIN. Whate'er some god ordains, or Fate or Fortune,
'Tis time to find either my throne or death.
We sacrifice too oft, to win the war.
The blood of men is needed, not of beasts.
In short, of all these gods whom men create,
To Victory only doth a king owe altars;
But she requireth human victims of us
Ere crowning with success our sweat and pain,
And the altar which she claims of fortunate
Kings is a battlefield and shattered walls.
Then let us nobly go to achieve a task
Whose outcome hangs but on a little courage.
PORSENA. I wait for the occasion that should speed us.
TARQUIN. Dost thou expect a god to come to announce it
To thee? Well then, and is not this a time
To conquer beyond question, if we attack
The enemy when he is without defense?
PORSENA. No, no, 'tis not the time to offer battle
When the contrarious gods restrain our arm.
TARQUIN. What, ho! Always the gods! These gods whom thou
Opposest to me are but a fine pretense
Which hideth something else. Junia abides
Within thy heart, and naught can drive her from it.
She is the sole god whom thou fearest to anger.
PORSENA. I am not astonished that in our situation
Thou, having assailed the gods, wouldst quarrel with men.
TARQUIN. I am not astonished that a very lover
Doth sacrifice his honor to his bliss.
To please a maiden who delights his eye,
He well may set free a whole guilty nation.
I really *am* astonished that an honored
Prince should make gifts so precious at the expense
Of others.
PORSENA.   Ill dost thou appreciate
Our toil and suffering.
TARQUIN.   I still owe nothing
For such vain favors.
PORSENA.   Feeling thus, thou plainly

SCEVOLE

Makest us see that thy proud heart would fain
Owe nothing to us. Truly, thou doest well.
Whatever one intends, it shames a king
To be in any's debt for anything;
And, sir, to spare thee this, we willingly
Will leave thee so that thou wilt owe us nothing.
                    [*Exit* PORSENA, *followed by his retinue.*
TARQUIN (*alone, gazing after him*).   Confess, then: Rome hath beaten
          thee. If mine
The loss thereby, the shame thereof is thine.
False to that tie which properly unites
Kings when rebellion would usurp their rights,
Do this great wrong to every monarch's crown
Of favoring those whose bold stroke hurled one down.
If *my* loss be a realm, more is thine own
By showing thyself unworthy of a throne.

ACT III

The scene is again the space before the tent of Porsena. ARUNS
and MARCELLUS *are discovered.*

ARUNS.   Yes, it is true; I like this quarrel, Marcellus,
          Which would rob Tarquin of my father's help.
          The Romans are a people dear to me.
          Alive or dead, Scaevola makes me fear
          For them. Alive or dead, Scaevola, whom
          I love because he saved my life, asks of me
          Mercy for them, and fain would, as repayment
          For what he did for me, have me bestow
          Upon his country what to him I owe.
MARCELLUS.   What! for a single man, wouldst spare a city,
          The refuge and protector of rebellion?
          That, surely, is a great reward.
ARUNS.   The boon
          Was greater. Wouldst thou have me do what honor
          Forbids? Wouldst aid a sacrilegious ruler
          Who tries to tyrannize over a king
          That shelters him?
MARCELLUS.   Nay, sir, but we must . . .
ARUNS.   Here
          The King is, coming out.

                    Enter PORSENA, *from his tent.*

                              184

SCAEVOLA

PORSENA.   Did ever monarch
Exhibit passions more mean-spirited?
Would he fain perish—make shipwreck of his fortunes?
We are restoring him to his high estate,
And the ungrateful man insults us! He,
Who is so proud, is driven from his own realm;
He comes and begs the succor of my arm;
And one would say, to see the arrogance
Which wraps him round, that it is I who ask
And he who gives!
ARUNS.   Oh, sire, abandon this
Insulting prince, who treats us as but vassals
And braves thee to thy face. Seize the chance given thee
To rid thy kingdom of a dangerous neighbor.
Let no one tell me that thou art obliged
By honor to restore his throne and fortunes.
Thou hast done quite enough for thy fair fame
By placing victory in his easy reach.
Thou hast done quite enough to show the Romans
Their walls would fall if thou shouldst lift thy hand.
What duty now, what sense of honor binds thee
To re-enthrone a monarch who insults thee,
And what excess of magnanimity
Can from thy mind blot such outrageous conduct?
   A sovereign can forget, without offense
Unto his honor, a wicked subject's blackest
Crime, but when kings at kings' hands suffer insult,
They must do everything to be avenged;
Or else, if they endure wrongs from their equals,
They cause themselves to be of fear suspected
Or helplessness—and more than the misfortunes
Of numberless disasters, helplessness
And fear dishonor kings. Show, then, that Fortune,
Hostile without thee, hath for the unjust Tarquin
Nothing but infamy. Let him fall and perish
With all his plans. To avenge thyself upon him,
Spare Rome, and let the Romans owe to thee
This day their freedom, which was promised them
By nothing but their manhood. If the crimes,
If the impieties of Tarquin drive
From his support all the offended gods,
His wicked pride, worthy of heaven's bolt,
Should also drive away all earthly kings.

SCEVOLE

MARCELLUS. These feelings are indeed noble and gallant,
But would be dangerous, methinks, to follow.
If thou shouldst spare Rome, and thy leniency
Should limit thy vengeance to thy freeing of her,
Could Tarquin not, by one of countless ways,
Make peace with Rome, return to power there?
And dost thou deem that then his might or fury,
Kindled by thee, would spare Etruria?
  Sire, pardon me: one takes revenge but ill
When after vengeance one remains in danger.
Rome hopes no more from any aid on earth;
Each blow we deal her is a thunderbolt;
And in their sorry plight, the Romans must
Stretch out to us their throats or suppliant hands.
But after all their efforts, their resistance
Which hath surpassed the power of human valor,
Can we still leave these walls which separate us
And not appear to give up this great siege?
Thus to withdraw, concedes to them the victory,
And less takes leave of Tarquin than thy glory.
  Sire, thou must be avenged—by greater deeds.
Thou must take Rome, and take it for thyself.
Thou must keep it, and all that it containeth,
As recompense for what this war hath cost.
Beguile the city with the joys of peace
And win the Roman people by thy kindness.
It hateth Tarquin, this it clearly showeth us;
And if it can change masters, will consider
Itself revenged. But better to win over
Rome and the Roman people, as thou didst love
Junia, carry out thine intentions; let
The noble bond of an illustrious marriage
Bind to thy destiny a Roman woman.
ARUNS. This counsel is strange and little just.
MARCELLUS.   I hold, sir,
That if 'tis useful to the King, 'tis just.
ARUNS. Then whatsoe'er is to a king's advantage
Is justice?
MARCELLUS.   Yes; his welfare is a law
For him with which he must comply; and where
One takes a crown from one who cannot reign,
'Tis rightly his who knoweth how to win it.
PORSENA. I do hate Tarquin and his tyranny,

And of your counsels twain . . .

                                  But what would Junia
With us?

                   Enter JUNIA.

JUNIA.   O king twice crowned, once by thy lineage
And once by virtues nobler than thy station,
Thy generosity gives me the boldness
To come to thee to ask another favor.
PORSENA. Ask freely all thou wishest; ask, besides,
Our hearts and thou shalt have them.
JUNIA.   I shall ask
For nothing which does not beseem thy honor
Nor signalize thy name e'en like a victory.
Thou seekest to conquer; and in harmony
With thy designs I come to ask of thee,
Porsena, the destruction of the Romans—
I come to ask of thee their shame and torture—
If their cause is not also that of justice.
    Consider, then, with a more curious eye,
For whom thou takest up arms obligingly.
If 'tis a righteous prince whom thou dost aid,
Wrong are the Romans; punish them, afflict them.
But if thou for a tyrant ravagest
Our fields, see if 'tis glorious to aid tyrants.
    Wouldst learn if Tarquin *did* love tyranny?
Let me be silent, sir; let his life speak.
Thou'lt learn that a great king, butchered by him,
Was his first step to a throne's usurpation,
And that with every reason to be loyal,
He foully slew this monarch who had made him
His son-in-law. To mount a winsome throne
The sooner, but all reeking with the blood,
Still, of her father, there shalt thou behold
The sanguinary wife of Tarquin make
Her chariot pass over that father's corpse,
Although at this sad sight her frightened steeds
Seem to respect the body of a king.
Even so, with a reign begun by violence,
The sequel might excuse its tragic opening,
But upon his unjust profanèd throne
Crime, under Tarquin, ever wore the crown.
If guiltily, then, he acquired a scepter,—
If worse he wielded it than he acquired it,—

SCEVOLE

When Rome expelled him, when Rome banished him,
Is this no tyrant whom her hate hath punished?
   Thus hath Rome given glorious indications
Of the just reverence that she feels for monarchs.
Can she show better how she honors kings
Than in thus punishing the man who wrongs them
And whose unjust, disloyal, bloody soul
Soils with such horror kingly majesty?
This town unconquerable hence deserves
That heaven's might should come to her assistance.
   Look on Horatius and his feat of arms:
Is there a semblance of the laws of nature
In having alone fought soldiers by the thousand;
In having stayed, alone, their raging steps;
In having alone, covered with splendid glory,
Snatched victory from the armies of two kings?
'Tis certainly an outcome that none rashly
Could to himself ascribe without impiety.
'Tis certainly an outcome that should teach thee
That all the gods uphold in him our realm.
   Yet, what a miracle! a king so glorious
Fights for a tyrant, against Rome and the gods!
He seeks unworthy victory for crime,
And makes the whole world doubt his claims to honor.
Seek, seek for names fairer and greater than
That of restorer of a wicked tyrant.
For my part, who wish honor's palm for thee,—
Who am beholden unto thee for thy kindness,—
I have believed that to discharge my debt
I ought to say these things to thee, which ought
To save thy fair fame and perchance thy life.

PORSENA.   If I have by some favors done thy worth
      Fit honor, thy good wishes now repay me
      And leave us quits. But truly it is time
      That we should make thee see how great a power
      Thy glance hath o'er our hearts. Rome is too little.
      Thy destiny requires of us with better
      Justice a grander glory.

JUNIA.   Sir, add nothing
      To this rare boon. It doth suffice thine honor;
      It is sufficient for my happiness.

PORSENA.   Rome is too little for thee, dear, noble foe.

JUNIA.   If it is little, what gift canst thou give me?

PORSENA.   Gifts worthy of thee, gifts which are so precious

That heaven makes none that are more glorious.
We wish to set a crown upon thy brow.
We wish to give thee all the power it giveth,
And make thee, by unheard-of blessings, own
One finds one's country where one finds a throne.

JUNIA. What! thou wouldst give me the delights of empire,
And thou refusest my country to my tears?

PORSENA. In truth, thou vexest me; I must be frank
With thee. My honor asks this and must have
Its will. Forget Rome, then.

JUNIA.   Forget my country!
Is this a king who speaks to me, or Tarquin
Enraged? For they are tyrants, not true kings,
Who such cruel laws prescribe for human hearts.
Forget my country! I cannot make myself!
What sayest thou, sir?

PORSENA.   Of what canst thou complain
If to thy fortunes, that now languish, I
Give for some ruined walls, a prosperous throne?

JUNIA. Perhaps that throne is nearer falling than
Rome's ruined walls for which thine arm contends.
Perhaps the gods, who to thy power set limits,
Have a support for them that shall o'erthrow thee.

PORSENA. Seeing that our greatness will be shared by thee,
Form wishes, now, more favorable to us.
Thy lot is dear to me, and thou mayest count
My love some day among thy foremost blessings.

JUNIA. Thy love!

PORSENA.   I know my age displeases thee;
But look upon this prince, decked with my power.
This is my son; this really is a crowned
Slave, whom thy glance shall win, if it hath not won him.

JUNIA. But only turn thine eyes; see Rome, and ask her
What I must do, and what she doth command.
To howsoe'er great marriage I be forced,
She, Porsena, is my mother; she must consent.
Speak, then, and answer us, O embattled Rome,
Should *I* give *my* hand to the hand that smites thee?
     What! wouldst thou fain establish hell in Rome?
What! wouldst thou cover her with blood and fetters?
Are these the charms with which wise Porsena
Thinks to attract a Roman woman's heart?
Wouldst *thou* love *thy* son if he loved the conqueror
Whose bloody hand had stabbed thee to the heart?

And seeing my country so assailed before me,
Should *I* give *my* hand to the hand that smites her?
Nay, nay, my lord.

PORSENA.   Farewell. Thou'lt hearken to me
Better when thou conceivest our righteous purpose.
    Marcellus, are all preparations made
For holding the review?

MARCELLUS.   Yes, sire, and all
Thy captains have received their orders.

PORSENA.   Let us
Go, then.
         My daughter, in the meantime, bethink thee.
Look on the blessings offered thee by a king.
When one is powerless to aid one's country,
One may without sin plan one's own protection.

              [*Exeunt* PORSENA, ARUNS, *and* MARCELLUS.

JUNIA (*alone*).   Then must he perish, but at the same time
He must in his destruction crush the tyrants.
O Scaevola! O my country! ye die matchless.
As I have for you both a like affection,
Rightly for both, alas, I have offered prayers
And made the same efforts to save you both.
But whether Fate here forms an obstacle
Or to save Rome hath still some miracle,
Ah, of two things that I love equally—
The one my land, the other him I love—
One must we hazard, yet not be certain that
His loss and death will end the other's woes!

Enter SCAEVOLA.

SCAEVOLA.   Well, what hast thou accomplished?

JUNIA.   I have put thee
In a position to obey exactly
The orders of the Senate, and no matter
With what dire blows thy rage may be displayed,
I have removed myself from the position
Of being ungrateful. I have tried to save
This hapless king and honorably repay
My debt to him, but I am now quits with him
Because he hath disdained my gratitude;
And though he has a great, staunch, generous spirit,
He merits death because he aids a tyrant.
Go, then. Go. . . . But alas!

SCAEVOLA

SCAEVOLA.   What! Brutus' daughter
Still wavers between Rome and Porsena?
She fears . . .
JUNIA.   Yes, I do fear; but oh, it is
For thee I fear! The peril that dogs thy steps
Dismays me, and thy manhood which impels thee
Where danger calls deserves at least that I
Should fear for it. If there is not one Roman
Who does not owe thee guerdon for this lofty
Deed which thine arm doth undertake, alas,
Since I am powerless, being here constrained,
For guerdon I at least give thee my fear.
SCAEVOLA. If great the peril, as I believe it is,
Fear not for me, but rather urge me on;
Or if thou fain wouldst amply recompense me,
Say that a little love begets thy fears.
I surmount danger, I already triumph,
If, when I go, I in thy heart remain.
JUNIA. What! when thy courage and thy noble anger
Would break with thine own hands thy country's chains,
Must thou ask of me to be cold no more
To thee? Must thou ask now my love and heart?
Couldst thou not guess that for thy manly virtues
Thou hast been given already what thou askest?
SCAEVOLA. What! thy love, Junia? Oh, dear, dear words!
JUNIA. Thou takest my heart with thee into the peril
To which thou hurriest.
SCAEVOLA.   Thou lovest me!
JUNIA. But let that urge thee, truly, to delay not
The risking of thy life, but make me see
By a fair death that I was justified
The better in acknowledging to thee
My feelings; for, indeed, whether thou dost
Vanquish Porsena or art vanquished by him—
In tears I say it—thou art sure to die.
Canst thou strike down a king amid his army,
Or canst thou fail to do so, and escape?
SCAEVOLA. Thus it belongs only to Roman manhood
To rush where doom is plain to see and sure.
My end is to be fair, proud, and renowned
If I shall die for Rome and die beloved.
I had supposed that only fame and honor
Could pay me for my death or victory;
But now thy love doth teach me verily

191

That love can well repay the noblest exploits.
Whether thou feignest love to spur me on
Or in thy lovely breast its flame doth burn,
I go with like firm step and the same fervor,
To seek from danger victory or death.
If thou dost feign to love me, matchless maiden,
I go to merit thy real love thereby;
Or if with a pure love thy heart is kindled,
I go to merit being loved still more.

JUNIA. I, I, to spur thee on, feign now to love thee?
Nay, Scaevola, 'tis true my love is great;
But when our country needs thine arm, if 'twere
Needful to spur thee on, I would not love thee;
For truly manhood loses all its worth
And is not manhood when it needs incitement.
I love thee and almost with envy see thee
Gloriously for our country defy danger.
It is not that my soul, laid bare to grief,
Doth not already sorrow for thy loss.
My heart already, reft of all good hope,
Is pierced with darts that soon will pierce thine own;
And it lacks little, Scaevola, at this moment,
That my love murmureth against thy manhood;
But to whatever dangers this may drive thee,
Far from complaining, I must imitate it.
Thou givest thy life, Scaevola, nobly, grandly,
And if I can do naught for Rome's salvation,
I would contribute to it by consenting
To the attempt which makes me lose my lover.
Thus, then, I shall do something for my country
By my consent to Scaevola's sacrifice.

SCAEVOLA. Consent most worthy of a gallant heart!
Without it I were loath to expose thy lover,
And by it thy fair soul shall share the glory
Of either my victory or else my death.
What, Junia! thou weepest?

JUNIA.   And Rome should weep
When to thy doom thou rushest that she may live.

SCAEVOLA. Farewell. I fear thy tears.

JUNIA.   Whate'er the gods
Prepare for thee, my hand shall urge thee on
If my tears stay thee. Go. Thou canst not die
Better. But can love lose thee and not sigh?

                    [*He goes out. She stands gazing after him.*

ACT IV

Scene One

*The scene represents the part of the camp shown in the first
scene of Act II.* JUNIA *and* FULVIA *are discovered.*

JUNIA. Porsena dead, thou sayest? Art thou sure, Fulvia?

FULVIA. Too loud the rumor swells. He is no more.

JUNIA. Knowest thou if he who stabbed him hath been captured?

FULVIA. Though bloody from his deed, he is thought to have
Escaped.

JUNIA.   Is thought to have escaped! Blest gods!
Is it possible?

FULVIA.   Why art thou so concerned
About his safety? Knowest thou what arm
Struck this mad blow?

JUNIA.   It could have only been
A glorious arm; and one should be concerned
About the fortunes of a man who hath
Delivered Rome from such a foe.

FULVIA.   And yet
'Tis said that the vile Tarquin instigated,
Himself, the assassin to kill Porsena.

JUNIA. And on what is this rumor based?

FULVIA.   'Tis said
That this cruel tyrant believed Porsena
Intended to facilitate Rome's freedom,
And fain would strike his own protector down
Rather than be uncertain about this.

JUNIA. So much the better if he hath struck down
The prop that held him up. The Romans' foe
Makes their cause stronger. He at least hath shown . . .

FULVIA. I hear some clamor.

JUNIA.   Gods! what do I see?
'Tis Scaevola who is pursued. He vainly
Defends himself, and numbers overpower him.

Enter MARCELLUS, *with* SCAEVOLA *a prisoner, and soldiers.*

MARCELLUS (*to* SCAEVOLA). Thou fleddest, but in vain, accursèd felon.

SCAEVOLA. Nay, nay, I fled not; I was going back
To give the Romans an account of what
My hands have done.

MARCELLUS.   Thou wilt not go so far.

SCAEVOLA.   It is enough for my fair fame that I
Have made my victory's noise reach even their ears.

Enter ARUNS.

ARUNS.   Is he taken?
MARCELLUS.   There he stands, this fuel for hell.
SCAEVOLA.   Here stands the scourge of tyrants whom thou servest.
ARUNS.   O gods! Whom see I? Scaevola!
SCAEVOLA.   'Tis he.
ARUNS.   Scaevola, unto whom I owe far more than
A crown; whose helping hand hath fought for me;
Whose heinous hand is lifted 'gainst my king!
The son's deliverer, but the father's murderer!
With reasons manifold for love and anger,
What shall I call thee?
SCAEVOLA.   Friend by preference,
Enemy only by necessity.
I love thee, Aruns; and if any danger
Hung o'er thy head still, threatening thy misfortune,
Thou still wouldst see me, armed for thy defense,
Pour all my blood forth to preserve thy life.
But if thou, like thy father, didst misuse
Thine arms and make us fear to lose our freedom,
And if thou madest thy power and authority
Serve to restore a tyrant to his throne,
I myself, burning with a noble wrath,
Would mingle thy blood with thy father's blood;
I, who prolonged thy life, would seek to end it,
And I, who was thy friend, would be thy slayer.
However powerful our friendship's tie,
Affection cannot live with tyranny.
In short, if thou becomest the Tarquins' champion,
A friend of tyrants cannot be my friend.
But if thy heart, more just, forsakes and hates
A cause so baneful to all potentates,
Even though thine anger doth decree my death,
I shall love thee always and shall not complain.
For, after all, 'tis right and necessary
For thee to avenge on me thy father's murder.
ARUNS.   The outcome hath defeated thine intentions,
Which proves thou wert unrighteous and not noble;
And thy fell heart, where hell hath kindled its flames,
Is much more guilty than thine erring hand.
Porsena liveth.

SCAEVOLA

SCAEVOLA.   The gods, leagued against him,
Guide the blows better which they have inspired.
Thy sire is dead, Aruns; mine arm attests it.
ARUNS.   He liveth, Scaevola; mine own eyes swear it;
And whatsoe'er death-blow thine arm hath dealt,
Porsena triumphs and is not even wounded.
SCAEVOLA.   Porsena is not dead?
ARUNS.   So far from suffering
That ultimate misfortune, he will have
The pleasure of taking vengeance for himself.
JUNIA.   How hath the blow miscarried that I hoped for?
SCAEVOLA.   By my not knowing who it was I stabbed;
By my not daring to learn which man was he,
For fear that if I asked, I would be noticed
And thus be held as one suspect, for having
Shown that I did not know the King by sight.
Hence I smote him whose proud demeanor made me
Believe and take him to be Porsena.
ARUNS.   O thou who, seeing my death nigh, didst prevent it,
Can I without ingratitude desert thee?
O thou who hast assailed my father's life,
How can I aid thee and not be unfilial?
SCAEVOLA.   Nay, nay, I am more just; I would not wish
That an impiety should avert my death.
Do a son's duty: in this situation
Be deaf to friendship; hearken to nature's ties.
Champion thy father's cause; to satisfy
His claims, I free thee now of what thou owest me.
I am guilty, Aruns; but whate'er men think,
My only crime is to have missed thy father.
O Rome, my country, pardon my mistake!
The fault lies in mine arm, not in my heart.
The fault lies in mine arm, not in my courage,
Which could make shipwreck of a thousand tyrants;
Or rather, if Porsena escaped death's clutches,
The fault is due to chance, not to mine arm.
I shall confess, though, noble Roman maiden,
That I should win thy hate by this great failure;
For when it is a question of achieving
Great things, chance errors become crimes in us.
JUNIA.   It is sufficient that thine arm hath shown
Porsena what he hath to dread from Roman
Heroism. He hath seen thy courage; he
Will dread it, though he vent his rage on thee.

195

For my part, if thy manhood, proved so often,
Had won me not, as thy deserved reward,
Thou wouldst o'ercome me by this memorable
Attempt which makes thee sacred in Rome's sight;
For thou couldst not appear more lovable
Or great than in this high endeavor which
Destroys thee.

ARUNS (*to* JUNIA).   Hide, at least, these cruel feelings,
And remain guiltless though but in appearance.

JUNIA. Nay, learn to know me better, and believe
That all my pride consists in seconding
This eminent crime. I shared in the great plan
Which Scaevola conceived; know that I wish
To share in the result. I pity thee,
However, that thou springest from a father
Whose murder is a blow that virtue prompts.

ARUNS. Do not make bad things worse.

MARCELLUS (*to* ARUNS).   Allow me, sir,
To carry out the King's desires and hest.

ARUNS. What hest?

MARCELLUS.   To bring the guilty man to him.

ARUNS. O father, friend, how wretched your claims make me!

SCAEVOLA. Thou payest too much for what I did for thee,
Being thus torn between thy sire and me.
Farewell.
(*To* JUNIA) And thou, whose great heart fain would be
My accomplice, love thy country without seeking
To share my doom; and if, perchance, to thee
Heaven is kindlier and some day allows thee
To dwell among the Roman people, tell them
That I am dead, not from the punishment
Which Porsena's rage wrongly prepares for me,
But from the regret, worse than a hundred deaths,
That ill I used mine arm to serve my country.
There, there my crime lies. Let us, then, go die.
I failed to help Rome, and I must be punished.

JUNIA. At least thou'lt die this day worthy to be
Brutus's son-in-law, and to have my love.

[*Exeunt* SCAEVOLA, MARCELLUS, *and guards.*

ARUNS. Her love! What have I heard? What! Scaevola
My rival? Wait; one word more, Junia!

JUNIA. I have said too much now, Aruns.

ARUNS.   O monstrous fate!
O gods! what shall we do?

JUNIA.   Dost ask the gods?
The gods will answer that, to satisfy them,
A son must needs desire his father's death
Rather than suffer it that, for still worse evils,
He should, by serving tyrants, be a tyrant.
Farewell. Do thou thy duty.   [*Exit* JUNIA.
ARUNS (*alone*).   If I do
My duty, whatsoever I may do
I shall do violence to mine own feelings.   [*Exit* ARUNS.

Scene Two

The scene is again before the tent of PORSENA. *Enter* TARQUIN
to PORSENA, *who is attended by his bodyguard.*

TARQUIN.   Because of a foul rumor, which some demon
Spreads everywhere to blacken my good name,
I come to offer myself to thee as hostage
Alike for thy security and thy profit.
Respecting not my title, do men accuse me
Of having sought some hand to shed thy blood?
No, no! if something roused my wrath against thee,
I could avenge myself without recourse
To crime; and when one wrongs my rank or honor,
I can engage in war and not in murder.
Hence I come now, either to satisfy thee
If proven guilty of this bloody act,
Or to seek satisfaction from thyself
If I am wrongly charged with this foul crime.
PORSENA.   The author of the attempt is hunted now,
And we shall both be well pleased by his capture.
TARQUIN.   There is no doubt that this atrocious deed
Is the vile effort of a Roman rebel.
He thinks that, having torn a crown from kings,
His work is incomplete if he attempts not
Their death. But how was this dire crime committed?
PORSENA.   I saw the blood but not the hand that shed it.
I was engaged in listening to the talk
Of certain of our men, when I beheld
A flash of steel, and Statius fell to earth.
TARQUIN.   What makes thee think, then, that *thy* life was aimed at?
PORSENA.   What the assassin said while stabbing him.
"Die, Porsena," he said; all men could hear it.
He struck, and at once fled.
TARQUIN.   And none could take him?

SCEVOLE

Enter MARCELLUS.

PORSENA. Well?

MARCELLUS.   Sire, he is captured.

PORSENA.   Let him be brought hither.
My sight must needs begin his punishment.

SCAEVOLA *is brought in.*

It must . . . But see him, full of pride and boldness.
His hand unarmed, his scowl at least still threatens;
And one would say he comes with the same purpose,
To accomplish with his eyes what his hand tried.
    Who art thou, wretch?

SCAEVOLA.   I am a Roman, Porsena.
Thou seest Roman freedom in mine aspect.
I with an arm which honor ever strengthened
Attempted, as a foe, to slay a foe;
And when a horrible, outrageous fate
Exposes me to the anger that I kindled
Within thy soul, I have a heart as fearless
To suffer and to die as I displayed
To take thy life. I had decreed thy death;
Wilt thou not order mine? I shall go thither
With the same step wherewith I went to slay thee.
For I am Roman, and with whatsoever
Doom thou canst manifest thy wrath against me,
Ever unconquerable is Roman spirit.
It is the spirit to do and to endure
Impossible things. Strike, then. Here is my heart.
But do not think to save thyself from death
By shedding *my* blood. Other hearts than mine
Will have the same thought. Other hands than mine
Will arm themselves to slay thee. And with fervor
Of courage no less great, a thousand others
Will seek like me the glory of thy death.
    Make up thy mind, then, Porsena, in thy peril
To battle every moment for thy life,
And to have foes, thy conquerors late or soon,
Everywhere in thy palace, nigh thy heart.
The youth of Rome, like lightning swift to strike,
Declare through me this fearsome war against thee;
They have no purpose save to kill thee. They
Find in thy heart's blood their one goal and glory.
Then dread no more our army's might, so often
Aroused to thy confusion, but let every

SCAEVOLA

Roman with fear inspire thee, because every
Roman has no aim but to stab thy heart.
If *my* hand hath not reft the light from thee,
'Tis not because the gods protect thy life,
But 'tis because these gods, who fight for us,
Desire thee to feel fear before thy death-blow.

PORSENA. Did ever murderer show greater boldness?
    'Tis he who ought to tremble, and 'tis he
    Who threatens me!

SCAEVOLA.   'Tis meet and right for tyrants
    To fear and tremble, as it is for Romans
    To vanquish them and crush them.

PORSENA.   Gods! what frenzy!

SCAEVOLA. It is not frenzy which inspires against thee
    My heart and hand. Whatever ardor fired me
    To such a glorious deed, I here am like
    The servants of the gods, who, quite unmoved
    And high-souled, slay the sacrificial victims
    For the public good, with neither hate nor fury.

TARQUIN. Traitor, who hast in rage defied my kingship,
    If thou must needs shed blood to profit Rome,
    Was it not mine thou oughtest to have shed,
    Since 'tis my wrath that shall lay Rome in ashes?

SCAEVOLA. Thinkest thou that *thy* blood, which my hand neglected,
    Is worthy of the work of Roman courage?
    Thy life was left thee after thy misdeeds,
    So that its length may be thy punishment;
    And none hath for Rome's sake decreed thy death,
    For Rome in all her troubles doth not fear thee.
    But if we plot the death of this great man,
    'Tis a clear proof he is esteemed in Rome.
    Yes, Porsena, my arm, which failed me, fain
    Would by thy blood show how thou wert regarded.
    Tarquin is looked on without fear or envy
    As a weak, lifeless body, but thou art
    Considered, with thy mighty deeds, the mind
    Which moves that hated body. We have thought,
    Honoring thee, that the far-famed Porsena
    Can for one day hold back the Romans' freedom,
    And that is all too long for such a noble
    People, who soon will make of kings their subjects.

PORSENA. How great and gallant are the Roman people!
    How fortunate it is that Rome esteems us,
    Since she decideth that today crowned sovereigns

Are worthy to be assassinated by her!
Are these the doings of that noble city
Which flees like shame unrighteous victory,—
Which would refuse prosperity and glory
When offered not by honorable hands?

SCAEVOLA. These are the doings of that noble city
Which thinks a tyrant's death is always just,
But which would wish to fight, as for her rights,
For the respect owed justly to true kings.
From such, Rome owes her being, and Rome reveres them
As well-reared children should revere their father.
Do thou, then, once a great king, whom we praised,
Usurp that name no more; thou hast renounced it.
Yes, thou hast lost it; for in thy high station,
Who aids a tyrant is himself a tyrant.
Be not surprised, then, after thy fine deeds,
That thou'rt not treated as a king is treated.
Be not surprised, then, that Rome sought not battle
But left to me the honor of killing thee.
Everyone equally, both great and small,
Hath naturally the right to punish tyrants;
And to destroy with them whoever aids them,
Is to slay victims for the good of all.

TARQUIN. Wilt thou permit this insolent fellow still
To scorn our might and brave us to our faces?

PORSENA. At least, to spare thyself unnumbered tortures,
Disclose, vile wretch, disclose thy accomplices.

SCAEVOLA. Ask not their names. They will not remain hidden.
They will disclose themselves soon by thy death.

TARQUIN. And thou delayest the fate of this base miscreant?

SCAEVOLA. He hath delayed too much. I myself blame him.

PORSENA *(to an officer of his guard)*. Light the flames. Go and immolate him for me.
Tortures will conquer him and make him speak.

SCAEVOLA. Add to them all the pain that hell can fashion,
He who knows how to die, knows well, besides,
How to keep silent.

PORSENA.   Then to this cruel man
Show yourselves cruel.
        (To another officer) Thou, bring Junia here.
She knew his plans. Her proud and saucy words
Show all too clearly her acquaintance with them.

SCAEVOLA

ACT V

The scene is again before the tent of PORSENA. ARUNS *is discovered, alone.*

ARUNS.   But to his valiant arm thou owest thy life. . . .
Yes, but he is thy rival. . . . But must the word
"Rival," thou wretch, arouse thine anger more
Than the dread words "thy father's would-be murderer"?
What! can I pardon this audacious spirit
Who hath attacked earth's likeness of the gods?
What! can I pardon him when I regard him
Thus as the enemy of my father's fortunes,
Yet cannot see him without hate and fear
When I perceive him as my rival here?
Is the wrong greater to love her whom *I* love
Than to have raised his hand against my father?
Ah, if that seems as great to noble souls,
To lovers' intellects it doth no less clearly.
O reason which I flout! offended nature!
Correct this fault of my insensate heart!
Let us allow the thunderbolts alike
Of gods and kings to fall upon a chieftain
Guilty a thousand times o'er. It may be
That heaven, which requires his punishment,
Made him my rival to incite my hate. . . .
Would heaven desire, though, that my base endeavor
Should use 'gainst him the life which he hath saved me?
He preserved me, and I with savage soul
Contemplate both his punishment and death.
Die, my love, rather, since it is thy passion
That made my rescuer odious in my sight. . . .
But to o'ercome a love so strong and dear,
Is Scaevola less my father's would-be murderer?
Did he offend less . . . But . . .

Enter soldiers, with JUNIA.

                      Where lead ye her?
JUNIA.   They lead a victim to thy wrathful father.
ARUNS.   Fear naught. My love assures thee of thy life.
JUNIA.   I am not troubled. I care for life but little.
My country thou destroyest. Me wilt thou
Defend?
ARUNS.   Accept my love and thou shalt save it.

I well know Scaevola fills all thy thoughts,
And that thy heart his prize and glory is;
But if his native land is dear to him,—
If he desires to see prosperity
And peace restored there,—thou shouldst nowise doubt
That, as 'twere some great medicine in sickness,
He would himself resign thee to his rival.

JUNIA.   I know that Scaevola is high-souled enough
To serve his country at his love's expense;
And following that precept which he would
Decree for me himself, I here, without
Deliberation, give up the man I love.
I heedlessly renounce mine own desires;
I shall compel my heart, nor heave one sigh.
To triumph over love without a struggle
And without difficulty is the least
Virtue that Rome imparts to us. I, then,
Shall sacrifice myself unto thy wishes.

ARUNS.   O words that ravish me with their delight!

JUNIA.   But if brave Scaevola preserved thy life
When with the shafts of death it was pursued,
Not willingly will I doubt that this great service
Hath charmed thy heart, since 'tis a generous heart,
And that the illustrious Aruns will agree not
To what I said, but if I give myself
To him, will give me back to Scaevola.

ARUNS.   Yes, I would give thee up to this true friend
If he were able to enjoy a boon.

JUNIA.   Wouldst thou display a noble, generous spirit,
Worthy that Scaevola should have fought for thee?
Rescue from ruin's brink a friend so true
And make him able to enjoy a boon.

ARUNS.   But can I honorably, to satisfy thee,
Embrace my father's would-be murderer's cause?

JUNIA.   How, then! Couldst thou with honor in his need
Refuse protection to thy rescuer?
Learn, Aruns, learn that a magnanimous heart
Hath in sore straits more ingenuity,
And that, to satisfy its noble instincts
It even will attempt the impossible.
I know it is no ordinary matter
To plead for one who sought thy father's life;
But by what act couldst thou bear witness better
That dear and precious is thy savior to thee?

SCAEVOLA

One thing more: do not think the interest
Of Scaevola, nigh shipwreck, prompts my words.
His interest consists in dying grandly.
His death will set him midst earth's demi-gods.
Because thou owest thy life but to his valor,
If I now urge thee to show gratitude,
It is to teach thee to deserve at least,
By some great act, what Scaevola did for thee.

ARUNS.   Ah, why canst thou not see my heart's sore torment—
How friendship, love, and natural ties contend there!
Thou'dst see more woes, thou'dst see more hampering chains,
Than one can picture when one painteth hell.
Thou'dst see that there-within, amid its tempest,
Those whom I love the most, cause me most pain.
'Tis pain to me that she who won my love
Contends with Scaevola and drives him thence.
'Tis pain to me that there mine angered father
Contends with Scaevola, Scaevola with my father.
But I can put no stop to these contentions,
And know not which side is the dearest to me.

JUNIA.   Take that of honor.

ARUNS.   But . . .

Enter MARCELLUS.

            (*To* MARCELLUS)   What can we do
Marcellus? Can we give him aid worth aught?
Shall *I* speak to the King?

MARCELLUS.   As thou hast bidden me,
I tried to learn what were his heart's true feelings,
But I have found there only rage and hatred.
Scaevola sees already the arrangements
Completed for his punishment. The fire
Is lit. He is prepared to die. If he
Is to be helped, 'tis time to hasten there.

ARUNS.   Then let us try.

Exit MARCELLUS. *As* ARUNS *is going out with him,* PORSENA
    enters hastily.

PORSENA.   O miracle! O marvel,
Incredible to mine ears if not attested
By mine own eyes! Ah, my son! Ah, my son!

ARUNS.   Hast thou not had thy vengeance? Could it be
That some god preserves Scaevola from it?

PORSENA. Yes,
  My son; his manhood, which defies my crown,
  Is the god who doth preserve him, and the god
  Who doth confound me.

ARUNS. May I ask of thee
  What is this great occurrence which will make me
  Share thy confoundment?

PORSENA. All things were already
  Prepared, the fire and implements of torture,
  To force this Roman to tell who were his
  Accomplices. I certainly could never
  Draw thee that picture without shuddering
  At mine own words no less than at what happened.
  "Speak, speak!" I said, showing the flames to him;
  "Tell us thy comrades in thy accursed plot,
  Or these fires and these irons which thou seest ready
  Will tear from thee the names of the conspirators."
  He laughed at this, and far from answering me,
  He, when I thought to daunt him with the tortures,
  Said to me: "Wouldst thou know how little do
  Strong men esteem their bodies, beside their honor?
  View with affright this excellent demonstration
  Thereof, which shows to thee my hand and heart."
  Then, as though on his hand he would take vengeance
  Because its blow had failed to find my breast,
  He thrust into the fire this guilty hand:
  The flames enveloped it; he withstood the pain.
  In short, he saw it burn with steadier glance
  Than if he had seen an enemy's hand consumed.
  Everyone quailed and shuddered at that sight.
  The man who suffered showed, alone, no feeling.
  I myself, whom his death, 'twould seem, should render
  Secure, forgot my wrath in wonderment.
  I know not what constrains my turmoiled soul
  To exalt the worth of him who seeks my death;
  But by a feeling either of fear or horror
  Moved for this noble foe more than myself,
  I had him dragged from his strange punishment
  Which rather honors him than avenges me.
  When his heroic conduct is reported
  And in what way he bore this punishment,
  'Twill be said—and I think so, too—that Porsena
  Tore him away from glory, not from pain.

JUNIA. Judge from this great act and from this high purpose

SCAEVOLA

How much the Roman people's hate should cost thee.

PORSENA.   What! boldness everywhere?

JUNIA.   And everywhere
Examples of greatness and of manhood, worthy
Of honoring with shrines.

PORSENA.   Nay, worthy of hell
And of a fate full to the brim with horrors.
If I should give free scope to righteous rage,
Thy words past doubt have shown me that thou wert not
Ignorant of this traitor's foul attempt,
Ungrateful woman; and at the very time
When *thy* prayers and *his* arm, equally cruel,
Sought my death, *I* was trying honorably
To build again thy fortunes and to give
A scepter to thee, who wouldst murder me!

JUNIA.   Yes, thou hast offered me this gift, this honor,
Wherein ambition bases all its joy;
But know that to my heart the estate of Queen
Is much below that of a Roman woman.
If thou a kindness didst me, 'twas in masking
The horror of a captive's lot with freedom.
But with whatever light this kindness shone,
Do not imagine me for this ungrateful.
I tried to recompense thee, but thy blindness
Made thee refuse my noble payment for it,
And whosoe'er refuses recompense
Ought to ask nothing more; no more is owed.
Wherefore did I, with words inspired by heaven,
Picture to thee the infamy of the Tarquins?
Why did I seek, as thy well-wishing foe,
To win thee from a cause most infamous
And worthy of eternal evils, which
Makes all its partisans the same as criminals?
Thus to reward thee for the semblance, even,
Of liberty, wherewith thou coveredst o'er
The chains into which war had brought me, I
Wished, as repayment, to give aid to thee
Which would save both thine honor and thy life;
For I had learned of this devoted purpose
By which our gods would make of thee their victim.
But finally seeing that thine evil star
Linked thee, for thy destruction, with the Tarquins,
I myself seconded the hate it showed.
I urged that great heart on, which fain would slay thee.

No more did I restrain that brave arm, now
Hapless in having failed in a brave deed.
No more did I prevent its noble anger
From dealing so great and so benign a blow;
For I call blows "great" and "benign" which hurl
To hell the friends of tyrants.

PORSENA.   Thou, ungrateful
For all my favors, shalt declare to me
The names of the accomplices, if not
As a result of kindness, as a result
At least of tortures!

JUNIA.   Gratify thy frenzy
And thy vindictiveness. My constancy
Would fain be shown, imagineth new torments.
That Roman burned his right hand, and thus triumphed.
If he stabbed not thy heart, he terrified it
At least. And I, to outdo his efforts, I
Will see my hand and body both made ashes.

PORSENA. Thou wishest, then, to make me act?

JUNIA.   Thou wishest,
Then, to constrain me?

PORSENA.   Recollect that I
Can do so, and that thou shouldst fear I will.

JUNIA. I fear no evils, chains nor tortures rude,
Which can exhibit my soul's fortitude.

PORSENA. Then I unwillingly shall make well deserved
Violence take the place of foolish pity.
I shall abhor the kindliness which put me
In danger, and shall love the cruelty
Which can remove me from it. Go, my son;
Have that abominable Roman tortured.
Show thyself pitiless to his perverted
Manhood. Stop not at cruelty, and beware
Of imitating, in this respect, my kindness.

ARUNS. Let a few words from me precede his torture,
And let me do, really, an act of justice.
Rememberest thou the time my evil fortune
Conducted me to Tarquin's Court in Rome?
There, sire, thou knowest, I was attacked and even
Unto the grave 'twas sought to bring my life;
And, by plots blacker than the blackest night,
Wherefrom 'twas basely schemed to pluck advantage,
All my men, scattered by affright, or darkness,
Left me a prey to caitiffs without number.

PORSENA. What then! Did he who sought my life seek thine?
ARUNS. If life is good, on him my good is founded.
Thou owest thy son to him, thy son, who hath,
Despite our trials, made many conquests for thee.
In short, without this Roman, armed to aid me,
Thine eyes would have shed tears for losing me.
Decree now what my hand must do. Decree
Whether my savior must endure my rage;
Whether I must forget the boon he did me,
To punish him for a wrong he failed to do.
For, after all, thou, triumphing o'er danger,
Despite him livest; I live because of him.
PORSENA. Then my assassin, my attacker, is
In thee mine aid and my deliverer.
O Scaevola! O my son! Ye gods, how should I
Treat such a dear defender and great foe?
But can I now, save to mine own dishonor,
Consider mercy for a king's assailant?
Nay, nay, he needs must die; those tenderest-hearted
Must needs be cruel to men with guilt like his.
Though they had saved our power and our children,
Though they had given us victory countless times,
The least attempts against our royal persons
Blot out all benefits done for our crowns.
But ah! . . . no matter. Let us think not of him.
It must, it must indeed be. . . . Bring him here.

SCAEVOLA *is brought in.* TARQUIN *also enters.*

TARQUIN. The traitor still lives, and thou lettest him live,
To repeat the blow from which the gods preserved thee?
Is thy hand, then, disarmed by fictive virtues
At the instant when it should defend thy breast?
This is in sooth to merit the harm meant us,
To leave alive those bent on our destruction.
There stands that savage man, as one victorious
By having caused fear in a king so glorious.
SCAEVOLA. Yes, Tarquin, thou beholdest him; and his heart's
Wrath at least did the deed his hand could not do.
Judge if I fear an executioner's cruelty;
See whether I repent so brave an effort—
I, who just punished this vile hand for having
Failed in the blow which Rome expected of it.
(*To* PORSENA) Thou, Prince, whom I esteem, and whom
mine error

        Alone saved from my furious blows today,
        Set free thy soul from one eternal dread.
        One hand is left me. Let it not find weapons.
        But despite all thy care, tremble; for know thou
        That Rome hath children worthier than I.

PORSENA.   Go hence, Scaevola; and have back thy sword,
        Which for my son erewhile was nobly used.
        I should indeed praise thee and praise thy manhood
        If thou hadst for my diadem done battle.
        Bethink thee, though, how highly I esteem thee,
        Since I, to honor thee, pardon thy crime.
        More barbarous towards thyself than cruel towards me,
        Thou art, meseemeth, Scaevola, enough punished
        By thyself. Go, then, and through our great mercy
        Bear hence the harm alone thou didst thyself;
        And go to show the Romans, by thy safety,
        That Porsena fears neither Rome nor thee.

SCAEVOLA.   Thou indeed couldst not, generous Porsena,
        Conquer or sway me by the fear of pain;
        But I must needs confess thou hast o'ercome me
        By this great act of magnanimity.
        Thus I shall tell thee truthfully, from love,
        What thou couldst not have wrung from me by force.
        I will disclose to thee the deadly straits
        From which I would save thee, should Rome so permit.
        Know that the flower of the Roman youth,
        Scattered amid thy camp, wait to do what
        I have left undone, and that three hundred heroes,
        Burning with eagerness to strike thee down,
        Prepare to deal the blow that *I* dealt vainly.
        The lot, which fell on me, gave me the honor
        Of being the first to attempt this great achievement.
        The rest will, in their turn, tread in my footsteps,
        Thus to repair the failure of my arm;
        And if thou canst against so many hands
        Impelled alike by one same thought, be still
        The victor and preserve thy life, I then
        Will make proclaim that heaven is on thy side
        And that Rome, in her danger, needs must fear
        So great a king.

PORSENA.   Go thou. Return to Rome.
        Enjoy the grace I show thee. I receive
        Thy news without a fear of what it threatens.
        My preservation from the doom which seemeth

SCAEVOLA

To hang above me will teach Rome to tremble.

TARQUIN. What, Porsena! thou thyself, false to thyself,
Wilt thus reward a foul, unnatural murderer?
Thou, his son, no less threatened by that blow—
Wilt thou have neither wrath nor thirst for vengeance?
Defend thy father in this ghastly moment
When he is false and harmful to himself.

ARUNS. He who obstructs the clemency of kings
Is, to my mind, guilty a thousand times.

TARQUIN. Blind son and father, I will give you justice.
Scaevola is my subject. I will punish him.

JUNIA. Thine honor, Porsena, compels thee now
To keep this tyrant from undoing thy kindness.

SCAEVOLA (to PORSENA). But, generous sovereign, to make thee know
That Rome is just, and that she hateth crime,
She formerly offered to thy kin, the Tarquins,
To place in thy hands, as an arbiter,
Her entire quarrel with them, and now she still
Wishes to place it there, if Tarquin will
Consent to this, and thou wilt let her do so.

TARQUIN. I? Deal with rebels otherwise than by using
The punishments which are prepared for them?
No, no; after their crimes and all they cost me,
My arbiter will be my wrathful sword.

PORSENA. Still thou couldst . . .

TARQUIN.   To myself could I be traitorous?
Could I to mine own subjects yield? Nay, nay!
I, to preserve thy honor and ours, desire
No arbiter, thou less than any other—
Thou, who assumest my aid and things so many
Hast promised me, yet favorest my foes!

PORSENA. Thou deemest me, then, unjust and impious?
Yes, Tarquin, so I am—when I aid thee.

TARQUIN. Then, to become again just, aid these rebels.

PORSENA. I shall pursue the right path. Thou hast left it.

TARQUIN. Why dost thou not command my hands to be
Bound fast with chains, and then abandon me
To the fury of the Romans? After having
Betrayed thy sovereign grandeur, that is all
Now left for generous Porsena to do.

PORSENA. I ought to, ingrate!

TARQUIN (as he goes out). Little I fear that danger,
And we shall live at least for vengeance on thee.

[Exit TARQUIN.

JUNIA.   Can there be any justice in a cause
　　　Whose leader dreads its trial by fair laws?
PORSENA.   The die is cast; my purpose now is changed.
　　　I wish to give the Romans life and peace.
　　　Then let that ingrate flaunt his arrogance.
　　　Rome's liberty is my revenge upon him.
　　　'Twill be his punishment—and thy reward
　　　For having defended and preserved my son.
ARUNS.   But, sire, vouchsafe that to this recompense
　　　From thee, I may on *my* part add some guerdon.
PORSENA.   What couldst thou do for him who saved thy life?
ARUNS *(indicating* JUNIA).   Give him, before thee, her whom he doth
　　　　　love.
PORSENA.   Doth he love Junia, then? Is he loved by her?
ARUNS.   Yes, sire.
PORSENA *(to* SCAEVOLA *and* JUNIA).   Then love with an undying ardor.
　　　I ne'er will break the bond created thus
　　　Which joins so nobly hearts so generous;
　　　And since they both have gained a victory,
　　　The one should be the other's prize and glory.
　　　Rome owes this marriage to thy just desires,
　　　And I give peace to her to celebrate it.
SCAEVOLA.   Rome, ne'er ungrateful for aught done for her,
　　　Will give thee fame eternal for this blessing.
PORSENA.   Because, then, of thy manhood, Rome doth triumph;
　　　Because of my affection, Rome surviveth;
　　　And I would have her count, with her woes ended,
　　　Among her founders Scaevola and Porsena.

Venceslas

(WENCESLAUS)

By

JEAN ROTROU

INTRODUCTORY NOTE

Jean Rotrou was born at Dreux in 1609 of an ancient and honorable family, which furnished three mayors to that town in the sixteenth and seventeenth centuries. He went to college there, and then was sent to Paris to continue his studies, but he soon began to write for the stage. He probably succeeded Hardy as the "poet" connected with the troupe at the Hôtel de Bourgogne, a relationship which required him to furnish them with a certain number of plays each year. Protected by the Count de Fiesque, by Chapelain, who was the chief literary critic of the period, and by Richelieu, he was one of "the five authors" whom the great Cardinal gathered about him to carry out his literary projects. In 1639, however, he purchased the office of Lieutenant of the bailiwick of Dreux; he retired to the city of his birth, married in 1640, and eventually had six children. He continued to write plays, but less hastily now, and was doing his best work so far, when his life came to an untimely end in 1650 under circumstances which have made him a figure of heroic legend. A deadly epidemic broke out at Dreux and he was urged to seek safety in flight, but he refused to go away in the absence or death of other officials who could deal with the situation, and so died at his post.

Rotrou was more prolific than any other seventeenth-century French dramatist after Hardy. Thirty-five of his plays survive, and some eighteen others have been lost. His best tragi-comedy, *Laure persécutée,* and his best comedy, *la Sœur,* have considerable merit. Poetically, he was far more gifted than any other French-classical dramatist save Corneille and Racine; indeed, he was the only one of the dramatists contemporary with these great men who was of stature as a poet comparable to the English dramatists contemporary with Shakespeare. But writing under pressure of haste as he did, during most of his career he was little more than a facile adapter of foreign plays. Towards the end of his life, however, he showed more originality; and it is to this period that his three most famous dramas, all tragedies, belong: *Saint Genest* (1645), *Venceslas* (1647), and *Cosroès* (1648).

Venceslas held the stage longer and was played more times than any other tragedy by any member of the earliest group of French-classical dramatists, who wrote during the great Corneille's youthful prime. It was performed 227 times at the Comédie Française between 1680 and 1857, and more than thirty editions of it appeared between 1648 and 1907. Its source was a Spanish play by Rojas; but though this supplied Rotrou with the story and the principal characters, and suggested many of the situations, the French dramatist's additions and amplifications make his work far more than that of a mere translator. H. C. Lancaster estimates that more than half of *Venceslas* may be considered original with him. His greatest improvement on his source is perhaps in the portrayal of Prince Ladislaus, his most impressive study of a single character and one that anticipates Racine in its depiction of a soul ravaged by frenzies of love and hate. Act IV is probably Rotrou's finest single act. But too much of the earlier part of this play is occupied with the misunderstandings about Duke Frederick's love which are somewhat artificially maintained between him and Ladislaus and the Princess Theodora, a figure evidently inspired by the Infanta in the *Cid;* and the working out of the striking problem posed in the later acts, which should have been decided solely on the merits of the issues involved, is vitiated by the intrusion of such factors as the Duke's claim of his promised reward from Wenceslaus and the rising of the populace in Ladislaus' behalf. The jarring suggestion with which the play ends, that Cassandra may eventually consent to marry her lover's murderer, is doubtless in imitation of the close of the *Cid.*

CHARACTERS IN THE PLAY

WENCESLAUS, *King of Poland.*
LADISLAUS, *the Prince, his son and heir.*
ALEXANDER, *younger son of Wenceslaus.*
FREDERICK, *duke of Courland and favorite of Wenceslaus.*
OCTAVIUS, *governor of Warsaw.*
CASSANDRA, *duchess of Königsberg.*
THEODORA, *princess, daughter of Wenceslaus.*
LEONORA, *attendant of Theodora.*
Guards.

The scene represents a room in the palace of Wenceslaus.

Wenceslaus

ACT I

WENCESLAUS, LADISLAUS, ALEXANDER, *and* Guards *are discovered.*

WENCESLAUS (*to* LADISLAUS). Be seated, Prince.
           (*To* ALEXANDER) And thou, child, leave us; go.
ALEXANDER. I am wronged, sire, if thou wilt hear me not.
WENCESLAUS. Leave us, I say. And do ye, guards, withdraw.
                  [*Exeunt* ALEXANDER *and Guards.*
LADISLAUS. What wouldst thou with me?
WENCESLAUS.   I have much to say.—
    (*Aside*) Prepare his heart, O heaven; touch it today!
LADISLAUS (*to himself*). How old age suffers and makes others suffer!
    Hear now the fine advice some flatterer gives him.
WENCESLAUS. Let me have, Ladislaus, not thine ear alone
    But thy heart also. I am waiting still
    For time to make that fruit ripe which my bed
    Produced to take my place, and I was wont
    To think thy mother would live on by what
    She left me of herself in thee. Alas,
    Not so! This image which she made is losing
    Much of its brightness and is blurred indeed;
    And viewing thee, the less I see of her,
    Grief for her death the more reneweth in me.
    Lo, all thine acts belie thy rank. I see
    Naught in them noble or worthy of my race.
    I seek for Ladislaus in them, and cannot
    Find him. In naught art thou a king save only
    The wish to be one; and that wish, 'tis said,
    Little considerate and too impatient,
    Scarcely endureth that *my* brow wears the crown.
    Thou hast deplored how sorely it weighs on me,
    And, not daring attack *me*, attackest mine age.
       Yes, I am old; but the result of being so
    Is my confirmed possession of clear reason.
    To reign is a high art, whereof the secret
    Only experience and age acquire.
    A king seems to thee happy; and his estate
    Seems a fair thing to thine ambitious thought.
    He swayeth human fortunes as he wills,

But dost thou know his sorrows, like his joys?
Whatever happy issue his plans aim at,
Ne'er doth he satisfy his subjects' wishes.
He is deemed cruel if he maintaineth justice;
If he is mild, timid—a friend of vice.
If he goes forth to war, he causeth misery;
If he doth cherish peace, he lacketh spirit.
If merciful, he is lax; if vengeful, barbarous;
If generous, prodigal; if frugal, miserly.
His purest and most innocent designs
Always in some minds take on a bad aspect,
And howso well his virtue may be known,
It never seems untainted to his people.
If to deserve, then, to rule o'er a kingdom,
Not even the purest virtue doth suffice,
What fortunes, thinkest thou, should attend the reign
Of worthless spirits given o'er to evil,
Capable only of licentiousness,
Slaves of their senses, ruling not even themselves?
       [LADISLAUS *shows impatience.*
 Here only fear of me curbs thy caprice.
Read thine own heart; appraise thyself but justly.
Canst thou lift hand against those I have chosen
To administer my laws and prop my throne,
And not outrage the reverence due my station
Nor at the same time lift hand against *me*?
Having my favor, the Duke offends thy sight.
Since he is dear to me, thou hatest him.
But take thou note, instead, how great he is.
See by what steps he hath achieved his fortune.
Think how his arm hath propped my throne,—and yet
My love for him gives him a foe in thee!
Nay, more than that: thy blind rage doth pursue him
Even in others, extending to thy brother.
Thy jealous nature cannot leave the young prince
The liberty of loving him I cherish.
His fondness for the Duke wins him thy hate.
Ah, seek some vent meet for thy haughty spirit;
Turn, turn thy fiery impetuosity
To quell the proud might of the Ottoman Turks.
Renew our never-ending quarrel against them,
And show thy courage in a righteous cause.
But 'gainst thy brother and 'gainst one I favor,
As needful to his king as he is dear,

WENCESLAUS

Who from the embattled hosts of Muscovy
Just now preserved my crown if not my life,
What feud is thine, forsooth—meet for great souls!
Thou wouldst control my favors at thy liking.
I can but ill dispense my love and hate,
And 'tis from thee that I must learn that art!
Time and experience must have taught me little!

LADISLAUS. Vouchsafe me . . .

WENCESLAUS.   One word more; then I will hear thee.
If I must credit manifold reports,
The sun doth rarely give light to the world
That the first beam it sheddeth here below
Doth not reveal some murder by thy hand—
At least thou livest in such bad repute
That thou art charged therewith rightly or wrongly,
And that, always the object of suspicion,
Thou art deemed guilty e'en in the arms of sleep.
From the idea that none needs to fear me
Spring private vengeance, killings, the reign of license;
And such disdain of my authority
Punishes me for leaving thee unpunished.
Thy manhood, then, of late so much extolled,
Through thy mad lusts declines as 'neath some spell,
And by its lessening thou in every heart
Losest fair fame and winnest contempt instead;
And yet I see that by some wondrous chance
In spite of all thy faults thou still art loved
And everywhere the star that guides thy fate
Receives at once for thy sake love and hate.
Because of some charm that I know not of,
Howe'er thou art despised, thou still art cherished.
Feared for thy crimes, thou hast the grace to please,
And those who murmur 'gainst thee pray for thee.
    Ah, my son, merit that this love should endure;
To keep the prayers, stifle the murmurings;
And reign in men's hearts as a consequence
More of thy character than thy fortune. Thus
Make thyself worthy of a diadem.
Born to give laws, first give them to thyself,
And let thy passions, like rebellious subjects,
Be ere all else brought to obey thy will.
Only on ruling these, shouldst thou rule others.
    By such steps will my throne be thine, my son.
My realm, my people, all will bow to thee

And thou shalt reign o'er them as o'er thyself.
But if thou, ever as thou art now, and ever
A slave to vice, acknowledgest no law
Except thine own caprice, and if, to win
Thy hate, one needs but some share of my favor;
If thy proud heart will not consider either
The deep respect with which the Duke reveres thee,
The genuine affection of thy brother,
A people's loyalty who smile upon thee,
Or the good counsel of a king and father,
Then, no more father, wholly king, will I
Let the law take its course with thee, and heedless
Of ties of blood, maintain my rightful power.

LADISLAUS.   Though all concerning me offends and shocks thee,
However much astonished by thy words,
I have at least this fruit of giving attention:
That I could please thee upon this occasion;
And on each point that seemeth to condemn me
I can defend myself and answer thee
If I may have, in turn, thine ear and heart.

WENCESLAUS.   Speak; I should gain more by defeat than victory.
I have a father's feelings towards thee still.
Convince me I am wrong; 'twill gladden me.

LADISLAUS.   Coming back yesterday from the hunt along with
My men, preparing the quarry for the hounds,
We talked, by chance, of the affairs of princes
And went on to discuss the art of ruling.
Then each made potentates as he desired,
And swayed thy realm according to his judgment,
And scarce on anything was there accord.
One to thy course adhered; another changed it;
It found its critics and its partisans;
But in the main they deemed thy years too many.
I, without any thought of disrespect,
Tossed into this free discourse my opinion;
And daring to speak my heart too openly,
Let slip these words, as I cannot deny:
"Why does my father, bowed with age," said I,
"And now with spirit ill-served by his strength,
Not rid himself, before he proves its victim,
Of a sore burden which must weigh him down?
Should he, who can make o'er to me his crown,
Risk whether or not the realm will give it to me?
And if he would retain the rank of king,

Will he not still if he to me resigns it?
How he complains that his age crushes him!
Deems he my youth cannot sustain this load?
Have I not learned, under his government,
Enough of policy and sagacity
To know what tasks a diadem entails;
What a king owes his subjects, realm, and self,
His allies, and the good faith of his treaties;
In what affairs his rights are limited;
Which war is harmful and which war is vital;
To whom, and when, and how he owes assistance;
And, to preserve his realm from evil chance,
How to dispose within it and without?
Know I not that a king who would be reverenced
Must be at need now gracious and now stern;
And, as the time and place demand of him,
Know how to speak with both his brow and glance,
Make use alike of frankness and of guile,
Show his face sometimes, sometimes but a mask;
Whatever advice is given him, be the same
Always, and often trust himself the most; —
But above all (upon this hangs the fate
Of thrones) to know what work to set for each,
Cause it that by judicious and wise choice
All offices fall into faithful hands,
Elevate few so high they can do mischief,
Be slow to make as well as to destroy,
Hold fast in memory good deeds and be
Swift to reward and late to punish? Is it"—
I said—"not with such art and by these maxims
The reigns of lawful sovereigns steer their course?"
    That is the truth concerning the first point.
I see thou hast been told of it, and nowise
Do I defend myself herein.

WENCESLAUS.   Go on.

LADISLAUS.   Touching my furious rage where thou art moved
    To take sides with my brother and the Duke,
    Of whom one is thy heart, one thy right arm,
    Of whom one sways thy soul, thy realm the other,
    I hate one, it is true: that insolent
    Minister who is precious unto thee
    As he to me is baleful—valiant
    (I grant him that) but vain, deceitful, flattering,
    And secretly usurper of thy power,—

This duke to whom thy heart, veiled to all others,
Yields itself without fear, and bares itself,
And who, under thy name more king than thou art,
Finds in ill turns to me his dearest joys,
Shows thee my deeds full of so many vices
And does me such bad offices with thee
That thy warped vision finds in me no longer
Aught like to thee or suitable in a king.
I would feign blindness and ignore the malice
Wherewith at every turn he slanders me
To thee if he had not appropriated
And taken from me the office which had made me,
When still so young, feared by so many monarchs
And in which, lately, he hath stayed the advance
Of the Muscovites and limited their boundaries.
At the outset of this great and famed campaign,
Thou gavest him the place to win its honor.
But if he is not too powerful to dread
My wrath, let him think well touching the choice
Of his reward, and if with the vast credit
He hath at Court, he cares naught for my rank,
Let him respect my love, or all his splendor,
Great though it be, will serve him not at all.
I speak not groundlessly; reports have told me
Whither his plans are aimed; and this, my lord,
Is one of the matters of which I complain.
WENCESLAUS.   Finish.
LADISLAUS.   As to my brother, after his
Insolence, my wrath cannot burn too hotly,
And the most frightful horror among all
Thy tortures cannot snatch him from my fury.
Why! when with heart incensed by conscious wrongs,
I plainly showed the Duke my cause of grievance,
And, rightfully made angry by his conduct,
Would put some check to his temerity,
My brother, heedless, mad, filled with misguided
Zeal, came up to assume his quarrel against me,
And yet more, dared clap hand upon his sword!
Ah! I call heaven, the sovereign power, to witness
That ere the sun, issuing from out the wave,
Darkens one half the world and lights the other,
He shall make flow my blood that he respects not
Or give me satisfaction for this insult.
Since I am so i' the people's ill esteem,

I needs must merit it by a great crime,
And, threatened with thy punishment so often,
Make myself worthy of the law's full rigor.
WENCESLAUS (*aside*). What more can I attempt with this proud spirit?
Try we a ruse where sternness is in vain,
Seeing that neither complaint nor coldness, threats
Nor force, could in the past bring him to reason.
(*To* LADISLAUS) My credence was no doubt a little hasty,
My son, and not unerring. I am glad.
Let us forget our quarrel in our embraces.
I cannot do a violence to nature;
I willingly yield thereto, and stifling anger,
Own myself vanquished, since I am a father.
Prince, 'tis now time that on a common throne
We reign together and be but as one.
Now, near the grave whereto I am declining,
I fain would see myself rise from my ashes
In thee, and thus, defying the ravages
Of time, begin a hundred years' more reign.
LADISLAUS. Upon thy peace alone my joy depends,
And if thy favor even so far extends,
I will accept it as a noble office
To be accounted king among thy subjects.

Enter the Prince ALEXANDER.

ALEXANDER. My lord!
WENCESLAUS.   What wouldst thou? Go!
ALEXANDER.   I shall withdraw,
But if thou . . .
WENCESLAUS.   What! still here? What wouldst thou say?
(*Aside*) How strange a role, O love, thou givest me—
To welcome sin and to drive virtue from me!
ALEXANDER. That if thou wilt not deign to hearken to my
Defense, thou wrongest him who was ill-treated.
The Prince is older; I respect his rank;
But we are of one heart and of one blood,
And for denial I have too much . . .
WENCESLAUS.   Thou,
Rash boy, with hand on sword, and 'gainst thy brother!
'Gainst my successor and my authority!
Beg, O thou insolent youth, beg his forgiveness,
And by repentance worthy of thy nature
Deserve the pardon I would have him grant thee.
Go, ask it of him. Open thine arms to him.

ALEXANDER.   Nay, think, my lord . . .

WENCESLAUS.   Speak not in answer to me.

ALEXANDER (*aside*).   Shall we, my heart, bow to his haughty mood?
Yes, to respect his age I needs must suffer.
How much my soul revolts at so great baseness!
Ah heaven!
(*To* LADISLAUS) Pardon then my rashness, brother.
My father bids me give thee satisfaction.
His order I obey: I ask forgiveness
Of thee. But by this order thou art in turn
Required to open *thine* arms unto me.

WENCESLAUS (*aside*).   O God! Cruel Ladislaus pays no heed to him!

LADISLAUS (*to* ALEXANDER).   Doth not thy pardon by the King
suffice thee?

WENCESLAUS (*to* LADISLAUS).   Prince, once again I order thee to
embrace him.
Let reverence for me vanquish thy wrath.

LADISLAUS (*embracing* ALEXANDER).   What ignominy, sire, thou
bringest upon me!
(*To* ALEXANDER)   Go, and ascribe my all-too-easy temper
But to the power that restrains my vengeance.

ALEXANDER (*aside*).   Ah, nature's ties! how cruel ye are to me!

WENCESLAUS.   Exchange these differences for mutual pledges,
And, when I am at peace with all the world,
Do not bring war into my house, my sons.
(*To* ALEXANDER)   Have the Duke come, my child.
                    (*To* LADISLAUS)   Remain here, Prince.
                                        [*Exit* ALEXANDER.

LADISLAUS.   Thou wouldst constrain me to more baseness yet,
Solicit still my pardon for this traitor!
But my heart hath no further room for foes.
Thy blood, which flows there, at thy hest revolts.
Love this presumptuous man; hold to thy choice;
And with the golden circlet 'round thy brows
Pay for his latest conquest, if thou wilt.
But suffer in me, sire, a frank disdain.
Leave my hate free to choose, even like thy favors.
Permit my obduracy, keeping thy love,
And do not bid me act in a weak manner.

WENCESLAUS.   My son, so near now to the throne where thou
Shalt mount, to fill my place and represent me,
Ruler over thyself as well as others,
Adopt my sentiments and have done with thine.
Take on, as I desire, conquering thine anger,

WENCESLAUS

This noble weakness, worthy of great hearts,
Which will but make thee loved throughout the land.
When thou'rt a king, forget a prince's quarrels.

LADISLAUS. Sooner than be one, I would keep my hate.
I pray, sire, spare me this humiliation.

Enter ALEXANDER, FREDERICK, *and* OCTAVIUS.

WENCESLAUS. Smother this hate, or I espouse his cause.
Duke, greet the Prince.

LADISLAUS *(aside)*. Oh, cruel necessity!

[LADISLAUS *and* FREDERICK *embrace.*

WENCESLAUS. And by close bonds united in the future,
Of your past discord lose all memory.

FREDERICK. To prove to him how far my zeal extends,
I gladly would lose blood and life for him.

WENCESLAUS. Often enough with blood and battles thou
Hast signalized for us thy heart and arm;
And thou too oft hast won by this famed zeal
All that gives deathless glory to a mortal.
But thy last expedition, which amazed me,
Surpasses all belief and claims its guerdon.
To have made our boundaries, with so small an army,
The bloody graveyard of so large a host
And by incredible feats in so few days
Reduced the Muscovite to sue for peace,
Are deeds whereof a due appreciation
Exceeds the power of the richest monarch.
Make no exception touching what I owe thee;
Ask; I have put all things within thy reach.
Prove that which I have promised to thy valor.

FREDERICK. I owe thee all, great king.

WENCESLAUS. Such deference
Is foolish. Kings' words are important pledges
Which they should, when they can, fulfil at once.
They are too precious to be hoarded up.
Such delay risks forgetfulness or loss.

FREDERICK. Seeing that thy grace compels me to receive
Pay for my service and reward for duty,
A bondage, sire, more sweet than empire's rule,
Love's flames and fetters are the prize I hope for
If of a heart consumed by violent love
The mouth dare utter . . .

LADISLAUS. Stop, thou insolent man!
Put limits to the flight of thy desires

And measure what thou wishest by thy deserts,
Or, though it cost the throne and mine own life,
In thy vile blood I shall thy love extinguish.
Where stands opposed my majesty, learn, rash duke,
To serve unhoping, suffer, and be silent,
Or . . .

FREDERICK. I am silent, sir; my hopes, if clashing
With due respect for thee, clash with my duty.

[*He goes out with* ALEXANDER.

WENCESLAUS. Prince, when thy·passions are thus yielded to,
Ill dost thou guard thy prospects of the crown
And thy head, too, whereon thou hopest to wear it.

LADISLAUS. Thou art king, sire; thou canst deprive me of it;
But I have just grounds for complaint, and neither
By king nor father can my wrath be governed.

WENCESLAUS. Still less should *I* be by a son and madman.
Look well to thine own safety. Heed my warning.

[*Exit* WENCESLAUS.

OCTAVIUS. O gods! Couldst thou conceal thy hate no better?

LADISLAUS. Wouldst thou I should conceal it and be frustrate,
And he should rob me of my hope's loved treasure
And for his prize should take her whom I seek?
What! Shall Cassandra be his victory's guerdon
Where he usurped my leadership and glory?
Cannot the State, o'er which he rules despite me,
The revenues which he at will controls,
His folk whom he exalts, the offices
Which he deals out, be judged enough reward
For him unless he takes love's recompense
From me besides and robs me of my life,
Robbing me of Cassandra? Do I not,
Thanks to thy pains and diligence, know the secret
Between them?

OCTAVIUS.   Yes, my lord; but she can be
Bent to thy wishes by the marriage which
Thou art to offer her. The Princess hath
Sent for her, and I hope *her* intervention
Will make her soon submissive to thy will.
But hide thy feelings better. Dread the power
Of a sire angered and a king defied.
Trust to our hands the love that doth possess thee.

LADISLAUS. He is my king, my father; it is true;
Passion transports me. But in two bright eyes

I find two kings more absolute than he,
And since my soul belongs now to another,
I am no longer master of myself.

A C T   I I

THEODORA *and* CASSANDRA *are discovered.*

THEODORA.   If, indeed, thy respect for neither him
    Nor me can move thee, all the realm, Cassandra,
    Speaks to thee through my mouth. If thou refusest
    Marriage with him, thou dost refuse the realm
    A queen and wouldst deprive it of a king.
    He whom thou floutest doth await a crown,
    Which all the people's voice already gives him;
    And he awaits it but to offer it
    To thee, and thy cruel heart cannot endure him!
CASSANDRA.   No, I cannot endure, however high
    He mounts, the enemy of my fair fame
    And lover of my shame, nor will I take
    For husband a seducer, who hath found
    That he assailed mine honor fruitlessly,
    Who, while he still could hope to win me vilely,
    Never desired me in the estate of wife,
    Who, with no goal except the basest lust,
    Limited his intent to my dishonor.
    In whatso aspect all the land regards him,
    I behold in him neither prince nor monarch;
    I see, beneath the regal pomp that clothes him,
    Only false lures to assail my chastity.
    After his feelings bent upon my ruin,
    His offered gifts, the efforts of his minions,
    His letters, plaints, corruption of those people
    Who he believed could serve his passion's aim,
    When all these wicked methods helped him little,
    He was at last reduced to virtuous ones.
    To gain his end despite my upright heart,
    He tried all things, both sin and piety.
    But he in vain would now have wedlock join us:
    This but calls virtue to the aid of vice;
    For, when a sovereign's desires are sated,
    'Tis well known he hath means at hand to free him
    From irksome marriage bonds. To break such ties
    And gild his crimes he lacks not plausible
    Maxims of State. His broken troth would follow

Close on his pledges. He considers only
Himself. He loves himself, not me.
THEODORA. His passions,
Somewhat unruly, make thee too suspicious.
CASSANDRA. 'Tis better to err less and to fear more.
THEODORA. Fortune smiles on thee. 'Twill not always do so.
CASSANDRA. I fear his fickleness and his brief loves.
What is a palace but an imposing house
Which cozening Fortune builds for our ambition,
Where the soul sighs in chains at every moment
And finds no peace on which it can rely!
THEODORA. More than a crown, I cannot proffer thee.
CASSANDRA. Thou'lt give me more, leaving me to myself.
THEODORA. Wouldst thou be less thy mistress, being less harsh?
CASSANDRA. Wouldst thou, then, call the loss of *my* heart nothing?
THEODORA. Thou wouldst not make a loss but an exchange.
CASSANDRA. And should I leave my injury unpunished?
What thou hast called "somewhat unruly passions,"
These criminal intents, insulting efforts,
These uncurbed words, infamous messages,
The hope, whose flames he fed, to ravish me
And all the offers that he thought could move me—
Can these defame the blood of Königsberg?
THEODORA. They have contended vainly 'gainst thy virtue.
CASSANDRA. That might be doubted, if I spoke not of them,
And if, consenting to this marriage yoke,
I gave to him what he would fain have stolen.
Forgive my grief. I know, sage princess, what
Submissiveness I owe unto thy Highness;
But in the choice my heart makes of a husband
My honor tells me I owe yet more to it.

Enter LADISLAUS

LADISLAUS (*aside*). Cruel tyrant o'er so strong a love, O thou
Respect which holdest me back, yield to mine ardor!
Is now my marriage or my grave prepared?
Weary of waiting, let me learn my fate.
(*To* CASSANDRA) Speak, lovely foe. 'Tis time now to decide
Whether to launch or stay the thunderbolt.
Either must thou destroy or succor me.
What is determined? Must I live or die?
Which of the twain wouldst thou: my heart or corpse?
Which shall I have of these: death or Cassandra?
Shall marriage join my lot to thy fair days,

Or wilt thou slay me by refusing me?

CASSANDRA.   Thou speakest to me of marriage? Wouldst have for wife
One whom vile lust hath burned for without shame?
I—gods!—I a king's, a sovereign's mate?
Ah, Prince, what present wouldst thou make the State,
Giving it for its queen a woman whose
Fame may be questioned? Wherefore should it reverence
One so ignoble and so ill respected
That thy impure desires sought after her?

LADISLAUS.   'Twill reverence, for this cause, the worthiest virtue
Whereof the proof hath ever signalized
A woman, and the most adorable
And divine being who hath ever made
A subject of her ruler. Only too well
I know (and never doth this heart come near thee
Unsmitten by confusion at its crime)
To how great insolence and indiscretion
My lawless youth carried at first my passion.
'Tis true that, dazzled by the lovely eyes
Which have enslaved and brought to grief so many,
O'erborne by charms so worthy of my vows,
I saw these only, aimed at these alone.
Forgotten was respect in seeing them.
But love new-born may follow errant courses;
Its blindness doth excuse it, and too sore
A penalty is banishment for this.
As soon as proper reverence cleared my vision
And in addition to thy store of charms
My glance on thy discreetness dwelt, thy station,
Thy noble ancestors, and thy rare virtues,
I curbed at once every offensive impulse
And made its violence subject to thy will.
Restrained by hopes that we shall wed some day,
My love is purged now of impurity.
The torch that leads, the ardor that impels me,
Seeks not a mistress but a wife in thee.
Be gracious, madam, to the deep repentance
Which loathes my crime and bows me at thy feet.
Vouchsafe that I should love thee in this manner
And rather of life rob me than of thee;
For if 'tis sin to worship thine attractions—
If one can please thee only by not loving thee—
Fain would I always of this fault be guilty
And sooner die than do as thou desirest.

CASSANDRA.   Both my desert, Prince, and my station also
    Are most unworthy objects of thy love.
    Yet even if I believed thy feelings real,
    And our respective ranks seemed to accord,
    No day should ever see us joined in marriage.
    Life will I lose, ere give consent to that.
    When first thy passion showed in its pursuit
    Of me such small respect or self-control,
    And when no object but a base intent
    Roused in thy mind the wish thou mightest possess me,
    I then saw in thee only the vile love
    Which did not seek to have me as a wife,
    Only the brutish efforts to seduce me
    With which thy lust assailed mine honor; and I,
    Observing naught about thee but thy vices,
    Conceived such horror of thee and of thy wooing
    That if I offend thee by not loving thee
    And though in me alone thou findest attraction,
    Fain would I always of this fault be guilty
    And sooner die than do as thou desirest.
LADISLAUS.   So be it! On him for whom thou feelest so great
    Horror, cruel woman, pour out all thy wrath.
    Take arms against me both of ice and fire.
    Invent unheard-of ways to torture me.
    Raise earth and heaven to oppose my passion.
    Enlist the realm to share thy hatred. Strip me
    Of the support it gives my aspirations
    Unto the throne. Do all things to destroy me.
    With all thine efforts and with all thine anger,
    Thou canst not end the love I feel for thee.
    I will be true to thee midst thine utmost scorn;
    I will adore thee, in thy wrath and cruelty;
    And to preserve still my love's flame for thee,
    Though in despair, I will preserve my life.
THEODORA.   Ah! we shall win naught from this haughty mood.
CASSANDRA.   'Tis needful he should understand me wholly,
    Having beset me, and should know my honor
    Is sensitive to the extent that I forget not
    And I forgive not insults done to it.
THEODORA.   But such a vengeance punishes thyself.
    Thou losest thus the chance to wear a crown.
CASSANDRA.   For me the crown would be devoid of charms
    Upon his brows that I have feared and love not.
THEODORA.   To reign cannot displease a noble soul.

CASSANDRA. Thrones often bear unhappy queens, who under
 The fair yoke of their royal power in sooth
 Have many subjects and scant liberty.
THEODORA. Dreadest thou a yoke which makes of thee a sovereign?
CASSANDRA. I do not wish to be a slave, but queen
 Over myself; or else if I should lose
 Indeed my freedom, I desire to choose
 My master and wear willingly his yoke.
THEODORA. To serve, with scepter held in hand, is worth
 More than thy freedom.
CASSANDRA.   Knowest thou if I have not
 Surrendered it already?
LADISLAUS.   Yes, I know that,
 Cruel woman, and know who my rival is.
 But I have deemed his station too much lower
 Than mine to give one grounds for hesitating
 To choose between my love and his presumption.
CASSANDRA. Thy rank is not among God's gifts to him,
 But his own blood cannot be shamed by thine,
 And he hath no great cause to envy thee.
LADISLAUS. Thou insolent girl, those words shall cost his life;
 And this sword, in his boasted blood so noble,
 Shall give me satisfaction for thy pride.
 Enough of laws, of laws too much respected!
 O prudence, reason, which I so have heeded!
 No more, my soul, persist in fruitless wooing;
 Let love die, now that hope hath ceased to live.
 Go, thou unworthy cause of my emotions!
 Thy thanklessness o'er-long hath made me suffer.
 I should have known thee, nor been further bound
 By the false sweetness of thy cruel charms,
 Or, being bound by them, begged not thy mercy
 But, asking naught, snatched ease from thee by force.
 My heart, however, curbed my power's license,
 And I repent not of an act of virtue.
 My intellect, now free, hath cured my feelings
 Of thy proud sway and thinks it but a dream.
 Of those base flames which did my breast consume
 There now is left but the red glow alone
 That shame and horror of my having loved thee
 Will leave forever stamped upon my brow.
 Yes, ingrate, yes, I blush for it, and my wrath
 Cannot forgive me what I did for thee.
 I would that from my life might be effaced

The memory of the time I was thy suitor.
Dead was I then to honor, and I lived not
While yet this abject heart called itself thine.
'Tis today only that I live and breathe,
Today, when I renounce thy empire's yoke
And when mine eyes, now in accord with reason,
Detest the sight of thee like death itself.

CASSANDRA. To rid thee of it, Prince, and not displease thee
I voluntarily will decree mine exile,
And, knowing the truth of what thou sayest, will take
Great care to show thee no more what thou loathest.
Farewell.   *[Exit* CASSANDRA.

LADISLAUS (*thunderstruck*). What wilt thou do, O craven soul?
Wouldst follow her that spurns thee? Art thou mad?
Nay, rather say, what has my blind rage done?
Thou cruel fair one! Alas, whither fleest thou?
Sister, in love's name, pitying the tears
Wherewith this heart bewitched pays her its tribute,
Still, if thou wouldst prevent a brother's death,
Seek that unfeeling woman; stay her steps.

THEODORA. Stay her, my brother, when thou drovest her hence?

LADISLAUS. Ah, serve her spell o'er me, against my reason.
I fain would disavow my heart's rebellion,
Serve her, adore her, die before her eyes.
Lacking her love, I will embrace her hate,
Love her disdain, and bless mine agony.
To make complaint of woes her charms have caused me,
Is to complain of undeserved disease.
Let me but see her if I may not have her.
My sickness hugs its source, grows by its balm.
When my heart feigned agreement with my voice,
'Twas 'neath a spell and I would fain deny it.
I was dying, burning; my soul worshipped her;
And heaven has wrought for me a destiny
Wholly of flame. Go.
        (*To himself*)   But what art thou doing,
Stupid, base lover? What caprice doth blind thee?
Hast thou thy senses yet? Prince without spirit,
Regain possession of thyself one instant.
        (*To* THEODORA)   My sister, dost thou leave me in this plight?

THEODORA. To stay her, was I going.

LADISLAUS.   What! seest thou not
What arrogant disdain impels her steps,—
With how great haughtiness she hath withdrawn,

The hate implacable she expressed for me,—
And that to expose me further to her lightnings
Is to give arms to one mad, in her frenzy?
Drive, rather, this cruel maiden from my mind;
Condemn the thoughts in me which speak of her;
Pretend she is unworthy of my rank;
And nourish in me the honor of thy race.

THEODORA.　I cannot hide from thee that the pain thou feelest
Shows too much weakness in one of royal blood.
I see what impulses contend within thee,
But difficulties are the field of manhood,
Where with a few wounds one can purchase glory.
Who fain would conquer is near victory
Already; he who sins against himself
Is vanquished soon; and nothing is so much
Ours as our will.

LADISLAUS.　　　　　Alas, 'tis very easy
To judge what pain is mine by the endeavors
Which at the same time sweep me here and there,
And by those impulses so swift and potent
Now o'er my reason, o'er my senses now.
But whatso strife they show to thee in me,
I fain, my sister, would believe thee and
Be mine own master,—fain would leave her free
To trust and think her blood forbids that she
Be raised to *my* state. Suffering her disdain
Of the rank which she rejects, in losing her
As mistress, I shall gain her as a subject.
I shall have absolute power o'er her who ruled
My heart. Her own refusal of me is
An ample punishment for her. Do not
Be born again, my stifled love, to augment
The triumph of the Duke of Courland. I
Am honored by his victory, and lose only
An obstinate caprice to love too basely.

THEODORA.　What, brother! does the Duke of Courland woo her?

LADISLAUS.　This, secret, sister, is no longer new.
Many observers whom I have commissioned
Have marked their love so well, 'tis hid no longer.

THEODORA.　Ah!

LADISLAUS.　　　'Tis from this love that my hate proceeds,
Not from his favor though it is so high
That I have grounds for saying with dismay
That scarce he leaves the King more than the name.

But since my plan is to forget this woman,
My pride must be expressed in serving his suit;
And, strikingly to retract my vows to her,
I shall go ask the King to grant their marriage.
My hand shall put my rival in my place;
And I shall look upon their love as coldly
As, when my ardor was most violent
And keen, this heartless maid was cold to me.

[*Exit* LADISLAUS.

THEODORA (*alone*).   O reason gone astray! O reason lapsed!
Did ever such unhappiness confound thee?
Doltish presumption, greatness which beguiles us,
Is there aught else false as your vanities?
The Duke doth love Cassandra! And I was vain
Enough to think that *my* glance caused his pain!
Nay, to be sorry for it and blame myself,
For thinking him a prize to be disdained!
The Duke doth love Cassandra! What! such tokens—
Such humble mien, honor paid, deference,
Ardor, attachment, tribute, fears—did they
Offer me but a heart no more its own?
Those sweet and heavy sighs which many a time,
Uttered without avowal, betrayed his silence,
His look, so frequently encountering mine,
Respect, attentions, care that he has shown me—
Did *they* come from a soul plighted another's?
Can I so ill interpret love's own language?
Mere homage do I take for heart's affection?
And is my confidence chimerical?
Yet with unconscious self-surrender I
Confess myself won, and believe I love him!
Though I could do so, would love have its will?
Do I not owe my hand to reasons of State?
And are we not the unoffending victims
A government sacrifices to its needs?
My heart, which shamefully stooped to a vassal,
Would it renounce for him his rivals' thrones?
But seek not to deceive me, pride of birth;
Love needs no scepter to confirm its sway.
It subjugates our hearts to secret charms,
Creates equality and does not seek it.
If the Duke has upon his brow no crown,
'Tis he who doth protect crowns and dispense them.

WENCESLAUS

By what achievement can one show himself
To be . . .

Enter LEONORA.

LEONORA.   Madam, the Duke would speak with thee.
THEODORA.   Admit him. Nay, after what I have learned,
Permit free access to Cassandra's lover,
Accept his homage and see him yet again:
How vile! must I do that?—Stay, Leonora.
A slight indisposition, felt just now,
Forbids the pleasure of my seeing him
Today. Make my excuses to him.   [*Exit* LEONORA.
                              Ah heaven!
What poison assails my reason without warning?
I wished to appear insensible to love,
And now I feel the loss of one indifferent
To me! I am unable to be his,
And, though without intentions towards him, cannot
Consent to his intentions towards another!

Enter ALEXANDER, *with* LEONORA.

ALEXANDER.   How now! Refuse the Duke a visit, my sister?
Whence this displeasure? What mischance excites it?
THEODORA.   A slight indisposition, which is transient.
ALEXANDER.   I gave him information which led him hither.
THEODORA.   What?
ALEXANDER.   Thinking that Cassandra was here with thee . . .
THEODORA.   Scarce have two minutes passed since she went out.
ALEXANDER.   And being aware how sweet he held her charms,
I have advised him to come here to thee,
To ask regarding her whom he adores
Thine aid, which Ladislaus, I have learned, implores.
Thou knowest the Prince, and thou canst judge if love
Can make him subject to the laws of virtue.
His bad deeds have too well declared his aims.
One can behold the future in the past
And easily tell that he attempts her honor,
Beneath these marriage offers, with false bait.
But speaking for the Duke, if I solicit thee
For her protection from a lawless passion,
Blame only me; ask of me satisfaction
For what may seem his treasonous presumption.
I, my dear sister, as regards Cassandra
Sponsor a fire which ne'er will turn to ashes

In him, the purest love wherewith a mortal
In Hymen's temple e'er made sweet the altar.
Against an impure love, aid love so perfect.

THEODORA (*leaning upon* LEONORA *for support*). My illness grows,
    my brother. Let me withdraw . . .
                         [*She goes out with* LEONORA.

ALEXANDER (*alone*). O hard constraint! O rigorous fate, to be
    Obliged to love under another's name!
    The while I live with spirit frustrate thus,
    What guerdon can my hidden love enjoy?
    What can I hope for in this ill-starred course,
    Which, though it shows the sickness, hides the sufferer?
    But whatsoe'er my brother may attempt,
    'Tis wrong to doubt Cassandra's faith in aught,
    And I can count upon the heart and arm
    Of one who will not spare himself for us.

A C T   I I I

FREDERICK *is discovered, alone.*

FREDERICK (*to himself*). Indiscreet thoughts, what have ye gained
    for me—
    Presumptuous desires, insensate passions,
    A mortal heart's yearnings for charms divine—
    When from a flight so high one falls so low!
    Hopes, which from earth were lifted up to heaven,
    Ought ye not to have known, the thunderbolt
    Which on your pride hath finally fallen would never
    Pardon the purposes ye dared to attempt?
    However deep respect thy suit hath shown,
    Thou seest that a refusal bids thee fly.
    Beware the contest which thou settest thyself;
    Judge of the peril of it, and withdraw.
    What right have I to hope, if my heart's ardor
    Offends the Prince and Princess equally,—
    If, when I wish to hazard speech or glance,
    I make one ill, the other mad with rage?
    Teach me, my soul, to love devoid of hope,
    And suffer all disdain with reverence.
    Resolve we without shame on such brave tameness
    Of spirit that no rejection can offend us.
    Bear we without reward a yoke so proper;
    Not daring to be a lover, let us be

WENCESLAUS

A slave—the victim, then, of all the harshness
Which haughty conquerors can exercise.

Enter ALEXANDER.

ALEXANDER. Duke, thy respect hath too long kept thee silent.
    Thou wrongest our friendship, which finds here a grievance.
    Thou dost not trust it or art false to it.
    Thou robbest me of what thou hidest from me.
    He who gives all his soul, wants all another's;
    And when whate'er concerns thee makes me eager
    To grapple with it, this heart, thy loyal friend,
    Is not content to unveil itself by halves.
    I have, with frank and genuine warmth of spirit,
    Done for thee all things that affection can do;
    Yet dost thou seem, ill assured still, to hold
    In doubt an oath sworn to so sacredly.
    I read upon thy visage secret passions,
    Feelings concealed, and wounds unspoken of,
    And with an eye that pities thee, yet is jealous,
    See that thou keepest a secret to thyself.
FREDERICK. When I have deemed my griefs remediable,
    I made thee share in them, I claimed thine aid,
    And saw results so prompt and so abundant
    That even the memory of them overcomes me.
    But when I think my woe cannot be succored,
    Enough that it crush *me* without thy sharing;
    Enough and too much that it make *one* wretched
    Without extending to thee and making *two* so.
ALEXANDER. That friend who suffers alone, wrongs his friend.
    Mine own share of thy grief will lessen thine.
    Speak out, Duke, and disclose to me thy secrets.
    Except in thy behalf, I have no interests.
    I now know that thy great and last achievement
    Thou wouldst have fain crowned by the hand of love,
    And when thou soughtest to tell the King, who owes thee
    This prize, what lovely lady charmed thy fancy,
    The wonted rudeness of my fiery brother
    Locked fast thy lips and forced thee to be silent.
    Grant, without telling me why he was concerned,
    That I may go and settle this quarrel for thee.
    Seek not to make me fear the consequences;
    Someone must finally needs curb his license;
    And since the King cannot have justice done us,
    I find my heart and arm thereto sufficient.

But when I offer thus to serve thy love,
Let me at least learn who its object is.

FREDERICK.   I am too much indebted to thy kindness
Without thy having new differences with him.
Whet not his hate; 'tis keen enough already.
He is the Prince, my lord; respect his anger.
Unto my evil star let us impute
Our trouble, and deem Fate guiltier than he.
Let my love keep the name unuttered which
Offends him; let considerations stronger
Still than his hest, which have beyond aught else
The right to bind me, bid me to forget it
Though it is precious above all things to me;
Let me avoid a field whence my retreat
Alone can rob the enemy of my rout.

ALEXANDER.   This stubborn silence teaches me thy secret,
But I, who learn it, am discreet and generous.
Hide it no more from me; thou lovest Cassandra,
Duke. To none else so worthy canst thou aspire,
Nor any whom the Prince, adoring her,
Would have such cause to make thee hopeless of.
The envoy of my love, thou too hast fallen
Beneath her spell, being taken unawares;
And my intentions towards her, set o'er thine,
Are the considerations thou deferrest to,
But thou fearest wrongly that a friend will blame thee
For crimes Cassandra causes and excuses.
However great the power her charms have o'er me . . .

FREDERICK.   Be not astonished that I have not answered.
Thy words surprise me, and this unworthy charge
Strikes me a blow so rude and so deep-wounding
That, dazed, I seek my wits and stand in doubt
If it is thou who speakest or I who hear thee.
I, to betray thee, sir? *I* seek Cassandra,
Towards whom I serve thee, for myself? *I* seek
To shake a love so steadfast and so strong?
Thou thinkest me vile indeed, or scarce thy friend.

ALEXANDER.   Thinkest thou thy loving her could change my
          friendship?

FREDERICK.   Couldst love me, were I guilty of this crime?

ALEXANDER.   My confidant or rival, I could not hate thee.

FREDERICK.   Sincere and generous, I could not betray thee.

ALEXANDER.   Love can surprise hearts and soon be their master.

FREDERICK.   His being surprised cannot absolve a traitor,

And any man of true heart who can die
Hath remedy at hand for love's surprisals.

ALEXANDER.   Forgive me a suspicion, not a belief,
Born of thy failure to confide in me.

FREDERICK.   I wish quite to forget it, but on condition
That this distrust be its own punishment,
And that for once to me be granted silence
Without thy friendship's plaint or alteration.
Besides (and if my care and loyalty
Have been suspected by thee, this advice
Should end all doubt of them) Cassandra so
Is persecuted by the Prince, and agents
So powerful beset her for his sake,
That if thou wishest to save her, 'tis no more
A time to love her 'neath a borrowed name.
Long enough and too long by my feigned wooing
Have I conducted thine affair; thy suit,
Under the pretext that thou servedst my love,
Enough hath hoodwinked all the Court. At length
'Tis needful to have done with trickery,—
To doff the mask and show the countenance.
Thou oughtest to assure Cassandra's peace,
Which every hour thy rival mars and troubles.
Her love hath given thee tokens of her troth;
'Tis time that marriage should work to your advantage
And make thee happy and leave him defeated.
From her comes this opinion; thou shouldst heed it.
I need not tell thee of all the reasons she gave me,
Going to the Princess, where I have just brought her,
Who, having espoused the interests of the Prince,
Hath summoned her, if what she saith be true,
To torture her once more in a new effort
In his behalf. Do thou beware the moods
Of her ambitious sex. A scepter's lure
Is dazzling to the eyes, and marriage now
Could set thee free from this anxiety.

ALEXANDER.   But would it free me from my father's power,
Who can . . .

FREDERICK.   If to his power thy love deferreth,
And if by filial duty thou art ruled,
Do naught in haste which may be harmful to thee.
But such tame passion cannot tear thy heart,
And thy impetuous brother's ardent suit
Denotes more love than one so circumspect.

ALEXANDER. Nay, I will reck not what is due my father
And in Love's hands will place my destiny.
Love rules my fortunes; let it rule my conduct.
I am Cassandra's; we this night shall wed.
But let us, Duke, still keep our doings secret;
Let us deceive, for some days, even her servants,
And (save for those most dear, entirely loyal)
Blind their suspicions, thou appearing her husband;
Then, with the marriage sealed and omens fair,
When time declares the truth and doeth its work,
We shall face nothing but the powerless rage
Of a surprised sire or a jealous brother.

FREDERICK. Though obviously I hazard my own standing,
This I am willing for thy sake to do;
And, being more thine than mine, I cannot well
Give thee my heart and yet refuse my name.
Thine own . . .

CASSANDRA *comes out of* THEODORA'S *apartments.*

CASSANDRA *(speaking to* THEODORA *within)*. Well, madam, we must
      needs resolve
To see this thunderbolt fall on our head.
A consequence of thine advice, if we
Are hurled so low, is that 'twill not surprise us.
(To ALEXANDER) Ah, sir, bring to an end my sad experience.
Shall my soul every day be put to torture?
Am I to suffer long so cruel a torment?
And can I not, at last, now love thee safely?

ALEXANDER. What outrage, madam, moveth thee to anger?

CASSANDRA. A sister's interest in a brother's cause.
She tyrannously seeks to dazzle me
By the bright splendor of a shining yoke.
They wish to blind me with a diadem
And make me reign and love despite myself.
So am I bidden to do now, or the Prince
Will make his power the instrument of his anger
And to posterity leave a tragic instance
Of the most awful vengeance for rejection
Wherewith was fortune ever signalized
And whereof all the ages yet have spoken.
These are the kindnesses which love breeds in them,
The sweet incentives which are offered me!

ALEXANDER. Peace, peace again possess thy loveliness!
Let thunders mutter; they will never strike,

Or else the author of those ills which Fate
Decrees thee will first fall beneath our ruins.
Base thy heart's calm on making me be happy.
Cut off this night all passage for his vows;
See without fear whatever he dares do
When thou hast given me a wife to shield
And openly, in my estate of husband,
My duty makes me answerable for thee.

FREDERICK. Forestall this night the ardor which transports him.
Dispatch is needful for such weighty matters.
Only how best to manage the affair
Remains to be considered. Let us go
Hence to discuss it.

CASSANDRA.   What anxieties,
What fear, and what distress fill all my heart!

Enter LADISLAUS

LADISLAUS. Madam, it cannot be that my suit fails.
I would be wrong to doubt or to dread aught
With two friends here who serve my cause so well
And whose affection springs from their souls' depths.
Surely, they spoke to thee in my love's behalf?

CASSANDRA. Thou, if they did, wouldst disavow their words,
Since in thy mind I hold so ill a place
That from thy life's course thou wouldst fain efface
The memory of the time when thou didst love me,
And since therewith thine eyes and heart alike
Abhor my presence no less than death itself.

LADISLAUS. Find here thy boast, and deem all that I said
As if it were but breath or idle tales.
Love made me say it; I was quite transported,
If such must be confessed to feed thy pride.
But if I am a good judge and should credit
My judgment, thou hast scant cause for vainglorying.
I do not see in thee such rare attractions
That thou shouldst be made eminent by them.
Nothing enhances very much thy beauty
Of face, or thou employest ill thy charms.
Thine eyes, those sorcerers fair, with all their lure
Cannot be charged with very numerous victims.
The yoke thou thinkest hath fallen on many necks
Bears not afar the rumor of thy conquests.
Save for one only, who rates his worth too high,
Thy sway extends over few other hearts.

As for mine own, which easily is wounded,
Thy beauty hath pleased me—I confess my weakness—
Hath cost me trouble, service, many steps;
But of my purpose well, I think, thou knewest.
Rightly thou didst not promise to thyself
A marriage which my rank could not permit me.
The interests of the State, which had to sway
My destiny, accorded not with my love.
Do what I would, Fortune was adverse to me.
Thou didst resist me—not a rare distinction.
Had I, refused, relied upon my power,
Success would easily have crowned my hopes.
To snatch my prize, would have assured me of it;
But I have not deemed that 'twas worth the trouble,
Still less to put thee in the place I claim
Or share with thee the throne which I await.
Such is the amount of love thou breddest in me.
If thou hast thought it more, be undeceived.
Thy disdain hath produced in me a like one.
I have resolved to trouble thee no further,—
Have lost desire at the same time as hope,—
And to disclose to thee with what indifference
I resign joys that I so long pursued,
I fain would do a service unto thee
For the disservice which thou didst to me.
I will not keep thee.—Brother, escort her hence;
And thou, Duke, bide here.

CASSANDRA.   Ah, that noble anger!
Preserve for me this generous scorn unchanged,
And may a throne, my lord, reward it soon!

[*She goes out, with* ALEXANDER.

LADISLAUS (*to himself*). Gods, with what effort and what agony
I let her go, tearing my heart in twain!
How sore a struggle frees me from her sway!
                    Duke, I was going to find thee, from the King.
FREDERICK. Whatever his command, 'tis pleasing to me.
LADISLAUS. Thou knowest that he loves thee and seeks thy good.
He gives thee but thy due when he exalts thee;
Thy virtues are the basis of thy credit;
And these same virtues, which rebuke my courses,
Require that for thy sake I suffer his justice
And let him recompense thy latest exploits
With that prize which his pledge leaves to thy choice.
Employ, then, for this choice, the power he gives thee.

Come choose thy bonds which are thy crown. The object
Of thine affections make thou known to him.
No more do I forbid the happiness
To which thou dost aspire; and I shall see
Thy valor recompensed without concern
And hence also without dissatisfaction.

FREDERICK. The hopes I rashly cherished have till lately
Flattered me that my suit might be successful;
But since 'twas my misfortune to displease thee,
Clearly displayed contempt hath quelled my boldness.
He who sees even his presence now forbidden
Were vain indeed to trust and boast his credit.

LADISLAUS. Far from opposing thee and crossing thee,
I go to ask thy marriage from my father.
I have his word already, and if 'tis needed,
I offer thee my service with this lady.

FREDERICK. That of his sovereign power would be futile
If from herself I still cannot win grace.

LADISLAUS. I deem the means are easy for thy doing so.

FREDERICK. Thy care hath ill disposed them in my favor.

LADISLAUS. My favor had no chance against thy virtues.

FREDERICK. My efforts had no chance against thy hatred.

LADISLAUS. My suit's withdrawal offers thee new hopes.

FREDERICK. My humbled love holds my allegiance sacred.
The soul that once hath been persuaded doth
Adhere too closely to the thought conceived there
Soon to replace scorn by esteem again
And easily be cured of its disliking.

Enter WENCESLAUS *and guards.*

WENCELAUS (*to* FREDERICK). Come, dear support which heaven
    hath given me,
Let me fulfil my promise, won by thy merit.
When thou hast served the State so gallantly,
Thou wrongest thy king, not letting him be grateful.
I staked my honor when I pledged my word.
One robs thee by withholding thy reward.
Let me do this no more; I owe it to thee.
Declare the name of her whom thou hast chosen.
Make trial of my justice in thy guerdon.
Reason hath healed the Prince of his caprice.
Thy interest is his; thy good delights him;
And he, who first opposed thee, now speaks for thee.

LADISLAUS (*to himself*). My rival hath my aid against myself!

Heaven, how thou puttest to proof my constancy!

FREDERICK.   To serve thee is so much its own reward
That 'tis a blessing none can snatch from me.
Sire, do not make, by offering recompense,
Of honorable deeds a hireling's task.
Are countless battles not repaid right well
If one can say: "This arm served Wenceslaus"?

WENCESLAUS.   Nay, nay, whate'er I owe to this resistless
Arm, 'tis unmeet thy king should be thy debtor.
Thy great heart troubleth mine by its refusal,
And asks too much of me in asking nothing.
Let us, by *thy* work and *my* gratitude,
Display the subject's and the master's virtues.
My fair fame cannot without stain permit thee
Such generosity as robs me of mine.

FREDERICK.   Stir not a fire which thou wouldst wish extinguished.
I love, my lord, where I cannot attain.
I know myself unworthy, and she I love
Would scorn my tribute, disavow my service.

WENCESLAUS.   Even the mightiest empires have no sovereigns
Whose love this arm would not deserve and honor.
Know, that unless my power be ineffectual
It guarantees the gift of her I give thee.

LADISLAUS *(to himself)*.   What! shall the marriage which was denied
my ardor
Now place my mistress in my rival's bed?

FREDERICK.   I dare no further to dispute thy will . . .

LADISLAUS *(to himself)*.   Nay, nay, base rival, I cannot consent to it.

FREDERICK.   And by thy orders forced to break my silence,
I shall obey thee, but 'tis by constraint.
Though certain to displease thee by obeying,
Much more than by not heeding thy commands,
I will confess, great king, that she who thrills me . . .

LADISLAUS.   Duke, once again, I stop thy mouth. I cannot
Permit thee this presumption.

WENCESLAUS.   Insolent youth!

LADISLAUS.   I have o'ercome my passion fruitlessly.
To endure his pride, my lord, and to please thee,
I have made every effort reason can prompt;
But my respect for thee hath vainly striven
To hold me in. My will cannot prevail
Over my feelings. I must let myself
Be led by passion; let thy wrath lead thee.
Lose for a wayward son a father's love.

Cut short the span of time allotted me,
And let the blood flow out thou gavest me;
Or if thy justice spareth still my head,
Reject the prayer of this presumptuous man
And humble his excess of insolence—
Else shall his death come on his triumph's heels.

[Exit LADISLAUS.

WENCESLAUS. Guards, seize him.
FREDERICK (*staying them*). Ah, my lord, what place of refuge
    Would not be useless to preserve my life
    And safeguard me from an uprisen people?
    Grant me his pardon or my removal hence.
WENCESLAUS. Let no care trouble thee or vex thee. Duke,
    I mean to make thy fortune mount so high,
    I shall endow with so much power thy hand,
    And thou shalt see this mutinous youth so humbled,
    That never any shaft of hate or envy
    Can make attempt against thy life, that henceforth
    The angry impulse of his passions shall not
    Set limits unto what thou canst aspire to,
    That he cannot do harm unto thy greatness,
    And that all things thou wishest lie in thy reach.

[Exeunt.

ACT IV

THEODORA *and* LEONORA *are discovered.*

THEODORA. Ah God! how utterly this fright o'erwhelms me!
    Thou seest thy story conformeth with my dream,
    And with such reasons for dread thou blamest my tears?
    I am too anxious, and have too many fears?
LEONORA. Thou hast them, certainly, a little quickly.
    Is that he hath not slept in his apartment
    So great a ground for being terrified
    And letting a dream in such degree torment thee?
    Thinkest thou the Prince, now at that fiery age
    At which the judgment rules so ill the body,
    At which the soul not yet controls the senses,
    At which the coldest always pines for someone,
    Lives that well-regulated, modest life
    On which *our* honor and good name depend?
    Seekest thou enlightenment touching a youth's nights
    Whom rest tormenteth and whom love consumeth?

245

That is to scan them with too curious care.
One must needs shut one's eyes to his behavior,
Must not be pained by it, or apprehensive,
And know not things which one would have to chide.

THEODORA. A dream cut short, disordered, dim, confused,
Which passes in an instant and can never
Return, casts o'er our spirits a light cloud,
And we are struck with fear no whit or little;
But dreams which are consistent, where throughout
Protesting horror doth forbid repose,
And in which all details stand forth distinctly,
Are heaven's warnings of events to come.
Alas! I saw the hand that pierced his side;
I saw the blow fall and his blood gush forth;
I saw another hand strike off his head;
I saw his grave made ready for his corpse;
And crying out with a voice that would have blenched thee,
I then dispelled my dream but not my terror.
Fright dragged me from my couch immediately,
And as thou sawest me, speechless and distraught,
Alone I hastened into his apartments
And found there that my fears were not unfounded,
For those who serve him told me . . . But what sight
Is this I see?

Enter LADISLAUS, *supported by* OCTAVIUS.

OCTAVIUS.　　　　　Ah, madam!
THEODORA.　　　　　　　　Yes?
OCTAVIUS.　　　　　　　　　　The Prince
Without me would have yielded up the ghost.
THEODORA. Was I afraid without cause, Leonora?
LADISLAUS. Permit me on this seat a moment's rest.
Weak and yet ill-recovered from the faintness
Which, through my fall and loss of blood, is mine,
I scarce can creep and know not where I am.
THEODORA. My brother!
LADISLAUS.　　　　　Sister! Thou! Knowest thou my plight?
THEODORA. O dream, precursor of some tragic thing,
How well this situation doth fulfil thee!
Through what misfortune, brother, or what crime
Do I behold thee in such sad, bloody state?
LADISLAUS. Love and Cassandra—thou seest what they cost me.
But take care no one heareth us.

THEODORA. See to it,

Leonora. [*Leonora goes to see that no one is listening.*

LADISLAUS. Thou, my sister, hast been shown
My secret thoughts, the bottom of my heart.
Thou knowest how I struggled with myself
To shake the yoke of this extreme love off
And pluck forth, from a heart pierced blamably,
The envenomed arrow her glance planted there.
Try as I might, unfaithful to myself,
My spirit still rebelled against my judgment;
My heart was so ill weaned from serving her,
That one thought would restore its old allegiance,
Such power, wretched beings that we are,
Hath love with us—not love, but man's fell foe.
To hide, no matter how, my baseness, I
Have feigned the healthier mind the more I suffered;
Disheartened by the scorn she showed her slave,
I acted like a king and played the bravo.
Nay, more, though frantic, fluctuant, confused,
I sought to use my influence for my rival;
But at the least thought my infatuate soul
Always revolts against the course I chose,
And that cold beauty whose fair charm enthralls me
Is stronger than my wrath or her disdain.
When from Octavius I learned yesterday
Of the marriage of Cassandra and the Duke,
Which then was being arranged and which that happy
Couple last night was to have consummated . . .

OCTAVIUS. O fatal news! Alas! thou bearest what fruit?

LADISLAUS. Succumbing suddenly to this crushing blow,
I then became incapable of reason,
Dismissed my people, shut myself up all evening,
And took no counsel save from my despair.
When night had fallen, by a secret door
I finally stole forth and gained the street,
Whence, quite bereft of prudence, honor, sense,
When I had reached the mansion of Cassandra,
I scaled the wall, got to a balcony,
And seeking some place suited to my frenzy,
Went down the stairs and in the shadows there
Prepared my angry heart for come what might.
At length at the Duke's name the door was opened,
And following then the fury that possessed me,
I ran, dashed out the light, and striking blindly

Thrice with my poignard, gave the Duke his death-wounds.

THEODORA *(dismayed, supporting herself with the help of* LEONORA).
The Duke? What do I hear! Oh!

LADISLAUS.   Thus attacked,
While on the staircase all was lamentation,
He, hearing me drop the dagger at his feet,
Seized it, pursued, and wounded me in the arm.
With this last effort his soul left his body.
He fell dead . . .

LEONORA.   O inhuman, barbarous rage!

LADISLAUS. And I, by devious paths whereof I know not,
Dragged myself through the hideous night until
I grew death-cold from having lost much blood,
And fell unconscious, and lay where I fell
Until Octavius, passing, gave me aid,
Bound up my wound, and brought me here, where I
Am coming to myself, though slowly still.

THEODORA *(leaning on* LEONORA *for support)*. I yield, dear brother,
to my extreme grief.
Weakness assails me and shows very plainly
How much concern I feel about thy hurt.—
(Aside) Upbear me, Leonora.—
                    (To herself) Art thou so soft,
My heart, as to lament Cassandra's husband
And to wish harm to him who rid thee of him?
This marriage insulted thee; his death requites thee.
                    [*She goes out, with* LEONORA.

OCTAVIUS. Already now, my lord, the first faint light
Of day, returning, makes the moon grow pale.

LADISLAUS. And will expose the night's crimes to all eyes.

OCTAVIUS. I hear a noise already in the King's
Apartments. Seek thy bed, ere someone comes.

LADISLAUS. Who wishes death, fears little, whatever happens.
But let us go. Help me.

Enter WENCESLAUS *and guards.*

WENCESLAUS.   My son!
LADISLAUS.   Yes, sire?
WENCESLAUS. Alas!
OCTAVIUS.   O fatal meeting!
WENCESLAUS.   Ladislaus,
Is it thou whose bloodless face and vacant gaze
Suggest a body whence the soul is fled?
Where bendest thou, so tranced, so cold, so bloody,

Thy trembling and uncertain steps? What is it
That hath so early drawn thee from thy couch?
What trouble fills thee and doth seal thy lips?

LADISLAUS (*sinking back into the chair he had quitted*).
What shall I say, alas!

WENCESLAUS.   Answer, my son.
What terrible thing . . .

LADISLAUS.   Sir, I will tell it thee.
I went . . . I was . . . Love hath such empire o'er me . . .
I am confused, sir, and can tell thee nothing.

WENCESLAUS. A soul beset with such confusion doth
Expose its guilt; for he who fears, hath sinned.
Hast thou not had a quarrel with thy brother?
Thy evil mood was always hostile to him,
And if my care did not avail to shield him
From it . . .

LADISLAUS.   Hath he not satisfied me? No,
I have not seen him.

WENCESLAUS.   What, then, awakened thee
Ere dawn hath launched the sun upon its course?

LADISLAUS. Hast thou not also risen before the sun?

WENCESLAUS. Yes, but I have good cause for shortened slumbers.
I see myself upon life's downward slope,
And knowing that death soon will take me hence,
I filch from sleep, death's image, all I can
Of the time, Ladislaus, that still is left me.
Being near the limits nature doth prescribe,
So that my foot is set on the grave's brink,
In these last moments that I walk my pathway
I to my days add what my nights are robbed of.
In rest, then, my weak eyelids carefully
Husband for me this remnant of life's light;
But what care can drive *thee* from bed so early
For whom thine age preserves so long a life?

LADISLAUS. If thou wilt of my life dispose with justice,
It now stands on the verge of the abyss.
This arm (since vain is all dissimulation)
Hath felled the chief sustainer of thy throne.
The Duke is dead; and I it was that slew him.
I had good reason to do it.

WENCESLAUS.   O God! The Duke
Is dead, foul villain?—is dead, thou barbarous wretch?
And for excuse, forsooth, thou hadst good reason

To be his murderer! Dost thou, O heaven,
Put to this proof my patience?

Enter FREDERICK.

FREDERICK. Good my lord,
The Duchess asks an audience with thee.
LADISLAUS. What do I see? What phantom, what delusion
Increaseth the disorder of my senses?
WENCESLAUS. What hast thou told me, Prince, and by what marvel
So quickly can mine eyes gainsay mine ears?
LADISLAUS. Have I not told thee that, confused and 'wildered,
I could say nothing and could reason no longer?
WENCESLAUS. Ah, Duke, 'twas time that thou shouldst rid my mind
Of a mistake which racked it mortally.
Hadst thou delayed one moment to relieve it,
A story of thy death would have caused mine.
Never hath heart experienced grief so strong.
But what was this thou toldest me?
FREDERICK. That Cassandra
Asks at the door to see thee.
WENCESLAUS. Let her enter.
LADISLAUS (*aside*). O ye just heavens! My hand, hast thou deceived
me?
Mine eyes, do ye deceive me? If the Duke
Is living, what life was it that I quenched,
And by what arm did mine receive a wound?

Enter CASSANDRA. *She throws herself, weeping, at the King's feet.*

CASSANDRA. Great king, the august shield of innocence,
Who meteth out rewards and punishments
Righteously, and of incorruptible
And perfect justice doth an example stand
For nations to admire now and hereafter—
King, father, both! avenge me! avenge us!
With thy compassion mix thy wrath, and furnish
Today, as an inexorable judge,
A precedent to all posterity.
WENCESLAUS. Madam, a truce to griefs that choke the voice,
And make thy tears speak.
CASSANDRA. Sire, thy Majesty
Knows well my family.
WENCESLAUS. Ursin of Königsberg,
Of whom thou art the daughter, was descended

WENCESLAUS

From ancestors derived from lineage royal,
And was my neighbor, honorable and loyal.

CASSANDRA. Thou knowest if to intend one of thy sons
To be his son-in-law, would have been too much
For one who held his station to aspire to.

WENCESLAUS. Love between equals maketh no offense.

CASSANDRA. They both have tried to change my free estate,
But with desires and thoughts of me quite different.
One deemed me upright; his intent was lawful.
The other, moved by wanton, self-willed love,
Doubted my virtue; his intent was vicious.
I, too, for them soon had quite different feelings.
Though both alike thy sons, they seemed not brothers.
I could not love or hate by halves; I held
The one my lover, and my foe the other.
The young prince by his virtues won my heart;
The elder by his vices lost that prize;
And for two different but proper reasons
I loved one of thy sons and loathed the other.
Alexander, seeing a rival in his brother,
And fearing too his sire's authority,
Made, though as ardent as discret and prudent,
A secret matter of our love, and under
The Duke's name veiling his own courtship, turned
Thy glance astray so skilfully that indeed
No one suspected till this day that he
Spoke for himself when speaking for the Duke.
His cleverness deceived our servants, even;
But fearing that the Prince, at his wits' end,
Would deem all things permitted to his power,
Follow the frenzy of a baffled love,
And dare attempt too much against mine honor,
We thought that only marriage could protect me,
And the hour ripe for us to join our hands
And, ending all his hopes, destroy his plans.
Last night already sleep gave balm to all. . . .
At this point, sire, let my tears flow; their course
Springs from a ne'er-to-be-exhausted source. . . .
The young prince, who expected joy from wedlock,
Came without escort, to avoid suspicion.
Scarce had he set foot o'er the threshold, when
He felt a barbarous hand, for his reception,
With three blows of a dagger pierce his breast.

WENCESLAUS. O God! the lad is dead.

LADISLAUS.   O my blind rage!
Thou art well glutted; now behold thy work!
[*The King sinks into a chair and buries his face in his
    handkerchief.*
CASSANDRA. Yes, he is dead; and I shall follow him
As soon as I have seen his death avenged.
I know his murderer, and I expect
Thy justice or thy wrath to punish him.
This is thine own blood, sire, that has been shed,
Thy living portrait that is blotted out.
I need a champion; I can choose no other.
The dead youth is thy son; my cause is thine.
Take vengeance for thyself, me, and a husband
For whom I weep here, widowed ere my marriage.
But though thou learnest, great king, of this fell deed,
Alas, couldst thou suspect the doer of it?
Yes, for thy heart avoucheth him for thee:
                          [*She points at* LADISLAUS.
It stirs; it speaks both for him and against him,
And feeling at once horror and affection,
Tells thee that Ladislaus slew Alexander.
His manner, too, my lord, his confused aspect,
His frightened face, his silence, tell it plainly,
And more than all, in truth, his hand still red
With this dear blood which maketh me lament.
    Which of the two will have more weight with thee:
Thy son the murderer, or thy murdered son?
Wert thou so weak and were thy blood so doting
That one could shed it with impunity,
Thou wouldst perchance behold the hand that spilled it
Turn against what is left of it in thee.
The murderer of his brother may be thine;
One crime may well be prelude to the other.
'Tis thus that crimes or virtues, linked in sequence,
Always or often lead from this to that one.
Beware to risk, by being too magnanimous,
Both throne and life and fame of being just.
If my keen sorrows have no power to touch thee,
Nor a son's loss who was so dear to thee,
Nor the grim thought of blows that robbed thee of him,
See, see the blood with which this dagger drippeth;
                          [*She draws a dagger from her sleeve.*
And if it moves thee not, learn whence it came.
Thy son withdrew it from thy son's breast. Yes,

A brother's hand, my lord, could launch the blow.
This blade doth bear the culprit's sign and name,
Tells thee of what arm 'twas the instrument,
As party to the deed, declareth its author.
This blade, still reeking, by a monstrous crime
Hath pierced the noblest victim of true love,
The purest being whom thou hast created,
And the most worthy heart thou wert beloved by.
This heart, this blood, this son, this victim, then,
Beg through my lips a rightly pronounced sentence.
   The monarch wrongs himself if he relents;
The father oweth justice to his son.
I wait for thine avenging hand to strike.
Either as thou art just or as thou lovedst;
Or if I can obtain no human aid,
The equity of heaven will lend me succor.
This sin against it seeks in vain for refuge;
Thereof 'twas witness, and 'twill be the judge.
To punish an arm black with such a crime,
Its own, which is not short, can be stretched forth
If thou dost leave to it our wrongs' repayment.
WENCESLAUS.   Hast thou, Prince, a defense against these charges?
LADISLAUS.   Nay, I am guilty. Noble king, abandon
This doomed life to the rigors of the law.
Let nothing sway thee to be less severe.
Let us suppress the names of son and father
And whatsoe'er can plead with thee for me.
Cassandra seeks my death; it must be granted.
Her hate commands it; I must needs be silent;
And I prefer a death that suits her pleasure
To a deliverance from doom and to
A never-ending life that would displease her.
Vainly would I conceal my boundless passion;
Until my death, my fate wills that I love her,—
Yes, to admit how hotly burns my heart,
Until my death, which she will bring upon me.
The stroke that kills me to avenge her wrongs
Will only be a slight and gladsome wound
Compared with that fell stroke which pierced my bosom
When her fair glances conquered and enslaved me.
They made me desperate till I would dare all things.
They robbed me of that peace which death would give me.
Since heaven decrees that I must be her victim,
Her mouth or eyes—what mattereth which shall slay me?

Sanction that doom wherewith she threatens me.
Lacking her favor, I desire no mercy.
Complete the work that love inaugurated;
Finish a death already well begun;
And if no other reason moves thy wrath,
Fear all things from an arm that killed a brother.

WENCESLAUS (*to* CASSANDRA). Temper the keenness of thine anguish
    madam,
And leave in *my* hands what concerns us both.
Today my mandates will display the marks
Both of a just judge and a worthy monarch.
I will divest myself of all emotion
And deal as law decrees with his confession.

CASSANDRA. My hopes, great king, have nowise been deceived,
    And . . .

WENCESLAUS.   Prince, arise. Give up to me thy sword.

LADISLAUS (*getting to his feet*). My sword? Ah, is my crime, then,
    so enormous
    That I . . .

WENCESLAUS.   Give it, I say, and do not answer.

LADISLAUS. Here it is.

WENCESLAUS (*handing it to* FREDERICK). Take it, Duke.

OCTAVIUS   O cruel abasement!

WENCESLAUS. And have him guarded in the adjoining room.
    Go.

LADISLAUS (*to himself*). Speed the end which thou hast destined for
    me,
Fortune. This is thy sport. Thy wheel hath turned.

    [*He goes out, under guard.*

WENCESLAUS. Duke!

FREDERICK.   My good lord?

WENCESLAUS.   Inform the Prince from me
That his head, once so dear unto the realm,
Must serve today as a far-famed example
To make his crime detested by our race.
    (*To* OCTAVIUS) Do thou escort this lady home again.

CASSANDRA. Great king, of all great kings the truest model,
Preserve unvanquished this inflexible heart;
Pursue this noble purpose to the end;
And hearken steadfastly, despite thy kindness,
To a son's blood that cries aloud for vengeance.

WENCESLAUS. Madam, this crime is not a thing to shield.
My business is to punish, not avenge.

    [*Exit* CASSANDRA, *with* OCTAVIUS.

Ah, heaven, thy providence with seeming bounty
Vouchshafed to make me father of two sons;
And one, of whom today the other reft me,
Requires me to destroy the one still left me!

A C T V

THEODORA *and* LEONORA *are discovered.*

THEODORA. How did he take my letter, Leonora?
LEONORA. With face and manner promising thee all.
In vain his modesty sought to dissemble.
On coming to thy name, he needs must kiss it,
As if constrained to imprint on those dear symbols
The tokens of a love fain to be silent.
THEODORA. How ill thou choosest thy time to try a heart
Which sorrow tries with such severity!
I mourned for the Duke's death as that of one
Who served my father's crown, and whom he needed;
And when I was relieved to find it false,
Learning he lived, I learned my brother was dead.
Still, though our hearts accorded in affection,
I cannot desire vengeance for his death.
I loved alike the slayer and the slain;
I pity equally the fate of both.
My grief has tears to give a brother murdered;
I find no arms against a murderous brother;
And if the blood of one aroused mine anger,
The other . . . The Duke comes. Leonora, leave us.

Enter FREDERICK. *Exit* LEONORA.

FREDERICK. Burning with zeal to serve thee, divine princess,
I come as bidden to thy Highness' feet.
THEODORA. Thou dost not flatter me? Can I trust in thee?
FREDERICK. 'Tis easy, madam, to make proof of this.
Blood to be shed have I. I wear a sword.
My hand is hot for service at thy hest.
THEODORA. I do not ask so much from thine affection.
I wish thee only to make one confession.
FREDERICK. What is it? Claim it.
THEODORA.   From thy lips to learn
What woman is so blest she moves thy heart
And will the guerdon be of those famed deeds
Which even into Muscovy extended

Our sway. I thought it was Cassandra's charms
That thou wert taken with; but since the young prince
Adored her, thou couldst not aspire to her.
FREDERICK.   Madam, my thoughts have dared a higher flight
Still, which my reason doth approve not of.
THEODORA.   Ne'er seek to find excuse in shamefacedness.
Name her, I bid thee.
FREDERICK.   I can make no answer,
But my voice yields this office to thine eyes.
Thou hast thyself named that illustrious name.
Thine own hand hath subscribed this letter with it.
                    [*He displays her opened letter to her.*
THEODORA.   Thy worth, Duke, gives great privileges to thee,
    But . . .
FREDERICK.   Daring to love thee, I condemned my love.
I hated mine own self for such presumption.
But, madam, blame a fatal star with raising
A hope which reason overthrows, with making
Thy subjects burn their incense at thine altar,
And with procuring their devotion for thee.
THEODORA.   If I have power o'er thee, can I rely
Upon a proof, this moment, of thy zeal?
FREDERICK.   The flame with which this heart doth burn for thee
Makes all things possible and the impossible easy.
THEODORA.   The task I set thee will be hard but noble.
FREDERICK.   It will augment the luster of my love.
THEODORA.   Far from it, for this proof is to keep hidden
A hope which for its daring would bring on thee
Reproach; to speak not, and permit thyself
Only respect and circumspection; finally,
For the reward of thy great services,
Which make thy name shine bright above all others,
To go and ask, for my sake, of my father,
Not my hand but a pardon for my brother,
Prevent his doom, and stay by thine assistance
The sharp steel ready to cut short his days.
Of this test, Duke, is thy love capable?
FREDERICK.   Madam, it is; and since 'tis so to blame,
'Twill exact vengeance on its own presumption
And sink, with me, into the tomb's dark night.
THEODORA.   Nay, I forbid that; leave reprisal to me,
And if I sway thy soul, do thou my bidding.
Farewell, Duke.   [*She goes out.*
FREDERICK (*to himself*).   What a storm beats down my hope,

And what a charge, my heart, hast thou received!
If I dare love her, I permit myself
Too great a license; and if I would punish
Myself for this, lo, she prohibits it.
Thus to forbid me death, yet to withhold
All cure from me, is not this to command me
At once to live and die? But . . .

Enter WENCESLAUS, *with guards.*

WENCESLAUS.   Oh, thou day
   Forever fatal unto my domains!
   Frederick!
FREDERICK.   What is it, sire?
WENCESLAUS.   Bring the Prince in.
FREDERICK (*to himself*). It will be needless to employ my influence.
   The ties of nature act; the King's wrath softens.
                          [*Exit* FREDERICK.
WENCESLAUS (*to himself*). A truce, a truce, my feelings, to that strife
   Which so unmercifully rends my bosom,
   Pierces my heart and seeketh to divide it
   Between my son to be destroyed and likewise
   My son to be avenged. All my affection
   Opposes itself vainly to my justice,
   And seeks a father's heart in a king's heart:
   I will divest myself of such a trait
   And hear no voice but that of equity.

Enter LADISLAUS *and* FREDERICK.

   But oh, vain constancy! Oh, imagined strength!
   At this sight I still feel myself a father
   And have not laid aside all human fondness.
   Go, guards! And thou, Duke, leave us for a moment.
               [FREDERICK *and the guards withdraw.*
LADISLAUS. Wilt thou preserve thy seed now or avenge it?
   Is this to announce my death or pardon, father?
WENCESLAUS. My son, embrace me.
LADISLAUS.   Sire, how great a mercy,
   What tenderness, and what unheard-of grace!
   But dost thou thus denote or dost remit
   My punishment? Are thine arms chains or shelter?
WENCESLAUS. Receive with this the last of their embraces,
   The last affection of my heart. Dost thou
   Know of what blood thou springest?
LADISLAUS.   I have given

Poor evidence of knowing, yet I know.

WENCESLAUS. Feelest thou the high impulses of this blood?

LADISLAUS. If I have not their deeds, I have their feelings.

WENCESLAUS. Then, feelest thou capable of a great act?

LADISLAUS. Yes; I resist the grief that crushes me,
And greater act than this no man can do.

WENCESLAUS. With manhood arm thyself, for thou shalt need it.

LADISLAUS. If it is time to go, my soul is ready.

WENCESLAUS. So is the scaffold; carry thy head thither.
More doomed than thou, my heart will follow thee.
I by thy death-blow will die more than thou;
Thereof my tears are ample proof for thee;
But to the State I owe this great example,
To mine own rectitude this noble act,
To thy dead brother this exalted victim.
I fear to utter, as much as thou to hear it,
The stern decree which these require and I
Have to pronounce. I have striven long to spare thee,
But either reigning is no more a virtue
And justice is to kings but a chimera,
Or to the realm I owe this sacrifice.

LADISLAUS. Well, make it; here, my neck is ready for it.
The culprit, mighty king, accepts thy sentence.
I proffer no defense; I know my crimes
Have often stirred thy soul to righteous wrath.
I could for this, my latest, urge the excuse
Of an arm's error through misunderstanding
And rage too credulous. Both my hate and love,
Which sought for satisfaction, aimed their blow
At not my brother but the Duke. I might
Claim also that this blow fell from an arm
Of which the earliest deeds served thy dominions
And won me place enough in history
To plead to thee with justice for my pardon;
But I have no wish to prolong my lot.
I have whereto I owe my death; thou owest it
To the nation, to my brother, to thyself;
I owe it to that cruel one whom I love;
I owe it to her hate, and wish to pay it.
'Tis a small tribute to relinquish life—
Little, to satisfy and please Cassandra,
To yield my head up and to shed my blood,
And, forced to love her to my latest breath
Without the power, in life, to meet her wishes,

Be ravished with the knowledge my death meets them
And I, in dying, please earth's loveliest eyes.
WENCESLAUS. To whatsoe'er thy heart devotes thy death,
Go and prepare thyself for this great test,
And though for earthly love thou dost abandon
Thy body, thus abandon not thy soul.
Dark though it be, the night hath many eyes
And did not hide thine evil deed from heaven.
[He embraces LADISLAUS *again.*
Farewell. Bring to the block a prince's heart
And make the whole land wonder there if, born
To rule and destined for so high a rank,
Thou diest on a scaffold or a throne.
[The King stamps his foot to summon FREDERICK.

Enter FREDERICK, *with guards.*

Duke, lead the Prince out.
LADISLAUS.   O too rigorous virtue!
Wenceslaus liveth still, and is no longer
My father!   *[He goes out with* FREDERICK.
WENCESLAUS *(to himself)*. O cruel justice, warring duties!
To keep my scepter I must slay my son!
But let the deed be done, stubborn affections;
And ye, mine eyes, conceal my tears and weakness.
I can do naught for him; ties yield to laws;
I cannot be both good king and good father.
See, Poland, in the horror which crime gives me,
If my selection was a fitting one
And if I to the duties of my station
Can give more than mine own son, mine own blood.

Enter THEODORA, CASSANDRA, *and* LEONORA.

THEODORA. By what law, sire, so barbarous and so harsh
Canst thou o'erturn the very laws of nature?
I hear the Prince, alas, is doomed to die
And for his punishment all is arranged.
What! shall we live (because of ruthless statutes)
The State without heirs, thou without a son,
And I without a brother? Ah, I beg thee,
Take counsel with thyself against thine anger.
'Tis too much that one fault should doom thy son.
A brother cannot be a brother's murderer;
The night alone is guilty of this murder.
He, quite as much as we, laments his fate

Fulfilled, and by the deed itself is punished
Enough. Compassion, which will pardon him,
No less than justice doth beseem a monarch.
With less rage thou wilt be more lenient to him.
Justice is often times the mask of anger,
And such a stern sentence will be ascribed
To a king's obligations less than to
A father's wrath. The people mutter 'gainst it;
The ties of nature speak; Cassandra keepeth
Silent. Her unexpected meeting here
With the Prince, the nation's welfare, and my tears
Have vanquished her; despite her grief she could not
Resist us; and thy son no longer hath
Aught but a father to prevail against.

CASSANDRA. I was returning, sire, to ask his death
And urge thy justice with becoming fervor.
My heart, impatiently awaiting vengeance,
Condemned each moment that delayed his doom;
But I cannot conceive by what reaction
The sight of him in chains hath in my soul
Silenced his brother's voice and quelled the fierce
Hate which I owe him for my loved one's blood;
And, wretched that I am, though my cleft heart
Adoreth still his victim, the laments,
The tears, the arguments of Theodora,
The murmurs of the people, and of all
The State, who take the part of the throne's heir
Against me and condemn the sentence which
Is grievous to thee, too—these in my breast
Abate my thirst for vengeance and reveal it
As a crime in me 'gainst the public good
And the realm's head. Hence I shall speak not, sire.
Dispose of that life as seems best to thee
Which thou didst promise me, and which I pursued.
    (*Aside*)   In the default, belovèd, of that blood
Denied thee, I have blood for thine appeasement.

WENCESLAUS. Duchess, thou canst not doubt—nor canst thou, daugh-
        ter—
That I, a father, fain would meet your wishes.
I, more than he, am punished by his doom,
And I would choose death sooner than my sorrow.
But I am king, and if I pardon him,
Disgrace will stain my crown eternally.
If I stand firm instead, my life and thy

Honor shall owe their safety to my harshness.
This lion is tame now, madam; but perhaps
He that hides thus submissively his passions
Tomorrow with more arrogant violence
Than ever will assail thy chastity.
Perhaps his hand, grown used to blood of mine,
Against my own breast will be armed tomorrow.
Thy pitying him befits a noble heart,
But if I wish to reign, this needs must be:
I must despite thee right the wrong thou sufferedst,
And, though thou yieldest, take up thy defense.
My wrath's continuance and thy wrath's abatement
Are the results of the same shining virtue.

Enter FREDERICK.

What of the Prince, Duke?
FREDERICK.   Sire, 'tis now that truly
He is a prince and such can call himself.
He seems, before all eyes, heroically
Preparing as for marriage, not for death;
And since, being now as calm as earlier violent,
He can no longer impose silence on me
And envy me a prize this arm hath won me,
I claim, great king, the guerdon of my labors.
WENCESLAUS.   That is most meet, and were it a whole province . . .
FREDERICK.   I ask, sire, but the Prince's pardon.
WENCESLAUS.   What!
FREDERICK.   I have thy promise, and this sacred pledge
Assures me thou wilt not refuse it. With
My blood I bought this boon that I dare hope for.
WENCESLAUS.   What! Frederick too plots to beguile my mercy?
What charm doth 'gainst a sire, in a son's favor,
Enlist and make plead for him his own foes?
FREDERICK.   A prince's fault is canceled easily.
The realm which he should rule owes him forgiveness.
Though by his crime the blood of the young prince
Was shed, his punishment would harm the State.
His cause, though unjust, is the public cause.
It is not always good to be too scrupulous.
Can one refuse that which the whole land wishes?
Canst thou, his father, be the last to soften?

Enter OCTAVIUS.

OCTAVIUS.   Sire, all the people, with a common outcry,

Speak in the Prince's favor and demand
Pardon for him; and a great multitude
Especially, assembled in the square,
In reckless zeal have overthrown the scaffold,
And with eyes full of tears, with one same purpose,
Vow to die with him or to save his life.
With single impulse and with single voice
All say he is exempt from the law's workings;
And if their hot hearts are not soon appeased,
Never would there be readier sedition.
In vain, to restore order and restrain them,
I have tried . . .

WENCESLAUS.   'Tis enough. Have him brought hither.
              [Exit OCTAVIUS.

LEONORA *(aside)*. Aid our prayers, heaven!
THEODORA *(aside)*.   Let us see what happens.
WENCESLAUS *(walking back and forth with great strides)*.
 Yes, daughter; yes, Cassandra; yes, my promise;
 Yes, ties of nature; yes, ye populace.
 What ye desire must needs be; and my will
 I must dispose according to your wishes.

   Enter LADISLAUS *and* OCTAVIUS.

LADISLAUS *(kneeling at the King's feet)*. By what good fortune . . .
WENCESLAUS *(raising him)*. Stand up, Prince. A crown
 'Neath which for forty years I ruled this land,
 Which must unsullied pass to the next reign,
 And all the jewels of which have such pure brightness
 (In which the assent of nobles and of commons
 Conserved for me the ancestral heritage),
 Is the sole means by which I could conceive
 How to disarm my power, in thy behalf.
 I cannot save thee while it still is mine.
 Thy head must either fall or wear it. I
 Must give it to thee if I am to pardon thee—
 Must punish thee for thy crime, or else must crown thee.
 The realm desires it thine. The people show me,
 By wishing thou shouldst live, that they are weary
 Of *my* reign. Justice is for kings the queen
 Of virtues; and to wish that I should be
 Unjust, is not to wish me any longer.
 Rule; 'tis by law my right to elevate thee
 And give my realm a father in my son.
LADISLAUS. What dost thou do, great king?

WENCESLAUS.   Call me that name
And thou beyond my power puttest thy pardon.
I want no more a rank that makes me be
Adverse to thee. Be thou king, Ladislaus,
And I will be a father. As a king,
I cannot tolerate the foes of law.
As a father, I cannot destroy my son.
A loss is easy when love urges it.
I lose a name only to save a life,
To satisfy the State, the Duke, Cassandra,
Who first have pardoned thee thy deed of murder.
The Duke for recompense requires thy pardon;
This rioting folk desire it granted to thee;
Cassandra grants it. I no more oppose it;
Only my dignity made me withhold it.
I without pain step from this rank supreme.
I fain would save a son more than a crown.

LADISLAUS. If thou canst not be both my king and father,
How can I be thy son and rule o'er thee?
I without pain renounce this rank supreme.
Abandon a son sooner than a crown.

WENCESLAUS. I want no more of it; restore it not to me.
He who forgives his king would punish Ladislaus
And make his head fall if it wears not that.

LADISLAUS. 'Tis ready here, my lord, at thy command.
I will preserve it, since I owe it to thee,
But will reign only to dispense thy laws,
And always, whatsoe'er I dare or plan,
Though with crowned brow, will be thy loyal subject.
(*To* FREDERICK) Duke, by what happy fate have I deserved
Both from thy courage and thy kindliness
The noble care thou tookest to save my life?

FREDERICK. I served the nation in preserving that.
But having paid the crown and thee my debt,
I beg one favor of thy Majesty.

LADISLAUS. Name it.

FREDERICK.   Thy leave, my lord, for my withdrawal,
To breed in thee no more this secret hatred
Which, understanding me but ill, made always
Suspect to thee my keenest loyalty
And deepest reverence.

LADISLAUS.   Nay, nay, Duke; thou owest
Thy help to my dominions. I as King
Inherit not the quarrels of the Prince,

And I should augur ill about my rule
If I must first remove its chief support.
He who finds whereupon his crown depends,
Who a firm prop discovers to his throne,
Who hath a subject worthy of this office,
Can boast his fortune and call himself a king.
Heaven gave us such a one; this nation hath him.
Through his work all smiles on us, burgeons, prospers;
By his device our neighbors, natural foes,
Seek only to be our allies, or vassals.
He makes our matchless power shine everywhere.
Through him all Europe either fears or loves us;
He is the strength and ornament of the State;
And by departing thou wouldst rob me of him!
The richest prize which I, in reigning, hope for
Is that thou shalt remain this empire's soul.
    (*Indicating* THEODORA)   And if thy will conformeth to my
      choice,
My sister will avail to bind thee to me.
FREDERICK.   I vainly would aspire thereto, when her
    Injunction hath forbidden me to serve her.
THEODORA.   I bade thee to conceal the love that bound thee;
    But the King's orders are above mine, and,
    Giving me to thee, end my opposition.
FREDERICK.   Oh, too great recompense of all my toil!
    (*To* LADISLAUS)   This is the prize, sire, which my favor sought.
    Thou who forbadest it to me, givest it to me.
LADISLAUS (*to* CASSANDRA).   For thee did I accept life and the crown,
    Madam. Command, and I relinquish them.
    Without thy favors, they possess no sweetness.
    I yield, renounce, detest them, without thee.
    On thee alone depends my fate, my life.
CASSANDRA.   After thy hand reft life from my beloved!
WENCESLAUS.   The scepter which I place there blots his crime out.
    In a new reign let us forget the past.
    Let him lose, with the name of prince, thy hate.
    When I give thee a king, give us a queen.
CASSANDRA.   Can I without too base and sore an effort
    Wed with a murderer, being his victim's widow?
    Can I . . .
WENCESLAUS.   Time, daughter . . .
CASSANDRA.   Oh, what can time avail!
LADISLAUS.   If I can win naught, let me at least hope

So great submissiveness will tire disdain
Till thou wilt be my love's prize finally.
WENCESLAUS (*to* LADISLAUS).   Let us go give our last tears to my child
And lock our grief up in his sepulcher.
Make me while yet I live praise my successor
And see my crown held by a fit possessor.

Cosroès

(CHOSROES)

By
JEAN ROTROU

INTRODUCTORY NOTE

Rotrou, to the average well-educated Frenchman of today and to the world at large in so far as it knows of him at all, is the author of *Saint Genest* and *Venceslas*. The former of these plays does not really deserve such distinction. It owes this to quite other factors than dramatic excellence. It is a martyr-play convenient to compare and contrast with Corneille's *Polyeucte*. Its hero and namesake, the head of a troupe of actors in the reign of the Roman emperor Diocletian, is converted to Christianity, and in the midst of a Court performance of a play about Christian martyrs suddenly departs from his lines, testifies to his new-found faith, and himself wins martyrdom. Justice is by no means done to the dramatic possibilities of this subject, but glimpses are shown of life in a dramatic company (really a French company of Rotrou's own day, not a Roman company) which are quite extraneous to the subject of the play but are interesting in themselves, and there are glimpses also of the affairs of the Emperor's family, equally irrelevant and also interesting. Moreover, some of Rotrou's best and most characteristic poetry is in *Saint Genest*, and style has always counted heavily in French literary appraisals.

In H. C. Lancaster's opinion, however, it is *Cosroès*, not *Saint Genest*,[1] that should be set beside *Venceslas*. He ranks it second among Rotrou's plays; but Reynier declares it not at all inferior to *Venceslas,* and Hémon would seem to rank it first. Some others definitely do so.[2] Hémon says:

"There is more imagination in *Saint Genest,* more intensity of feeling in *Venceslas,* but *Cosroès* is somehow better worked out, more mature, more powerfully tragic." [3] Reynier points out that "this fine play" is the sole drama of Rotrou's that is really original, and reveals what great capacities were his and what injustice he had done himself customarily in writing so hastily and not depending more on his own creative ability.[4] There was no previous play on the story of Chosroes, which is told by Baronius in his *Ecclesiastical Annals,* except a dull, ponderous Latin tragedy by Father Cellot; Rotrou has utterly

[1] *Op. cit.,* Part II, p. 550.
[2] E.g. Person, *Histoire du Véritable Saint-Genest de Rotrou,* Paris, 1882, p. 19.
[3] Translated from his *Rotrou: Théâtre choici,* Paris, n.d., p. 75.
[4] In Petit de Julleville's *Histoire de la Langue et de la Littérature française,* Paris, 1897, Vol. IV, p. 380.

transformed this. His *Cosroès,* instead of being heavily indebted to the work of others, has the especial interest of being
itself the inspiration of a still finer play by a greater man.
It appeared in 1648-9, and either late in 1650 or early in 1651
Corneille presented his *Nicomède,* which deals with essentially
the same situation of an aging king in the Near East and his
second wife and her efforts to supplant with their son the rightful heir to the throne, the son of his first marriage. But
whereas Corneille makes of this theme a heroic comedy, Rotrou
more logically gave his play a tragic outcome, with the question
posed of a son's right under any circumstances to revolt against
his father, and with the grim suggestion of the eternal recur-
rence of the same situation, when once created; for Chosroes
had similarly destroyed his own father, and Siroes at the end
of the play seems destined for similar remorse.

Cosroès contains no act that is the equal of the fourth act
of *Venceslas,* but it is better sustained throughout, and its
entire first half is of a really notable excellence. True, in the
latter part of Act III and in Act IV it deteriorates, chiefly
because of the intrusion here of the unnecessary and conventional figure of Narsea, with the hackneyed story of children
exchanged in infancy; this was doubtless prompted by an ill-
advised desire to supply the play with a "love-interest," but
Narsea at least serves the function of showing yet another distressing complication which may result from such violence to
family ties as the *coup d'état* of Siroes entails. Act V, however, returns to something like the standard of the first two
and a half acts. Though *Cosroès* does not possess the emotional intensity of *Venceslas* nor any figure so vivid and vital
as Prince Ladislaus, it is written with naturalness, firm imagi-
native grasp of detail, and restrained power, and has an unusual number of well conceived and clearly presented characters.

CHARACTERS IN THE PLAY

CHOSROES, *King of Persia; son of Hormisdas, the preceding King, whom he murdered.*

SIRA, *wife of Chosroes and Queen of Persia; formerly wife of Sapor, King of Armenia.*

SIROES, *son of Chosroes by his earlier wife, Abdenede.*

NARSEA, *reputed daughter of Sapor and Sira; the betrothed of Siroes.*

MARDESANES, *son of Chosroes and Sira.*

SARDARIC, *captain of the palace guard.*

PALMIRAS, *a Persian nobleman.*

HORMISDATE, *female attendant and confidante of Sira.*

ARTANASDES, *brother of Hormisdate.*

PHARNACES, *a Persian nobleman.*

Satraps.

Guards.

The scene is a room in the palace of the King of Persia.

"Chosroes" and "Siroes" are three-syllable words, accented on the first syllable as are "Pharnaces" and "Sardaric." "Abdenede" and "Hormisdate" are four-syllable words. The accent is on the penult in "Hormisdas," "Abdenede," "Narsea," "Mardesanes," "Palmiras," and "Artanasdes"; on the antepenult in "Hormisdate."

Chosroes

ACT I

SIROES *and* SIRA *are discovered.*

SIRA. What! thou against my son! thou, his base brother!
Thou, insolent man!

SIROES. Madam, be not so angry!

SIRA. And to include me also in your difference!

SIROES. I honor thee as queen, him as a kinsman;
But if he invents a phantom to contend with . . .

SIRA. I know the way, wretch . . .

SIROES *(aside)*. Ah, my cruel step-mother!

SIRA. To make whoe'er offends him lose his life,
And show my love for him 'gainst all who hate him.

SIROES. If the blood-tie, madam, which binds him to me
Did not assoil me of such blame as this,
To teach how far I owe respect to him
The love thou plainly bearest him doth suffice,
And that we in thy son behold thine image,
And that we cannot reverence him enough.
By these considerations governed, I
Have the respect for him he owes to me.

SIRA. He, to thee!

SIROES. Yes, to me. The mood in which
I find thee tries my patience all too sorely;
And thou, thy Majesty, if thou spokest calmly,
Wouldst praise my self-control and my discretion.
My sire is Chosroes, and my mother was
A princess: and my age compared with his,
The rights of primogeniture, and the fact
That I have shed my blood in the State's cause,
Give me, without conceit, some rank above him,
And make sufficient difference between us
To obligate him to show to me some deference.
But, madam, let us leave this graceless theme.

SIRA. Comparest thou Abdenede's blood and mine?

SIROES. I well know that her birth, to thine not equal,
Could nowise boast it was from royal stock,
And that, ere Persia owned thy sway, thou wast
Already the sister, child, and widow of kings.
But still thou knowest my mother, before thee,

273

Possessed the power and my father's heart;
And that is, doubtless, the more glorious honor
Which makes all eyes be turned towards thee, today.

SIRA.   When he made me the sharer of his splendor,
I in alliance bore my crown to him.
I purchased thus the estate that here is mine,
And like my life I joined my realm to his.
I with a diadem must needs seem fair,
While Abdenede brought him but herself
And yet that treasure was of no great worth.

SIROES.   Only through my profound respect for thee
Can I endure thy words of bitter scorn.

SIRA.   Thou still complainest, after thine insolence?

SIROES.   Thou canst not speak except with violence.
This frenzy ill befits the rank thou holdest.

SIRA.   It well befits my quelling of mutinous spirits.
I am right to avenge thy insults to my son
And keep myself informed of thy distempers.

SIROES.   I know it only injures me with thee
That I can have the hope to rule this realm;
And if my sire would hearken to what thou sayest,
My ruin would ere long prove my fears just.
Thanks to his grace to thee, in which thou trustest,
Thy son e'en now has one foot on the throne,
And by thine aid he soon would have the other
Also, if his ambition matched thine own.
But in this great design that busieth thee
He sees the perils which attend usurpers;
He sees before their feet dire precipices
And knows that tyrants oft are immolated.
He knows a supreme Lord dwells in the skies
Who tears the scepter from their guilty hands
And hath his thunder for this kind of crime
To fall in the defense of lawful princes.
The sin might please thy son; the punishment
Makes him close fast his ears to thine ambition.

SIRA.   This is indeed to declare war against us,
Thus threatening us with heaven and with earth.
We shall see what will be the consequences;
I will die, traitor, or my son shall reign.

SIROES (*laying his hand on his sword*).   Then must this blade prove
           useless to me, first,
This heart cold, and this right arm powerless.

CHOSROES

Enter MARDESANES, *with the baton of a commanding general.*

MARDESANES.   What is it, Siroes, that angers thee?
    How now? thou hast thy hand upon thy sword,
    And the Queen stands before thee! Gods!
SIROES.   I laid
    My hand there, but without ill will except . . .
SIRA.   Except just merely to attempt my life!

                              [*Exit* SIRA, *furious.*

SIROES.   Sun, to whose sight our hearts are nowise hid,
    Witness and judge of all, thou knowest the truth
    And guardest it too well to leave unpunished
    So foul and odious a calumny!
MARDESANES.   Was it I that was the subject of your quarrel?
SIROES.   She told me of her diligence for thee
    Which is to set the crown upon thy brow.
MARDESANES.   Can anyone destroy thy right to it?
SIROES.   I showed this sword to her, as my defense
    If in my life I saw another have it.
MARDESANES.   But were we not at one about this matter?
SIROES.   I was, with thee, but not with her; and her
    Ambition, if her influence be not futile,
    Will put the scepter in thy hands despite thee.
    But do not wish that she may be successful;
    She cannot render thee a less good service,
    And I do more for thee, turning thee from it,
    Than she in offering it and crowning thee.
MARDESANES.   Art thou disquieted by a mother's zeal
    Who loves to please herself with this vain hope?
    Let her beguile her heart with such delusions
    And find her joy in fashioning fair visions,
    Nursing a lovely dream. Leave her that comfort,
    And laugh at plans which can bring no result;
    And yet the while, trusting the faith I owe thee,
    Respect in her the passion of the King.
    Spare thou his madness and the griefs that crush him,
    That make him careless of all other matters,
    Whence in his woe all things but vex and pain him.
SIROES.   I have for him respect that gains me naught;
    But whether I shall win his love or hate,
    I needs must let the Queen's wrath take its course,
    And learn what time and the event shall teach.
MARDESANES.   Unchanged are thy suspicions and my feelings,
    And I esteem too little a crown's glory

To rack my spirit with the cares it gives thee.
'Tis but a splendid yoke. Repose is sweeter.

SIROES. Thou needest do naught; another works for thee;
And thou canst judge if empire hath its charms
By those thou findest in our host's command.
This truncheon, which the King has given thee,
Hath made thee lord already o'er the soldiers;
But when a little time hath taught to thee,
By this authority, the joy of ruling
And seeing a whole State beneath thy sway,
'Twill please thee better changed into a scepter,
And the trial which thou thus wilt make of empire
Will lead thee without difficulty where
Thy mother wishes. Thou'lt deny her nothing.

MARDESANES. That is but thy opinion; 'tis not mine.
I feel myself, indeed, in spirit and lineage
Fit to possess and use this noble power;
But howso fair may be the circlet royal,
It would not please me on a brow disloyal.
Europe, that hath so many sovereign kingdoms,
Offers enough crowns to my princely blood,
To die for nobly or not be without one,
Whatever charms they may possess for me.
But make assurance doubly sure; enlist
Thy friends; have vengeance ready to fall on me;
Set up thy standard; form so strong a party
That it will quite dispel this new-born specter,
This usurpation, this my reign, which thou
Canst not excuse in a fond mother's fancy.

SIROES. Since thou so wishest, I must needs excuse it
And on thy honor dare repose my faith.
But keep this counsel in thy memory:
If, after having forced me by thy protest
To trust thee, thou dost find ambition sweeter
And yieldest to its seduction, spare me not;
Yes, to confirm thy destined fortune, ere
Thou joyest in thy prize, be sure to slay me.
Remove all obstacles, and make my tomb
Serve as foundation of the usurpèd throne.
Let my blood bathe it ere thou sittest thereon,
Or think not that thou long shalt be my master.

Enter PALMIRAS *in the background.*

MARDESANES. It is indeed not easy to convince thee.

Palmiras, seeing me, dares not accost thee.
He blames me, too, for his humiliation.
(*To* PALMIRAS)   Approach. I shall withdraw and yield to thee
My place. My presence is inopportune
For thee.   [*Exit* MARDESANES.
PALMIRAS (*coming forward and gazing after his retreating figure*).
        Thou dost not well, to yield it to me,
E'en as thou didst not well to sue to have
Mine office and to dispossess me of it.
But now when Sira reigns, what boots it me
To make complaint? What can I hope from her
Or what must I not fear? A woman's wrath
Abideth long, and my weak influence
Tried quite in vain to fortify itself
And overcome those efforts that could blast it,
Seeing that it struggled to maintain itself
'Gainst the King's wife. Because I dared to oppose
Their marriage, she hath nursed this project long
Within her breast, and when all power is hers
Now, when she is supreme, her hate bursts out.
    (*To* SIROES)   This my experience, Prince, speaks to thee
        plainly.
Be warned by my example, and avert
Such blows of fortune; profit by my ruin;
It should instruct thee; and, made wise, destroy
Quickly whoso is able to destroy thee,
Or the same thunderbolt shall fall on thee.
SIROES (*walking back and forth, and meditating*).
    "I will die, traitor, or my son shall reign."
After this threat, what have I still to ponder?
Yes, Mardesanes will sit on the throne
Instead of me! and his proud mother will
Before mine eyes beguile my father's mind,
Which madness hath impaired, and by the power
Her influence o'er him giveth her will set
My crown upon the brow where she desires it!
What crime or what defect is mine, that one
May snatch my scepter and bestow it elsewhere?
My birth, my mother, is there blame in them?
Are we unfit to fill a glorious station?
Would any, after twenty years, besmirch
E'en in the tomb a virtue once so fair?
Nay, nay, my mother, time with too much honor
Still keeps thy memory living in men's hearts.

For centuries it will be a thing illustrious
Which hate shall reverence and cannot stain.
My sole crime lies in having a proud step-mother
Who loves her son, and whom my father worships.
The marriage that placed her in Chosroes' bed
Robbed Siroes of his ancestral right!
    Celestial guardians of the power of kings,
Ye gods who o'er the fate of crowns preside,
Sovereign upholders of the cause of sovereigns,
Sustain this day the laws' authority,
Destroy the power of bourgeoning usurpation,
And 'stablish, firmly propped, a tottering throne!
PALMIRAS.   Thyself sustain it, Prince; lend it thine arm.
Heaven helps not him who doth not help himself.
When thou canst act, reserve the thunderbolt.
Before the aid of heaven, use that of earth;
Use thy friends' aid, thine own, and the occasion's,
And furnish discontented souls a leader.
    Thou'lt see a faction formed for thee with ease.
Within it see already the whole army,
Whom our refusal twice of peace with Rome
Makes mutinous in righteous indignation,
And who, preferring me to the general sent them,
Will joyfully obey my secret orders.
The angered satraps in a body also
Offer support to thy authority;
For all, though cleaving to thee with one consent,
Have various different matters to avenge.
Some of them, thinking on Hormisdas' death,
Are still offended by that monstrous crime,
And would with joy and eagerness behold
A second parricide repay the first.
Others, deposed from office, are awaiting
The least occasion to declare themselves;
And others yet, whose family honor hath
Been touched by wrongs done to their wives or daughters,
Too weak for vengeance, have till some fit day
Concealed alike their hatred and dismay.
    The people see thee as a rising sun,
And, ill enduring him who holds thee back,
Detest the sight of one so far declined
Prolonging thus his witless, feeble age.
His mind, wracked by his murder of his father,
Hath undergone a total change through brooding,

And since he is no longer sane one instant,
He remains king only in name and lineage.
A woman is in all things else the ruler;
All Persia acts and moves by her caprice,
And soon shall through her son, whom she will crown,
Receive from her the laws which thou shouldst give.
Bethink thee, for thine own sake do thyself
Justice; seize what is thine lest it be snatched
From thee. Whoever dareth to thy place
Pretend, by the same crime desires thy blood.
The Queen, who fears thee, is too politic
To leave one who could feed men's hate of her,
And to dare, when she drives thee from the throne,
To spare thee. 'Tis a case of die or reign.
    Do thou but authorize our proffered aid.
When one can strike first, to delay is weakness.
All the King's influence will ne'er suffice,
When he hath been dethroned, to form a faction.
Persia, revolting 'gainst his policies,
Will show her hate for public wrongs and private,
Avenge her palaces and strongholds burned,
Her proscribed satraps, her exhausted riches,
And the blood vainly poured out by her people
So many times against the Roman legions.

SIROES. *(thoughtfully).* To let one's throne be stolen is craven, but
    To drive one's father thence is impious.
PALMIRAS. Which he, to teach thee how, himself hath been!
SIROES. Alas, doth his example justify me
    Better, and shall it cause me less repentance?
PALMIRAS. Thou dost not drive him from the throne, since he
    Desires to leave it, or since thy step-mother,
    To speak more accurately, drives him from it
    So that her son shall occupy thy place there.
SIROES. He gave me life.
PALMIRAS.   He gives away thy birthright.
SIROES. Yet 'tis my father.
PALMIRAS.   Hormisdas was *his* father;
    And if thou art so faint of heart, beware
    Of being the victim of his second crime.
    He who spares not the blood from which he sprang
    May well not spare that which proceeds from him.
SIROES. O bitter destiny! O cursèd fortune!
    Upon my side are reason, right, and nature;
    And by a sad fate, like no other's, they

Are 'gainst me, if I follow their advice.
Though lawful heir unto my father's scepter,
I cannot hope to have it, save by crime.
Guilty, I stain it; innocent, I lose it.
If my right crowneth me, my sire must wear
Chains, and I risk my life if I do not
Impiously quench the source from which 'twas mine.
O father, mine own blood, can I not spare thee?
Can I not innocently either live or reign?
Can I not sit on our ancestral throne
Save by my sire's imprisonment or death?

PALMIRAS.　My lord, I see these thoughts must be allowed
　　Some while yet to thy piety.
SIROES.　　　　　　　　　　What can
　　The wrath which animates me 'gainst Sira do
　　When I adore the Princess, her fair daughter,
　　Whose power o'er me can bring to naught my plans
　　And in the midst of all my rage disarm me?
PALMIRAS.　What! dost thou love Narsea?
SIROES.　　　　　　　　　　　I worship her.
　　Our love is secret; the Queen knows not of it;
　　But in us both its flame burns.
PALMIRAS.　　　　　　　　Reign, and I
　　Promise thee happiness in thy love. But what
　　Would Pharnaces with thee? He serves thee well.

Enter PHARNACES.

PHARNACES (*to* SIROES).　O gods! Knowest thou the news, sir, from the
　　　　camp?
SIROES.　What news?
PHARNACES (*looking around him cautiously*).　That thou'rt betrayed,
　　　　and that the King
　　　　Means ... but ...
SIROES.　　　　　　　Speak without fear. None heareth us.
PHARNACES.　Disdaining *thy* rights and the Persian law,
　　To crown, before the army, Mardesanes.
PALMIRAS.　Behold if I was right, great prince, and if
　　I gave too soon my counsel, ere 'twas needed.
　　(*To* PHARNACES)　But what effect had this upon the host?
PHARNACES.　'Tis scarce believed, and all men murmur at it.
　　They think this rumor spread to try their hearts,
　　Reveal their thoughts, and learn how strong their feelings;
　　But to it everyone is found ice-cold.
　　Yet 'tis a rumor, sir, which threatens thee

And nowise ought to leave thy wrath unstirred.
All hearts are thine, as justice bids. Howe'er
They feign, they cannot see without distress
The King permit so much to the Queen's pride,
Act as her subject, and unworthily
Leave all the government unto her care.
"Is it strange," they say, "if nothing prospers with us?
Insanity or Sira ever rules him.
What might he do, thus frenzied or enchanted,
By one bereft of reason, by the other
Disarmed?" Loud runs this murmur through the host,
Which still is shaken by its leader's loss:

                            [He indicates PALMIRAS.
And if 'tis brought to give thee its allegiance
And hear the treaty which the Romans offer,
Vain are the Queen's plots for her son against thee.
I stake my head, sir, that the throne is thine
When all would give their lives in thy support.

SIROES. *(to himself)*. "I will die, traitor, or my son shall reign."
    (To PHARNACES)   Yes, let her die, and us reign, Pharnaces.
I will debate no more after this threat.
If from her wrath the throne can shelter us,
I place myself in your hands, faithful friends.
Clear me the road there; climb we to its refuge.
Render her pride and hatred ineffectual.
To uphold the majesty of the law we must
Forget our blood-ties and maintain our rights.
Persia, by them, demands me of myself;
She rejects Mardesanes, and desires
That I command. Yes, Princes; yes, my rights;
Yes, Persia; yes, my country. 'Tis your wish
That I be king, and I obey you. Fain
Am I to hold through you the hoped-for scepter,
And I will recognize no more my father
Against your counsels; nay, I wish to hold it
In order to avenge you, to avenge
Myself, and share it with you—yes, with you,
Worthy inspirers to this noble boldness,
Who call me to the throne and show me there
My place.

PALMIRAS.   I vainly sought for Siroes
In one so sluggish and so chill of mood.
I recognize him by this high-souled ardor.
'Tis with such manly aspect, sir, that he

COSROES

Must needs appear. Persia will know her master
By this great heart. The occasion beckons. Come;
Let us lose no more time; let us seek out
The nobles, win the citizens, enlist
Our friends, and, the conspiracy once formed,
Keep watch on Mardesanes, to the army
Declare ourselves, and promising to hearken
Unto the terms the Romans offer, move
Aemilius to lend to us his aid.

ACT II

CHOSROES, SIRA, SARDARIC, *and guards are discovered.*

CHOSROES (*to himself, in a seizure of madness*).
    Black deities, pitiless maidens, frightful ministers
    Of heaven's vengeance, cruel fiends, redouble
    Or stay your efforts to leave life to me
    Or to give death. No longer has this body
    A spot you have not wounded yet; no longer
    Is there a place left for your snakes to bite;
    And among all the paths which ye have shown me,
    I can find none to lead me down to hell.
    It is in sparing me that death is cruel;
    I cannot come whither my father calls me.
    Complete ye my destruction; in his tomb
    Shut up with him his son and slaughterer.
SIRA (*to* CHOSROES).   Drive from thy soul these melancholy cares
    Which bring such unreal things before thine eyes.
    'Tis by hallucinations thou art frightened.
    Thou seest naught of all that thou dost see.
CHOSROES.   What! Hearest thou not from the depths of yon abyss
    A fearful voice reproach me for my crime,
    Picture the horror of that monstrous deed
    To me, and 'gainst mine own breast urge my hand?
    And canst thou not espy in yon thick mist
    The shadowy image of my dying father,
    Who orders that I quit his throne usurped
    And shows to me the place where fell my blow?
    Seest thou not, issuing from yon dreadful chasm
    Which belches fire and sulphur and bitumin,
    A fleshless ghost stretching an arm to me,
    Who bids me to descend there, following him?
    O deadly poison, malady of great souls,

Cursèd ambition, unto which I hearkened
And which, to glut thyself, canst stop at nothing,
How dearly hast thou sold me kingship's joys!
To achieve thine aims and give thee satisfaction,
Cruel voice, I had to sacrifice my father.
With the same stroke I sacrificed my peace,
Which endless remorse thwarts at every turn.
There still remains to sacrifice myself
To thee, and in the skies I hear already
The rumblings of the storm that will fall on me,
And its approach makes all the horizon dark.

[He seems to recover his sanity.

SARDARIC *(to* SIRA*)*.   This seizure long hath held his mind in thrall.
SIRA *(to* SARDARIC*)*.   He speaks no more, and now regains his reason.
   (To herself)   Advantage must I take of this occasion,
Strengthen his purpose, learn the precise time
Which is to crown my wishes when it crowns
My son.
   (To CHOSROES*)*   Wilt thou nurse always this remorse
Which still is thine? Unless thou stiflest it,
'Twill work thy death. My lord, forget this ill thing.
To cherish twenty years the memory of it,
Is to be punished for it too severely.
CHOSROES.   The whole realm, where my station is unlawful,
Keeps my thoughts fixed and shows my crime to me.
The hatred of the people and the soldiers
Bears witness to me of Hormisdas' death;
And more than all, alas, my fits of frenzy,
When they possess me, bid me follow him.
Sorrow is mine that they so trouble thee,
And also shame because thou seest them,
But shame yet greater for their monstrous cause,
Which to all showeth me parricide and madman.
SIRA.   While thou yet holdest the reins of government,
Thou still must look on that which caused thy deed.
Yes, neither crown nor scepter canst thou see
Without recalling that a crime bestowed them
Upon thee. Clearly is thy peace impaired,
Still, by the cares of State which still thou hast;
Thy woe makes thee less fit to deal with them.
Cast off this burden ere it crushes thee.
It is a load I must resign with thee,
But I will give up all to save my husband.
Release thy spirit from what afflicteth it.

COSROES

Dearer to me is Chosroes than the King
Of Persia; without him I cannot live,
And living with him I can still be queen
And reign through someone else. The power which passeth
Into our other self leaves in our hands,
Still, the supreme authority, and we
Lose nothing when, though with another name,
Our blood yet holds the same rank.

CHOSROES.   I have too much
Experience, too much evidence have I seen,
O generous physician and support
Of kings, of the close tie our love hath fashioned,
To expect to lose thee if I lost my realm.
I know thy love is to myself attached;
That it regardeth me and not my crown.
So hath this burden long been sweet to me
Because thy bearing it hath done it honor.
I love its splendor only on thy head.
I well know how unworthily I won it.
I cannot wear an ornament so precious
When I recall from what brow I dared snatch it
And know that all that makes it gleam on mine
Is the distinction of a monstrous crime.
If thou wouldst place it, then, on thy son's forehead,
I strip it off with joy; 'tis promised thee.
I cannot guard it by ancestral right,
Since I have stained my hand with my sire's murder.
More justly Mardesanes will succeed;
Let us possess him of his grandsire's throne.
If my acquirement of it was unlawful,
I have enjoyed it without right to do so
And now retain it wrongfully, as I
Wrongfully won it. I despoiled my father
Of it; I balk my sons' hopes of it now.
Let us debate no longer; let us choose
Before the camp a sovereign for the Empire.
Calm and rid of a weight that wearies me,
Without regret I in chill age shall see
My scepter wielded by an abler hand,
My guilty self replaced by innocence.

SARDARIC.   But can he, sire, accept this without sin
Against the first-born's claim and the realm's laws?
(To SIRA) Madam, forgive the freedom of my zeal;
The rights of birth belong to Siroes.

CHOSROES

(*To* CHOSROES)   Wouldst thou see Persia armed against her-
    self?
Wouldst give her war in giving her a king?
Think! of what woes thou makest her the target!
A place so lofty is well worth defending.

SIRA.   Thou whom we worship, Sun, thou art my witness
If my son's interest is at all my care,
And if the ambition which a crown excites
Would take it from myself to adorn another!
Thy good alone, sire, could deprive me of it.
I yield it willingly when I must to save thee.
But putting off the load that weighs thee down,
Consider on which of these two it is better
That it should rest. The advantage of the first-born,
While thou art living, is obscure; as yet,
Doth his seniority have no actual rights.
A king who fleeth care, whom age bows down,
Can lean upon whomever he may please to,
And, that his laws may be dispensed by others,
Can give a king's prerogatives to his agents.
Siroes, with the rights which he can claim,
As soon as he is reigning will not wish
To be dependent longer, and whilst thou
Thinkest to share the throne with him, thou'lt be
Unto his reign a vexing obstacle.
Thou soon wilt see him, if he finds the chance,
Remove those objects which are irksome to him,
And I can fear yet worse, after the fact
That, if it had not been for Mardesanes,
He would have been my murderer this morning,
And that to this end he had drawn his sword.

CHOSROES.   O gods! what sayest thou?

SIRA.   This did not surprise me.
Deeming my influence fatal to his hopes,
He ne'er hath ceased to assail my power; and all
His grounds are that with thy affection I
Am blest; the son's hate springs from the sire's love.
What can I, then, expect from his enthronement?

CHOSROES.   I will provide for thy security.

SIRA.   Raise Mardesanes to the supreme station,
And thou wilt reign, thyself, sire, in another.
Under the rule which he will see made his,
The State, the King, all will look up to thee,
And for thy comfort, which concerns us most,

His mouth shall utter only thy commands.
Through him wilt thou reign; he will reign through thee;
And it will be thy laws which he will give us.
The cares be his; the glory will be ours.
I know his worth; he is my son and thine,
With whom thy true love honored this my body
And for whom I dare stake my life as surety.

CHOSROES. Now, by the tears I owe my father's ashes,
By the bright chariot of the god I worship,
By the old age still left me, which he lights,
Madam, this day shall Mardesanes reign!
So have I promised thee; and my peace doth urge me,
No less than doth my love, to keep that promise.
Assemble for form's sake the council, Sardaric,
But make all ready for the coronation.

SARDARIC. Where the Queen, sire, seemeth so much concerned,
I dare no more disclose my thought to thee,
But . . .

SIRA. No one wishes to hear thy advice.

SARDARIC. No one hath done amiss who followed it,
Madam; and this design is so important
That it should not too rashly be pursued.
If I foresee its issue, 'tis far-reaching.

SIRA. I will accept thy counsels when I need them.
Yet, to attempt naught to our own confusion,
Arrest thou Siroes; guard him well for me.

SARDARIC. Great king, if thou wouldst see thy people rage,
The army and the whole realm rise against thee,
Lay this command on me; have him arrested.

CHOSROES. Not to obey, will cost thy head.

SARDARIC (*to himself*). O gods,
Ye whose decrees are past our understanding,
Bring unto naught the horrors I foresee.

[*Exeunt* SARDARIC *and guards.*

SIRA. If great men heeded everything said to them,
They would resolve on nothing and fear all things.
The populace speak much, but they do little,
And after its first blaze, their fire dies down.
In any case, a terrible example
Made of one leader in this insurrection
Will all the rest disarm.

Enter MARDESANES.

CHOSROES (*to* MARDESANES). Come here. This realm,

Weary of bending to my governance,
And my own peace, both, ask of us a king.
Prince, let us give them one. Collect thyself.
MARDESANES (*aside*). Fatal ambition, hide thy lure from me!
CHOSROES. My days of life, which draw near their last night,
    And those infirmities which trouble them
    And which will call me soon to meet my Judge,
    Permit me even in death to serve my realm.
    The cares and labors which have aged me so
    Still cannot quite engulf me in the grave.
    Despite the attempts of time and Fate, I have
    Means to prolong my honors and my years,
    Whence, though I cease to reign, I will extend
    My reign, and start it o'er by seeing the next one,—
    Will quit the throne and still be master here.
    And, Mardesanes, 'tis in thee I fain
    Would be reborn and start it o'er again.
    Staunchly support the arm that is to crown thee.
    'Tis the reward I owe to Sira's love.
    Fulfil aright thine office and our hopes,
    And represent him well who hath preferred thee.
MARDESANES. I am thine, mighty prince; I would be jealous
    If any were in serving thee more zealous.
    I know how much I owe to thy great love;
    I am myself the pledge and witness of it;
    And even if thou hadst crowned me in the cradle,
    Thou gavest me more in giving life to me.
    How can I, then, make better use of it,
    Choose better work, than to sustain thine age?
    Employ me, sire; thereby shall I be honored;
    To bear thy burden will be dear to me:
    But, setting me that task, remain the sovereign.
    Depute the power to me, but keep thy rank;
    Or if thou layest aside both rank and power,
    Bethink thee unto whom thou oughtest to give them.
    By the realm's law, the hereditary scepter
    Should from thy hands be passed on to my brother's.
    Make his that bounty which thou hast for me.
CHOSROES. A father's mandate is the highest law.
SIRA. Vain mother-love, affection that but vexes,
    How tamely are thy gracious gifts received!
    I have brought forth a child unworthy of me
    And cannot recognize in him my blood.
    Though nobly reared, and born to govern, he

Has not acquired the feelings of a prince.
The offer made to him of sovereign power
Finds in his breast a heart irresolute!
MARDESANES.   Rouse not the fires of one who lacks not ardor!
I have all feelings that befit great souls,
And my ambition summons me full loudly
To the station I refuse and thou'dst force on me.
Too much a throne allures; one mounts it gladly;
But one should scan the road which leads one to it
And not press on thereto, only to leave it
Soon, and to find there naught save great repentance.
If I might dare, sire, to name thy example,
The proof that I speak truly, would be ample.
    Enough my hand by this baton is honored
Without a scepter. Great king, by the Genius
That watches over States; by all his cares
Which make thine prosper; by the blood of Cyrus,
The noble source of our blood; by the ghost
Of Hormisdas; by thine own unconquered arm,
Which Heraclius stands in dread of, still;
And by the worth and merit of the Queen
Herself, whose love solicits thee for me,—
Minister not to the fires of her affection,
And, deaf for my sake once unto her prayers,
Permit in me a wise disdain of empire;
Save from a mother's love my rectitude!
    Thou makest me the target of what perils,
If thy consent approveth her design!
The Greeks and Romans even to our walls
Will the whole body of the State devour,
And with their fortunes thus triumphant always,
In this last refuge will attack its heart.
My brother has the good will of the satraps,
And the occasion offered them for vengeance
Supplies for their revolt a pious pretext
And will make all their enmity burst forth.
Can a Palmiras, swollen with his renown,
Dismissed from office now and from the army,—
A Pharnaces, a Saïn, in whose breasts
Hate burns because their fathers were proscribed,—
Neglect so rare an opportunity
When it presents itself, nay, cries out to them?
If the enemy, justice, and our great men
Are all against me, to my luckless cause

Who will stand loyal? The authority
Which thou wilt have laid down, will be by whom
Feared or respected in this time of strife
If I must break the law when I dispense it?
Beware lest thou, in honoring me, destroy me.
He who would lawlessly usurp a right
Is crowned oft-times a victim, not a king;
Oft is the State a shrine, the throne an altar,
Where that poor wretch awaits the mortal blow.

CHOSROES.   Thou fearest to reign because of inexperience.
Of confidence and boldness there is need.
A scepter greatly loses weight, when borne.
Thy rule, established once, will seem legitimate.
My orders have kept factionists from gathering.
The arrest of Siroes will check their intrigues.
If some disturbance rises, I will quell it.
Against all rebels shall my power support thee;
I can consign my crown to whom I please to,
And this is reason enough: I bid thee wear it.

MARDESANES.   Since 'tis a gift from thee, I cannot spurn it.
Thou willest that I reign. I must obey thee;
But with regret I rise, sure of my downfall.
Pray heaven, may only *my* life be imperilled!
(*To* SIRA)   Ah, madam, thy love bears for me what fruit!

Enter SIROES.

SIROES.   What rumor, sire, is spreading through the Court?
What blind rage, what unconquerable hate
Maketh the Queen complain against me always?
I know too well how much thou prizest her
To fail in reverence towards one thou lovest.
If truthfully her memory will bear witness,
She knows how well I honor thee in her,
And oft would I have o'ercome her dislike,
If by submissiveness all hearts were softened.
If 'twere not ill to boast my services,
I could have mentioned to her, among other
Service, the blood I shed not long ago
To save her son, surrounded by the foe.
Prince, thou rememberest it. And thou, too, madam.

MARDESANES.   I keep that memory cherished in my breast.

SIRA.   Frequently thou hast cast this up to us,
And hast informed us of it quite enough.
But I have now the right to disregard it

When thou hast threatened me, and I am doubtful
Whether thou wouldst have shed thy blood for him
When thou wouldst fain take *my* heart's blood in turn.

SIROES. So rare a deed would be well worthy of me,
And thou wouldst set me in the King's good graces
In sooth, if this vile story won his credence.
But I have greater trust in his discernment.

SIRA. The intended blow, forestalled by Mardesanes,
Was that of a vile soul; my story was not.

SIROES. O heaven, against this false charge defend me!

SIRA (*to* CHOSROES). Thou seest, each word he uttereth insults me.

SIROES. Thy son, who speaks not, serves thy wishes ill,
And . . .

CHOSROES. We shall learn the whole truth at more leisure.
Important business takes me to the camp.
Meantime, bow to the mandate which concerns thee,
Prince. 'Tis from me.
    [*He goes out, followed by the Queen, who looks at*
    SIROES *triumphantly.*

MARDESANES (*to himself*). Thou virtue fraught with perils,
Fatal obedience, whither dost thou lead me!
        [*He goes out. Enter* SARDARIC, *with guards.*

SIROES. What mandate, Sardaric, hast thou from the Queen?
The King does naught except to serve her hate.
'Tis she who speaks in all that he commands.

SARDARIC. Ah, my lord, hold in fear this perilous spirit!

SIROES. The mandate?

SARDARIC. 'Tis that I am to arrest thee.
Not to obey it, hazards mine own head;
But I have not so soon forgot thy favors.
I lay my head and office at thy feet.
Seed of great Cyrus and so many sovereigns,
Preserve thou, Prince, the traits of thy forefathers.
'Tis time to stand forth, to see thy decrees
Govern the destinies of thrones and peoples.
The King will in the camp proclaim thy brother.
Destroy his faction with a hostile faction.
If thou declarest thyself, their plans are vain.
Fortune will aid thee; but lend helpers to it.
'Tis time to wrest from a step-mother's hands
The realm which calls to thee and worships thee.
There is no deference which should restrain
The gallant boldness which must needs uphold thee.
Besides the crown, thy life is now at stake.

The populace are thine; thine is the army.
At the first order Pharnaces and Palmiras
Will arm those men whose hearts they have won over.
For thee, the whole realm is in one vast plot.

SIROES (*embracing* SARDARIC). And best of all things, Sardaric is mine.
For guarantee against a dolorous fate
I have the arm on my side that was chosen
To be the instrument of my destruction.
Come, let us launch, and not await, the lightning;
Weigh well the means by which we must succeed;
But make me reign to reign with me, and give
Thyself a comrade rather than a king.

ACT III

SIRA *and* HORMISDATE *are discovered.*

SIRA. Now, as I vowed, despite the laws of Persia,
On Cyrus' throne I have placed Mardesanes.
Palmiras, whom I had had thrust from office,
Had not the influence to oppose my choice,
And I have taken the power to do harm
From those concerned who could have slain my son.
Above all, Siroes, seized by my command,
Can raise no obstacle to our control,
And Mardesanes, finally, as successor
Of Artaxerxes, reigns and doth today
Administer the destiny of Persia.

HORMISDATE. Madam, forgive me if I say again
Thou hast accomplished a design most daring.
Thou knowest my heart; pray heaven that the result
Be of the nature which thou hast conceived.
But, if my thoughts have any weight with thee,
I glimpse great perils in this great success.
A State so loyal to its rightful sovereigns
To see without regret its laws o'erthrown,
To see a government affecting all men
Pass for no reason to what hands thou choosest,
And without wrath to suffer it that chains
Bind him who lawfully should hold the reins,
To accept such yoke as thou art pleased to give it—
These things I am unable to imagine.
In the bewilderment caused by surprise,
One may not combat a bold enterprise:

But viewing it with more collected spirit,
One, if he can, undoes what he permitted.
A great success may end in great misfortune,
And matters quickly wear a different face.
Treacherous is Fate, fickle the populace.

SIRA. The arrest of Siroes rids me of this fear;
It chills the ardor of his partisans.
But if thou carest to keep him from escaping,
And holdest dear my peace, and this day darest
To prove the consequences of my favor
(As my affection wishes to believe),
Make thine my fortunes, my Hormisdate,
And in my cause enlisting thyself blindly,
Lay the foundations of a great career.

HORMISDATE. Love loseth value when one sues for it.
If mine, dear madam, is of any worth,
Regard its naked self, and be concerned
With but its purity, which enough is shown thee.

SIRA. Can I depend upon thy brother?

HORMISDATE. Madam,
He is all thine, and would do all to please thee.
I answer to thee for his loyalty,
Which for thy sake would make him give his life.

SIRA. I ask its proof, and if I am ungrateful,
May I see brought to naught the hopes I cherish!

HORMISDATE. What proof?

SIRA (*giving her a dagger and a cup*). By his hands let the Prince in
prison
Be given from me this sharp blade and this poison
And choose his death by one of these two means.

HORMISDATE. Just gods! what insults hast thou borne from him,
To carry to this point thy hatred of him?

SIRA. Or if he will not, let thy brother be
The means of it.

HORMISDATE. Madam, when I but think
Of such a fell design, I seem to see
The wrath of heaven descend upon me; I
Stand speechless, and I shake with horror at it.

SIRA. I need a hardier soul to serve my hate.
One pays a cheap price for that State whose conquest
And assured sovereignty cost but one head.
I will exalt thy brother to such station
That no one, save mine own blood, will be higher;
And the place which he will hold in the ministry . . .

CHOSROES

HORMISDATE. Subjects must needs be silent and obey.
    By such a strong bond thou hast bound me to thee
    That in thine interests I make no question.
    Madam, I serve thy wrath without delay
    And bear this gift and order to my brother.
    Yet do I fear it is a fatal service
    I do thee, and I dare say further, that
    I auger ill thereof.   [*She goes out.*
SIRA (*alone*).   That one who trusts
    The gods' decrees, trusts not in auguries.
    They have ere this determined all my fortunes.
    I dare all, laughing at those prudent cowards
    Who tremble at the thought of what may chance.
    In great designs vain is so much precaution.
    I mean to rid the State of him I loathe,
    And seek my vengeance rather than my safety.

    Enter SARDARIC *and guards. She sees them.*

    Hath the charge given thee, Sardaric, been performed?
SARDARIC. Nay, I perform another with regret,
    Madam.
SIRA.   What?
SARDARIC.   To arrest thee.
SIRA.   How audacious
    Thou art! Me, rash man?
SARDARIC.   Thee.
SIRA.   For whom?
SARDARIC.   The King.
SIRA. Impostor! Chosroes lays this charge on thee?
SARDARIC. Hath Chosroes not resigned the crown?
SIRA.   What, then?
    Is it my son who thus commands thee, traitor?
SARDARIC. Thy son command me! In what capacity?
SIRA. That of thy king, thy master, insolent dog!
SARDARIC. Siroes is my king; he is my master.
    Persia hath just acclaimed him with these titles.
SIRA. Gods!
SARDARIC.   And to bring thee to acknowledge him
    With us, we are expressly bidden to seize thee.
SIRA. Thou, faithless man, to seize me?
SARDARIC.   Thee, none other.
SIRA (*looking around her*). And this effrontery is left unpunished!
    A traitor, a false wretch, my assigned guard,
    Lays hand upon me, serves mine enemies!

With all my influence and all my power,
I find none to defend me in my need.
Ye flatterers, weak friends, vile pests of Courts,
Base adulators, I await your help;—
Where now is your importunate multitude?
Offer ye sacrifice to Fortune only?
And, to be instantly abandoned by you,
Need we receive but one shaft of her anger?
What! not one loyal soul, not one true subject,
Here in Persepolis, in the royal palace?
My moan is useless and my cries are vain,
And in the Court the Court is found no more!

SARDARIC.   Come, on thy side no one is to be found.

SIRA.   Gods will espouse it, if Fate turneth from it.
They watch too well over the cause of kings
To let the majesty of the law be outraged.

SARDARIC.   'Tis in their justice Siroes puts his trust.

SIRA.   After he has usurped his father's throne?

SARDARIC.   After thy son would fain have usurped his.
But, madam, I obey and question nothing.

SIRA.   Unless quite all be lost, my vengeance, traitor,
Will give me thy head and thy master's head.

SARDARIC.   The weaker side will bow before the stronger;
But news of thine imprisonment is awaited,
Madam, and thou canst see that some last deference
Forbids my hesitant arm the use of force.
Most loath to treat thee with indignity
Am I. Come, spare us this necessity.

SIRA.   'Tis nowise marvelous that a faithless subject
Still hears the voice of his weak, faltering honor
When by a vile, perfidious act he fain
Would wound in me the body of the State,—
When, in the State's employ, he turns his rage
Not 'gainst the offender, but 'gainst his employer.
Siroes bids thee to imprison me!
The recreant has cloaked his treason long,
Has cleverly seduced hearts and bribed traitors,
Has envied long the power of his masters.
The plot which a whole Court and city share
Is neither one man's task nor one day's work.
Those unto whom in pity I have left
Their heads, have brought this tempest upon mine:
But if its cloud doth dissipate itself
In lightnings' glare; if Fortune (oft inconstant)

Can change, the executioners shall leave,
After this treachery, so memorable
And great a tragedy that never faction
Shall lift itself hereafter without trembling
For dread of the reverse which may o'erwhelm it.

SARDARIC.   I leave these things' disposal unto Fortune;
        But time . . .

SIRA.   Approach; come, drag me if thou darest;
        And if the name which yesterday I saw thee
        Worship, today entirely lacketh homage,
        Tread under foot all reverence, drag me hence,
        And do not expect, traitor, that I shall
        Obey thy master's orders and with broken
        Spirit accept my prison.

    Enter SIROES *and* PALMIRAS. *They hear her last words.*

SIROES.   A truce to pride.
        'Tis now unseasonable, Princess. Grandeur
        Which is no more, is no more to be thought of.
        When it was thine, Queen, I paid reverence to thee.
        Thou as a subject must revere the King,
        Obeying my decrees when I command thee.

SIRA.   Traitor, my place usurped upon my throne!

SIROES.   Rightfully taking my place on my own.

SIRA.   Thine, while thy father lives and while I live?

SIROES.   Mine, though thou seekest to set thy son thereon.

SIRA.   When the King lays the scepter's load on him?

SIROES.   When the land's laws consign it otherwhere?

SIRA.   The King not being dead, thou hast no rights.

SIROES.   He owes me the King's title when he doffs it.

SIRA.   He thinks to serve the nation by his preference.

SIROES.   The nation has decided differently.

SIRA.   Pharnaces and Palmiras are the nation?

SIROES.   They, when my ruin was sought, lent me their aid.

SIRA.   And gave the counsels which have poisoned thee!

SIROES.   The advice they gave me nowise did me harm.

PALMIRAS.   Sire, it beseems thee not to talk so much
        With criminals whose arrest hath been decreed.

SIRA.   Criminals? thou insolent man!

PALMIRAS.   Such insults, madam,
        Are in despair the weapons of a woman,
        They harm us less than they arouse our pity.
        Do thou thine office, Sardaric.

SIRA (*to* SARDARIC).   Let us go.
  Deliver me from the sight of these fell men,
  These loathsome objects, these abominations.
  No matter where I flee, they are more frightful
  Than the blackest cell which will remove me from them.
  Come.   [SARDARIC *and his guards lead out* SIRA.
SIROES.   With sad auspices my reign begins
  If it has birth by blood and punishment.
PALMIRAS.   The blood of enemies is the best foundation
  For thrones where one would seat himself securely;
  Proof of one's power must be shown at outset,
  And pity is in monarchs not a virtue.
  The camp resents denial of thy rights.
  Voices acclaim her son; all hearts are thine.
  In this great strife, one must prevail or die,
  O heir of Cyrus, heir of his dominion!
  What made that mighty king so feared and potent
  Save the proscriptions ushering in his reign?
  Each quarter's chief assures thee of the city;
  Pharnaces and Sarbaras treat with Aemilius;
  I have released the Roman prisoners;
  The Queen is in thy hands, the palace quiet.
  Little is left to do, and by the fall
  Of two heads thine will be made safe from storms.
  Their doom secures thee, and 'tis to this end
  That thou must prove thy mettle, must be strong,
  Must with a manly and rare forcefulness
  Assist the revolution Fate began.
SIROES.   I would be more severe towards other foes,
  But still, though king, I feel myself a son.
PALMIRAS.   Son of a sire who feels himself no longer
  Thy father, knows no son except thy brother,
  And to defraud thee sets him on thy throne!
SIROES.   Reason is on my side; blood's tie is not.
  What destiny is mine that crime alone
  Can preserve for me what is my just right!
  But vain indeed now is all reasoning.
  I shall lament only, and think no more.
  I sorrow for a father's death or flight,
  Yet though I sorrow, still must I pursue him.
  Save on the throne, my life no more is safe.
  All my security lies in my reigning.
  Whereas, before this wrong and outrage done me,
  I lived to rule, I now must rule to live,

And only with the scepter in my hand
Can I ward off the shafts of cruel Fortune.
    Send back the citizens. Make sure of the city,
That it may be, in this great time of change,
Our certain refuge.

PALMIRAS.   If thou arm thy soul
With manhood, all will prosper.

SIROES.   Do thou make
Sure of the leaders' loyalty—neglect naught—
While I subdue a last remaining frailty
Which keepeth still some softness in my heart.

                                [Exit PALMIRAS.
    Would thou hadst given me, Fate, a lowlier rank
And let me taste of peace more calm and pure!
Cruel goddess, the bright stones that crowns are set with
Symbolize well the cares thou givest us,
And such vain ornaments show well the hardness
Of those sharp griefs with which thou stabb'st our hearts.
The crown of which it was proposed to rob me
Is scarcely on my head. But gods, for what
Encounter must I now prepare myself!

               Enter NARSEA.

NARSEA.   Tell me, my lord, by what name I should call thee.
Speak I to him who loves me, or my sovereign;
And seeing thy state as high as I could wish it,
Am I now thy heart's mistress or thy subject?
What is my duty towards thee in thy greatness?
Owe I to thee my homage or my troth?
Tell me what place mine is, and by its distance
From thine, in making our positions clear
Thou wilt make clear what deference I must show thee.

SIROES.   Thy lot is mine; our love hath so decreed;
Nor hath the royal diadem obscured it.
Thou rulest my fortunes, and my heart beats only
In bondage dearer than mine empire is.
Love's chains I value as I do my crown.
I reign, my princess, and I serve thee still.
The land makes me its king; love, thee my queen;
I am its sovereign, and thou art my sovereign;
And all my power, which name of "king" increaseth,
Will not impair the power thou hast o'er me.
E'en those are our positions.

NARSEA.   What blind anger

Makes thee forget, then, that the Queen is my
Mother?

SIROES.   The anger, Princess, or the reason,
Rather, which made me put my sire in prison.
In whatso station Persia this day sees us,
We cannot reign save by this well-known method;
We cannot, save by it, enjoy our love;
We cannot, save by it, keep safe our life.
Kinship or Fortune must be disregarded;
One works our harm, the other makes us prosper.
The ills which we would heal must not be played with,
And 'tis our would-be murderers I arrested.

NARSEA. Our murderers, the authors of our being!

SIROES. The authors of the wrong they wish to do us.

NARSEA. Is empire worth this inhumanity?

SIROES. Was it worth threatening us with such ill treatment,
Or that a blind sire should select for victim
Of the usurper him who should be master?
Power devolveth ill upon faint hearts;
Let us with a king's name have a king's traits.
Even in our own blood let us root out crime,
But above all strike down what strikes at us.
Do I owe aught to one who would arrest me?
Must I thank him for life who would take mine?
Or must I thank thy mother who detests me,—
Who employs all her influence, all her skill,
To balk me of a right which birth has given me,
And having dispossessed me, crown her son?
Thou art my sovereign, Sira is a criminal;
Choose which of us thou wilt espouse the cause of—
A mother in custody or a lover thoroughly
Prepared to hear his enemies pass sentence
Upon him, dooming to the scaffold him
Whose heart, swayed by thy glance, thou hast accepted.

NARSEA. Fearest thou naught more? hath thy provident care
No power to foresee all the misfortunes
The anger of a woman can bring on thee?

SIROES. 'Tis true that someone may smile at us who
Betrays us in his heart and seeks to find
A malcontent to whom to lend his aid
For insurrections and assassinations.
On whatsoe'er foundations it may rest,
New-born authority is always envied,
And people oft, renouncing all allegiance,

Love those distressed whom they have hated prosperous.

NARSEA. A queen in chains, then, is not in distress?

SIROES. She is not likely to be freed from them
Nor given a chance to use the power still hers
Which could elicit servile loyalties.

NARSEA. Hope not for answer, O unwelcome prayers!
Mistress no more am I where Fortune reigns.
Love rules no more where interest is concerned.
Hear me in naught; State policy forbids.
It forces thee to sacrifice all ties.
At least the daughter must with her mother die.
The two, my lord, need but one executioner,—
One prison, one judge, one sentence, and one tomb.
I, born of her, have had all blessings from her,
And I deserve from heaven the same misfortunes.
We are but one blood and one single heart.
I might accomplish that which she began,
Might make my brother's cause mine own against thee,
Devote myself as she did to thy ruin,
Undermine thy authority, and that throne
To which thou hast ascended overthrow.
If thou hast found me fair, beware lest arms
I win against thy power by my charms
And purchase thus some offered heart and hand
With courage to end for me thy life and reign.
Forestall alike all that can injure thee;
Destroy, forewarned, whoever might destroy thee;
Fear thou the blindness of love turned to rage,
And think but of thine own security.
Wouldst thou force me to love my foe? Could I
Endure my mother's murderer in my bed—
Share without horror with her enemy
A power that was cemented by her blood?
   Lead me forth, guards; his safety bids you do so.
Protect his life and crown from my fell fury.
Ah, kinship's ties, to what do your claims drive us
That by my lover my vows grow distrusted,
And to obtain my doom or your indulgence
From him, I threaten that one whom I worship?
From such wild outbursts, judge, sir, of my woe.
I could have gained more with the help of tears,
But in the deepest sorrow they are few.

SIROES. Soldiers, attend your mistress and find Sardaric.
Let him obey the orders which she gives him,

Especially to deliver Sira into
Her keeping. Go.

NARSEA.   This boon costs thee too much.

SIROES.   No, no; I bare my breast to the Queen's rage,
And think no longer of my lawful rights
Nor of the place I hold, save as things lost.
I give thee preference o'er the gods whose grace
Hath sought to save my father's throne for me;
Thou wishest to take it from me, and I must
Obey thee and in blind allegiance to thee
Betray my interests and thine own. I have
But one regret: that my unmeasured love,
In hazarding my life, hazards itself
And at the moment when success smiled on me
I lose the assurance thou wilt e'er be mine.

NARSEA.   Whatever is thy risk, I run the same.
The same couch shall be ours, or the same grave.
I promise to be thine alive or dead.
Marriage shall join our flesh or death our souls.
But if thou wilt consent to trust my love,
I guarantee thee life, the throne, and me.
Mine eyes shall watch the Queen with all the care
Demanded by place, time, and circumstance;
And I dare promise thee a shield of proof,
A heart's guard vigilant and understanding,
Which will protect thee from the swords of foes
Or which they needs must pierce to reach thy breast.

SIROES.   Rule as thou wilt the fortunes of the State.
Use as thou pleasest a despotic power.
Destroy this heart o'er which that power is thine.
It must endure it, truly. Guards, obey her.

A C T   I V

Enter SIROES *and* ARTANASDES.

SIROES (*reading a letter*).
    "This letter voucheth to thy Majesty
      That he confidently may
    Believe the things its bearer comes to say,
    And that I answer for his loyalty.
                         PALMIRAS."

What is it, Artanasdes?

ARTANASDES.   Ah, the mere thought,

Sire, of my dreadful tale doth freeze my blood.
The Queen somehow contrived to look to *my* hand
To execute a hideous plan for her.
Believing thee arrested, through my sister
Thy fell foe bade me give a gift to thee,—
Bade me see thee die to appease her hate,
Or, if thou wouldst not slay thyself, then slay thee.
(*Displaying the dagger and the poison*)   This blade, or else
       this poison . . .

SIROES.   Oh, vile woman!
ARTANASDES.   Were to cut short thine unoffending life.
SIROES.   O gods!
ARTANASDES.   And I accepted the commission
For fear another hand would have discharged it.
She plied my sister with whatever means
Might shake the firmest constancy; and we
As a reward for this great crime, should have
So fine a portion in the posts of State
That all things would be ours, and, save herself,
None would have stations nearer to the crown.
My sister, though, opposing to ambition
One's virtuous recoil from heinous deeds,
And shuddering, horrified, at such a crime,
Embraced this task but to deceive her. I
Feel the same horror for her odious purpose,
And since the matter appertaineth to
Thy Majesty, upon whose life I know
The destiny of Persia doth depend,
I sought Palmiras to come and tell thee of it;
But he, being busy elsewhere, could not do so,
As saith his letter which I have given thee.
SIROES.   Be assured that my gratitude will end,
Good Artanasdes, only with my power,
And that I can repay a service better
Than Sira promised to reward a crime.
Preserve these instruments of mortal hatred
Which is resourceless now, and which we shall
Make impotent, if the gods, hostile to those
Who are so unrelenting, are indeed
Protectors of the interests of kings.
O formidable spirit, cruel step-mother!
Too pious Narsea and her unworthy mother!
ARTANASDES.   No, not her mother, sire. Hereof I have
A secret which will set thy mind at rest.

SIROES. What secret, Artanasdes? Prithee, tell me!
ARTANASDES. Since Persia's fortune takes another face,
   Learn of a thing most happy for thy love,
   Which more than twenty years dared not reveal,
   And by the truth of which it will be seen
   Narsea hath no real tie with the Queen.
SIROES. O gods!
ARTANASDES. When Fate had cut short the third decade
   Of Abdenede, still in her life's morning,
   Soon afterwards the thoughts of Chosroes,
   On banishing his sorrow for her loss,
   Aspired unto Armenia's throne. He planned
   To take up arms; his purpose was accomplished.
   To tell thee of what followed would be needless;
   Enough to say a marriage joined the two crowns,
   And that the age, the rank, and the estate
   Of those concerned found such consent in Sira
   That from one treaty came both peace and nuptials;
   Enough that it is well known that into
   Thy family Sapor's widow brought a daughter
   Of age the tenderest, whose budding life
   Had scarcely beheld six moons wax and wane,
   And that by good chance or by ill the nursing
   Of her was delegated to my sister.
   But of this precious charge the care was hardly
   Accepted when (this secret has been kept)
   A quite unlooked-for seizure of convulsions
   Cut short the little flower's destiny.
   It chanced I then was at Palmiras' house,
   And thither came my sister with a face
   Full of dismay. "Ah, brother, where," she said,
   In sore distress, "can I betake myself
   For shelter from the anger of the Queen?
   Narsea, alas, is dead! She has just died."
   Palmiras, then appearing, heard her sighs
   And had no sooner learned what woe possessed her
   Than instantly he found the remedy,
   And seeing his baby girl there in a cradle,
   Said to us: "Try what fair fate may be hers.
   Let us now seize our chance and watch the outcome
   When Fortune plays a trick on nature thus."
   Narsea so resembled Sydaris
   That not alone their faces were alike
   But similarity of hair and age

Was fortunately theirs, just as of features.
So, to conclude, the care of Sydaris,
Now called Narsea, was given to my sister.
Palmiras, on the other hand, as his daughter,
Buried the Princess and deceived her family,
And sees in this young star-like beauty shine
One whose death twenty years believed and mourned.

SIROES.   O gods! if these words do not cheat mine ears,
What can I ask of you after this marvel?
'Twas justly my reproach, throughout the Court,
That Sira's blood had given love to me;
And hate of her, so natural to my breast,
Forbade me to love aught that came from her.
Too kindly was my heart to think this strange,
Yet in my blindness it made no mistake;
It did naught base and, against my belief,
Loving Narsea, it loved naught of Sira's.
But can I build my faith on one man's story?

ARTANASDES.   If the respect one owes to a king's ears;
If the sincerity of one so loyal
That he hath dwelt long in the royal palace;
If the word, too, of my sister and Palmiras,
Who wrested from an unjust yoke thy kingdom;
If my abandonment of the Queen's cause,
Whose hate I did not serve but held in loathing;
And finally if my life, which I dare stake,
Do not suffice, great prince, to win thy credence,
Put this weak body to the test with tortures.
Thou wilt draw from it naught more wholly true.
My entire life ere now should have established
My probity.

SIROES.   What thanks, kind gods, and what
Good fortune do I owe to you! And thou
Who bringest peace unto my struggling love,
Thy blessings, Artanasdes, will surpass
Thy expectations and will make thy house
Be envied. Come. Keep for me this blade and poison.

Enter SARDARIC *and guards.*

SARDARIC.   Thy greatness, sire, hath no more obstacles.
Each hour, each moment, works new miracles
For thee; and the peace-treaty which Aemilius
Agrees to now, binds Heraclius to thee.
But one more piece of news, much more important,
Which may surpass thine expectation, sire,

Is that the troops, all with one common will,
Are bringing Chosroes and his son as prisoners.

SIROES. Chosroes! I tremble, and despite my wrath,
I know at this sad name my father still.
But in their seizure what command was followed?

SARDARIC. None, save the ardent zeal with which all serve thee.
Scarce had the faint sound of a few forced voices,
Proclaiming Mardesanes, sought to win
The soldiers' minds and hearts, most ill prepared,
When Pacor and Sandoces, whom I had
Suborned, aroused the two corps they command,
Crying out: "Let us see this king of ours!"
Mardesanes at these words, pale, chilled with fright,
Hardly yet reigned ere he was king no more.
Sandoces was the first to seize his person;
Chosroes took alarm; some stir there was;
But both being once arrested, it died down
And instantly a "Long live Siroes!"
Was heard throughout the camp and, testifying
To boundless ardor for thee, offered thee,
United like their voices, every heart.
 Marvel at the good fortune which attends us:
Two kings found in their army not one subject;
Their rally-call was stilled as soon as raised,
And thy name only rang through all the camp.
Pharnaces brings them, and the whole host following,
Expects of thee their loyalty's reward.

SIROES (*bursting into tears*). How vain your splendors, mighty
 sovereigns,
If scepters are so soon exchanged for shackles!

SARDARIC. Relish the boon of such a swift change better,
Nor be ungrateful to the gods who grant it.

SIROES. Sardaric, let my grief exhibit to thee
Not only a king's feelings, but a son's,
Pitying a sire in chains who reigned this day.

SARDARIC. For Persia more than for himself he bred thee.
Think of his crimes and not his wretchedness,
And being thy country's father, mourn not thine.

SIROES. O hapless father, whom I formerly
Obeyed, who wouldst be dear to me if thou
Wert not king, and whose fortunes otherwise
I would respect . . .

SARDARIC.   By the loud noise outside,
I take it that they now are here, my lord.

CHOSROES

One who will let a great plan's outcome lapse
May see time snatch his weapons from his grasp
And give them to the guilty when he cannot
Prevent it. Shall they be brought in?

SIROES.   Stay, stay!
Let me recover first a king's fit temper.
Since I must quench the pity that is in me,
Let me prepare myself for this cruel strife
In which, against the counsels of ambition,
The tie that binds me to my father seeks,
Though I do not confess it, to protect him.
Alas! can I without sin launch this bolt?
What god can pardon me when my tears condemn me?

SARDARIC.   Such weakness, sire, doth not beseem thy station.

SIROES.   To end it, make this tie of blood be silent.
Against its promptings, vain is my resistance. . . .
    Hold them some moments in the adjoining room,
The while I put on that severity
Which now, against my wishes, I must use—
Yes, while my heart prepares itself to hate them
And while I school it to be barbarous.
An odious tyrant, my accurst self-interest,
Demands, O hapless sire, thy doom. In vain
Have I resisted its authority;
The steel that slays thee is thy golden crown!
    Cursed ambition! fatal eminence!
How dearly dost thou sell thy hollow grandeur!
What blessings can ills bring which cost such pain?
    (*To* SARDARIC)   Lead Mardesanes to the tower where
The Queen is, and see to it the King does nothing
While I take counsel briefly with myself.
            [*Exit* SIROES, *followed by* ARTANASDES *and guards.*

SARDARIC (*to himself*).   Fortune, how absolute is thy dominion
Over us all, fatal to those who are
The greatest of mankind, as to the humblest!
All moves by thy caprice, and from thy strokes
Naught in the world can call itself exempt.

Enter NARSEA *and guards.*

NARSEA.   Go with me, Sardaric, and set free the Queen.

SARDARIC.   I deem thee, by thy coming marriage, my sovereign
And, questioning naught, would bow to thy command.
But this is a thing, madam, which concerns
The King too greatly for . . .

305

COSROES

FIRST GUARD ATTENDING NARSEA.   I bear his order
For this and come to inform thee of it.

Enter PALMIRAS.

PALMIRAS.   *I*
Bear one to the contrary; *I* come to forbid it.
NARSEA.   Prince, knowest thou who I am?
PALMIRAS.   Madam, I do,
And know what thou owest me and I owe thee.
But this is not a time to explain myself.
                              [SARDARIC *goes out with the guards.*
NARSEA.   The State is much advantaged by thy counsels.
The strife which troubles it and which thou hast sown,
And the strong factions which thou hast created,
Have in the royal house caused a division
Which from thy zealous loyalty hath being.
PALMIRAS.   By this division thou art so exalted
'Twill be ungrateful of thee not to thank me.
NARSEA.   The Queen in chains, greatness is naught to me.
PALMIRAS.   The realm now knoweth, and hath, no queen but thee.
NARSEA.   Indeed, thou showest me this by thine obedience!
PALMIRAS.   I have done more for thee than thou supposest.
NARSEA.   This last boon proves, especially, thy zeal.
PALMIRAS.   Thou wilt know, some day, whether I am faithful.
NARSEA.   If 'tis the King thou fearest for, I will answer
For his life's safety.
PALMIRAS.   I will answer for it
Without thy care or aid.
NARSEA.   I marvel how
Ardent thou art in his defense.
PALMIRAS.   Time yet
Will teach thee that to be so is a virtue.
NARSEA.   Despite mine anger, I revere the King.
PALMIRAS.   And when thou knowest me thou'lt revere me.
NARSEA.   What a thing to revere! my mother's foe!
PALMIRAS.   *Thy* mother hath been always dear to me.
NARSEA.   At least thou keepest her guarded with great care!
PALMIRAS.   I will explain this better, when 'tis needful.
NARSEA.   And all mine influence, O piteous queen,
Cannot o'ercome thy persecutors' hate;
And the sole answer which my plaints receive is
That he who holds thee now in fetters loves thee!
O cruel affection which results in bondage,
Whereof the fruit is chains, the token fetters!

306

PALMIRAS. Sira's captivity or death is not
    Of any consequence to thy Majesty.
NARSEA. Ah, how endure the grief which overwhelms me!
    The imprisonment of Sira or her death
    Is not of any consequence to me!
    Can he who dares propose so false a code
    To me have lain in any woman's womb,
    Or sucked he from a lioness's breast
    The cruelty that my woe inspires in him?
PALMIRAS. Thy sorrow touches me. O nature's ties,
    'Tis time for me to bare unto the light
    Of day a secret kept for twenty years,
    That ye may be revered e'en where ye should be,
    And that unto his daughter's eyes a father
    May show himself. Nay, nay, my child (this name will
    At first surprise thee) thou hast no least part
    In Sira's evil fortunes, and if I
    Have in some small degree thy credence . . .

Enter ARTANASDES.

ARTANASDES.   Sir,
    Thy presence is impatiently desired.
    The spirit of the King is so irresolute
    He changeth his entire determination
    With each new instant. At the sight of Chosroes,
    Who now is in his frenzy, such keen fear
    Seized Siroes, that, in his perturbation,
    Uncertain and confused, within the space
    Of one same moment he both would and would not.
    Our work is vain, unless his mind, reduced
    Now to this state, regains a firmer seat,
    And there is hope in none but thee to help him.
PALMIRAS. O heaven, from our heads avert thy wrath!
    Save a too pious king from his own weakness
    And save those who have made his fortunes theirs.
    (*To* NARSEA) I go to the King, madam; Artanasdes
    Will, with his sister, finish in my place
    The revelation of my heart to thee,
    And being less concerned than I, will make
    The matter clearer to thee than I could.
                    [*Exit* PALMIRAS, *hastily.*
NARSEA (*to herself*). Gods! what is this enigma, and therefrom
    What am I to infer? What light can I

Find in such darkness, and with how much faith
Ought I to trust the truth of what I hear?

A C T   V

Enter SIRA, SARDARIC, *and guards.*

SIRA.   I, dastard, I, so fear him as to entreat him?
I, whose soul is free in a captive body?
I, to be seized in spirit with some terror
When I have 'neath my sway seen Asia tremble,
And seen my stock, fertile of potentates,
Rule with such splendor o'er so many States!
I, after vain attempts of rage and arms,
To try to touch his heart with sighs and tears?
My son to be subservient, who should govern—
To live a subject, who should die a king?
My rage is frustrate, all my hope is vain,
Yet though without effect, my hate found utterance;
A timorous minion failed to strike him down,
But it was I who armed the hand that spared him,
And the honor that I die at least his foe
Will rob of infamy the death that I
Expect. If in the time still left to me
I should desire a little liberty,
'Twould be that I might kill him ere I died;
And if I struck with weak and timid arm
Like that base spirit whom I sought to charm,
Then he might boast my failure. But . . .

Enter SIROES, PALMIRAS, *and* PHARNACES.

SIROES.   We now
Come to provide against the violence
Of both thy fury and thine insolence.
Well, madam?
          [*He seats himself, and* PALMIRAS *and* PHARNACES *with him.*
SIRA.   Well, thou traitor, thou art king!
The shafts I aimed at thee have turned against me;
And by those means by which I hoped to set
My son in thy place, I have in mine own
Set thee and wrought my fall instead of thine.
I have done more; I tried without avail
To deal thy death-blow by my servant's hand.

CHOSROES

I have (or knowest thou this?) desired my freedom
That I myself might then attempt the deed.
Be not astonished; life do I disdain.
I swore to die or see mine offspring reign,
And still, if liberty were granted me,
Would use it to achieve for him thy ruin.
Is this enough? Witnesses here are needless.
My trial is soon ended. Pronounce sentence.

SIROES. I must admire this lofty spirit, madam,
And we should make such strength of heart renowned.
Through thy great hatred thou hast in the State
Made changes great but fatal to thyself.

SIRA. Little I reck of what to me is fatal.
My sum of bane is what thou hast of blessing.
I little should weep life, should die content,
If thou survivedst me subject to my son
Or if thy life-thread I had cut in twain.

SIROES. These are great projects for a woman's hand
And merited more careful pondering
Than with the ambition which sealed fast thine eyes.
More power or luck was needed than thou thoughtest
To banish from the throne its rightful heir.
Such deadly plots contrived against his life
May have success but do not always have it.
This, madam, thou hast proved. With thy great courage
Which hath left naught untried to overthrow me,
With all thine efforts, what hast thou accomplished?
On whom does this bolt fall? Where hast thou hurled it?
Upon the head whereon thou laidst my crown,
Upon my father's head, and upon thine.
How wast thou blinded that thou didst not deem,
With gods in heaven, that I would be protected?
Doubt'st thou that what most claim their care august
Are a king's interests if his cause is just?

SIRA. They ill avouched it in deserting our side
And granting thine the things they have let happen.
But whether or not they watch o'er men's affairs,
As it turns out, questions like these are futile.
Pronounce my doom; dismiss me from this spot.
Tyrant, deliver me from thy hateful sight.
Thy features all torment me; each look stabs me.
My greatest punishment is to behold thee.

SIROES. I needs must free thee from such dreadful tortures.

COSROES

(*To the Satraps*)   Princes, release her from them by your
judgment.

[*He talks with the Satraps, in low tones.*

SIRA.   Consult, thou cruel wretch, with thy ministers.
Our woes are the result of their ill counsels—
This remnant of proscribed men, who escaped
The executioner, who can mount by no means
Except upon our tombs, and can recover
Only by our misfortunes their high stations,
From which we have deposed them, in the realm.
The death which I await concerns them much.
Fear not; their counsels will be as thou wishest!
Well, traitor, and ye base support of traitors,
Ye what decide, my judges and my masters?

SIROES (*showing her the dagger and the poison which a guard hands
him*).   It was from thee that these gifts were brought to me.

SIRA.   Well?

SIROES.   Dost thou find them witnesses sufficient,
Or is aught else yet needed to confound thee?

SIRA.   Having avowed all, I have naught to answer.
I make myself my law, and my great crime is
Not that I dared, but that I, daring, failed.

SIROES.   The tools of evil will serve for punishment.
Choose one of them. Do justice on thyself.

SIRA.   This is some grace still, which I dared not hope for.
I choose the poison; have it ready for me.
I deem it less a poison than a cure
Which I should take for sickness that hath seized me.
'Twill taste sweet, since I cannot have thy blood,
Of which with joy I would have drained thy body.
Rather than life I choose a healthful death
Which shall deliver me from a foe's hands.
But add one favor to my choice of end:
Let my son go before me to it, tyrant,
That I may see him by his death preserved
From the disgrace of bending as a subject
Beneath his enemy's yoke. If he should live,
Well wouldst thou fear what he might yet accomplish.

SIROES.   Thy prayer is noble, and it shall be granted.
Bring him in, Sardaric, and lead out the Queen.

SIRA (*vehemently*).   Queen is my essence, though thou knowest 'tis
futile!
Till now I was thy step-mother; I am glad

310

To die this day to be naught more to thee.
                    [*She goes out with* SARDARIC *and the guards.*
PALMIRAS. Allow despair these vain recriminations.
SIROES. She is a woman; she is soon to die;
          And these are only words. Indeed, moreover,
          If the interests of my authority
          Allowed me to dispense with that severity
          Which vengeance rightfully incites me to,
          I would with pleasure suffer her still to live,
          And, despite all her hatred's consequences,
          Would rather pardon her than punish her.
PALMIRAS. Wholly aside from what concerns his person,
          No king can yield in what concerns his crown,
          But if he seeth the State to be endangered,
          Is bound to punish, though he wish no vengeance.
          Justice for him lies in his country's good.
          That which a subject could do, a prince cannot.
          And the indulgence which doth risk his realm
          Is of all faults a mighty sovereign's greatest.

          Enter MARDESANES, SARDARIC, *and guards.*

SIROES. 'Tis he. His whole crime is a mother's pride
          And my resentment ill sustains mine anger.
          (*To* MARDESANES)   Indeed, thou hast observed my counsel
              poorly,
          Prince; thou with profit wouldst have followed it.
          See how ambition robbed thee of all sense.
          Well I foretold thee what thou wast to come to,
          And that it much behooved thee not to spare me
          If, finding these false splendors too appealing,
          Thou shouldst permit a mother's plans to sway thee,
          Who, loving thee too much, did thee scant kindness.
          Well, am I rightly jealous of an empire,
          And is the throne of Persia, then, not sweet?
MARDESANES. To taste the sweetness to be found therein
          Needs longer trial.
SIROES.   Ere accepting it,
          Thou shouldst have taken some counsel with thyself.
          Didst thou not know a scepter is like fire,
          Which, carried in thy hand, can do thee scathe?
MARDESANES. The proof thereof is manifest in thyself,
          When, having touched it, thou dost burn with anger.
SIROES. But by what right tookest thou possession of it?
MARDESANES. The right to obey the mandate of a sire.

SIROES. What sire can bar me from a natural right?

MARDESANES. What sire? Thine own and mine, who, knowing his offspring,
Bequeathed his throne according to his will.

SIROES. He doubtless based his choice upon thy merit!

MARDESANES. I have not probed the orders which he gave me.

SIROES. Thou hast but ill observed thy plighted faith.
I would have kept mine better unto thee.

MARDESANES. I much prefer to acknowledge a fault, nobly,
Than to defend myself with fear and trembling.

SIROES. I have more reason to have thee punished, justly,
Than tamely to forget an outrage done me.

MARDESANES. At least thou hast not, in avenging it,
The glory of being prayed to to forget it.

SIROES. Thou art too great of heart.

MARDESANES. I am enough so
To show great courage in a great despair.

SIROES. But 'tis revealed too late.

MARDESANES. Quite soon enough
To displease one who, flushed with arrogance,
Beholds his wrath defied. If thou couldst think it
Unsuited to my rank, Prince, thou thus offerest
An insult unto those of thine own blood.
Hapless or fortunate, guilty or innocent,
I can feel everything which thou canst feel;
And even if I could hope to avert thy wrath,
I have thy pride too much to bow before thee.
The instant when I held the regal power
And felt the diadem upon my brow
Gave me, like thee, the spirit of a king,
Which ne'er will leave me, but will die with me.
Only with sore pain could I have restored
The scepter to thee, if I might have kept it,
Which, when a subject, I was loath to grasp;
And, having been a king now, I have learned
That its possession, which makes love grow cold,
Dilates ambition. Thou hadst better fortune
As well as prior birth, and we have fallen
Before thy might. But I, although still stunned
By this vicissitude, will ever keep
A heart unbowed, and would begrudge one prayer
Unto thy pride even to save my life.

SIROES. So be it. Death will tame thy haughty spirit.

MARDESANES. From the throne one falls best into the tomb.

CHOSROES

The zest of governing lives in me too strongly
To let me lose it while my life is left me.
One born to reign is capable of all things;
I would not stop at aught to gain that end,
To bring to pass my mother's plans for me,
And to avenge my shackles and my father's.
I reverenced thee when of thy rights despoiled.
I scarcely could consent to rule o'er thee,
And might perhaps have had the basic virtue
To come and kneel and give thee back thy crown.
But now, after the faction formed against us
And the sanguinary plots which thou hast woven
In open scorn of every natural tie,
I will not hide it from thee that if chance
Were to restore the scepter to my hands
Today, all claims henceforth on me to give it
To thee would be in vain, and casting off
All feelings of a brother unto thee,
I would have justice and avenge my father.
That is my attitude concerning thee,
And that is all the fear thou canst find in me.
I leave the verdict to thy tyrant power.

SIROES.   I was moved not to punish thine offense,
But thou opposest thyself too arrogantly
Unto my pious impulses of mercy,
Guarding too ill the safety of thy head.
Remove him, Sardaric.

MARDESANES.   Come. My head is ready.

SIROES.   To punish also the inordinate pride
Of one who so desired to see him crowned,
Make Sira's eyes witness the spectacle.

MARDESANES.   Proceed; reign, tyrant; reign without a hindrance.
Part of the power which my father gave me
Was that of meeting death without despair.
                            [*He goes out with* SARDARIC.

PALMIRAS.   I praise the virtues which a scepter brings us.
It is thy due, sire, for such strength of soul;
And one can recognize in this great spirit
The heir of Artaxerxes and the blood
Of Cyrus. Thou wilt overcome all, Prince,
In mastering thyself. But there remains
One proof to give still of this strength, and here
It is that Siroes must show all his manhood.
(*To a guard*)   Soldier, with Sardaric bring Chosroes.

313

SIROES. Stay, soldier.

PALMIRAS.   'Tis important, sire, for thee
To join . . .

SIROES.   Ah, it is here my resolve weakens;
Speechless, aghast, I know no more my station;
And in my foe I still love mine own blood.
O nature's ties!

PALMIRAS.   Thy victory is at stake,
And rarely, sire, does one attain to greatness
By common highways and well-beaten paths.

SIROES. Ah, too much have I practiced your cruel virtues!
I cannot buy the sweetness of a throne
At his expense who gave me life and breath.

PHARNACES. This softness of thy heart cometh ill-timed.
For the realm's peace, thy rule must be assured.

SIROES. And I resign it, cruel men; reign; I leave it.
Not at this price my brow desires a crown.
'Gainst mine own blood my heart revolts in vain;
Love makes it reverenced if power does not.
Give my sire, savage lords, another judge,
Or let him in a son's arms find a refuge.
O thou whose virtue merited his love,
Mother, alas! what fruit thou borest to light!
Why heldest thou not my funeral in thy side
And gavest me not thy womb for monument
If I must take his life and rank of king
From the dear other half yet left of thee?
Shall I reign blithely? Will either heaven or earth
Favor one's own sire's executioner?
To prop my throne and make my station firm
Shall I exhaust the source whence flowed my being?
Who will keep faith with a perfidious prince
Whose first decree hath been a parricide?
No, no, I do not want a throne befouled
With blood, the very blood whence I took life.
Trusting that passion common in great spirits,
I, against nature, heard ambition's voice.
I deemed my tenderness of heart false virtue;
With sovereignty the stake, my heart was silent;
But when a father must be sacrificed,
Ambition speaks no more and sonship counsels.
It presses me; it makes me take his part,
Whom well it knows its source and origin.
Here he is! Gods! I tremble. My voice fails

And in deep reverence falters on my lips.
But what await I?

Enter CHOSROES, SARDARIC, *and guards.*

CHOSROES.   Nature and ye gods,
Its authors, witness an unheard-of sight.
The horrible novelty invites your view.
My son, upon my throne, is now my judge
And doth not think himself secure unless
My head supports it and my blood cements it.
Then sacrifice my life to serve thy statecraft;
Make the realm surely thine by this great crime,
Tyrant; allow full scope for rage to act
And leave no room for ties or piety.
    (*To* PALMIRAS *and* PHARNACES)   And ye, so proud and brave
        in my misfortune,
My masters now, who were this morn my slaves . . .
SIROES (*kneeling*). Sire, deign to hear. O nature! and ye gods!
Ye can turn here your vision without horror.
He whom thou dost contemn reveres thee still.
I am no tyrant nor my father's judge.
Those feelings are all mine which thou hast taught me,
And I renounce my rights, remain thy son.
Nay, father, neither kingship nor all maxims
Thereof can force me thus to reign by crimes.
Over my life thou hast too sovereign rights
For me to sacrifice thee to my wrath.
Is there a son's hand that a father's sigh
Or tear or glance cannot disarm with ease?
If against thee I hearken to mine anger,
Alas, thy advocate is in my breast!
There, in mine own despite, thou findest a refuge,
And, criminal or not, thou hast no judge.
Possess unvext the realm which I restore
To thee. Thou only, sire, canst heal this strife.
Arbitrate 'twixt thy sons; end their dispute
By making thine again the rank they fought for.
Do not resign it at my rights' expense,
But rule in peace thy children 'neath thy power.
CHOSROES. Can Mardesanes' sentence and the Queen's
Allow my mind to entertain such thoughts?
Addest thou fraud to cruelty, thou traitor?
SIROES. Make trial of my good faith and of thy power.
CHOSROES. Revoke their death, then, and restore them to me.

SIROES. Soldiers, follow the King; do what he orders;
And, not considering the consequences
To me . . .
SARDARIC.   Sire!
SIROES.   Bring the Prince back, and free Sira.
         Go.   [*Exeunt* CHOSROES, SARDARIC, *and guards.*
PALMIRAS. Thou forgettest that Palmiras, Pharnaces,
And all thy friends will shortly take their place
And wear the chains which we have made them wear,
And thou thyself not easily wilt escape them.
Yes, think not, without peril to thyself,
To spare their lives and put in hazard ours.
We shall not shun the arrows of their rage;
But fear thou lest these shafts pierce also thee.
As they shall owe their lives less to thy mercy
Than to thy doubts and to thy weakness, Sira,
Judging the future by the past, will know,
As a good politician, how to o'er-reach thee,
And will take measures skilfully that the crown
No more shall press the brow that quickly doffs it.
SIROES. I cannot better guard a shaken heart
Where ties of blood have gained despotic power.
Thou shouldst have made the voice of nature mute
Which murmured secretly against thy counsels
And forced me to prefer the risk of death
To the inhumanity of deeds so cruel.
Such strength of soul requires too stern a manhood.
PHARNACES. Sire, let us not expect a dismal fate.
The throne itself will fall ere thou shalt fall,
And so great piety will be rewarded.
But wherefore comes the Princess?

Enter NARSEA.

NARSEA.   Oh, sad fortune!
O prince as lofty-hearted as unhappy!
SIROES. What is it, madam?
NARSEA.   Alas, sire, Mardesanes
Hath lost both crown and life, but like a brave man.
The gallant blow with which his soul was sped
Came from a noble hand and not a base one.
Knowing his death to be in preparation,
And taking, in his need, a high resolve,
He chose his time to snatch a soldier's sword
And drove it to the hilt into his bosom;

The blood gushed from his breast in a swift flood,
And sooner was his death seen than his purpose.

SIROES. Cruel men, that is the outcome of your counsels!

NARSEA. I was attending Sira, as in duty;
And though the secret which had cloaked my lot
Had just now been revealed so clearly to me,
Still I could not except unworthily,
I thought, have any part in her misfortunes.
The station which was mine because of her
Procured for me the honor of thy love.
If not her daughter, I am what she made me,
And owe at least my nurture to her care;
But seeing her in tears above the body
Of her dead son call Fates and gods her foes,
I was distressed and stunned by this sad sight,
And, powerless to speak a word, withdrew.
I also saw the poisoned cup borne to her
Which thou didst order for her punishment.

Enter SARDARIC *and guards.*

SARDARIC. Ah, sire, in spite of thee the guardian spirit
Of Persia shields thee and destroys thy foes!

SIROES. What new thing now?

SARDARIC. When Chosroes had re-entered
The prison, and saw the Queen had taken poison,
Swiftly, despite his escort's care and watch,
Before she drank it all he seized the cup
And drained the rest. "I must," he said to us,
Seeing with sad eyes Sira give up the ghost
And Mardesanes bathed in blood and lifeless,
"I must placate the wrath of Persia's fate,
Pay to my sire that tribute which he waits for,
Leave Siroes the throne which he aspires to,
And end the quarrel of so many tyrants."
Then, when he fell, a guard upbore him falling,
And we . . .

SIROES (*in a frenzy*). Well, are ye satisfied, cruel men?
Does my reign bear unhappy fruits enough?
The crown at this price costs me all too dear.
Come, madam; let us save or join my father.

[*He rushes out.*

PALMIRAS. Let us not leave him. [*All follow except* SARDARIC.

SARDARIC (*to himself*). Futile are his efforts.
The poison is swift, the tyrant dead already.

Laodice

By
THOMAS CORNEILLE

INTRODUCTORY NOTE

Thomas Corneille, the brother of the great Pierre Corneille, was nineteen years his junior. Born in Rouen, in 1625, he attended the same Jesuit college there; similarly he afterwards studied law and was admitted to the bar but presently became a dramatist; his literary career was begun under the tutelage of his brother. He married the younger sister of his brother's wife; and for long periods, first in Rouen and later in Paris, the two families lived under the same roof. On the death of Pierre Corneille in 1684, Thomas was elected to his place in the French Academy. He wrote few plays after 1680, but was prodigiously active as a journalist, grammarian, translator, and encyclopedist during the remainder of his long life, which did not end till 1709. Of all the French dramatists of the seventeenth century, too many of whom were oversensitive, jealous, or spiteful, he had the most admirable and lovable character.

His dramatic work was the most varied, the most widely representative, of all of these, and next to Rotrou's (and, of course, the pre-classical Hardy's) was the most copious. He wrote, alone or in collaboration, forty plays—comedies, tragedies, and spectacle plays—and four operas. He began by writing comedies of intrigue based on Spanish models; later he wrote comedies of character. In *Timocrate* (1656), which had more sensational immediate success than any other play of the century, he created the vogue of what is called romanesque tragedy because the inspiration of all such plays can be found in the interminable and preposterous pseudo-historical romances of Madeleine de Scudéry and La Calprenède. The distinguishing mark of these tragedies is their complete lack of "local color," even of the meager sort attainable in the dramas of those days. The names of the dramatis personae might be well known to history or legend; the names of the places involved might be clearly indicative of Asia, or of classical Greece or Rome, or of the Gothic Dark Ages; but the real setting in every instance was the world of extravagant adventure, romance, and gallantry depicted in *le Grand Cyrus* and *Clélie*. Most, but not all, such plays were characterized also by great complexity of plot and by problems of identity. Thomas Corneille wrote eight tragedies of this type, his most influential contribution to French drama though hardly a creditable one. He also wrote six tragedies which were more or less in imitation of those of the great Corneille—

la Mort de l'empereur Commode (1657), *Stilicon* (1660), *Camma* (1661), *Maximian* (1662), *Laodice* (1668), and *la Mort d'Annibal* (1669) —and two others, *Ariane* and *le Comte d'Essex,* which have been thought to be in imitation of Racine.

These last two are generally considered his best plays; but they stand apart, being unlike any of the rest. Whatever their relative merit compared individually with his six "Corneillian" tragedies, those six, taken together, constitute his most important characteristic achievement in tragic drama. True, in every instance their author is patently the author of *Timocrate;* gallant love holds a larger place in them than in the tragedies of his brother, between which and his own romanesque plays they stand midway. Though *Stilicon, Camma,* and *la Mort d'Annibal* have each been preferred by some critic or critics, *Laodice* is here selected as the best of them. If Thomas Corneille is the most genuinely representative dramatist, this play is perhaps the most characteristically typical single specimen of French-classical tragedy that can be found in the entire period.

The wicked queen who gives *Laodice* its name is evidently patterned after the "Cléopâtre" of his brother's *Rodogune.* Thomas Corneille's greatest dramatic gift was his ability to devise striking if somewhat melodramatic situations, of immense effectiveness on the stage. It is best exemplified in *Laodice* by the scene in Act III in which the Queen solicits her son, of whose identity she is unaware, to murder her supposed son, revealing gradually to the horror-stricken youth the real depth of his mother's depravity. The piquant situation in which Axiana is offended by her lover's apparent willingness to see her married to another is one that the author used repeatedly in his plays.

Thomas Corneille possessed no share of the poetic genius of his great brother. The average quality of his verse is probably inferior to that of any other dramatist included in this volume, except Campistron.

CHARACTERS IN THE PLAY

LAODICE, *Queen of Cappadocia.*
ARIARATHES, *disguised under the name of "Orontes"; son of Laodice and rightfully king.*
AQUILIUS, *a Roman ambassador.*
ANAXANDER, *a subject prince under Laodice.*
PHRADATES, *a subject prince under Laodice.*
AXIANA, *princess of Cilicia.*
CLEONE, *confidante of Laodice.*
ALCINA, *confidante of Axiana.*
THEODOTUS.

The scene represents a room in the palace of Laodice.

The names "Laodice," "Aquilius," "Phradates," "Cleone," "Alcina," and "Theodotus" are accented on the second syllable; "Axiana" on the third syllable; "Ariarathes" on the first and fourth syllables. The final "e" in "Laodice" and "Cleone" forms a syllable.

Laodice

ACT I

Axiana and Alcina are discovered.

AXIANA.   What! doth the Senate send an embassy;
    And without even waiting till the envoy
    Hath time to reach here, doth the Queen consult
    Only herself about the choice, and wish
    To give a king at last to Cappadocia?
ALCINA.   Art thou surprised at this when Rome takes interest
    In whom she chooseth for the Princess' husband?
    For a long time already have the people
    Urged loudly such a step, desired a king;
    And as Aquilius, whom this matter brings here,
    Might arrive suddenly and take the Queen
    Unawares, to forestall his mandate, she
    Wishes today by her sole choice to give us
    A master and to gain thus a support
    For herself. Jealous of the splendor which
    A crown irradiates, she beyond question
    Finds difficulty in giving it to her daughter;
    But he whom she alone selects at least
    Will owe Rome nothing and her everything.
AXIANA.   But Rome will take offense at this procedure.
    If the late king died fighting in her cause,
    Even so, he was in death rewarded for it
    When Rome enlarged the kingdom of his sons
    And when to Cappadocia was added
    Cilicia entire and Lycaonia.
ALCINA.   Why did his hapless sons not live, through whom
    All of these realms were destined to be thine!
    The marriage that with the eldest of these princes
    Was to have joined thee would have made thee reign
    Over all these domains, and thy Cilicians
    Would have beheld their princess in the station
    Of her ancestors, through this glorious union.
AXIANA.   Heaven, whose harshness towards me is thus shown,
    Deprived me of Cilicia where my fathers
    Reigned, but since I was sent here by Rome's orders,
    I could expect a lofty destiny.
    At least, in giving to the Queen my lands,

Rome seemed to keep for me the rank of sovereign,
And, to see them more surely joined to her,
Chose me to wed the eldest of her sons;
But they no longer live, and though 'tis claimed
That heaven hath preserved young Ariarathes,
Arsinoë, his sister, hath sole right
Now to possess the rank I hoped from him.

ALCINA.　Whate'er Arsinoë's wish to gain that rank,
A subject still can Ariarathes leave her.
The hope that smiles the fairest oft deceives us.
Who knoweth if this brother be not living?
If we believe the Queen about it, he
Is ready to appear.

AXIANA.　　　　　　Knowest thou whence cometh
The rumor which doth raise him up anew?
The Queen, whose soul the throne could ever charm,
Regretfully maketh a king of him
Whom she is now about to name. Her flimsy
Assurances that her son yet lived put off
Continually the marriage of her daughter,
Who still would for her brother's reappearance
Wait if the wearied populace had not hastened
This great day. They believe the Prince is dead,
And fain would have a master.

ALCINA.　　　　　　　　　Ah, if he were
Alive, and let himself be recognized,
The throne assured for thee . . .

AXIANA.　　　　　　　　　It hath its charms
But at this price might be too costly for me.

ALCINA.　What! thou'dst refuse to marry Ariarathes?

AXIANA.　He alone from an unkind fate can free me,
But howsoe'er a throne may dazzle us,
Can one be happy where one's heart is not?

ALCINA.　O gods! and could it be that, to touch thine,
Love . . .

AXIANA.　　　　It can do with me what it can do
With others, and the obstacles which one
Sets up against its shafts, which he feels pierce him,
Augment sometimes what he had thought to lessen.

ALCINA.　Thy words surprise me, but whom am I to think
That love hath wished to destine for such glory?
Our princes who could even to thee aspire
Address their sweetest prayers to their ambition.
Arsinoë's hand confers the diadem,

> And in their eagerness for sovereign power,
> Each for this marriage that creates a king
> Courteth Orontes, trying to win his aid.
> This noted stranger hath great influence
> Over the Queen.

AXIANA.   And great are his deserts.

ALCINA.   He obtains all things without difficulty,
> And the high honor which he now enjoys . . .

AXIANA.   'Tis high; but thinkest thou too much could be done
> For him?

ALCINA.   I know he is so necessary
> Unto the realm that not enough can be
> Done to retain him. Since the kindly gods
> Sent him to us more than two years ago
> And kept him here, the mark of his least exploits
> Hath been the quelling of the insolence
> Of our proud foes; and what they boldly planned
> Or put in practise was at once defeated
> By his wise counsels. But these rare achievements
> Of valor and of prudence give him glory
> And not high birth, and the inferior station
> Where heaven placed him, none the less prevents him
> From hoping to be loved by thee.

AXIANA.   Perhaps
> Within his heart that hope dares not be born;
> But why, Alcina, might it not? Doth love
> Always result from reason, and doth no one
> Ever love without knowing what he doeth?

ALCINA.   I should suppose that the great difference
> Between his rank and thine . . .

AXIANA.   And have I not
> A heart and eyes like any other woman?
> And when true merit shines in anyone,
> Is it possible for me not to esteem him?

ALCINA.   Esteem is innocent, and was always sanctioned;
> But love . . .

AXIANA.   Dost thou not know how love disguiseth
> Itself? Being free to see and to esteem,
> When one does love, does one perceive that fact?
> The most beguiling lure of love's vague sweetness
> At first is but a tribute to which virtue
> Compelleth us. The brightness that it shines with
> Before the eyes of countless witnesses
> Cannot expect less of a heart which sees it.

The soul in vain is troubled and confounded.
Reason consents to this; 'tis merit's due;
And one does not desire to recognize
That this great merit, in spite of all one's efforts,
Pleases one so that one thinks of it always.
'Twas thus that, dazzled by such stainless manhood,
I hid from mine own self my heart's subjection,
And that too well I trusted that heart's judgment
And came to love, thinking I but admired.
All things that history tells us about heroes,
All greatness that is theirs, I have beheld
In this Orontes. To his latest battles
The realm which tottered till his arm sustained it
Owes its whole victory. Through him alone
The Queen sits more securely on the throne;
And if he in his birth found Fate unfriendly,
Though one should hence wish to decry his deeds,
Upholding kings is more than being king.

ALCINA. I fain would think so. But Orontes, madam—
Is he so happy as to read thy heart?
Knows he its secret?

AXIANA.   I have sought to hide
From him what vainly I would pluck therefrom.
I ever watch myself 'mid all its promptings,
But love says much when thinking it says naught,
And whatso care one takes to mask one's feelings,
If the lips speak not, the eyes often speak.
Also I shall confess, this victor bold
Seems to feel sure of not displeasing me.
I see him sometimes with a yearning glance
Ask my acknowledgment of his attentions.
His love, which rigorous respect keeps silent,
Borrows of sighs the aid to explain itself;
And I have often known he was assured
That if they spoke to me, I understood them.
Alcina, judge . . .

ALCINA.   See how love leads him to thee.

Enter ARIARATHES, *going under the name of "Orontes."*

ARIARATHES. Madam, thou knowest of the Queen's intention.
Taking her subjects' wishes as a mandate,
She is about to give a king to us.
In her son's stead, whose loss is much lamented,
Arsinoë, her daughter, takes her place

Today, and the husband whom she chooses for her
Will mount the throne thereby and govern here.
How sweet 'twould be to me if on this day
Thou, not Arsinoë, wert to be crowned!
When Rome made disposition of thy conquered
Domains, the Queen meant for her son to be
Thy husband, and in Cappadocia
Thou wast brought up to have the glory which
Her choice destined for thee. Would to the gods
That this son would appear, and he was ready . . .

AXIANA.　Orontes always takes an interest in
My destiny, and cannot, without sorrow,
Behold my glory clouded by the fate
Which made me lose Cilicia. As that
Is the domain where my forefathers reigned,
I should have wished to reign there after them,
No doubt; but since the gods have otherwise
Decreed, in taking from me Cappadocia
They have taken little from me; and at least,
Now owing neither heart nor troth, if I
Live without state, I *can* live for myself.

ARIARATHES.　What! would thy heart's gift to Prince Ariarathes
Be a fate for thee . . .

AXIANA.　　　　　　　　Freedom pleases me,
And this proud heart of mine finds an affront
In whatso makes it bow to reasons of State.

ARIARATHES.　I praise the pride which doth oppose such reasons;
But if I dared, madam, to probe its cause . . .

AXIANA.　What wouldst thou say to me?

ARIARATHES.　　　　　　　　What thou concealest
From us: that someone else hath secretly
Entered thy heart, no doubt, and thus . . .

AXIANA.　　　　　　　　　　　Too far
Doth thy suspicion go, for my fair fame.
But what grounds, after all, hast thou to have it?
Have I been seen to value any man's
Vows or attentions?

ARIARATHES.　　　　　Madam, in the name
Of the gods, do not conceal this from me. Such
Strong interest impels me to discover . . .

AXIANA.　Thou? And what interest hast thou reason to take
In it?

ARIARATHES.　Madam . . .

AXIANA.   Explain thyself. Thou hast
    My full permission.

ARIARATHES.   Thou knowest the influence
    Which graciously hath been allowed me. I
    Can sway the Queen's mind as I please; and while
    The choice for king still keeps her soul uncertain,
    Name whom thou lovest, and thou wilt not be vexed
    With fear that e'er on him this choice may fall.
    I could contrive to spare thy heart such tortures.

AXIANA. Perhaps I should be less unjust to him,
    And feel my honor outraged if my heart
    Should rob him of the happiness of reigning.
    But I herein find little ground for dread,
    And, to acquaint thee fully with the reason,
    If some true worth were bound to charm my heart,
    'Twere through thine eyes that I should wish to love.
    The man whom thou wouldst choose ought to attract me.

ARIARATHES. And thou couldst trust, madam, regarding this,
    A reckless wight, who, to crown someone's fortunes,
    Would seek, whate'er thy rank, rather for love
    Than princely blood? How quickly I should see thee
    Forced to recant!

AXIANA.   Choosing through thee, I little
    Should fear the outcome. He who by his virtues
    Hath always shown himself . . .

ARIARATHES.   What serveth this
    Advantage where the rest is lacking? What
    If I proposed to thee some man whose lineage
    Differed too widely from the blood of kings,
    Some man whose worth was dimmed by this ill fortune?

AXIANA. Such a defect should be ascribed to Fate.
    A hero gives proof only of great merit,
    Only . . .

ARIARATHES.   And if I dared speak for myself
    To thee, if I dared swear that ne'er such ardor
    Mixed with such homage seized on any heart,—
    That mine, entirely thine, would sacrifice . . .
    But name the punishment for this mad daring.
    Possessed therewith, I wander and am lost.
    Is it for me to wear such glorious chains
    Of love?—to hope for aught where my presumption
    Aspireth? Madam, speak.

AXIANA.   Adieu.

ARIARATHES.   What! wilt thou
    Not tell me . . .
AXIANA.   Leave me some due share of pride.
    To have listened was to say too much to thee.
ARIARATHES. It sayeth much, 'tis true; but if this homage . . .
AXIANA. What use to urge me to say more about it?
    Thou knowest the obligations of high birth
    And who I am. Judge thou accordingly.
ARIARATHES. What thou objectest is not what impedes me.
    Be true to this high birth; that will not pain me.
    Tell me but this: whether my love offends thee;
    Whether thy heart . . .
AXIANA.   I know not what this means,
    But I am conscious that it is disturbed
    With the desire to listen to thee, and that
    Whate'er love forces thee to undertake,
    Thou couldst expect the happiest success
    If pride of birth in me did not oppose thee.
            [*Exeunt* AXIANA *and* ALCINA. *Enter* PHRADATES.
PHRADATES. Wouldst thou confess it? The Princess Axiana
    Seeks to make void, through thee, a choice she censures.
    The marriage of Arsinoë must disquiet her.
ARIARATHES. The hope to wed a crown is hard to part with,
    But Axiana frets not. Far from fearing . . .
PHRADATES. So she is placid, and I am to be pitied!
    Though all Arsinoë's preference is for me,
    Orontes, I have rivals, and I tremble;
    For well thou knowest that their jealousy,
    Taking Arsinoë, will take life from me.
    Thou only canst sustain my hopes against them;
    Thou hast complete control over the Queen;
    And oft-times when confusion filled my soul
    Thou hast assured me of my love's success.
    At last 'tis time to speak, my dear Orontes.
ARIARATHES. I owe thee too much, sir, to wish to fail thee.
    This service is the least that honor sets me.
    Without thine aid I should have died in battle,
    And oft thy kindness, championing me, hath deigned
    To strengthen me in the rank which I attained.
    About thy love, hence be in no distress.
    I answer for the Queen; love thou Arsinoë,
    And thou canst deem thyself at fortune's peak
    If thou canst be made happy by her hand.
PHRADATES. Many aspire to the honor of this choice,

But I especially fear Anaxander.
This vaunting rival's claims lack not support,
And of his partisans . . .
ARIARATHES.   Fear naught from him.
The blind ambition which his pride breeds in him
Gives him but little of the Queen's good graces.
She seeks a kindly, docile, pliant spirit
To serve as her support in reigning always,
One who, being nobly born yet subject to her,
Will leave the power to her and be content
With the mere title.
PHRADATES.   I abandon it—
That power—entirely to her fervent wishes.
Arsinoë's heart is all that I desire;
And if her hand . . .
ARIARATHES.   What, sir! her person hath
Charms for thee stronger than her royal crown?
PHRADATES.   Yes, I call heaven to witness: no ambition,
But she alone, hath kindled all my longings;
And quite as dear to me without a throne . . .
ARIARATHES.   I have always thought thee able to love nobly.
'Twas well thou couldst. This will explain my words:
Ariarathes will appear here soon.
PHRADATES.   Ariarathes?
ARIARATHES.   What! His return irks thee?
PHRADATES.   Nay; but I fathom ill the Queen's designs.
Why feigns she now to choose another king?
ARIARATHES.   I alone know the secret of her son.
She herself knows it not; and, to hide nothing
From thee, who honorest me with a true friendship,
Aquilius, whom Rome sends expressly here,
Comes to restore this prince to his forefathers'
Throne.
PHRADATES.   We all know that since his earliest years,
During the late king's day he was Rome's hostage;
But scarcely was that king deprived of life
Than Rome said that he had been carried off;
And if we should believe what she declared,
None knew the perpetrators of this crime.
ARIARATHES.   Alas! they now are only too well known.
Excuse me, sir, from speaking about this,
And sooner to conclude a talk that pains me
Remember the sad tales told of the Queen.
The death of her five sons—all children—left

In her hands, stained her name with blackest crime.
Poison removed them; at least, everybody
Told this against her, wishing to believe it.
But if suspicions were uncertain here,
The crime was soon apparent to the Romans.
    As fear of giving up the crown some day
Had armed her hand 'gainst her own flesh and blood,
Young Ariarathes' being a hostage with them
Was a hard obstacle to her will's fulfilment.
To carry him off from Rome, she chose Orcamus,
Who, shocked and filled with horror by her frenzy,
Feigning to serve her, came to tell the Senate
The plan of this accursèd, final crime.
Rome, then engaged in a grim war, withheld
The lightnings of her anger for some time,
And thought that one lone witness did not give her
Fit warrant to destroy a queen and take
Her realm. But to expose the Prince no longer
To such wrath, she pretended that somebody
Had carried off her hostage, while she reared him
Under a false name elsewhere, thus avoiding
Any suspicion of the ruse which saved him.
    Orcamus, meanwhile, went back to the Queen,
And made her sure her luckless son was dead;
And his own death, which followed, left her free
To profit by her crime with perfect safety.
That she might always reign alone though hated,
She would not have Prince Ariarathes live;
Yet, feigning to doubt this son of hers' demise,
Of that pretense she made the throne the prize.
But now 'tis time at last to break the silence;
Rome's envoy is much nearer than 'tis thought;
And it must be, this very day, made clear,
Before all else, that which hath brought him here.
PHRADATES.   Ah, let the whole secret be plain to me!
What thou hast told me shows me Ariarathes.
Since with a false name he deceives us all,
Thy rare worth makes me deem that thou art he.
Have complete faith in my fidelity.
ARIARATHES.   Yes, Prince, I must confide in thee entirely.
Son of a wicked mother . . .
PHRADATES *(about to kneel)*.   Ah, sir!
ARIARATHES *(preventing him)*.   This
Deference, if we were seen, might rouse suspicions.

'Tis best thy fealty now be hidden. Treat me
But as Orontes till the Roman comes.
He only has the right to tell my secret.
PHRADATES. But why, sir, for two years disguise thyself?
ARIARATHES. Rome has allowed this time to me to let me
Attempt to soften the hate my mother feels
And see if I can make her understand
She need not fear her son when he is crowned,—
That, far from having ambition to be king,
Even when ruling I would fain obey her.
I have succeeded, so 'twould seem; she loves me,
Or she at least appreciates my efforts
To uphold her power. I have the happiness
Besides, to have been able, without a throne,
To form a tie, myself, with Axiana
And see my vows heard, while my love discreet
Has ne'er, to make them please, betrayed my secret.
I wish to keep it carefully till she learns
That Ariarathes lives and comes to crown her
And I have proved whether, midst this sweet prospect,
Orontes, the forsaken, will not grieve her.
It will be then . . .
PHRADATES.   Sir, I see Anaxander.
ARIARATHES. Let me learn what his aspirations are.
His intrigues need no more alarm thy love.

Enter ANAXANDER. *Exit* PHRADATES.

ANAXANDER. Phradates takes great pains to court thy favor,
Nor do I doubt that he hath some advantage
Over whoe'er would ask for thy support.
The secret friendship which men note between you . . .
ARIARATHES. This friendship, sir . . .
ANAXANDER.   I am not jealous of it.
Speak to me only quite without reserve.
Thou knowest my hopes. Is the place filled? Hast thou
Proposed Phradates? Wilt thou make him king?
ARIARATHES. I know not if this choice depends on me,
But if the throne hath charms which rouse thy hopes,
Be sure thou ne'er shalt see Phradates on it.
ANAXANDER. If truth thou tellest me, every hope is mine.
All will be happy to declare for me;
And whatsoe'er my rivals may attempt,
If thou'rt against them, they have naught to hope for.
But since 'tis thou through whom I wish to gain

The throne, if I mount thither 'twill be thine
Rather than mine; I give my word to thee
Concerning this, and, better to assure thee,
I will join to it now bonds of close union—
A marriage with my sister . . .

ARIARATHES.   Ah, sir, dost thou
Not see what distance heaven hath set between us?

ANAXANDER.   If heaven hath made thee spring from lowlier blood,
That is no fault to one who knows thee truly.
This brilliant match is but the least reward . . .

ARIARATHES.   I am surprised at such excessive honor.
Like thee, I feel ambition's charms in secret;
But how wilt thou oppose Prince Ariarathes?
He liveth, 'tis said, and comes for his ancestral . . .

ANAXANDER.   Let me but mount the throne, and we may leave
The rest unto the gods.

ARIARATHES.   What! thou'dst refuse
To give the crown up?

ANAXANDER.   We shall know what rights
Attach to it when marriage gives it to me;
Then we shall see, as time decideth all things,
Whether it should be given up or defended.

ARIARATHES.   Of Ariarathes' race, fond are the memories;
And 'gainst thee for his sake I fear that proudly . . .

ANAXANDER.   Were he supported by a million swords,
Wielding the scepter, I should fear him not.

ARIARATHES.   But if he showed the kingliest marks to thee
Which heaven e'er set upon the brows of monarchs,
Couldst thou without remorse, his throne usurping . . .

ANAXANDER.   Thunder would I without remorse see smite me!
Be it about to fall, 'tis good to await it.
But we lose time, and may be overheard.
Go to the Queen, and, be assured, the throne
Is really thine if she makes choice of me.

                          [*Exeunt.*

A C T I I

Laodice *and* Cleone *are discovered.*

CLEONE.   Madam, it is surprising that this very
Day thou shouldst wish to share the royal power
And choose a husband for Arsinoë
Before Rome can confer with thee. Aquilius

Comes only for this marriage.

LAODICE.   And can Cleone
Herself be thus astonished at me—she
To whom my conduct should have made it plain
That I have but one choice: to die or reign?
Long did I vainly make dead Ariarathes
Live again. A presumptuous populace
Exhibited its impatience, and our princes
Found in my daughter's marriage a sweet hope
And of the power of Rome availed themselves.
Thereby they think to force me to a choice,
But I shall not await what I should fear
If one of them, made by Aquilius king,
Could see himself reign lawfully despite me.
If I must share the throne, I shall at least
Be sure, in setting there a king, to see
My creature on it, and to remain always
For those who fain would make of me a subject
Sole mistress of the realm they would take from me.

CLEONE.   This king whom thou wilt choose ought to care only
To please thee, but to gain the daughter's love
He will forget the mother, and when once
Arsinoë has taken him as her husband
I question who will have the greater power,
Thyself or she. Naught is there which in time
Will not be sacrificed to love.

LAODICE.   And being
Now able to foresee this, dost thou deem
That I shall trust myself thereto and suffer it
That given by mine own hand today, my daughter
Shall have the joy of making someone king?

CLEONE.   For whom, then, is this husband who shall mount
The throne—whose choice thou promisest?

LAODICE.   For whom?
For me, Cleone.

CLEONE.   For thee, madam! Will Rome
Consent to this?

LAODICE.   What, then? Must I needs bow
Before her pride, and when I ought to show
My royal capabilities, shall this
Mistress of kings decree my course of action?
Whether or not she murmurs, I can make
A king who shall disdain her and take orders
Only from me, and, fully satisfied

With the bright splendors of so great a title,
Shall save me from the humiliation of
Obeying mine own daughter. The pretext
For such a step is plausible; my son
Is thought to be alive, and with the lucky
Mistake of this false story, I shall pretend
That my hand gives the populace a master
Only while waiting till this son shall please
To come here and take o'er at last from me
His kingdom, which a husband of his sister
Would not resign to him.

CLEONE.   Whate'er Phradates
Expects or Anaxander hopes to have,
I ask no longer who thy choice will be.
The many honors lavished on Orontes
Tell me enough without thy naming him.
His pure and perfect loyalty, his valor,
His prudence . . .

LAODICE.   Rather say, he is an alien
With no support of birth, and policy
Requires me to make someone king whose fate
Depends entirely, in the last resort,
On me. He is a man whom I at will
Can cherish or destroy, ruin at the least
Project that he might form to injure me,—
Who would be dutiful, would fear, would have
No rescuers if it ever were my pleasure
To order that his days should end. But now,
After these haughty words, this revelation
Of my ambition's lofty policy,
Dare I confess to thee, in shame, that love
Almost entirely sways my choice today?

CLEONE.   Love, madam? Thou?

LAODICE.   Be thunderstruck, Cleone.
Thou knowest I ne'er loved aught except the throne,
And that a vast, insatiable ambition
Made me feel scorn for every other passion.
To slake its thirst, I treated as a weakness
The tender feelings born of natural ties;
And though the death of five sons was the cost,
I could see naught but the delights of reigning.
My sixth son, who was held at Rome a hostage,
Still caused my jealous heart anxiety.
Fearing that he might some day take the throne

From me, with neither pity nor remorse
I had him carried off, and sought to have
His death appear uncertain still, that thus
The rights which make my daughter queen might be
Held in abeyance, and that I might use
Whatever means I needed to prevent
Her marriage, under the pretense of keeping
The crown for this son. Midst the burning ardor
Of my desires which centered all my soul
Upon the throne, I scarcely can imagine
What abject quality prompts me to seek
A lover in a king of mine own making.
    I feel this shameful, and it irks my pride.
I in my heart call myself weak and vile,
And yet I cannot pluck from out my breast
The sweet thoughts that too charmingly beguile me.
Ever I see Orontes, diligent,
Spirited, loyal, eager to display
By numberless attentions his devotion,
To make my pleasure his sole interest
And comply blindly with whate'er I wish.
I feel myself touched by it, and his deference
So brings my soul into accord with his
That I should now distrust myself if I
Were forced to choose between the throne and him.
    Such feelings are unworthy, craven, base;
I hate myself for them, but cannot cast them
Out of my heart. It seems that for my shame
The harsh decree of heaven hath made of them
A needful thing for me, and that the love,
Unworthy of a queen, which burns in me,
Is the inevitable penalty
Of my o'erweening pride, and that the wrath
Of heaven hath wished deliberately to kindle
A flame within me at the age when one,
Whate'er one *can* feel, ought to blush at loving.
Pretexts of policy will cloak my shame;
I can conceal it even from Orontes' eyes,
But I must needs with thee relieve my heart
Of the too heavy burden of its ardor,
That, being with my pride familiar, thou
Canst help me find what hath become of it,
And pity me at least . . .

CLEONE.   Madam . . .

L A O D I C E

Enter ARIARATHES.

LAODICE *(aside to* CLEONE*)*.　　　　　　　Now listen
And see if I speak as I ought to speak.
　　Orontes, I must make a great decision,
For I lack skill to cancel for my daughter
The marriage urged for her, and can no longer
Oppose the insolent projects which the princes
Who are my subjects have conceived against me.
The prospect of the crown's inheritance
By her beguiles them with the hope of having
A splendid outcome end their undertaking,
And all who could aspire unto the honor
Of being chosen have intrigued in secret
For the support of Rome. Aquilius
Comes to make choice among them of our master,
And one can see how I, though born to greatness,
Am shamed if, in this choice which I expressly
Desire to hasten, I must needs respect
The mandate of the Senate. But although
Refusal of the yoke of mighty Rome
Is not an act unworthy of a queen,
Heaven is my witness that a dearer interest
Begets the pride for which I may be censured
And that in this pride, proper to my rank,
All that I think of is a mother's duty,
Which always bids me keep safe for my son
The scepter of which some desire to rob him.
　　'Tis this that I would fain do, with that love
Which ties of blood require, which nature urges;
And since his throne's support is seen in thee,
'Tis by thy hand that now I finally
Hope to accomplish everything for him.
He surely lives, and heaven, which inspires me,
Promises me the happiness of giving
The kingdom to him if Orontes, ever
Possessed by a true zeal, wishes to be
Still such a one as I have always known him.
ARIARATHES.　Forgive me, madam, if my chagrin finds words
When I perceive thou doubtest the zeal that fires me.
Surely my dearest wish will be fulfilled
If I can see the Prince, thy son, made king;
But so extreme my zeal is for thine interests
That notwithstanding the respect one owes

A crown, if this son should forget his duty
When on the throne and should abuse against thee
His sovereign power,—if he did not still leave thee
All the rights that the diadem now gives thee,—
He would see me myself take arms to drive him
From off that throne where thou alone couldst place him.
Then judge if I would always be the same
As hitherto thou knowest I have been,
And if I have deserved that thou shouldst be
Unsure of me and bind me with new oaths.

LAODICE. I looked for no less from that noble heart
Which I enlisted in this realm's defense.
Besides, when with uncertain powers I must
Consign the throne to faithful hands in trust,
Seeing how arrogant our princes are,
I fear the worst if one of them becometh
Master, and since ambition blinds them all,
For this choice I feel sure of none but thee.
Not that my daughter yields to my behest
So far that as a sister she desires
What *I* seek as a mother. Jealous pride
Of royal blood maketh her heart revolt
Against me, against thee. Thy marriage means
Disgrace to her, and whensoe'er I urge her . . .

ARIARATHES. Wouldst have Arsinoë stoop to me? No, no!
Whatever scorn she may display, my fortunes,
Too far below hers, make me well deserve it.
Her pride is just, and if when she is queen
Her greatness irks thee for thy son's sake, thou
Hast other means by which to risk no whit
The throne which thou wouldst for thy son preserve.

LAODICE. There *is* one, yes, without constraining her,
Which can prevent her being feared some day
And spare thee all necessity of ever
Serving as target for her loftiness.
Thou knowest the furor stirred up by the princes;
They roused the people, who demand a master.
Well, they shall have what they have asked of me
If I invest thee with the rank of king.
This plan surprises thee, and fifteen years
Of widowhood have banished all suspicion
That I would ever make a second marriage;
So 'twill seem strange that with my eminence
A queen would choose a husband suddenly.

But though this should belie mine own proud nature,
My chief pride is in being a good mother,
And I should deem I reached the peak of this
If I had made the throne sure for my son.
As on all sides ambition threatens, 'tis
To save it for him that I set thee on it
And choose in thee, 'neath this great name of "king,"
His guardian, who will wed me for his sake
And, filled with the same thought which governs me,
Will have the selfsame zeal to rule this realm
And be like me ready to give up, always,
What anyone else would surely try to keep.

ARIARATHES. Ah, for such goodness one life is too little
For me to offer thee anew today,
And all my blood a thousand times shed for thee
Could not discharge the debt I owe to thee!
Having, in proof of thine esteem, already
Raised me to an exalted, glorious rank,
Thou wishest (no matter how the people might
Object or what the Senate of great Rome
Might think) to add the splendor of a throne
Now to my lot with all things else which this
Bestows on kings, and to complete thy work
In this thy creature! Fathom if thou canst,
Madam, what ardor humble loyalty
Keeps in my breast; then see 'tis necessary
That I shall finally explain to thee . . .

LAODICE. My heart shares somewhat in my policies.
I love the reasons that seem to force on me
The marriage to which I wish to stoop for thee.
The people, who have long owed life to thee,
Without regret will see thee as their master,
And if Rome feels aggrieved, we e'en shall let her
Assail a hero who protects my son.

ARIARATHES. Ah, since the interests of this son alone
Make thee not trust the Princess with the throne,
It must no more be hidden . . .

LAODICE.   Yes, 'twould be futile
To wish still to conceal my purpose from thee.
Since all is settled, I speak willingly.

Enter ANAXANDER.

Prince, I hear ever talk of Ariarathes.
'Tis said he is about to show himself,

And this report hath too much weight for me
To think it right I should decide thy future.
Among great rivals whom fair hopes induce
To offer their devotion to my daughter,
This son whom Fate reserves to be your king
Will choose, when crowned, better than I can choose.
The people, though, day after day declare
That, while he waits to show himself, they wish
A second master, who will give commands,
Act, and be able notably to aid me
In bearing the great burden of this realm.
By gift of mine own hand I must content them,
And I believe my choice will rightly please them
When they shall learn that by my side Orontes . . .

ANAXANDER.   What! is it by *thy* marriage thou wilt give us
A king, and on the strength of a mere rumor
Which was deliberately circulated
Must we accept a stranger as our master?

LAODICE.   Prince, do not abuse my too great kindness
Which makes me bear thy forwardness. I know
What to myself and to this realm I owe.

ANAXANDER.   Orontes! Will the Senate grant him to thee,
Which at thy subjects' plea demands for them
A worthy, not a fortune-favored, ruler?
Will it allow a throne where for so long
High birth has been the warrant of its kings,
Where lordly blood . . .

LAODICE.   Silence! Thou goest too far.
Orontes is of unknown origin.
His lineage may be lowly; that I know
As well as thou, but be it what it may,
Despite thee and despite Rome he shall be
Thy master, and if any insolent man
Should murmur at my choice, I am the Queen.
The scepter is the thunderbolt of monarchs.

                                    [*Exit* LAODICE.

ANAXANDER.   Flattered by such hopes as the Queen hath given thee,
Thou couldst be sure about Phradates' fate
And rid me of all grounds for fearing him
When I supposed that he would have thine aid
To rule this land.

ARIARATHES.   This honor she accords me
Is out of keeping with Orontes' fortunes.
It is too great, but I shall use it well!

Her aims in this choice shall not be defeated.

ANAXANDER.   So thou wilt guard the crown, then, for her son?

ARIARATHES.   That will be my attempt, and in my place
Others might give it up with less good grace;
But truly, as I would fain keep faith in all things,
When Ariarathes is produced, Orontes
Will be no longer king.

ANAXANDER.   Thou thinkest thyself
Already that, and clutching avidly
The precious remnant of a woman's reign,
Thou willingly agreest to give nobly
The throne to this youth who thou knowest is dead.

ARIARATHES.   If heaven accords me any claims to reign,
I will not trench on those of Ariarathes.
Time will show whether he is dead or not.

ANAXANDER.   Thus should a hero win a glorious name,
And with whatever eye the Senate views thee,
Thy marriage will outstrip its mandate to us,
And I believe, when such dear ties are formed,
Its justice is so great that it will leave thee
In happiness. Unless it should disturb thee,
Thy honored place is sure; but in the end
Thou wilt be the Queen's consort, while her daughter
Arsinoë will vouchsafe to give her hand
To one of us and choose thereby a king.

ARIARATHES.   I know what charms that marriage hath for thee.
Much doth it promise thee, but I little fear it
And pity thee if, thinking thus to have
Claims to the throne, thou findest no support
More powerful than her choice.

ANAXANDER.   What! art already
So far supreme as to dispose of her?

Enter THEODOTUS.

THEODOTUS (*to* ANAXANDER).   Ah, knowest thou, sir, the great news?

ANAXANDER.   Tell it quickly.

THEODOTUS.   Aquilius even now is close at hand.
All go to meet him but three miles away.
The populace in their surprise and joy . . .

ANAXANDER (*to* ARIARATHES).   Dost thou still think Arsinoë will obey
            thee,
Sir, and the Senate will be powerless?

ARIARATHES.   Aquilius is here. We must receive him.

THEODOTUS.   'Tis not for him alone such joy bursts forth.

He comes accompanied by Prince Ariarathes.
He brings him with him.

ANAXANDER.   What! this prince still lives?

THEODOTUS.   No more is that report deemed false. He now
Is seen, is spoken to. He himself gives orders . . .

ARIARATHES.   'Tis through him only that Arsinoë
Bestows her hand. Gain it, sir.

ANAXANDER.   And through him
Also will a presumptuous man be foiled.
Go, sit on that throne where the Queen awaits thee.

ARIARATHES.   I know not which of us is more chagrined.

ANAXANDER.   Before I learned thou wert a vile false friend
My heart was fired by some ambition. Then
I would have been much vexed to find the Prince
Balking me; but the punishment of thy pride
Is such a sweet sight to me—it assures me
Of savoring a pleasure so delicious—
That if I can enjoy it, I shall have
Naught to regret. Flatter thyself with all
The happiness which the crown doth promise thee.
Thy fortunes will be fair, whatever heaven
Decrees, and for a moment's space, at least,
Phradates, whom I see, can worship in thee
The phantom of a king.

      [Exeunt ANAXANDER *and* THEODOTUS. *Enter* PHRADATES.

PHRADATES.   Sir, whence arises
This rumor which hath suddenly been noised?
Aquilius, it is said, brings Ariarathes.
He shows himself, is seen.

ARIARATHES.   Be not surprised.
From secret sources I had learned all this.
Impelled by wicked daring, an impostor
Who knew the trials of my earliest childhood
And had heard no more said of my abduction,
Has taken my name—taken it publicly.
As son of the late king, and by long woes
Made to live doubtful of his father's rank,
That he might find the means to end their course,
He came to beg for Rome's assistance. Rome,
Which always had had knowledge of my fate,
Hath feigned to be deceived by his false claims
And sends him hither only to be punished
Here for the shameless fraud which he has dared
Maintain. I shall derive hence this advantage

At least: that if there is some traitor here,
To this knave's peril he will be revealed,
Though after the kind feelings which my mother
Hath shown towards me, my secret enemies
Cause me scant fear.

PHRADATES.   Thou thinkest her vanquished?
ARIARATHES.   Yes.

Natural ties are strong; such is the warmth
Of feeling for her son which dominates her
That she, for fear someone might dare abuse
The power of the scepter, forced herself
To choose me for her husband! Knowing me,
Judge what I should expect from this. However,
Watch Anaxander carefully, and I
Shall go now to discover, where it is
A question that involves a throne, what secret
Sentiments Axiana has towards me.

A C T   I I I

ARIARATHES *and* AXIANA *are discovered.*

AXIANA.   I shall acknowledge that despite thy love
I had expected this nobility,
Ne'er doubting that vicissitudes so cruel
Would see the hero triumph o'er the lover.
But I insist that heaven's bequest to me
Did not oblige Orontes to exhibit
Such joy. A heart that really loves, when losing
The object of its love, could have excused
Itself from being so magnanimous.

ARIARATHES.   To see a loved one in a rival's arms
Is truly a worse woe than death itself.
I know that; yet despite my jealous anguish,
I, who dared love thee, think but of thy interest.
Thus, when my princess gains the name of queen,
I make no question if my loss be certain;
The sight of her raised to this lofty station
Affords me all I need for my contentment.
That alone strikes mine eyes; and when I think
Thereof with soul obsessed by thy good fortune,
A tender rapture leads me to imagine
That 'tis I, 'tis my hand which is to crown thee,
That if the throne shall end thy woes, 'tis I,

Despite all envious men, who place thee on it!
Dost thou condemn my joy in this sweet dream . . .

AXIANA.   Yes, cruel man, since thou dost not place me on it!
I have told thee more already than is seemly.
Exult to thy heart's fill over thy conquest
And see a princess at her pride's expense
Lament a blessing which comes not from thee.
When the Queen seemed about to crown thee, when
I had to force myself to see her take thee,
I wished, I tried to quell my heart's desires,
But could not do so without many a sigh.
Against *thy* interests I urged *my* love;
I longed for thee to have this regal glory,
And in my soul I trembled at the prospect.
What makes *thy* heart less stricken at *my* lot?
A lack of love? or an excess of virtue?
Either on thy part is an insult to me;
And if thou'st offered me a true love's homage,
Oughtest thou to force me to grieve secretly
To see thou dost not grieve at losing me?

ARIARATHES.   Ah, if this love which thou didst waken in me
Could not till now reveal itself enough,
How could I better prove to thee its ardor
Than by the great joy that fills all my heart?
Thou reignest, and as I have no lot but thine,
This triumph means more than all else to me.
To enjoy it wholly and without distraction,
Turn, as I do, thine eyes from me. Behold
Only the greatness to which heaven calls thee,
Only this throne.

AXIANA.   How *can* I, thou false man?
Whoe'er would have a heart fixed on a throne
Betrayeth a loved one or hath never loved.
How I deceived myself when I imagined
That the Queen's offer of her hand to thee
Had caused thee some distress! Thou wert to reign,
And the bright splendor of a lot so glorious
No longer let thee turn thine eyes towards me.
Thou gavest thyself up to the charms of empire,
Conquering thy love . . .

ARIARATHES.   What do I hear thee say?
I? *I* consented, in the hope of reigning,
To lose . . .

AXIANA.   And what hath caused thee to disdain it?

ARIARATHES. Love, that true love whose fervor is revealed
When I resign thee unto Ariarathes.
Am I to snatch thee from a great king's marriage?
AXIANA. Nay, not for this do I complain of thee.
I have already said that thou art noble
To give up, for my sake, all hope of me.
But would it be unworthy of thy greatness
Of soul to show at least a little grief?
Couldst thou, unfeeling man, not let a princess,
For her love's sake, cost thee some human frailty,
Or dost thou deem that thou wouldst have to blush
If thou shouldst dare regret thy loss of me?
Ah, why against thy love, so arrogant,
Have I not made my pride of birth be felt;
And why have I permitted a confession
To be extracted from me which doth cause me
Such bitter pain and touch thy heart so little?
ARIARATHES. Therein lies all my joy, all my good fortune,
But when the gods dispense their favor to thee,
Would it be love to mingle my regrets
With the splendors of a lot which crowns thy wishes?
AXIANA. Which crowns my wishes?
ARIARATHES.   So I tell myself.
Before thou doubtest it, see Ariarathes;
And if, on knowing him, thou art displeased
That Rome obliges thee to reign with him,—
If, when my princess gives her hand to him,
She still can find something to be regretted,—
The greatness of my sorrow then will show her
To what despair this qualm of hers can bring me.
Then my despair unceasingly will make her
See if I fear her costing me some frailty
And if I have rejoiced at her good fortune
Save when assured that this would cause her joy.
AXIANA. Go; thou shalt have thy wish. Since thou so willest,
I needs without regret, without a murmur,
Must satisfy thee. I shall give up all
To gain the throne, and see no more in thee
Save that which renders thee unworthy of me.
Be sure that when I reign with Ariarathes,
There is naught elsewhere that beguiles my heart,
And that his hand brings me a bliss so perfect
That I would so have chosen had Rome not done so.
Moreover, even though I should have to sigh

Unceasingly, it is enough that once
I stooped to baseness, and I would deprive thee
Of any opportunity to plume
Thyself on having caused my heart to suffer.
Thou wouldst behold me placid, calm, and steadfast,
Showing, whate'er my woe, a soul contented,
Hiding all pangs thereof, disclosing naught
Which seemed to mar for me the joy of reigning.

ARIARATHES. If I may credit what thou seemest to mean,
This joy will always be without a shadow,
And, to conceal no more what all will learn,
Know . . .

AXIANA.   The Queen comes, and I will hear thee not.

Enter LAODICE *and* CLEONE.

LAODICE. Princess, heaven at last by striking tokens
Shows us that ever it preserveth sovereigns.
This son of mine so longed for, he of whose
Return my love was sure by secret instinct,
Hath come, fills all the land with rapture, opens
For thee a radiant pathway to the throne.
To keep it safe for thee, what care I took!
Thine eyes have long been witnesses thereof—
Seen me oppose the marriage of my daughter
And ever await this miracle's glad day.
And now, when I was forced to yield at last
To the wishes of the populace, the gods
Have vouchsafed to accord me what I wished for.

AXIANA. If 'tis a wondrous miracle, it doubtless
Was brought about by that unceasing care
Which this sweet hope ere now hath cost thee, madam.
I owe too much to thy exceptional kindness
Not to share all thy feelings. For thyself
Alone in the return of this thy son
Whom heaven sends back to thee, my cup of joy
Would have been full; to make it overflow
With sweeter rapture, thou permittest me,
Besides, to hope that he will be my husband.
So great an honor is indeed a blessing
At which the gods will let me show myself
No less delighted than surprised. Most happy
Were I if for my dowry I could make
All the world subject to thy noble son.

LAODICE. Thy prayers had power to give him back to me.

They joined with mine; that, Princess, is enough.
Let us have now no thought but to give thanks
To heaven for a return which constitutes
This land's one happiness. Thou art awaited
In the temple, where thou wilt, by sacrifices,
Discharge thy duty to the gracious gods,
While I will see to it that everyone
Shall show his loyalty by going forth
With ceremonious pomp to meet his king.

AXIANA. Madam, I shall obey, and my obedience
Will say better than I all that I think.
I swear it to thee; thou shalt find it so.

[*Exit* AXIANA.

LAODICE. Let me be left alone here. Thou, Orontes,
Stay. [*Exit* CLEONE.

ARIARATHES. I was waiting, madam, to declare
What joy thine own had wakened in my heart
When I had learned heaven gratifies thy wishes . . .

LAODICE. The more they seem fulfilled, the less, Orontes,
They are satisfied, and since I after all
Must needs hide nothing from thee, I have wanted
My son, and now he fills me with despair.
By his return my hopes are all defeated.

ARIARATHES. What! thou art sorry? thou who lovedst only
This son? thou who didst guard the scepter for him,
And who by virtue of the name of mother . . .

LAODICE. Yes, mother of a son to whom I should
Be dear, and who would come without assistance
To take the royal power from my hands.
But I cannot endure the slave of Rome,
A puppet of those tyrants whom our ancestors
Used to defy. He comes to make us bow
Before his haughty masters—make us share
Those chains which he is base enough to wear.
Could I feel any joy to see him crowned?
No, no; in vain the hope of reigning fills him.
No Senate's mandate if he seeks to do so!
No foreigners can force me to obey.

ARIARATHES. Then wilt thou thine own flesh and blood betray?
If the Senate sends him, is he made its slave
By using it to vouch for who he is?
Without it, without word from Rome that reared him,
Would not thy son's identity be doubtful?
Couldst thou on *his* word know him Ariarathes?

LAODICE. 'Tis true that Rome must needs identify him;
But really, if she had knowledge of him,
Why were his fortunes so long hidden from me?
When she informed me, sending deputies,
That she desired to help me choose a king,
For what strange reason was I not informed
That her ambassador would bring my son?
Aquilius comes with so great secrecy
That he appears before he is expected,
As though the people, if surprised completely
In seeing their king, might better turn against me.
To this, to this tends all Rome's policy!
It is revealed to me by these precautions.
She in the vilest way seeks to wrest from me
What she assumes that I would not surrender.
She with my daughter's marriage forced on me
Supposedly wished first to fill my mind,
And when Rome learns that I have chosen *thee,*
Her jealous heart will fancy this a crime
And wish to punish thee for deserving it.
But though the people rise or Rome be angry,
To destroy thee or lay down laws to me,
My son is not yet sure of being king.

ARIARATHES. Truly would I, like thee, condemn the course
Whose too great secrecy doth anger thee.
Ere now should Ariarathes have appeared.
But think of what it means to offend the Senate.
Having sent him back to thee, will it, deemest thou,
Let thee presume to mar his destiny?
'Twill surely take up arms. Any but thee
Would fear great power impelled by righteous wrath.

LAODICE. If the realm wants a king, requires a man,
With thee for husband why should I fear Rome?
With this great title armed, consort and king,
Wilt thou lack spirit to do battle for me?
Wilt thou be less the invincible Orontes
Whom our proud neighbors to their shame have known,
And is the storm of war thou seekest to shun
More dangerous when it comes from farther off?

ARIARATHES. My spirit would be the same; yet howso brave,
What hope hath one against a lawful king
Who can, despite thee, despite all our plans,
Win, when he shows himself, his subjects' hearts?

LAODICE. Well, if thou fearest that he will conquer all,

LAODICE

That is an ill which may be remedied.

ARIARATHES.   How can it, when his mere name here already . . .

LAODICE.   Thou dost not understand me; I must better
Explain myself.
                            Severity is painful
To me, and in my reign, if for my safety
I let myself be feared, I have attempted
Always to use the mildest methods 'gainst
Unnumbered enemies jealous of my greatness.
As slow to punish as I am quick to pardon,
I oft have been content to disarm boldness,
Such horror from my earliest years have I
Felt at the harshness exercised by tyrants.
But where it means a throne, I must confess—
Since to that only all my heart aspires—
That if I must resort to arms to keep it,
A little bloodshed will not frighten me.
What! this dismays thee? Thou dost blench, 'twould seem.

ARIARATHES.   Yes, madam, it is true: I blench, I tremble,
And where a son's blood is the only means . . .

LAODICE.   Thou'dst rather, then, see shed thine own and mine?
That is the one choice to be made. Decide.
We must expect, or launch, the lightning's bolt.
'Twill surely fall upon whichever of us
Dares not, because of scruples, use it first.
If my son does not die, our death is certain.

ARIARATHES.   Thou hearkenest to those feelings which misgivings
Breed in thee. But can nature's ties be broken?
Thinkest thou that this son . . .

LAODICE.   I must tell thee all.
Truly, with thee, whose heart is still too tender,
To half explain makes one misunderstood.
Knowing me wholly, thou canst judge of me.
   The late king at his death left me six sons.
By different strokes of fate, five of them died.
Perhaps thou'st heard some ugly rumors whispered;
I have disdained their insult and believed
These slanders, while I reigned, not worth my tears.
With my heart charmed by such a brilliant fortune,
I used all means to make it mine more surely.
Carried to Rome as hostage, Ariarathes
Could rob me of it, were he not removed.
I ordered him to be—decreed his death—
But now I see the gods have not allowed it,

That a vile knave betrayed me, and that Rome
And Ariarathes learned my secret aims.
Thou canst from this judge what a son too surely
Convinced of all his mother's pride, can do.
If I would sacrifice his life to reign,
Would he, to reign, in his turn wish to spare me?
He is of mine own blood, a blood too eager
For empire's throne to tremble at the prospect
Of a mere matricide, and if this son
Of mine be not destroyed by me, he soon
Will show himself well versed in mine own lessons.
He must, he must be killed; I have no choice.
'Tis said he comes unguarded with Aquilius.
Thou hast no foes but mine, and he who wishes
To rid himself of them can find a way.

ARIARATHES. Ah, no! To make thee lay aside a purpose
So deadly to him, grant that he may cherish
The hope which still is his, and that this hapless
Prince may through me oppose thee with the ties
Of blood that birth has given him. Believe,
In hearing me, that it is he who pleads,
That he would fain soften his mother's heart,
And that he kneels and through my voice says to thee:
"Give life to me a second time. I know
Thou hatest me. But what inspires thy feelings?
To be thy son is not so great a crime.
Consent to pardon it since I so revere thee
That thou shouldst never be suspicious of me.
Take for thy warrant the true, pure loyalty
Which my love pledges thee in the face of heaven,
That loyalty which no vicissitudes . . ."

LAODICE. With thrones at stake, does one put faith in oaths?
Do not deceive thyself; though it should be
That crime was odious to him, as to thee,—
That virtue had for him the same attraction,—
With what he knows of me, I would not trust
Myself in his hands. Nay, if I should have
Complete assurance that he would leave the throne
Always in my possession, and would always
Be my submissive subject, I would feel
Still the same ardor to achieve his death.
To make my ordering it just and lawful,
'Twould be enough to see that he forgave
My crime, and that I needs would die if he,

Because of noble fears and scruples, did not
Refuse to be as wicked as myself.
Therefore I cannot see him dead too soon,
Though he were but a witness of my shame;
Therefore I always must attempt his life,
I needs must fear his crime or hate his virtue,
And in his blood seek our security,
To save me from the one or to avenge
Myself upon the other. That is all.
Contend no more! Thou must declare thyself
And choose which of these two things thou preferrest.
If to shed blood disturbs thee, gives thee pain,
I know who without qualms will hear a queen,
And for one crime exacted of their fealty,
Will not disdain to rule with me. But ere
I borrow any other arms than thine,
Reflect that one crime oft compels another
And that, when I have told thee my resolve,
Only the throne can be a safe place for thee.

ARIARATHES.   Well, take my life, then, madam; it is thine.
Virtue alone hath ever swayed my soul;
And if I needs must die, then I shall die
Well satisfied to give my blood because
Of my refusal to do a heinous deed.

LAODICE.   'Tis too much! Let us say no more about it.
Such an excess of virtue wearies me.
   Here, someone!

                    [She claps her hands. CLEONE *appears.*

CLEONE.   Madam?

LAODICE.   Listen.
    [She speaks in a low tone to CLEONE, *who afterwards with-*
      draws.

ARIARATHES.   Oh, I beg thee,
By my devotion to thee shown so often . . .

LAODICE.   'Twas great, I know, but I have well repaid thee.
Howe'er a stubborn envy might oppose thee,
Through me thy fortunes have defied all hazards.
Exalted swiftly, thou hast now a station
Which ne'er was given but to the noblest blood.
Master, for two years past, of power supreme,
Thou clearly lackest but the name of king.
I offer this to thee, and for reward,
Ungrateful man, of all my favors to thee,
Thou wouldst fain tear me from the throne whereon

I seek to place thee? thou wouldst fain that I
Should serve as victim of the Romans?
ARIARATHES.   I?
Say that I wish to spare thy hand a crime—
To see this fell intent withstood by ties
Of nature.
LAODICE.   Go. Till needed, keep thy virtue.
I shall reward as usual him who serves me.

Re-enter CLEONE.

(*To* CLEONE)   Well?
CLEONE.   The command is given.
ARIARATHES.   Madam!
LAODICE.   Go,
I say. I know thy heart; thou knowest mine.
Enough, then.   [*Exit* ARIARATHES.
CLEONE.   What new turmoil agitates
Thy soul again, madam? If I dared speak
Without displeasing thee . . .
LAODICE.   Alas, Cleone!
This son of whom I thought to rid myself
And whose return I feigned that I awaited . . .
Gods!
CLEONE.   Such a sudden turn indeed doth change
This great day. But it seemeth that some other
Misfortune is combined with the harsh fate
That threatens thee. Meseemed that when Orontes
Went from thee, I perceived thee hold in check
A violent rage. Before he quitted thee
Thou gavest me to understand 'twas needful
That Anaxander should be found at once,
As if alone able to relieve thy woe . . .
LAODICE.   Come, follow me. Learn what I wish of him.   [*Exeunt.*

ACT IV

LAODICE *and* CLEONE *are discovered.*

LAODICE.   Thou vainly pointest out to me that the people
Are to be feared. The enterprise is daring,
But I have had to force myself to launch it,
To stifle nature's voice, nor hesitate
To reap the fruit thus of my earlier deeds.
He who can make his seat firm on the throne

By crime, deserves to be hurled thence if he
Shrinks from committing it, and although a thousand
Offenses render him detestable,
The last absolves him and is always glorious.
Unless I choose to perish, he must die.

CLEONE. I see what thy security requires.
This son, informed from childhood of thy schemes,
To save himself will do as Rome advises,
And in her natural distrust of thee
To take thy life alone will satisfy her.
That is what thou wilt surely have to frustrate.
Anaxander gave his word, but can he keep it?
See what he risks in promising this deed.
The Prince will surely have some guards about him,
And though thou dost not fear their feeble succor,
Will he who sees the blow not know the hand?
His minion seized, what then of Anaxander?

LAODICE. What interest have I in his fate? The blow
Struck, let him perish; little do I care.
I shall completely disavow his crime,
Nor do I deem that I need later fear
Ill fortune if the Romans wish to rid me
Of an ambitious man. 'Tis not that he
Hath failed to take every precaution, though:
He hath compelled me to consent that those
He uses, if they find themselves arrested,
Shall say they are the agents of Orontes.

CLEONE. What, madam! such prompt hate for this poor man?
Thy love, then, can give in so soon?

LAODICE.   To him
Who does a crime for us, we must grant all.
Anaxander hates him and would ill have served me
If I had not feigned to have cast him off
And to desire to impute to him the deed
Which, despite *his* refusal, will soon be witnessed.
But though Orontes hath deserved my hate,
My heart is still futile and weak against him.
After all that he owes me, to refuse
To do a crime when I was its reward
Was to join insult to disdain; and yet,
With feelings which I vainly disavow,
Against my interests, I praise him for it
Myself! A strange confession for a heart
Sunk deep in guilt, to feel itself constrained

To appreciate virtue! Yes, such as I am,
Bound fast to wickedness by the ruling passion
Which a harsh fate hath given me, I see
Myself, despite myself, forced to respect
That which my fatal tendencies forbid me
To imitate. The more Orontes spurns
Temptation to do evil, the more strength
My love for him appeareth to acquire.
He disappointed me by his refusal,
And far from hating him for this, I would
Have loved him less if he could have obeyed me.
My passion grew in seeing his glory grow,
And if he could so soon make me admire him,
If I attempt a crime opposed by him
'Tis really to reward thereby his virtue.
I make the throne its guerdon, where, whatever
Any accuse me of, I wish to purchase
For him the place which he refuses—there
To watch his glory shine—and let ambition,
This great day, serve as pretext for my love.
Thus only can my shame be blotted out.

A far-off uproar is heard. Enter AXIANA.

AXIANA.   Ah, madam! there has been a strange disaster.
Only confused reports of it as yet
Are heard, but if 'tis true, the Prince is dead.
LAODICE.   What! my son?
        (*Aside*)   All goes well, Cleone.
                    (*Aloud*)   Oh, Princess!
AXIANA.   This report turns the common joy to sighs.
All, equally surprised by this misfortune,
Uplift a wail that echoes even here.
Men mourn, men weep, and in their rage the people
Ask heaven the reason for its cruelty
And swear they will avenge this precious blood.
LAODICE.   O too sore outcome of the gods' fierce wrath!
After a long reign full of woe and fears
Is this the happiness they offered me?
That son on whom their hatred chose to fall—
Did they restore him to me but to snatch him
From me? But if he really is dead,
Doth any know the traitor who hath dared
To soil his hand with such black villainy?
He owes his blood to him; our tears are useless.

AXIANA. Prince Ariarathes hath been slain; no more
Is known. Men speak of insults and dissension
Which in the ranks caused unforeseen disorder,
But naught is clear, and if it can be doubted . . .

Enter PHRADATES.

LAODICE. What am I told, and what have I to fear,
Phradates?
PHRADATES.   The blind frenzy which is bred
In a great people by their master's death.
Their despair rages, and by their confused
Outcries . . .
LAODICE.   Alas! is it true, then, that my son
No longer lives and that unto my prayers
Heaven hath seemed responsive but the better
To double the bad fortune which o'erwhelms me?
I have felt too great joy, and all my senses,
Enraptured, have too much that triumph tasted
In which I waited for my son. 'Twas fated
That by his death his glory should be followed.
PHRADATES. It was that triumph alone that cost his life.
By thy command, madam, all did their best
To put themselves into a proper state
To go forth and receive him. All the people
Under their chief men, richly dressed, were burning
To render this first homage to their king,
And left the city with the eagerness
That such a great event inspires in subjects.
Scarcely had we yet gone a thousand yards
Across the plain than we beheld, far off,
The Roman eagle shining, which seemed to come
Toward us at a slow pace, and thus allowed
Our squadrons time enough to arrange themselves.
We stopped, and while the attempt was being made
To curb the fervor which the soldiers showed
When they beheld him, Ariarathes came
And trusted himself to us, followed by
Aquilius and a large part of the Romans.
He had at once in proof of our true fealty
Both our deep reverence and our humblest homage;
He gladly suffered us to crowd around him,
And when respects were paid, we all began
To move on. Then it was that 'twixt two chieftains
A point of honor gave birth to a quarrel

Which scarce can be believed. They both were near
The Prince and wished to guard him and disputed
The privilege of doing so, which neither
Of them would give up, and in their blind ardor
For this distinction, while Aquilius
Was still proceeding forward with Orontes,
Such was the heat with which they pressed their claims
That after threats were made, they came to blows.
The troop took sides for one or for the other;
In spite of us they grappled, struck, and slew;
And with a fatal thrust at random given,
The Prince was pierced early in this sad strife.
He fell, and with no strength to speak a word
Scarcely had heaved two sighs when he expired.
His death filled all the combatants with terror,
The chieftains and those foremost were arrested,
And wishing to clear up this crime before thee,
Aquilius will come here to ask for justice.

LAODICE. And he shall have it. I shall make him see
The horror which I feel for this vile murder.
Such unexpected strife involves some mystery.
Rome hath a mother's aid to clear it up.
She reared my son and she, too, is his mother
With the same claims that ties of blood give me
And moved by the same interests to seek justice;
And in whatever way a monarch dies,
Though by ill chance which could not be prevented,
This accidental crime must needs be punished.
(*To* AXIANA) Princess, to *my* grief add thine own as well.
To avenge my son the better, let us urge
Each other on. He would have seated thee
Upon the throne; and to repair the injustice
Of Fate which cannot allow this to be,
If Rome will suffer me to dispense her gifts,
Thou canst not hope for aught that in my woe
I would not grant; obtain but her consent
And I will give thy realm back to thee.

AXIANA.   Madam,
Thy generosity doth not surprise me,
But I should deem my soul no less ungrateful
Than base, if I so soon forgot the death
Of Ariarathes. Let us avenge that,
Punish his treacherous murderer, and later
The Senate will decide my destiny.

LAODICE

Enter ANAXANDER.

LAODICE. How now, then? Is my son dead, Anaxander?
ANAXANDER. Yes, madam. In the Romans' arms he hath
    Just given up the ghost. His triumph brought
    About his death, nor has there ever been
    A stroke of Fate more sudden or unforeseen.
LAODICE. I see the secret cause of this chance blow.
    This is the cost I pay for a rash people
    Which, seeking to compel me to select
    A king, lends arms against me to ambition.
    My grief names none among you, but my son
    Being no more, the crown goes to my daughter,
    And her hand's gift, which breeds such jealousy,
    Hath charms full sweet for him who can aspire
    To it. If no one had this guilty hope,
    My son would still be living.
PHRADATES.   There may be
    Reasons I know not of for thy suspicions,
    But as mine honor is besmirched thereby,
    I yield myself up as a prisoner
    Until they be looked into. Innocence
    Puts itself willingly to the test.
ANAXANDER.   'Tis bitter,
    Madam, to see that anyone suspects us;
    But if the hope of reigning could inspire us
    To undertake a murder which thou must
    Avenge, what of Orontes, unto whom
    This very day, by thy resolve to wed him,
    Thou thyself profferedst the crown? I do not
    Accuse him, but it is astonishing
    That, having gone to meet the Prince, he left him,
    And hastening towards the city with Aquilius,
    Thus made his help be unavailable,
    Seeming expressly to have put himself
    Where he could interpose no obstacle
    To this foul crime. There is much murmuring,
    And many hold him guilty.
AXIANA.   Of such falseness
    Orontes is incapable. His virtues,
    His noble heart, all speak sufficiently
    For him.
ANAXANDER.   I well know that his character
    Must argue strongly for his innocence,

That **a true** hero is unalterable,
And **ne'er** forgets himself. Aquilius,
However, knows what is the common talk;
And dealing with this horrid crime, sheer treason,
Can he do less than demand thorough proof?

LAODICE. Orontes' constant zeal to serve this realm
Should banish all suspicions of his guilt.
His honor shines too bright to let them linger.

ANAXANDER. Madam, Aquilius speaks for the Senate,
And when we have to render an account
To him for Ariarathes, if he should
Demand that unto Rome we send Orontes,
To dare dispense with carrying out a bidding
So urgent, dost thou think it is enough
To deem him innocent?

AXIANA.   Here he is, now.
Permit me to withdraw. An obvious
Concern to punish must incite thee, madam,
And I should fear that in a situation
So cruel, I ill could know the criminal.

Exit AXIANA. *Enter* ARIARATHES.

LAODICE. Come, speak, Orontes. It is vain for us
To try to exculpate thee, when on the strength
Of a report now bruited, Anaxander
Accuses thee. Is it by thy contrivance
That this crime has been so successful?

ARIARATHES.   Madam,
Aquilius is not twenty paces distant.
He knows about the crime, and if he thinks me
To be accomplice to it, I have blood
To shed; thou shalt do justice at his bidding.

LAODICE. With the proud hope which I have given thee,
To be suspected is to be judged guilty.
Murmurs and plaints are heard. What canst thou say
In thy defense?

ARIARATHES.   Perhaps somewhat too much
Credence is given to Anaxander's charges.

ANAXANDER. I have told what is rumored, and I have not
Intended to lend strength to a suspicion
Which thou dost not deserve. But it is futile
Indeed to war against thy innocence.
The arrested rioters will be thy defenders,
And having nowise shared their guilty rage . . .

LAODICE

ARIARATHES. Finish thy speech before the ambassador.

Enter AQUILIUS, *with a bodyguard of Roman soldiers.*

LAODICE (*to* AQUILIUS). Who would have thought, sir, that so glad
    a day
Was destined thus to cost me sighs and tears,
And when thou camest here to end my woes
The honor of seeing thee could make me weep?
Must I, as all my thanks to thy republic,
Express my grief to her and show the value
Of her long kindness by the agitation
My son's death causes me? Thou broughtest him back
To us, taught by great masters how to walk
In the footsteps of his noble ancestors,
And by a harsh blow of the grimmest fate
The moment of his glory is that in which
He died. At this cruel sight my senses fail me,
Yield to the frenzy of my stricken soul,
And take flight when I find I must avenge
Both the offense to Rome and our king's blood.

AQUILIUS. Madam, I grieve for thee. The magnitude
Of thy misfortune seemeth so unusual
That scarcely could thy fortitude give way
Less utterly before the blow that fells thee.
'Tis surely cruel, and when its violence
Leaves thy heart thoroughly inclined to vengeance,
If it will comfort thee to tell thee now
That I desire to share that task with thee,
Trouble thyself only with choice of tortures.
Accomplices suffice to show the guilty,
My search to find him hath not been in vain,
And thou canst deem him in thy hands already.

LAODICE. 'Tis only thus that I expect some cure,
After my son's death, for the griefs that crush me.
To give Rome satisfaction and fulfil
This hope, assume here, sir, absolute power.
I know thou canst not err or be unjust
In judging who is innocent, who guilty;
And those whom envy fain would persecute
Have naught to dread in being at first suspected.
Perhaps my grief would have in its impatience
Vision less clear and greater violence.
'Tis thou whom it will trust. Give orders. Punish.

AQUILIUS. The offense to Rome is great as well thou knowest;

But howso sternly this may arm her wrath,
Madam, she still remains less stern than just,
And though I ever must uphold her interests,
When I presume to sentence anyone
I am answerable for it. But yet more:
I only at the peril of my head
Can see a great disturbance imminent
And still take no precautions; and I myself
Would be suspected of a crime if I
Neglected aught to save the realm from this.
I have some strong suspicions which can be
Only revealed when those who gave them birth
Are in our hands. These people shall be heard
In their legitimate defense; but I
Will nowise speak until they are arrested.
I ask thee, in the Senate's name, to seize them.

ANAXANDER.   In *thy* realm, innocence hath naught to dread,
Madam; and if men still suspect Orontes . . .

LAODICE.   Whate'er the Senate bids must needs be done.
Speak, sir: whom dost thou wish to be arrested?

AQUILIUS.   Anaxander.

ANAXANDER.   Me!

AQUILIUS.   If 'tis a wrong I do thee,
The blood of certain criminals can repair it.

ANAXANDER.   Madam . . .

LAODICE.   This is no time, Prince, to protest.
(*To* THEODOTUS)   Let him be led to prison.

ANAXANDER.   What! such in-
       justice?
If Rome but wills a thing, must it be done?

AQUILIUS.   Rome never is unjust. When thou insultest her . . .

LAODICE.   Theodotus, obey!
       (*To* ANAXANDER)   And thou, submit.

ANAXANDER.   And in my rank's despite . . .

LAODICE.   Submit, I tell thee.
Thou thyself knowest to what Rome constrains me.
'Gainst thee, 'gainst all, I needs must do her bidding.
If thou art accused falsely, thou canst prove it.
Go.
       Let his guard be strict.

ANAXANDER (*surrendering his sword*).   I must yield, madam.
But be consoled: thou knowest my heart and wilt not
Let me be driven to extremities.

AQUILIUS. Follow, and see to all, Lucilianus.

> [*Exeunt* THEODOTUS, *with* ANAXANDER, *and a Roman soldier.*

LAODICE. Sir, does my frank compliance satisfy thee?

AQUILIUS. Madam, my act was by the Senate's warrant,
And thou canst pay thy debt to Rome no better
Than by thy seconding whate'er it orders.
'Twill doubtless learn of this with joy; but now
The time has come for *thy* joy to be shown
And a knave's death, unworthy of thy tears,
To. be no more reckoned among thy woes.

LAODICE. What sayest thou, sir?

AQUILIUS. That heaven, always just,
Hath let crime slay only a guilty wretch
Who stole thy son's name and supposed his fraud
Had won the throne already. Rome had sent him
To thee to punish his audacity.

LAODICE. 'Twas not my son? Ah, sir! But tell me, please,
Is Fate more kind to Ariarathes? Can I
Believe he lives and thou wilt bring him to me?

AQUILIUS. Madam, he lives. The story of his death
Was a deception, used successfully,
Which Rome, anxious to guard thy son for thee,
To avoid exposing him, thought justified.
She hath always taken care of him and, ready
To restore him to thee such a one as thou
Canst hope for him to be, she has wished first
To frustrate here some plots that she suspected.
Thou seest the result; and being expended
Upon a fraud, their fury will perchance
Be difficult to rouse again, when, warned
That some have sought his life, the Prince will find
Help in precautions.

LAODICE. What! it then can be
That I again shall see him, after all?
(*To* PHRADATES) Go and proclaim this glad news to the
people!
Calm their despair by drawing them from error.

> [*Exit* PHRADATES.

(*To* AQUILIUS) But let me see him soon, sir. This attempt
Defeated, he has nothing more to fear.

AQUILIUS. 'Tis hard to check a natural eagerness.
Thou presently shalt see him come in splendor.
In the meantime, learn the justice of the Senate.
If it so wrought that this thy son shall reign

Whom heaven gives back to thee, it is not willing
To see thee left without a crown or be
Reduced by this day's changes to dispense
No laws except as someone else consents.
Live no man's subject; be a monarch always.
Thou shalt be queen of Lycaonia.
It is Rome's conquest; she can give it to thee.

LAODICE.   I know that vainly would my son object.
If Lycaonia to this realm belongs,
It is the price of a great woe for which
I still sigh. The good fortune of the Romans
Cost me my husband. But permit my son
To decide this for us. Concerned for him
And far less queen than mother, I desire
His greatness; it alone is dear to me.
Let him allow me near him, let him choose
To send me far away from him, my wishes
Are satisfied if I behold him reigning.
That triumph is all to which my love aspires.
To that end, assume here complete control.
Go, see to all things, and as thou preferrest,
Give orders in the town as in the palace.

ACT V

ARIARATHES *and* PHRADATES *are discovered.*

ARIARATHES.   What! despite all attempts to abate their fury,
Could they not be restrained from slaying him?

PHRADATES.   Sir, the attempt was made to avert this outcome;
But, full of rage and grief, the populace
In their wild frenzy sought but how to seize him,
And despite all Theodotus could do,
Laid hold on Anaxander and refused
To let him be conducted to the prison.
"Prince Ariarathes' death must be avenged,"
They cried, and instantly, as though assured
That he was guilty, without further question
They took him for their victim. Anaxander
In dying cried out loudly that the Queen
Herself alone had caused her son to perish,
And the impatient anger of the people
Would even on her have made its work complete
If everywhere the story had not spread

Of the erroneous crime, and disabusing
Their minds of their mistake, disarmed their wrath.
To witness in their transports what keen joy
They felt on learning that they had mourned only
For a false Ariarathes, one would think
That they already knew with full assurance
That heaven would give them for their king a hero
Such as they could expect in thee alone.

ARIARATHES. Thus have I caused the death of Anaxander,
Whom I arrested through Aquilius
Only to frustrate what he might attempt.
But if his end has rid me of one foe,
What must I not dread always from my mother?
Her wishes all have but a single goal:
To see me perish.

PHRADATES.   Heaven will protect thee
To the very end. It has declared itself
Too clearly 'gainst her turpitude. Meanwhile,
Admire her cleverness. All the joy that could
Be manifested for a son preserved
From treachery is shining in her eyes.
She with Aquilius directs, arranges
Who shall be escort for King Ariarathes,
What guard he is to have, and how to balk
New crimes like that which now she seeks to punish.
No troubled glance reveals her heart's vexation.
By that which this great day hath brought, her prayers
Are granted. Heaven has given her back her son.

ARIARATHES. I cannot bear the hell of being hated
By her. If my submissiveness serves only
To breed still greater hate, let us confound her
By telling who I am, and find out whether
This son whom her ambition hath betrayed,
When known for who he is, will still be hated.
Here she is; let me make a last attempt
To overcome the hardness of her heart.
Perhaps the hour of victory has arrived.

Exit PHRADATES. *Enter* LAODICE.

LAODICE. Orontes, thou hast won. My son is saved.
Heaven hath twice defended him already
Against the fell schemes of my jealous envy.
Twice it hath turned aside my fury's blows
But ne'er could it have triumphed without thee.

'Tis thou who, with more power o'er my heart
Than heaven, couldst make less great my eagerness
To wear the crown and couldst compel the pride
Which by my very station hath been swollen,
To think of ties of blood and to respect them.
The past is past. This pride no more inspires me.
By virtue thou hast torn me from crime's ways.
Despite my many vows to stop at naught,
My son shall live and reign, now. My ambition
Consenteth. He has nothing more to fear.

ARIARATHES.   My heart yearns to believe thee; I am trying
To make myself believe thee; but forgive me,
Madam, for being forced to feel a doubt
Which my respect for. thee gainsays. In vain
Do I desire to keep it from arising.
Thou askedst Ariarathes' blood of me,
And if, despite the gods who show themselves
His helpers, the same spirit were to arm thee
Once more against him, wouldst thou then disclose
To me thy terrible intent?—to me
Who by refusing served thee ill, and who
By seeking to avert thy cruel purpose
May have become a criminal in thy sight?
How can I judge whether sincere repentance
Hath given the victory to natural ties
And finally restored his mother to him?
What proof can *he* have of so great a change?

LAODICE.   That heaven which shields him, and my own departure.
I can be just, and I can see too clearly
How great distrust the knowledge of my schemes
Must cause him, to require of him that he
Should feel assured of me or should endure
My presence and reign without anxiety.
I plotted his destruction, and to punish
Myself for this, I shall impose my exile
To Lycaonia upon myself.
There hath the Senate said that I may reign.
I take its offer and e'en now am ready
To go. But with this remnant which it leaves me
Of honor and of glory now, I have not
Lost from my heart the memory of thy virtues,
And if I still presume to mount a throne
'Tis less for love thereof than to crown thee.
Yes, having promised thee a mighty marriage,

I nowise shall revoke my plighted word.
My one wish is to take thee for my husband.

ARIARATHES. I know my debt to thy exceptional kindness,
But when it was thy pleasure to permit me
To aspire to a great marriage so beneath thee,
Fearing the worst from Rome in that dilemma,
Thou soughtest aid. This have the gods provided.
From such humiliation they have saved thee.

LAODICE. They changed my fortunes; they have not changed me.
My son, so long the target of my hate,
Would still be hated if thou wert not loved.

ARIARATHES. If *I* were not . . . *loved?*

LAODICE. I have wished to keep
Silent to thee about it just as long
As a convenient pretext let me do so
And what love's flame has made me dare for thee
Could be concealed beneath some reason of State.
But now this flame, fanned higher by thy worth
Always, no longer can compel itself
To such restraint, and hardly will my son
Find mercy on this day if I do not
Let thee know that he owes it to that love.
'Tis this which makes me live for thee alone,
Which saves from me the blood I sought to shed,
And which, despite my jealous pride, that I
May give myself to thee, quells my ambition.
'Tis this, this love whose ardor overcomes me . . .
What now! Thou'rt shaken. Explain thyself, Orontes.
Whence come these troubled, hesitating glances,
This cold astonishment?

ARIARATHES. Alas!

LAODICE. Thou sighest?

ARIARATHES. 'Tis true, I sigh; and would to heaven, madam,
That I might hide what agitates my soul,
And that the evils which I foresee would not
Result from this dread secret thou hast told me.
My secret will crush thee as thine crushed me.
I sighed at one; thou'lt tremble at the other.
The more thou seest the error of thy love,
The more will hate give thee a horror of me.

LAODICE. Thou lovest, then, elsewhere; and to wed a queen
Is not worth breaking other bonds for her.
Such constancy is worthy of a hero.

ARIARATHES. My prayers are too well granted for my peace.

3 6 7

Madam, how cruel a blow! Who could have dreamed it!
I sought for glory that I might make thee love me,
And now I find myself forced to lament
A blessing which I have so much desired.
Hate an ill-doer, destroy a foolish man.
I have too long concealed what I must now
At last conceal no longer; but when love
For me hath seized upon thy heart, oh, how
Can I confess to thee I am thy son?

LAODICE. *Thou . . . my son?*

ARIARATHES.   If nature's voice, still silent,
Dares not inform thee of my origin,
Spare not my blood, this blood too odious,
Which may in flowing make thee know it better.
'Tis thus that thou wilt doubtless learn with pleasure
The woeful truth so dreaded by thy soul.
To crown the ills of this accursed day,
Satisfy hate instead of love. 'Twill be
Sweeter to me . . .

LAODICE.   Be not afraid. I *will*
Satisfy this unconquerable hate.
Thy sighs are powerless to plead against it.
If thou astoundest it, thou dost not shake it.
What! by false loyalty thou couldst have made me
Confess the haughty pride which sought thy death,
Couldst have been shown the crimes my heart conceals,
And the result shall be thy prayers' success?
Nay, between us this hate must needs decide.
It challenges us both to monstrous deeds;
And if the gods have cheated me of love,
At least 'twill cost thee innocence or life.
To save thyself one, thou must lose the other,
Become my victim or else make me thine,
And in a word, decide, whate'er the future,
To perish at my hands or slay me first.

ARIARATHES.   These violent feelings needlessly possess thee.
Whate'er may happen, madam, thou shalt reign.
If all my wishes centered on a throne,
I would not for two years have been a subject;
I would not for two years have tried to merit
My mother's fondness by respectful **care;**
I, sword in hand and fearing not her anger,
Would have come boldly . . .

LAODICE.   Oh, why didst thou not?

Then would my hate with open force have tasted
Freely the joy of seeking thy destruction,
Nor would I have been torn at hearing of it
Nor had to dread my weakness against thee.
But thus disguised, thou hast contrived to make me
Cherish the one foe whom I had to fear.
Thy winning virtues, with too sweet a charm,
Have forced my wrath to heed them, and the attractions
They offer to my heart are such that when
It fain would hate thee, it can nowise do so:
Thou turnest it from all that it resolveth.
    Ah, this crime is too great e'er to be pardoned!
Five children by my secret intrigues slain
Still leave me not so guilty as thou art.
By countless services which thou hast done me,
Thou hast roused in me love for mine own son;
Thou hast enkindled in a mother's breast
A passion at once horrible and sweet,
Whose consequences I must dread the more
Because it seeks to rob me of the fruits
Of all my crimes. It vainly doth aspire;
I must have these, must sacrifice once more
The ties of blood; and that ambition which
I was about to stifle must resume
The pride which made it triumph over them.
Though outraged nature were to cost me grief
Untold for this deed, I have gone too far
To tremble at the rest and basely fear
To immolate thee to attain my ends.

ARIARATHES.   Well, take this sword, then, if thou needest its help.
If 'twill be sweet to thee to see my death,
Hasten to taste that joy; I shall not stay thee.
Strike! pierce this breast whose dying sighs have been
Always the object of thy dearest wishes.
Wash away in my blood the tenderness . . .

LAODICE.   Leave in me, then, thou wretch, the power to do so;
And when all seems to inspire my heart to hate thee,
Tear out of it what makes me love thee. Take
From me those flames which, though I loathe them, make me
See in my son a lover I adore,
And which, despite the pride that seeks his death,
Can vitiate my wrath and stay my hand.
In vain I cruelly plot against thy life:
Motherhood seeks it, love accords it to thee;

And when the one consents to blot it out,
The other comes to charm me and thus save thee.
O harsh malignity of Fate revealed
In that accursed love which rules my soul!
Ever have crimes accompanied my hatred,
And I am linked with sin so fatally
That when I cease to hate I still commit one
In loving thee. The ungovernable madness
Of violent love inflames me with a criminal
Passion for mine own son; and he is saved
Only by those unholy fires which blind
Infatuation kindled in my bosom.
The gods have willed it; vain is my resistance.
Live, Ariarathes, and make someone queen,
Whilst I surrender to the need of seeking
Peace for myself, security for thee.

ARIARATHES.   Where wilt thou find it for a son who loves thee
Except by thy consent to share my power?
Be with thy counsels the land's chief support,
And reigning with me . . .

LAODICE.   Do not trust that thought!
Whatever I might promise thee, ambition
Perhaps would kill the love which overcame it,
And in another's arms the one we love
The best becometh hated by us soon.
Let us protect ourselves from such a danger.
The Senate, through its envoy, urges me,
Opens the way for me, and I can do it.

ARIARATHES.   The prayers of a son will have some power.
If time does all things, I can still believe . . .

Enter AXIANA *and* ALCINA.

LAODICE.   Princess, enjoy at last thy promised greatness.
The gods will grant it when a happy bond
Unites thy fortunes with my son's career.
Their kindness to thee is completely shown
When they in famed Orontes make him known.
Taking this hero from my hand as husband,
Thou canst not doubt that he is worthy of thee.
I leave thee now to share this joy with him,
And he will tell thee more.   [*Exit* LAODICE

AXIANA.   What must I needs
Believe? After I gave up, to be queen,
My fondest dreams, could it be that Orontes . . .

Oh, please, please, speak! Whate'er the Queen hath told me,
  I fear my love wanted to hear too much
  And was too credulous of what beguiled it . . .
ARIARATHES. Nay, trust that love; 'twill not deceive thee. I
  Am Ariarathes; and if I have hidden
  The knowledge of my birth from thee till now,
  It was because I wished, by my devotion,
  To merit being loved, without the throne
  Having a share in thy sweet love for me.
  Besides, I sought to learn the Queen's true nature.
AXIANA. The hatred of the people roused against her
  Is to be feared. They gather fast; they threaten
  And cry with a loud voice that they abhor
  The sway of an unnatural murderess,—
  That when her hate is shown against her offspring,
  To pardon her means death for Ariarathes.
  Danger impends, and in this situation . . .
ARIARATHES. The people have already taken vengeance
  For my mistakenly reported death,
  And this uprising to which fear incites them
  Gives me new proof of their fidelity.
  But they must now be pacified, and I
  Can pacify them.

Enter AQUILIUS.

     (*To* AQUILIUS) Sir, the time has come
  To hide no longer my identity.
  The Queen has learned it, and the Princess too.
AQUILIUS. All was nigh lost, sir, by too long a silence.
  I saw the Queen, and shall confront the people
  To tell them all that she was told by thee;
  But that is not enough: thy sight is needed
  To appease at once the maddened populace,
  Who, gathering numbers in the palace court,
  Expect new crimes by her against her son.
  They cry out that she is her children's murderess,
  And would perchance obey the rage that fills them
  If we should still delay to show their king
  To them, to check them and to calm their fears.
  Time presses. Quick! or we must dread the worst.
AXIANA (*to* ARIARATHES). Come, sir. These flames cannot be
      quenched too soon.
  Without thee, every effort will be vain.
ARIARATHES. I fly! But . . .

Enter PHRADATES.

PHRADATES. Ah, sire, the Queen lives no longer.
ARIARATHES. Gods!
AQUILIUS. What! the blind, swift rage of the rioters . . .
PHRADATES. Nay, sir; learn the whole truth of this misfortune.
Though she had heard the populace were gathered
About the palace and were already eager
To look on their new master, she insisted
On coming out upon a balcony
And showing herself to the unruly mob.
The sight of her at once aroused their fury.
All with one voice declared their loathing of her.
Boldly combining insults with their threats,
They soon dared fling at her the vilest taunts,
When with a voice that could be heard far off,
She cried: "Begone! I know what is my due,
Base people, who till now with timid maxims
Have feigned to have no knowledge of my crimes.
Did I not wish to lend to you my arm,
Ye would forever tremble, and not punish!"—
Then raised a dagger which she had seized upon
And fell, ere any saw it, without life.
One blow, despite us, hath cut short her days.
ARIARATHES. O too unhappy son! O piteous death!
AQUILIUS. Heaven is just, and showeth well its justice.
But, sire, the populace yearn for their sovereign.
Constrain thy grief, and to reward their fealty,
Go, let them see their king, and their queen also.

Le Comte D'Essex

(THE EARL OF ESSEX)

By
THOMAS CORNEILLE

INTRODUCTORY NOTE

Ariane (1672) and *le Comte d'Essex* (1678) enjoyed far greater and more lasting fame than any of the other, quite short-lived tragedies of Thomas Corneille. They were often included in old editions of the plays of his illustrious brother, and were acted more frequently than any other tragedies written in seventeenth-century France except some of Pierre Corneille's and Racine's, *Ariane* being given at the Comédie Française 258 times between 1680 and 1793, *le Comte d'Essex* 281 times between 1681 and 1812. The former has generally been the more highly esteemed, and has continued to be revived at intervals; for its subject, the desertion of Ariadne by Theseus, is the more appealing and offers greater opportunities for an emotional actress. But love is the sole concern of all the important characters, and with none of them is it hindered or thwarted except by some other love. The impression which this gives of an artificial society occupied only with love-making is incompatible with great drama or even good drama except in the field of comedy. *Ariane* was written the year after Racine's *Bérénice,* which it closely resembles in dealing similarly with the piteous disappointment of a loving and trusting woman's hopes of marrying the man she loves, and in so many other ways that to doubt the paramount influence here of Racine, then at the height of his fame, is surely gratuitous; but it is State polity, not love, that Racine opposes to love.

In dramatizing the story of Queen Elizabeth and the Earl of Essex, Thomas Corneille was preceded by La Calprenède, whose own *Comte d'Essex* is one of the best tragedies written in the interval between the *Cid* and *Horace.* Thomas Corneille's *Comte d'Essex* is only partially "Racinian." Elizabeth, whom he does not represent as an old woman such as she really was at the time of the death of Essex, resembles the heroines of Racine in her intense emotionalism and fluctuating impulses, but nothing could be more characteristically "Corneillian" than her desire to love and to be loved by her favorite without the hope of marriage, and Essex himself is Corneillian in his overweening pride. But though this pride makes him at first incredulous of the danger threatening him and afterwards unwilling to stoop at all to avert it, the chief factor in his fate is his savage desire to hurt those who love him but have wronged him: the woman he adores, who has presumptuously taken it upon herself to decide what is best for him, and "for his sake" put herself beyond his reach; and the Queen, whom he has served so well but who believes in his guilt. This is a truly notable piece of characterization; for though the determination to let oneself suffer harm that others may be made sorry is perhaps somewhat childish, it is undeniably human and, latently, almost universal, and it has received little treatment elsewhere in literature.

But there is a sobriety, an air of reality, about this play throughout; the distinctive flavor of *Timocrate*, which persists in all other tragedies of its author, is absent here. The romanesque element, which all French-classical tragedies share to some extent, is much smaller than in most of them; there is a minimum of gallantry, for such a theme in that day. All the important characters are complex, and their psychology is sound. Indeed, one of the chief faults of *le Comte d'Essex* results from the realism of their portrayal; they (Elizabeth especially) go over and over the same ground, as tortured people who do not know their own minds are wont to do, and this does not make for the effective progress of dramatic action. The other serious flaw is that the death of Essex, effected by his enemies without authorization by the Queen, is not really a solution of the dramatic conflict between him and her. She risked such an outcome, however, when in obstinate pursuance of her heart's desire that he should humble himself before her, she left him under sentence of the law after she had learned that he was guiltless; and though she finally declared, too late, that she would set him free unconditionally, her entire previous behavior indicates that she would never have brought herself to do so, but would have perpetuated an indecision which must eventually have cost him his life, as it does immediately in the play.

CHARACTERS IN THE PLAY

ELIZABETH, *Queen of England.*
THE DUCHESS OF IRETON, *loved by the Earl of Essex.*
THE EARL OF ESSEX.
CECIL, *Lord Burleigh, the Queen's chief minister, an enemy of the Earl of Essex.*
THE EARL OF SALISBURY, *a friend of the Earl of Essex.*
TILNEY, *the Queen's attendant and confidante.*
CROMMER, *captain of the Queen's guards.*
Guards and attendants.

The scene is laid in London.

The Earl of Essex

A C T I

*The scene represents a room in the palace of Queen Elizabeth,
in London.* ESSEX *and* SALISBURY *are discovered.*

ESSEX. No, my dear Salisbury, there is naught to fear.
However great her anger, love will quench it,
And in the plight into which Fate has plunged me
I am too wretched to obtain death's boon.
Not that it would not irk me sore for envy
To be allowed to blot my life's fair fame.
A man like me should by his very name
Be not more free from crime than from suspicion.
But countless exploits on both land and sea
Indeed have made me known sufficiently
Throughout all England, and I have served too well
To dread aught that my foes dare charge me with.
Thus, even though fraud should have deceived the Queen,
The nation's welfare makes my pardon certain;
And only too well is it known, by what
Mine arm hath done, that whoso loses men
Like me, does not recover them again.
SALISBURY. I know what augmentation of her glory
England hath gained from thee by more than one
Victory. Thy services are great, and never
Hath realm or throne been by a stronger arm
Supported. But despite thy valiant deeds,
Do not be blind through too much confidence.
The more our queen, whose favors match thy merit,
Hath put thee where thou ne'er shouldst fall, the more
Thou needest to tremble lest her pride should stifle
A love that she with shame beholds rejected.
To see thine honored state end suddenly,
Her gracious hand needs but to be withdrawn;
And what security does the rarest service
Give him who treads the verge of an abyss?
One false step is enough; countless examples
Of such great downfalls fill the world with awe.
Permit the friendship that so closely binds us . . .
ESSEX. I made all tremble; wouldst thou have me tremble?
Fraud, it is true, attacks me; but this arm

379

Makes England dreaded by the strongest nations.
It has done everything for her, and I
Have reason to think that the long favor brought me
By so much glory will avail for me
Against my vile foes without difficulty.
It costs me enough for me to expect all things
From it.

SALISBURY. Because of thee this realm is prosperous;
Because of thee 'tis dreaded. But indeed,
Whatever blood its glory costs thee, since
A subject owes his all, if he one time
Forgets himself, people behold his crime
And not his exploits. Men say that thy friends
With secret intrigues have involved themselves
For thy sake in conspiracies and plots,
That thou hast written often to the Earl
Of Tyrone, contriving with that dangerous spirit,
And that thou hast supported him and the Irish,
The cause espousing of that rebel people.
They produce witnesses, and the evidence
Is weighty.

ESSEX. And what profits them their story
If I am innocent? The Earl of Tyrone
Whom the Queen dreads, wishes to be restored
To favor, and to win like grace for Ireland;
And I would think that I had served the realm
Better than ever, if my counsel should
Be followed, and peace be assured thereby.
Because he hates the vile, he would be useful
To me to drive hence Cobham, Raleigh, Cecil—
A pack of men low-born, base flatterers
Who reckon it their glory to be authors
Of public discord. They will ruin all.
The Queen, whom they delude, does not desire
That honest folk should tell her what they are.
They rule her thoughts and cause her to approve
Of all that best can serve to set them higher.
Their greatness waxes by the fall of others . . .

SALISBURY. They have their interests; let us speak of thine.
Four or five days ago, for what good reasons
Didst thou besiege the palace of the Queen
When the Duke of Ireton, wedding Henrietta . . .

ESSEX. Irreparable error, made too late!
Instead of a base rabble, soon dismayed,

Why could I bring no army to mine aid?
By sword, by flame, by any means whatever,
I would have fain been master of that palace.
'Tis over; riches, honors, rank, employment—
My purpose failed, and all is lost for me.

SALISBURY. What does this frenzy tell me?

ESSEX.   That a secret
Love linked my fate with that of Henrietta,
And that her maiden heart, won by my love,
Did not pretend that this was not returned.

SALISBURY. The Duke of Ireton wedded her; she forsook thee.
And canst thou deem . . .

ESSEX.   Her marriage mystifies thee;
But learn now from what hidden motives she
For my sole interests sacrificed herself.
As the Queen's confidante and lady-in-waiting,
She knew the fondness for me that possessed her.
Daily she had to talk to me for her,
Who fain would win my heart but could not move it;
And seeing that her own love, because I loved her,
Armed me with sheer indifference towards the Queen,
To take the cause thereof, and all hope, from me,
She wedded . . . Who, alas, could have foreseen it!
While she continually blamed my coldness
To the Queen, she was preparing me for this
Dire blow, but after threatening to inflict it,
She made me, by a swift and tender change
Of heart, sure that she would be true to me.
At last she in my absence found the courage
To lose me,—was perfidious to herself.
She loved me, past all doubt, and gave her hand
Only to snatch from me a heart that needs
Must love me. At this fatal news how great
My fear was! I took arms to stay her marriage;
I rushed, with headlong uproar, to the palace;
My madness was displayed in all its frenzy.
I sought to save a precious thing of which
I most deceitfully was being robbed;
But, warned too late, I failed in my endeavor.
The Duke, sole object of my jealous transports,
Was my belovèd Henrietta's husband
Already. If my outburst was too violent,
If it is held a crime in me, then I
The innocent victim of my love shall die,

Grieving to know that after this vain effort,
The Duke will in my death be ever happy.

SALISBURY.   I doubt not this young duchess was well worth
The cruel sorrows that her loss hath cost thee;
But midst thine undertakings' great success,
Why, when she loved thee secretly, wert thou silent?
The Queen, whose boundless grace towards thee outstrips
Thy wishes . . .

ESSEX.   Therein lies her tyranny.
Alas! what serves me this excessive favor,
Which lets me not dispose of mine own heart?
Loved by her too much always, I could not
Be forced to feel for her such love as that
Which Henrietta vainly strove to stifle.
Not to endanger one so exquisite,
I feigned to be in love with Suffolk's sister.
The Queen's implacable, jealous anger quickly
Removed her and her brother from my sight.
Exiled, though guiltless, from the Court, those two
Taught me still better to conceal my love.
Thou seest the consequence, and my disaster.
What agony! A rival has my loved one!
She faithlessly could wed the Duke of Ireton!
Ah heaven!

SALISBURY.   She is to blame. Thou must forget her.

ESSEX.   Forget her! Could my heart grow able to?
Oh, no, no! let us see this fair, false woman.
Here I await her. I could ne'er talk with her
Since the sad day on which her fatal marriage
Betrayed my love, but now I come to tell her . . .

SALISBURY.   She is at hand. Farewell. I shall withdraw.
What'er thou hopest from so dear a meeting,
Remember that thy ruin is attempted,
And neglect nothing.   [*Exit* SALISBURY.

Enter the DUCHESS.

DUCHESS.   I have been the cause
Of thy misfortunes; and thy agitation
Tells me what plaints thou makest 'gainst my marriage.
I make them to myself for thee. Thou lovedst me,
And never could a love more beautiful
Have had a right my wishes to fulfil.
All of the strength and tenderness that love
Can have I saw in the solicitude

With which it made thee treat me. Wholly mine,
Thy heart deserved that mine should find its treasure
In the sole happiness of being thine.
To this its inclination would have led it,
But thou hadst made the Queen love thee too much.
Such kindness lavished on thee till this day,
Paying her debt to thee, declares her love.
That love is jealous. She who crosses it
Commits a crime which makes her ruin certain.
Thine would have followed. Blinded by thy love
For me, thou didst not fear the yawning chasm.
I had to lend thee aid against the weakness
Which mastered thy charmed senses. Just as long
As thou beheldest me able to be thine,
Thou wouldst have scorned all that her wrath could do.
The countless secret foes who wish to harm thee,
Attacking thy fair fame, could have destroyed thee;
And their vile efforts would have made her think
Thy crime of love to be a crime of State.
To take from envy every weapon 'gainst thee,
I had to sacrifice my life's contentment
For thee. My marriage was of great importance
To thy security. I had to be untrue
To thee. My heart resisted such a course;
I cleft that heart in order to constrain it.
Bemoan *my* lot, if thine thou darest bemoan.

ESSEX.   Yes, mine I do bemoan. Thou vainly thinkest,
Madam, to justify this cruel course.
If thou hadst loved me, thou wouldst of thyself
Have known that when one loses one's beloved,
One loses everything, and that the anguish
To which thou wast condemning me surpasses
All those misfortunes which dismayed thy soul.
Thine unkind pity, with a crushing blow,
Through fear of a calamity imagined,
Gave me a real one. What can now avail me
The fairest fortune? Had I the desire
For any other blessing than thyself?
I had deserved, perhaps, despite the Queen,
That thou shouldst take some pains to guard it for me.
Another would have refused to sacrifice
A lover; thou hast thought it right to do so.
My heart would fain revere the hand which rends it;
But I shall still dare once to say to thee

That 'gainst this heart of mine thy hand was hostile.
'Twould not have been the case if thou hadst loved me.
DUCHESS. Ah, would to heaven, sir, to complete my torture,
That this reproach had had a little justice!
I should not feel with such intensity
All calmness leave my agitated soul.
My love for thee had reached the highest peak—
I need not blush thereat, thou hadst deserved it—
And the Earl of Essex, so renowned and mighty,
Loving me to excess, could well be loved
In turn. This is to tell but half: I vainly
Belong now to another; with the same
Fervor I still am conscious that I love thee,
And that the change involved in being a wife,
Despite my duty, has no power against thee.
Judge how much harder is my lot than thine.
Naught obligates thee to love someone else;
And when thou losest me, though the loss be great,
At least, forgetting me, thou canst love no one.
But 'tis not merely that in my misfortune
My heart, to do its duty, tears itself
From that one whom it loves; it needs must by
An effort worse than death attempt to join
Itself to someone whom it does not love.
If the necessity, for honor's sake,
Of my self-conquest makes thee see what struggles
The victory must cost, if thou conceivest
Their direness, do not rob me of the fruit
Of my heart's sufferings. It is to preserve
The Queen's grace towards thee that I have been willing
To treat myself so cruelly. She has made me
Witness her love for thee. Contrive to keep it
As thy support. Thou wilt have need of it.
To blacken, to decry thy services
A thousand tricks join with imposture's shafts.
Honor engages thee to o'erlook nothing
To repulse calumny and to clear thyself.
ESSEX. I? Clear myself? Mine innocence alone
Ought to defend me 'gainst the envious.
The imposture will miscarry, unopposed,
And I should wrong myself if I could doubt it.
DUCHESS. Thou'rt great and famous; ne'er hath victory
Better assured a noble subject's glory;
But by as much as thou art highly favored

Should fear that thou mayst fall make thee submissive.
Besides its being believed that thou intriguest
With Ireland, thou art charged with manifest
Revolt. To have beset the palace, armed . . .

ESSEX. O love's misfortune, ne'er to be forgotten!
The Duke is taking thee to wife; I learn it;
And yet my love cannot prevent thy marriage!
Why did I not know earlier that thou wouldst
Be false to me? In vain wouldst thou have been
Bidden to obey. I would have . . . But 'tis done.
Whatever the Queen thinks, I shall keep silent
About the reasons for my violent conduct;
For, were the secret of my love for thee
Revealed, to crown my woes thou wouldst be banished.

DUCHESS. But thou forgettest that the Queen suspects
That this was a bold plot to seize her crown.
Witnesses heard in secrecy against thee
Make their false accusations seem the truth.
Raleigh accepts their story, and vile Cecil . . .

ESSEX. Ever have both had base and servile souls,
But vainly doth their malice plot my death.
The Queen knows me and will not credit them.

DUCHESS. Do not rely on that. A deadly insult
Does her chagrin regard thy coldness towards her.
By her express command they probe this matter.

ESSEX. The storm, in any case, will be all noise.
Its threat is vain and troubles not my soul.

DUCHESS. If someone should arrest thee . . .

ESSEX. None would dare,
Madam. Were this rash act to be attempted,
Its consequences might undo the realm.

DUCHESS. Though dear thy person to the Queen, beware,
In braving her, of making her wrath greater.
She wants to talk with thee. If thou offendest her
I put no trust in all her kindness to thee.
It was to tell thee what thou needs must fear
That I have driven myself to this sad meeting.
My duty, frightened at my agitation,
Forbids my seeing again one whom I loved
Too much; but having already done the hardest
Thing to preserve thy life, I now must do
The rest, and not permit . . .

ESSEX. Ah, to preserve it
There was an easier means that could be found.

It was to spare me the dire agony
In which thou knewest . . . Oh, what a wrong thou didst me!
Thou fearest my destruction, and thou didst not
Fear it when thou wert signing my death-warrant.
This love to which my heart is wholly given . . .

DUCHESS. Sir, think no more of that; my honor bids thee.
To have refused a marriage which the Queen
Decreed for me would have revealed our secret.
The storm is violent; to calm its fury
Constrain thy lordly heart, 'tis I who beg thee,
And though mine still in secret sighs for thee,
Remember me, but see me nevermore.
A love so sweet . . . Farewell. I grow confused.
Cecil approaches. I shall have to go.

[Exit the DUCHESS. *Enter* CECIL.

CECIL. The Queen hath charged me with informing thee
That thou shalt hold thyself in readiness
To see her in an hour. If thy conduct
Has given rise in her to some slight suspicions
Of which thou shouldest know, it is for thee
To find some way whereby thou mayest obtain
Her alarmed heart's consent to banish them.
I doubt not that it will be easy for thee
To put her mind in a more tranquil state.
Whatever the impression which disturbed her,
Innocence always can prevail before her.
In view of the esteem in which I hold
A hero to whom crime must be abhorrent,
I could not grudge this counsel, and I would
Count myself happy if its honesty
Might safeguard thee against thy foes.

ESSEX.   This friendly
Ardor surprises me; 'tis rare and noble;
And as, perhaps, there is a scheme to crush me,
I see that it should be most comforting
To me in my misfortune to be able
To hope that I may have a judge like thee.
I know the value of it. But, pray, go on.
Thou needs must know of everything that happens.
Seeing that my hate is dangerous to thy friends,
What crimes dare they invent to ruin me?
And as I am about to be accused,
Regarding what impostures must I take
Measures to answer them? Naught is concealed

From thee. Speak out. I am discreet, and I
Some interest have in keeping this concealed.

CECIL. Ill dost thou thank the good will which induced me
To give thee counsel to avert the storm
Threatening thee. If the pride that leads thee on
To projects too ambitious makes some faults
Observable amid thy virtues, those
Who dread the consequence thereof for England
Are justified in censuring thy blind course.
Though their opinions differ from mine own,
These people are without reproach—and fearless.

ESSEX. Those zealous for the realm no doubt deserve
To be, without distrust, heard by the Queen.
Such, I believe, is just, and that indeed
Some speak disinterestedly against me.
But Raleigh, Cobham, and perhaps thyself,
Serve their own interests when they call me "traitor."
So long as I lose not my present post,
Your grasping schemes will always be defeated.
I shall prevent you from amassing fortunes
By the increase of public misery.
The populace, reduced to sighs and sufferings,
Perhaps will find, despite you, how to breathe.

CECIL. What we have seen thee do, not long ago,
Indeed shows well thy popularity.
But howso high the station where thou mayest
Be placed, the most successful oft fall thence.
This office hath its perils.

ESSEX.   I admit that
Frankly. As it is high, all things must needs
Be feared there. But though dangerous for one
Who makes a false step, I perhaps shall still
Not fall immediately; and I shall have
Abundant leisure, after long abuse,
To teach who I am to some venal flatterers
Who, seeing me a too constant foe to crime,
Can rise up only if they cast me down.

CECIL. For an opinion stated . . .

ESSEX.   It favored me;
But as affection makes thee so considerate,
Since when, and why, dost *thou* think that thou mayest
Believe that time could make us friends? Is it
Because I have been seen, with shameful weakness,
To love the cowardly, support the vile,

And take the part of those false, faithless men
Who make the art of treachery their sole practice?

CECIL. I suffer, temperately, talk which insults me;
But, forced to yield, I have at least the advantage
That, fearing the most monstrous crimes, the Queen
Treats *thee* as guilty, and does not accuse *me*.

ESSEX. I know that thou incitest the Queen against me.
Perhaps thou wilt not easily beguile her,
And when I shall have spoken, whoe'er asperses
My loyalty will need me to win her pardon.   [*Exit* ESSEX.

CECIL (*to himself*). 'Tis time to act. I have played the slave too long.
Let us undo an arrogant man who flouts us,
And hesitate no more, since act we must,
To anticipate the blow he seeks to deal us.

A C T   I I

The scene represents another room in the palace. ELIZABETH
and TILNEY *are discovered.*

ELIZABETH.   Vainly wouldst thou deceive the grief that whelms me.
He embraced guilt because he hated me,
And the fair Suffolk, to his heart denied,
Makes him to his indifference to my love
Add crime. To excuse him, do not try to tell me
That he is ignorant to what extent
Love's poison ardently devours my heart.
My words, mine eyes too well have made him know,
The ingrate, that 'tis he whom best I love.
When I blamed his heart's choice, did this not tell him
That I would have him sigh for me alone?
And have my troubled glances not explained
What my refusal had already shown?
Yes, he knows how intense my feelings are,
But Suffolk's exile arms him for revenge.
He dares for *her* sake to give up his soul
To crime—seeks *my* life only to crown her.

TILNEY.   However just may thy suspicions be,
'Tis hard for me not to defend him 'gainst thee.
His saving of the realm, his valor, exploits,
Glory, and lordly heart—all plead his cause.
'Tis true thou thinkest that he grieves for Suffolk,
But, madam, should a subject love his queen?
And though such love be born, is it to triumph

Where respect, even stronger, strives to quench it?
ELIZABETH.   Ah, when one's heart, surprised, yields to love's charms,
The majesty of rank hath feeble arms.
Love, shackled by respect, becomes the more
Ardent, the more it finds itself restrained.
But the Earl, if he loved me, would have had
Nothing to fear. I gave him grounds enough
Not to restrain himself; and that is why
I blush, when after so much favor shown him
His coldness should be my reward for this.
TILNEY.   But I maintain that still he seeks to please
Thee only. What can *he* hope from this passion?
ELIZABETH.   What can he hope! And what can *I* hope from it
Except the sweetness to see, love, and yearn?
Ah, sad, strange pride that robs me of him I love!
My happiness, my peace is sacrificed
To my exalted station, and I would die
A hundred times rather than make a king
Of one who, on the throne, would be beneath me.
I know 'tis much to ask his soul to burn
Forever with a fruitless flame for me,
And 'tis a cruel woe to love hopelessly;
But mine own share therein should make his easier,
And when my rank oppresses me, if he
Knows it and sees it, little is the pain.
Let him commiserate himself and me
And, satisfied with loving me . . . But what
Say I? He lets another charm his heart,
And his mad ardor breeds such blindness in him
That, to appease it, he would fain destroy
His queen. But let him fear to anger me
Too much. I force my wrath not to break out;
But sometimes love, outraged by long disdain,
Tired finally of suffering, turns to wrath.
I shall not guarantee . . .

Enter the DUCHESS.

Well, Duchess, what
Have served the pains thou takest for my sake?
Hast thou talked with the Earl? Will he be ruled?
DUCHESS.   He shows a reverence inviolable
For thee; and if thine interests need his arm,
Command its service; danger will not daunt him.
But he cannot endure without impatience

Anyone's daring to defame to thee
His innocence. Guilt and crime are hideous words
Which rouse a noble anger in his soul.
He takes it ill that anyone should accuse him
And that his queen should hearken to what impostors . . .
ELIZABETH.   I doubtless wrong him—when he dares besiege me
Even in mine own palace! His sedition
Is nothing, and I ought to disregard it;
And the correspondence that he has with Ireland
Shows the complete innocence of his projects!
Ah heaven, must this heart, which feels its wounds,
Tremble to speak 'gainst an ungrateful subject?
What! when his purposing my death demands
His own, does an unworthy pity stay me,
Confound me? And do I, always too weak,
After his baseness still not dare protect
My majesty? If love once gives place to hate,
He will see what it means to insult his queen.
He will see what it is when I suppress
That love in which my heart was softened towards him.
Till now I have borne all; howe'er he wronged me,
I always let his services speak for him;
But since his arrogance extends to crimes,
I must abase him and dismay all ingrates.
To the whole world, which sees me, notes me, I
Must give a great example of stern justice.
He seeks to make me do so. Thus he wills it.
Enough, then!
DUCHESS.   What! thou takest his foes' part,
Madam? Dost know not that his life's distinction
Arms secret envy 'gainst his eminence?
Guilty in semblance . . .
ELIZABETH.   Ah, say in reality.
The evidence hath been heard, the indictment drawn,
And if I choose no longer to defend him,
Only his sentence waits to be pronounced.
Let him consider that; otherwise . . .
DUCHESS.   Can he not
Have been suspected of imagined crimes?
ELIZABETH.   Ah, would to heaven . . . But no, the proof is clear.
Did he not seek to force the palace doors?
If the great throng of folk that followed him
Had given his rage support, he would have triumphed.
My throne no longer mine, 'twould have been his.

DUCHESS. One is not always guilty when one seems so.
But granted that he be, will thy charmed heart
Decree his death? Thou hast so greatly loved him!
ELIZABETH. Ah, hide that love from me which too high esteem
Kindled! To cause me to remember it
Is to augment his crime. I must confess it,
For to my shame 'tis true, I felt . . . I had
For him . . . But of what use to think of it?
Suffolk has snatched him from me; Suffolk, whom he
Prefers to me, demands my blood of him.
The wretch would fain content her. Ah, but wherefore
Amid the sorrows to which love exposed me
Did I do naught but banish her that caused them?
I ought with more, more violence to have let
Myself take bolder vengeance on this rival.
My mildness hath sustained her guilty hopes.
DUCHESS. But had this love some power over her?
Hath she betrayed thee, and with heart disloyal
Incited 'gainst thee . . .
ELIZABETH. She caused all my woes.
She made herself beloved, she made me hated,
And this a hundredfold is to betray me.
DUCHESS. I do not dare oppose . . . But Cecil comes.

Enter CECIL.

CECIL. No greater care, madam, could be observed.
The signature of the Earl hath been examined.
The documents are his; we know the hand.
For aid proposed, all Ireland now is ready
To make the storm burst when the word is given;
And thou wilt soon see the whole realm o'erthrown
If thou dost not forestall this monstrous scheme.
ELIZABETH (*to the* DUCHESS). Art thou so zealous still to exculpate
him?
Thou seest.
DUCHESS. I see that Cecil doth accuse him.
He pictures him committed to a wicked
Project; but I know why. He is his foe.
CECIL. I, his foe?
DUCHESS. Thou.
CECIL. Yes, I am one to traitors
Whose rash pride lifts their hands against their masters;
And while those masters' safety is entrusted
To me, my boast is that I have no friends.

DUCHESS.   The Earl, however, hath not so little glory
         That thou shouldst soon destroy the memory of it.
         The realm, for which he often took up arms,
         Owes him enough, perhaps, not to forget him.
CECIL.   If he at first chose to show loyalty,
         The Queen hath well repaid his services.
         The greater her esteem for his rare talents,
         The more she ought to punish a false ingrate.
DUCHESS.   If the Earl dies, whatever envy deems,
         The blow that slays him falls on innocence.
         Ne'er with the slightest guilt . . .
ELIZABETH.   Well, we shall see.
         (*To* CECIL)   Convoke the council. It shall be the judge.
         Await my order.   [*Exit* CECIL.
DUCHESS.   Ah, what wouldst thou do,
         Madam? Dost thou give credence to thy wrath?
         The Earl . . .
ELIZABETH.   Have no anxiety for his life.
         This is the hour appointed. He comes hither.
         The love I had for him makes his first judge
         Himself. He can find here a sure protection.
         But if he dare persist in being proud
         And flout this love, he must expect the worst.
         I weary of seeing . . .
TILNEY.   Madam, the Earl is here.
ELIZABETH.   Bid him to enter.
         (*To herself*)   What strife distracts my soul
         Already! It is *he* who from *my* kindness
         Must seek for aid; the danger concerns *him;*
         And I am more afraid than he is.

Enter ESSEX.

                                              Earl,
         I have learned all, and I now speak to thee
         Knowing into what abyss thy blind course hurls thee.
         I know the madness of that course, and what
         Interests have made thine aims extend as far
         As to the throne. Thou seest that for the sake
         Of my original esteem for thee
         The most enormous crime is called but madness,
         And it depends on thee whether thy queen
         Today shall not forget what thou attemptedst.
         For such a great compulsion of herself,
         All that she asks is a sincere confession.

      If this offends the pride which made thee dare
Too much, consider that to refuse it to me
Is to risk everything; that when too much kindness
Moves me to mercy, he who dares disdain it
Must fear my vengeance; that my hand is armed
With thunderbolts for him who mounts too high;
And that one word can send thee to the scaffold.

ESSEX.   Madam, thou canst decree my punishment.
I know a subject's duty to his queen,
And well know that the throne where heaven seats thee
Gives thee despotic power o'er my life.
Whatever calumny decrees through thee
For it, 'tis odious to me—take it, thou!
In the sad state to which I am reduced,
To snap its thread will be a favor to me.
But my fair fame, which vile deceit assails,
I cannot without indignation see
Outraged. 'Tis glorious enough for me
To have a right to see with grief the affront
It suffers. If thou hast reason to complain
Of any crime, if the result thereof
Is it be feared for the affrighted State,
'Tis to see flatterers strive now to pull down
Its chief support by rendering me suspected.

ELIZABETH.   The pride which makes thee boast thy services
Shows very little signs of virtue in thee.
If thou believest my words, thou'lt seek in me
A means more certain . . .

ESSEX.   Madam, I can see
That traitors, wicked men, inured to crime,
Have by their lies robbed me of thy esteem,
And 'gainst their baseness all my rectitude
Tries vainly to avouch my loyalty.
Had I been capable of belying it,
Thou wouldst have seen me guilty without fear
Of thee. 'Tis on the throne, to which I might
Perhaps ere now have mounted, that I could have
Displayed my power. To rise to that high station
Would have absolved me of the sin of doing so,
And those who seek to ruin me when guiltless
Would have beheld my crimes but to applaud them.

ELIZABETH.   Traitor, didst thou not arm the populace
And try, though vainly, to assume my place?
What! does not thy investment of my palace

Convict thee of the greatest, of the blackest
Of all attempted villainies? But tell me
(For verily the wrath which animates me
Cannot, because of thy foul crime, compel me
To lose my fondness for thee; and if I
Try to confound thee with thine infamy,
I make thee see this only to forgive thee),
Why wish my death? and what has thy queen done
Which should incite thy hate to seek her ruin?
Perhaps I showed some harshness towards thee when
I interposed a barrier to thy love.
Suffolk had won it; but if thou canst complain
Because, on learning of this love, I sought
To quench it, think, thou ingrate, at what price
And with how many honors my esteem
Has lavished boons on thee. 'Tis not enough
To say "esteem," and well thou knowest it.
A stronger feeling ruled my breast. For whom,
Cruel man, for whom have I refused so many
Princes and kings and heroes scornfully?
To wed them would, past doubt, have raised my power
To the height to which 'tis known that I aspire;
But whatso'er it promised, that which would
Of thee deprive me had no charms for me.
Thy heart, whose conquest I then held so dear,
Was the sole blessing that could make me happy,
And if my regal pride had not forbidden
I would have offered thee my hand to gain it.
Take hope, and try to o'ercome a qualm of honor
Which doth oppose my wishes and thy victory.
Deserve that, softened by thy solicitude,
My heart should fain be deaf to irksome warnings.
Make me surrender wholly to my love.
Make this Elizabeth, so proud, so haughty,
Her whom the world could ne'er reproach with having
Let anyone see her pride unbend, at last,
To set thee where her love invites thee, cease
To think no subject can be worthy of her.
Sometimes my dignity resolves to yield.
How knowest thou if that time will long continue?
How knowest . . .

Essex.   Nay, madam; I can tell thee this:
My queen's esteem must needs content my wishes.
If love should lead her to unworthy aims,

394

I should in fealty to her honor stay her.

ELIZABETH. Ah, I perceive too well thine infamy.
The throne would please thee only with my rival.
Whatever lure the passion which corrupts thee
May have, take care; thy death may be its fruit.

ESSEX. With loss of thy support, I am defenseless,
But death has never daunted innocence,
And if, to satisfy some secret foe;
Thou cravest my blood, without regret I give it.

ELIZABETH. Go. 'Tis enough. Thy wish must be indulged.
To thy base lot do I abandon thee,
Consenting, since in vain I sought to save thee,
That without seeing . . .
                    Tremble, ingrate, when
I do not dare go on. My kindliness,
Which always stubbornly defends thee, tries
For the last time to make its voice be heard.
While for thy sake I still consent to hear it,
A pardon is offered thee; thou canst accept it.
But if . . .

ESSEX.   Accept a pardon, madam? I?

ELIZABETH. To do so, wounds thy spirit's pride, I see;
But if that galls thee, thou shouldst have been careful
To avoid ever having need of it.
Thou shouldst have followed righteous maxims only,
Refusing . . .

ESSEX.   True; great crimes have I committed.
Those which mine arm wrought for thee on the sea
Make me indeed worthy of all thy wrath.
Thou knowest it, madam; and crestfallen Spain
Will vindicate a conqueror whom England
Indicts. 'Tis not to boast of my achievements
That I will add my voice to their acclaim.
Anyone who fought bravely for his queen
In like case would have met with like success.
My good luck has accomplished all; but truly
This luck would elsewhere have assured my fortunes.
Elsewhere if fraud had plotted my disgrace,
None would have been allowed to dare . . .

ELIZABETH.   Well, Earl,
By the law's strictness it must be decided
What recompense is due for such rare exploits.
If I have ill requited thy great service,
Thy judges will not be unjust like me,

And thou'lt receive from them the right reward
Of all thy proofs of zeal and loyalty.
                              [*Exeunt* ELIZABETH *and* TILNEY.
DUCHESS. Ah, Earl, desirest thou in the Queen's despite
        To serve the wicked hate of thine accusers?
        Dost thou not realize that thou art lost
        If thou shouldst undergo judicial sentence?
        What judges couldst thou have who would protect thee?
        They are thy foes, Raleigh one, Cecil one;
        And canst thou deem that in thy mortal peril
        Those who desire thy death will judge thee guiltless?
ESSEX. What! If my tarnished honor I defend not,
        I shall be treated as a traitor to
        My country? If there was in my behavior
        A seeming crime, thy marriage was its cause.
        Little does it concern the realm. Thou knowest
        How innocent I am in this respect;
        And since by thee my honor is not doubted,
        Whate'er my foes wish to suppose about it,
        Whate'er their hatred dares, cannot alarm me.
        Their fraud will presently be made apparent;
        And, wicked as they are, if they are bent
        Upon my death, though gathered for the sentence
        Which must condemn me, they perhaps will tremble
        Before pronouncing it.
DUCHESS.   If the disturbance
        My marriage made thee raise before the palace
        Were my sole reason to fear too harsh a sentence,
        I could of this crime clear thy loyalty
        By telling of the love thou hadst for me.
        But testimony given on what 'tis claimed
        Thou hast with Ireland . . .
ESSEX.   That is no great crime;
        And if our love, kept hidden from the Queen,
        Let my misfortunes fall on none but me . . .
DUCHESS. What! fearest thou that our love will be revealed?
        This danger daunts thee? Why, 'tis of thy making!
        The Queen, if thou wouldst let her, would relent
        And pardon all, without examining aught.
        'Tis thou, who by refusing . . .
ESSEX.   Say no more.
        He who accepts a pardon is the object
        Of vile suspicions; and I have a heart
        Too proud to stoop to the unworthy suppliance

To which it is desired that I be forced.

DUCHESS. If I with any hope may soothe my anguish,
I see that in the Queen such hope must rest.
I still wish, with new efforts, to attempt
For thy sake to o'ercome her wrath, despite thee;
But if I can do nothing, recollect
That thy life, long exposed to envy's rage,
Too much hath cost me for me to deserve
That thou, seeking to die, shouldst cause my death.
I have said too much to thee. Farewell.

ESSEX.   Ah, madam!
After thou hast of all hope robbed my love,
By what care for my life . . . What! leave me thus?

[*Exit the* DUCHESS.

Enter CROMMER *and guards.*

CROMMER. 'Tis most unwillingly that I come hither;
But a cruel order, which I regret with all
My heart . . .

ESSEX.   However irksome it be, thou
Canst tell me what it is.

CROMMER.   I am commanded . . .

ESSEX. Well, to do what? Speak without hesitating.

CROMMER. To take thy sword and to arrest thee.

ESSEX.   What!
My sword?

CROMMER.   This order I must needs obey.

ESSEX. My sword! Is insult added to injustice?

CROMMER. Not without reason art thou astounded. I
Am loath to obey, but I must do so.

ESSEX (*giving him the sword*).   Take it.
Thou holdest in thy hands what all the world
Has more than once beheld serve England well.
Let us go. Whatsoever grief is mine,
The Queen desires her ruin; so must it be.   [*Exeunt.*

ACT III

The scene represents the same room as in Act II. ELIZABETH,
CECIL, *and* TILNEY *are discovered.*

ELIZABETH. The Earl hath been convicted?

CECIL.   With regret,
Madam, his name with an ignoble sentence

Is seen besmirched. His judges sorrow for him,
But they have all alike found him so guilty
That they have spoken with a single voice.
As though to vitiate all our procedure,
He hath o'erwhelmed me from the first with insults.
Anxious to aid him if I had been able,
I wished to be excused from judging him.
The law forbade, and 'tis despite myself
That I have cast my vote in the high council,
Which, 'wildered by the blackness of his treason,
Have deemed that the realm's peace must cost his head.

ELIZABETH. His perfidy appears, then, evident?

CECIL. The blow would have been deadly to thee, madam.
With Lord Tyrone's help and an Irish following,
He sought the throne and would have snatched it from thee.

ELIZABETH. Ah, well I read him when the populace
Supported his bold insolence against me.
He thought to win their aid to take my crown.
What can excuse his crime? what cleanse him of it?
How answered he?

CECIL. That he had naught to say;
That for his whole defense it should suffice us
To see his mighty exploits take his part,
And that he could be judged according to them.

ELIZABETH. What arrogance! Though he sees the lightning's bolt,
He cannot in the least degree repent?
Exposed to my revenge, he braves my power?
He dares . . .

CECIL. His arrogance is beyond belief.
One would have said, to see his self-assurance,
That 'twas his judges who had perpetrated
His crime and they feared from him in these straits
That which he was too proud to fear from them.

ELIZABETH. His arrogance, however, needs must stoop.
He seeth the pass to which his crime hath brought him.
The stoutest heart is shaken by death's decree.

CECIL. This dire blow hath not daunted him at all.
As with one who maintains a fatal boldness,
I have sought to lead him to ask mercy of thee.
What said he not to me! My face burns crimson.
I cannot tell thee.

ELIZABETH. Ah, though he should ask it,
He ne'er shall have it. He could have obtained it
From me, a little while ago, with ease.

I was disposed to show him kindness, then.
I saw regretfully that he wished to force me
To seek that sentence for him which has now
Just been pronounced. My arm was slow to punish
And held the lightning back till he compelled me
To loose it 'gainst him. That will cost his head.
Make all arrangements. To prevent his death
The commoners, who fear this, may attempt
Violence. He has won their love. Forestall them.
Station guards where'er the risk is greatest.
Forget naught. Go.

CECIL.   Thou knowest my fealty. I
Will answer for all rioters. Trust in me.   [*Exit* CECIL.

ELIZABETH (*to herself*).   Now, faithless man, now is thy death resolved
     on.
The end has come, despite me; thou thyself
Hast made it sure. Thou fearedst the result
Of my ignoble pity. No more kindness!
Thy wishes shall be granted. My affection
Was winning an unworthy victory.
I stifle it. 'Tis time to have some care
For my fair fame; 'tis time that in just anger
I taught the world the greatness of my pride.
Ah, thou hast made this captive heart th' accomplice
Of thy black crimes, upholding what is wrong!
And I shall know the blow impends, shall see it;
Thou wilt disdain me; I shall let it fall!
Nay, since the loving woman in me always
Irked thee, I must, to please thee, show myself
A queen, and reassume the pride I dared
Forget so that love might exculpate thee.

TILNEY.   With too great readiness to believe this pride
Perhaps, thou hast allowed the Earl to be
Arraigned. He hath received his death-sentence.
All tremble for him, but he will not die.

ELIZABETH.   Not die? He? Credit me; thou art mistaken.
Thou knowest his crime; dost thou excuse him for it?
Dost thou condemn the indignity he suffers,
Or deem too swift his sentence, or unjust?
Thinkest thou that though the ungrateful man declared
Himself against me, he hath not deserved
The death which is prepared for him, and that I,
In leaving him to perish, am too vengeful
For that which I have suffered from his scorn?

TILNEY.   Whether his doom be just or wrought by envy,
    Thou lovest him, and that love will save his life.
    He hath so closely knit thy days with his
    That by the same blow they will both be ended.
    Thy blind rage doth in vain conceal this from thee.
    Thou wouldst lament the death which thou wouldst sanction,
    And the bloody sequel of this anger would
    Avenge thy woes on him less than on thee.
ELIZABETH.   Ah, cruel woman, why make my hate afraid?
    Is it a passion unworthy of a queen?
    And doth the love that wishes to impede
    My reign not tire of seeing itself disdained?
    What serves it me that I, feared as a foe,
    Should fortify my power abroad by peace,
    If, with my sorely wounded heart, I cannot
    Enjoy the calm for which I yearn so greatly?
    My smiling fortune seems to hold e'en victory
    Itself in thrall; I everywhere have triumphed;
    All men talk of my glory—and my insistent
    Kindness cannot, even though joined to prayers,
    O'ercome the pride of an ungrateful subject!
    More doomed than he is by the death decreed him,
    Unhappy princess, what dost thou resolve?
    Wilt thou let perish, without aid or pity,
    Thy glory's prop, thy life's support?
TILNEY.   Canst thou
    Not do thy will? Thou weepest!
ELIZABETH.   Yes, I weep,
    And feel sure that if *he* dies, *I* must die.
    O monarchs whom my love rejected for him,
    Turn your eyes on me; ye are well avenged.
    A queen undaunted in the midst of dangers,
    Trembling for love's sake, dareth to shed tears!
    Yet were it certain that those tears shed by me,
    The while they make me blush, would not be vain,—
    That the base wretch, assailed by keen remorse . . .
    What thinkest thou? tell me. The most fearless quaileth;
    The shape of death, whose equipage is ready,
    Makes all things seem legitimate to avert it.
    Reduced to see his head pay for his guilt,
    Will he not, deemest thou, wish to beg my mercy?
    Sure that my kindness doth surpass his crime . . .
TILNEY.   He should appeal to it. But if he doth not?
    He is proud, madam.

THE EARL OF ESSEX

ELIZABETH.   Ah, thou drivest me frantic.
Whatever his rash schemes have dared against me,
Though by my fall the realm must be o'erthrown,
Let him but soften, and 'tis enough; I shall
Forget the past. But though, fain to hold back
The thunderbolt, I shudder to destroy him
And tremble to make up my mind to do so,
If he defies me always and constrains me
Thereto, I being queen and he a subject,
Can I exempt myself from this stern course?
Despite him let us save him. Speak, and make him
Hearken to thee. See him, but hide from him
The fact that it was I who sent thee to him.
Preserve my honor in explaining thyself
For me; picture to him my heart aware
Of what I owe him; make him see that I
Regretfully abandon him to his fate,
That on the least remorse he will be pardoned;
But if, to sway him, thou must needs go further,
Let my love's care become thy only care.
Forget my fair fame; tell him that I love him
(All guilty as he is) a hundred times
More than myself; that if he fain would end
My miserable life, he only has
To let the course of *his* life be cut short.
Urge, beseech, offer him all to melt his heart.
In short, if true zeal for thy queen is thine,
By fear, by love, by pity for my fate,
Prevail on him to spare himself and snatch him
From death. Let him not perish, and thou wilt
Have served me well. I say no more to thee.
Mine own life is at stake. Lose no time. Run!
Make haste, and let me see what things a friend
Is going to try to do in his defense.

Exit TILNEY. *Enter* SALISBURY.

SALISBURY.   Madam, excuse the greatness of my grief
If, coming for one who is my other self,
Trembling, and seized with terror for thy sake
And for the realm's sake, I now dare to beg thee
Not to undo thyself. I nowise seek
To learn what his crime is; but if the sentence
Rendered appears legitimate to thee,
Will it appear so when thou deignest to see

Whose head it strikes off with a fateful blow?
'Tis that famed hero who a hundred times
Hath crowned his victories by the noblest exploits,
Whose lot was e'er so glorious and so fair,
That is consigned to a vile executioner.
After the world hath served as a great stage
For his high qualities which all adore,
Couldst thou permit a scaffold to be reared
To show to all how he is recompensed?
When I thus come to picture unto thee
His great worth and his grievous fate, it is not
Friendship alone that brings me here; it is
The afflicted realm; it is thy sorrowing Court,
Which fears disasters, losing his support.
I know that in his conduct he was somewhat
Imprudent; but crime does not attend always
Its semblance, and in the exalted station
To which his talents raised him, for possessing
His queen's esteem, he hath his enemies.
For him, for thee, for us, beware the cunning
Of those who undertake his death. Remember
That clemency hath always had its claims
And is the virtue worthiest of monarchs.

ELIZABETH.   Lord Salisbury, I appreciate thy zeal.
I love to see a friend so true and gallant,
And praise in thee the spirit which thy concern
Gives thee to murmur against a righteous sentence.
I feel thereat, like thee, much grief; but I
Owe to the realm still more than to myself.
If I have let the Earl's crime be made known,
'Tis he who forced me to do what I did.
Ready to forget all if he confessed
His crime to me, I have assuredly
Desired to reinstate him in my graces.
My kindness hath served only to redouble
The pride by which ambitious men most often
Meet shipwreck. He is outraged at the care
Which he hath seen me take to avert the storm
From him, though he is sure to perish by it.
If for his pride his head atones to me,
'Tis *his* fault; he will have what he deserves.

SALISBURY.   He does deserve a shameful punishment,
Seeing that his pride opposeth his queen's kindness.
If aught in him can or must needs offend thee,

'Tis that heart's haughtiness which cannot bow,
That haughtiness to which he would give ear
At his life's risk. But with his being too proud
Has he the less well served thee? the less well
Shown thee in countless combats for thy sake
That nothing is impossible to his arm?
By his blood lavished, by his glory's brightness,
If any memory of them doth remain
Still thine, vouchsafe to accord to the misfortune
That overwhelms him now the pardon which
I kneel to beg for him. Remember that
If he was ever necessary to thee,
What he hath done already, he again
Can do; and that our foes, now trembling, hopeless,
Have never triumphed more than they will triumph
When thou shalt lose him.

ELIZABETH.   I shall with regret
Lose him. But I am queen; he is a subject,
Guilty, and meriting his punishment.
His sentence now hath been pronounced, and all
The world will fix on him, on me, its eyes.
When his sheer pride, whose insolence thou hast blamed,
Made me desire that he should sue for pardon,
If he could thus have snatched himself from death
Yet scorned to do so, is it for me to weaken?
Is it for me to suffer that a subject
To impotent outbursts should reduce my anger,
And that he should be able, to my shame,
To inform the future that I knew his crime
And dared not punish it?

SALISBURY.   There is much talk
Of a revolt and secret plots. But, madam,
People make use of counterfeited letters.
The witnesses by Cecil heard and questioned
Are witnesses who may have been suborned.
The Earl doth challenge them, and when I suspect them . . .

ELIZABETH.   The Earl is sentenced. If his doom dismays him,—
If he would do something to lighten it,—
Resuming fealty, he might be heard.
Go. My fit pride, which his presumption angers,
May show him kindness still. Let him deserve it.

Exit SALISBURY. *Enter the* DUCHESS.

Come, Duchess, come, and pity my distress.

I seek to pardon, I wish to, I have power to;
Yet ever must I tremble lest a stubborn
Guilty man should himself hold out against me.
Thou heaven, which gavest me a heart so high
And great, why madest it not be unfeeling?
Why must an ingrate, haughty as his queen,
Have won my love so and deserved my hate?
Or if thou wast resolved he should betray me,
Why hast thou not permitted me to hate him?
If this grim sentence nowise daunts the Earl,
Dire loss I needs must suffer, or else shame.
His death will kill me; and if I preserve him,
The wretch will have defied me with impunity.
What woe is mine!

DUCHESS.   One must indeed be pitied
When one abhors severity yet sees
One's self constrained thereto. But if the Earl
Dares, though condemned, to accept his sentence rather
. Than any pardon, to requite his intrigues
At least instead of capital punishment
A prison could . . .

ELIZABETH.   No; I would have him bend.
My honor is involved. He must submit.

DUCHESS.   Alas! I fear that he will to thy goodness
Not yield; that in thy wish to abase his spirit
Thy efforts . . .

ELIZABETH.   Ah, I have a means unfailing.
Naught equals the dire suffering it will cost me.
'Tis of all pangs the worst; I may die of it;
But if his pride goes ever with his boldness,
He must be saved at the expense of *my* life.
That is my firm resolve. O frustrate longings!
O my heart! Is it thus that thou betrayest me?

DUCHESS.   Great is thy power; but I know the Earl.
He will desire . . .

ELIZABETH.   I cannot conquer him
Save to my shame. I know it; but I at last
Shall easily prevail, and that I shall
Thou wilt thyself agree. He worships Suffolk;
'Tis she who led him to seek satisfaction
For the indignity of her being exiled.
Whate'er this fatal purpose costs my heart,
I am willing—I shall suffer it—that on him
Her hand shall be bestowed; and the ungrateful

THE EARL OF ESSEX

Wretch who opposes me with rebellious pride,
Sure now of happiness, will wish to live.

DUCHESS. If only thus thou thinkest to move him, learn
A secret which must be concealed no longer.
Needlessly anxious o'er his love of Suffolk,
Thou hast punished her too much. He loved not *her*.
'Tis I alone—none other's charms are guilty—
Who have entrapped his heart, unsought by me.
From fealty, from respect, I tried to extinguish
A love to which thou couldst so rightfully
Object. With heart bewildered by his wooing,
I futilely attempted to resist him.
As love is hopeful, so would he fain hope.
He deemed that pity could be sovereign in thee,
That time would make thee kindly to his love,
And although Suffolk had no charms for him,
To avoid exposing me, he feigned to love her.
Her exile shocked him, warned him against rashness;
But if my interests forced him to be silent,
His heart, in which constraint but fanned the flames,
Hath not less given me the most ardent sighs.
I, who usurped it, banished thee therefrom.
    I wronged thee, madam, and I am punished for it.
To restore unto thee what I had thus
Taken from thee, my hand's gift was required
And this I chose to give. He heard that news
When absent from the Court. He came back raging,
Aroused the populace, made it follow him
Unto the palace at the fatal moment
When marriage gave me into the possession
Of someone else. He came to prevent that,
And this it is which he concealed from thee.
'Tis hence that crime attaches to his glory.
A fit of frenzy, which may be forgiven
A distressed lover, is misdeemed sedition.
If it be thought treason—if such its aspect—
This my confession proves its innocence.
    Then, madam, then, by all that e'er could capture,
Affect, enkindle thy desires, I swear—
By the most tender vows that thou couldst make,
By his own self, that which is dearest to thee—
On doubtful evidence which could not daunt him
His judges have presumed to sentence him
To death. Accord to me his life, to pay me

    For mine own sacrifice that snatched me from him
    And righted the wrong done thee. I have suffered
    Enough now to deserve that thou shouldst show
    Somewhat less wrath against so dear a criminal.
ELIZABETH.   Have I heard rightly? the false man loves thee,
    Scorns me, defies me; and to mine own hurt
    I would, in helping him, secure for thee
    The joy of being loved and seeing me suffer!
    Nay, he must perish and I be revenged.
    I owe this dire course to my outraged love.
    He well deserves the punishment decreed him.
    Guilty or not, he loves thee. 'Tis enough.
    If he did no real crime, as some would have it,
    With his supposed crime I will save mine honor,
    And reasons of State, to take his life, will serve
    As pretext for my reasons of love.
DUCHESS.   Just heaven!
    Thou couldst thus sacrifice him to thine anger?
    Nowise do I repent of having served thee;
    But oh, what more against my interests could I
    Have done, in order to restore him to thee
    And to reject his vows? All testified,
    All made me sure, of his love's fervor. What
    To take me from him better wouldst thou have done,
    Thyself?
ELIZABETH.   Less than thou didst. For him alone,
    Come what might, always all my love would have
    Been kept. In vain would any other's heart
    Have been enthralled by me; no marriage mine!
    But after all I am not loved; my heart
    Can nowise tolerate his disdain, and in
    Such despair, one who can do all, will do it.
DUCHESS.   Ah, show to him a heart more generous!
    Must *my* conscientiousness be made a crime
    In him, and doth the aid I deemed that I
    Should give thy love, cause him to seem to thee
    More to deserve to perish?
ELIZABETH.   I was wrong,
    I own; and though I fly into a rage,
    My love is always strongest, well I know.
    Heaven, which reservest me for endless sorrows,
    Naught more was lacking in my cruel fate
    Than not to suffer me, in this fatal passion,
    To have the power to hate my rival. Ah,

How mighty is the charm of virtue! Duchess,
'Tis over. Let him live. I give consent.
With one concern thou fearest and I tremble.
Let us unite against him for his sake,
And draw him from that peril which he dreads not,
That both of us may see him and both love him.
Very unlike will our rewards be for it:
His whole heart will be thine, mine his hate only.
No matter—he shall live; his crime is pardoned.
I will oppose his death. But 'tis decreed
Already. England knows this; all the world
Will have just cause herein to be surprised.
My fair fame, which he always hath upheld,
Would have him ask forgiveness of me. Win him
To do so. Thou hast every power o'er him.
Go; employ violent means to make him yield.
Save him, save me; in my distress, to put
My trust in thee is all that I can do.   [*Exeunt.*

ACT IV

The scene represents a room in a prison. ESSEX *and* TILNEY
are discovered.

ESSEX.   I doubtless owe much to this care which brings thee,
But thou couldst well have spared thyself the trouble.
Though my death-sentence seemeth dreadful to thee,
I would much rather undergo it than
Deserve it.
TILNEY.   Let me chide thy fortitude.
Although death ne'er dismays a lofty soul,
When we must see it under this dire sentence
Slowly approach with its sad equipage ...
ESSEX.   I shall admit that I believed the Queen
Would have felt some distress at slaying me.
I came into the palace with no fear
Of being arrested, deeming it a place
In which my life would be secure. I mean not
That if she finds such pleasure in my blood,
I feel regret at satisfying her;
But since I shed that blood so oft for her,
Perhaps a scaffold was not my desert.
It now requites more than one victory for her.
She wishes to forget that; and I feel

Regret for her fair fame. I feel regret
That in her blindness she brings on herself
The shame which she thinks to make fall on me.
God is my witness that a faithful subject
Ne'er for his sovereign had a heart so zealous.
I have displayed it in a hundred battles.
Silence thereon is vain; *they* are not silent.
If, when I served her well, I did my duty,
My life at least she ought to have protected.
To make her rise up so in arms against me,
My crime is merely that I cannot love her.
Attraction always comes unsought, like illness.
If it o'erwhelms the heart, Fate is to blame;
And any other woman would have forgot
So slight a grief and not have punished me
For that which is the fault of destiny.

TILNEY. Thy coldness, I confess, angered the Queen,
But if thou wilt consent to placate her,
Her wrath will come to naught. 'Tis thou thyself,
Thou, who by hearkening too much to a pride
Whereof the exhibition doth offend her,
Now dost pronounce thy doom. Through thee, men say,
Ireland revolts. Though the crime charged be false,
It is accounted as a real crime;
And when she extends her hands to thee to save thee,
Her honor would have thee take at least one step,
Would have thee . . .

ESSEX.   Ah, if it is true that she
Thinks of her honor, to ensure her name
Against too black a stain, she still hath choice
Of courses to which justice can assent,
Rather than stoop to slay the innocent.
Men dare to accuse me; let her anger smite
Those witnesses suborned who find me guilty.
Cecil hearkens to them; he hath produced them.
Raleigh hath furnished them with all their falsehoods.
Let Raleigh, Cecil, and all others like them,
These miscrants who make worthy people tremble,
Wash out, in their vile blood, their faithlessness,
Beneath the headsman's hand, as they deserve;
Then, shedding thus such really guilty blood,
The Queen will execute a righteous judgment;
Then will the dread display of her stern justice
Make safe her honor, having saved the realm.

But to permit these wretches' proper doom
To fall on me, who uphold her royal grandeur!
To suffer that against me some forged letters . . .
No, no, posterity will not believe it:
Never can it be credited that, with
All memory vanished of all debt to me,
Imposture was allowed the power to crush me.
Yet the Queen sees this, and unmoved she sees it.
The peril to the realm does not disquiet her.
I needs must be content, since she is pleased,
And not be daunted by a shameful death
Which stains her honor yet does not dismay her.

TILNEY.   Does not dismay her? She is in despair!
She blames thy hard heart; she condemns her anger.
To give her soul once more the peace it pines for,
Would uttering one word cost thee so much?

ESSEX.   I think my death will be a blow to her,
And she will feel herself somewhat ungrateful.
I indeed have not merited my misfortune;
But time makes mild the bitterest of griefs.
Though by her keen remorse my death be followed,
More would she suffer if she let me live.
She cannot win this heart now held suspect.
I could feel nothing for her but respect.
If I, because 'tis filled by her who sways it,
Am criminal, I should wish to be so always;
And it is better, doubtless, that by taking
My life, her unjust hate should quench her love.

TILNEY.   Shall I accomplish naught?

ESSEX.   Thou dost augment
My pain. That is enough.

TILNEY.   But what, then, shall
I tell the Queen?

ESSEX.   That I have just been warned
That ready stands the scaffold; that the sentence
Is in a moment to be carried out;
That, although innocent, I hold this death
Dear which will make me soon cease to displease her.

TILNEY.   I shall go back to her. But oh, once more,
By what thou owest . . .

ESSEX.   I know what I owe.
Farewell. Seeing that my honor must oppose
Thine efforts, leave to me my life's last moments.
They are so few that I at least should have

The privilege to savor them alone.　　　　　　[*Exit* TILNEY.
(*To himself*)　O Fortune! Greatness, whose beguiling lure
Surprises, moves, and blinds ambitious souls!
This is the fruit, then, of so many honors!
Long was I gaining them; one moment ends them.
All that the destiny most to be envied
Can join of glory to the fairest life
I to myself could promise, and to deserve it
There was no task too great for me to try;
Yet today—can it be believed?—'tis unto
A scaffold that the Queen doth send me! there
That before all men's gaze I, charged with crimes . . .

Enter SALISBURY.

(*To* SALISBURY)　Well, the result thou seest of my favor!
This haughty Earl of Essex, whose high fortunes
Drew an importunate throng of flatterers,—
Who saw the whole world jealous of his blessings,—
Brought low, condemned, couldst thou have recognized him?
The hapless victim of vile, wicked men,
I have indeed changed in a single moment
My lot! All things are fleeting, and if someone
Had told me, after what I have been, what
I was to bear, I would not have believed him.
SALISBURY.　Although thou findest that all things change and pass,
For thee will naught change if thou'lt spare thyself.
I have just seen the Queen, and what she told me
Shows plainly that her love pleads for thee still.
Thy pride alone, which she would fain o'ercome,
Resists her kindness, struggling stubbornly.
Constrain thyself; one word which shows submission
Will set thee above all thine enemies.
ESSEX.　What! when their lies o'erwhelm me infamously,
Shall I, to prove them right, act as though guilty?
And shall the amazed world, through my base compliance,
Infer that I with justice was condemned?
SALISBURY.　I urged thine innocence, in pleading for thee;
But still she seeketh grounds for clemency.
She is thy queen; and when, to assuage her anger,
She wishes but one word, wilt thou refuse it?
ESSEX.　Yes; for that word would cover me with shame.
I have lived proud, and I will die the same,
Always unshaken, and disdaining always
To merit the doom which is to end my days.

410

SALISBURY. Thou wilt die proud! Ah God! and canst thou deem
  That on a scaffold thou canst keep thy fame?
  That 'tis not shameful for a man once mighty . . .
ESSEX. The crime, and not the scaffold, makes the shame;
  Or if my doom brings any infamy,
  It falls on an ungrateful queen, who would
  Forget a hundred proofs of my devotion
  And ne'er deserved a subject such as I.
  But since I find death more to be desired
  Than feared, her harshness is a favor to me,
  And I have been wrong in complaining of it.
  When I have lost that which I loved the best,
  Confused and in despair, I find existence
  Hateful. What serves it me, this irksome life,
  Save better to acquaint me with misfortune?
  The Duchess only could have made it sweet
  To me . . . Alas! another is her husband,
  Another in whom love less true, less tender . . .
  But she must know of this my fate. What says she
  Of it? or do I flatter myself, in thinking
  That some affection still will make her feel
  Compassion for my lot? Robbed of her love
  So full of witchery for me, I would fain
  Have at least some share in her tears. The virtue
  Austere which holds her faithful to her duty
  Seems to forbid all hope to my sad prayers;
  Yet whatsoe'er it undertakes against me,
  I pay most dearly for aspiring to her,
  And she can, without doing aught too shameful,
  Weep for a hapless man consigned to death.
SALISBURY. What! can this perfect love, this pure affection
  Which made thee live for so long for the Duchess,
  Not turn thy soul from this resolve to die,
  When thou foreknowest how much 'twill make her suffer?
  For having loved thee, see the cost to her
  Of this cruel sacrifice . . .
ESSEX.   Past doubt, she loved me;
  And had it not been for the Queen, I had
  Good reason for thinking that she would have found
  Felicity in always loving me.
  All of the love fair lady e'er expected
  From truly faithful heart, I felt for her;
  And perhaps my care, my constancy, my faith
  Deserved the sighs which she hath heaved for me.

411

No happiness could e'er have equaled ours;
Heaven barreth it, she liveth for another.
Another hath won all I thought to win.
Marriage assures his bliss; I can but die.

SALISBURY. Ah, if to satisfy this sinful wish,
Thou must find joy in being done with life,
Lose it; but at least do so as a hero.
Go and make crimson with thy blood the waves;
Go into battle where thine honor calls thee;
Seek glory, follow it, and die for it.
'Tis there that men like thee confront death proudly,
Which elsewhere even the bravest rightly dread.

ESSEX. Though 'gainst a whole world armed for my defeat
I were to go alone in search of death,
I vainly should approach it without fear;
Such is my misery that 'twould flee from me.
Since here it surely offers me its aid,
Why not take now the remedy of my woes?
Why, base and timorous, try to stay the wrath . . .

Enter the DUCHESS *and her attendants.*

SALISBURY. Come, madam, come; thou'rt needed here. The Earl
Is bent on dying. Reason, justice, honor,
Affection—naught can make him listen to me.
If thou wilt speak opposing his despair,
He will yield, surely, and thou wilt prevail.
Disarm his pride, thy victory will be easy.
He beareth a sentence which he can make vain;
To thee I leave him to have his life in care,
And fly to seek yet other aid elsewhere.   [*Exit* SALISBURY.

ESSEX. What honor, madam! and how much must envy
Begrudge this blessing in my life's last remnant,
That I am allowed, here, before I die,
The joy of seeing thee and of saying farewell!
The fate which falls on me would ne'er have found me
If heaven had made me worthy to be thine.
I merit death only because it did not;
Hence springs my sentence, nor do I murmur at it.
I hasten to carry it out, however hard,
Well content if my death will make thee know
That never till this day a burning heart
Had loved so greatly in its self-surrender.

DUCHESS. Were this love such as I have wished to think it,
More surely should I know it when, intent

On thy fair fame, thou wouldst protect thy head
From persecution, and live to be dreaded
By flatterers vile. 'Tis with the memory
Of such a noble ardor that I dare,
While trembling at the perils into which
My evil fate hath brought thee, and quite rightly
Afraid, to beg thee to preserve thy life,
Which I have claimed belonged to me—ah, sweetness
Too briefly tasted and forever ended!
My pride I made it; heaven hath punished me.
Enough its rigor sets itself to crush me
Without thine own seeking still more to do so.

ESSEX. 'Tis true that my love's fervor dedicated
My life to thee and made thee mistress of it.
I gave thee utter power over it,
And thou wouldst have that still, hadst thou so wished.
But now in this disaster fraught with woe
What can I do with a possession useless
To thee? What can I do with a possession
Which thy selection of a husband lets thee
No more regard as thine? I treasured it
For thy sake only; and thy fatal marriage,
To make my life be longer, hath destroyed
Whate'er remained of it. Ah, what a deed!
If I cannot endure the insulting pardon
Which so insistently is offered me,
Do not say, madam, that I am too proud.
Thou wert the first who didst to death condemn me,
And I, a hapless lover, refuse mercy
And carry out the doom dispensed by thee.

DUCHESS. Cruel man! Is it a small thing, then, if I
Forget self and think only of thy interests?
To see how far thy power o'er me extends
Wouldst thou fain triumph o'er my duty also?
It wavers, and I feel that, torn with fears,
It cannot stay me from the shame of tears
Which, now about to flow from my sad eyes,
Will have more power to plead and make thee yield.
Nay, though they spring from feelings all too tender,
If they will profit thee, I wish to shed them.
By these tears, which on this disastrous day
I shed much less from pity than from love,—
By this heart, pierced by every shaft which fear
Can launch for that one's sake who is most dear,—

And lastly by those oft repeated vows
To follow blindly all my will, oh, save
Thyself! save me from that which threatens me!
If thou'lt submit, the Queen will pardon thee.
Her kindness, which she is prepared to show thee,
Desires not . . .

ESSEX.   Ah, the man who loses thee
Has nothing to preserve! If thou hadst flattered
The hope which now I lack; if, though not mine,
Thou still wert no one's; and if thy love at least
Had been less cruel to *my* love and had spared me
The horror of seeing someone else possess thee,
To save this heart for thee in which thou only
Hast place, I would a hundred times, though guiltless,
Have asked for mercy. But to live and see
Continually a hated rival . . . Ah,
Madam! at that word I grow mad. If, then,
Some frenzy marks my madness, it may be
To him permitted who takes leave of life.

DUCHESS.   Leave of life! Ah, if not for thine own sake,
Live for thy friends' sake, for the Queen, for all;
Yes, live to save me from a peril which
Bewilders me. If 'tis of scant avail
To beg, I will it and I so command.

ESSEX.   Cease, cease to wrong thyself, commanding this.
Thou wouldst esteem me less, dared I obey.
I have not merited the reverse which fells me,
But I die innocent; and if I should live,
'Twould be in guilt. Filled always with a love
Whereof the crushing grief would endlessly
And everywhere appear before thine eyes,
I would attempt to take thy heart, thy love,
From the happy man . . . Why this unworthy weakness?
Let us without dismay behold the mandate
Of heaven against me, madam, carried out.
If it allows me to be sacrificed
To envy's rage, at least it cannot find
Any blot on my life. The entire time
Which it allowed me, I have given to thee
And to my country. That calamity
Above all others unto me, thy marriage,
Showed me that I had not been worthy of thee,
That I had wrongly dared to seek thy hand;
And my ungrateful country is unworthy

414

Of me. I have not in its service spared
My life, and this it takes from me. Some day,
Some day, perhaps 'twill know its error. 'Twill
See by the evils it will have to suffer . . .

CROMMER *enters, with guards.*

But, madam, I must now take thought of dying.
They come, and I behold on these sad faces
The certain proof of what is wanted of me.
Let us go. I am ready. Farewell, madam.
To satisfy the Queen, I mount the scaffold.
DUCHESS.   Ah God! the scaffold! What, to touch thy heart,
    Pity . . .
    (*To her attendants*)   Support me . . .
ESSEX.   Thou lamentest o'er me,
Madam. May heaven, to reward thy kindness,
Crown thee with honors and prosperity,
And shed on thee all the fair fame which now
Envy takes from me by a shameful death.
(*To the guards*)   Come, I am yours.
(*To an attendant of the* DUCHESS, *supporting her fainting
    form*)   Be careful of her. She hath
Need of help in the state in which I leave her.
[He goes out, under guard.

A C T   V

*The scene represents a room in the palace, the same as in Acts
II and III.* ELIZABETH *and* TILNEY *are discovered.*

ELIZABETH.   The approach of death in no wise daunts his heart?
    With neck bared for the axe, he still is fearless?
    And the ingrate doth disdain my helping hand,
    And can be calm when *I* tremble for *him?*
    Oh! . . . but in talking with him didst thou picture
    All I can do and all he ought to fear?
    Knoweth he what sore anguish *my* heart feels?
    What saith he?
TILNEY.   That his life was ever guiltless,
    And that if fraud can make itself believed,
    He will die rather than betray his honor.
ELIZABETH.   At the expense of mine he wants, the wretch
    Wants, to display his power o'er his queen.
    Countless new crimes would follow his proud triumph;

415

He knoweth that my love will shield his life.
Using all means to end his arrogance,
I wished to send him even to the scaffold,
Trying this medicine as a last hope.
But too great is the shame of that; 'tis better
That I should yield; that on me, on my fame,
So swift a change should make the humiliation
Fall for a sentence wrongly given him.
But when for him I act against myself,
For whom do I preserve him? For the Duchess.
He loves her.

TILNEY.   Loves the Duchess?

ELIZABETH.   Yes, a name,
Naught more, was Suffolk, borrowed to conceal
A love which they did not disclose. The Duchess
Loved him, but she was not disloyal to me.
Her marriage proves it. I can blame her not.
'Twas to stop this that, rushing to the palace,
He went so far as to foment rebellion.
Although his frenzied action was unlawful,
That outbreak had no criminal intent;
And Ireland's being, 'tis said, favored by him
Has rendered him suspected of some bargain.
He hath his foes, fraud hath its stratagems,
And envy sometimes . . . Ah, weak woman, thou
Excusest him! Although no crime had blackened
His fealty, even if he be innocent,
Can he be so in *thy* sight? Is he not—
Yes, he—that headstrong subject who considered
That to have pleased thee well was his misfortune
And stubbornly preferred a shameful end
To the honors with which thou wouldst in thy love
Have crowned his destiny? It is too much!
Since he desires to perish, let him perish!

Enter the DUCHESS, *hastily.*

DUCHESS.   Ah, mercy for the Earl! He is being led
To execution now.

ELIZABETH.   To execution?

DUCHESS.   Yes, madam; and I greatly fear, alas!
That at this very moment he meets death.

ELIZABETH (*to* TILNEY). Stop them! Run—fly—and have him
brought back here.   [*Exit* TILNEY.
It is my will, my will, that he shall live.

At last, proud queen, his own unconquerable
Pride makes thee yield! Without his having asked
For aught, thou wishest to accord him all!
He shall live, and not owe to the least prayer
The life that he will use only to shame thee—
Only to make thee better realize
The abasement into which a love unworthy,
That with impunity he defieth, brings thee.
No more art thou that queen once great, august.
Thy heart is now a slave. Obey; 'tis just.
   Cease to heave sighs, Duchess; I have surrendered.
My grace doth guarantee to thee his life.
'Tis done: I pardon him.

DUCHESS.   Ah, how I fear,
Madam, that his misfortune hath too late
Softened thy heart! A secret horror makes me
Anticipate it. I was in the prison
Whence I beheld him issue. Then my anguish
Robbed me of consciousness, and lost me time
In reaching thee; and, what especially
Increases my anxiety, I encountered
Cobham not far from here. When he beheld me,
He lacked not much of trying to forbid me
An entrance to thy cabinet. No doubt
He was there only to avert the counsels
Which he feared somebody would come to give thee.
He hates Lord Essex, and lends formidable
Aid to the faction which assails the hapless
Earl. They will take thee by surprise; and such
Is of my lot . . .

ELIZABETH.   Ah! if his enemies
Have hastened to go forward with his death,
There is no blow, no vengeance swift enough,
Which can . . .

Enter CECIL.

(*To* CECIL)   Come here. What hast thou done to the Earl?
I am told that he is led to execution.

CECIL.   His death is of importance to thine honor
As well as to thy realm; and we cannot
Too soon enforce the penalty and thereby
Forestall revolt by those to whom he was
A powerful support.

ELIZABETH.   Ah! I begin
To see that it was not my interests only
Which were the basis of this cruel sentence.
So, then! ye know that *I* shrank from allowing
It to be carried out and I only wished
To see if his proud heart would be dismayed;
That sentence should have been referred to *me*.
And ye without my signature have dared
To execute him! I have just dispatched
An order to desist; if it arrives
Too late, somebody's head will pay for that,
And for the offense to me and to the realm
Other and viler blood shall make atonement.

CECIL.   This death must needs at first be sad for thee,
But thou wilt soon see it was necessary.

ELIZABETH.   Was necessary! Get thee from my sight,
Wretch, whose pernicious counsels I have heeded
Too much. My grief no more can be contained.
The Earl's death will leave *thee* to fear the worst.
If *his* blood hath been shed, tremble for thine.

CECIL.   I can fear nothing, having done my duty,
Madam; and when time makes thee realize
That in the Earl a traitor hath been punished,—
That a false subject . . .

ELIZABETH.   He was less one than thou
Who, in assailing him, hast me assailed.
Too late mine opened eyes perceive thy purpose.
Thy shameful counsels took me unawares.
Thou owest me satisfaction for it.

CECIL.   These transports . . .

ELIZABETH.   Begone! Out of my sight! Answer me not!

[*Exit* CECIL.

Duchess, they have deceived me. My stunned soul
Seeks vainly to cast off its load of horror.
What I just learned explains my whole misfortune.
Those witnesses heard with such eagerness,
The sentence soon pronounced, soon carried out—
All shows me plainly the Earl's innocence
And, to add infinite torment to my misery,
Shows it to me perchance too late! O bitter
And vain remorse! Begin my punishment
By treating me as thy rival; hear hate's voice;
Condemn, detest, my barbarous cruelty.
My blind love cost thee his heart's wedded troth;

My jealous frenzy, aiding envy's schemes.
May yet perhaps, alas, cost thee his life!

Enter TILNEY.

(*To* TILNEY)   What! back already? Hast thou stopped every-
  thing?
Hath my command been heard? Is it obeyed?
TILNEY.   Madam . . .
ELIZABETH.   Thy looks increase my dread. What is it?
  What hath been done?
TILNEY.   Imagine, from my tears.
ELIZABETH.   Thy tears! I fear the greatest of misfortunes.
  Thou knowest of my love, and sheddest tears.
  Would anyone, when I wished the Earl to have . . .
  Tell me not of his death, if mine thou seekest not.
  Nay, vain the frenzy of a distracted soul!
  'Tis done, thou'rt sure?
TILNEY.   Yes, madam.
ELIZABETH.   He is dead!
  And thou couldst let this be?
TILNEY.   Torn by my fears,
  I ran, but everywhere saw only tears.
  His enemies, madam, had done all things swiftly.
  The sentence was already carried out.
  His death, despite thee wrought, which so afflicts
  Thy sorrowing soul, can only be avenged.
ELIZABETH.   At last my cruelty has thus reached an end!
  Duchess, I ought to leave thy grief free scope.
  Reproach me, rail at me; what thou canst say
  Perhaps will speed the death for which I long.
DUCHESS.   I shall give way to grief; I cannot hide it;
  But wifely duty will not let me speak;
  And since it shames me to reveal by tears
  That this in vain struggled against love's sweetness,
  I go to weep elsewhere, after this blow,
  What I have lost because of thee and for thee.

                                   [*Exit the* DUCHESS.
ELIZABETH.   He lives no more. O queen! O unjust queen!
  If thy love slew him, what could thy hate have done?
  No, no! the fiercest tyrant throned in blood . . .

Enter SALISBURY.

Well, it is over. Thou hast thy friend no longer.

419

SALISBURY.   Madam, thou hast now lost in the Earl of Essex
      The greatest . . .
ELIZABETH.   I know it—know it to my shame.
      But if thou thoughtest that I wished his death,
      Ill hast thou known the madness of my heart.
      'Gainst me, 'gainst everyone, to save his life,
      Thou shouldst have dared all; thou wouldst then have served
         me
      Right well. Didst thou not see that my poor pride
      Sought for a little safety for my honor?
      Thy weak affection did not understand it.
      Thou didst not stay me—and thou hast destroyed me.
      Sending me word of what was taking place,
      Thou wouldst have saved us both.
SALISBURY.   Alas! How guess it!
      Never hath deed so promptly followed menace.
      Unable to persuade him to ask mercy
      Of thee, I was assembling all his friends
      To come and kneel before thee and show to thee
      What ills would from his death fall on thy head,
      When countless confused outcries told us plainly
      Of an attempt to speed his execution.
      I sent thee word at once from every side . . .
ELIZABETH.   Ah, the vile Cobham stopped all messengers!
      I see the foul plot.
SALISBURY.   I unconsciously,
      Full of my grief, and master of myself
      No more, advanced and swiftly ran towards him.
      I found him standing at the scaffold's foot.
      He saw me, he embraced me; undismayed,
      He said: "Although the Queen suspects me wrongly,
      See her for me, and let her know that nothing
      Has ever shaken my fidelity;
      And if I some audacity have shown
      In my rejection of her grace, 'tis not
      Because of pride that I have refused mercy.
      Weary of life, crushed by the bitterest griefs,
      In welcoming death it is from them I flee;
      And if I shall have aught of them hereafter,
      'Twill be when I behold how my base foes,
      Who now exult o'er me, will make her feel . . ."
      He was not given time to finish; he
      Was wanted on the scaffold. He climbed thither.
      As he declared himself devoid of guilt,

So did he seem quite unashamed to stand there.
The crowd, which he saluted, he saw weeping
And more distressed than he by his misfortune.
I tried meanwhile to win delay until
Thou shouldst know what was being done. I raised
Continual outcries, hoping to be heard.
These only hastened what I sought to stay.
He knelt; the axe awaited him already;
With fearless mien he offered to the blow
His head, which, severed from his body . . .

ELIZABETH.   Ah,
No more! My death will follow his; I know it.
'Tis but through him that I now reign so honored;
Through him that naught is too exalted for me;
Through him, his valor, that the greatest sovereigns
Have begged for peace, beaten or else afraid—
And yet I could resolve . . . Ah, vain remorse!
He dies—through thee alone, O queen too pliant!
When thou hadst owed all to his deeds renowned,
When he had for the realm oft shed his blood,
Who would have e'er dreamed that so grim a sentence
Should make him on a scaffold shed the rest?
A scaffold! God! How horrible! What a downfall!
    Come, sir; let us at least before the whole
World's eyes with funeral honors seek to amend
The injustice of a cruel and shameful death.
If heaven can by my prayers be touched, thou wilt
Not long be able to reproach me for it.   [*Exeunt.*

Andronic

(ANDRONICUS)

By
JEAN-GALBERT
CAMPISTRON

INTRODUCTORY NOTE

Jean-Galbert Campistron was born at Toulouse, probably in 1656, of a noble family. He went to Paris at an early age, became interested in writing, and found notable friends and patrons. Most of his literary work was done between 1683 and 1693, after which he was given official employment as *secrétaire général des Galères*. He received the marquisat de Penango after being with Vendome at the battle of Steenkerke, and various honors culminating with his election to the French Academy in 1701. He retired to the city of his birth, made an excellent marriage in 1710, from which five children were born, and died in 1723.

Seven of his tragedies survive: *Virginie* (1683), *Arminius* (1684), *Andronic* (1685), *Alcibiade* (1685), *Phocion* (1688), *Adrien* (1690), *Tiridate* (1691), and *Pompeïa* (written before 1698). Two others, *Phraate* (1686) and *Aëtius* (1693), are lost; and of a tenth, *Juba,* only two lines remain. He also wrote two comedies and three operas.

Campistron was the most important tragic dramatist between Racine and Crébillon at least—more probably, between Racine and Voltaire. He was regarded as in some measure the disciple of Racine and the continuer of his work. Modern estimates of him vary widely. Lanson, for example, considered him not worth reading, and pronounced his inventions commonplace, his characters featureless, and his style invertebrate, languid, and a perpetual echo of Racine.[1] But H. C. Lancaster admits only his stylistic weakness, and asserts that his *Andronic* and *Tiridate* "are, among the tragedies of the century, surpassed only by those of Corneille and Racine."[2]

Certainly these two plays had much the greatest success of all in their day, and are by far his best; aside from occasional passages, the others possess little merit. Of the two, *Andronic* is by universal consent the superior. As compared with the best plays of Du Ryer, Rotrou, and Tristan, it is somewhat lacking in vigor and in grasp of realistic detail; it is more artificial and conventional; it is essentially elegiac. Yet except for an undeniably weak fifth act, it is competently fashioned, is not blemished by any glaring absurdity, and is notable for consistent, complex, subtle characterization which will sustain a searching analysis.

---

[1] *Histoire de la Littérature française,* ed. of 1903, p. 548, and *Esquisse d'une Histoire de la Tragédie française,* New York, 1920, p. 104.

[2] *Op. cit.,* Part IV, Baltimore, 1940, p. 277.

ANDRONIC

This play has little action; it rather presents, in the main, a situation—one indeed most unusual, but entirely possible in an absolute monarchy, thoroughly human, and poignantly conceived in all its aspects by the imagination of the dramatist. Stereotyped gallantry obtrudes only in the hero's raptures on receiving Irene's letter.

Andronic takes its plot from the well-known story, later made the subject of tragedies by Alfieri and Schiller, of Philip II of Spain, his wife, and his son Don Carlos; Campistron transfers this, with changed names, to the Byzantine Empire in the days of the Palaeologi.

CHARACTERS IN THE PLAY

THE EMPEROR, *Calo-John* (*more properly, John V*) *Paleologus,
ruler of the Byzantine Empire.*
ANDRONICUS, *the Emperor's son by his first marriage.*
IRENE, *the Emperor's recently wedded wife; daughter of the
emperor of Trebizond.*
LEO, *a minister of State.*
MARCENUS, *another minister of State.*
LEONTIUS, *envoy of the Bulgarians to the Emperor.*
EUDOXIA, *chief attendant and former nurse of Irene.*
NARCEA, *another attendant of Irene.*
MARTIAN, *confidential attendant of Andronicus.*
ASPAR, GELAS, *officers of the Emperor's guards.*
CRISPUS, *officer of the Emperor.*
Guards.

*The scene represents a room in the palace of the Emperor at
Constantinople, called by its earlier name Byzantium.*

The name "Andronicus" is accented on the third syllable;
"Marcenus," "Leontius," and "Eudoxia" on the second. The
name "Irene" is given the modern, two-syllable pronunciation.

Andronicus

ACT I

Marcenus and Crispus are discovered.

MARCENUS.   What! despite all our troubles and long hate
Leo, thou sayest, would fain speak with Marcenus?
With me? Is this the truth? Can I believe it?
CRISPUS.   Yes, noble lord; and he should be here soon.
MARCENUS.   Hath aught sufficient influence o'er my soul
To curb the wrath one moment that enflames me,
When he who for so long took pains to offend me,
And who was quick to cross me in all I planned,
Has tried a hundred times to usurp my power
And the noble place I fill here in Byzantium?
For my part, I confess, firm in my hatred,
I see in him only a mortal foe;
And the favor I enjoy, thwarting his own,
Avenges well the harm he wished to do me.
I shall receive him, though, and to learn clearly
The secret feelings of a man . . .
CRISPUS   (*interrupting*).   He comes.

Enter LEO.

LEO.   Let us be left alone.   [CRISPUS *withdraws.*
(*To* MARCENUS)   May I, sir, hope
That thou wilt please to listen to me calmly
And that, with thy suspicions in abeyance,
Thou unconstrainedly canst hear my words?
MARCENUS.   I cannot hide my real surprise from thee;
But howsoe'er this colloquy disturbs me,
Speak, and fear nothing when thou layest bare
Thy thoughts. I swear an oath, sir. Trust my word.
LEO.   It is enough. This pledge dispels my fear.
I shall explain with frankness and directness.
For more than twenty years, thou knowest well, sir,
'Tis we two that have swayed the Emperor's mind.
Between us he divides his heart and power,
And we dictate the orders that he gives.
To rob thee of the station which thou holdest,
Chagrined and desperate I have oft conspired;
And thou, impelled against me by like envy,—

429

Thou hast assailed my favor and my life.
I feared thee only; thou didst fear me only;
And since we needs must now speak honestly,
It was with reason that, jealous of each other,
Thou fearedest my power and that I feared thine,—
For each of us, appraising well his rival,
Quaked lest the other should o'erthrow his fortunes,
Alike assured, fain to destroy each other,
That one of us sufficed to rule the Empire.
    Oft, when our strife was ready to subside,
The Emperor has been careful to maintain it.
Our quarrel hath served him better than our zeal;
Each of us was a faithful minister,
Whose eyes, fixed on a single enemy,
Would keep him ever constant in his duty;
And thus, so long as lived our mutual hatred,
The Emperor has enjoyed the fruit of it.
    It needs must end; the time for that has come.
Thou knowest how matters stand, sir, in this Court:
That the Emperor, nearly two months ago,
By marrying Irene, assumed new ties;
That from his hapless son he snatched this princess,
Breaking the bonds their plighted troth had formed.
To wrath now Andronicus gives his soul up,
And if he spares his father in his rage,
If he respects him still, ah! do not doubt
That he will let its lightnings fall on us.
He thinks that his sad fate was our contrivance;
He thinks that in resolving on a second
Marriage and forming thus a tie that wronged him,
The Emperor followed thy advice and mine.
We stand in equal peril, have fears in common.
Let us unite our hearts, sir, and our fortunes;
And let us hasten to build for our defense
Bulwarks which Andronicus cannot shatter.
MARCENUS.   I do not know how certain I can be, sir,
Of banishing distrust from our discussion.
But none can overhear us in this place.
We are alone. What would I have to dread?
Shouldst thou accuse me, thou as one sole witness
Canst on my loyalty cast no suspicion.
Concerning that, I know the Emperor's mind.
Hence I shall answer thee, and lay bare my heart.
    I see too well how true is what thou sayest.

E'en more than thou supposest, the Prince should be
Feared. He will reign. How can we save ourselves?
I, who was given the task of rearing him,
Have long, for my part, made an arduous effort
To probe the reasons for his disquietude.
Thou knowest that ever restless, solitary,
And sullen, he seemed to live but with regret.
Thanks to my pains I have read his inmost soul,
Seen his despair; his heart burns with ambition.
Given over wholly to the wish to reign,
He finds naught pleasing while he wears no crown.
Despite the care employed to bow his spirit
And curb his haughty pride by long subjection,
Each day beholds him, far from growing humbler,
Resist us more and haughtier still become.
Too conscious of his rights and of his lineage,
He cannot bear in the least to be a subject;
But above all, I learned his soul was mastered
By his aversion for the Emperor's favorites.
He views our power in his father's Court
As something, sir, we dared to filch from him;
And if the Emperor's death be his desire,
'Tis more to punish us than change his lot.
　　Such is the Prince; and I can tell thee further
That he is dear to the Court and is adored
By the populace. From childhood he pretended
A kind heart, winning the whole Empire's love.
Thou seest how he supports the rebel Bulgars.
Daily the envoy of this barbarous people
Consults him, talks with him; and Andronicus
Aids him with all his influence with the Emperor.
　　Ah, let us make these plans for peace be fruitless!
What could we two be in a tranquil realm?
The Emperor, freed then from fears and care,
Being more supreme, would listen to us less.
Vainly he gives us tokens of affection.
He—doubt it not—is like all other sovereigns:
They cherish men like us with the same ardor
And buy our counsel with the highest favors,
So long as discord or contrarious fate
Renders such help essential to their greatness;
But danger past and they safe from misfortune,
Their ardent friendship loses all its warmth.
We are suspected when no longer useful.

Our former services are scant protection;
We are no longer seen with the same eyes;
What was praised earlier is an odious crime;
And exile, prison, nay, a speedy death
Confirms our shame to future generations—
So much the more unfortunate we that when
Woes crush us, a whole angry world denies us
Its tears; that 'mid the wrath that falls upon us,
Our sorrows are the cause of public joy,
The populace exult, and, far from pitying,
Complain that death for us is too much kindness.

LEO.   Yes, let us, sir, prevent the wonted course
Of things, which would afflict us with the anger
Of an unworthy fate. Let us beset
The Emperor. Let us never let him savor
Wholly the happiness of untroubled peace.
Thus we, being masters here, will have no master,
And haughty Andronicus . . . But I see him.
The envoy comes with him, and Martian also.

Enter ANDRONICUS, LEONTIUS, *and* MARTIAN.

ANDRONICUS (*to* LEONTIUS). I shall speak to them of it; they both
    are here.
Leontius, thou shalt see with how much fervor
I take the part of those who are oppressed.
(*To* MARCENUS *and* LEO) Ye whose sole counsel and high
    favor with
The Emperor sway him to what course ye will,
Incline him to be merciful. Make him yield.
Let him accord the peace for which Leontius
Asks, and no more crush 'neath the cruelest lot
A folk not wicked but unfortunate.
Urge him; spare nothing; second what I seek.
Let it be granted that I may go forth—
May go into Bulgaria—and I will
Secure the loyalty of this restless people.
I promise it, if trust be only given me.
Consider that your counsels caused my woes;
But if by means of you I win my father's
Consent, I can forget all else for this.
I even abase myself to beg it of you.

MARCENUS. Ah, my lord.

ANDRONICUS.   'Tis enough. I shall but say
That some day I shall be the Empire's master.

Leave me.   [*Exeunt* MARCENUS *and* LEO.

LEONTIUS.   In hoping to obtain thine aid,
     Sir, we have flattered ourselves . . .

ANDRONICUS.   Ah, what can I
     Do now? Alas! more wretched still than ye,
     I nowise can regain what I have lost;
     But ye can some day through a kindly peace
     Forget the wrongs that have been done to you.
     The Emperor is to see you here and hearken.
     He hath so promised. He is coming now.
     I shall make every effort, and shall be
     Too happy if my pains give to your lands
     That longed-for peace which I do not enjoy.

           Enter THE EMPEROR *and guards.*

     (*To* THE EMPEROR)   My lord, Leontius still begs audience of
         thee,
     Which thou hast deigned to promise.

THE EMPEROR.   Let him approach.

LEONTIUS (*kneeling before* THE EMPEROR) .   Permit me, sire, to clasp
         thy knees and venture
     To beg that thou wilt hear my . . .

THE EMPEROR.   Rise,

LEONTIUS (*rising*) .   Vouchsafe
     Thus much, just heaven, that my plea may move him!
     (*To* THE EMPEROR)   Sire, a whole people speaks by my lips
         to thee,—
     A people ever obedient to thy mandates,
     That was the strongest rampart 'gainst thy foes
     And often made its rightly renowned valor
     Feared throughout Europe. When thy illustrious father,
     Performing his great exploits, saw himself
     The terror and the arbiter of kings,
     Thou knowest well, sire, that this gallant folk
     Was always honored by his fond esteem.
     This noble hero, for his most famous battles,
     Chose among us his officers and soldiers.

       That happy time is gone. These valiant warriors
     Are now despoiled by greedy governors;
     By odious fetters are their spirits broken;
     The rigor of their lot o'erwhelms their manhood.
     All moan, all sigh in our sad provinces,
     Chieftains and soldiers, populace and princes.
     Daily our rights are ruthlessly infringed,

And justice and the laws are held as nothing.
Vainly our tyrants try to tell our people
That 'tis from thee their edicts come to us.
Nay, thou dost not approve their bloody crimes.
I will say more: thou dost not know of them.
Ah, if thou couldst thyself see for one moment
For what ill deeds thy name is made the cloak,
How that revered name serves but to oppress us
And better bind the yoke 'neath which 'tis sought
To bow us, then wouldst thou, who to thy subjects
Art emperor less than father, think no more
Of aught except to end their miseries
And soon to punish with severity
Such foul abuse of thine authority.
   Then, if our people have been seen in madness
To take up arms to uphold their country's laws,
Our governors, sire, are guiltier than we.
They have instructed us too well in cruelty.
For thee we cherish the most unshaken fealty.
Must we needs give some signal proof thereof?
Must we, to vindicate thy royal honor,
Pour all our substance out, shed all our blood?
Must we expose our bodies to war's horrors,
And follow thy standards to the ends of the earth?
Thou'lt see us, cheerful even amid deserts,
Defy to serve thee every peril met with,
And merit of thee, in trying to do thy will,
The favor which of old thy father showed us.
But if we needs must daily see new tyrants
Pillage our homes and massacre our kindred,
And the wealth taken from our provinces
Make these cruel wretches mightier than our princes,
I will confess it, sire, our folk in wrath
Will ever clamor against their depredations.
It is for thee to judge, our lawful master,
If we should be absolved of crime or punished.
If thou condemn'st us, full of reverence for thee,
Sire, without murmuring, we shall bear thy blows.
But spurn at least the sanguinary counsels
Of the perfidious authors of our woes;
Thyself pass sentence and do not consult
With those concerned in troubling thy domains.
THE EMPEROR.   'Tis thus thou hopest by artifice to shield
   Thy head from punishment full well deserved.

What say I? Thou wouldst dictate laws to me,
So that to reign I needs must have thy sanction.
'Tis thine to obey, with no excuses offered,
Commands thou hearest given in my name;
And if I listened to my indignation,
I would not answer thee save by chastisement.
But I indeed wish still to curb my anger,
And to determine whether to be indulgent
Or rigorous is best. Go. I have heard
Thy suit, and thou shalt soon learn my decision.
          [Exit LEONTIUS.
 (*To* ANDRONICUS) Well, wilt thou speak again, Prince, for
  these rebels? ·
ANDRONICUS. None of thy subjects are more faithful; and,
 Despite thy favors to their persecutors,
 Sire, thou wouldst shudder if thou knewest their woes.
 The Emperor my grandfather, whose keen insight
 Equaled his great heart and his warlike virtues,
 Admired their valor, found pleasure in their fealty.
THE EMPEROR. What he then did, proves naught for me today.
ANDRONICUS. So be it! Since thy heart is still too angry
 To grant their plaints the grace which they deserve,
 Entrust their fate to me. My labors must
 Assure the peace of the abused Bulgarians.
 I must go . . .
THE EMPEROR. Thou?
ANDRONICUS.   Permit me to set forth.
 Suffer me to be absent for a time.
 Everything urges me to this course, sire:
 A people whom I pity, and who are eager
 To see their destiny in my hands, the wish
 To calm the unrest of the Empire, and a number
 Of other reasons of which I cannot tell thee.
THE EMPEROR. Thou, from Byzantium go, and leave this Court?
ANDRONICUS. Yes, I implore of thee this mark of love.
 Wilt thou refuse me the first boon I ask?
 If the result can equal my assurance,
 Thou wilt soon learn from this achievement what
 The Empire should expect of me some day.
THE EMPEROR. I know not how to judge of words which stun me.
 To what strange task thou dost consign thyself!
 Why leave a place where everything is thine
 To cast thy lot among our enemies?
 Thou'rt in Byzantium, where my Court adores thee.

What a strange project, I again repeat!
Must thou bestir thyself for thankless peoples?
Consider, Prince. I leave thee to thy thoughts.

[Exeunt THE EMPEROR *and guards.*

ANDRONICUS. Fixed is my purpose; naught can turn me from it.
Let us, dear Martian, speed this necessary
Departure, leave this spot where I can see
Nothing which does not drive me to despair.

MARTIAN. What! dost thou dream that, far off from this city,
'Neath other heavens thou wilt be more tranquil?
Nay, sir! thy discontent will leave thee not.
Wilt thou, then, change thy heart by changing climes?
Thinkest thou to feel, by going from Byzantium,
Less keen emotions, more indifference?

ANDRONICUS. No, no! I dare not hope for any peace.
The past is past; my torments ne'er will leave me.
Far from healing the wounds that pierce my soul,
I cannot even conceive the thought thereof.
Too strong is Irene's spell. I feel my love,
Hopeless and purposeless, grow more each day.
I saw her, loved her, from her earliest childhood;
This love hath by five years of hope been nourished.
Her glance can move me even more than earlier,
And I would strive quite uselessly against it.
But this unhappy flame that I can quench not
Perhaps no longer could control itself.
I cannot with a calm mien see my father
Possess a treasure which I had deserved.
He did me too much wrong in taking Irene
From me; within my heart he kindled hate
Which all my rectitude cannot suppress.
Only by absence can I triumph o'er it.
I know how much respect I owe my father,
And heaven witnesseth my reverence for him.
I fain would do still more; but he has robbed me
Of all. His choice . . . But let us speak no further
Of this. I am too deeply moved. I know
Myself no longer, and I fear myself.
I am young and jealous; I have lost her I love.
Let us fly, and not expose my shaken virtue
To the remorse of having striven but ill.

MARTIAN. Sir, how I pity thee! how unfortunate
Thy fate became, with this disastrous love!
Without it, content always, honored, glorious,

ANDRONICUS

Assured from birth of thine ancestral station,
Thou wouldst have tasted, with a heart at peace,
The happy lot which heaven gives earth's masters.
ANDRONICUS. How sayest thou? I was born to be unhappy!
Love did not alone make my lot a harsh one.
What! to divine how miserable I am,
Is it not enough for thee to know my father?
The Emperor, suspicious and the slave
Of his own rank, has never shown to me
A parent's tenderness. The holiest feelings
Instilled by nature would to his heart austere
Seem criminal, and 'tis not permitted me,
Being born a prince, to know a father's love.
MARTIAN. What, sir . . .
ANDRONICUS.   Here my heart murmurs at its fate.
I was not fashioned for a life obscure.
Thrilled by the heroes of my race from childhood,
Their virtues I esteem more than their rank.
Especially my grandfather's example
And glory always have incited me
And filled my thoughts. These, fixed on that famed warrior,
Can be diverted by naught else. I look
On his career with eyes of envy. I
Compare my life with his effulgent days.
Nothing presents itself unto my sight
Through his life's course but noble undertakings
And triumphs achieved; nothing but walls demolished,
Cities surprised, peoples subjected, lands
Conquered, kings humbled, rebels punished, peace
Maintained with all his allies; or if ever
Destiny said his courage nay and mingled
Some bitter thing with his prosperity,
He seems to me the greater in misfortune;
I see him even 'gainst angry Fate prevail,
And plucking a new glory from disaster,
By force of manhood bring back victory.
    But I, forever penned within these walls
And occupied till now with frivolous trifles,
I do not know an army's care or marshaling
Except in a vague way or by report.
Ah, this one thought, more than my sum of woes,
Chafes me, consumes me, and draws tears from me!
Come; let us obey the impulse which directs me,
And take so swift a flight towards glory's goal

That my deeds, blent one day among the number
Of my lost days, will for them all atone.
　　Yet find Eudoxia; she knows my anguish
And oft has urged me from Irene to fly.
She must be told of what I have resolved.
Go find her. Say to her that before departing
I ask above all else to see the Empress,
And that she ought to do me still this kindness,
And that I dare to tell myself she will.
Adieu; run; hurry. I shall wait for thy
Return to make my final preparations.　　　[*Exeunt severally.*]

A C T I I

IRENE *and* EUDOXIA *are discovered.*

IRENE.　I will not see him; no; my mind is made up.
　　　Darest thou to advise this fatal meeting?
　　　Eudoxia, knowest thou not his lot and mine?
EUDOXIA.　But why refuse to speak with him a moment?
　　　Dost thou desire that he should be made angry
　　　By thy reluctance and no longer hasten
　　　To leave Byzantium? Harken to me, take care
　　　That thou dost not make bitterer his despair;
　　　And since he gives up seeing thee forever,
　　　Accord him, madam, the favor that he asks.
IRENE.　To what sighs, what regrets wouldst have me listen?
　　　Thou who didst take me from our happy clime
　　　And leddest my footsteps to this baleful place—
　　　Thou whose advice, zeal, prudence ought at every
　　　Moment to fortify my constancy,
　　　Which might succumb beneath my mortal woes—
　　　Wouldst thou expose me to the peril I shun?
EUDOXIA.　Madam, hast thou less cause to fear that peril
　　　If thou wilt not hear this unhappy prince?
　　　Resolved that thou shalt hearken to his farewell,
　　　Everywhere, always, he will follow thee,
　　　Hoping at least to owe to favoring chance
　　　The pleasure of his sorrow's utterance to thee.
　　　What say I? Dost thou think that, thus o'erburdened
　　　With love, he can resolve to leave the Court?
　　　Vainly one plans to part from one beloved.
　　　Thou must thyself confirm him in this purpose.
　　　Show him the danger ye both run: that someone

Would soon or late see of his love some sign;
That the Emperor would, in keeping with his nature,
Forget the holy names of spouse and father,
And would destroy you both for a mere look
In which perhaps love might have little share.
Augment the innate pride of Andronicus;
Point out to him the path where honor calls him;
Command him above all never to see thee;
Let him no more approach these palace walls;
Let him think always that his fate and thine
Must needs divide you even unto the tomb.
   O heavens! what wouldst thou do if Andronicus
Should, by returning here some day to see thee,
Baffle thy hopes and wake by his sad presence
The memories which his absence will have dimmed!
Then what new battles, secret sighs! Alas!
Spare thyself this keen anguish. If the Prince
Once promises thee to disturb no more
Thy soul's peace, madam,—to go far from thy sight,
Hopeless of coming back, and there to stifle
Or cherish his hapless love,—whatever burning
Desire, whatever ardor importunes him,
I guarantee that he will keep his promise.
See him, and quail not at his cruel fate,
But sentence him to an eternal exile.

IRENE. Can I impose so harsh a sentence on him?
Ah, let me flee him; ask naught else of me.
I caused his woes by causing him to love me.
Shall I beset him still to leave the Court
And go to endure among a barbarous people
The strange caprices of a hostile fate?
What say I? thinkest thou that in my sad bosom
My virtue can resist my grief before him?
On hearing his sighs, on seeing his tears—no, no!
The very thought makes me too much afraid.
   To this sad interview I cannot expose
Myself. My torture is too great without
His own being added to it. Alas, it shakes
My constancy too much to have left my birthplace,
The place where all things seemed to anticipate
My wishes, where my heart knew never aught
But happiness! O fortunate abode!
Dear Trebizond! O walls wherein I lived
In peace profound! Why did I not, when I

Lost you, by speedy death cut short the course
Of my sad days? I left you, carried hither
By the false prospect of a happy marriage.
I deemed that Andronicus, linked with me
In fortune, would be always my companion.
So said our fathers; Trebizond and Byzantium
On this illustrious marriage based their hopes.
I came with joy to celebrate the nuptials.
The Prince was lovable; he was in love.
    Vain plans, vain transports, futile expectations!
At length I arrive; but scarcely have I entered
This city, when I find myself consigned
To infinite ills. I needs must wed the sire
Instead of the son. Our destinies are changed.
An order from my father in one instant
Destroyed the happiness for which I hoped.
A victim of State policy, and bound
To obey, I had to be for duty's sake
Mine own betrayer.

EUDOXIA.   Well, but why recall
Thy past afflictions, occupying thy mind
With these sad thoughts? Make a brave effort, madam;
Fulfil thy destiny with fewer pangs,
And hide with care from the whole Empire's eyes
The secret sorrows . . .

IRENE.   Ah, what darest thou tell me?
Who hath e'er better hid her grief than I,
And better bowed to Fate's injurious mandate?
Yet who hath ever had a fate more adverse?—
Scrutinized closely by an austere Court
In which the dearest eyes seem foes to me;
In which I have naught good that I was promised;
In which, committed without cease to anguish,
My sore oppressed heart fights against itself—
What shall I say? in which this heart so wretched
Is oft less strong, despite me, than I wish.

EUDOXIA.   Double thine efforts. Time and thy constancy
Will quell the violence of thy deep woe,
And with the Prince gone shortly from thy sight,
Thou canst . . .

Enter NARCEA.

NARCEA.   Prince Andronicus is approaching.
He seeks thee, madam.

IRENE.   Ah! I dare not await him.
Eudoxia, thou canst speak to him and hear him.
See him, and tell him that in my present state
I can but flee from him and banish him.

Enter ANDRONICUS.

ANDRONICUS.   Thou fleest from me, madam? Ah, how unjust!
Wilt thou be an accomplice to my woes?
Alas, to crush a luckless heart, wilt thou
Help Fate, which is determined to afflict me?
IRENE.   What dost thou ask, Prince? and what darest thou say?
Scornest thou the commands I laid upon thee?
What is thy purpose when thou comest hither
To make me hear adieus against my will?
Since thou art ready now to leave Byzantium,
Couldst thou not go still innocent of wrong?
Hast thou forgotten that a solemn vow
Imposes on us, both, eternal silence;
That no more talk between us is legitimate;
That one word, one glance, one sigh is a crime;
That, ever careful to perform my duty,
I staked my honor nevermore to see thee;
And be whate'er they may the ills thou facest,
That I can do nothing but pity thee?
ANDRONICUS.   What do I hear? Just heaven! of what dost thou
Accuse me, madam? What have I done deserving
This anger? Do I come to thee to ask
That thou shouldst give some tears from sorrowing eyes
To the woes that crush me? Do I come to thee
To ask thee to allow me, since I needs
Must die, to perish at thy feet? More jealous
For thy peace than art thou, I have taken pains
To exile mine own self, because I love thee.
Forgive my saying those words, for the last time.
Note well that I awaited not thy bidding
To go,—that thou hast needlessly resolved
To banish me, because I have already
Anticipated thy decision. Since
That fatal day when thou, torn from me, madam,
Gavest thy life to someone else, although
Love's flame hath ever burned deep in my heart,
Thou knowest if mine eyes have spoken of it;
If the least sign, if an imprudent sigh,
Hath caused thee to suspect some wrong desire.

441

I have in all respects kept strictly silent.
    But human hearts are not made to be done
Such violence. I well know all the struggles
Of which I needs must be the prey if under
The same sky we should dare to breathe. I know,
I know only too well, all that thy foes
And mine, and the whole realm, mayhap, might say.
They have known I loved thee, and should know that he
Who loves thee for one day must love thee always.
They would perchance dare to suspect us both.
Let us save from suspicion my fair fame
And thine. I seek to go away. Urge thou
The Emperor to grant me this one favor.
Ah joy, if by thy help mine aim succeeds!
    I go to appease the rage of some insurgents.
They want me as their chieftain, and I doubt not
That I shall soon be master in their lands;
That, with their valor ever prompt to serve
My wishes, there is nothing which they will
Not undertake, if I march at their head.
I come to offer thee their swords, my power.
Heaven, which condemns me ne'er again to see thee,
Which bids me to suppress a love so fair,
At least can in such zeal find no offense.
If it forbids my heart thoughts all too sweet,
It lets mine arm do battle for thy sake;
And if that arm should e'er be needed by thee,
Either to go to serve the Emperor
Thy father, or to slay or to drive hence
Any whose presence here offends thine eyes,
Summon me, madam; and I can do all this.
I wish but honor or death for my reward.
I seek no blessing save to give my blood
To thee, since 'tis forbidden me to give thee
My heart.

IRENE.   Thou vainly flatterest me with these
Distinguished services. My wishes do not
Aspire to such great sacrifices. When thou
Hast left this baneful place, what shall I have
Further to fear, Prince, in this Court? Alas!
I shall see all here with indifference.
To practice virtues worthy of my birth,
Accustom my too oft rebellious heart
To cherish a husband given me by heaven,

Obey his hest, seek only how to please him,
Wholly devote myself to my stern duty,
Lighten those subjects' lot whose lives I rule—
That will be mine employment till I die.
Yet I confess (and without sin I can)
That thou wilt always have my highest esteem,—
That to commend thee and to praise thine exploits,
Unto the general voice I shall add mine,—
That all my joy, the only one I picture,
Will be to see the great deeds for which heaven
Destines thee, and a hundred monarchs' envy
Prove right the choice which I had made of thee.
   After this, go. Stay faithfully in exile,
Nor e'er come back unless I should recall thee.
Achieve a happiness in other climes
Which thou wouldst never find where I would be.

ANDRONICUS. E'en yet? This happiness thou paintest to me—
Alas! in losing thee I have lost it, madam!
And I no longer know where I can seek it;
My loss is one which I cannot repair.
If any purpose still is in my soul,
It is to put injurious Fate to shame;
To show the world by some illustrious act
That hearts like mine deserve a different lot,
And, buying my first victory with my blood,
Make from my wrongs a monument to mine honor.
Do thou forget, however, my misfortunes,
Madam, and while my lamentable days,
Nourished with sighs and tears, speed towards their end,
Reign, and . . .

IRENE.   Dost think my fortitude so great?
This cruel slur, more than all of thy repinings,
Dismays my courage and confounds my purpose.
Ah, Prince! supposest thou that inhuman, heartless,
I look unmoved upon thy pain,—that midst
The horrors of thine exile, thou alone
Art to be pitied and art alone unhappy?
But what say I? Where doth some power sweep me?
Oh, why didst come again, trying to see me?
Go, Prince. Too long have lasted our farewells.

EUDOXIA. Ah, madam! I espy the Emperor here.

Enter THE EMPEROR, LEO, *and* MARCENUS.

THE EMPEROR. Madam, what was his talk and thine about?

My presence, unforeseen, disturbs you both.
I see it; all your pains cannot conceal it.

IRENE.　E'en here had Andronicus come to seek me,
Sir; he has thought my help is necessary
To win consent from thee to what he hopes for.
He has just been begging me to speak for him.
Each moment that he loses irks him more.
Permit a free rein to his martial ardor,
And suffer that to his suit I add my prayer.
　I have done what I could, Prince; thou hast heard me.
Mayest thou obtain the boon which thou desirest.

　　　　　　　　　　　　[Exeunt IRENE *and* EUDOXIA.

THE EMPEROR.　What, Prince! thou givest way to thine impatience?
Thou art resolved to leave Byzantium?
Thou makest others urge me to consent?

ANDRONICUS.　Yes, sire, and I already burn to go.
I cannot curb the ardor that impels me.

THE EMPEROR.　I hear reluctantly these words that grieve me,
And I should have preferred that this unhappy
Project had never, Prince, entered thy breast.
I told thee, more as father than as ruler,
That I approved not of this rash forth-faring.
'Twas overmuch, I think, to have convinced thee
That thou'dst displease me by its further mention;
But since despite me, since unduteously,
Thou askest me again for what offends me,
Do not, then, wonder at my just refusal.

ANDRONICUS.　Ah, sire! wouldst thou . . .

THE EMPEROR.　　　　　　　　Reply to me no further.
Learn to obey me with a more submissive
Spirit. Let us forget this enterprise
And give no food to dangerous suspicions
Of which we both hereafter might repent.

ANDRONICUS.　Very well, sire; I take leave of thy presence.
But thou imposest too much constraint on me.
I can no longer feign in such a plight,
And the instigators of thy harsh refusal
May yet for all my sorrows pay me dearly.

　　　　　　　　　　　　　　[Exit ANDRONICUS.

THE EMPEROR.　What words! what boldness! what audacity!
Before my face . . .

LEO.　　　　　　Thou seest, sir, how he threatens us.
His anger, which cannot be aimed at thee,
Will fall with the more fury on our heads.

444

What say I? Deemest thou that this prince will stop
At making the storm break on us alone?
What evils I foresee for our poor sons!
How hard a fate for them doth Andronicus
Prepare!

MARCENUS.   I fear not all that he can do.
I reck not of my son when I can serve
My emperor. Though it be I whom Andronicus
Will crush first, thou hast need too, sire, to fear
His purpose. He would have been less confounded
In spirit at thy refusal if he had not
Been meditating some great enterprise.
Would he, then, go to seek rebellious peoples
Except to further their disloyalty?
What draws him from the bosom of his country
Unless the wish to vent thereon his fury?
Perhaps, pledged to Leontius, he means
To disobey and go without permission.

THE EMPEROR.   He, go without permission!

MARCENUS.   Sire, I fear it.
'Twas Andronicus only whom Leontius
Sought, and to wheedle this ambitious prince
The better, he caressed him with a title
Which here he has not. The Bulgarians,
Armed against thine authority, will soon
Be brought beneath thy sovereign sway again.
But what distress and trouble they will cause thee
If, with a chief like him, they march against thee—
If they can henceforth brave thy wrath by setting
The son up to oppose the father's threats
And publish widely that their care and courage
Conspire to render thy successor safe!

LEO.   Alas, to what excesses he might go
If in a situation to dare all!
Dissatisfied, and followed by those warriors
Whose triumphs have already made them bold,
After he had secured his power among them
He well might come to establish it e'en here.
A youth, successful in his first wrong-doing,
Without fear gives himself to blacker projects,
And heeding only flatterers who praise him,
Comes even to think that heaven approves his crimes.
He deems that all he undertakes will thrive.
There is no scheme that seems too great for him.

He rushes on, self-assured, triumphs, slays;
Fate does his will and victory flies with him.
He wins the soldiers' hearts and confidence;
The people at his name are frozen with terror.
Thus he obtains supreme control o'er all men;
All flee from him or honor him, dread or love him;—
Till by his valor to the skies exalted,
He sees his most outrageous deeds become
Glorious.

THE EMPEROR.   How thou astoundest me! But let us
Prevent his flight. Let us unceasingly
Note what he does. Have all his steps watched closely.
Double your care. Put faithful spies around him.
Thus let us try to catch him setting out
If this he dares despite my prohibition.
Go.   [*Exeunt* LEO *and* MARCENUS.
(*To himself*)   This is not all. In this fatal moment
I feel my heart disturbed by a new fear.
How Andronicus still alarms and irks me!
Why does he bring Irene into his projects?
What interest has she in my son's schemes?
What say I? they were talking when I found them;
I noticed their confusion when they saw me.
Ah heaven! What dread! But I may be mistaken.
Let us drive hence this thought and spare our eyes
The cruelty of such an odious image.
But not so—let us rather probe the secrets
Of this strange enterprise. Love in all hearts
Stifles the voice of natural ties. Hence let us
Not be too certain that a son is duteous.
When love is great it deems all things permissible.
I know that Andronicus loved the Empress;
And though my marriage snatched her from his longings,
The fires with which he burned may not be dead.
Irene perhaps listens to him and pities him.
Ah, if I thought it! . . . A stern punishment . . .
Come, let us clear up this distressing mystery.
Vainly they hide it and, to fathom all,
It is sufficient that my heart begins
To be suspicious. Let us wait no longer;
And if I find a crime, let it be punished
Without considering whether I love the victim.

ACT III

ANDRONICUS *and* MARTIAN *are discovered.*

MARTIAN. What doest thou, sir?
ANDRONICUS.   Ah, speak to me no more
  Of this. Thy words here, Martian, are in vain.
  I am too much incensed to stop complaining.
MARTIAN. What! canst thou not control thyself one instant?
  Temper thy frenzy. Is it in this palace
  That thy repinings must break forth so loudly?
  Thou mayest be watched.
ANDRONICUS.   Hast found Leontius?
  Is he ready? What did he say? What is his answer?
MARTIAN. He makes of thy commands his highest duty.
  But here he is.

Enter LEONTIUS.

ANDRONICUS (*to* LEONTIUS).   It is in thee I place
  My hopes. To endless woes hath Fate consigned me.
  Friend, I am lost if I may not go with thee.
  The Emperor forbids me to depart,
  But the ardor which I feel cannot be daunted.
  If I can by thine aid escape securely,
  My wishes are fulfilled, I am content.
  Speak. Shall we go forth from this hostile place?
  Can this fair hope be granted unto me?
LEONTIUS. Yes, all is ready, sir; thou need'st but follow me.
  Come; let thy flight deliver thee forever
  From all the woes and perils that threaten thee.
  Accept the succor of our armèd people.
  They want thee only; they will rival each other
  Giving their blood in the defense of thine.
  Shatter a fatal yoke. Let thy first blows
  Attract all eyes and every heart to thee.
ANDRONICUS. Yes, no more wavering! With too much violence
  My heart hath been assailed, my patience wearied.
  Now let us open our eyes, too long deceived,
  And in our turn repay the ills endured.
LEONTIUS. Avenge thyself and us. Our tribes await thee.
  Refuse to them no more the arm they beg for.
  Thou hast the plan agreed on in thy hands
  As a sure proof of our fidelity.
  Sir, thou wilt find the troops in readiness,

The soldiers proud their victories are famous,
True to their leader, full of fortitude,
And resolute to conquer or to perish.
Fly to command them, and make trial of Fortune.
But above all, put irksome fear aside.
In setting hand to this great undertaking,
Be sure to steel thy heart against remorse.
Reflect no longer midst thine enterprise
If exact justice blames or sanctions it.
Enter the race, and with no stop or stay
Hasten to mount to the highest eminence.
    Scrupulous care and rigid obligations
Are virtues, sir, for ordinary men.
He who perceives himself shocked easily
Should never follow in the steps of heroes.
Those men whose fate it is to rule the world,
Carrying war and terror with them, far
From having hearts accessible to remorse,
Measure their virtue by how great they are.

ANDRONICUS. But for my flight, friend, what course must I take?
LEONTIUS. Martian knows. I go in haste, to expect thee.
    As soon as the Emperor hath dismissed his Court
And hath himself withdrawn to await the day,
Martian will lead thee carefully in my footsteps
And make sure the escape for which thou yearnest.
I have, on all the roads along which thou
Wilt pass, some faithful friends and trusty hearts,
Who, burning with complete devotion to thee,
Will furnish thee the means for a swift flight.
Then hasten, sir. I without more delay
Go to prepare all to fulfil thy wishes.   [*Exit* LEONTIUS.

MARTIAN. So thou hast chosen, sir. Despite my prayers
    Thou yieldest to a frenzy of blind rage.
There is naught, henceforth, that can stay thee. Into
What perils thou rushest to throw thyself! Dost thou
Not know the abyss where this departure leads thee?
I shudder at it. Thou seekest thy certain ruin.
The Emperor will no longer see in thee
His son, and thou art lost if thou art taken.
Wilt thou not calm this ardor that betrays thee?

ANDRONICUS. Cruel man! dost thou dare to condemn my going?
    Oh, let me, let me flee! Is there a place
More to be feared for me than this dread Court?
I know what woes my plans prepare for me,—

That to go hence unbidden risks my head,—
That now detected, I would die tomorrow,—
That neither blood-ties nor the realm can shield me.
But thus my fate decrees; I must obey.
   Well, what then, Martian, wouldst thou have me do?
Canst thou indeed conceive, in these sad moments,
The rigor of my lot, my fears, my torture?
I lose forever all that I adore.
I see raised high two men whom I detest,
Both bent on injuring me; their wicked power
Makes me loathe, almost, my own parentage.
Despite so many grounds, so much coercion,
Have I once let some plaint escape from me?
My sighs I stifle, my regrets I stifle;
I punish but myself for evils done me;
And, as my heart feeds on its melancholy,
My life is poisoned by my eternal sorrow.
At last, now, tired of seeing things so cruel,
To fly from deeds or wishes that are wrong,
Of life less careful than of my innocence,
I ask to leave Byzantium, as a favor,
And to go try my courage and my arm
To subjugate and pacify some lands
That have rebelled. The employment which I ask for
Is still refused me; my own loyalty
Is doubted, and I see that I am feared.
   My wish to go away is laid to criminal
Intentions. I am thought consumed with longings
To reign, and ready to attempt, through pride's
Excess, that which I did not even do
When robbed of her I loved. For these false reasons
I am kept here. I see my father harden
His heart against my tears. I see my foes
Triumphing o'er me in my anguish. They
Have bound me to my woes with stronger chains;
They wish to see me suffer; and they would not
Be satisfied if I should suffer elsewhere.
MARTIAN. But, sir . . .
ANDRONICUS.   I cannot listen to thee further.
I yield to the frenzies of the rage I long
Kept hidden. No more counsels! I must hence,
Or perish. To the field which waits for me
I burn to rush. I have nursed a timorous grief
Too long. I wish my wrath henceforth to guide me,

To make the Emperor fervently repent
Of having treated his own son so harshly.
　But a deep silence reigns already here.
Make haste; conform thyself to my impatience.
Watch for the moment when we can depart,
And when that time has come, return and tell me.

　　　　　　　　　　　　　　　[Exit MARTIAN.
(Alone, to himself)　　At last, now, in a moment my cruel fortune
Shall take on, with my flight, another aspect
If heaven grants the prayers which I have uttered,
Approves my going, and supports my projects.
O places where so long I loved to dwell,
Dear to my heart, Byzantium's hallowed walls,
And palace of my fathers, where I first
Beheld the light of day, I rob myself
Forever of your blest abode. I flee.
But when I go, my love entrusts to you
A treasure dearer far to me than life.
Yea, blest are ye to hold her in your close!
I love, I worship, and I dare not name her. . . .
To give her pleasure, double all your charms.
See her days pass untroubled, unafraid.
May heaven expend on me alone its harshness,
And may ye nevermore behold her tears.
At last . . .

　　　　　　　　　Enter MARTIAN.

MARTIAN.　　　　　Come, sir. The time is ripe. Set forth.
ANDRONICUS.　Let us go. Heaven, guide our undertaking!
　May we, unseen, escape hence.
　　　　　　　　　　　　　But someone
Is coming. 'Tis the Emperor that I see!
Can my intent be known?

Enter THE EMPEROR, LEO, MARCENUS, ASPAR, CRISPUS, GELAS,
　and guards.

THE EMPEROR.　　　　　　　Seize them, guards!
ANDRONICUS.　Ah, by my death I shall at least forestall
　His justice!
　　　　　　　[He tries to kill himself, but is disarmed.
THE EMPEROR.　　　But reflect, Prince, that a purpose
　So grim can make thee seem to me a criminal.

One does not slay one's self when one has nothing
  To fear.

ANDRONICUS.   Since thou knowest all, what use to feign?
If none took on themselves to warn thee of it,
Would I have been arrested when I sought
To go away? I am a criminal, yes.
Thou knowest my crime. I wanted from thy grasp
To steal thy victim; to satisfy at once
My heart and thy suspicions; to spare thee
The trouble of seeking reasons to condemn
A son whom thou believest disloyal to thee,
And save thee from the horror of his murder.

THE EMPEROR. Can guilty arrogance go further? Let him
Be taken from my sight and guarded well;
                        [Exeunt guards, with ANDRONICUS.
And let Leontius and Martian,
His miserable accomplices, expire
In the midst of torments. Do thou, Leo, hasten;
Lose not a moment; follow the Prince. Go,
And learn, precisely, everything that can
Help us to prove his guilt and justify
My wrath against him.
               [Exeunt LEO, ASPAR, CRISPUS, *and* GELAS.

MARCENUS.   Thou hast seen it, sire;
But for us, but for our advice, the faithless
Leontius would have taken hence thy son.
They both were going, together. This quiet palace
Seemed to assure them of an easy flight.
But one of my men, sire, following them closely,
Learned all their plans, marked all their preparations,
And told me all. Our care balked their escape
And the deplorable results thereof.
Thus, do not doubt, the schemes of the rebellious
Peoples are frustrate, their disorders checked.
No longer fear the efforts of their arms.

      Enter IRENE, EUDOXIA, *and* NARCEA.

IRENE. What have I heard, my lord? What rumors, fears,
Unforeseen dangers, odious designs
Trouble thy peace and bring thee to this spot?
Trembling for thee, most anxious and distracted,
I seek thee, headlong; nothing meets my sight
But tears, sighs, glances filled with consternation,
Soldiers struck dumb, and guards amazed. What causes

        This dreadful alteration in the Court?
THE EMPEROR.   Madam, my peril moves thee overmuch.
        I have averted it. Fear naught for me.
        My hand can punish a disloyal son.
IRENE.   What, my lord . . .
THE EMPEROR.   Andronicus brazenly
        Flouted my wrath and sped to take up arms
        Against me, going hence though I forbade it.
        He sought to join the rebels in their madness;
        But heaven, which ever leads and guides my footsteps,
        Cheated the hopes of this perfidious prince
        And, as it rightly watches over kings,
        Hath bowed a recreant son to the law's rigor.
        I have him in my power; and for his guilt
        A memorable example must be made
        Of him to awe insurgent spirits.
IRENE.   Ah, couldst thou
        Form this dire purpose? Couldst thou be so cruel?
THE EMPEROR.   Madam . . .
IRENE.   To push thy wrath to this excess . . .
        How horrible! Forgive my frank words. Sir,
        I fear for thee the inevitable recurrence
        Of natural impulses, of strong affections,
        Which would with mortal wounds transfix thy heart
        And cost thee sorrows for thy son destroyed.
        I fear for thee that shame, those woeful titles,
        Which this grim sacrifice would give to thee.
        Such notable examples of strict justice
        Bring in their train eternal retribution.
        Hate falls upon the one who punishes,
        Pity and love upon the one who dies;
        And he who lays cruel hands upon his sons
        Seems not to have deserved their loyalty.
        I may have said too much, sir; but my zeal
        Seeks only to prevent thy keen remorse,
        Which thy repentance would bring on thy head,
        And save from all unworthiness thy memory.
THE EMPEROR.   Madam, that is enough. I can take care
        Of mine own honor. I see what is the meaning
        Of this officious zeal which has been just
        Displayed before mine eyes. I know thy heart;
        I know its every thought. Come; have no doubt
        Of my appreciation.   *[Exeunt all except* MARCENUS.
MARCENUS *(to himself)*.   Now at last

The Prince stands on the brink of ruin. Shall we
Inflame the Emperor still more against him?
Or shall we seek to save him? Ah, without
Fear let us take this offered opportunity.
He threatened us; he would some day destroy us.
Let us not wait for that dire turn of fortune.   [*Exit.*

ACT IV

Leo and Aspar are discovered.

LEO.   Yes, it is thou I seek. I come to give thee
An order vital to the Empire's safety.
To thee alone the Emperor dares entrust it.

ASPAR.   To please him I am ready to do all.
Command me.

LEO.   The Emperor has already seen
The letter which was intended for the Prince.
Thou knowest that that one who had undertaken
To give it to him, was near by when we
Surprised him. But the Emperor wishes him
To see it. He sets thee this task; he sends it,
Aspar, to thee. Let it be given the Prince,
And with such skill deceive him that he will not
At all suspect the trick.

ASPAR.   Have confidence,
Sir, in my zeal.

LEO.   But above all, employ
A faithful agent. Instruct him carefully
When thou hast chosen him. Remember thou
Shalt answer for it. Adieu.

ASPAR.   Fear nothing. I
Shall make thee know that Aspar, when he chooses,
Chooses no traitor.   [*Exit* LEO.
                    I see Andronicus.
He bends his steps this way.

Enter ANDRONICUS, *guarded.*

ANDRONICUS.   Let me be left
Alone a moment. Let no one disturb me.
                    [ASPAR *and the guards withdraw.*
(*To himself*) Plans ill-devised, vengeance ill-fated, whence
My heart with too much hope was flattered, sweet
Illusions which beguiled my spirit, projects

Vanished as soon as formed, no more provide me
With your vain fancies; let me contemplate
My misery without you. O great heaven,
To what state do I find myself reduced!
In this plight everyone betrays or shuns me.
Friendless, with no help in this fatal hour,
What must I needs expect? What hope is left me?
The sacrifice already of Leontius
And Martian just now to the Emperor's wrath,
The strengthening of my guard from hour to hour,
The black presentiment which afflicts my soul,—
A thousand doleful things make me imagine
In what way these beginnings must conclude.
Yes, I can doubt not that my doom is sealed,
Since all the plans I made have been discovered.
I am betrayed and I shall die; harsh Fate
Invests my death with the dark hues of crime.
    Let the Emperor punish me as his frenzy pleases;
But let him also judge himself, and do
Justice upon himself. Let him remember
The paths of both, and which one of us two
Is the guiltier or the more unfortunate.
Carried away by heat of a rash spirit,
I formed vain schemes, gave vent to my heart's rage,
Yielded to hopes which someone came to rouse—
These crimes are all that I can be accused of.
My father . . . but what say I? he refuses
To be that. How am I to know him that?
He robs me of my lady, and the Empire,
And life: I have but this proof of his love!
    Let us not strive to rouse affection in him.
Naught would disarm his vengeful wrath, and even
If I could by my efforts touch his heart,
My life is not worth what one sigh would cost me.
But what is wanted with me?

Enter GELAS.

GELAS.   This is a letter,
    Sir, which I promised I would give thee secretly.
ANDRONICUS.   But hast thou naught to say? Can I not know . . .
GELAS.   Nay, sir. I go, for I have done my duty.   [*Exit* GELAS.
ANDRONICUS.   Is it some remedy for the ills that crush me?
    Does heaven cast on me a kindly glance?
    Who can be moved by my cruel fortune? Let us

Read this. I do not recognize the hand,
But scarce have I set eyes upon this writing
Than suddenly my soul is agitated.
I do not know what presage, what unconscious
Turmoil, evokes these unexpected feelings.
(*Reading*) "Make peace, by one last effort, with thy father.
Spare naught henceforward, Prince, to save thyself.
Save a life necessary to the realm.
Remember that in dying . . ." I can read
No more.
              Unequaled goodness! Adored princess!
What! is thy heart concerned still for my life?
Yes, I no longer doubt; my soul finds light.
To speak thus to me, thou hast the sole right.
I know thy voice. It seems to me I hear it.
Would I have dared put trust in this last effort?
By all forsaken . . . Ah, too favored prince!
How canst thou merit such solicitude?
     No more shall I lament my father's cruelty.
What kindness could have done so much for me
As did his wrath? Irene, I make thy wishes
My sovereign law. Thou wishest me to live;
That is enough for me. I am prepared
To lend myself unto thy least desires.
Alas, though! will the Emperor care to hear me?
No matter! to content thee, all must needs
Be risked. My pride, my rage must yield to love.
Then be resolved, my heart, to do thyself
This violence. Bow, though it seemeth useless.
Accept this token, Princess, of my fealty,
The hardest for a man like me to give;
But after this, beware of making other
Efforts for me. To save my life, do not
Expose thine own. Risk nothing more to help me,
And leave my fate to its sad course.
                    (*Calling*)   Ho there,
Guards! One of you!

                    Enter Aspar.

Aspar.   My lord, what is thy need?
Andronicus.   Find out if I can have speech with my father;
     If he will stay the course of his resentment
     And deign once more to hear me for a moment.
                              [*Exit* Aspar.

A N D R O N I C

(*To himself*)   What is it I do? Ah heaven! how hard a
   meeting!
What can I say to him? What shame to see him!
I go, then, basely to implore the grace
Of him who treats me with indignity,
Who ne'er bestowed on me caress or kindness,
Who hates me in his heart, whose coldness chills me,
Who bars all access to paternal love
And in his son sees but a guilty subject.
Shall I be able even to bear his presence?
He will not answer me, save with icy silence.
His brow will show me naught save stern disdain.
'Twill be my task to abase myself in vain.
Is there a woe, is there a punishment,
Bitterer to me than this self-immolation?
O rigorous yoke of a triumphant victor,
How fearsomely thou fallest upon my heart!

Enter ASPAR.

ASPAR.   Prepare thyself, my lord. Thy father comes.
ANDRONICUS.   My king, say rather. What sore strife! What oppro-
   brium!
I more than ever feel my heart rebel.

Enter THE EMPEROR.

THE EMPEROR (*to* ASPAR).   Leave us here.
   (*To himself*)   Will he fall down at my feet?
ANDRONICUS (*to himself*).   Ah, how shall I begin? What is it I hope
   for?
THE EMPEROR (*to himself*).   At sight of him I feel my wrath re-
   doubled.
ANDRONICUS (*to himself*).   Come, be submissive; hesitate no longer.
   (*To* THE EMPEROR)   My Lord, thou seest me confused,
      abashed . . .
THE EMPEROR.   What, Prince, dost thou expect of me? What hope
   Has made thee wish my presence in this place?
ANDRONICUS.   Ah, my lord, do not crush me; reassure me.
   My soul is seized with trouble and affright.
   My humbled heart succumbs to my distress.
THE EMPEROR.   Can such a heart as thine be, then, so weak?
ANDRONICUS.   My lord, remember that I am thy son.
THE EMPEROR.   And the most dangerous of all my foes.
ANDRONICUS.   Dost thou think that? Ah heaven! What darest thou say,
   sir?

456

THE EMPEROR. The things that reason and a just wrath inspire.
ANDRONICUS. How miserable I am!
THE EMPEROR.   Guiltier by far.
ANDRONICUS. Wilt thou not put aside this heartless mood?
  Wilt thou be towards thy son stern and unbending?
THE EMPEROR. And hast thou shown thy father more affection?
ANDRONICUS. Well, that is settled, then. I can no more
  Give to myself the name, sir, of thy son.
  And yet, alas! in this unhappy moment
  That name alone is left me of my blessings.
  Yes, my lord, I oppose to thy just anger
  Only this blood, these lineaments that I have
  From thee. I dare, with this defense, to expect
  That thou wilt ne'er deem me entirely guilty.
THE EMPEROR. This makes thee the more criminal in my sight.
  Thou joinest names too vile to that name. Ingrate,
  I cannot without shuddering recognize
  My blood in a rebel and my son in a traitor.
ANDRONICUS. My lord . . .
THE EMPEROR.   These are no longer, now, suspicions.
  We have uncovered all thy treachery.
  Go, Prince; proceed where honor urges thee.
  Incite against me all Bulgaria.
  Signalize in this noble task thine arm.
  With other crimes still . . .
ANDRONICUS.   Ah! do not believe it.
  With no imaginary crimes reproach me.
THE EMPEROR. What! to become a headstrong people's leader;
  To negotiate with rebels secretly—
  Tell me: are these crimes only my inventions?
  What doubt is there of thy ingratitude?
  If I had still the least uncertainty,
  Quickly would I deceive myself for thee.
  I would defend thee, not as now accuse thee.
  But I have seen thine own base signature.
  That sight makes nature silent in my breast.
  To what, then, do these treacherous agreements
  Tend, this asylum offered, help accepted,
  These mutual pledges, and this guilty compact,
  Save to the throne whereon thy father long
  Hath wearied thee? Answer me if thou canst.
  Hast thou some explanations? Or are these,
  I should ask, all thy treasons? Speak out. Thy
  Embarrassment suffices to convict thee.

ANDRONICUS.   Nay, sir. I cannot answer thee, or dare not.
   I am less guilty than I seem to be,
   And yet thou knowest not all my secrets.
THE EMPEROR.   What!
ANDRONICUS.   The outrageous conduct of thy favorites
   Could justify the purpose of my flight.
   Under the galling yoke of their harsh sway
   The most submissive spirits sometimes murmur;
   And in a young man's heart one should ascribe
   Such errors to the frailties of youth.
   But I would rather owe to naught but thee
   My safety. Let me kneel again before thee.   [*He kneels.*
   Art thou not moved at all in my behalf?
   What! far from listening, thou avertest thy face.
   Thy heart is closed to feelings of affection
   Which ought to master it in this sad hour.
   Sir, look upon me with a father's eyes . . .
   Alas! I only make thy wrath the bitterer!
THE EMPEROR.   Prince, hast thou nothing more to say to me?
ANDRONICUS (*rising*).   No. To have said so much makes me ashamed.
   Ah! 'twas no horror of what threatens me
   Which has abased me thus to beg for mercy,
   And I did not indeed expect from thee,
   After such sternness, any kindlier treatment.
   I know well that thy heart is hard towards me,
   And death has nothing terrible to show me.
   If someone had not made me make this effort . . .
THE EMPEROR.   Enough! I understand thee.
ANDRONICUS.   Sentence me.
   Hasten the fatal blow of tardy justice.
   Life is henceforth my cruelest punishment,
   And I would soon die of regret and shame
   That I have humbly kneeled to thee in vain.
                                     [*Exit* ANDRONICUS.
THE EMPEROR.   Ye heavens! how far doth his blind insolence
   Carry him! 'Tis too much that I should do
   Violence to my feelings, for his sake.
   "If someone had not made me make this effort,"
   He said. . . . Ah, that one phrase decides his death.
   Only too well I see the Empress loves him.
   No, no, none other can this be but her.
   'Twas Irene's hand that wrote the odious letter
   Which filled my soul with fatal agitation.
   A-tremble for his life, crossing my wishes,

ANDRONICUS

She has risked all for my rash son. I can
No longer doubt it; the traitor has betrayed
Himself. Whom would he have obeyed but her?
And had it not been for the hope to please
Her whom he loved, would he have e'er constrained
Himself to take this course? And with what manner
Did the insolent youth put on humility?
It was my hate he roused, and not my pity.
I saw this haughty spirit, e'en at my feet,
Retract the homage of his forced respect.
He could not persevere in feigned repentance.
His lips betrayed the arrogance of his heart.
At what time? At the very moment when,
Despite my wrath, the traitor made me conscious
I was a father; and when all my anger
Was on the point of leaving me—say rather,
When I would have been able to pardon him!
   How clearly does this letter prove they share
An understanding of some sort! Ye shall
Abuse no further my too great indulgence,
Traitors! But by what magic could they blind me?
How have they dared to dream they could deceive me—
Me, who with so great pains and perseverance
Have learned the science of probing hearts; who by
The art which I employ to cloak my projects
Know every highway, every secret path;
Who by my policy and skill in feigning,
Force all my neighbors, all the kings, to fear me?
In mine own palace and amidst my Court
I see myself the dupe of a rash love.
A false pair, without art, without experience,
Hoodwink my reason, cheat my care, gainsay,
By their love, deadly to my honor, all
That which the universe proclaims is mine.
Alas! they tricked me without difficulty
Or forethought. I felt no disquiet about them.
My heart was not beset by dark suspicions,
But slept, quite trustful of their seeming virtue.
O wretched husband! O unhappy father!
   Where shouldst thou stop? to what point carry anger?
Their just deserts cannot too soon be given them.
In their false blood, then, let us drown this outrage.
But above all, let us contrive with prudence
Their death. By diverse paths let us achieve

459

My vengeance. Let us for mine honor's sake
Prevent all rumor dangerous thereto.
Let us for crimes of State doom Andronicus,
By secret means destroy the Empress, and
Conceal at once her guilt and its requital.

ACT V

Andronicus is discovered, alone.

ANDRONICUS.   Shall I be long, still, in this cruel state?
Why is a guilty prince allowed to live?
This ominous delay and this uncertainty
Have made me bear already too great tortures.
Each moment added to my hapless days
Doubles the horror that I feel of them.
Will no one come? After our interview
Can the Emperor leave my fate still in suspense?
If he believes that what I have attempted
Insults him, by my shame and my chagrin
He is too well avenged. Ah, how I suffer!
But I give way to my impatience. Heaven,
That seest how I strive, make me more constant.
I cannot cope with all the things I feel.
    But here at last is the order and the death
Which I await.

Enter ASPAR, GELAS, *and* CRISPUS.

ASPAR.   My lord . . .
ANDRONICUS.   I understand thee.
'Tis wished that I should die. Then let us go.
ASPAR.   Thou art to choose the manner of thy death.
The Emperor permits it.
ANDRONICUS.   By his kindness
I am surprised. I thought him not so tender
And my offense too great. Indeed I shall not
Abuse his goodness, and the blow shall follow
Its promise closely. Have a bath prepared
For me. When the time comes to go hence,
Thou'lt find me ready. Come back and let me know.
                                        [*Exit* ASPAR.
But ah! what seizure, what emotion grips me?
Give me a chair.
                        [CRISPUS *brings him a chair. He sits.*

ANDRONICUS

Enough! Let me be left
Alone. . . . Then go. Show not your sorrow to me.
How shall my ills be served by sighs and tears?

[*Exeunt* GELAS *and* CRISPUS.

(*To himself*)   'Tis time to put on a brave constancy.
What end, alas, have all my hopes! Descended
From the most noble blood, which all men reverence,
Lord of a hundred peoples from my cradle,
When I would free myself from ghastly thralldom
Whose yoke so long has made my spirit groan,—
When blessings, honors, glory, and every pleasure
Ought to come flocking to my earliest wish,—
I die; and for the crown of misery
I hear my father's lips decree my doom.
    So be it! Always a victim of Fate's harshness,
Only by death can I escape my woes.
Only thereby may I find peace, for heaven
Can work no miracle to give me that;
And while I lived and while the same fires burned,
I needs would be a criminal or unhappy—
In fruitless rage, a lover without hope,
Held back both in my love and in my vengeance,
Pierced through with tender pangs, shaken with anger,
Yet never daring to either woo or strike!
    Ah, heaven should have been a little less
Adverse to me; at least have left my love
Or my wrath free; have offered me a heart
For which mine own could burn unchecked, or else
A rival's blood that I could sacrifice.
After all, in such strife I cannot live,
And I should thank the fate that frees me from it.
    Yes, I am resolute; but what, Irene,
Is to become of thee? Shun my father's wrath.
My death will cost thee dangerous tears. The Emperor
Will at the sight of them take great alarm.
How do I know? perhaps in this dread hour
Less was it as my father that he doomed me
Than as my rival. Ah, the o'erwhelming thought
To which my mind gives itself up! O heaven,
What peril for Irene if he suspects her!
How I fear, Princess, that his arm's dire blows
Will fall on thee next, after smiting me!
That is what stuns me, not my death. But I
Have reached the time, now, for my slaughter. Heaven,

461

I offer thee my life. Abate thy sternness.
Mayst thou stretch far from me thy vengeful hand!
Shield innocence against a barbarous husband;
And ne'er grow weary of defending it!

Enter ASPAR *and* GELAS.

Why dost thou show me a dumbfounded face?
Hast thou done, Aspar, what I bade thee do?
ASPAR. Yes, all is ready, sir. I quake to say it.
ANDRONICUS. All is ready! Then let us go.
ASPAR.   How I
Admire thy courage! Gelas, escort the Prince.
                              [*Exeunt* ANDRONICUS *and* GELAS.
(*To himself*) Ah! in his sad fate I have hidden from him
Evils more cruel, even, than his death.
Disastrous issue! Terrible occurrence!
O loss to the Empire, ever lamentable!
With what things are we threatened after this!

Enter IRENE *and* NARCEA.

IRENE (*to* NARCEA). No, to thine anxious care I cannot yield
Myself up. I must needs see Andronicus,
Narcea, in this dreadful hour and give him
All of the time still left me.
                              What doeth the Prince,
Aspar? Shall I learn this, in my turn?
ASPAR (*hesitating*). Madam . . .
IRENE.   Explain thyself. Speak to me frankly.
ASPAR. A direct order calls me to the Emperor.
Thou wilt know all.
IRENE.   Go. Be sure to say to him
That I am here; in fact, that I await him,
Ready to tell him some important secrets.   [*Exit* ASPAR.
NARCEA. But what is thine intent? What is it thou doest?
Madam, rememberest thou what plight is thine?
Ah, how I pity thee! My affrighted heart
Regards thy fate . . .

Enter EUDOXIA.

EUDOXIA.   Oh, what is this I see!
What is thy purpose? Thou hast, then, deceived me?
What, madam! Didst thou from mine arms escape
Only to rush here, with unworthy grieving
To show that thou hast merited thy woes?

ANDRONICUS

<table>
<tr><td></td><td>What hath my care availed? Ah, could I think
That thou so ill wouldst cherish thy fair fame?
What will folk henceforth say? this realm? thy husband?</td></tr>
<tr><td>IRENE.</td><td>O heavens! What time thou choosest for thy counsels!
Alas, be more indulgent for my sake.
Eudoxia, I am about to die—die guiltless.
Thou hast ever seen me so obedient
To thine authority that it ought to be
Permitted me to fail one time in this.
Abate thine anger; stifle thy reproaches.
I now begin to feel death drawing near.
That is the prompt work of the deadly draught
Which crowns the horror of my cruel lot.
Thine eyes beheld with how great ingenuity
The recreants sought to hide their fury from me.
But all their pains could not one instant dupe me,
And avidly my hand and lips have taken
The unlawful vessel and the fatal drink
By which the course of my sad days shall end.</td></tr>
<tr><td>EUDOXIA.</td><td>Ah, turn from this design and seek for help!</td></tr>
<tr><td>IRENE.</td><td>Wouldst have my woes go on and on forever?
No; let me be a victim of the Emperor.
He thinks the same crime stains his son and me.
Hie we to Andronicus. He is nigh.
Come mingle with our sad farewells thy tears.
Let the last glances of this loyal prince
Show him the greatness of my mortal grief.
Ere he dies, let him learn now that Irene
Will not one instant more live after him;
That, from an irksome yoke set free, my soul
Will show itself wholly concerned with his;
That in the moment when death breaks our bonds,
Our spirits, issuing thence, will meet each other;
And that, restored to him for whom alone
I e'er was born, I finally shall accomplish
My entire destiny!</td></tr>
</table>

Enter GELAS.

<table>
<tr><td>GELAS.</td><td>Where art thou hastening,
Madam, and what is it that thou art seeking?
Ah, rather needest thou to be carried hence!
Avoid a spectacle which rends my soul.</td></tr>
<tr><td>IRENE.</td><td>Is Andronicus dead, then?</td></tr>
<tr><td>GELAS.</td><td>He no longer</td></tr>
</table>

ANDRONIC

Is living, madam. I just saw him die
In the bath which he himself had had prepared.

IRENE (*to* EUDOXIA *and* NARCEA). Support me. After this blow, my
    strength fails.
    (*To* GELAS) And thou, of the Prince's death, tell me the rest.

GELAS. Without lamenting his cruel fate an instant,
He followed us. Unflinchingly he entered
The bath, and he himself held out his arms
And let his veins be opened. He displayed
A heart indifferent to his pain, and soon
He saw the water of the fatal bath
Turn crimson with his blood, which ran in streams.
In the meantime he grew pale, his eyes grew dim,
And as the moments passed he became weaker.
His soul, too fain to slip forth with his blood,
Speeds to the fated end . . .

IRENE.   I am o'ercome.
Vouchsafe a brief time to my stricken spirit . . .
That is enough. Finish these words that kill me.

GELAS. He raised to heaven his eyes for the last time,
And uttered these words with a dying voice:
"O death, the one sure refuge from misfortunes,
With eye serene would I observe thy coming
If the whole fury of the vengeful rage
By whose decree I suffer should fall only
On me. I fear . . ." At this, his soul was greatly
Moved, and he cast a restless glance about him.
He said: "Cruel father of a hapless son,
I give thee back the blood thou gavest me.
Seek none elsewhere to satisfy thy rage."
Thereon he almost lost the power of speech.
No more did he preserve in his confused
Talk any sequence. 'Twas but broken words.
His mind was now beclouded and bewildered;
Vague purposes possessed it, and it wandered.
He spoke to thee and to the Emperor,
Sometimes seemed tranquil and sometimes in frenzy.
Drained finally of his blood, he lost all strength.
His head sank toward his breast, nodded, and dropped.
He died; his bleeding body, pale, ice-cold,
Showed to us nothing more than some blurred portrait.
As for me, with a heart pierced by this dreadful
Vision, I loathe his persecutors' fury,
And fearing lest my tears be deemed a crime,

464

I shall go elsewhere, to conceal my grief.   [*Exit* GELAS.

IRENE.   'Tis done. The light hath from his eyes been ravished.
Burst forth, my sighs; his death gives you the right to.

EUDOXIA.   What then . . .

IRENE.   Regrets, transports till now restrained,
Be manifest. 'Tis time. I shall no longer
Keep you pent up within me. He is dead!
Ah heaven, what blood did they dare spill! Receive
At least the tears which now I give thy ashes,
Dear prince. See how, on hearing of thy fate,
Irene can nothing more, and dies of sorrow.
But ah, the effects of the poison have increased!
I feel my weakness and distemper grow,
And the noxious workings of the mortal venom
Take from my grief the honor of my death.
Nay, nay, I was mistaken; they act together.
The two at once . . . The Emperor comes. I tremble.
My pain redoubles at the sight of him.

Enter THE EMPEROR.

Sir, ere I died, I wished to speak to thee.
Thou hast punished Andronicus. I die of poison.
Thou hast suspected him, suspected me.
A letter which fell today into thy hands
Unquestionably sealed our cruel fate.
It came from me. I could have hidden this from thee,
For the handwriting was unknown to thee.
Without shame I avow it. Well, why conceal it?
'Tis the sole crime with which I can be charged.
This do I swear by heaven, that heaven whose power
Rewards or punishes us as we deserve:
Neither thy son nor I, till our last breath,
Has ever had a criminal desire.
His going was to flee me. With a duteous
Heart, I imposed on him eternal absence.
'Twas then that both of us were sacrificed
Horribly to thy miserable suspicions.
This day shall furnish history with a ghastly
Page that posterity can scarce believe.
I say no more. I have fulfilled my lot.
I pass without regret into death's arms,
Because it breaks the marriage-bonds that join us.
       Eudoxia, let us use discreetly this
Last moment of my life. Remove me hence.

465

Let me at least be able as I die
To have no eyes but thine for witnesses.

        [*Exit* IRENE, *upborne by* EUDOXIA *and* NARCEA.

THE EMPEROR.   What have I heard! What dread, what sudden pity,
    Seizes my heart, frightens and tortures me!
    Were both of them guilty or innocent?
    I know not. . . . But alas, what woe is mine!

Manlius Capitolinus

B y
ANTOINE DE LA FOSSE

INTRODUCTORY NOTE

Antoine de La Fosse, the son of a goldsmith and nephew of a painter of some note, was born about 1653. He received an excellent classical education and served as secretary successively to three distinguished men, Foucher, who was the French envoy at Florence, the Marquis de Créqui, and the duc d'Aumont. He was with Créqui when the marquis was killed at the battle of Luzzara, in 1702. He died in Paris in 1708.

Besides some translations, notably of the odes of Anacreon, he wrote four tragedies. Good workmanship can be found in *Polyxène* (1696), in *Thesée* (1700), and in *Corésus et Callirhoé* (1703), for La Fosse wrought carefully and might have gone far if he had begun dramatic composition earlier in life; but it is solely for his *Manlius Capitolinus*, the second of his four plays, that he is remembered at all. *Manlius* is important in several respects. Appearing in 1698, it remained in the repertory of the Comédie Française for a century and a half, with 250 performances in that period. It is the last French tragedy of any merit in the seventeenth century; it thus brings to a close the golden age of French drama. And it is the first French tragedy that was based on an English play. Though it purports to depict the downfall of the haughty and ambitious savior of Rome from the Gauls as told in the sixth book of Livy, and takes thence the setting, the names of the chief characters, and some of the material of its first and last acts, its plot is substantially that of Thomas Otway's tragedy, *Venice Preserved,* transferred to early Rome much as Campistron transferred the story of Philip II and Don Carlos to the late Byzantine Empire in his *Andronic.*

Comparisons between the English play (published in 1682) and *Manlius* have been vitiated by the strange, wholly unjustified traditional reputation of the former. William Archer completely demolished its pretensions to excellence—for all time, one may hope—in his book *The Old Drama and the New*.[1] *Manlius,* on the other hand, is one of the very best tragedies written by others than Corneille and Racine in seventeenth-century France. La Harpe considered it and Rotrou's *Venceslas* the best of all these. It possesses a wealth of detail and allusion, giving a lifelike sense of background, that can hardly be matched in any of them except *Cosroès*. Interest

[1] New York, 1929, pp. 160-164.

is well sustained throughout; its characters are well drawn; its forceful, competently fashioned verse is probably superior to that of any other minor French tragedy between Quinault and Crébillon, if not between Rotrou and Voltaire. The alien influence, less of *Venice Preserved* than of English drama in general in so far as La Fosse was acquainted with it, may be seen in two ways—one good, one bad. Here perhaps for the first time in French tragedy we encounter a depiction of connubial love's growth and ripening with continued association. But we also find at times a too-hurried development, an inadequacy of preparation or motivation, which is unfortunately common in Elizabethan and Restoration drama but is hardly paralleled in French tragedies between 1640 and 1700. Too precipitant, for instance, are the disclosure of the conspiracy to Servilius, the proposal that he shall join it, and his eager assent; they do not quite achieve verisimilitude. But the chief blemish in this play is the separation of Servilius from Valeria without explanation or even leave-taking; this was unnecessary, and was certain to excite her suspicions, and the disaster which overtook the conspirators is thus made the result of their incredibly bad judgment at this point.

CHARACTERS IN THE PLAY

MANLIUS CAPITOLINUS, *a Roman nobleman.*
SERVILIUS, *his friend.*
VALERIA, *wife of Servilius.*
VALERIUS, *Consul of Rome; father of Valeria.*
RUTILUS, *one of the chiefs of Manlius' conspiracy.*
ALBINUS, *confidante of Manlius.*
TULLIA, *confidante of Valeria.*
PROCULUS, *one of the household servants of Manlius.*

The scene is a room in the house of Manlius, on the Capitoline Hill, in Rome.

Manlius Capitolinus

ACT I

MANLIUS *and* ALBINUS *are discovered.*

MANLIUS. Thou knowest, Albinus, how important such
    A secret is, and thy proved loyalty
    Assures me of thy silence. Before thee
    Mine anger can without fear be displayed.
    Just gods! when will the time for action come?
    When can I punish all the wrongs at once
    With which Rome's tyrants have repaid my service?
    I thank their enmity, Albinus, which,
    Divesting me of useless pity, makes me
    Able to envisage without qualms today
    The thought of building upon their destruction
    My greatness. For indeed, when I, so often
    Cheated of my desires, espoused the cause
    Of the populace against them, I wished only,
    By showing them my power, to contrive
    To teach them to behave more prudently
    Towards me. But after the affronts wherewith
    They have made my face burn scarlet, my rage cannot
    Act either too soon or too much. I wish
    To make them see, by one dread lightning bolt,
    How ill does Manlius bear contumely,—
    How vital 'twas, Albinus, to spare naught
    To win me or, if not that, to destroy me.
ALBINUS. Yes, but whatever eagerness impels thee,
    Is an inconstant, doubtful, timid people
    (Whose zeal, at first impetuous and ardent,
    Lends ostentatious aid to its protectors
    And who in danger trembles and deserts them)
    An assured warrant for the hope it gives thee?
    When a dictator's wicked tyranny
    Made thee thyself, who couldst believe this people
    Forever bound by hundreds of kind deeds
    Unto thy fortunes, bear a prison's shame,
    Were not its rabble, that in thy behalf
    Gathered, confused by terror at his voice?
    Who of them undertook then thy defense?
MANLIUS. At least they forced the Senate to release me.

Their zeal and my hope grow from their repentance.
Breaking my chains revealed their power to them
And this fact, that to end an unjust yoke
Their whole success depends on perseverance.
How many of the efforts they have made,
Oft even without a leader, have succeeded!
They have won tribunes, whose good aid supplied
A needed curb unto the consuls' pride.
They have been seen to engage in nobler tasks:
The haughtiest Romans have been exiled by them;
They have compelled those of the highest station,
In wedding with their daughters, to permit
The union of their families thus with them.
They have acquired a share in conquered land;
And what, Albinus, do they need to make them
Dare more, except to show to them a leader
Whose skill and courage will aid the undertakings
In which their ardor may engage them?

ALBINUS.   Then, sir,
'Tis on this hope that thou, with a loud voice,
Denouncest everywhere the Senate's laws?
Art thou not fearful that such haughty boldness
May give to their suspicions too much light?

MANLIUS.   No; in their arrogance they defy me ever
And deem that my ill feeling all finds outlet
In empty words. They know too well that Manlius
Bends not. They would suspect me if they saw me
Quieter. By disguising least my hatred,
I best deceive them. Under my presumption,
Albinus, I conceal myself from them;
And while preparing all those things against them
Which they should fear, I even have the pleasure
Of not controlling myself.

ALBINUS.   I say no more.
Thou hast foreseen all, and I think thy wisdom
Will likewise have provided against all.
What happy omens for so just a purpose!
This rock on which the Gauls were wrecked, this towering
Capitol, the asylum of our gods,
The hope of Rome—thou thyself holdest it;
Its fate is in thy hands. And what may we
Not augur from the courage and the zeal
Of friends so many, armed for the same quarrel?
And most of all from Rutilus, that brave soldier

Who, crushed by the decrees of a stern Senate,
Would without thy prompt aid, thy kindly care,
Have ended woes and life alike in prison!
And what good fortune also that Servilius
Returned here unexpectedly today!
How zealously he acts as a friend should!
Distant from Rome, he scarce learned, as he fled,
Of the wrong done thee by the Senate's action,
Ere he came back, to bring assistance to thee.
The love, the fright, the tears of his Valeria,
Whom he presumptuously snatched from her father,
Vainly—and vainly also all his friends—
Have sought to stay him. And what joy he showed
When, clasping thee, he saw his fears were needless!
What pleasure he must take in thy designs!

MANLIUS. He still knows nothing of them, and I wish,
Albinus, with no witness to unbosom
Myself thereon to him this morning. But—
Wouldst thou have thought it?—poor Valeria,
Trembling for him and following his steps,
Has fortunately entered Rome unnoticed
And reached my house this very hour, to join him.
But I shall all the sooner for this secret . . .

ALBINUS. Someone is coming.

Enter PROCULUS.

PROCULUS.   Valerius is here
To see thee, sir.

MANLIUS.   Valerius! What weighty
Matter compels this consul to seek *me?*
Could he yet know that his abducted daughter,
Following Servilius, has come to *my* house?
(*To* ALBINUS)   Go, run to warn them; bid them have no fear.
Find Rutilus after thou speakest to them.

Exeunt PROCULUS *and* ALBINUS. *Enter* VALERIUS.

VALERIUS. I come to learn from thee, sir, what to think
Of a report, injurious to thine honor,
Now circulated. Servilius, 'tis said,
Sheltered within this house, thinks to enjoy
Through thee a sure asylum here; he dares
To flatter himself that thou wouldst even wish
To assume, against my vengeance, his defense.

MANLIUS. Yes, it is true, sir, that he dares to flatter

    Himself thus. I should take it as an insult
    That anyone could doubt it. I can surely
    Preserve myself from that too common error
    Of being false to friends misused by Fortune,
    Regulating by its caprice my hate
    And love. What he hath done, sir, seems to thee
    A dreadful crime. That is not how one sees it
    When one with ample evidence weighs his reasons
    For it a moment. But whate'er he be
    Therein, by what law, after all, must he,
    If criminal towards thee, be so towards me?
VALERIUS. By this law, sir, dear to the noblest souls,
    Of having no friend dearer than one's country;
    Of giving all up to maintain its justice.
    Thy friend hath by his crime sinned 'gainst its laws.
    In thy sight as in mine he thus is guilty.
    Not to disturb thee with our secret doubts,
    How long wilt thou so promptly and so gladly
    Espouse the cause of every malcontent
    And lavish favors on him?—as the wont is
    Of one who would become his country's master.
MANLIUS. And how can I allay, sir, thy suspicions?
    What are the hidden reasons for thy fears?
    Must I regard as foes all whom a Senate,
    Cruel and unjust and violent, assails?
    And am I criminal when my kindly welcome
    Softens the blows launched by their angry pride?
    'Tis I, 'tis *my* aid, that preserves them here.
    Thou askest whence a Roman, one sole man,
    Assumes the burden of the woes of others,
    And offers all men a hand prompt to aid them?
    Is it for thee to object to just compassion?
    Is that a virtue to be feared in me?
    If one can thus gain favor with the people,
    Why does none practice it today but me?
    Why do ye not begrudge me this advantage?
    Why does not each of you, to end suspicions,
    Apply himself, by the same kindnesses,
    To attract and hold the friends which they have won me?
    Is there no way to lull the Senate's fears
    Save to mistreat the people, mock their tears?
    Are avarice, arrogance, and the harshest measures
    The basis of the safety of a nation?
    My kind deeds make you fear, yet tranquilly

MANLIUS CAPITOLINUS

Ye view the excessive power of Camillus!
In the army, city, Senate—everywhere—
Before mine eyes ye load him down with honors.
He is sole arbiter of peace and war.
His docile colleagues, satisfied with titles,
Leave all authority in his hands alone
And seem to fix it there to excite his hopes.
  Why such respect and love for what he does?
The Gauls' flight ye ascribe unto his arm.
Your flattering eulogies speak but of him.
Yet what had been your fate, with all his aid,
If when Rome, given up to the barbarians,
Running with blood, ravaged by flames, awaited
The help which he was gathering far away,
They had become the masters of the Capitol?
'Twas I, anticipating your vain efforts,
Who hurled the Gauls down from its ramparts' height.
This proud Camillus conquered after me
A foe already stricken, seized with panic.
'Twas I who by my deed prepared his victory,
And in his glory many had a share;
Mine is mine only, I then fought alone;
And while Rome honors eagerly his valor,
This Senate and these consuls, whom my courage
Saved from cruel death or ignominious slavery,
On first suspicion blush not to undo me,
Make me repent my service, in their prison,
And with affronts unnumbered, to reward me,
Disgrace my consular descent and name.

VALERIUS. Sir, with less anger thou couldst better judge
Our motives, which appear unrighteous to thee.
If now Camillus gives us no offense,
It is because we see what spirit fills him.
To heed his counsels, certain of good issue,
Is to obey the gods who have inspired them.
Have we a reason for shame at this obedience
By which our glory and our freedom grow?
Are not these things the goal of truly Roman
Hearts? When 'tis reached, what matter by whose guidance?
Thou hast like zeal for Rome and for Rome's glory;
Thy aims are similar, I would fain believe.
But to speak frankly, is it without grounds
That Rome is anxious, thinking otherwise?
And what suspicions were not born perforce

That day when thou wert bidden to come before us,
And thy great crowd of followers and the Senate's
Seemed two armed camps determined to do battle?
What streams of Roman blood would then have flowed
If to the end the populace had dared
Defend thee! One would think that after this
Thou wouldst be careful to refuse to see
Any unsavory person. But in giving
Aid to the insolent Servilius . . .

MANLIUS.   I see him, sir, coming to speak with thee.
Perhaps on hearing him, more kindly feelings
Will take the place of wrath within thy breast.
I leave you both.

Enter SERVILIUS. *Exit* MANLIUS.

VALERIUS.   What would this knave with me?
SERVILIUS.   Sir, if thy sight confuses and dismays me,
I know how odious I am to thee.
I swear to heaven, that is my only woe.
To end its cause, I have come here to throw
Myself upon thy mercy. Without anger
Wilt thou consent to hear me for one moment?
VALERIUS.   What is thy hope? What darest thou to expect?
That I, I, patiently could listen to thee?
That I, I, could forget that day when thou,
Having prepared for flight and being sure
Of the compliance of my deluded daughter,
Camest in thy mad love to snatch her e'en
At the altar from her husband's arms before
My face? With what wrath, by what cruel death
Ought I to . . .
SERVILIUS.   Ah, couldst thou with any justice
Reward my rival with a prize which thou, sir,
Knowest was due to me alone? Vouchsafe
To think more fitly of my rights and honor,
And if that fatal day comes to thy mind,
Remember too that fearsome night on which,
Amid the carnage, flames, and din, already
The raging Gauls had bound Valeria's hands
With fetters, before thy distracted eyes.
What was my rival doing at that dread moment?
He served Rome elsewhere; I served Rome and her.
I fought for the one; I saved for thee the other.
All covered with my blood, shed for thy sake,

I dared to ask of thee my deed's reward,
And driven to despair by thy refusal,
I did against a proud, incautious rival
What the Gauls saw my arm do against them.

VALERIUS. And so to have saved her from the Gauls thou deemedst
Gave thee due grounds to impose thy will on me!
Thou thoughtest through them to triumph over me
And on my lost rights base thy right supreme!
For of what use to me is what thou didst?
The Gauls were taking her; thou takest her.
In vain my word had pledged her to another.
Him, even like me, thou thinkest to have conquered.
In short, thou treatest me like a vanquished foe.
How canst reproach me, earning me this name?
If promising Valeria elsewhere gave
Thy disappointed love cause for complaint,
Did then my offer of her sister to thee,
My help, my boons, reveal my scorn of thee?

SERVILIUS. Ah, sir, on me thy boons were vainly lavished!
Thou tookest more from me than thou couldst give me.
Valeria had, alone, my heart and vows.
Whate'er was not she, was beneath their notice.
Far from contenting me, thy gifts without her
Were . . . But to what does a rash ardor bear me?
All that I argue only makes thee bitterer.
Then I shall give myself into thy hands.
To owe my pardon but to thy kind heart,
I here beg for myself thy former goodness.
The more I seem, sir, wicked in thy sight,
The nobler wilt thou show thyself if thou
Forgettest my crime. Thy ancestors and mine,
Joined by this marriage, can without shame . . .

VALERIUS.   Well,
Let us discuss a reconciliation.
Wouldst thou do something worthy to appease me?

SERVILIUS. To be so happy, what can I refuse?
Speak, sir! oh, speak!

VALERIUS.   Thy valor and thy birth
Can make, 'tis true, connection with thee prized;
But this I deem wrong, and no more will know thee,
Since friendship unites thee with Manlius,
That haughty spirit, distrusted by his country.
Be constant, if thou wilt, to indulge his rage,
But join not *my* blood with the crimes and fate

To which his schemes some day might carry thee.
Undo now freely what thou didst by force;
In short, vouchsafe my daughter a divorce.
To put it better, choose to have henceforward
Him without her, or else her without him.
See which of these two choices pleases thee.
Thou canst not otherwise disarm my anger.

SERVILIUS.   If thy proposal could for a single instant
Have made me waver, I should want to kill
Myself with this knife, here, in front of thee.

VALERIUS.   Enough! Farewell!   [*Exit* VALERIUS.

SERVILIUS.   I, to escape thy fury,
I, betray Manlius or lose Valeria!
That aim, cruel man, is beyond all thy efforts.
Too strong the bonds that bind them to my heart!
To tear them thence, it must be rent in twain.
Storm, thunder, satiate the rage that fills thee;
No matter how cruel blows it rains upon me,
What can they . . .
                    But I see Valeria coming.
O just gods, who behold my deathless love,
Judge, seeing her, did I do too much to gain her?

Enter VALERIA.

VALERIA.   Well, hast thou seen my father, now? Of all
Your talk, what is the outcome? Do his love
And approbation of our marriage tie
Fulfil at last the wishes of Valeria?
But what concern is this thy face exhibits?
What evil . . .

SERVILIUS.   Dost thou see these honored walls
Wherein so many heroes have been born,
Wherein the favor of the gods hath made
Their presence felt, and whence, if we must needs
Believe their words, the subjugated peoples
Of the entire world will some day be governed?
This Rome, in short, my country and thy country—
Neither of us hath in its destiny
A portion any more. Its sight henceforth
Is not permitted us, and we have no hope
Hereafter save among its enemies.

VALERIA.   I understand thee, sir: nothing can bend
My father. We must leave Rome, to escape
His wrath. But I am not surprised at this.

O cruel fate! A mortal woman's lot
Would else have been too blest. But let us hasten;
Let us begone before the tempest comes
With which his vengeance menaces thy life.
Let us not vex him more by staying longer.
Nothing should keep us here, sir, any further.
Whate'er misfortunes Fate assembles for us,
United we shall suffer them; together
We flee. All places have unnumbered charms
For hearts that love each other truly. Ah,
Can one be happy without any cost?
Manlius, sir, freed from his cruel prison,
Hath here no longer need of thy devotion.
Thy debt paid to a friend so dearly loved,
Let us both give ourselves now to each other
Completely. Let us go and flee the prospect
Of staying here to breed suspicion of us.
Come; let thy love, convinced by mine, learn this:
With thee my heart finds everywhere its honor,
Its happiness, its country, and its gods.

SERVILIUS.   O faithful heart! O virtue that I worship!
With thee what exile can afflict me further?
What blessing can I lack? I have for thee
A lover's fervor in a husband's breast.
What do I say? thy beauty and thy goodness,
Seen intimately, make my love flame higher;
And every day, enthralled by countless charms,
I always see more than mine utmost dreams.
Yes, let us go, Valeria; let us flee
This fatal place. But let us, first of all,
See the friend left me still, and in our plight
Of which he is a witness, let us both
Ask him for his advice and his assistance.   [*Exeunt.*

A C T   I I

MANLIUS and SERVILIUS are discovered.

MANLIUS.   No, I do not approve of this new flight,
Thy change in fortunes ought to change thy course.
SERVILIUS.   What secret motive makes thee censure me?
Thinkest thou that with gladness I shall leave thee,
When, shaping all my aims to please Valeria,
I offer up our friendship to her love?

Would to the gods that, joined forevermore,
Our three hearts . . . But vain thought, unfruitful longings!
Thou seest with what influence and power
Valerius can hasten here his vengeance.
Thy kindly care would vainly seek to aid me
Against a Senate openly his friends;
And when an easy flight can make me safe
From them in some asylum far from Rome,
Ought I to involve needlessly a generous
Friend in the perils of a luckless love?

MANLIUS.   But wilt thou flee thy fortune, fleeing hence?
Where thinkest thou to drag out a weary life,
And what resources canst thou find there still?
Dost thou know what just happened in the Senate?
How far Valerius' anger hath been carried?

SERVILIUS.   No. And what hath he done?

MANLIUS.   All that he could do.
'Tis a small matter that the cruel Senate
Condemns thee to eternal banishment.
To make the days left thee a torment to thee,
Thou art despoiled of chattels, titles, rank,
And thy home, too, whose precious treasures soon
Will be the spoil of a fierce soldiery,
And which unnumbered hands will now pull down
At once, to be in its foundations buried.
The order for the carrying out of this
Decree hath been already given, and
Haughty Valerius himself hath signed it.
In short, thou hast lost all; and in this plight
Judge if it be enough for thee to share
The residue of my property, which, like
The blood I shed in combat, I have vainly
Lavished in serving these ungrateful men.

SERVILIUS.   Thus, barbarous father, thus thy cruelty
In striking me hath fallen on Valeria.
Her lot and mine, united, must . . . Ah, Manlius!
Thou knowest how in danger I behave;
Thou knowest if injurious Fate till now
Hath driven my spirit to the least abasement:
But when I think, alas! that this my plight
Will soon expose to the severest trials
A fair young girl whose love, whose constancy,
Cannot demand too much in turn from me,
I lose at such a prospect all my firmness.

But pardon me this cowardice, I pray thee,
Which, making me foresee such dreadful things,
Makes me bedew thy generous breast with tears.

MANLIUS. With tears! Ah, rather may these treacherous Romans
Be in their blood drowned by thy valiant hands!
Tears! tears! Doth grief in such degree possess thee?
There is a nobler remedy to heal it,
An eminent privilege, a glorious right
Which men like thee share with the gods themselves:
Revenge. My hand will second thine. Our lot
Is one. Thy wrong is mine. It is at me
They aim, and in Servilius they think
To humiliate the pride of Manlius.
Let us associate in a common vengeance
Those who associate us in the same trespass.
Let us avenge all our cruel wrongs, and rid
Ourselves of senators and consuls.

SERVILIUS.   What
Sayest thou? With these dark words thy voice and look
Revive my hope, reanimate my courage.
Thou seemest to meditate some mighty project.
Go on, go on, dear friend; tell me thy secret.

MANLIUS. Since thy plight is the same as mine, thy anger
Ought to have taught thy heart what mine can do.
Learn, then, that soon our tyrants will consign
The fate of Rome to my hands, by their death.
I have brave friends to lead this enterprise,
And won by *my* efforts or theirs, the people
Have chosen Rutilus to devise with me.
Thou knowest his prudence and fidelity.
To speed the tardy hour of my vengeance
I have admonished him to come at once.
All smiles on me. To carry out my aims
I have found sundry means, each independent,
Which can assist, but cannot balk, each other,
And any one of which alone can bring me
Success in my designs. And if I can
Attain it, I leave thee to judge what share
Thereof my friendship will assign to thee.
This is the plan, Servilius, which fires me
And upon which thou oughtest to base thy hopes.
Not that it blinds me so that I conceive
That no caprice of Fate can make it fail.
I know too well how sudden is disaster;

But is it not better, friend, that Rome should see
Manlius die while seeking his revenge,
Not Manlius alive, enduring insults?
If thou couldst but requite thy lot's dishonor,
Wouldst thou view otherwise mere loss of life?
SERVILIUS. No, Manlius; no, no. Thy vows are mine.
I hear with ecstasy thy noble purpose,
And from my life's ills I derive this good thing,
That they can to my fervor add my rage.
Only command. On which one of those ingrates
First must the fury of mine arm descend?
Must I go in broad daylight with my followers
To face the Senate's cohorts and break in
Their doors, or pull their burning palaces
Down on their heads? Thou seest my will entirely
Disposed to obey thee.
MANLIUS.   I desire, before
All else, to present thee to Rutilus.
As he is an exacting, careful man,
An oath, which all are bound by, will be needed
To assure our friends, through him, of thy fidelity.
And thou, without being warned, knowest enough
To conceal all this carefully, even the slightest
Signs of it, to all others afterwards
And make thine eyes and face keep it a secret.
SERVILIUS. Thou knowest me too well, to fear that any
     Reproach . . .
MANLIUS.   Let *me* speak to him. I see him coming.
But go not hence, for I shall call thee soon.

     SERVILIUS *walks aside. Enter* RUTILUS.

(*To* RUTILUS)   At last it is too late, sir, to draw back.
By careful pains and craft, we have made harmless,
As far as possible, the caprice of Fortune.
Action is needed now, no more debate.
In such designs, 'tis fatal to delay.
Perhaps my efforts with the aid of thine
Would add in time new means to those already
Adopted; but when a sufficient number
Can once, as now, be gathered, lest some turn
Of fate may scatter or divide them, one
Should seize the offered chance and undertake
The task proposed. How well the time, moreover,
And place are suited to our resources!

MANLIUS CAPITOLINUS

The Senate declares war on the Circeians,
And must, to start it with fair auspices,
Come to the Capitol to sacrifice.
How suitable for us the time and place,
I say! A time when that whole body puts
Itself in our hands! and a place where I
Am master, where the fastened gates expose it
Without its armies to our unleased fury!
The day is not yet chosen, but to be ready
We must know certainly the people's mood.
By our redoubled efforts we must rouse them
Against a Senate whose great power they hate.
They must not see me, lest suspicion waken;
But in thee, sir, I put my trust completely.
I know that thy devotion to our cause
Will prompt thee to say all that need be said.
    There is one thing more. I believe thou knowest
That yesterday Servilius joined me here
And that my heart conceals no secret from him.

RUTILUS.   What, sir! He learned through thee of our designs?
MANLIUS.   Yes. What surprise . . .
RUTILUS.   I with regret explain.
Gladly would I suppress my heart's misgivings
If the betrayal of thy plans exposed
My life alone. But unto me a great
People entrusts its fate. Sir, in displaying
My faith in thee, I must be careful not
To sacrifice its safety to discharge
The debt I owe thee. 'Tis not by its blood
That I must satisfy that debt. I know
Thy friend. I know why he is wroth, and how
By aiding us he can repair his fortunes.
But marriage still unites him with the consul,
With that proud consul whom our hate proscribes;
And though to placate *him* attempts were vain,
Though hopeless seems the task to make him kindlier,
Is he so proud and of his wrath so full
As to refuse, sir, to forget his vengeance
If he could learn a secret so important?
However strong the basis of the friendship
Whose claims now make thee certain of Servilius,
Hath love less power? Is it less his master?
What do I say? If chance should bring to birth
Some issue where his heart must choose between them,

Thinkest thou that it would be love's part to yield?

MANLIUS.   To dissipate this doubt, which does him wrong,
His presence here before thee is sufficient.
Come here, Servilius.

[SERVILIUS *comes to them.*

SERVILIUS (*to* RUTILUS).   What glorious fate,
What unforeseen blessing was waiting here
For me! Sir, how the plan whereof I learned
Should . . . But what coldness thou displayest to me!
Can I be doubted by thee? Have I vainly
Aspired . . .

RUTILUS.   Why dost thou ask that? Thou hast heard me.

SERVILIUS.   I have; and very far from being offended
Thereat, sir, I myself praise thy distrust.
I myself blame like thee the confidence
Of my too ardent friend, too partial to me.
Nowise do I wish here, by a vain oath,
To make the gods witness my pledge to thee.
For faithless souls, that is too weak a bond.
I can assure thee in another way.
(*Indicating* MANLIUS)   In *his* hands I shall place, to answer
          for it,
Far more than all the scepters in the world,
The only blessing that an envious Fate
Hath left me. Sir, Valeria here hath shelter.
There is the pledge of my fidelity.
I give her to our mutual friend, as hostage;
And mine own self, to assure thee better still
Of my good faith, I put into *thy* hands
That thou mayst watch over both it and me.
Seeing my every step, observe my conduct;
And if my constancy should flag hereafter,
At once before mine eyes draw forth this blade,
Say to Valeria, while thou stabbest her breast,
"For guerdon of thy virtue, of thy love,
Servilius by my hand, himself doth slay thee,"
And then in the same moment, turning on me
Thy blows, rip out my heart. Let it be shown
To all eyes as a coward's heart, a perjurer's,
And feed it to the vultures after that.
(*To* MANLIUS)   Thou, sir, go to prepare her, in my place,
To see Fate separate us for some days,
Vouchsafing, that I may be spared her tears,

To bear her my adieus and calm her fears.

[Exit MANLIUS.

RUTILUS. Sir, I now realize that my doubts were wrong.
I with delight behold thy noble rage.
This is the surest hostage thou couldst give us,
And I should not require another pledge,
Were there no need of proving thy good faith
To others more distrustful than myself.
For this design in which our zeal unites us
Is such that everyone doth guarantee
In vain his own arm faithful. He will bring
Only a wavering courage into danger
If he is not as sure of all the others.
Impressed, however, by thy fervent ardor,
Sir, I shall leave thee thine own master still.
Consult with Manlius; let him choose with thee
The post at which thy hand will smite beside us.
Meanwhile, to speed the day of our rejoicing,
I shall go quickly where his bidding sends me.

SERVILIUS. And I, to avoid useless grief, shall flee
Valeria's presence and no more behold her.
Manlius will take pains to assuage her sadness.
Far from me shall I banish all vain affection,
And in my heart I wish to leave henceforward
Only the hope of triumph which makes glad
My rage.   *[Exit* SERVILIUS.

RUTILUS *(to himself)*. His look and words show a fine spirit,
And he could not do more to reassure me.
However, this may be but a first impulse
That fierce resentment wakens in his heart.
Full of his vengeance, he takes thought no whit.
Let us go execute our orders promptly
And come back soon to test whether he knows
The greatness of the cause he hath embraced.   *[Exit.*

ACT III

VALERIA and TULLIA *are discovered.*

VALERIA. No, naught can calm the anxiety I feel.
Why, without seeing me, doth Servilius leave me
And someone else bring his farewell for him?
To what mysterious place doth he now go?
What plans are his when Rome hath banished him?

He has just talked with Rutilus and Manlius.
Is it by their advice that he doth leave me
And for the first time hides his secrets from me?
What hope remains to me and lets me live?
He is with Manlius; thou hast just been told so.
I want him to come here. I shall await him.

TULLIA. But wherefore, madam, art thou so disturbed?
Fearest thou that such a great and noble hero
Would leave thee to the lot in which thou sufferest?
Knowest thou so little such a lofty soul?
Ah, quell these fears unworthy of his love!
Thy woes make certain his fidelity.
And how canst thou find such offense herein,
Thou who so manifestly showeth today
That Fate is powerless against perfect love?

VALERIA. Already, reasoning thus, I have condemned
My fears; but scarcely doth my heart repulse them
Than other dreadful doubts arise to trouble
The peace which it begins to feel, and rend it.
I can no longer live in this cruel pain,
Tullia. Before he goes, he must explain.

TULLIA. I hear the door open. 'Tis he, madam.

VALERIA.   Leave us.

Exit TULLIA. *Enter* SERVILIUS.

SERVILIUS. Yes, thou shalt fall, proud Senate, 'neath my blows.
I have just chosen the station where my fury . . .
But what is this?   [*He turns abruptly to leave the room.*

VALERIA.   Ah, sir! thou fleest Valeria?

SERVILIUS. How now! What is thy wish? Comest thou here
To make my grief more by sad words of parting?
Thinkest thou to shake my purpose with thy tears?

VALERIA. Nay, sir; I have no longer hopes so sanguine.
'Tis true that hitherto the love which joined us
Submitted all thy wishes to mine own.
My least unhappiness disquieted thee.
But that time is no more; thy heart is wayward.
The lordly rights of marriage make it bold
To scorn at length my sweet dominion o'er thee.
Thou shunn'st me, leav'st me a prey to countless fears,
To cry to heaven, to drown myself in tears,
And showest in grieving me a stouter heart
Than if thou tookest revenge on some cruel foe.

SERVILIUS. What do I hear, Valeria? Is it to me

That thy heart uttereth this harsh reproach?
Is it I whose ardor marriage hath made cold?
Am I this recreant, callous to thy tears?
VALERIA.   Nay, when I hear thy voice, thou'rt that no longer.
I can no more cherish a doubt of thee.
Thy sight restores peace to my troubled soul.
But, to abuse not my credulity,
Give me the reasons which can justify thee
When I can see thee not nor hear thy voice.
Being about to leave me, hide naught from me.
Tell me . . .
SERVILIUS.   No more, Valeria! Let us cease
To talk. Whatever thy dominion o'er me,
Respect a secret that I cannot tell thee.
VALERIA.   "Cannot"? What canst thou fear? Ah, know me better
And let my sex deceive thee not herein.
Do not look on me as some common soul
Whom peril dismays, on whom a secret weigheth,
But as a hero's wife, a Roman's wife,
A faithful friend taken unto thy bosom,
Who learned long since, by happy studiousness,
To make habitual in herself thy virtues,
With noble ardor, with disdain of death,
Constant in loyalty, whate'er her lot.
My heart is equal now to all that thine is,
And howso heaven threatens either of us,
For thee I can with ease defy its blows,
Or even, if necessary, share them with thee.
SERVILIUS.   Ah, too apparent is thy goodness to me
Nor could my life sufficiently repay it.
But wherefore ask so fervently of me
That which mine honor cannot grant to thee?
Allow my duty to set bounds to thy
Dominion over me. The secrets which
I hide from thee are such . . . But whither stray
My wits? Farewell.
VALERIA.   Vainly thou fliest from me.
I understand now, everything. The postponement
Of our departure, thy concealed distraction
Which thy fierce, gloomy look shows plainly to me,
Thy eagerness to avoid me—all betrays thee.
Thou seekest revenge upon my father.
SERVILIUS.   Who?
I?

VALERIA. Thou. In vain thou wouldst not tell me of it.
Only too well my troubled love can see.
Manlius and Rutilus, for whom thou fleest me,
Are linked with thee by like dissatisfactions.
Therefore these talks at which ye fear my presence;
And if I must explain all that I think,
The vast collection of all sorts of arms, sir,
Which Manlius hath carefully concealed here,
After the stories of his plans 'gainst Rome,
Indicates other schemes than one man's death.
Still furious at the recent outrage done him,
He doubtless will against the Senate . . .
SERVILIUS. Gods!
What darest thou to divine? Knowest thou, Valeria,
What danger, from this hour, threatens thy life,
Or that its safety in the future hangs
On blotting out this talk from thy remembrance?
If any had the least suspicion of it,
Thy life and mine, both, would be at an end.
Thou art a hostage here for my good conduct;
I am for thine.
VALERIA. Ah, with affright I shudder!
I, a base hostage for a frenzy blind
By which must perish my father and my country?
SERVILIUS. Oh, stay thy cries! Is this that vaunted heart?
VALERIA. Yes, that which can for thee defy misfortune
But shudders for thee at so black a crime.
Thou, sacrifice thy fair fame to thy vengeance!
Conceive against thy country such designs!
Dare with my father's blood to stain thy hands!
'Tis true that on this day his deadly anger
Hath crowned the sum of ills which overwhelm us;
Yet still he is my father, sir. Canst thou
Thyself shed blood which is the source of mine,
E'en with that blood allied whence thou wert born?
Not fearing names like "traitor" or "assassin,"
Thy heart till now so lofty, so magnanimous,
Plans with delight so many dreadful murders?
Whatever charms revenge at first presenteth,
'Tis always fatal unto those that seek it;
With the remorse which follows its dark deeds,
Those best avenged are oft those least content.
SERVILIUS. Thou judgest me ill. I seek, Valeria,
To avenge my wrongs less than to save my country.

This is no savage effort to destroy it.
I let bad blood to purge the State thereof.
VALERIA.　And with what purer blood canst thou intend,
Forsooth, to replace that which thou wilt shed?
From whom to save thy country? From the Senate
And from the consuls, hated by the people?
Ah, followest thou the insensate people's whims?
Howe'er unjust to thee hath been the Senate,
Whate'er the wrath within our hearts can urge,
Is it not better and more worthy of us
To endure alone those ills which trouble us
Than to see all our native land in tears?
But think not that I would, after such words,
Betray a secret whereon hangs thy life.
That life is precious beyond all things to me.
But if my father in my tears can find
No aid against thy fatal rage, I call
The gods to witness, I shall perish with him.
I leave that thought with thee.　　　　[*Exit* VALERIA.
SERVILIUS.　　　　　　　　By what ill chance
Hath she divined this perilous secret's truth?
Fatal dilemma! Naught could I deny.
To do so, would have been a vain, crass lie.
To keep her silent I was forced to make
Her loving heart conceive the need of silence.
And how fear, after all, a heart like hers?
But I, have I no reason to doubt mine own?
What qualm, in hearing her . . . what sudden pity
For our doomed tyrants now hath shaken my hate?
I? I to feel misgivings about anger
So just? I could . . . No, ingrates, ye shall all
Die. Mine eternal hatred so decrees.

Enter MANLIUS.

MANLIUS.　My friend, I come to bring thee happy news.
The Senate, as we secretly have hoped,
Orders a solemn sacrifice tomorrow.
'Tis then that it must come here, to perform it.
Knowledge of this from Rutilus just reached me.
Meanwhile, full freedom is Valeria's here,
And thou mayest every hour enjoy her sight.
Forgive me if my hand hath held her hostage.
I had to allay thus Rutilus' distrust.

491

Only take care that before him today . . .
But he is here now.

Enter RUTILUS.

RUTILUS *(to himself)*.   I see Manlius with him.
 'Tis what I wished for. Let us test his mettle.
MANLIUS. What joy, sir, doth thy face display to us?
 What should be hoped for from our friends?
RUTILUS.   All, all, sir.
 It seems that everything conspires with us.
 No more delay to accomplish what we wish!
 How gladsome a surprise when I reached home!
 I found those of the populace to whom I
 Can safely trust the secrets of our plans.
 Hearing of the sacrifice, they came themselves
 To warn me I should seize the occasion offered.
 O'ercome with joy, to see that at this crisis
 Their own impatient eagerness outstripped me,
 I told them: "Yes, dear friends; yes, noble band;
 Fate shall fulfil the hope which animates you.
 All is in readiness, and, as ye wish,
 After tomorrow there shall ne'er be consuls.
 How great was the imprudence of our forebears,
 Who, having first destroyed the haughty power
 Held by one king, under a name less lordly
 Made for themselves two tyrants who, to oppress us,
 Change each year, and who all, inheriting
 Their hate of us from one another, busy
 Themselves by turns in tightening our chains!"
 With these and other words doubling their anger,
 I deemed it meet to make a clean breast to them,
 Showing our preparations and our various
 Stratagems, secretly backed e'en by some senators;
 That which their own arms had to do in Rome
 While on the Capitol thy soldiers wrought;
 The posts to be surprised, others to be given us;
 The forces one will have, leaders to follow;
 Where to unite and where to separate;
 All those to be got rid of by the sword;
 The homes of the proscribed, which, as we pass,
 We shall at once consign to flames and pillage;
 That, above all, no pity unworthy of them
 Must leave our slaughtered tyrants an avenger.
 Wives, fathers, children—all have shared their crimes;

All are the rightful objects of our rage;
All ought . . .
    (*To* SERVILIUS)   But whence, sir, comes it that at this
Account thy look doth change and thou dost tremble?
SERVILIUS. Yes, when so near to achieving our great purpose,
    I tremble with surprise and joy before thee.
    My heart, were it less moved, would not believe
    Sir, that it felt the happiness it should feel.
RUTILUS. Forgive my error, and hear me. I then added:
    "They glimpse not, they suspect not our intentions.
    From this repose in which these proud men sleep
    The thunder must awake them, at their graves.
    And when before our eyes the flames and carnage
    Shall everywhere display our fury's work—
    All of these palaces, built by our toil,
    Consumed forever by devouring fire;
    These judgment seats, where insolence held sway,
    So often bathed with tears of innocence,
    O'erthrown and broken, lying in the dust;
    Terror and death ranging on every side;
    The cries, the tears, in a word all the violence
    Into which license leads victorious soldiers—
    Let us remember, friends, in those cruel moments
    That with weak mortals nothing can be blameless,
    That even their best designs have different faces,
    And that we can no more, after so many
    Failures, restore in any other way
    To the troubled land innocence, peace, and freedom."
    All on hearing my words, which made them bolder,
    With triumph near, applauded and embraced.
    All with unnumbered prayers would speed its moment
    And vied in swearing oaths to thee anew.
MANLIUS. Then Fortune, thus responsive to our prayers,
    Hath led our tyrants to the chasm's verge.
    I have but one day more to bear their scorn.
    But what, sir, can I do, what reward is there
    Which can discharge my obligation to thee?
RUTILUS. I cannot keep silent to thee about it.
    There *is* a favor which thou couldst do for me.
    But this thy friend will let me in regard
    To my affairs explain to thee alone
    My secret feelings.
               I shall leave thee, sir.   *[Exit* SERVILIUS.
MANLIUS. By what blest fortune can I . . .

RUTILUS. Doing me
This favor, thou wilt do thyself a favor.
Sir, thou rememberest the oaths I took
When I espoused thy projects, with our friends.
I then swore before all that if I had
A brother who was very dear to me—
Though both of us were born in the same hour,
Were reared with the same care, in the same place,
And heaven had with the strongest bonds united
Our wishes, sentiments, pleasures, and pains—
If this dear brother, showing the least dread,
Could make me fear some lack of faithfulness
In him, I would myself immediately
Punish his cowardice and would prevent
Thus our undoing and his ignominy.
Thou, sir, didst praise this noble resolution,
And all took, after thee, the same oath.

MANLIUS. Well?

RUTILUS. This is the time when an essential act
Must prove thine oath's sincerity.

MANLIUS. Upon whom?

RUTILUS. Upon thy friend. I had foretold this to thee.
The while he heard me, rapt, sad, and dumbfounded,
With wavering glance, too well did he reveal
He secretly repents despite himself.
The horror of Rome burning made him shudder
With dread. Didst thou not see this, like myself? . . .
(*As* MANLIUS *shakes his head*) These proofs are not plain to
thine eyes; but they,
According to our oaths, are quite sufficient.
We have agreed that in this sort of project
Suspicions oft must pass for certainties,
And that 'tis better in a doubtful case
To slay the innocent than to spare the guilty.
Servilius falls under this agreement.
It argues death for him and for his hostage,
And if some pity seizing on our souls
Compels our wrath to spare a woman, let her
In a safe place be closely guarded, and
Let him be slain, him who hath broke the oath.

MANLIUS And who shall slay him?

RUTILUS. Thou.

MANLIUS. What darest thou tell me?
What is this madness which a doubt breeds in thee?

Know that his honor, outraged before me
By any other man, would by this arm
Already be avenged. But I do justice
To thee, and deem that this offense results
From thine excessive cautiousness. Do me
Like courtesy, and calm thine anxious fears.
Rely on me as to my choice of friends.
Reflect that this suspicion is a subtle
Fear and hence ill befits the heart of Rutilus.
                              [*He turns to go out.*
RUTILUS. In vain thou leavest me. I must make thee see
Without delay how right is my suspicion.
                    [*Exeunt,* RUTILUS *following* MANLIUS.

A C T   I V

SERVILIUS *enters, alone.*

SERVILIUS.   Where do I rove? Where am I? What confusion
Makes my steps random, robs me of self-control?
How swift the change! O vengeance! O my wrath!
Do ye abandon me to base remorse?
Have I, then, constancy only in suffering?
And must I fear to punish those who wrong me?
Vainly my heart seeks to grow firm again.
Ah, if the mere recital makes me shudder,
What shall I do, great gods, at the dread sight
Of all that can make vengeance horrible!
Oh, let us fly; keep from these crimes our hands.
Fly whither? In what place henceforward hide
Where Rome all drowned in seas of blood will not
Rise endlessly before my soul aghast?
    Letting her perish, dost thou not betray her?
But thy friends, too, who counted on thine arm?
Towards either cause thy flight is criminal.
No, no, to one of them thou must be loyal.
To keep thine oath, thou needs must immolate all;
Or else, to save Rome, thou must needs reveal all.
Immolate all! Thy heart shows too much weakness.
Reveal all! That, thy heart sees is too base;
Thou wouldst destroy thy friends. Which wilt thou choose?
Two opposed stumbling-blocks threaten thy virtue;
Avoiding one, thou'lt lose it on the other.
    O ye whose equity is our example,

Ye who give us precepts of righteousness,
Just gods, great gods, will ye now let this heart
So faithful to the honor which impels it
Fall, despite that, into the snares of crime?

Enter VALERIA.

VALERIA.   Heaven, that inspirest in me this upright purpose,
Lend me, even to the end, thy sovereign aid!
(*To* SERVILIUS)   Sir, I well know how great is thy disquiet
Which makes thee in this spot seek solitude.
What diverse cares must needs divide thy soul!
But wouldst thou fain indeed be rid of them?
Wouldst thou today that a successful shift
To save thy country should save all thy friends?
It can, sir, without danger and with ease.
Friendship may make thee shrink from it at first;
But honor, duty, pity authorize it.
SERVILIUS.   The means?
VALERIA.   We must disclose what is intended,
But not till we have been assured the Senate
Will pardon all of the conspirators.
Saved by our efforts from a fearsome fate,
Can it with less reward repay such service?
SERVILIUS.   What do I hear? What thinkest thou me, Valeria?
VALERIA.   The man thou must be for the safety of all.
I know what pledges bind thee to thy friends.
I perceive all the plight which thou perceivest,
What names they in their rage may give to thee;
But should so trifling a consideration
Daunt us? Is it wrong to break rash oaths
Which wrath has prompted, and which 'twas wrong to swear?
Is true repentance, then, no more permitted?
What! to avoid blushing before some friends
Seduced and carried away by their blind rage,
Thou wouldst prefer to blush before thy country!
Before the whole world! Canst thou reasonably
Waver one instant between these two courses?
See better now what must result from each.
If we do not speak, Rome will be destroyed.
If we dare speak, what evil can we fear?
All Rome is saved, and pardoneth all of them;
And when, remembering thy holy deed,
She makes resound the glorious story of it,
Midst all the honors which will unto thee

Be paid, will *their* reproaches then be heard?
Trace for thyself the terrifying picture
Of all the cruelties to which thou art sworn.
Conceive, sir, that amid the dreadful wreckage
Thou hearest the cries of children 'neath the sword-edge;
That with disheveled hair and tear-stained cheeks
A bleeding mother comes, fleeing her slayers,
To show to thee her son, whom in her arms
She bears, and fall upon her knees before thee:
Is thy rage stayed then? an inhuman soldier
Kills her before thine eyes, and at the same time
Makes the blood of her son, whose side he pierces,
Spurt over thee together with her milk.
Wouldst thou endure the horror of this sight?
SERVILIUS.   By the immortal gods, this realm's support,
These words are lightnings that invade my heart
And make a fearsome day there which with horror
Fills me. O'ercome with pity . . . What, cruel Rome,
Wilt owe thy safety unto those thou hatest?
I could betray all a friend's acts of kindness?
Force him . . . No, no, my heart will never dare.
VALERIA.   Hast thou a friend more precious than Valeria?
SERVILIUS.   No. For my life's whole joy thy love suffices.
Thou alone satisfiest my heart's wishes.
Ah, why, just gods, is happiness so sweet
Not given to me unalloyed and peaceful?
What storms relentless Fate doth mingle with it!
VALERIA.   And why, then, not avert them, sir? Thou must,
Must decide finally about it. Thou
Hast naught to dread; and, since all must be told thee,
I have the pledge I wished for from the Senate.
Fearing to be surprised, they have accorded
All to me.
SERVILIUS.   Gods! what hast thou undertaken
Without my leave?
VALERIA.   I promised thee to keep
Silent. I feared that the conspirators
Would seek revenge on thee. But by such means
Now everything is safe. I have done all,
Sir, without thy consent. I saw 'twould be
Too hard to win that from thee. Thus 'tis I
Alone who to their anger am exposed;
And though I acted in thy name for both,
Thou canst lay all the blame on me, to them.

SERVILIUS. What hast thou done! O heavens, with what dreadful
    Reproaches will their terrible anger crush me!
    What shall it serve me, pray, to disavow thee?
    After they are betrayed, that would but mock them.
    Will they not see at once I must have told thee
    The secret which the Senate learned from thee?
    And can they doubt that we were in accord?
    'Tis o'er and done, Valeria. Shun their rage.
    Fly from this fatal spot whereon the tempest
    Shall fall. I wish to expose no head but mine
    To it.

VALERIA.   Go. Fear naught. But someone comes.
    We must beware of eyes that are distrustful.
    Let us begone, and keep all well concealed.

                                  [Exit VALERIA.

SERVILIUS *(to himself)*. In my dismay, whom do I see again!
    Is he aware of what hath taken place?
    How bear to meet him, wronged so, face to face?
    No matter; let us stay. In such disaster,
    After our sorrow, let us show our courage.
    But in what meditations is he sunk?

Enter MANLIUS.

MANLIUS. Knowest thou the hand of Rutilus?
SERVILIUS.   Yes.
MANLIUS *(holding out a letter to him)*.   Here; read.
SERVILIUS *(reading)*. "Thou wouldst not heed my justly-felt suspi-
    cions.
    Their object hath disclosed our whole design.
    'Tis by a senator in concord with us
    That now this information is made mine.
    Flee unto Veii, where our fate directs us;
    But to assuage our misery from this blow,
    'Twere well if death at thy hands robbed the traitor
    Of all his crime's reward, ere thou didst go."
MANLIUS. What sayst thou?
SERVILIUS.   Strike.
MANLIUS *(astounded)*.   What!
SERVILIUS.   Thou must needs have
    heard me.
    Strike, I say; for thine arm thus cannot err.
MANLIUS. What sayest thou, wretched man? Where stray thy wits?
    Knowest thou indeed what thou hast dared to tell me?
SERVILIUS. Yes, I well know that thou canst justly pierce

This vile heart offered to thee as a victim;
That I with faith forsworn betrayed thy plans.

MANLIUS *(after a pause)*. And in thy breast I do not sink my dagger!
Why must my hand, too backward, recognize
A friend still in a traitor's countenance?
Who? thou? thou hast betrayed me? Heard I rightly?

SERVILIUS. It is true, Manlius. 'Twas perhaps my duty.
Perhaps, when tranquil, thou'dst have grounds for thinking
That without me thou wouldst have stained thine honor.
But still the reasons that have impressed my mind
Would not avail to allay thy bitterness,
And naught care I that Rome, approving, doth
Declare me innocent when thou deemest me guilty.
I come, then, at thy hands to expiate
My crime. Strike. I shall die content with my
Fate, since my treason, which hath saved my country,
Saves for thee at the same time life and honor.

MANLIUS. Thou, save my life!

SERVILIUS.   And even thy friends' lives.
The Senate hath been forced to sign their pardon.
They all are safe.

MANLIUS.   And what consent, what warrant
Made thee the arbiter of their fate or mine?
Who told thee that life had such charms for me?
What wouldst thou I might henceforth do with it?
See myself here the Romans' scorn and byword?
Lose it perhaps in a most wretched lot
Or in a quarrel while showing confidence
In some new friend, perfidious like thee?
Gods! when at every point my wariness
Made me foresee the very smallest dangers,
By thee our purpose had to be defeated
And by the unworthy one whose love seduced thee!
For thy crime is her work, I have no doubt,
Thou base, unworthy Roman, born for slavery,
Who savest proud tyrants bent on wronging thee
And dost betray the friends that would avenge thee.
How fierce will burn their rage against me! I
Have guaranteed thy staunch fidelity,
Have laughed at their distrust, have stayed their hands
Which by thy deserved death would have forestalled thee.
Why could I not accept their wisdom's counsel?
Thy blood was worth the trouble, then, to shed it.
'Twould have assured my plans' accomplishment;

But now it fruitlessly would soil my hand,
And since it is too vile to wash out thine
Offense, I leave to thy remorse my vengeance.

[*Exit* MANLIUS.

SERVILIUS.   At these reproaches direful, what confusion,
What doltishness doth hold me witless here?
What course now take? He flees me like some monster.
Shall I go and again show him a sight
He loathes? O wrath too just! O voice that daunts me!
Terrible names, heard called me for the first time!
I "base," "perfidious"! and I still would live?
As much as he, I hate, abhor myself.
He has inspired me with his wrath against me.
Come, let us not endure such names of horror,
But in the tomb's night hide their infamy;
And seeking him, despite his settled anger,
Force him to question, seeing what I do,
Which ruleth in my breast, crime or remorse.

Enter ALBINUS.

ALBINUS.   Sir, all is lost, and in affrighted Rome
The news is broadcast of our plans betrayed.
I came in great haste to warn Manlius of it,
But 'twas too late. Valerius already,
Who, in this perilous strait, for greater safety
Himself had undertaken to carry out
The orders of the Senate, without warning
Had entered suddenly with his followers
And had arrested Manlius in his rooms
And at the very instant when blind frenzy
Had armed his hand to take his life, himself.
They left him, sir, this mansion for a prison;
For it was to be feared, 'twas said, that if
They were to take him from the Capitol,
His secret friends would arm the populace,
O'erwhelm his escort, and assure his pardon.
SERVILIUS.   Just heaven!
ALBINUS.   I go to follow his fate's course.
Thou, save thyself; fly to seek aid for him.
I shall inform him.   [*Exit* ALBINUS.
SERVILIUS (*to himself*).   Let us ourself go learn . . .
But here Valerius is.

Enter VALERIUS.

MANLIUS CAPITOLINUS

(*To* VALERIUS)　What hath been told me?
Wherefore is Manlius arrested by thee,
Sir? Have I paid too little for his freedom?
Hath not this pardon for all been ratified?
Surely, the Senate keeps its word when pledged?

VALERIUS.　I give no reasons for its secret orders.
Whether or not thou knowest them, matters little,
Since for thee, sir, they are not to be feared.
Its kindness leaves thee no right to complain.
It fully pardons thee, and in oblivion
Wishes its sentences 'gainst thee to be buried.
It restores all to thee, and in our annals
Would fain preserve the memory forever
Of thy devotion. This is what I come
To say to thee for it; and for myself,
Also, I come to assure thee that, renewing
A sincere friendship with thee, I give thanks
Unto the gods, whose salutary care
Has made thy marriage, far from my intentions,
The secret source of safety for all Rome.

SERVILIUS.　And for my part, that is what here my soul
Doth disavow. I shall detest forever
This Senate which doth praise me; I give back
Its favors, whereof it accords but half;
I give back to thee, too, thy useless friendship.
I find herein my woe and ignominy
If this shall cost the life of Manlius.
'Twas not my purpose, in betraying him,
Either to sell his blood or to spare mine.
For his own interest, I took care of yours,
And my compassion wished to save you both.
What! shall I gain naught from my treachery,
For which remorse doth hound me, except its shame?
Shall ye gain all its fruits? Shall I destroy
All for me only, saving all the realm?

VALERIUS.　I have already said all I could say,
Sir. But restrain these unjust feelings. We
Go to the Senate to decide his fate,
And whether he be pardoned or condemned,
Believe me, honor doth henceforth command thee
To abandon him, as well as his designs,
And wish for nothing but the public good.
I must begone. Farewell.　　　　　[*Exit* VALERIUS.

SERVILIUS (*alone*).　　　　　In what disquiet

The uncertainty of these dark words doth leave me!
Is it the Senate's wish . . . But canst thou doubt it?
From what one sees of thee, should one respect thee?
Thou play'st thy friends false; thy foes play thee false;
And thou hast broken the same oaths that they break.
   Thus, then, will Manlius charge me with his death.
I shall see . . . But let us not abandon him,
At least. To save his life, let us endure
Ours still; and whether success crowns my efforts
Or cheats my care, after his fate is settled
Let us at once die for our honor's sake.
Above all, let us not bear to the tomb
His hate, and try . . . But here the cause of all
My anguish is.

Enter VALERIA.

VALERIA.   Sir, I have seen my father,
And I cannot describe the kindness which
In a few words he manifested towards me,
But pressed for time, he left me suddenly
To seek thee, so he said, with the same thought;
And doubtlessly . . . Ah, sir, cast not on me
These looks so stern that chill me with affright.
What makes them wild? What horror unforeseen . . .
SERVILIUS. Darest thou indeed still show thy face before me?
Dost thou not see the risk thou runnest here?
VALERIA. But why?
SERVILIUS.   To what fate has thy tongue reduced me!
Manlius is where? What hast thou done, false woman?
Thou vainly tremblest at the wrath that fills me.
Thou shouldst have thought of that, before thy treachery.
Thou hast just plunged him in the worst of plights.
Arrested, threatened, humbled as he is,
He has but death to hope for. Thou hast made me
The object of his hate forever. But
Indeed, when I first shared in his designs,
I gave thee as a hostage for us both,
And thy life was the warrant of his safety.
Thou hast betrayed him; thou hast made Rome triumph:
What stays my fury to avenge him, then?
VALERIA. Well, wherefore, sir, this passioning, these insults?
If it requires my blood to still thy conscience,
Have I refused it to thee? Is it not
All thine? I can bear death, but not thy anger.

Sacrifice a fond victim without rage.
Let this be only a magnanimous act.
When thou dost pierce my heart, ah, do not hate me!
Pity, at least, this heart which, even till death,
Loved thee and died by thy stern hand alone
For having saved my country and my father.

SERVILIUS.   I pierce thy heart? Ah, give me back, then, mine
Such as I gave it thee to merit thine,
True to its pledges, gallant, fearless; thou,
Alas, hast made it cowardly, perfidious,
And whatsoe'er a just wrath counsels it,
'Tis thine asylum, where thou canst defy me.
Nay, at this moment, on thy face the gods
Have set their hall-marks, which my rage respects,
Or else the tutelary spirit of Rome,
Which thou hast saved today, is also thine.
Well, then, 'tis thou to whom I must appeal.
By all the affection that for thee I feel,
By thine eyes, by thy tears, whose power to charm
Can so well take from crime its punishment,
Show now thy power in my friend's behalf,
And while I go to speak in his defense,
Before the Senate hath decided aught
Go, swiftly go, unto thy cruel father;
Fall at his feet; weep; make his obstinate heart
Feel an unwonted pity for our woes.
Let him appease the anger of the Senate;
Let Manlius live, or all of us shall die.

ACT V

MANLIUS *and* ALBINUS *are discovered.*

ALBINUS.   Yes, I confess I feared the worst for thee, sir,
When I beheld the Senate, keeping ill
Its word, reserve the right, in pardoning all,
To decide the fate of Rutilus and thee.
I feared to see thee made its hate's one prey,
Punished alone, now Rutilus hath escaped.
But since it is not quick to assume this task,
But to the tribunes gives the right to judge thee,
Showing that it cannot decide about thee,
Dares not condemn thee, is ashamed to acquit thee,
Its fear in leaving thee to kindlier judges

Should hearten them to disappoint its wrath.
'Tis to Servilius that thou owest this boon,
For since thou fain wouldst see him here, at last
I dare to tell thee of him; far from angry . . .

MANLIUS.   O gods! must he needs force my heart to hate him?

ALBINUS.   What! talkest thou still of hate and anger after
All that his true repentance hath attempted?
Thou seest it. Who else dared speak for thee
And feared so little the all-powerful Senate?
While the whole people, frightened by the doom
To which the knowledge of thy plans exposed
All thy accomplices, withdrew themselves
From thee, and thought by thus deserting thee
To prove their innocence or buy their pardon—
While all were silent, even thine own brothers—
He opposed stoutly the stern senators
And showed to them four hundred citizens
Snatched from a prison's horrors by thy kindness,
As many more saved by thy hand in battle.
And many honors won in storming ramparts,
Ten crowns, the prize of ten renowned encounters,
And thy blood, shed hundreds of times for them.
Especially what ardor fired his heart,
What blushes suddenly suffused their faces,
When, pointing out to them, who saw that deed,
This hill wherefrom thine arm smote down the Gauls,
He invoked the vengeance of the gods, of whom
Thou then wast the defense, upon these ingrates!

MANLIUS.   Vain cure for these mine ills, help unavailing!
Even though his zeal and pains should save my life,
Can he retrieve my hopes for what I sought?
Can I love life when I have lost my vengeance?
Why should I hide, though, from thy faithful heart
How I feel drawn towards him despite myself?
Yes, I confess it, to my secret shame
My hatred for this treacherous friend disturbs me,
Embarrasses me; and while, unmoved, indifferent,
I see all that he undertakes to save me,
My heart disdains his care yet finds a charm
Therein which, notwithstanding all its bitterness,
Touches it and disarms it. Not that now,
Careless of my fair fame and without wishing
Aught more, I quench mine anger; I intend . . .
But he is coming. Go, Albinus. Let me

At least conceal my weakness from his eyes.

Exit ALBINUS. *Enter* SERVILIUS.

(*To* SERVILIUS)   So thou expectest, then, to triumph despite me,
In my confounded heart, over a wrath
Which is thy due? I see that thy repentance
Impels thy boldness to oppose unnumbered
Efforts unto the fate which threatens me.
But though thou canst not of success be certain,
Thou, who betrayedst me, now dishonorest me.
It seems to my oppressors that 'tis I
Who, trembling for my life, humble myself,
Asking thine aid. Thine ill-considered ardor
Exposes me to their contempt, and thou
Little dost know the price of my affection.
If *its* loss doth so much disturb and pain thee,
Thy efforts all are vain save at the price
Which I exact, and which can better prove
Thy loyalty to me, by its lone self,
Than all that e'er thy zeal dared do for me.
Could I this time rely upon thy courage?
SERVILIUS.   I have deserved the insult of this doubt,
In thine eyes, but without desiring vainly
To explain myself about it, or to take
Oaths which thou wouldst no more believe, if I
Have still done little to blot out that wrong,
Only remember well that in a noble
Heart smitten by remorse, after such falseness,
Shame o'er its downfall maketh its virtue stronger.
MANLIUS.   Well, hearken, then. Thou knowest how much the Senate
Is, in its fury, bent upon my death.
Bound by my pardon which it signed for thee,
It still can prosecute me and keep faith
With thee. It turns me over to the tribunes,
And by this stratagem to them committeth
Its hatred, sure that they will take my life;
For docile to its mandates, envious
Of my distinction as they are, their blows
Will be directed by its hand against me;
They will decree only as it inspires them,
And the cowed populace dares not gainsay them.
What hopest thou, then, from thy attempts to save me?
Dost think the Senate, by thy words beguiled,

Will have the imprudence to leave me alive
After the things my hate hath twice attempted?
No, no, Servilius; my death is certain.
And what shame mine, what fury in my bosom,
To see my foes, according to their whim,
Decree my fate and choose my punishment!
Wilt let thy friend conclude before thine eyes
A life so glorious at hands so vile?
Indeed, 'tis thou, Servilius, who hast brought me
The assured infamy of such a death.
I ought to be saved from that shame by thee.
Disarmed, watched closely, I can for myself
Do naught; my guards disarmed thee on thine entrance;
But to deceive this vigilance 'tis needful . . .

SERVILIUS.   I understand. But someone comes.

Enter ALBINUS.

ALBINUS.   A tribune
Is hastening here to tell thee what hath happened.
Thou'lt see him, sir; he mounts the Capitol.

MANLIUS.   When all is known, what serves this useless task?
(*To* SERVILIUS)   Thou seest 'tis time indeed to play thy part.
Waste not a moment after he has gone.
Know that without this favor all thy show
Of zeal for Manlius only wrongs him further.

SERVILIUS.   Go. I will serve thee even beyond thy wishes.

                     [*Exit* MANLIUS, *with* ALBINUS.
(*To himself*)   Yes, 'tis the end. I must blot out forever
The vile reproach 'neath which my honor pines.
The future must . . . But I behold Valeria.
A steeled and constant heart must brave her sight.
This is the ghastliest moment for my love.

Enter VALERIA.

VALERIA.   I shall now see thy wrath burst forth against me,
But the most speedy death will be the dearest.
I come here to deliver myself up
To thy just rage. With my hard-hearted father
My efforts have been vain, my tears . . .

SERVILIUS.   I know it;
But fear no more the violence of my passions,
Valeria. I have softened Manlius' mood.
Thy crime was mine, and thou must share the pardon
Which I obtain. I thank thee for those efforts

Which thou hast made to win thy father's mercy
And save my friend. In turn vouchsafe to pardon
The outburst of my anger. As thou seest,
Fate rules our hearts. It can, when it desireth,
Trouble the concord of those most united
And make them conscious of their helplessness.
But stay the course at last, now, of thy tears.
Hear, with a soul more resolute, my words,
And show a courage worthy of thy birth.

VALERIA. I will obey thee, if 'tis in my power.
Speak.

SERVILIUS. Dost thou recollect that ill-starred day
On which the gods' hate kindled first our love?

VALERIA. Ill-starred? Just heaven!

SERVILIUS. What! e'en now thy courage . . .

VALERIA. And can I hear without dismay such words?
So that day, which beheld my happiness,
Is now a day ill-starred and hateful to thee?
Alas, with names how different, sir, thy love
Recalled it in thy unfeigned ecstasies!

SERVILIUS. That mad love had no thought but of itself.
It ne'er foresaw the miseries that the Fates
Would bring on thee after that baleful day,
Nor that it was itself to be their agent;
That it would make thee leave thy tranquil, happy
Lot, to attach thy life to my grim fortunes;
That through it—for its sake—thou'dst undergo
The wrongs of exile, the hard toil of flight;
And that at last today my savage passions
Would against thine own blood incite my hands.

VALERIA. Oh, whither tends this talk? Why uselessly
Recall that vanished memory to my mind?

SERVILIUS. Thou knowest the peril of my hapless friend.
The tribunes' court is ready now to try him.
I go to undertake there his defense
Before the eyes of all; but if the outcome
Should cheat my hopes, it is for thee, Valeria,
After so many trials, to lose without
Regrets the author of all thy ills. Farewell.

[*Exit* SERVILIUS.

VALERIA. What said he to me? What new thunderbolt!
What cruel course doth he intend for me?
I, to prepare to lose him on this day
When everything appears to make it sure

That he is to be mine! And what, then, would he?
Break off our marriage? Flee me? Or cut short
His life with his own hands? What will become
Of me? O gods! Whatever be his purpose,
Vainly would I fain tear it from his breast.
To my confounded gaze how dread a calm
Showed in his face a soul unshakable!
Under a vain pretext of going out
Did he not say farewell to me forever?
Ah, heaven! if that be so! If it be needful
That my soul . . . Let us run and find the truth
About it.

Enter TULLIA.

(*To* TULLIA)   Oh, come; follow me!
TULLIA.   The guards
Here have been ordered by thy husband, madam,
To stay thy steps and keep watch over thee.
He himself gave that order, in my presence,
When in hot haste Albinus came to say
His master, in departing, wished to see him.
VALERIA.   Ah gods! what dost thou tell me? What good reason
I have to tremble! Dost thou know if his
Sentence . . .
TULLIA.   I could not learn of it. Already
One of the tribunes, sent to bring him, hath
Mounted the Capitol, letting it be thought
That he came there only to question him.
He feared lest a forewarned band of the people,
To rescue Manlius, waited for their going.
Soldiers were stationed, though, along their route
And others followed in their footsteps soon
Who very shortly formed a numerous escort
To assist in haling Manlius to the tribunes.
Servilius thereupon, distracted, desperate,
Left suddenly and from my sight was gone;
But he beyond doubt, madam, hastened into
The tribunes' presence and boldly undertook
His friend's defense.
VALERIA.   When he left here, he said
To me, himself, he would. And what, if Manlius
Dies, will become of him? I shudder even
To think of it; and meanwhile, like a prisoner,
I should wait . . . No, I needs must follow him,

Tullia—must in this mansion, torch in hand,
Light me a pyre or open a path for me . . .
   But I espy Albinus. Why is he
Confounded thus?

Enter ALBINUS.

                Albinus, whither fliest thou?
ALBINUS. I myself know not; and when so bewildered
   With blind emotion . . .
VALERIA.   Hath Manlius just been
   Condemned to death? Servilius . . . Speak; explain
   Thyself without evasion. Thou wilt tell me
   Naught that my fears have not already told me.
ALBINUS. Alas! 'twould be but useless care to hide
   A woe from thee which many eyes have witnessed.
   Learn, learn from this exact account the deeds
   Of a magnanimous and ruthless virtue.
   With hasty step Servilius eagerly
   Joined Manlius not far distant from this mansion,
   Near that famed spot which saw the victory
   That on the Capitol displayed his glory,
   And which now saw, right in the face of heaven,
   The gods' defender laden with shameful fetters.
   Thy husband, shocked, stood quivering at this outrage,
   But the proud Manlius, with countenance
   Composed, addressed then those who formed his escort.
   He told them that he knew a weighty secret
   Which he desired to tell Servilius
   Alone, to inform the Senate and the realm.
   They instantly withdrew a little from him;
   None feared to leave him with his friend unarmed.
   I only remained near him; I heard all,
   And marveled at the words his courage prompted.
   "All is now over; doubt it not. My judges
   Have signed my death-sentence," he said. "I have
   Sure information of it. If my misfortune
   Touches thee, spare me the indignity
   Of hearing it from them; and helping me
   With the encumbrance of my shackles, toward
   That brink thou seest yonder speed my steps.
   Let us at least leave Rome the eternal stigma
   Of seeing me perish where I conquered for her."
   Thy husband answered: "Yes, by this fit act
   Must thou be snatched from thy dire fate. But this

509

Is not enough to save thy memory
From that cruel slight which thy fair fame ascribes
To me. I wish by imitating thee
Today to avenge thee." Over the hill's verge
He in a twinkling threw him with himself.
There was a cry, a rush there. But all care
Was vain now. Both plunged headlong to the foot
Of the Capitol. In each other's arms they died,
A woeful spectacle of horror, where
One sees affection hallow passion's rage.

VALERIA.   So be it! All is over. O cruel Fortune!
And I am still the plaything of thy hate!
But 'gainst thy rigors which I have foreseen
I secretly found arms for my despair,
And I in spite of thee, by this kind blow,
End all thy schemes against a wretched woman.

[She stabs herself.

TULLIA.   Great gods! What frenzy . . .

VALERIA.   Do not pity me.
I go to join forever him whom I
Have lost—whom I, I only, have destroyed.

Rhadamiste
et Zénobie
(RHADAMISTUS AND ZENOBIA)

By
PROSPER JOLYOT
CREBILLON

INTRODUCTORY NOTE

The real name of the dramatist known as Crébillon was Prosper Jolyot. He was born at Dijon in 1674; and twelve years later his father, a city official there, purchased an estate near by called Crais-Billon, from which the name Crébillon was derived. Prosper was educated by the Jesuits at Dijon, studied law, and became a lawyer at Paris, where he entered the office of a prosecuting magistrate for further legal studies. This magistrate discovered the young man's literary aptitude and encouraged him to write tragedies. His first play, *la Mort des Enfants de Brute* (1703), was rejected and never printed, but in the next fourteen years he produced six other tragedies —*Idomenée* (1705), *Atrée et Thyeste* (1707), *Electre* (1708), *Rhadamiste et Zénobie* (1711), *Xercès* (1714), and *Sémiramis* (1717)—and three more at much longer intervals: *Pyrrhus* (1726), *Catalina* (1748), and *le Triumvirat ou la Mort de Cicéron* (1754). He was elected to the French Academy in 1731, and held several offices in the course of his life—among them that of censor, which won him the ill will of fellow dramatists whose plays he refused. Voltaire was not the least active of his enemies. Their attacks added to the unhappiness caused by his pecuniary embarrassment; he had at one time (especially c. 1715) been prosperous as a result of financial speculation, but later was reduced to penury. In his old age this was somewhat relieved by royal favor. A man of strong constitution, he lived till 1762.

Crébillon was the most important French tragic dramatist in the eighteenth century before and except Voltaire. He deliberately sought themes of extreme violence and horror, best exemplified by his dramatization of the story of Thyestes' unwitting feast on the flesh of his own murdered sons. In his efforts to interest his audiences, he made much use of surprise and recognition. A frequent detail in his plays, as too often in other French tragedies of the eighteenth century, is what is known as the *voix du sang*, an impulse of attraction or affection which one is alleged to feel instinctively towards one's unrecognized kindred when one encounters them. Though *Atrée et Thyeste* has had its admirers, Crébillon's fame rests on *Rhadamiste et Zénobie* almost as completely as La Fosse's on *Manlius Capitolinus*.

Rhadamiste et Zénobie has had widely different appraisals. Boileau is said to have thought it unspeakably bad. Though all have recognized its clumsiness and lack of clarity in setting forth the highly involved situation in the first act, the older critics, from La Harpe in the eighteenth century down to Nisard and even Dutrait near the end of the nineteenth, admired the play greatly. But Petit de Julleville called it more bizarre than beautiful and more violent than powerful, the work of a man who observed the world only through a dream; and later critics in general have found it essentially a strained, factitious, romanesque melodrama. To H. C. Lancaster, however, it seems "to deserve neither the enthusiasm nor the scorn that it has received." [1]

[1] *Sunset,* Baltimore, 1945, p. 119.

CHARACTERS IN THE PLAY

PHARASMANES, *king of Iberia.*
RHADAMISTUS, *king of Armenia; son of Pharasmanes.*
ZENOBIA, *wife of Rhadamistus; going under the name of Ismenia.*
ARSAMES, *brother of Rhadamistus.*
HIERO, *Armenian ambassador, confidant of Rhadamistus.*
MITHRANES, *captain of the guards of Pharasmanes.*
HYDASPES, *confidant of Pharasmanes.*
PHENICE, *confidante of Zenobia.*
Guards.

The scene is laid in Artanissa, capital of Iberia, in the palace of Pharasmanes.

The names "Pharasmanes," "Rhadamistus," "Arsames," "Mithranes," "Hydaspes," and "Phenice" (three syllables) are accented on the next to the last syllable. "Ismenia" is accented on the second syllable.

Rhadamistus and Zenobia

ACT I

ZENOBIA, *under the name of Ismenia, and* PHENICE *are discovered.*

ZENOBIA.   Ah, leave me to my mortal cares, Phenice.
Thou multipliest the horrors of my position.
Leave me. Thy pity, thy advice, and life
Are evil fortune's crown for poor Ismenia.
Just gods, avenging heaven, dread of the wretched,
Is not the fate which hounds me dire enough?
PHENICE.   Shall I behold thee, always bathed in tears,
Frightening my soul with endless paroxysms?
Sleep vainly scatters poppies here; the night
No more has either rest or sweetness for thee.
Cruel woman, if love finds thee unrelenting,
Be at least conscious of my grieved affection.
But what are thy misfortunes? Captive here
Where love bows to the power of thy glance,
Thou leavest the bonds in which thou grewest up,
Only to make Iberia's king thy slave.
What does this conqueror of the Romans ask for?
He fain would put his scepter in thy hands.
If, when his loving service is rebuffed,
He finally wearies of his fruitless deference,
By what disdain, pain given, and harsh refusals
Hast thou thyself not kindled his fierce wrath?
Beguile him; crown his wishes, not resist them.
Thou soon wilt see him tenderer and humbler.
ZENOBIA.   Better than thou I know this savage conqueror
For whom, but vainly, thou wouldst bend my heart.
Whatever the great names which victory gives him,
And that proud brow whereon such glory shines,
In spite of all his exploits, the world offers
Naught which should be more hateful to my sight.
I have deceived too long thy faithful friendship.
Thy loyalty must not be thus rewarded.
I must speak out. When thou knowest all, at least
I shall no more see thee oppose my death.
Phenice, thou'st beheld me relegated
To slavery's chains, in which I was not born.

517

I number in my line as many kings
As ancestors, and the family whence I sprang
Yields only to the gods. This Pharasmanes,
This monarch who makes Asia tremble, who
Defies the futile jealousy of Rome,
This cruel king, whose love thou'dst have me favor,
Is that king's brother who gave life to me.
Would to the gods the fate which binds me to him
Had by no other ties e'er bound Zenobia!
But joining sweeter ties to ties so sacred,
Fate made him, too, the father of my husband—
Of Rhadamistus.

PHENICE.   Great is my amazement.
Zenobia, thou! O gods!

ZENOBIA.   Yes, she herself,
The daughter of so many kings, the last
Scion, Phenice, of a noted line—
Illustrious, but alas, yet more ill-starred.
After long strife, my father, Mithridates,
Lived with his brother in the midst of peace.
Both the Armenias, subject to our sway,
Set midst the greatest kings this happy prince—
Too happy indeed, if his perfidious brother
Had been less covetous of a throne so mighty!
But far from lending him support, this cruel
Man preyed upon him, striking at his heart.
To blind my father and entrap him better,
He put into his hands his infant son.
Pleased, Mithridates reared him in our midst—
For him, as one he loved; for me, a husband.
I shall confess that, seeing his great affection,
I deemed it right to match this with mine own,
Not knowing that beneath fair outward seeming
One may conceal one's criminal inclinations.

PHENICE. Yet never has a king in Asia earned
A name more glorious, worthier of envy.
The terror now of other kings, already . . .

ZENOBIA. Only too well did he display his valor.
I scarce had entered on my fifteenth year
When all had been prepared for our great marriage.
Rhadamistus thought himself assured of it,
When his cruel father, in a plot against us,
Entered our realm, followed by Tiridates,
Who burned to wed the child of Mithridates.

This Parthian, wroth at being deprived of me,
Sowed everywhere fear, horror, and confusion.
O'erwhelmed by his false brother, Mithridates
Made on the son recoil the father's cruelty,
And better to avenge himself on his
Unnatural brother, he promised Tiridates
His scepter and my hand. Then Rhadamistus,
Enraged by an affront so mortal, ravaged
In his turn all that of the realm was left,
Despoiled my father of it, drove him out, too,
And setting bounds no longer to grief's fury,
Despite Numidius and all Syria,
Forced Pollio to yield up my father to him.
    To save a hapless father I attempted
To move my lover's heart, which I thought generous.
He promised to forget the outrage done
His love, if with my hand he was rewarded—
To give the realm back to its former ruler
The moment that our marriage bound me to him.
Impelled to the altar by a hope so sweet,
I myself wished to speed this fatal marriage,
And my false lover dared to consummate it,
Stained with the blood which thus I thought to save.
But heaven, incensed at such unholy rites,
Lighted our nuptials with the Furies' torch.
Just gods! what nuptials! what a barbarous husband!

PHENICE.   I know that the whole land, indignant with thee,
Ascribed to thee the King's unhappy fate
And but with horror viewed this wicked marriage.

ZENOBIA.   They did not know his fate was hidden from me,
And cruelly would avenge his death on me.
Troubled by his remorse, at this great danger
Rhadamistus seemed o'erwhelmed, himself;
But soon this prince, again possessed with frenzy,
Spread round him in his turn carnage and horror.
He told me: "Follow me. This insulting rabble
Thinks vainly to deny my valor passage.
Follow me." From the altar he went swiftly,
Raging and terrible; in his arms he bore me,
Fleeing with his retinue through Artaxata,
Which took revenge for Mithridates' death,
Albeit too late. My husband, on all sides
Assailed, then cast on me a baleful glance . . .
    But far from e'er recounting deeds so dark,

Let us respect a wretched husband's memory.
Exempt my virtue from this odious story;
Against a hapless man I have said only
Too much. I cannot wake these recollections
Without lamenting Rhadamistus' fate.
Let this suffice thee, then, to know, Phenice:
That I, the victim of a love reduced
To desperation, was, by a dear hand
And reeking with my blood, plunged 'neath the waves
Of the Araxes, at the point of death.

PHENICE. What! 'Twas thy husband . . . Gods! how barbarous!

ZENOBIA. Death's horrors were already darkening
My sight, when heaven by someone's helping hand
Saved me from otherwise inevitable
Destruction. But I scarcely had escaped
From such dire peril when I had to mourn
A luckless husband. Not without a shudder
I learned that his cruel father, feigning anger
Over his brother's death, but really jealous
Of his son's greatness, had by his sole efforts
Aroused our people 'gainst us; and that, coming
Into Armenia secretly, he himself
Had cut short his son's days. Allowing then
A free course to my grief, I cursed the pains
That had been taken to preserve my life;
I left without regret my rank and country,
And roamed through Media under a false name.
At last, aften ten years of woe and slavery,
A stranger everywhere, without help or stay,
When I was hoping for some fate more tranquil,
War in one moment robbed me of all shelter.
Arsames, bringing terror in his wake,
Came, armed with thunder, to lay waste those regions:
Arsames, of a blood so guilty in
My sight, Arsames in my sight so dear,
Son of a faithless, cruel, and jealous sire,
And brother of Rhadamistus—of my husband!

PHENICE. Whatever obligation may be thine
To that tie, will it flout thy husband's ghost
To give thyself to a magnanimous prince
Whose love has been displayed by so much kindness?

ZENOBIA. If only a cruel absence did not snatch
Our sole hope from us, in our misery! . . .
Arsames, taken hence by a sad duty,

Leaves my distracted heart naught to expect;
And I, to crown my woe, learn that Armenia,
Which is so rightfully Zenobia's,
Will fall into the power of Rome or Parthia
Or possibly into less worthy hands.
With savage heart flattered by lure of conquest,
Now Pharasmanes plans to leave these climes.

PHENICE.   Well then, escape from his unjust dominion.
Hast thou not on thy side Rome and thy rights?
Rome must determine, through an ambassador
Who has left Syria, Armenia's fate.
As that land's queen, induce this Roman envoy
To act for thee against a barbarous prince.
He is expected within Artanissa
Today. Beg Caesar's help and Caesar's justice.
Win the support of his ambassador.
Compel him to defend thee, or flee with him.

ZENOBIA.   How shall I break the chains which hold me here?
Will anyone believe me, furthermore—
A fugitive, unknown? How . . .

Enter ARSAMES.

                                        What is this?
Arsames here!

ARSAMES.   Is it allowed me still
To show myself before thine eyes?

ZENOBIA.   Is it
Thyself, sir? What, Albania already . . .

ARSAMES.   Is wholly subdued, madam. The fair Ismenia,
When glory seems to deck my brow with favors,
Alone appears desirous to o'erwhelm me
With harshness. Sure that my return will bring
The wrath of an inexorable father
Upon a guilty son, jealous and desperate,
I yet have dared, that I again might see thee,
To leave the lands committed to my charge.
Ah, madam, is it true that a proud, terrible
Monarch has learned to know thy glances' charm?
And marriage is to crown his suit today?
Forgive the frenzy of a hapless lover.
My grief annoys thee. I see that with constraint
Thou hearest of my anxious love the plaint.
Not without reason dost thou blame me for it.
Reproaches ill become rejected lovers;

And I, always a target for thy rigor,
Whom hopeless love devoured and persecuted—
Yes, I, always submissive to thy sway—
Of what can I complain, alas! and what
Was I e'er promised? Indignant at the portion
Prepared for thee, however, I do complain
Alike of thee and of a cruel rival.
The love, the tender love I feel for thee,
Rejected though it is, is not less jealous.

ZENOBIA.   Sir, 'tis too true that a most baleful love
Has here expressed a passion that I loathe;
But whatsoever the King's pomp and power,
He vainly thinks to make disposal of me.
But this is not to say that I, aware
Of the ardor which possesses thee, commend
These transports into which thy love impels thee.

ARSAMES.   Ah, despite all the love wherewith I burn
Make me alone the target of thy wrath.
Impose the harshest sentence on my passion,
Provided thou wilt not accord thy hand
Unto my father. If thy heart must burn
For others than myself, let me have rivals
Whom I can immolate, against whom my fury
Can act without a murmur. Love has not
Always respected natural ties. I know it
Only too surely from my jealous frenzy.
How can I, if the King becomes thy husband,
Be certain to what lengths his cruel injustice
Will drive me? Thou art not the only blessing
His hand has snatched from me. Armenia,
Concerned with choosing for itself a king,
Through Hiero's influence has declared for me.
Burning to end a shameful slavery,
I in my turn was coming to do homage
To thee; but a jealous father, a cruel rival,
Would rob me of this scepter and thy hand
Alike. Ah, let him at his pleasure take
Both the Armenias from me; but let him leave
The beautiful Ismenia to my suit!
I found my happiness in pleasing her.
'Tis the one gift I pray for to the gods.

ZENOBIA.   And why, then, is it that thou hast brought me here?
Whatever my sad fortunes elsewhere were,
They held their course at least amid quiet shadows.

'Tis thou who with too much attention crownest
My woes. Moreover, what canst thou expect
From such strong passions? Is so great a love
Appropriate for a captive's lot? Thou still
Knowest not the extent of my calamities.
Nothing can stanch the fountain of my tears.
Ah, even if love joined my heart with thine,
Marriage would not unite our destinies.
In spite of all his power and fatal love,
The King is not thy deadliest rival, sir.
A duty stern, from which naught can release me,
Must force thy love forever to keep silent.
I hear a noise. The door is opening.
Ah, 'tis the King, sir! How I fear his presence
Alike for thee and me!

Enter PHARASMANES, MITHRANES, HYDASPES, *and guards.*

PHARASMANES.   What do I see!
It is my son. Arsames in this city!
What purpose brings him here? Thou'rt silent, madam.
Arsames with thee, Arsames in my Court,
When I myself knew not of his return!
Of this confusion what am I to think?
(*To* ARSAMES) Thou to whose care did I entrust my
          vengeance,
And whom I honored with a choice so glorious,
Speak, Prince; what object brings thee here again?
What need, what purpose could conduct thee hither
Without mine orders, without informing me?

ARSAMES.   Thine enemies subdued, was I to think
That my return, sir, could alarm thee? Ah,
Thou knowest too well my heart and my devotion,
To doubt the purpose which recalls me to thee.
Be sure, when thou hast given me my task,
That since thou seest me, it hath been discharged.
When I have bought thee glory with my blood,
When everywhere my victory's fame resounds,
I will confess, sir, I did not expect
Such a reception to reward my exploits.
I hear on every side that Rome and Syria,
With Corbulo in arms, threaten Iberia.
Thy son, led here by duty, told himself
That gladly, then, wouldst thou again behold him.
Not once did I suspect that my impatience

Was to implant distrust in thy great heart.
I thought the door would open to show thee to me,
When 'twas Ismenia, sir, whom here I found.

PHARASMANES.   I fear not Corbulo, or Rome, or Syria.
My soul is steeled against these names renowned;
And I do not approve of this solicitude
Which, without my consent, has brought thee home
From such a distance. And what of more importance
Than the duty of a son and faithful subject
Has this great zeal done or resulted in?
Whatever thy past services, doubtest thou
That criminally to return has blotted
Them out? Know that thy king recalls them still
Only to spare from punishment the projects
Of which he is ignorant. In any case,
Depart ere this day ends, and fly to Colchis
To stifle thy love's flame. I above all
Forbid thee to behold again Ismenia.
Know that her lot is to be linked with mine;
That marriage is this day to crown my love;
That this sole object of my tenderest vows
Has only too well merited royal grandeur—
Thy slave aforetime, but today thy queen.
This plainly enough tells thee that my jealous
Transports wish here no witnesses like thee.
Go.   [*Exit* ARSAMES.

ZENOBIA (*to* PHARASMANES).   And by what right does thy jealous love
Aspire to bow my soul to its desires?
Vainly thou offerest me the mightiest grandeurs;
It is not at this price that one shall win
My heart. And how dost *thou* know, sir, if marriage
May not have linked my fate with someone else?
How knowest thou if the blood to which I owe
My being lets me listen to thy suit
And love?

PHARASMANES.   Indeed I know not of what blood
Thou art; but if it be as fair as it
Deserves to be, the name of Pharasmanes
Is glorious enough to dare to join
Itself with even the gods' blood. Vainly thou
Combinest trickery with thy unkindness—
Vainly, because in the end thou must obey me.
I have neglected naught to win thy favor.
Less as a king than as a lover, I

Have spoken of my love; but now my heart,
Angered by pride so frivolous, in its turn
Gives scope to sovereign power, and because
I must as a king explain myself with thee,
Dread my authority or at least my wrath,
And know that, despite love and all its power,
Kings are not wont to be so much resisted;
And that, whate'er thou hopest from my madness,
All, even love, must be submissive to them.
I see thou wilt refuse me. 'Tis to Arsames'
Return here that I owe the scorn wherewith
Thou dost reward my passion. But beware
Lest, ere this day's end, by thy tears my love
Shall be revenged on a presumptuous son.

                  [*Exeunt all but* ZENOBIA *and* PHENICE.

ZENOBIA.   Ah, tyrant, since my fondness must take arms
And for thy frenzy my hate punish thee,
Beware lest love, armed with my feeble charms,
Requite thee soon with all the woes it caused me.
Why should I fear, then? Shade of Mithridates,
Is it not time my vengeance struck for thee?
Come to my aid, too, spirit of my husband,
And with thy jealous transports fire my heart!
Avenge thyself through me upon a deadly
Enemy. Nay, do thou avenge us on him
Rather through his remaining son. The crime
Against thee which thy father has committed
Can only by his other son be punished.
The gods reserve his punishment for that son
Alone. Then let us arm his 'venging hand.
Phenice, go and find him. Tell him that
He and his pity are my one recourse;
But beg his help without his knowing I sent thee.
Bid him to interest Rome in taking my
Defense, to save me from a tyrant's power,
And if he can, win the support for me
Of her ambassador, expected here
Today. Dazzle him with Armenia's throne.
Review to him the woes of sad Ismenia.
With hope of a scepter shake his loyalty.
Finally, to touch his heart, paint my despair.
Since love has caused my life's calamities,
What else but love is to avenge Zenobia?

A C T   I I

Enter RHADAMISTUS *and* HIERO, *meeting.*

HIERO. Is it thou I see? Shall I believe mine eyes?
Rhadamistus living! Rhadamistus here!
Can it be that heaven, for our tears' sake, restores thee
And grants my heart a day so full of joy?
Is this, sir, indeed thou? By what good fortune
Dost thou belie the story of thy death?

RHADAMISTUS. Hiero, would to the gods that the foe's hand
That took my scepter had cut short my life!
But heaven has left me, to reward my frenzy,
Days which are woven of sadness and of horror.
Far from exhibiting thy zeal or joy
For a hapless king whom Fate sends back to thee,
No more look on me save as on a madman
Too worthy of the wrath of men and gods;
Whom heaven's vengeance has long since proscribed;
Of crimes and of remorse a fatal mixture;
Unworthy of life and thy affection; one
Deserving horror, but compassion also;
Traitor 'gainst nature, recreant towards love;
Usurper, ingrate, perjurer, monstrous villain.
Save for the dire remorse which rends my heart,
Hiero, I would forget that heaven takes vengeance.

HIERO. I love to see regrets born of thy virtue;
But, sir, is duty at all times one's master?
Mithridates, by bad faith towards thee, himself
Seemed to impose on thee the law of vengeance.

RHADAMISTUS. Ah, let not thine affection gild my crimes.
Paint the full horror of Mithridates' death
For me; recall that day and those dread oaths
Which I befouled with so much hapless blood.
If thou still knowest the number of my victims,
Reckon if possible my remorse thereby.
I grant that Mithridates, for betraying
My love, deserved indeed a harsher fate;
That to my cheated love I owed his blood;
But 'gainst that love, how had Zenobia sinned?
Thou shudderest, I see. Thy hand, thine own hand,
Would plunge a dagger in my faithless breast
If thou couldst know how far my savage spirit
Carried the frenzy of my jealous rage.

Learn all my monstrous deeds, or my misfortunes
Rather; but unrecounted, by my tears
Judge of them.

HIERO.   Touched as deeply as art thou
By the fate that crushes thee, I do not seek
To learn if thou art culpable. Little guilt
Accompanies so great remorse; and I
Am only sorry for thy frenzied anguish.
Calm this despair to which thy heart surrenders
Itself, and tell me . . .

RHADAMISTUS.   How shall I dare go on?
How dare talk with thee of my madness, when
All my blood freezes at the very memory?
Without my grief repeating it here now,
Thou knowest all that my criminal hand has done.
Thou sawest how a rebellious populace
At the altar snatched from me the happiness
Destined for me; and well knowest how, despite
The perils threatening my life, I carried
Zenobia off before their eyes. Vain efforts!
I fled without avail. Paint to thyself
My desperation at this fatal moment.
    I longed to perish; but Zenobia, weeping,
Bathed with her tears these arms felonious
And twenty times clung to my knees to thwart
My purpose, saying to me the tenderest things
That love inspires. Oh, Hiero, what a sight
For my distracted soul! Nothing so lovely
Ever displayed itself before mine eyes.
So many charms, however, far from softening
My heart, did but increase my jealous fury.
"What!" said I, quivering with it, "shall the doom, then,
To which I hasten assure to Tiridates
His spoil?" Zenobia's tears increased my madness,
And to reward such love I gave her death.
Yes, hearing no more aught save my utter frenzy,
I myself dragged her into the Araxes
Forthwith. 'Twas there that my hand chose for her
A tomb and quenched our hymeneal torch.

HIERO.   What fate for a queen so much concerned for thee!
RHADAMISTUS.   More formidable after this shocking deed,
Stripped of all followers, without aid, pursued,
I gave myself up wholly to despair.
Unworthy now to live, I hurled myself

Among my eager, fierce pursuers, whom
A sire more cruel than all my enemies
Urged on to slay his hapless son. At length,
Pierced through with swords, I was about to perish
When a large force of Romans, come from Syria,
Full of just anger at these savage men,
Snatched me, all bleeding, from their barbarous hands.
This Corbulo, who had taken arms to crush me,
Having now reached Artaxata's walls too late
For the purpose of avenging Mithridates,
Rescued the enemy whom he came to slay.
Touched, without knowing me, by my sad fate
Or by some valor which I had displayed,
This Roman, by care worthy of his great soul,
Saved me despite myself from mine own frenzy.
    Knowing his goodness but not thankful for it,
I long concealed from him my name and lineage—
Bearing the horror of my unhappy life,
Ever beset with ghastly memories,
And for a crown of woes, deep in my heart
More than erewhile consumed with fatal flames
Which to requite my crimes, love, outraged by me,
Relit there, again waking without hope
The tenderest paroxysms of keen longings
For dust devoid of consciousness. Possessed
Thus by regrets, remorse, and love, and dreading
Equally night and day, I have dragged out
A weary life in Asia. But attaching
To Corbulo alone my fortunes, eager
For dangers, and always, by a sad fate,
Finding but glory where I sought for death,
And never thinking of my former greatness,
I learned, when ten years seemed to have effaced it,
That my Armenia after various choices
Was soon to come beneath an odious sway:
My father, planning secretly its conquest,
Was to crown there his brows with a new circlet.
    At this report I felt my pride and anger
Again wake jealousy in my heart. At last
I made known my identity to Corbulo.
Perchance too bitter 'gainst a savage father,
In *my* turn secretly jealous of his greatness,
I had the Romans name me their ambassador.

HIERO.   And what, sir, is thy hope, bearing this title?

What project can thy vengeance here devise?
Hast thou forgotten in what fearsome danger
The ardor to avenge thyself has plunged thee?
Beware of listening to so rash a frenzy.
Thus crushed with horrors, what dost thou think to do?

RHADAMISTUS.   How do I know, Hiero? Crazed, bewildered,
Criminal without intent, good to no purpose,
The unfortunate puppet of my unmeasured grief,
Can I in my position know myself?
My heart, torn ceaselessly with divers cares,
A foe to crime, yet without loving virtue,
The piteous victim of a hapless love,
Yields to remorse without renouncing sin.
I give way to repentance, but in vain,
And know myself only to loathe myself.
How say what hales me to this cruel spot—
Whether it be despair, or love, or hate?
I have lost Zenobia; after that dire blow
Canst thou still ask me what it is I wish?
Desperate, proscribed, loathing the light of day,
I fain would take revenge on the whole world.
I do not know what poison fills my breast,
But all is frenzied there, even my remorse.
I seek here for the author of my misery,
And nature vainly tells me 'tis my father.
But it is here perhaps that angry heaven
Wishes to justify itself for slackness—
Here that the inevitable bolt awaits me,
Too long suspended o'er my guilty head;
And would to the cruel gods that this suspended
Bolt might indeed no longer be awaited!

HIERO.   Flee, flee, sir, from this fatal region. Far
From drawing the celestial wrath upon thee,
Let nature's tie at least assuage thy fury.
Remember that all here is sacred for thee;
That if thou must avenge thyself, it should be
Far from Iberia. Take the Armenian road
Again with me.

RHADAMISTUS.   Nay, nay, there is no longer
The time for that. I must fulfil my fate—
Avenge myself, serve Rome, or soon meet death.
With policies ever adverse to my father,
Rome has made me the guardian of her interests,
Sure that I shall neglect naught to restore

Her power and mine, against a king she fears.
   She would avoid a war of doubtful issue;
For war against him has been more than once
Humiliating for her; would protect
Armenia, or by jealous care would make it
A very torch of discord for us. I
By gift of Caesar am Armenia's king
Because he thinks to destroy through me Iberia.
My father's fury has been shown too clearly
For Rome to fear between us any compact.
Such are the lofty schemes in which her greatness
Takes pride; such is her boasted policy.
'Tis thus, undoing through the son the sire,
That Rome becomes fatal to all her foes.
Thus, to confirm an unjust power, she dares
To trust her interests to my revenge
And send me here, under a sacred name,
Less as ambassador that as a madman
Who, sacrificing all to the rage that drives him,
May carry his frenzy even to parricide.
I glimpse her purpose, but my angry heart
Gives itself up to the despair that wrings it.
Thus I today, both Rome's foe and Iberia's,
Behold again the palace of my fathers.

HIERO.   A deputy like thee, but chosen by others,
I am entrusted with Armenia's interests.
I came from her to offer to thy brother
A throne to which in spite of us thy sire
Would mount, and to declare to that proud king
That he in vain wishes to rule Armenia.
But dost thou not fear that, despite thine absence . . .

RHADAMISTUS.   The King ne'er saw me since mine earliest childhood,
And nature's voice speaks in his breast too faintly
For him to remember features long forgotten.
I feared thine eyes alone; and but for me,
Thou mightest, despite thy fondness, not have known me.
   The King draws near. How hardly can my heart
At his first sight restrain a fatal frenzy!
Let us control, though, all its violence,
And practice an ambassador's discretion.

Enter PHARASMANES, MITHRANES, HYDASPES, *and Guards.*

(*To* PHARASMANES)   A race triumphant, master of many
   kings,

Which deigns to use my voice to address thee here,
Knowing thy secret plans as thou thyself dost,
Proclaims to thee this day its sovereign will.
'Tis not that Nero, jealous of his greatness,
Knoweth not what he owes to kings like thee;
Rome is aware to what point victory
Exalts thy glory among names renowned.
This people, then, so oft a conqueror,
Thereby admires not less thy haughty valor.
But thou knowest, too, how far Rome's power extends;
Hence take good care not to awake her vengeance.
    Ally, or rather subject, of the Romans,
Armenia to their choice looks for her sovereigns.
Thou knowest it, sir; yet from the Caucasus' foot
Thy soldiers are advancing towards the Phasis.
The banks of the Cyrus, thronged with warriors,
Display thy waving banners everywhere.
Rome, shocked and restive at such preparations,
Has ne'er accustomed kings to so great boldness.
Though she, perhaps at her own rights' expense,
Did not cut short the course of thy achievements,—
Though she abandoned Media and Tigranes,—
She does not mean to yield to thee Armenia.
Hence I declare that Caesar does not wish
For thee to bend thy steps towards the Araxes.
PHARASMANES.   Though I defy the menace of vain words,
I shall confess surprise at thy audacity.
Soldier of Corbulo, how darest thou bring
Orders to me from Nero, in my Court?
And since when does he think that, scorning honor,
Though taught by victory to fear Rome no more,
Forgetful henceforth of the highest greatness,
I shall have more respect for her ambassador?—
I, who yoking together invincible peoples,
Have so many times defied these terrible Romans,
And have made tremble, also, those famed sovereigns
Of Parthia, today the dread of Rome.
Ne'er has that city in a triumph seen
My likenesses, borne in a chariot, made
The target of her insults. The disgrace
With which my mighty deeds have covered her
Hath truly with proud steel avenged all kings.
    But what care brings thee to this barbarous land?
Is it, then, war that Nero now declares?

Let him not be deceived; no splendor here,
As thou canst see full well, dazzles one's eyes.
Even the courtiers who pay homage to me,
My palace—all here has but a savage pomp.
Nature, a step-mother in these harsh climes,
Produces only iron—not gold—and soldiers.
Her shaggy breast offers to men's desires
Naught which can tempt the avarice of Rome.
But, to have done with useless talk now, Rome
Wishes to block the course of my designs.
But if she really is informed of them,
Why has she not assembled yet her army?
What are your legions doing? Do these haughty
Conquerors no longer fight except by envoys?
Ye needs must in Iberia, torch in hand,
Change my intent to go into Armenia,
Not by vain words unworthy of Romans, when
I go to open with the sword a road
For myself thither, and perhaps yet more,
Disdaining Artaxata, to defy
Corbulo even on the Euphrates' banks.

HIERO (*to* PHARASMANES). E'en if the Romans should respect our laws
    And leave to us the choice of our own kings,
    Sir, do not hope, with wishes governing thoughts,
    To make Armenia declare for thee.
    The envious Parthians and the jealous Romans
    Would then on all sides arm themselves against us.
    Absorbed with weeping for her woes, Armenia
    Asks but a king who would be as a father
    To her; our wasted folk need only peace,
    And under thy sway, sir, we ne'er should have it.
    Thy virtues Artaxata doth respect,
    But thy ambition is no less suspect;
    And we sigh only for a sovereign
    Towards Parthia unconcerned, to Rome submissive.
    Indeed, to seek to bring us 'neath thy power
    Is less to conquer us than to wish our ruin.

PHARASMANES. In this speech, filled with pretexts so absurd,
    Prompted by reason less than by the Romans,
    Too well I see the interest which guides thee.
    Well then, since 'tis so wished, let war decide.
    Ye shall soon learn whether from Rome or me
    Ye must expect, sir, to receive your laws,

And whether, despite your fears and your false maxims,
Anyone else has rights more valid o'er you.
Who should succeed my brother? who my son?
To whom have claims more sacred been transmitted?
RHADAMISTUS. Who? Thou, sir, who alone didst cause their ruin?
Should one be heir to those whom one has murdered?
PHARASMANES. What do I hear? Insult me in my Court?
What, ho! guards . . .
HIERO (*to* PHARASMANES). Sir, what thinkest thou to attempt?
PHARASMANES (*to* RHADAMISTUS). Thank the name wherewith Nero
honors thee.
Without that sacred name, which I respect still,
Were I to die for it, the grossest outrage
Would soon avenge me on an insolent minion.
Believe me, though: despite the dignity
Of the role which thou dischargest, shun my wrath.
Return this very day; report to Corbulo
How here the orders of Nero are received.
[*Exeunt all but* RHADAMISTUS *and* HIERO.
HIERO. What hast thou done, sir? when thou shouldst fear all . . .
RHADAMISTUS. What wouldst thou, Hiero? I could not hold in.
Besides, in angering him I gain mine ends.
This outburst will commit the Romans to them.
To do the task which Rome entrusted to me
I now have only to stir up Iberia—
Only to form a faction which will keep
A king here whom his exploits make too proud.
Chafing at Pharasmanes' yoke, abhorring
The war which he alone makes them endure,
His subjects all are secretly his foes.
Let us yet more inflame their hearts against him
And, to requite my father's rage the better,
Try to involve my brother in our plans.
I know a way certain to catch him. Let us
Make him at least a partner in crime with me.
A king both a cruel father and a tyrant
Deserves indeed no progeny unlike him.

ACT III

RHADAMISTUS *is discovered, alone.*

RHADAMISTUS. My brother wants to see me secretly!
Gods! can he know me? What intent is his?

No matter. I needs must see him. My revenge
Begins, I feel, to cherish flattering hopes.
He cannot risk meeting me secretly
If not forced by his father to be recreant.
The door opens. . . . I see him. . . . Hapless victim!
Not me alone a cruel king oppresses.

Enter ARSAMES.

ARSAMES.　If I can trust the wrath his eyes reveal,
　　The King goes hence ill pleased with Rome. Too well
　　I know the pride of him who gave me birth
　　To think that Rome has grounds for pleasure, either.
　　　Sir, without disrespect to thine high office,
　　May I on this occasion speak in secret
　　And hope that Rome will hearken to my prayer
　　Nor with the father will confound the son?
RHADAMISTUS.　Although he failed to accord me the respect
　　Which is my due, look for all things from Rome
　　And from thy virtues. Not beginning with
　　Today does Rome respect them.
ARSAMES.　　　　　　　　　　　　How those virtues
　　Will soon be doubted by thee! How I dread
　　Destroying in this very colloquy
　　All that thou thinkest of a heart like mine!
　　Whate'er, then, the regret which crushes me,
　　Indeed I feel this heart is not less guilty;
　　And by whate'er remorse I am assailed,
　　The more deliberately I am false to virtue.
　　When war 'twixt Rome and us is once declared,
　　Or even when it is openly prepared for,
　　I know I cannot speak with thee or see thee
　　Without betraying my father and my duty
　　Alike. I know this; yet, more criminal still,
　　'Tis but thy pity that I now implore.
　　A harsh sire, jealous of my happy fortune,
　　Forces me now to have recourse to thee.
　　　I seek not, for mine own justification
　　When all condemns me, to picture Pharasmanes
　　To thee by spewing poison on his life.
　　Nay, though he be towards me so stern, so haughty,
　　Though I be the sole victim of his anger,
　　He is not less great hereby, nor less magnanimous.
　　The voice of nature in his heart, 'tis true,
　　Could never tell his own sons from his foes.

5 3 4

Not I alone of his invincible seed
Have been proscribed from birth by his relentless
Harshness. I had a brother, sir, illustrious
And gallant, worthy of the happiest fortunes.
How I regret, still, his sad destiny!
Never was anyone more unfortunate.
A father, who conspired against his own
Child, himself plunged the dagger in his bosom.
Sharing in that young hero's loss of favor,
Perhaps I now shall suffer the same fate.
Truly the guiltier, I expect no less.
But this is not the greatest of my cares.
Nay, death henceforth holds naught that frightens me.
How different a care disturbs and prompts me!

RHADAMISTUS. Whate'er thy purpose, thou canst fearlessly,
Sure of pledged aid, declare thyself to me.
More shocked than thou by this cruel sire, I feel
My wrath redouble at his very name.
Touched by thy virtue, and entirely thine,
E'en knowing not thy woes, I share them all.
Soon wouldst thou calm this grief which weighs upon thee,
Didst thou but know how far extends my interest
In thee. Speak, Prince. Must the whole Roman Empire
Fly to take arms against an inhuman father?
Be sure that *my* heart, in accord with thine,
Today longs only for the selfsame vengeance.
If it but needs to bring here Corbulo,
Whatever be thy plans, I dare make oath
That we shall satisfy thy wishes soon,
Though we for thee alone must conquer Asia.

ARSAMES. What dost thou offer me? What counsels! Ah, sir,
How ill dost thou divine my inmost heart!
What? I? Betray my father and my country,
Bringing the Romans into Iberia?
Ah, if to this extent I must be recreant,
Let Rome herself henceforth expect naught from me.
I ask for naught from her, since crime is needed
To buy a favor which I deemed legitimate;
And well I see, sir, that I must today
Seek elsewhere aid for the unfortunate.
Dazzled by Rome's great name, I had supposed
That like the gods themselves she rescued mortals;
And to obtain her noble help I thought
That it sufficed for one to be in need.

I dare to think so still, and with this hope
Let me implore the succor of the Romans.
   'Tis for a captive, by our power enslaved;
She makes use of my voice to touch thy heart.
'Tis for a captive, lovable, ill-starred,
Who, with her charms, deserves a different fate.
Indeed, to judge her station by her virtues,
None ever sprang from more illustrious lineage.
This tells enough of her exalted birth
To interest Rome in taking her defense.
She wishes to speak here with thee in secret,
And ne'er was anyone worthier of thy care.
Seized by a fatal love, sir, Pharasmanes
Would snatch from me this one thing that is left me,
The single blessing in which I found my joy,
And the sole one which I could dispute with him.
'Tis not that I, grown bold in the hope of aid,
Would carry her off in *my* turn from my father;
Even if he resigned his captive to me,
My lot would not be happier or sweeter.
I only seek to send away my loved one,
E'en without hope of seeing her again.

RHADAMISTUS.   With but few followers, with no power here,
   I can do naught but offer my protection.

ARSAMES.   'Tis all that I desire; I am content.
   I go, sir, to arrange for her escape.
   I know not why; but for some hidden reason
   I give Ismenia up with less regret.
   To calm the sorrow of my troubled soul
   It is enough that in thy hands I place her;
   Yet would that I might at my life's expense
   Repay my debt to thee for this kind succor!
   But I can offer only, in my plight,
   For such a good deed, the good deed itself.

RHADAMISTUS.   I do not ask, dear Prince, for a more pleasing
   Reward. 'Tis meet for me, if not for thee.
   Let me henceforward serve thee like a brother.
   How I regret thou hast so cruel a father!
   But why alarm thyself about his vain
   Passion? Why leave her who has charmed thy heart?
   Vouchsafe to trust her fate and thine to me.
   Follow me, both of you, to a safe asylum.
   Touched by his woes, I cannot leave Arsames
   Without fear to the anger of his king.

Prince, thou rejectest counsels which displease thee;
But if thou knewest who urges them upon thee . . .
ARSAMES.   Give to me counsels which are nobler, worthy
Of what I owe and worthy of us both.
The King will leave tomorrow for Armenia.
The point is how to save Ismenia from him.
This very moment he can take her from us;
And she, his tearful captive, has no hope
But thee. Already trusting in thy kindness,
She waits impatiently for the sight of thee.
Adieu, adieu, sir; I should fear to intrude
On secrets which she means for thee alone.   [*Exit* ARSAMES.
RHADAMISTUS.   Thus, jealous father, unjust and barbarous father,
'Tis upon all thy seed that thou dost turn.
Beware lest that same seed, so often flouted,
May rise at last, indignant with its source;
For love already rules Arsames' heart,
Where it secretes a deadly, burning poison.
    However great this virtuous son's respect,
Can men be rivals without being foes?
Nay, there is no heart so magnanimous
Nor great that its unhappy love cannot
Lead it to crime. But vainly I aspire
To arm my brother's hand against his king.
He is not used, like me, to deeds of wrong.
Didst thou deserve, cruel man, a son so loyal?
Thy harshness seems to augment his zeal the more.
Nothing can shake his duty or devotion,
And always more submissive . . . What an example
For me! Gods, do ye with so many virtues
Adorn my brother, then, to make me only
Too like my father? What is the intention
Of the madness which assails me? To corrupt
The virtue of a duteous son? Nay, let us
Now imitate it, rather; let us yield
To natural instincts. Have I not long enough
Stifled their murmurs? What am I saying? Ought
My heart to hearken, rather, to a father's
Voice, and be less rebellious 'gainst his sway?
Cruel fathers, have ye rights which we have not,
And are our duties sacred more than yours?
Someone is coming. It is Hiero.

Enter HIERO.

(*To* HIERO)   Dear friend, 'tis useless. All my utmost efforts
Have been without result. Wholly unhappy
Although he is, the virtuous Arsames
Almost without a murmur sees his love
Thwarted; and how expect aught of him still
When love has thus no power over him?
How different, Hiero, is his heart from mine!
I have lost hope that I can shake Iberia,
And soon the King will set out for Armenia.
Let us precede him there, flying to do
The monstrous deeds for which I seem reserved.
To go with thee I wait but for Ismenia.
Thou knowest she is to marry Pharasmanes.

HIERO.   What! my lord . . .

RHADAMISTUS.   She can serve my purposes.
She is of a race, 'tis said, allied with Rome.
Could I refuse to my unhappy brother
Help which begins to make her dear to me?
Besides, to carry her off, is it not enough
That my cruel father's heart burns for her charms?
That is my warrant. I shall await her here.
Watch where we might be taken by surprise.
Farewell. I think I see her. Aid my care
And leave me briefly with her here alone.

Enter ZENOBIA. *Exit* HIERO.

ZENOBIA.   My lord, is it allowed a hapless woman
Whom Fate holds chained to a proud tyrant's yoke,
To dare appeal, though shamed by slavery's bonds,
Even to the Romans, masters of the world?
Yet for these masters of the world what task
Were better than to solace my great woe?
Heaven, which 'neath their laws august bows all . . .

RHADAMISTUS.   What do I see? Ah, wretched man! Those features—
That voice—Just gods, what sight do ye present
Before mine eyes?

ZENOBIA.   Whence comes it that thy soul
Is so disturbed at sight of me, my lord?

RHADAMISTUS.   Ah, had my hand not robbed of life . . .

ZENOBIA.   What is it
I hear? Regrets? And what is it I see
In turn? Sad memory! I tremble, shudder.
Where am I? and what sight is this? My strength
Abandons me. Ah, sir, dispel my terror

And my confusion. All my blood is frozen
Even to my bosom's core.

RHADAMISTUS (*aside*).   Ah me, the passion
That fills my being leaves me no more doubt.
Didst thou, my hand, commit but half the crime?
(*To* ZENOBIA)   Victim of a cruel man's contriving 'gainst thee,
Sad object of a jealous, desperate love
Driven by my rage to the utmost savagery,
After such frenzy, is it thou, Zenobia?

ZENOBIA.   Zenobia! great gods! Cruel but dear husband,
After such woe, Rhadamistus, is it thou?

RHADAMISTUS.   Can it be possible that thine eyes can fail
To recognize him? Yes, I am that cruel,
That monstrous man; I am that traitor to thee,
That murderous husband. Would to heaven that
Today thou hadst forgot his crimes as well!
O gods, who to me in my grief restore her,
Why do ye not restore her to a husband
Worthy of her? By what kind grace does heaven,
Touched by mine anguish of regret, permit me
To see once more such loveliness? But alas!
Can it be, too, that at my father's Court
I find a wife so dear in slavery's chains?
Gods! have I not bewailed my crimes enough
Without your crushing me again with this
Sad sight? O victim dear of my despair!
How all I see augments thy husband's guilt!
What, thou art weeping?

ZENOBIA.   Woe is me! But wherefore
Should I not weep at such a fateful moment?
Ah, cruel man, would to heaven thy hostile hand
Had never struck save at Zenobia's life!
Then would my heart, disarmed at sight of thee,
Find joy in my reunion with my husband,
And love, as honored by thy jealous frenzy,
Would to thine arms with joy restore thy wife.
Yet do not think that, without pity for thee,
I can with enmity see thee again.

RHADAMISTUS.   What! far from crushing me with her reproaches,
Great gods, it is Zenobia who fears
To hate me and who justifies herself!
Ah, rather punish me; thy fatal kindness,
Even in pardoning me, smacks of my cruelty.

Spare not my blood, dear being whom I worship;
Deprive me of the bliss of seeing thee
Again.   [*He throws himself at her feet.*
     Must I, to urge thee to this step,
Embrace thy knees? Remember at the price
Of whose blood I became thy husband. All—
Yes, even my love—requires that I should perish.
To leave a crime unpunished, is to share it.
Strike! but remember that, despite my frenzy,
Thou ne'er hast for one instant left my heart;
That if repentance could make innocence,
I would no more urge thee to hate or vengeance;
That in that wrath's despite which ought to stir thee,
My greatest frenzy was my love for thee.

ZENOBIA.   Arise! too much is this. Since I forgive thee,
What serve regrets to which thou yieldest thy soul?
Go. It is not to us the gods have given
The power to punish enemies so dear.
Tell me the climes where thou desirest to dwell.
Speak. From this moment I will follow thee,
Assured that the remorse which grips thy heart
Springs from thy virtues more than thy misfortunes,
And happy if my fealty to thee
Could some day set Armenia an example,
Make her like me obedient to thy sway,
And teach her, if no more, her duty towards thee.

RHADAMISTUS.   Just heaven! can it be that lawful bonds
Unite so many virtues with such crimes;
That marriage fastens to a madman's lot
The nearest perfect being to whom the gods
Have given life? Canst thou again behold me
Without thy father's death, without my cruelty,
Without my brother's love—that prince, that lover,
So great and noble—making thee detest
A hapless husband? And can I tell myself
That thou, indifferent to his love, disdainest
The virtuous Arsames' proffered vows?
What words are these? 'Twould be too great a blessing
For me if even, within thy breast, today
Fidelity might stand in place of love.

ZENOBIA.   Quiet the vain doubts with which thy soul is seized,
Or hide at least unworthy jealousy.
Remember that a heart which can forgive thee
Is not a heart to doubt—not without crime!

RHADAMISTUS. Forgive, dear wife, my fatal love; forgive
    Those doubts which all my soul abhors. The more
    Thy barbarous husband is unworthy of thee,
    The less his unjust fears ought to offend thee.
    Give me again thy heart, thy hand, O dear
    Zenobia mine, and deign this day to follow me
    Into Armenia. Caesar has made me its king.
    Come and behold me henceforth blot my crimes out
    By dint of virtues. Hiero is here.
    He is a faithful subject. We can trust
    To his hands our escape. As soon as night
    Has veiled the skies, come and await me here
    Assured of seeing me again. Farewell.
    Let us not linger till a savage foe,
    When heaven has reunited us, shall part us
    Forever.
           Gods, who give her back to me
    To crown with joy my longings: oh, create
    A heart within me worthy of your goodness!

ACT IV

Zenobia and Phenice are discovered.

PHENICE. Ah, madam! stay. What! am I not to learn
    Who makes those tears flow, that I see thee shed?
    After so many secrets trusted to me,
    Hast thou still any which are not for me?
    Arsames is about to go. Thou sighest!
    Wouldst thou lament noble Arsames' fate?
    Does he make flow those tears which bathe thine eyes?
    He goes; and, knowing that thou disdainest him,
    This hapless prince goes, banished from Iberia,
    To mourn at Colchis for Ismenia's loss.
ZENOBIA. Far from telling thee of my guilty grief,
    Would I might with my tears efface its shame!
    Phenice, leave me; I no more will hear thee.
    The ambassador of Rome will soon return.
    Leave me alone here.   [*Exit* PHENICE.
           Whither am I going?
    What is my hope? O foolish woman! Where
    Does a blind sense of duty drag me? I
    Come ere 'tis night. For whom? A prejured man
    Whom nature's voice hath outlawed in my heart.

Have I forgotten, then, that his cruel hand
Made all my race fall 'neath a murderer's steel? . . .
What am I saying? With a heart in which
Unlawful fires are kindled, have I virtue
Enough to point out crime in him? Would he
Appear to me so culpable today
If I did not burn with a sinful love?
Let us without regret stifle a shameful
Passion. 'Tis for my husband, and none else,
To reign over my soul. Although he is
Entirely barbarous, he is heaven's gift,
Which I am not permitted to find odious.
Alas! despite my woes, despite his cruelty,
I could not see him without softening towards him.
What power marriage has o'er virtuous hearts!
Someone is coming. Gods! what object do ye
Offer unto my sight!

Enter ARSAMES.

ARSAMES.   What! I behold thee
Again! It is thyself, madam. What god
Restores thee to the prayers of poor Arsames?
ZENOBIA.   Ah, fly from me, my lord! It means thy life.
ARSAMES.   Should my cruel father end the course of that,
Alas! when I lose thee, beloved Ismenia,
Would I wish still to snatch some remnant of it?
Crushed by my woes, I ask of the gods only
The sad delight of dying before thine eyes.
With heart so pierced by losing her I love,
If thou wouldst to my love extreme respond,
I fain would only die. I see thy tears.
Madam, couldst thou be touched by my misfortunes?
The direst fate no more has aught which daunts me.
ZENOBIA.   Instead of giving up thy heart to love,
See my confusion and in what state I am.
My lord, have pity on my mortal anguish.
Fly; do not worsen the torment which o'ercomes me.
Thou hast a rival, the most deadly rival.
If he surprised thee in this fatal spot,
Oh, I should die of grief because of that.
Farewell, my lord, farewell! If e'er my prayers
Had over thee some power, far from hearkening
To the ecstasies which love inspires in thee . . .
ARSAMES.   Who is this rival, then, so deadly for me?

Have I some other than the King to fear?
ZENOBIA. Without desiring to pierce so sad a mystery,
Hast thou not, sir, enough in having thy father?
Fly, Prince. Yield to my tears. Be satisfied
With seeing me touched by thy woes, and go.
Take thyself hence, too noble-souled Arsames.
ARSAMES. Has a disloyal friend betrayed my love?
What turmoil rises in my fearful breast!
What! always rivals, and be loved no whit!
Fairest Ismenia, thou vainly wishest me
To flee. I cannot, were my life the price.
I see thy tears flow, which are not for me.
Who is this rival, then? Dispel my fears.
Why do I find thee in this palace still?
Was I refused the help which I implored?
Have the false Romans not kept faith with me?
Ah, vouchsafe to explain thy agitation. . . .
Speak; do not fear to tire my constancy. . . .
What! thou wilt nowise break this cruel silence?
Do all forsake me on this fatal day?
Gods! must one have no pity, having no love?
ZENOBIA. So be it, my lord; so be it! I must content thee.
I owe this necessary avowal more
To mine own self than thee. 'Twould ill requite
Thy generous care if I should any further
Deceive thy hapless love. Fate has disposed
Already of Ismenia's hand.
ARSAMES.   Just heaven!
ZENOBIA. And the husband to whom marriage binds me is
That very Roman whose support and succor
Thou earnestly didst beg for me today.
ARSAMES. Ah, were he Caesar's self, in my despair . . .
ZENOBIA. Restrain thy frenzy's violence. But I have
Too much exposed him to thine enmity.
Deserving hatred not so much as pity,
This is a rival, sir, who, although deadly
For thee, will nowise find thy heart unfeeling;
Who by the tenderest ties is linked with thee:
'Tis Rhadamistus.
ARSAMES.   My brother?
ZENOBIA.   And my husband.
ARSAMES. Thou, thou Zenobia? Gods! Is it in *my*
Soul that a guilty flame had to be kindled?
After what I experience, what heart

Will dare to boast of being without foul sins?
Madam, what secret hast thou told me? Didst thou
Reserve this guerdon for the tenderest love?

ZENOBIA. I have withheld it, sir, as long as possible.
But now that I have spoken, respect my virtue.
My name alone tells thee what thou must do.
My secret known, thy love must needs be silent.
My heart was ever jealous of its duty . . .
Someone is coming. Ah, fly, sir! 'Tis my husband.

Enter RHADAMISTUS *and* HIERO.

RHADAMISTUS. What do I see? How now! my brother . . . Hiero,
Go and await me.   [*Exit* HIERO.
     (*To himself*)   Scarcely can my soul
Preserve itself from fearful turmoil.
                    (*To* ZENOBIA)   Madam,
All is in readiness. The shades of night
Will soon efface the light that shines on us.

ZENOBIA. Sir, since I give myself into thy keeping
Henceforth, naught stays me here, and I am ready
To follow thee. Sole master of my fortunes,
Whatever be the climes where heaven wished
To guide my steps with thee, thou canst command;
I follow thee.

RHADAMISTUS (*aside*). Ah, the false woman!
                    (*To* ARSAMES)   Prince,
I had supposed thou hadst set out for Colchis.
Knowing too well thy father's frenzied rage,
I did not think to see thee in this place;
But when thou leavest Ismenia soon forever,
Thou art concerned about thy life but little,
And whatso'er be a cruel father's anger,
'Tis easily forgot in such sweet moments.

ARSAMES. A heart recks little of impending dangers,
When duty bids it to renounce its passion,
And those sweet moments wherewith thou reproachest me
Cost very dear a heart which love has touched.
'Tis time, I see, for mine to give them up.
Howe'er it be, at least thou tellest me that.
     But ere night separates thee from us, sir,
Permit me to object to thy behavior.
To what must I ascribe thy frigid speech?
What can bring on me such a discourteous greeting?
This day, this very day, I well recall,

And here, thy keen affection spoke not thus.
This rival, pictured as inexorable,
Is not, sir, the most deadly of my rivals.
Despite his wrath there is among them now
One, for my love and me, more cruel than he.
These words surprise thee. 'Tis no more a time
To feign. The voice of kinship in my heart
Can be repressed no longer. Would to heaven
That with like ardor it could have been able
To expound itself in thy heart's very core!
No cruel secret then would have snatched from me
The joy of knowing my brother and clasping him.
Do not withhold thyself from my embrace.
Why frustrate, sir, such tender moments? Ah,
Again look on me with a brow less stern.
Do not afflict me with an unjust anger.
'Tis true my heart burned for her charms divine;
But then, sir, then I knew not who she was.

RHADAMISTUS.   Gods! what is this I hear? What! Prince, Zenobia
Put in thy hands the secret of my life?
This secret, in itself, is so important
I cannot even admit it here too loudly.
Thou knowest the value of what she trusted with thee,
And I believe thy heart devoid of treachery.
Yet I can sanction only with regret
The disclosure of this weighty secret to thee;
At least this should not have been made without
My consent; and by my example truly
She ought to have kept silent to thee of it.
If I had wished to see thee thus informed,
Mine own affection for thee would have made me
Reveal it here. She who can so betray
My secret, be the outcome what it may,
Cannot be otherwise than culpable.
I know, 'tis true, how great thy virtue is;
But doubts, in spite of that, assail my heart.

ARSAMES.   What! the black frenzy of thy jealousy
Extends thus even to Zenobia, sir?
Canst thou insult . . .

ZENOBIA.   Leave a free course, my lord,
To doubts indeed so worthy of his heart.
Thou dost not know the husband of Zenobia
Nor all the paroxysms that seize his soul.
To dare, though, to insult my rectitude,

Rhadamistus, answer me: of what complainest thou?
Thy brother's love? Ah, cruel man, if indeed
My heart had yielded to the greatness of it,
Would not thy death's report, confirmed so often,
Have left me mistress of my choice? What rights
Over me does a marriage give to thee
Which one same day saw broken as well as made?
Dare, dare to boast of that grim day on which
My blood was poured out to requite my love!
Recall the fate of my whole family.
Think of the gore thy murderous frenzy shed,
And then consider on what to base thy claim
That I should harbor love or faith for thee.
'Tis true that, pitying thy brother's woes,
I have revealed the secret of thy lot
And mine. I am ignorant if this indeed
Is to betray it; but understand, thine honor
Was my sole aim therein. I sought to extinguish
His passion's hope, and to expel a love
Which wronged me from his breast. But since thou wishest
To give thyself up thus to thy suspicions,
Know, then, this heart entirely which thou doubtest.
I mean to make thee know it with one utterance,
And then I leave thee master of my fate.
I loved thy brother; I cannot deny it.
I do not even seek to justify it.
But this prince, who, despite his love, ne'er knew it,
Would still not know it, but for thy base doubts.
   (*To* ARSAMES)   Prince, after this avowal, I say no more
To thee. Thou knowest too well a heart like mine
To think that love has any mastery o'er it.
My husband lives; hence my love's flame expires.
Cease, then, to hearken to a love now odious,
And above all keep thyself from my sight.
   (*To* RHADAMISTUS)   As for thee, when night so permits, I
   shall
Return and place myself, here, in thy hands.
I know the madness of thy jealous doubts,
But am too virtuous to fear my husband.   [*Exit* ZENOBIA.
RHADAMISTUS.   Barbarian that I am! My jealous madness
Insults alike my brother and my wife!
Farewell, Prince. I shall fly, shamed by my fault,
To expiate at Zenobia's feet my frenzy.   [*Exit* RHADAMISTUS.
ARSAMES.   Dear object of my vows, beloved Zenobia,

'Tis over. Thou art snatched from me forever.
Love, cruel love, to augment my woes didst thou
Have to choose rivals of my own blood for me?
Ah, let us flee hence . . .

Enter MITHRANES *and guards.*

Heavens! what would Mithranes

    With me?
MITHRANES.   Sir, I obey regretfully;
    But Pharasmanes, whose anger I in vain
    Have tried to soften . . .
ARSAMES.   Well?
MITHRANES.   Desires that I
    Secure thee here. Permit . . .
ARSAMES.   I understand.
    And what, then, is my crime?
MITHRANES.   I do not know
    The reason for this, unjust or just. But I
    Fear for thy life. The rages of the King
    Have never roused more terror in my heart.
    Savage and restless, he is much distraught,
    Muttering thy name. He menaces, together
    With thee, the ambassador of Rome. Indeed,
    Ye are accused of secret conference.
ARSAMES. That is enough, Mithranes, and I am
    Satisfied.
        My life do I abandon,
    O Fate, unto thy blows; but save, if this
    Be possible, my brother and Zenobia.

A C T   V

PHARASMANES, HYDASPES, *and guards are discovered.*

PHARASMANES. Is it then true, Hydaspes, that my son,
    Arsames, is in concord with my foes?
    What! is this son, formerly so submissive,
    So loyal, and so worthy to be loved,
    Only a traitor, an insurgent? What!
    This son, my only hope against the Romans,
    Was able to forget so far his duty?
    False youth, 'tis all too much to love Ismenia,
    Dare to betray thy father and Iberia,
    Oppose at once my glory and my love . . .

For crimes less grievous thine unhappy brother . . .
But thou in vain seducest a rash prince,
O Rome! Think not to turn me from my projects.
Defeat or death alone can discompose them.
One foe the more can never make me tremble.
In the just rage that fills me 'gainst thee, Rome,
This only offers me another victim.
My son concerns himself in thy behalf;
That is enough. Where I must needs take vengeance,
Everyone is a Roman in mine eyes.
But what says Hiero? Hast thou made thyself
Understood clearly? Does he indeed know
All that he can expect of me if he
Will in Armenia support my plans?

HYDASPES.   Moved little by the hopes of rarest favors
And ever the more steeled against thine offers,
Hiero's heart proves incorruptible,
Whether he wishes to display his staunchness
Or sets a higher price upon his power.
Knowing how he can serve or injure thee,
I have o'erlooked, sir, nothing which might tempt him.

PHARASMANES.   Well then, 'tis vain to speak to me of peace.
Though I should faint, unhonored, 'neath the burden,
I wish to bring war e'en to the Romans' home,
Avenging all the world on these proud tyrants.
How I hate Rome! I do not know what horror
Seizes me at their envoy's name alone.
His visage has brought turmoil to my soul.
Ah, it is doubtless he who has corrupted
Arsames. Both arrived here the same day . . .
The traitor! 'Tis too much. Let him appear
Before me. But I see him. He must needs . . .

Enter ARSAMES, MITHRANES, *and guards.*

False and ungrateful son! what am I saying?
Perhaps within thy heart a parricide!
Minion of Nero, what is thine intent?
(*To* HYDASPES)   Let Rome's ambassador be brought here to
    me.   [*Exeunt* HYDASPES *and two of the guards.*
(*Again to* ARSAMES)   Traitor, I will confound thee before
    him.
I wish to know at least what thou canst answer;
I wish to see with what mien thou canst face
The evidence of a plot which I forestalled;

And we shall learn then if thy base accomplice
Can still be haughty, even under torture.
Thou vauntest to me no more thy loyalty
Nor zeal.
ARSAMES.   'Tis not less genuine for my king.
PHARASMANES.   Son most unworthy of life! to make me think so,
Make me lose all the memory of thy projects.
Great gods, who know my hate and my designs,
Could I have brought to birth a friend of Rome?
ARSAMES.   Shameful reproaches, which are vainly heaped
Upon me, make thy son no guiltier, sir.
What serves it thee to abuse me thus with insults?
Give death to me if that is my desert,
But flatter not thyself that I shall fear it
So much that, trembling, I shall beg for life.
Could he grow tenderer who really seeks
To make me die only because a rival?
I know that in thy mind the least suspicion,
Legitimate or unjust, convicts of crime,
That to be doubted is to be proscribed,
And that thy heart, moreover, never pardons.
Who could defend me from thy jealous frenzies,
O thou who e'er condemnest me unheard?
PHARASMANES.   In thy defense, well, what canst thou say to me?
ARSAMES.   All that my character should say to thee:
That this suspected son ne'er came to seek thee
Here in Iberia to betray his country.
PHARASMANES.   Whence, then, today this secret colloquy
If thou in truth hast nothing here in mind?
When I vow deathless hate against the Romans,
Is seeing their envoy being loyal to me?
Is it to punish him for insulting me
That here my son engages him in converse?
For he could nowise see an enemy
Who has insulted me, save to avenge me
Or to betray my vengeance. One of these
Two motives could alone have prompted him,
And I must needs decide which one it was.
Solve this for me. I am prepared to hear thee. . . .
Speak.
ARSAMES.   I have nothing more to tell thee, sir.
'Tis not a secret which may be revealed.
Sacred considerations seal my lips.

Enter HYDASPES, *hastily.*

HYDASPES.   The Roman envoy and the Armenian . . .

PHARASMANES.   Well?

HYDASPES.   Are carrying off Ismenia from the palace.

PHARASMANES.   Gods! what is this I hear?

(*To* ARSAMES)   Traitor, is that
Enough?

(*To* MITHRANES)   Assemble here my scattered guards.
Go. Be ready to follow me at once.

(*To* ARSAMES)   Wretch, hope not to survive this crime attempted!

HYDASPES.   Thy guards collected, though by various paths,
Already from all sides pursue the Romans.

PHARASMANES.   Rome, would that thou couldst see their punishment
And here receive the first-fruits of my fury!

[*He starts to go out.*

ARSAMES.   I will not leave thee, though I must perish for it.
Nay, listen to me. I will tell thee all.
'Tis not a Roman whom thou wilt pursue.
Far from inviting by his race thy wrath,
He springs from parentage the most illustrious,
Respected even in this Court. His death
Would by thine own regrets be followed. This
Ravisher is the husband of Ismenia.
'Tis . . .

PHARASMANES.   Go on, thou impostor! Thinkest thou
To stay, by shameful tricks, my fury's course?

ARSAMES.   Ah, let me at least follow thee. I pledge
My word to bring thy captive here to thee.

PHARASMANES.   Back, traitor! Do not answer me.

Mithranes,
Keep him here.

(*To his guards*)   And ye soldiers, follow me.

[*Exeunt* PHARASMANES, HYDASPES, *and most of the guards.*

ARSAMES.   Gods, who perceive the madness he intends,
Will ye abandon him to his savage frenzies?
What fate requires that this disastrous day
Shall burden love and kinship with such horrors?
I should have spoken; the name of "son" perhaps . . .
Alas! what would to make it known have served me?
That sweet name, far from having stayed his cruelty,
Would but have made him the more criminal.
Nay, woe is me! what do laments avail me?

In my position, what can I still fear?
Die, yes; but let my death be useful here
To those unfortunates whom the gods abandon.
(*To* MITHRANES)   Friend, if 'tis true that my relentless father
Leaves thee a heart touched by his son's misfortunes,
In my last hour I can but turn to thee.
I do not ask that thou shouldst save my life;
Fear not that I dare attempt aught for that.
But if thou knewest the blood soon to be shed,
Thou fain wouldst save it, though it cost all thine.
Follow me. Let thy pity help me shield it.
(*As* MITHRANES *shakes his head*)   Disarmed, unaided, am I formidable
Enough still to alarm thy heart unyielding?
Indeed the only favor that I ask
Is but to lead me where the King has gone.
MITHRANES.   I love thy virtues; I shall not deny it.
But I must needs obey thy father, sir.
Thou seekest in vain to move me from my duty.
ARSAMES.   Well then, since naught can move thee for my sake . . .
Alas, though, all is over! I see him coming.
Just gods! of what race have ye given us birth!
My brother is no more.

Enter PHARASMANES, HYDASPES, *and guards.*

(*To* PHARASMANES)   What hast thou done, sir?
PHARASMANES.   Avenged the outrage done me. I am content.
At the palace gates I found the faithless villain,
Whom his ill fortune made still more intrepid.
A rampart of my guards, slain by his arm,
Held back the boldest, chilled the hearts of all.
I saw the false wretch twice, disdaining death,
Try even before mine eyes to take Ismenia.
His eagerness to regain so great a treasure
Had made him twice renew the attempt already,
When at last, angry at such boldness, I
Sought him myself amid his followers.
They all quailed; and my hand, despite his valor,
Plunged this avenging sword into his breast.
Go, see him dying in Ismenia's arms.
Go, share with him thy perfidy's reward.
ARSAMES.   What! he is dead, sir? After this dire deed,
Strike; spare not thy unhappy son.
(*Aside*)   O gods,

551

Did ye restore to me my ill-starred brother
For him to perish at my father's hands?
Thine arm, Mithranes!
PHARASMANES *(to himself)*.   Wherefore does the fate
Of a cruel ravisher so touch his heart?
The Roman whom this sword has just cut down
Was, if I may believe his words, Ismenia's
Husband; and yet my son so felt his charm
As to lament his death—his rival's death!
What still can make this death so grievous to him?
What means the mystery of my son's tears?
But why, for mine own part, after such fury
Do I, despite myself, share in his grief?
By what strange spell, despite the wrath that fires me,
Does pity find a way into my heart?
What plaintive voice assails my mind in secret
And can within me speak in such sad accents?
Why do I shudder? What, then, is my crime?
Could I have been mistaken in my choice
Of victim, or is Roman blood so precious
That he who makes it flow offends the gods?
To serve ambition, I have cut illustrious
Careers short without pity or regret;
And when I punish one who outraged me,
Does my weak heart fear it has been too vengeful?
Whence can the agitation have been born
Which his death causes me? I do not know;
But his demise alarms me and disquiets me.
When I had shed the blood of this proud foe,
All mine was chilled. I trembled and I shuddered.
It even seemed to me that this fierce Roman
Suddenly grew indifferent to his fate,
Careful to spare my blood while I shed his,
And though it cost his life, would not take mine.
Quaking, I recollect Arsames' words.
Clear up the turmoil into which thou'st thrown
My soul. Hear me, my son; resume thy senses.
ARSAMES.   What serve, alas, these impotent regrets?
Mayest thou, forever ignorant of this secret,
Forget therewith of whom thou wert the father!
PHARASMANES.   Ah! this too much dismays me. Explain thyself,
My son. With what new dread dost thou assail me?
But to redouble it in my heart aghast,
What sight, great gods, present ye to mine eyes?

RHADAMISTUS AND ZENOBIA

Enter RHADAMISTUS *carried by soldiers,* ZENOBIA, HIERO, *and* PHENICE.

(*To* RHADAMISTUS)   Poor wretch, what purpose brings thee
    here again?
What seekest thou?
RHADAMISTUS.   I come to die before thee.
PHARASMANES.   What agitation grips me!
RHADAMISTUS.   Though my death nears,
    Fear not, sir, an unwarranted reproach.
At thy hands I receive my crimes' reward.
May the just gods be satisfied thereby!
I did not merit life and its enjoyment.
    Beloved Zenobia, dry thy tears. Farewell.
Mithridates is avenged.
PHARASMANES.   Gods! what do I hear?
    Mithridates? Ah! what blood, then, have I shed?
Miserable me! Can I mistake him? With
My heart so shaken, what other could it be?
But if 'tis he, alas! what crime is mine!
Nature, avenge thyself. This is my son's
Life-blood.
RHADAMISTUS.   Did not the thirst which thou didst feel
    To shed it, sir, suffice to tell thee so?
I saw thee with such wrath pursue it that
I deemed that I indeed was known to thee.
PHARASMANES.   Wherefore conceal it from me? Oh, wretched father!
RHADAMISTUS.   Always thou madest thyself to be so dreaded
    That ne'er could thy proscribed or miserable
Children regard thee as a father to them.
Happy am I, when thy hand immolated
A traitor, not to have shed the blood from which
I sprang; that nature's bond could cheat my fury
And in this fearful hour rule my soul—
And finally, when I lose a wife so dear,
Happy, albeit in death, to find again
My father. Thy heart softens. I see thy tears.
    (*To* ARSAMES)   Brother, draw near; embrace me. I am dying.
                [ARSAMES *embraces him.* RHADAMISTUS *dies.*
ZENOBIA.   Heaven, if thy justice must be done by crimes,
    Wherefore avenge the death of Mithridates?
PHARASMANES.   O my son . . . Are ye satisfied, ye Romans?
    (*To* ARSAMES)   Thou, whom I beg to avenge me henceforth
        for him,

Go quickly to possess Armenia's throne.
To thee I lovingly resign Zenobia.
I owe this sacrifice to my hapless son.
But take yourselves hence, both of you; my offspring
Must be protected from my jealous frenzies.
Fly; tempt no more thy father's heart to slay thee.

Zaïre

B y
VOLTAIRE

INTRODUCTORY NOTE

An account of the life, career, and works of the great Voltaire, whose real name was François Marie Arouet, can be found in any history of French literature or general encyclopedia. A brief statement of important biographical facts and some consideration of him as a dramatist are sufficient here.

He was born of affluent bourgeois parents in Paris in 1694, was educated at the Jesuit college Louis-le-Grand, and under the guidance of the worldly Abbé de Châteauneuf acquired an entrée into brilliant, dissolute social circles, and developed literary tastes and ambitions. From the first his own writings got him in trouble with the authorities, partly because of his natural bent and partly because of ideas bred by republican and Protestant contacts which he made during a youthful visit to Holland. Banished to England in 1726, he was greatly impressed by the comparatively enlightened way of life in that country—and by the plays of Shakespeare, whose art, so alien to French traditions, first attracted but later repelled him as barbarous, yet still influenced his own dramatic work to some extent. He was allowed to return to France in 1729, but was continually giving offense there to Church or State or both, so that he often could not live in Paris. For three years he was a guest at the Court of Frederick the Great; and for more than twenty years he lived in or near Geneva, most of that time just inside the French border, continually carrying on his crusade against intolerance and injustice. At last, in 1778, public insistence compelled the government of Louis XVI to let him come to Paris, but the excitement of his triumph was too much for the frail old man, and he died on May 30 of that year.

Voltaire wrote twenty-three tragedies that were acted, of which *Zaïre, Alzire, Mahomet,* and *Mérope* are generally considered the best. In his own times his reputation as a tragic dramatist was immense; he was thought by many the equal of Corneille and Racine, if not their superior; and even today his fame resulting from quite different work, as the ironic champion of enlightenment and humanity, makes him remembered also as a dramatist, and the reflected light which illumines his tragedies exhibits them in a false perspective. Like Crébillon's, they are essentially melodramas, with incogniti, recognitions, and misapprehensions important factors in almost all of them.

Zaïre (1732), which shows plainly the influence of *Othello,* is almost universally regarded as Voltaire's best play. Coming to it after reading the chief tragedies of the contemporaries of Corneille and Racine, one is instantly struck by its extraordinary, sophisticated technical competence, hardly matched by those great men themselves, in the superficial aspects and minutiae of drama. But one will also note the presence here of the stock devices of melodrama: recognitions and misapprehensions, unfortunate promises of silence imposed with doubtful necessity, and sheer ill chance. And worse than all this, the very essence of the play is in contradiction to human nature.

Voltaire was at some pains to justify the credibility of Zaïre's conversion, on which all depends. She had already felt an attraction towards Christianity. But having also already decided, despite this fact and the probability that her parents were Christians, that she would not embrace the religion of Orosmanes' foes, it is incredible that the turning of that probability into a certainty should effect an immediate complete reversal of her attitude; that the chance discovery that Lusignan was her father should instantly transfer all her loyalty and obedience to him, practically a stranger to her; that she should cringe before him guiltily when he inquired what faith was hers; that she should yield at once to his exhortation and be persuaded forthwith to accept Christianity; should deceive, disappoint, perplex, and torture the man who loved her, who granted all her desires and was raising her from slavery to be his queen, and whom she is alleged to love fervently; should wish that she had died before she loved him or should ask for death now, regardless of what anguish her loss would mean to him; should without even a protest hear her brother speak of him abusively and threateningly. It is only in a stage world, not in real life, that people are bowled over and hypnotically obsessed by the mere name of "father," in the complete absence of endearing habitual contact.

It is not clear why Nerestan, in Act III, received with astonishment as well as rage the news that Zaïre had intended to marry Orosmanes, when he had already known, and spoken regretfully at the beginning of Act II, of the love between them; but it creates a theatrically effective scene.

The fact is that in France, as in England, there is a fundamental difference—indeed, much the same difference—between the tragedies of the great national dramatic period and those of the period that followed it. Despite their mannerisms and artificialities—or, we may say, through the distorting prism of their mannerisms and artificialities—the French dramatists of the seventeenth century were trying to depict human life as they conceived it was or had been or might be. But the writers of tragedy in eighteenth-century France, like those in Restoration and post-Restoration England, endeavored to put on the stage not a representation of life, however idealized or conventionalized, but some concoction of stereotyped theatricalities. In England, even when so great a man as Dryden is at his best in *All for Love,* his characters are lay figures in a stage world; and just as even Dryden failed in England, even Voltaire could not succeed in France.

Yet in spite of all their faults—the invariable melodrama, the stock stage devices, the conventionalized psychology— Voltaire's greatness appears now and then in his dramas. The influence of Shakespeare upon him is strikingly shown in the scene in which Orosmanes awaits the coming of Zaïre, that he may kill her, where the deliberate creation of "atmosphere" and of suspense produces effects hitherto unknown in French tragedy. Occasionally Voltaire displays a breadth of historical vision, a firm grasp of the essence of a matter, and a sweep of imagination which it would be difficult to find even in Corneille or Racine. Orosmanes' depiction of the weak, sensual Moslem rulers whom he refuses to imitate is an instance in point. Lusignan's eloquent appeal to Zaïre is likely to seem, to an unthinking audience, adequate for her conversion; for, since it occurs before the second act is concluded, the audience itself has known of her love for Orosmanes only a little longer than it has known that Lusignan is her father, and there are few finer pieces of rhetoric in French drama.

CHARACTERS IN THE PLAY

OROSMANES, *Sultan of Jerusalem.*
LUSIGNAN, *the last Christian king of Jerusalem, now a prisoner of Orosmanes.*
ZAÏRE, *a young slave-girl of the Sultan.*
FATIMA, *a slave-woman of the Sultan.*
NERESTAN, *a young French knight.*
CHATILLON, *one of Lusignan's knights, like him a prisoner.*
CORASMIN, *chief officer of the Sultan.*
MELEDOR, *another officer of the Sultan.*
Slaves.

The scene represents a room or inner court in the seraglio of the Sultan, in Jerusalem.

The names "Orosmanes" and "Corasmin" are accented on the next to the last syllable; "Lusignan," "Nerestan," and "Chatillon" on the first syllable. "Zaïre" rhymes with "Hah, here." The name "Fatima" is properly accented on the first syllable, but so much more customarily on the second syllable that care has been taken in this translation to use it so that it will accord fairly well with the metre if pronounced either way.

Zaïre

ACT I

ZAÏRE and FATIMA are discovered.

FATIMA. Fair young Zaïre, I did not think to see
The change of feelings which this place breeds in thee.
What flattering hopes or happy fortunes turned
Thy gloomy days into unclouded days?
Thy heart's peace, like thy charms, grows ever greater.
Thy bright eyes are no longer dimmed with tears,
And look no longer towards those blessed climes
Where that brave Frenchman was to lead our steps.
Thou speakest to me no more of those fair lands
Where women, reverenced by a courtly people,
Receive the homage due their loveliness,
Companions of their husbands, and queens always,
Pure though unwatched, prudent though unconstrained,
And virtuous not because of any fear.
Dost thou no longer yearn to have such freedom?
Is the seraglio of a Sultan, is
Its strict seclusion, is the name of "slave"
Not bitter to thee? Dost thou, then, prefer
Jerusalem to the borders of the Seine?
ZAÏRE. One cannot yearn for what one knows not of.
Heaven stayed our footsteps on the Jordan's banks.
An inmate of this palace from my childhood,
I every day grow more accustomed to it.
Earth's other regions, blotted out for me,
Have left me subject to the Sultan's power.
I know but him, his glory and his might.
With life 'neath Orosmanes my one prospect,
All else is a vain dream.
FATIMA.   Hast thou forgotten
That noble Frenchman who with tender fondness
So often promised he would break our fetters?
How greatly we admired his lofty courage!
What honor his in those disastrous battles
The Christians lost before Damascus' walls!
Victorious Orosmanes praised his bravery
And let him leave this country on parole.
We wait for his return; his generous purpose

561

Was to come back and buy our liberty.
Can we have cherished but an empty hope?

ZAïRE.　Perhaps he promised more than he could do.
Two years have passed, and he has not returned.
A foreigner, an unknown prisoner,
Promises much, Fatima, and keeps little
Of it. He lets himself make rash vows, hoping
Thus to escape from his captivity.
He was to bring ten Christian knights their freedom,—
Strike off their chains or reassume his own.
Wrongly have I admired such fruitless zeal.
Think of him not.

FATIMA.　　　　　　But what if he kept faith,—
If he appeared here and fulfilled his oaths?
Wouldst thou not wish . . .

ZAïRE.　　　　　　　Fatima, 'tis too late.
All is changed . . .

FATIMA.　　　　　　How now! What dost thou mean?

ZAïRE.　I cannot hide my destiny from thee.
The Sultan's secret still should be preserved,
But 'tis my heart's joy to confide in thee.
Whilst thou, with other captives, wert compelled
To leave for some three months the Jordan's shores,
Kind heaven, to end our lives' unhappiness,
Hath chosen to save us by a mightier hand.
Great Orosmanes . . .

FATIMA.　　　　　Say on.

ZAïRE.　　　　　　　Our own Sultan,
The Christians' conqueror . . . dear Fatima . . . he
Loves me. . . . Thou blushest . . . I understand thee . . . Think
　　　not
That I could stoop to trying to win his love
Or that a haughty master offered me
The shameful honor of the rank of favorite
And I would bear the indignity and dangers
Of mere indulgence of his transient passion.
That pride which breeds our maidenly reserve
Has not been brought to naught within my breast.
Rather than to abase myself so much,
I would not blench at shackles or the grave.
I shall amaze thee now: his lofty soul
Offers to my poor charms a true devotion.
Amid so many who are fain to please him
I keep his glance fixed upon me alone,

And marriage will confound their threatening intrigues
And make me queen over his heart and them.
FATIMA. Thy charms, thy virtues, deserve this reward,
And I am more delighted than surprised.
May thy felicity, God grant, be perfect!
I shall be glad to be among thy subjects.
ZAÏRE. My equal always! Sharing my good fortune
With thee, I shall the better know its sweetness.
FATIMA. May heaven allow this marriage to be sealed!
Oh, may this greatness which is destined for thee,
So often falsely declared happiness,
Leave in thy bosom's inmost core no turmoil!
Is there no secret qualm that holds thee back?
Does naught now tell thee thou wert once a Christian?
ZAÏRE. Ah me! what sayest thou! why recall my troubles?
Do I, alas, know who I am, Fatima?
Has heaven e'er permitted me to know?
Has it not veiled from me my origin?
FATIMA. Nerestan, who was born not far from here,
Told me thou wert of Christian parentage.
Nay, more than this; the cross which was found on thee,—
Childhood's adornment, since preserved with care,—
That Christian symbol which the art that shaped
The lovely ornament withheld from notice,—
That cross with which I countless times have decked thee,—
Perhaps hath still remained in thy possession
As secret evidence of the loyalty
Thou owest to that God thou hast forsaken.
ZAÏRE. Without more proof, can my untutored heart
Accept a God whom he I love abhors?
Custom and laws of State inclined my youth
Unto the faith of the triumphant Moslems.
I see this: that according to our rearing
Our feeling, conduct, and beliefs are formed.
Beside the Ganges I could but have served
Idols, in Paris Christ, and here Mahomet.
How we are taught does all; our father's hand
Writes in our childish hearts those earliest lessons
Which time and those about us write again
And which perhaps God only can efface.
Thou wert not made a captive in this land
Till reason, strengthened by maturity,
Left thee its torch to light thee to thy faith.
I from my very cradle was a slave

Of the Saracens; too late did I learn aught
Concerning the religion of you Christians.
Yet, far from being prejudiced against it,
I oft have by that cross, I shall confess,
Been moved, despite myself, to fear and reverence.
I even dared invoke it, ere the image
Of Orosmanes filled my secret thoughts.
I honor, I hold dear, those laws of love
Which Nerestan so often told me of—
Those laws which, ridding earth of misery,
Make those whose hearts are softened be as brothers.
Sweetly united thus, they must be happy.

FATIMA.　Why dost thou range thyself against them, then?
Today thou art to assume the yoke forever
Of Moslem law and be the foe of Christians.
Thou art to wed their haughty conqueror.

ZAÏRE.　Who would refuse to accept his offered heart?
My frailty I must needs admit. Perchance,
Had I not loved, I would have been a Christian.
Perchance I would have bowed unto your law.
But Orosmanes loves me, and all else
Now is forgotten. I see but Orosmanes,
And my enraptured soul is ever filled
With happiness, knowing I am adored.
Before thine own eyes set his charm, his exploits.
Think of his arm, victor o'er many monarchs,
His gracious countenance girt round with glory!
I speak not of the throne he offers me;
Nay, gratitude is but a feeble thing,
Offensively inadequate for love.
My heart loves Orosmanes—not his crown,
Dearest Fatima, but himself alone.
Mayhap I cherish too fondly this sweet fancy,
But if toward him heaven had been cruel and doomed him
To slavery's chains like those that I have worn,
And had placed Syria beneath my sway,
Either my love deceives me or today,
To raise him to me, I would stoop to him.

FATIMA.　Someone approaches. Doubtless 'tis himself.

ZAÏRE.　My prescient heart informs me it is he:
After his two-days' absence from the palace,
His love restores him to my longing eyes.

Enter OROSMANES.

ZAIRE

OROSMANES. Sweet, pure Zaïre, before the rites of marriage
Forever join our fortunes and our hearts,
I think I ought to speak about my plans,
My love, and thee quite frankly, as a Moslem.
  Our sultans, unto whom earth bows, their customs
And privileges, I take not for examples.
I know our laws, indulgent to our pleasures,
Open a boundless field to our desires.
I can be prodigal of my caresses,
With concubines to serve me, if I choose,
And at my ease in the seraglio can
Declare my will and rule my realm from there.
But if effeminate indolence is sweet,
Grievous are its results. I see about me
A hundred kings brought low by it. I see
Degenerate successors of Mahomet,
Caliphs who tremble midst their tawdry splendors
Upon the wreck of altar and of throne,
Powerless in all but name, in Babylon—
Those who would still be, as their sires had been,
The masters of the world if they were like them!
  Bouillon took Jerusalem and Syria
From them; but soon, to punish our faith's foes,
God armed the hand of mighty Saladin.
After his death, my father regained Jordan.
Now I, the weak heir of his new-won greatness,
The doubtful lord of an unstable kingdom,
See these bold Christians, all athirst for rapine,
Drawn from the shores of Europe to our shores;
And when the trumpet and the voice of war
Reverberate from the Euxine to the Nile,
I will not be the slave of sensual passions,
Abandoning myself to the soft life
Of a seraglio. By mine own fair fame
I swear, and by Zaïre and my love's flame,
To have but thee for wife and my heart's mistress,
To be thy friend, thy lover, and thy husband,
And to devote myself to war and thee.
  Deem not that to preserve my honor I
Entrust thy virtue to those Asian monsters,
Those odious guardians of a sultan's harem
And vile abettors of their master's lusts.
I have no less esteem than love for thee,
And, confident of thy chaste nature, leave

565

My honor in thy hands. Such an avowal
Hath shown thee all my heart. Thou knowest that I
Have placed my happiness wholly in thy keeping.
Thou knowest well what bitterness would infect
The rest of my thenceforth abhorrent life
If thou didst not receive the gifts I give thee
With other feelings than mere gratitude.
Zaïre, I love thee, and I expect from thee
A love that answers to my own's white heat.
I shall confess, naught else would satisfy me.
If I were loved but little, I would imagine
That I was hated. All of my emotions
Are violent. I beyond measure wish
To love thee and find favor in thy sight.
If with an equal love thy heart is filled,
I come to wed thee, but on this condition
Alone, and if our ventured marriage bond
Does not make thee happy, 'twill make me wretched.

ZAÏRE. Thou, my lord, wretched! Ah, if thy great soul
Can find its happiness in my love,—if truly
Thy fate depends upon my inmost feelings,—
What mortal e'er was happier than thou art?
Those dear and holy names, beloved and lover,
Belong to both of us, and I have, moreover,
This joy, so sweet to my unbounded love,
Of owing all to him whom I adore,
Of seeing his kindness the sole architect
Of my good fortune, of being the work of his
Noble hands, and of reverencing and loving
A hero I admire. Yes, if among
The hearts that were submissive to thy sway
Thou couldst discern how much mine worshipped thee
And if thy choice august . . .

Enter CORASMIN.

CORASMIN.   That Christian slave
Who was paroled, my lord, and went to France
Has just returned, and asks an audience.

FATIMA. Ah, heaven!

OROSMANES.   He may enter. Why does he
Not come?

CORASMIN.   He stayed his steps in the outer court.
I did not think that in this privy place
A Christian should appear before thy face.

OROSMANES.   Nay, let him come. Anyone, anywhere,
 Can henceforth without disrespect appear
 Before me. I despise those laws which make
 Invisible tyrants of so many sovereigns.

 Exit CORASMIN. *He re-enters with* NERESTAN.

NERESTAN.   Most noble foe, esteemed by every Christian,
 I come back to acquit us of our oaths.
 I have fulfilled all mine; the rest is thine
 To do. I bring the ransom unto thee
 Of Zaïre and Fatima and ten knights,
 Illustrious captives in Jerusalem.
 Their freedom, which I have delayed too long,
 Was to be given them on my re-appearance.
 Keep thy word, Sultan; they are thine no more,
 For at this very moment I have freed them.
 But when their fetters, thanks to my endeavor,
 Are broken by the payment of their ransom,
 My fortune will be wholly spent, and I
 (To hide naught) must forego the hope of doing
 Then for myself what I have done for them.
 Nothing but poverty is left me. I
 Have saved these Christians from their dolorous prison,
 Have satisfied my honor, oaths, and duty;
 I am content, and come to place myself,
 A prisoner and a hostage, in thy hands.
OROSMANES.   Christian, thy lofty spirit pleases me,
 But shall it now be flattered by surpassing
 In magnanimity great Orosmanes?
 Take back thy liberty; take home the gold
 Thou broughtest for ransoms and yet more, my gift.
 Instead of the ten Christians that I promised,
 I will accord to thee a hundred; choose them.
 They shall go hence with thee, to teach thy country
 That there are virtues to be found in Syria,—
 That they may judge, in going, who deserve
 (The French or I) the lordship o'er this land.
 But Lusignan was never meant to be
 Among those Christians whom I would set free.
 He alone cannot be surrendered to thee.
 His name would be a menace to my throne.
 He is of that French line that ruled Jerusalem.
 His right to wear my crown is known; this right
 Must be adjudged a crime—such is the cruel

Decree of Destiny, that shapeth all things.
Had I been vanquished, I would be the criminal.
Lusignan needs must end his days in chains
And never look upon the sun again.
I pity him; but blame thou necessity
For this one act of cruelty and vengeance.
As for Zaïre, credit me, without taking
Offense: no price within thy power can buy her.
All your French knights and all their overlords
Would league themselves in vain to take her from me.
Thou mayest depart.

NERESTAN.   What! She was born a Christian.
I have thy word, and hers, that she should go.
And Lusignan, that hapless, agèd man—
Could he . . .

OROSMANES.   I have made known to thee my will,
Christian. I honor thy nobility,
But this proud mood of thine, while it compels
Esteem, begins to be displeasing to me.
Go. Let the sun, rising o'er my domains
Tomorrow, find thee nowhere near the Jordan.

                           [Exit NERESTAN.

FATIMA.   Save us, O God!

OROSMANES.   And thou, Zaïre, now go
And assume power over the seraglio
As the Sultana. I must give my orders
About the marriage rites that are to crown thee.

                   [Exeunt ZAÏRE *and* FATIMA.
What is it, Corasmin, that this infidel
Slave seeks? He sighed. His eyes were fixed on her.
Didst thou not see?

CORASMIN.   What sayest thou, my lord!
Dost thou give heed to jealous false suspicions?

OROSMANES.   I, jealous? Stoop, with all my pride, so low?
Endure the misery of such shameful torture?
Love with a love that is like hatred—I?
Suspicion and distrust invite betrayal.
I see her whom I love swayed by love only.
I idolize her, my Corasmin,—love her
With love far greater than my favors shown her.
I am not jealous . . . if I ever were . . .
If my breast . . . Ah, hence with such hateful thoughts!
Happiness pure and sweet reigns in my soul.
Go; prepare all things for that blissful moment

Which will unite me with my heart's desire.
I shall devote one hour to my realm's care
Today—its other hours all to Zaïre.

A C T   I I

NERESTAN *and* CHATILLON *are discovered.*

CHATILLON.   O noble Nerestan, brave knight who hast broken
    The shackles of so many wretched captives,
    Saver of Christians, sent by God who saved us,
    Come forth and show thyself; taste the sweet pleasure
    Of seeing our comrades, weeping, kneel and kiss
    Thy blessed hand, which hath delivered us.
    They clamor for thee, thronging at the gates
    Of the seraglio. Come, do not deprive them
    Of all sight of the hero they await.
    May they, united under their deliverer . . .
NERESTAN.   Illustrious Chatillon, praise me not so highly.
    I have but done my duty as a Frenchman—
    What thou wouldst do if thou wert in my place.
CHATILLON.   True. Every Christian, every worthy knight,
    Should sacrifice himself for his religion,
    And the felicity of hearts like ours
    Lies in self-sacrifice for the good of others.
    Happy are they to whom God gives the power
    Of doing such a duty as thou didst.
    We, the poor playthings of relentless Fate,
    Unhappy Frenchmen, prisoners in Jerusalem,
    Forgotten in our chains, to which the father
    Of Orosmanes doomed us long ago,
    Save for thee never would see France again.
NERESTAN.   God deigned, sir, to use me. His providence
    Softened the heart of this young Orosmanes.
    But what ill fortune with the good is mingled!
    What fearful bitterness the false clemency
    Of this proud sultan mingles with his favors!
    God sees me, hears me; *he* knows if my heart
    Cherishes any aims but those that seek
    His glory. All I did was in his service.
    I hoped to lead to him a lovely maiden
    Who in her infancy was made a slave,
    As I was, by the cruel Noureddyn
    When, after bathing Syria with our blood,

The enemies of the true faith surprised
The vanquished Lusignan in Caesarea.
Rescued by Christians from the Sultan's palace,
Once more a prisoner here three years ago,
Sent back to Paris on my word alone,
Sir, I beguiled myself with the vain dream
Of bringing back Zaïre to that blest Court
Which Louis makes the sojourn of his virtues.
The Queen already, at my prayer, was stretching
Her own hand from the throne for her protection
And finally, when the longed-for moment came
Which should release her from captivity,
She was refused me—nay, Zaïre herself,
Forgetting Christians for the Sultan's love . . .
Let us think no more of it . . . Sir, a crueler
Refusal further crushes me with woe.
The unhappy Christians' hope hath been betrayed.

CHATILLON.   For them I offer thee my liberty,
My life. Dispose of it. It belongs to thee.

NERESTAN.   Our Lusignan, held in Jerusalem,
This last of all his line of mighty heroes,
This warrior whose fame once filled the world,
This hapless king descended from great Bouillon,
Is not to be surrendered to the longings
Of Christendom.

CHATILLON.   Sir, if thus matters stand,
Thy boon to me is futile. What base soldier
Would break his fetters when his lord still lies
In chains? Thou never knewest Lusignan,
But I did. Sir, thank heaven, whose clemency
Has for thy happier fortune placed thy birth
Long after those forever cursed days,
Those days of slaughter and calamity,
In which I saw our savage masters' yoke
Fall on these sacred walls our fathers conquered.
Ah, hadst thou seen this temple yielded up,
The sepulcher of the God we serve profaned,
Our sires, our babes, our daughters, and our wives
Perishing in the flames before our altars,
And our last king, bowed with the weight of years,
Slain without pity, on his dying sons!
Lusignan, sole survivor of that race
Restored our courage in those ghastly moments.
Amidst the wreckage of the shrines o'erthrown,

The conquerors, the conquered, the heaped dead,
Terrible, grasping in one hand a sword
Which every moment bathed in Moslem blood
And in the other carrying, held aloft,
The dreaded standard of our holy faith,
He cried with a loud voice: "Frenchmen, be steadfast . . ."
Then certainly the power of the Most High,
Which saves us now, sheltered him with its wings,
Made smooth his passage-way, and went before him;
And the sad multitude of rescued Christians
Bent their steps, following us, to Caesarea.
    There Lusignan was, by the common voice
Of all our knights, chosen to rule o'er us.
Ah, my dear Nerestan, God, who humbles man,
Beyond doubt did not wish in this short life
To give us the reward deserved by virtue.
Vainly had we done battle for his sake.
Dire memory, whose horror still o'erwhelms me!
Jerusalem, laid in ashes, was yet smoking
When our fierce foes attacked us in our place
Of refuge, and a vile Greek's treachery
Delivered us into their hands. The flames
By which of late Zion had been consumed
Now raged in Caesarea. There did thirty
Disastrous years come to their final climax.
There I saw Lusignan, bound with shameful gyves,
Great in defeat, unheedful of his downfall;
He was moved only by his brethren's woes.
    Sir, since that time, this father of his people,
Confined apart from us, grown grey in chains,
Has languished in a dungeon, without light,
Forgotten by all Asia and all Europe.
Such is his fearful lot. Who can, when he
Suffers for us, be happy without him!
NERESTAN.   Happiness, it is true, would prove one cruel.
How I abhor the fate that keeps him from us!
How thy words make my heart go out to him!
I know his woes—have known them since my birth.
I ne'er have heard them told without fresh pangs.
Thy shackles, his, and Caesarea in ashes
Are the first sights, the first unhappy things,
That smote upon my still scarce opened eyes.
I grew to manhood; these dread pictures still
Rise up before me at thy harrowing story.

ZAIRE

> From Christians slaughtered in a certain shrine,
> Some children, sir, were gathered, I among them,
> Torn from blood-spattered arms of trembling mothers
> By hands that reeked with carnage. We were brought
> Into this royal palace, into this
> Seraglio in which I behold thee now.
> Noureddyn reared me beside this Zaïre
> Who since—forgive my heart-felt sigh—who since
> Hath gone astray in this accursed place
> And for a barbarous master hath forsaken
> Her God!

CHATILLON.   Such is the Moslems' baleful practice,
> Corrupting Christian captives while yet children;
> And I give thanks to heaven, propitious to us,
> That in thy first years saved thee from their clutches.
> But after all, sir, this Zaïre herself,
> Who hath renounced Christ for the Sultan's love,
> Might lend us succor with her influence.
> What matters it of what arm God makes use?
> Wilt thou not credit me? Just men as well
> As wise men know how to avail themselves
> Of crime and of calamity, to help them.
> Thou mightest employ the favor of Zaïre
> To bend the will, to touch the lordly heart,
> Of Orosmanes to restore to us
> A hero whom he ought, himself, to pity,—
> Whom doubtless he admires, and who no longer
> Is to be feared.

NERESTAN.   But would that hero wish us
> To stoop to such vile means to break his bonds?
> And if he wished this, is it in my power
> To gain one moment's audience with Zaïre?
> Thinkest thou that Orosmanes would consent?
> Would the seraglio open to my voice?
> And if I finally could appear before her,
> What could be hoped for from this recreant woman
> Who ought to feel affronted at my sight,
> Reading her shame inscribed upon my face?
> Sir, 'tis indeed hard for a lofty heart
> To look for aid from those whom it despises.
> One dreads rebuffs; one blushes at their boons.

CHATILLON.   Think of Lusignan! think of serving him!

NERESTAN.   Well . . . But what way to reach that faithless girl?
> Could . . . Someone nears. What see I? Heavens! 'tis she.

ZAIRE

Enter ZAÏRE.

ZAÏRE (*to* NERESTAN). 'Tis thou, brave Frenchman, whom I come
    to speak with.
  The Sultan grants me leave; have no misgivings.
  But reassure me, who, when I approach thee,
  Tremble; and with mute gaze no more reproach me.
  We fear each other, sir; our cheeks burn crimson.
  I both desire and dread to meet thine eyes.
    We were from birth attached to one another.
  A horrid prison held us in our childhood.
  Fate crushed us with the burden of like chains,
  Which our affection's dearness made less heavy.
  Later, I had to sorrow o'er thine absence.
  Heaven bore thy footsteps to the shores of France.
  Finally I saw thee here again a prisoner;
  Freer association then was ours.
  One of a throng of slaves and lost among them,
  I lived unnoticed by the Sultan's glance.
  Whether 'twere from nobility or pity
  Or rather the result of sincere fondness
  For me, thou soon vouchsafedst to return
  To the fair kingdom of the French, to seek there
  The ransom of the unfortunate Zaïre.
  Thou bringest it; but heaven hath made vain
  Thy efforts. In Jerusalem, far from thee,
  It stays my steps forever. But no matter
  What splendors or what charms my fortune has,
  I cannot leave thee without shedding tears.
  I shall think always of thy kindness to me,
  Cherish the tender memory of thy virtues,
  Like thee alleviate human misery,
  Protect all Christians, be a mother to them.
  Thou makest them dear to me, and these unhappy . . .
NERESTAN. Protect them? thou, who dost abandon them,—
  Who spurnest the ashes of the Lusignans . . .
ZAÏRE. I come to honor them and restore to you
  The last of all that line, for whom ye sigh.
  Lusignan is released, and ye shall see him.
CHATILLON. What! we shall see again our king, our father?
NERESTAN. We Christians owe to thee one we so love?
ZAÏRE. I ventured, with scant hope, to beg his freedom.
  The generous Sultan grudged him not to us.
  He is led hither.

ZAIRE

NERESTAN.   How my heart is moved!

ZAÏRE.   My tears, despite me, hide him from mine eyes.
Like this old man, I, too, have pined in chains.
We feel for one with woes that we have suffered.

NERESTAN.   Great God! what goodness in a paynim's soul!

Enter LUSIGNAN, *supported by Christian slaves.*

LUSIGNAN.   What voice recalls me from the abode of death?
Am I with Christians? Guide my trembling steps.
My woes, more than my years, have made me weak.
[He sinks into a seat.
Am I indeed free?

ZAÏRE.   Yes, sir. Yes, thou art.

CHATILLON.   Thou livest, thou allayest our ceaseless sorrows.
All our sad Christians . . .

LUSIGNAN.   O glad day! that voice!
Chatillon, is it thou? Again I see thee!
We both were martyred for our fathers' faith,
And does the God we serve now end our woes?
In what place are we? Aid my feeble eyes.

CHATILLON.   This is the palace of thine ancestors.
Noureddyn's son profanes it, dwelling in it.

ZAÏRE.   The master here, the mighty Orosmanes,
Can recognize true worth and love it, sir.
(*Indicating* NERESTAN) This gallant Frenchman, who is un-
known to thee,
Led here by honor from the shores of France,
Just now has paid the ransom of ten Christians.
The Sultan, moved like him by honor, would
By freeing thee match his nobility.

LUSIGNAN.   Such is the nature of French knights. Their greatness
Of heart was always dear and useful to me.
Thou worthy knight! didst thou cross o'er the sea
To succor us in our woe and break our bonds?
Oh, speak! whom must I thank for such a deed?

NERESTAN.   My name is Nerestan. Fortune, long cruel,
Which placed me here in chains, almost at birth,
Soon let me leave the empire of the Crescent.
Led by my heart to Louis' court, I served
Under him my apprenticeship in war.
My wealth and rank were given me by this sovereign
So great in valor and greater still in faith.
I followed him to the banks of the Charente,
Where the proud English, with their dreaded prowess,

574

Succumbing to our might held long in leash,
Bowed to the lilies which they had defied.
Come, sire, and to earth's greatest monarch show
The scars of chains which do thee honor. Paris
Will reverence the martyr of the Cross,
And at the Court of Louis kings find refuge.
LUSIGNAN.   Ah, once I knew the glory of that Court.
When Philip at Bouvines made victory his,
I fought beside Melun, sir, Montmorency,
D'Estaign, de Nesle, and the far-famed Coucy.
But I must not hope to go back to Paris.
Thou seest how I stand on my grave's brink.
I go this day to ask the King of kings
For the reward of all the woes I suffered
For him. Ye witnesses of my last hour,
While there is still time left me, hear my prayer.
Nerestan, Chatillon . . . and thou whose tears
Honor my misery in these precious moments,
Madam, have pity on the most wretched father
That ever hath endured the wrath of heaven,—
Who sheds before thee tears of which time hath not
E'en yet been able to drain his dying eyes.
A daughter and three sons, my hope and pride,
Were taken from me in their infancy.
Ah, my dear Chatillon, thou shouldst remember!
CHATILLON.   I shudder still at thy misfortunes.
LUSIGNAN.   Captured
Like me amid the flames of Caesarea,
Thou sawest my wife and two of my sons perish.
CHATILLON.   Laden with chains, I could not succor them.
LUSIGNAN.   Alas! and I, a father, could not die!
Dear children mine in heaven, watch o'er, I beg you,
My other children if they still are living.
My youngest son, my daughter, saved to wear
The yoke of slavery by cruel hands, were both
Carried off from their father to this same
Seraglio in which heaven reunites us.
CHATILLON.   'Tis true. Amid the horrors of that final
Disaster, in mine arms I held thy daughter,
Who had not long been born; and since I could not
Save her, my liege, I was myself about
To sprinkle on her brow the holy water
Of baptism, when the Saracens came, reeking
With blood, to snatch her from my bleeding grasp.

575

Thy youngest son, to whom Fate had permitted
Scarce more than four years yet, but who e'en then
Was all too able to realize his plight,
Was with his sister taken to Jerusalem.

NERESTAN.   With what sad memories my soul is torn!
I at that same age was in Caesarea,
Alas, and, smeared with blood and bound with fetters,
I followed there the throng of Christian captives.

LUSIGNAN.   Thou, sir? . . . Thou wert brought up in this seraglio?

[*He looks searchingly at* NERESTAN *and* ZAÏRE.
Ah me! did you have knowledge of my children?
They were of your age, and perhaps mine eyes . . .
(*Spying the cross which* ZAÏRE *wears*) What a strange orna-
ment, madam, to wear here!
'Tis thine since when?

ZAÏRE.   Ever since I was born, sir.
How now! whence comes it that thou sighest so?

LUSIGNAN.   Ah, to my trembling hands deign to entrust . . .

ZAÏRE (*giving him the cross*).   Into what turmoil now is my mind
thrown?

[LUSIGNAN, *weeping, raises the cross to his lips.*
Sir, what is this thou doest?

LUSIGNAN.   O God on high!
Mine eyes, do not beguile my timorous hopes.
Could this be . . . ? yes, it is the same. I see
The very gift which to my wife I gave
And which adorned the heads of all my children
When we would celebrate their natal day.
I well recall . . . But feeling overcomes me.

ZAÏRE.   What do I hear? and what conjecture now
Makes my heart throb? Ah, sir . . .

LUSIGNAN.   Let the sweet hope
I glimpse not fail me, God, who seest my tears,
Who diedst upon the cross and livest again
For us! Speak. Make all clear. This is Thy doing.
What, madam! it hath been always in thy hands?
Ye both were prisoners, taken in Caesarea?

ZAÏRE.   Yes, sir.

NERESTAN.   Is it possible?

LUSIGNAN.   Their speech, their features,
Are living counterparts of their dear mother's.
Great God, thou wishest, makest, me to see it.
Strengthen me. For such joy I am too weak.
Madam . . . Nerestan . . . thine arm, Chatillon!

Nerestan, if by that name I must call thee,
Hast thou—God grant it!—on thy breast a scar
Which mine eyes saw a sword in a fierce hand . . .
NERESTAN.   Yes, I do have one, sir.
LUSIGNAN.   Just God! Glad moment!
NERESTAN.   Oh, sir! Oh, Zaïre!
LUSIGNAN.   Come to me, my children!
NERESTAN.   I, thy son!
ZAÏRE.   Sir!
LUSIGNAN.   Glad day that gives me light!
My daughter! my dear son! embrace your father.
                                  [*They embrace him.*
CHATILLON.   How much so great good fortune moves my heart!
LUSIGNAN.   I scarce can tear myself, now, from your arms,
My children. I at last again behold you,
Dear hapless remnant of my family.
Thou, my son, worthy heir . . . thou . . . alas, thou,
My daughter, free me from my dread suspicions.
Dispel their horror, which makes my senses reel,—
Which crushes me amidst my crowning bliss.
    Thou who alone hast ruled her fate and mine,
My God, who givest her back to me, dost thou
Give back to me a Christian?
                          Wretched girl,
Thou weepest! Thou avertest thine eyes! Thou'rt silent!
I understand. O guilt! O righteous heaven!
ZAÏRE.   I cannot lie to thee; 'neath Orosmanes . . .
Punish thy daughter . . . she was a Mahometan.
LUSIGNAN.   May thunder's bolt fall only upon me!
Ah, my son, without thee I should have died
At those words. For thy glory, God, have I
Fought sixty years. I have seen thy temple fall
And the memory of thee perish. Languishing
For twenty years within a fearful dungeon,
With tears I have implored thee to protect
My hapless children; and when through thy power
We are again united and I find
A daughter—lo, she is thine enemy!
    I am indeed most wretched. 'Tis thy father,
'Tis I, 'tis my imprisonment, naught else,
Which reft thee of thy faith. Dear daughter mine,
Thou source of my last cares, think, think at least,
What blood flows in thy veins. It is the blood
Of twenty kings, all Christians like myself;

It is the blood of heroes, the defenders
Of heaven's law; it is the blood of martyrs . . .
O daughter still so dear! knowest thou what portion
Was thine? Dost thou know who thy mother was?
Dost thou indeed know that within the moment
When she gave birth to this sad final fruit
Of our ill-fated love I saw her slaughtered
By a fell hand, the hand of the same brigands
With whom thou joinest thy destiny? Thy brothers,
Those martyrs slain before mine eyes, hold out
Their bleeding arms to thee from heaven's height.
Thy God, whom thou betrayest, whom thou blasphemest,
Died in this very place, for thee, for all men—
Here, where mine arm so often served his cause!
Here, where his blood calls to thee by my voice!
    Behold these walls; behold this sacred temple
Seized by thy masters—all proclaims the God
Thine ancestors avenged. Look round about thee:
His tomb is near this palace; yonder stands
The mountain where, to wash our sins away,
He perished at the hands of impious men;
Yonder he rose, victorious, from his tomb.
Thou canst not walk within this holy place—
Thou canst not take one step—and not find there
Thy God; and neither canst thou here remain
Without denying thy father, and thy honor
Which claims thee, and thy God who lights thy path.
    I see thee in my arms, sobbing and trembling.
In thy white face the Lord shows thy repentance.
I see his truth implanted in thy heart.
I find once more my daughter I had lost,
And am possessed again of peace and pride
In having saved my child from unbelief.

NERESTAN.   I rebehold my sister, then. Her soul . . .

ZAÏRE.   Father, dear author of my days, oh, tell me,
    What must I do?

LUSIGNAN.   With but a single word
    Rid me of shame and misery. Say this:
    "I am a Christian."

ZAÏRE.   Yes . . . I am one . . . sir.

LUSIGNAN.   God, in thy realm above, hear her confess thee.

Enter CORASMIN.

CORASMIN.   Madam, the Sultan bids me say to thee

That thou must withdraw hence immediately
And, above all, have done with these vile Christians.
     Ye, Frenchmen, follow me. I yet must hold you.
CHATILLON.   How now! What thunderbolt, Lord God, confounds us!
LUSIGNAN.   Our courage, dear ones, must be greater still.
ZAÏRE.   Alas, sir!
LUSIGNAN (*to* ZAÏRE).   O thou whom I dare not rightly
     Call, swear to me to keep this dangerous secret.
ZAÏRE.   I swear it.
LUSIGNAN.   Go, and leave the rest to heaven.
       [*Exeunt*, ZAÏRE *on one side, the others on the other.*

A C T   I I I

OROSMANES *and* CORASMIN *are discovered.*

OROSMANES.   Thou wert deceived, Corasmin, by thy fears.
    No, Louis hath not turned his arms against me.
    The French will henceforth have had quite enough
    Of seeking climes which Fate ne'er made for them.
    They nevermore will leave their native land
    To languish in the deserts of Arabia
    And come to water with their cursed blood
    These palms which God made flourish here for us.
    They cover with their ships the seas off Syria.
    Louis hath from the coast of Cyprus caused
    Much fear in Asia. But I am informed
    That this king hies himself far from our ports,
    Threatening instead the shores of fertile Egypt.
    I have just now heard the first news of it.
    Against the Mamelukes his courage calls him.
    My secret foe, Meledin, is his quarry.
    My throne is made securer by their strife.
    I need no more dread either France or Egypt.
    Thus our two enemies join in cementing
    My power and, lavish of the blood they should
    Conserve, are at great pains, by slaughtering
    Each other, to avenge me on them both.
     Release these Christians, friend. I grant them freedom.
    I wish to please their king and let them live.
    I wish them to be sent to him at sea
    That Louis may know me and respect my pledges.
    Take Lusignan to him. Tell him I give him
    One who by birth was to his crown allied,

One whom my father vanquished twice, and whom
He held in chains till he himself was dead.

CORASMIN.   His name, to Christians dear . . .

OROSMANES.   Need not be feared.

CORASMIN.   But, sir, if Louis . . .

OROSMANES.   I can feign no longer.
Zaïre so willed; that was enough. When I
Surrendered Lusignan, 'twas to my conqueror.
Of Louis I reck little; all I do
Is for Zaïre. None else could thus have had
Dominion o'er my heart. I have just brought
Pain to her, and 'tis now my task to lessen
The sore distress which she must needs have felt
When, on false tidings of the French king's plans,
I did these Christians some small violence.
Nay, more—the moments wasted with my counselors
Have stayed the preparations for our marriage.
By a whole hour my bliss must be deferred,
But 'twill at least be spent in pleasing her.
She asks to have a private conversation
Here with this Nerestan, this noble Christian . . .

CORASMIN.   And art thou so indulgent as to grant it?

OROSMANES.   They both were slaves in childhood; both have worn
My chains; and they will never meet again.
Zaïre, besides, would hear to no refusal.
I cannot say her nay. I cast aside
For her the harsh restraint of the seraglio.
I have disdained those laws whose stringency
Makes of sad virtue a necessity.
No Asiatic blood flows in my veins.
Born in the rocky heart of Tauria,
I have the fierce pride of my Scythian fathers,
Their habits, passions, magnanimity.
I shall let Nerestan, ere going, see her.
I in my joy wish happiness for all.
After these moments stolen from my love,
Her every hour is mine irrevocably.
Go, friend; this Christian waits. Thou mayest admit him.
Speed their meeting, as Zaïre desires.   [*Exit* OROSMANES.

CORASMIN *opens the door and admits* NERESTAN.

CORASMIN.   Here for a moment thou again canst bide.
Zaïre will soon appear before thy sight.

                                    [*Exit* CORASMIN.

NERESTAN. In what a state and what a place I leave her!
Oh, my religion! father! sister dear!
But here she is.

Enter ZAÏRE.

My sister, I can, then,
Talk with thee. Ah, under what circumstances
It hath pleased heaven to reunite us now!
Thou wilt no more behold thy hapless father.

ZAÏRE. O God! Lusignan . . .

NERESTAN. His last hour hath come.
His joy, in seeing us, hath snapped the cord
Of his weak being, by his too great exertions;
And the emotions with which he was filled
Have quickly drained his inmost springs of life.
But 'tis the crowning horror in his last moments
That he knows not his daughter's sentiments.
He now is dying, full of bitterness,
And in his mind's uncertainty he asks,
With his last gasps, whether thou art a Christian.

ZAÏRE. What! when I am thy sister thou canst think
That to my blood and faith I will be false?

NERESTAN. Sister, that faith, alas, is not yet thine.
For thee, the light which guides us is but dawning.
Thou hast not undergone that precious rite
Which washes off our sins and opens heaven
To us. Swear by our woes and by thy sires—
Those holy martyrs of whose blood thou art—
That 'tis thy wish to receive here today
That seal of the true God that makes us his.

ZAÏRE. Yes, by that God I swear whom I adore,
Whose will I seek to know, but know not yet,
To live henceforth obedient to his precepts . . .
But, brother dear, alas, what would he of me?
What must I do?

NERESTAN. Abhor thy captor's sway.
Serve, love this God whom thy forefathers loved,
Him who was born hard by and died here for us,—
Who reunited us,—who has brought me to thee.
Is it for me to instruct thee? Less well taught
In matters such as this than fervent, I
Am but a soldier; faith alone is mine.
A holy priest will come to thee, e'en here,
To bring life to thee and unseal thine eyes.

Be mindful of thine oath, that the baptismal
Water may not bring death and God's curse on thee.
Arrange that I, too, may come back with him.
    But on what grounds, O heaven, can this be done?
Of whom in this unhallowed palace ask it?
Thou, born of twenty kings, a sultan's slave!
The kinswoman of Louis, and the daughter
Of Lusignan! A Christian and my sister,
And Orosmanes' slave. Thou knowest what
I mean. . . . I cannot speak more of it. God,
Hast thou reserved this final blow for us!

ZAÏRE. Nay, cruel man, go on! Thou knowest not
My inmost heart, my torments, hopes, rash deeds.
Brother, have pity on a sister gone
Astray, torn, wretched, dying of despair!
I am a Christian . . . eagerly I await
That holy water which can cleanse my heart.
I will not be unworthy of my brother,
My lineage, mine own self, my hapless father.
But speak to Zaïre; conceal nothing from her.
Tell her . . . what is the code of Christendom?
What punishment awaits an ill-starred woman
Who, left in slavery far from all her kindred,
In a barbarian found a noble champion,
Won his heart, and would be united with him?

NERESTAN. O God! what sayest thou? The swiftest death
    Ought . . .

ZAÏRE.   Enough! Strike! Forestall thy shame.

NERESTAN.   Who . . .
    thou?

    My sister?

ZAÏRE.   'Tis myself of whom I spoke.
Orosmanes loves me. I was going to wed him.

NERESTAN. Wed him? Is this the truth, my sister? Thou,
    The daughter of kings?

ZAÏRE.   Strike, strike, I say! I love him.

NERESTAN. Wretch who disgracest thy ancestral blood,
Thou beggest for death and thou deservest it;
And if I hearkened only to thy shame,
My honor, and the honor of my house,
My father and his memory,—if thy God's
Law, which thou knowest not, if my religion,
Did not restrain mine arm,—e'en in this palace
I would go, yes, would go this very moment,

And slay this savage, with my sword, who loves thee
And, after his breast, plunge it into thine
And thence then pluck it only to pierce mine.
Ah heaven! while Louis, setting an example
To all men, brings war to the trembling Nile,
Only to come soon, striking shrewder blows,
To free the holy sepulcher and city,
Zaïre, meantime, his kinswoman, my sister,
Weds with the tyrant lord of a seraglio!
And I go now to tell poor Lusignan
His daughter taketh a Tartar for her god!
And in this same dread hour thy dying father,
Alas, is praying for Zaïre's salvation!

ZAÏRE. Stop, stop, dear brother . . . look into my heart.
Perhaps Zaïre is not unworthy of thee.
Spare me these horrible reproaches, brother.
Thy wrath, thy words are more injurious,
Bitterer to me, more painful than that death
Which I implored of thee and did not win.
The estate in which thou findest me o'erwhelms thee.
Thou sufferest, I can see. I suffer more.
I would that heaven, in kind severity,
Had made my blood flow through my veins no longer
On the first day when, poisoned with a love
Profane, though pure and Christian in its source
That blood, my heart beat fast for Orosmanes,—
Or on the day when first he loved thy sister!
Forgive me, Christians! Who would not have loved him?
He gave me all; his heart had chosen me;
I saw its pride subdued for me alone.
'Tis he who hath let Christians have new hope.
'Tis he to whom I owe this blessed meeting.
Forgive . . . Thy rage, my father, my heart's feelings,
My oaths, my duty, my remorse, my weakness—
All torture me, so that today thy sister
Dies of repenting rather than of love.

NERESTAN. I blame thee and I pity thee. Believe me,
God will not let thee die till thou art spotless.
I pardon thee, alas, these shameful throes.
He has not lent thee, yet, his mighty aid.
That aid, which maketh strong the feeblest souls,
Will strengthen this frail reed, shaken by the stormwind.
He will not suffer it that, pledged to Him,
Thy heart shall be shared by Him with a savage.

Baptism will extinguish its love's flames,
And thou wilt live in Christ or die a martyr.
Finish the promise thou begannest to make,
And while thou'rt still full of remorse and horror,
Swear to King Louis, to Europe, to thy father,
And to thy God, whose voice thou hearest already,
Never to celebrate this odious marriage
Before the priest unseals thine eyes,—before
He in my presence makes of thee a Christian
And from his hands God takes thee as His own.
Dost thou swear this, Zaïre?

ZAÏRE.   Yes, I do swear it.
Make me a Christian, guiltless. I consent
To all. Go, close our dying father's eyes.
Go. Would that I might follow thee, and die first.

NERESTAN.   I go. Adieu, dear sister. Since my prayers
Can snatch thee not from this vile palace, soon
Will I return to snatch thee from hell's clutches
By baptism and restore thee to thyself.   [*Exit* NERESTAN.

ZAÏRE.   Here am I, God, alone! What shall I do?
God, do not let my heart be false to thee!
Alas, am I, then, really French or Moslem,
Lusignan's daughter or Orosmanes' bride,
A Christian or a girl in love? The oaths
I swore! My father and my native land,
Ye shall be satisfied. . . . Fatima comes not.
In my extremity has everyone
Abandoned me and left me to myself?
Alone, with none to help me, can I bear
The burden of the tasks now laid on me?
To thy law, mighty God, my soul bows—yes,
But make my lover stay out of my sight!
Dear lover, could I have foreseen this morning
That I today would dread to look on thee—
I who, so rightly given o'er to love,
Had then no other happiness, no other
Concern, no other thought than to speak with thee,
To hear thy love, to see thee, to long for thee,
To wait for thy return! My heart adores thee
And—woe is me—to love thee is a crime!

Enter OROSMANES.

OROSMANES.   Come; all is ready, and my spirit's ardor
Can bear no more, madam, the least delay.

ZAIRE

The marriage torches burn bright for thy lover;
The perfume of sweet incense fills the mosque;
The power of Mahomet's god, invoked,
Confirms mine oaths and consecrates my love.
My subjects, prostrate, offer prayers for thee,
All stretched before thy feet. Thy haughty rivals,
Who once strove for my heart and went thine equals,
Now needs must learn to bow unto thy will,
Happy to follow thee and to obey thee.
The throne, the marriage feast, the ceremony,
All wait. Let my life's happiness begin.

ZAÏRE. Where am I, wretched maid? O love! O grief!

OROSMANES. Come.

ZAÏRE.   Where to hide myself?

OROSMANES.   What sayest thou?

ZAÏRE.   Sir . . .

OROSMANES. Give me thy hand. Deign, beautiful Zaïre . . .

ZAÏRE. God of my father! Oh, what can I tell him?

OROSMANES. How dear to triumph o'er this sweet confusion!
How it augments my love and happiness!

ZAÏRE. Alas!

OROSMANES. It makes thee still more precious to me.
It but bespeaks thy virtuous modesty.
Worthy and winsome being, to whom I cleave,
Delay no more.

ZAÏRE (calling).   Fatima, come; upbear me.
(To OROSMANES)   Sir . . .

OROSMANES.   Heavens above! What means this?

ZAÏRE.   Sir, this marriage
Was the supreme bliss of my soul entranced.
I cared not for the throne nor for its grandeurs;
A better love indeed filled all my breast.
Fain would I that, thy noble heart made mine
And scorning for thy sake the crowns of Asia,
Alone and in a desert, beside my husband,
I might have trod them 'neath my feet with thee.
But . . . sir . . . these Christians . . .

OROSMANES.   What! these
Christians . . . Madam,
What has this sect to do, then, with my love?

ZAÏRE. Lusignan, that old man weighed down by sorrows,
Concludes his life and woe this very hour.

OROSMANES. So be it! What concern so keen and tender
Can thy heart feel about this agèd Christian?

Thou art no Christian. Brought up here, thou long
Hast held my father's faith. Shall an old man
Who to the burden of his years succumbeth
Now trouble thy fair fortune? The kind pity
Which he elicits from thee ought to be
Forgotten in this happy hour with me.

ZAÏRE.   Sir, if thou lovest me . . . if I was dear
To thee . . .

OROSMANES.   Art "dear"! Ah God!

ZAÏRE.   I beg thee, let us
Defer . . . Allow these rites prepared for by thee . . .

OROSMANES.   What sayest thou! Gracious heavens, is it thou
Who speakest? Zaïre?

ZAÏRE *(to herself)*.   I cannot bear his anger.

OROSMANES.   Zaïre!

ZAÏRE.   It wracks my heart, sir, to displease thee.
Forgive my grief. . . .
    (To herself)   Nay, I forget at once
All that I am and all that I must do.
I cannot bear to see his face. 'Twill kill me.
I cannot . . .
    (To OROSMANES)   Oh, suffer that far from thee,
Sir, I may go to hide my tears, my woe,
My prayers, despair, and horror at my plight.

            Enter CORASMIN. *Exit* ZAÏRE.

OROSMANES.   I stand here motionless, and my frozen tongue
Aids not the tempest in my outraged soul.
Is it I to whom she speaks? Heard I aright?
Is it I she flees? Ye heavens! what have I seen?
Corasmin, what, then, can this great change mean?
I let her go. I know not mine own self.

CORASMIN.   'Tis thou alone that causest her confusion,
And thou complainest of it. Thou accusest,
My lord, a heart in which thou reignest supreme.

OROSMANES.   But why these tears, then, these regrets, this flight,
This grief so utter written in her glance?
If 'twere that Frenchman . . . ! What a thought! How ghastly!
What fearful light hath shone into my mind?
Alas, I put aside legitimate
Distrust! A slave could dare so to presume?
My dear friend, I could see a heart like mine
Reduced to dreading now a Christian slave!
But tell me—thou couldst well observe his face,

Couldst understand the language of his eyes.
Hide nothing from me. Is my love betrayed?
Let me know my misfortune. . . . Thou art trembling . . .
Shuddering . . . Enough!

CORASMIN.   I fear to excite thy fears.
True it is that his eyes have shed some tears;
But after all, my lord, I have seen nothing
Which ought . . .

OROSMANES.   For this affront I was reserved!
But no, had Zaïre herself wronged me, she
Would with more cleverness have hoodwinked me.
Had her heart been perfidious, would the secret
Sorrow that troubled it have been disclosed?
Listen: let not thy thoughts suspect Zaïre. . . .
But, sayest thou, the Frenchman groaned, wept, sighed? . . .
What does it matter to me why he wept?
Who knows if love caused, even in part, his grief?
And what can I dread from an unbeliever
Who will tomorrow go, to come no more?

CORASMIN. Hast thou not, sir, despite our customs, let him
Enjoy the sight of her a second time?—
Is he to come a third time?

OROSMANES.   He? that treacherous
Knave show himself again to my heart's mistress?
Yes, I would send him to her—punished, dying,
Shedding before her his perfidious blood—
Mangled and torn there—and my reeking hand
Would mingle *her* blood with her lover's blood. . . .
Forgive the transports of an outraged heart.
'Twas violent from my birth; it loves; 'tis wrung.
I know my frenzy, and I fear my weakness.
I feel I lower myself by these unworthy
Suspicions. Nay, I go too far when I
Fix them upon Zaïre. Nay, nay, her heart
Was never fashioned for unfaithfulness. . . .
But think no more mine will degrade itself
By suffering at her coldness, by lamenting
O'er her caprices, by complaints, by taking
Pledges anew and giving them anew.
Such courses are unworthy of me. 'Twere
Better I should regain a fit and proper
Control over my feelings. It were better
I should forget the name, e'en, of Zaïre.
Let the seraglio be shut fast forever.

Z A I R E

Let terror dwell within the palace gates.
Let all here feel the reins of slavery.
Let us observe the ancient usages
Of Oriental monarchs. One of these
Can towards his slave forget his pride, withal,
And let a gracious glance upon her fall.
But it is base to cringe to a mistress. We
Should leave to the Occident such servility.
That dangerous sex, which would o'er all hold sway,
May rule in Europe, but must here obey.

A C T   I V

ZAÏRE *and* FATIMA *are discovered.*

FATIMA. How much I pity and admire thee, madam!
  'Tis God, the Christians' God, who doth inspire thee.
  To thy weak heart he will give power to break
  The ties so dear and strong that bind thee here.
ZAÏRE. What! could I make so dire a sacrifice?
FATIMA. Thou askest grace of Him. He owes it thee.
  To an obedient soul he must lend aid.
ZAÏRE. Never had I such need of his support.
FATIMA. If thou canst see no more thy noble family,
  The God thou servest will be a father to thee.
  Thou'rt in his hands, he speaks within thy breast,
  And if the holy priest, his instrument,
  Cannot come into this accursèd palace . . .
ZAÏRE. I have stabbed Orosmanes to the heart.
  Oh, could I bring despair to him who loved me?
  How monstrous! Ah, the horror of that moment!
  God, 'tis thy will. . . . I would have been too happy . . .
FATIMA. What! still regret thy shameful bonds? Now hazard
  Thy victory, after thou hast fought so hard?
ZAÏRE. Unhappy victory! Inhuman virtue!
  Nay, nay, thou knowest not what I sacrifice,
  Fatima. This great love, my life's delight,
  From which I hoped, ah me, such happiness,
  Had shown to none its full intensity.
  I offer up to God my heart's cruel wounds.
  Before his eyes I wet with sinful tears
  This very place in which, thou tellest me,
  He chose to dwell. Weeping, I cry to him:
  "Divest me of my love. Take my heart's wishes

588

From me, and fill me wholly with thyself."
But then, Fatima, instantly the face
Of him I love, that dear and handsome face
Which I continually behold, appears
Before me in my soul 'twixt heaven and me.
Ah, line of kings from whom God gave me birth,
My sire, my mother, Christians, God my master,
Ye who today take from me him I love,
End now my life, which can be his no longer.
Let me die innocent, and let his dear
Hand at least close the eyes he loved!

                          But what
Is Orosmanes doing? He does not seek
To know if I await here life or death.
He flees me, leaves me, and I cannot bear it.

FATIMA. What! thou? the daughter of kings, whom thou wouldst
        follow,
    Thou, in God's arms, thine everlasting stay . . .

ZAÏRE. Oh, why could not my lover have served Him?
    Was Orosmanes born to be His victim?
    Could God hate so magnanimous a being?
    Noble, just, kindly, full of every virtue,
    Were he a Christian, what more could he be?
    Would to God that my reverend instructor,
    The holy minister whom my soul desires,
    Might come soon and deliver me from this
    Bewilderment of soul in which thou seest me!
    I know not, but in sooth I still dare hope
    That this God, of whose mercy I have been
    So often told, will frown not on our union.
    Perhaps, if worshipped by Zaïre in secret,
    He will forgive the strife in her torn heart.
    Perhaps, by giving me the throne of Syria,
    He would through me bring succor to the Christians
    Of Asia. As thou knowest well, Fatima,
    The mighty Saladin, who took the lands
    Along the Jordan from my ancestors
    And made his clemency admired like that
    Of Orosmanes, had a Christian mother.

FATIMA. Ah, seest thou not that to console thyself . . .

ZAÏRE. Let me alone. I can see everything.
    I soon shall die, but blind myself to naught.
    I see well that my native land, my lineage,
    And all things else condemn me, that I am

A Lusignan, that I love Orosmanes,
That all my vows, my life-days, are with his
Linked. I sometimes would fain fall at his feet
And tell him everything about myself.

FATIMA. Remember that to do this might destroy
Thy brother and endanger all the Christians,
Who have no help but thee, and thus would be
Treasonous to the God who calls thee to him.

ZAÏRE. Oh, if thou only knewest the noble heart
Of Orosmanes!

FATIMA.   He is the protector
Of the Mahometan faith; and hence the more
He worships thee, the less he can endure
That one should dare to tell thee of a God
Whom he must hate. The priest will come to thee
Secretly, and thou gavest thy promise.

ZAÏRE.   Yes.
I must await his coming. I have given
My promise; I have sworn to keep this secret.
With what regret I tell it not, alas,
To him I love! and he, to crown all horrors,
No longer loves me.

Enter OROSMANES. *Exit* FATIMA.

OROSMANES.   Madam, there was a time
When my enthralled soul listened without blushes
To love's sweet accents and considered it
Noble for me to pine in bondage to thee.
I thought myself loved, madam; and, indeed,
Thy master, laying at thy feet his heart,
Would needs expect to be. Thou wilt not hear me
Burst out like an unmanly, jealous lover
Into reproaches, shamefully, against thee.
Hurt deeply, but too proud still to complain,
Too great, too high of soul to stoop to feign,
I come to tell thee that my coldest scorn
Shall worthily repay thy vain caprices.
Prepare not to deceive my tender love,—
To seek for reasons with which thy cleverness
May guilefully show the rebuff I suffered
In a new aspect to my blinded eyes
And thus bring back to thee a lover who
Knows thee no more and who, above all, fears
To be humiliated, and fain would never

Discover why he was insultingly
Rejected by thee. All is over, madam,
Between us, and another in thy stead
Shall mount unto the station which my love
Vouchsafed to offer thee. She will have eyes
And know at least the price at which my heart
And hand are to be had. 'Twill cost me dear,
But as to this I am resolved. Learn now
That Orosmanes will not stop at aught,—
That I would rather lose thee, and far from thee
Die of despair at losing thee, than ever
Possess thee if to give thyself to me
Should make thee heave one sigh except from love
Of me. Go. Never will mine eyes again
Look on thy beauty.

ZAÏRE.   God, who seest my tears,
Thou hast now taken all from me. Thou wishest
To reign alone in my distracted soul . . .
     So be it! Sir, since thou dost no longer love me . . .

OROSMANES. It is too true that honor bids me not to,
'That I adored thee, that I now renounce thee,
Abandon thee, even as thou desirest,
And in another's love . . . Zaïre, thou weepest?

ZAÏRE. Oh, dear lord, oh, at least never believe
That I regret the glory of thy throne.
I know that I must lose thee; 'tis my fate;
But thou divinest little, sir, my feelings.
May heaven, which dooms me, punish me forever
If I regret the loss of anything
But Orosmanes' heart.

OROSMANES.   Zaïre, thou lovest me!
ZAÏRE. Love him? Oh, God! Woe's me!
OROSMANES.   What wondrous turn
Is this, which I can fathom not! Thou lovest me!
Then why didst thou compel thyself, cruel woman,
To lacerate so true a lover's bosom?
I knew myself but ill. In my despair
I deemed I had more mastery o'er myself.
Nay, far less of grim strength my soul possessed.
     Zaïre, may heaven's vengeance never give
Thy lover, whom thou holdest in love's bonds,
'The power to forget his love for thee!
What! seat another woman on my throne?
I? Nay, I never had that dreadful thought.

Forgive this feigned disdain, so well belied;
Born of mine anger, born of my stunned mind,
'Twas the sole sorrow that in all thy life
Heaven will wish thy gentle breast to bear.
I will love thee always. . . . Why, though, did thy heart,
Sharing my love, defer my happiness?
Speak. Was it some caprice? or sudden dread
Of having a master, though I would not be one?
Or might it be some ruse? Spare thyself that.
Thou needest not artifice; it becomes thee not.
Let it ne'er shame the holy tie between us.
Even the most innocent ruse partakes of falseness.
I have ne'er known it, and my tortured heart,
Full of a love so true . . .

ZAÏRE.   Thou drivest me frantic.
Indeed I love thee, and it is the greatness
Of my love for thee that makes great my woe.

OROSMANES.   Ye heavens! Explain thy words. What! always rack me?
Can it . . .

ZAÏRE.   Why, mighty God, may I not tell him!

OROSMANES.   Zaïre, thou hidest what strange secret from me?
Is there some Christian who conspires against me?
Does treachery assail me? Speak.

ZAÏRE.   Why, were there
Some treachery that assailed thee, thou wouldst see me
Throw myself between it and thee. Against thee
None conspires. There is naught to fear for thee.
My grief is for myself. 'Tis I alone
Who should be pitied.

OROSMANES.   Thou? pitied? Great God!

ZAÏRE.   Suffer that at thy feet I, trembling, ask
A favor of thee.

OROSMANES.   A favor? It is thine.
Ask even my life.

ZAÏRE.   Ah, would to heaven thy life
Were linked with mine already! Orosmanes . . .
My lord . . . grant that this day, alone, far off
From thee, and wholly given o'er to woe,
I more collectedly may view my lot
And trouble not thine ears with my laments. . . .
Tomorrow, all my secrets will be told thee.

OROSMANES.   With what anxieties, O heavens, thou fillest me!
Couldst thou . . .

ZAÏRE.   If love for me still speaks within thee,

Refuse me not the boon which I implore.

OROSMANES. Well, then, all that thou wishest, I must wish.
I give consent; 'tis at a heavy cost
To my tormented mind. Go, but forget not
That for thy sake I sacrifice the sweetest
And the most lovely moments of my life.

ZAÏRE. In speaking thus, thou stabbest me to the heart.

[*She turns to go out.*

OROSMANES. What! even now thou leavest me?

ZAÏRE.   Alas, sir!

Enter CORASMIN. *Exit* ZAÏRE.

OROSMANES. Ah, 'twas too soon to seek this lone retreat,
Too quickly to abuse my easy kindness. . . .
(*To* CORASMIN)   The more I think of it, good friend, the less
Can I imagine the reason, so well hidden,
Of such despair. Behold her, by my love
Raised to the throne, midst all the happy fortune
Her soul desires, near him she loves, who loves her
And at her feet waits with impatient ardor:
Her eyes, so full of love, are drowned in tears!
I am indignant at such veering moods. . . .
    But after all, have I myself been less
Unjust to her? Have I been less to blame
In her offended sight? Is it for me,
Then, to complain? She loves me; 'tis enough.
I must atone, by some indulgence of her,
For the insulting wrongs my jealous transports
Did her. I will complain no more. Her heart,
I see, is without guile. Her artless nature
Appears in all her words. She is at present
Of that blest age when innocence reigns supreme.
I should have faith in her sincerity.
She loves me, past all doubt; yes, in her tender
Glance I have read the love she hath for me,
And her heart, kindling to my love, a score
Of times flew to her lips to tell me hers.
Whose soul could be treacherous and base enough
To exhibit so much love and feel it not?

Enter MELEDOR, *with a letter.*

MELEDOR. This letter, sire, addressed unto Zaïre,
Seized by the guards and to my hands consigned . . .

OROSMANES. Give it . . . Who brought it? Give it here.

MELEDOR (*giving him the letter*).   One of those
    Christians, my lord, whose bonds thy mercy broke.
    He was about to enter the seraglio
    Secretly. He was put in chains.
OROSMANES.   Alas,
    What is it that I shall read? Leave us.   [*Exit* MELEDOR.
                      I tremble.
CORASMIN.   The letter, sire, may make all plain to thee
    And calm thy heart.
OROSMANES.   Ah, let us read. My hand
    Is shaking, and my affrighted soul foresees
    That my whole fate depends upon this letter.
    Let us read.
    (*Reading*)   "Dear Zaïre, 'tis time to meet.
    Facing the mosque, a secret exit will
    Permit thee, swiftly and unseen, to cheat
    All watchful eyes and thus our hope fulfil.
    Reck not of risks. Thou knowest my fervor. I
    Wait there. If thou art faithless, I shall die."
      Now, then! What sayest thou, my Corasmin?
CORASMIN.   I, sir?
    I shudder at such utter heinousness.
OROSMANES.   Thou seest how I am treated.
CORASMIN.   Oh, what treachery!
    To such a wrong, my lord, art thou indifferent—
    Thou, whose heart just now, on a mere suspicion,
    Was poisoned with so keen a grief? Ah, clearly
    The horror of such infamous behavior
    Hath cured thee of a love that wounds thine honor.
OROSMANES.   Rush to her instantly; go, fly, Corasmin!
    Show her this letter. Let her tremble. Then
    'Neath countless dagger-blows let the false woman
    Die. But before thou strikest . . . Ah, dear friend, wait,
    Wait; it is not yet time. I wish this Christian,
    Before her led . . . I wish no longer aught . . .
    I die . . . succumb to my excessive rage.
CORASMIN.   None ever suffered such a cruel wrong.
OROSMANES.   This, then, is what it was—that dreadful secret,
    That secret which so weighed on her vile heart!
    Under the borrowed veil of artless fears
    She fain would for a while avoid my sight.
    I forced myself to agree; I let her go;
    She went out weeping . . . and 'twas to deceive me!
    What! Zaïre!

CORASMIN. All aggravates her crime.
　　　Sire, do not be the guileless victim of it,
　　　But calling to thine aid thy loftiest instincts . . .
OROSMANES. This is that Nerestan, that noble hero,
　　　That much-praised Christian, who paraded so
　　　His sublime virtues in Jerusalem!
　　　Even I admired him, and my heart was piqued
　　　That any Christian equaled me in them.
　　　Ah, he shall pay for his foul knavery!
　　　But Zaïre—Zaïre is far guiltier.
　　　A Christian slave, whom I could have allowed
　　　To do the lowliest tasks without injustice!
　　　A slave! She knows what I have done for her!
　　　Oh, wretched me!
CORASMIN. Sire, if thou wilt permit me,—
　　　If midst enormities that must overwhelm thee
　　　Thou wouldst . . .
OROSMANES. Yes, I will see her, speak with her.
　　　　　　　　[*He claps his hands. An attendant appears.*
　　　Go, haste thee, slave, and bring Zaïre to me.
　　　　　　　　　　　　[*Exit the attendant.*
CORASMIN. Nay, in this state what couldst thou say to her?
OROSMANES. I know not, friend, but I intend to see her.
CORASMIN. Alas, my lord, thou wilt in thy mad grief
　　　Reproach her, threaten her, make her tears flow.
　　　The kindness of thy heart will give her weapons
　　　'Gainst thee, and notwithstanding thy suspicions,
　　　Beguiled, thou wilt seek ways to exculpate her.
　　　Wouldst heed my counsel? Show her not this letter.
　　　Let it be given her by an unknown hand.
　　　Thus, despite all concealment and deceit,
　　　Thou wilt discern her hidden thoughts and feelings
　　　And every purpose of her inmost heart.
OROSMANES. Deemest thou Zaïre indeed is false to me?
　　　Come; be the truth whate'er it may, I mean
　　　To try my fate and find the strength of soul
　　　For this last effort. I wish to see how far
　　　A brazen woman can carry perfidy.
CORASMIN. My lord, I fear for thee this fateful meeting.
　　　A heart like thine . . .
OROSMANES. Nay, fear thou naught! Although
　　　I cannot feign as she, alas, hath done,
　　　I have the firmness to control myself.
　　　Yes, since she forces me to perceive a rival . . .

ZAIRE

Here, take this missive, to all three so fatal.
Go, choose a faithful slave to give it to her.
Put in sure hands this cruel letter. Go;
Be quick. . . . I will do more, will shun her sight.
Let her not come near . . . It is she, just heavens!

Enter ZAïRE. *Exit* CORASMIN.

ZAïRE. Sire, thou astoundest me. What urgent reason,
What sudden command calls me back to thee?
OROSMANES. 'Tis necessary, madam, that thou shouldst
Enlighten me. This command is more important
Than thou supposest. I have taken thought. . . .
Made wretched by each other, we have need
With one word to decide my fate and thine.
Perhaps, indeed, what I have done for thee,
My pride forgotten, my scepter at thy feet,
My kindness, deference, attentions, trust,
Have compelled in thee some appreciation.
Thy heart, besieged without cease by thy master,
Overcome by my favors, hath believed
That it was overcome by love. 'Tis time
That I should look, with thee, into thy soul.
'Tis necessary that in response to *my*
Frankness its inmost depths should be disclosed.
Bethink thee. Answer with the truthfulness
Which my sincerity, at least, deserves.
If the resistless power of some other
Love doth outweigh my boons, or even offsets them,
Thou shouldst so tell me, and in that same instant
Thy pardon is in my heart. Speak. I await
Thine answer. Shield not from my honest love
Now the presumptuous man who loves thee madly.
Remember that I see thee, speak to thee,
Still,—that thy words can stay mine anger's lightning,—
That this is the last moment in which I can
Forgive.
ZAïRE.   Thou, my lord? thou canst talk thus to me?
Thou, cruel man? Learn that this heart, which thou wrongest,
And which heaven fain would test by such dread trials,
Save that it loves thee, would from pride defy thee.
I fear naught but my fatal love for thee.
Ascribe to that love's flames, which still consume me,—
To that love only, which I should forget,—
The fact that now I stoop to justify

Myself. I know not whether heaven, always
Hostile to me, destined my ill-starred life
For thee. Whate'er may happen, by my honor,
Which in my breast hath no less part than love,
I swear that Zaïre, of her own free choice,
Would loathe the sight of even the mightiest kings.
Having known thee, I could endure none else.
    Wouldst thou hear more and understand me better?
Wouldst thou this heart in all its grievous pain,
This desperate heart, should bare itself to thee?
Learn, then, that secretly, despite itself,
It had felt, long since, everything it told thee
Earlier today,—that it had yearned for thee
Ere yet thy tender love gave any sanction
To its first impulse of surrender to thee,—
That it awaited not thy favor shown me
To lay itself before thy feet—in short,
It loved thee when thou paidest me no heed,
And ne'er had, and will ne'er have, any lord
But thee. To this do I call heaven to witness,
Which I perhaps offend, and if I have
Merited its eternal wrath,—if I
Have sinned, thou ingrate,—'twas because I loved thee.

OROSMANES (*to himself*). What! of the truest love she still assures
     me?
    Such treachery! Zaïre! . . . The perjured woman;
    When I have in my hands proof of her falseness!

ZAÏRE. What sayest thou? What turmoil fills thy breast?

OROSMANES. There is no turmoil. Dost thou love me?

ZAÏRE.   Canst thou
    Speak to me in these fierce tones of a love
    Avowed so fondly every day? Thus speaking
    To me of love, thou makest me cold with fear.

OROSMANES. *Dost* thou love me?

ZAÏRE.   Thou canst doubt my love!
    But still I ask, what frenzy masters thee?
    How dreadful is the glance thou dartest at me!
    Alas! Dost thou doubt what is in my heart?

OROSMANES. No; I do not have any doubt about it.
    Go. Withdraw, madam.

Exit ZAÏRE. *Enter* CORASMIN.

                Friend, her perfidy,
E'en at its hideous climax, is well masked.

Calm midst her guilt, gentle midst all her baseness,
She to the end continues her deception.
    Foundest thou the slave? Hast thou served well mine anger?
Shall I confirm alike her wickedness
And the wrong done me?

CORASMIN.   Yes. I have obeyed thee;
But thou canst care no more for her false charms.
Surely, thou wilt now see her with indifference,
With no recoil on thee of thy revenge
Because of any love.

OROSMANES.   Corasmin, I
Love her more madly than I ever did.

CORASMIN.   Thou? Good heavens! Thou?

OROSMANES.   I see one ray of hope.
This odious Christian, this apt son of France,
Is youthful, hasty, frivolous, and vain.
He easily can believe what he dares wish.
Impulsive and self-confident, he would
Have the presumption to declare his love.
One glance of Zaïre's would have dazzled him.
No doubt it pleases him to let himself
Be thus enthralled. He thinks that he is loved,
And it is he alone who sins against me.
Perhaps they do not have an understanding
Between them. Zaïre has not seen this letter,
And I gave way to mortal pangs too quickly.
    Corasmin, hearken: when night's blackest hour
Hath come to lend its shadows to men's crimes,
So soon as e'er this Christian upon whom
I lavished kindness, Nerestan, appears
Beneath the palace walls, do thou see to it
That instantly my guards shall seize him. Let
The direst punishment be prepared for him,
And let him, laden with chains, be brought to me.
Leave, above all, leave Zaïre wholly free.
Thou seest my heart and how o'ermuch I love her.
My frenzy mounts. I myself tremble at it.
I blush at being so crushed with grief, but woe
Unto the ingrates who have wronged me so!

ACT V

It is night. The scene is very dimly lighted. OROSMANES, CORAS-
MIN, *and a slave are discovered.*

OROSMANES (*to the slave*). She has been summoned; the thankless
    woman soon
Will come. Remember that thy master's fate
Is in thy hands. Give her that treacherous Christian's
Letter. Report all to me. Mark her closely.
Tell me her answer. Someone nears. . . . 'Tis she.
(*To* CORASMIN) Come, dear true friend of an unhappy ruler,
Come, help me to conceal my grief and rage.
    [*Exeunt* OROSMANES *and* CORASMIN. *Enter, a moment later,*
    ZAÏRE *and* FATIMA.

ZAÏRE. Who, then, can speak to me in my present plight?
Who, alas, from its horrors can extricate me?
Shut now is the seraglio. God! if 'twere
My brother! If God's hand, to uphold my faith,
Brought him here, by some hidden way, to me!
What unknown slave appears before mine eyes?

THE SLAVE. This letter, secretly put in my hands,
Will make thee sure of my fidelity.

ZAÏRE. Give it me.   [*The slave gives her the letter.*

FATIMA (*to herself, while* ZAÏRE *reads it*). Mighty God, display
    thy goodness!
E'en in this palace let thy grace descend!
Rescue my princess from the cruel Orosmanes!

ZAÏRE (*to* FATIMA). I wish to speak with thee.

FATIMA (*to the slave*).   Go hence. Withdraw.
We will soon call thee back. Be ready. Leave us.
    [*Exit the slave.*

ZAÏRE. Read this letter. . . . Oh, tell me what to do!
I want to carry out my brother's bidding.

FATIMA. Say rather, madam, the eternal bidding
Which God before his altars lays upon thee.
'Tis nowise Nerestan, but God, who calls thee.

ZAÏRE. I know it and rebel not when He calls.
I took an oath. But can I place myself,
My brother, and the Christians in such danger?

FATIMA. 'Tis not their danger that so much disturbs thee.
Thy love alone speaks in thy shaken soul.
I know thy nature: thou wouldst think as they do,
Wouldst hazard all, if thou wert not in love.

Ah, at least recognize the error which
Ensnareth thee. Thou tremblest at the prospect
Of angering the lover who hath wronged thee.
What! seest thou not how fierce his nature is
And how a Tartar's soul lurks 'neath his kindness?
This tiger, still ferocious when he loves,
Even though he adores thee, threatens thee. . . .
And can thy heart still not detach itself
From him? Thou lovest him?

ZAÏRE.   For what can I
Reproach him? It is I who wronged him—I
Whom he had seen, this very day, myself
Desire this star-crossed marriage. Lo, the throne
Awaited me; the temple was adorned;
My lover loved me—and then I deferred all!
I, who had formerly had to fear his power,
Have recked naught of the fervor of his feelings.
I curbed his love; he did as I desired:
He sacrificed for me his passion's ardor.

FATIMA.   This wretched love with which thy soul is smitten—
Even at this moment can it fill thy thoughts?

ZAÏRE.   Ah, everything, Fatima, makes me desperate.
I know that the seraglio holds me fast.
I fain would see the Christians' happy land,—
Would leave this place where I have gone astray,—
And I am conscious that I then straightway
Desire the opposite and in my heart
Vow that I ne'er will from its walls depart.
What plight! what torture! nay, my troubled soul
Knows not what I should do, nor what it wishes.
I feel naught but a dreadful terror. . . . God,
Let not my black presentiments come true!
Protect our Christians and watch o'er my brother.
From heaven above, watch o'er his precious head.
Yes, I will go to meet him, will obey him;
But when he shall have left Jerusalem,
Emboldened by his absence, then, to speak,
I will reveal unto the man I love
The secret of my birth; I will avow
Unto him the religion which is rightly
Mine; he will read my heart and will have pity.
But though I were to be condemned to torments
Now, I would not betray the blood from which

I sprang. Go; thou mayest bring my brother here.
Call back that slave. [*Exit* FATIMA.
    (*Alone*)   God of mine ancestors!
God of my kindred, of my hapless father!
May thy hand guide me, may thine eyes observe me!

Enter FATIMA *and the slave.*

(*To the slave*)   Go, tell the Christian who hath followed thee
That I will not be false to him today,—
That soon Fatima will admit him here.
(*To herself*)   Come; be reassured, wretched Zaïre!

Exeunt ZAÏRE *and* FATIMA. *Enter* OROSMANES *and* CORASMIN.

OROSMANES.   How slow the moments seem unto my rage,
    Great God!
    (*To the slave*)   Well, what was said? Speak. Tell me.
THE SLAVE.   Sire,
    No one has ever seen such perturbation.
    She blenched, she trembled, and her eyes shed tears.
    She made me go out; then she called me back,
    And with a faltering voice and heart much troubled
    She promised to await, sir, near this spot,
    The man who was to come to her tonight.
OROSMANES.   Go; 'tis enough. [*Exit the slave.*
    (*To* CORASMIN)   Get thee, too, from my sight.
    Leave me. All mortals have become odious to me.
    Leave me, I say, alone with my great rage.
    I hate the whole world; I loathe even myself.
                              [*Exit* CORASMIN.
    Where am I? O God! Where am I? What do
    I wish to do? Zaïre, Nerestan, oh,
    Ungrateful couple, treacherous couple! Monsters,
    Take from me this life-breath I breathe, this air
    Polluted by you. . . . Miserable Zaïre,
    Thou nowise shalt enjoy . . . Come back, Corasmin!

Re-enter CORASMIN.

    Ah, too cruel friend! what! thou abandonest me!
    Come here. Has he appeared, this rival of mine,
    This guilty wretch?
CORASMIN.   No one has yet appeared.
OROSMANES.   O night! O fearsome night! Canst lend thy veil
    To cloak such crimes? Zaïre! . . . The faithless woman! . . .
    After such favors! With an eye serene,

A countenance unmoved, I could have seen
My fall, however terrible, from my throne.
I could in the most dire captivity
Preserve my courage and tranquillity.
But to behold myself to this extent
Deceived by her I love!

CORASMIN.   What dost thou mean
To do in such a ghastly situation?
What is thy purpose?

OROSMANES.   Dost thou not hear cries?

CORASMIN. My lord . . .

OROSMANES.   A dreadful noise sounds in mine ears.
Someone is coming.

CORASMIN.   Nay, none yet approaches.
O'er the seraglio utter silence broods.
All are asleep, all is quiet, and night's shadows . . .

OROSMANES. Alas, crime sleeps not, and its horror haunts me!
To carry to this point her guilty daring!
Thou didst not know my heart and its fond love!
How I adored thee—ah, how passionately!
    Corasmin, one glance from her could decide
My fate. I can know naught of happiness
Nor suffering except through her. Take pity
Upon my frenzy. Yes, run . . . Ah, cruel woman!

CORASMIN. Is it thou who weepest? thou, Orosmanes? Heavens!

OROSMANES. Those are the first tears that mine eyes have shed.
Thou seest my lot; thou seest the shame to which I
Surrender. But those tears are cruel, and death
Will follow them. Pity Zaïre; pity me.
The hour draws near. These tears are harbingers
Of blood that is to flow.

CORASMIN.   Alas, I tremble
For thee!

OROSMANES.   Yes, shudder at my suffering,
Shudder at my love, and shudder at my vengeance.
Come hither. Come. I hear . . . I am not mistaken!

CORASMIN. Someone is walking close 'neath the palace walls.

OROSMANES. Go and seize Nerestan. Go, I say, and bind him.
Loaded with chains, let him be dragged before me.

Exit CORASMIN. *Enter* ZAÏRE *and* FATIMA, *walking amidst the
shadows near the back of the scene.*

ZAÏRE. Come, Fatima.

OROSMANES (*to himself*). What do I hear? Is this

That voice whose sweet tones have so oft enthralled me,
That voice which hath deceived so honorable
A love, that treacherous voice, the instrument
Of wickedness? The false wretch! . . . let us take
Vengeance. . . . Is this, then, she? O Fate! Zaïre!

[*He draws his dagger.*

Ah God! my hand can scarcely hold this dagger!

ZAÏRE (*to* FATIMA). Here is the place. Come, help me to be brave.

FATIMA. He will come soon.

OROSMANES (*to himself*). Those words revive my fury.

ZAÏRE. Quaking, I go; my heart is sore dismayed.
(*Seeing the figure of* OROSMANES) Is it thou, Nerestan, whom
I so await?

OROSMANES (*rushing upon her*). 'Tis I, to whom thou art false!
Die, faithless woman! [*He stabs her.*

ZAÏRE (*falling*). I die, O God!

OROSMANES. I have revenged my wrong.
Let us go hence. I cannot . . . What have I done? . . .
What is just, only . . . punished her great crime.
Ah, here her lover is! Fate sends him to me
To make my vengeance and fierce joy complete.

CORASMIN *and slaves bring in* NERESTAN, *bound.*

Draw near, thou wretch, who camest to snatch from me—
To rob me of forever—what was so dear
To me. Contemptible foe, who still displayest
A hero's boldness with a villain's soul,
Thou wonnest here my esteem, to bring shame on me.
Go; thy reward awaits thee. Be prepared
For it. Thy pangs will equal those which thou
Hast caused me—equal thy ingratitude
And the horror which thou broughtest to pass!
(*To* CORASMIN) Hast thou
Given orders for his torture?

CORASMIN. Yes, my lord.

OROSMANES (*to* NERESTAN). It hath begun already in thy heart.
Thine eyes seek everywhere and still ask to see
That faithless girl who loved thee and shamed me.
Look! There she is.

NERESTAN. What sayest thou? What mistake
Is thine?

OROSMANES. Look there, I say.

NERESTAN. Oh, what is this
That I behold? Alas, my sister! Zaïre . . .

> She is no more. O monster! O dread day!

OROSMANES.   His sister? What do I hear? God! Can it be?

NERESTAN.   Barbarous man, it is too true. Come; drain
> The last blood that is left of that ill-fated,
> August race from my bosom. Lusignan,
> That aged man, was her unhappy father.
> His sorrows have just ended, in my arms,
> And from her dead sire I was bringing her
> His last admonishments and last farewell.
> I came here to implant Christ's pure religion
> In her too weak, too tender heart. Alas,
> She had offended 'gainst our God, our Law;
> And God has punished her for loving thee.

OROSMANES.   Zaïre! . . . She loved me? Oh, is that true, Fatima?
> His sister? . . . She did love me?

FATIMA.   That, cruel man,
> Was her sole crime. Tiger athirst for blood,
> Thou hast just slain one who despite herself
> Persisted in adoring thee and ever
> Told herself that her fathers' God, accepting
> The sincere tribute of her repentant tears,
> Might look with pity on her hapless love
> And grant that ye twain yet should be united.
> Alas, her wish to this extent misled her;
> She cherished this fond hope and her distressed
> Mind and heart wavered between her God and thee.

OROSMANES.   Thou tellest me enough. Ah heaven, she loved me!
> Go; I have no need now to know aught more.

NERESTAN.   For what, then, dost thou wait to slake thy fury,
> Fell tyrant? Of that glorious blood wherewith
> Thy father's arm and thine have drenched this spot
> None is left, save in me. Come, re-unite
> A luckless man with his sad family—with that
> Hero whose daughter thou just now hast murdered.
> Thy tortures—do they wait? I can defy them.
> Thou hast already tried me with the cruelest
> Of all of them. But does the thirst which ever
> Consumes thee for our blood permit the voice
> Of honor still to speak to thee? In taking
> My life, do not forget those Christians whom
> Thou sworest unto me thou wouldst release.
> Will thy relentless heart, despite its anger,
> Be capable of that magnanimous act?
> Speak. At this price I shall be glad to die.

ZAIRE

OROSMANES *(approaching the body of* ZAÏRE*)*. Zaïre!

CORASMIN.   Alas,
      my lord, where bendest thou
Thy steps. Go within. Too great grief hath mastered
Thy soul. Let Nerestan . . .

NERESTAN.   What is thy will,
      Savage?

OROSMANES *(after a long pause)*.   Unbind him. Hearken, Corasmin:
        let
All his companions be set free at once.
Lavish my largess on these wretched Christians.
Crowned with my favors, loaded with my wealth,
Let them be guided to the port of Joppa.

CORASMIN.   But, sire . . .

OROSMANES.   Obey, and do not answer me.
      Fly; be not faithless to the last desire
Of a Sultan who commands, a friend who loves thee.
Go. Lose no time. Away. Obey.   *[Exit* CORASMIN.
              (To NERESTAN*)*   And thou,
Warrior ill-fated, but less so than I am,
Leave this dire place. Carry back to thy country
This body, which my blind rage deprived of life.
Thy king, all Christians, hearing of thy sorrows,
Will never speak of them except with tears;
But if the truth should be made known by thee,
Loathing my crime they yet may pity me.
Bring them this dagger, which my misguided arm
Plunged in a breast I ought to have held sacred.
Tell them that I have slain atrociously
The worthiest, the most virtuous of women
Whose innocent beauty heaven ever shaped.
Tell them that at her feet I laid my realm;
Tell them that with her blood my hand was dyed;
Say that I worshipped her—and have avenged her.
        (To his slaves)   Respect this hero and conduct him hence.
                              [He kills himself.

NERESTAN.   Guide me, almighty God; I do not know
      What to think. Must thy frenzy, Orosmanes,
Awaken admiration now in me,
And in mine own grief must I grieve for thee?